SECOND EDITION

MIS

Managing Information Systems in Business, Government and Society

SECOND EDITION

MIS

Managing Information Systems in Business, Government and Society

Rahul De

Hewlett-Packard Chair Professor
Decision Sciences & Information Systems Area
Chairperson, Centre for Software & IT Management
Indian Institute of Management Bangalore

WILEY

MIS

Managing Information Systems in Business, Government and Society

SECOND EDITION

Cover Image: Peshkova/Shutterstock

Other Wiley Editorial Offices:

John Wiley & Sons, Inc. 111 River Street, Hoboken, NJ 07030, USA

Wiley-VCH Verlag GmbH, Pappellaee 3, D-69469 Weinheim, Germany

John Wiley & Sons Australia Ltd, 42 McDougall Street, Milton, Queensland 4064, Australia

John Wiley & Sons (Asia) Pte Ltd, 2 Clementi Loop #02-01, Jin Xing Distripark, Singapore 129809

John Wiley & Sons Canada Ltd, 22 Worcester Road, Etobicoke, Ontario, Canada, M9W 1L1

First Edition: 2012
Second Edition: 2018
Reprint: 2022
ISBN: 978-81-265-7122-2
ISBN: 978-81-265-8537-3 (ebk)
www.wileyindia.com
Printed at: Yash Printographics

DEDICATION

This book is dedicated to my late father Dr Rajat De, and to my mother Sonali De.

This book is also dedicated to my family – wife, Sharmila and daughter, Riya – without whose support and encouragement this book would not have been possible.

PREFACE TO THE SECOND EDITION

The first edition of this textbook released six years ago. Much has changed since then and much has remained the same. Predictably, the changes are the massive innovations brought about by IT. Innovations in cloud computing, internet-of-things, artificial intelligence, analytics, machine learning and blockchain technologies, to name a few, dominate markets. Managers across all industries and organisations have to understand these new technologies and have to grasp how to manage and mould them to their advantage. What have remained the same are the core concepts of managing technology and the strategic use of technology in business.

This second edition builds on the core themes of managing IS, with four additional chapters – on *innovations, cloud computing and internet-of-things, green IT and smart cities, and artificial intelligence*. The earlier chapters are re-arranged and also upgraded with fresh caselets and key points. Data, figures and tables are updated, wherever necessary.

Students who read and learned from the book are the main inspiration for the changes in this edition. It is their questions in class that inspired me to update the content of the chapters and also add the new chapters.

PREFACE TO THE FIRST EDITION

I began my career as a professor of information systems in the USA, in the early 1990s, where I taught undergraduate and graduate students at several different universities. One of the things that used to impress me, and also helped me immensely as I started out as a teacher, was the quality of the available textbooks. I found that each of the textbooks was very carefully written and prepared for a specific audience – the student of MIS. The books were relevant and contemporary, and students could easily relate to them as they had many examples from the American context and culture. It was easy to adopt such books as texts for a class, as they had ample scope for both setting the tone of the course and also for letting the instructor design the course according his or her own preferences.

When I moved to India, and began teaching MIS at IIM Bangalore, I found that the textbooks available here were the same ones that I had seen and used in the USA. Initially, this seemed like good fortune as I already knew these books and could easily adapt my course around them. However, it soon became clear that the examples, cases and context of the textbooks were entirely different from anything Indian students were used to or familiar with in their daily or work lives. For example, students in India can read about and understand the general issues related to using an information system for parcel delivery in New York city, however, they are much more interested in reading about such a system in Bangalore or New Delhi.

As I began to write this textbook, these experiences were paramount on my mind. The overall plan and content of the book was driven by the following concerns, which have become the most important features of this text.

1. A majority of the examples, data, cases and illustrations are drawn from India – covering areas such as use of information technology in businesses, in state or central government departments, and by people in remote parts of India, etc.
2. The emphasis in the writing and exposition is on understanding how to make decisions regarding and about information systems, as opposed to the specifics of the technology. The text does not dwell on the details of any specific technology, but only on how it is used, what are its capabilities, and what are the challenges in managing it.
3. The discussion of different concepts is from the perspective of the user of IT, and not that of the creators or manufacturers of IT.
4. New and emerging concepts and technologies, such as open source or cloud computing, are covered, both to provide relevant content to the reader, as well as to inspire and build interest in the topic of the book.

ABOUT THE BOOK

This book extensively covers the operation and management of information systems as they are used by businesses, by government and by individuals in society. Written with a view to understand and manage information systems and their applications, the book will be of use as a course text on Management Information Systems, as well as a text for all readers interested in the topic.

The central viewpoint of this book is managerial decision making. This perspective informs the discussions on information technology and information systems, their use and management and their role in organisations. This viewpoint underscores the need to understand and make sense of the myriad information technology tools and systems available in the modern era, before they can be managed effectively.

The book has a special emphasis on Indian businesses, and the Indian government and social context. Most of the examples in the book are drawn from case studies of Indian business organisations, government departments, NGOs, and people in all walks of life who interact with and use information systems. The text also draws upon examples from other parts of the world to understand information technology in different contexts, and to show its future prospects.

The text emphasizes networking and telecommunications technology, both wired and wireless, which has become the dominant mode of access to the information age for people. This material lays the foundation for understanding the future of information systems and the manner in which they are shaping the world around us.

To understand information systems it is important to see not only what they are but also how and why they are used. When people use and interact with technology they learn a lot about the technology, and then begin to change or shape the technology to their needs. It is the same with information systems also - people change the way they do work as well as change the technology to help them do their work. An important goal of this text is to show how people adopt technology and manage it to meet their needs.

This book has separate chapters on important and emerging topics in IT, such as open source software, social networks, ICT for development and electronic governance.

Acknowledgements for First Edition

This book was written over a period of several years, during the course of which I had the opportunity to discuss both material in the book and the process of writing with several friends and colleagues. Murali Patibandla of IIMB and Alfonso Duran-Heras of University Carlos III of Madrid gave me consistent advise and encouraged me to stay on the course. Having written books themselves, their advice was practical and simple.

I would like to thank summer interns Shreya Modi and Meera P. Jacob for helping collect data for many of the cases. I am indebted to students of an MIS class at UCIII of Madrid for having read and commented on early drafts of three chapters of the book.

I am grateful for the periodic advise, commiserations and encouragements of Praveen Settigere of Wiley India. He met me at opportune moments to fill up my sagging sails. Thanks also to Meenakshi Sehrawat of the editorial team of Wiley for an excellent job of editing the text.

I must acknowledge the comments, questions, criticisms, challenges and insights that I have obtained from PGP students at IIMB, over the years, who have taken my MIS class. These inputs have been invaluable in developing the arguments and overall flow of this text.

Many thanks to Supriya Dey of IIMB for writing the Stuxnet case and to Uma Bharath for helping with creating the review questions, the additional online resources, and the slides for use in class. Their help is priceless.

And finally, many thanks to my wife, Sharmila Chakravarty, for supporting me throughout these long years of writing, frustration, struggle and eventual relief.

Acknowledgements for Second Edition

I am indebted to students in the PGP programme at IIMB for pointing out needed corrections in the first edition. Some also discussed with me how certain sections could be improved, and also commented on the overall design of the book.

TEACHING WITH THIS BOOK

This book is designed to be used as a text for a 20-session semester course on MIS or a related topic. Each chapter can then act as the basic reading material for the classes for each week. However, the book can be used for shorter courses also. Each chapter in this text can be read independently and does not depend on any earlier chapter. Instructors are thus free to design their course in any manner they think fit - they could use chapters from the different themes in any order, depending on their priorities.

A shorter than 20-session course could be designed in different ways:

1. Include all the eight chapters from the first theme, to cover the central ideas of MIS and then select relevant chapters from the other two themes.
2. Include select chapters from the first theme (Chapters 1–3 are recommended), and then select all or few from the other two themes. This will give a more technology-oriented flavour to the course while including important MIS concepts.
3. Although the third theme appears in the end, chapters from this theme may be included earlier in the course to bring a flavour of new and emerging ideas in MIS up front.

The lead cases may be used as discussion material in class. Each case provides material on a specific example of MIS use and design. Instructors can require students to read the case in class, or have them read in advance, and draw inferences from the case while discussing MIS issues. The caselets can be used in a similar manner. The cases can also extend the discussion to issues beyond those covered in the text material.

SPECIAL FEATURES OF THE BOOK

Learning Objectives and Chapter Summary

Each chapter in the text starts with a listing of the learning objectives. These statements highlight the key takeaways for the reader from reading the chapter. This is followed by a chapter summary that provides the major ideas of the chapter in slightly more detail, but all in the space of a few paragraphs.

Learning Objectives

After completing this chapter, you will be able to:

- Get an overview of the modern organisation
- Understand information systems in organisations
- Learn to manage information systems in organisations

Leading Case

Each chapter includes a lead case. These cases highlight an important real-world problem in a business setting, in government or in the society, that is solved by using information systems. The cases are brief in nature, so that students grasp the essence of the problem and IS solution quickly, and highlight issues that are covered in detail later in the chapter. The cases thus serve to foreground the issues discussed in the chapter.

CASE STUDY: mJUNCTION

Metaljunction (mJunction) is one of the largest e-commerce firms in India. mJunction was started by two very large industrial steel production houses in India – the Steel Authority of India (SAIL) and Tata Steel. The initial goal of the steel giants behind the mJunction idea was to sell steel to industrial consumers through a common website. However, the idea grew into new dimensions, and today mJunction deals with metals and minerals, steel, auto components, coal, books, equipment and other products. They allow buyers and sellers of all these industrial products to list their needs and offerings on mJunction. In this manner, mJunction has grown tremendously and is currently one of the largest e-commerce sites in India, and the largest steel-selling site in the world.

As stated earlier, mJunction started out as a site for selling raw steel (it was called 'metaljunction' then). At that time steel was sold manually in India. Producers made steel of various types and qualities that were stocked in their manufacturing plants to be picked up by dealers and wholesale merchants. Pricing was ad hoc and often subject to stiff bargaining as manufacturers were keen to reduce inventories and offload their products. Merchants purchased steel at prices much lower than their fair value thus realising huge profits.

When Tata Steel and SAIL decided to create an online site for selling steel, their goal was to regularise the market to increase sale volumes and realise better prices for their products. They started hesitantly in times of the infamous *dotcom bust* when many e-commerce ventures had failed, without being sure of the outcome of their venture. However, they were able to enrol

Mind Map of Topics

Each chapter also contains a mind map of the topics covered in the chapter. This is a graphical depiction of the topics and how they are related. The mind map helps readers see the key ideas and concepts on a single page, and enables their overall understanding of the chapter contents.

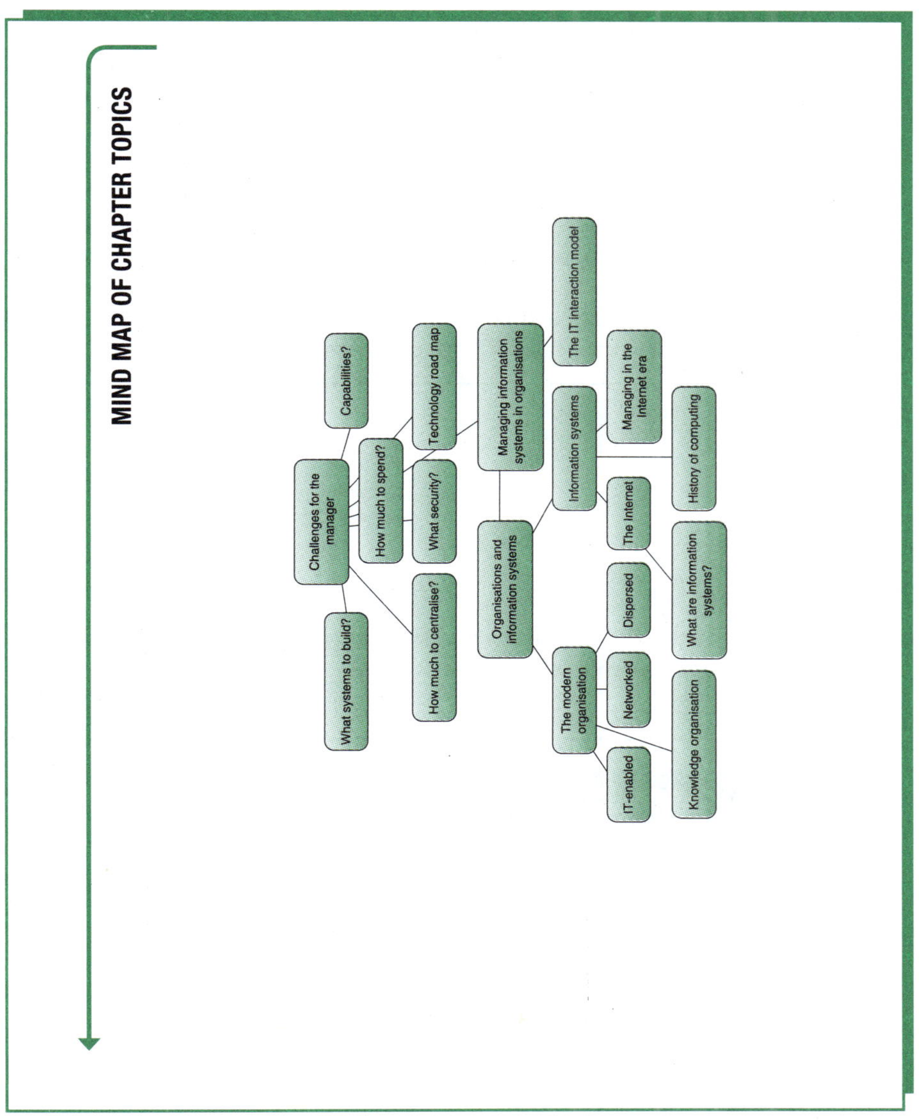

Real-World Examples

The text relies heavily on real-world examples, cases, anecdotes and data to illustrate issues and concepts. The examples are drawn mainly from the Indian context; however, examples from other nations and cultures are also provided. These examples help to clarify issues and point to complexities that are otherwise difficult to explain in a brief manner.

> purchased with each other. In a famous case, a large retailer found from a market basket analysis that men in a certain part of the USA were likely to buy beer and diapers on Thursday evenings. This was an unusual finding and the retailer sought to explain why. It was later learned that many families with young children planned their weekend trips on Thursday evening, at which point the women would ask men to go and buy diapers from the store. The men would take this opportunity to buy beer, also for the weekend. The retailer used this information to announce promotions and increase sales of both these products.

Caselet

Each chapter includes a caselet, a shorter case write-up that dwells on a real-world application or illustrates a concept.

> **Caselet** **ID Fresh Foods**
>
> ID Fresh Foods is a firm that sells ready-to-cook ingredients for making traditional Indian foods. Their business proposition is to market ingredients that can be cooked easily for freshly made meals. For example, one of their earliest products was batter for idlis and dosas that could be taken from a packet and cooked on a stove or steamed. Their batter retained its freshness and enabled users to prepare fresh meals without the labour of preparing the ingredients. Starting out in 2005, ID Fresh was able to establish a presence and reputation in the Bangalore market,

Review and Research Questions

Several review questions are included at the end of each chapter to help the student revise the material covered. The questions can be answered based only on the material in the chapters. The research questions, on the other hand, are designed to make students seek information and answers elsewhere, on the Internet, in the library, or from visits to neighbouring organisations. The objective of these questions is to encourage the student to explore issues over and above those covered in the text.

Review Questions

1. What are the basic features of a modern organisation?
2. How are information systems (IS) and information technology (IT) different?
3. How did information systems evolve?
4. What difference does the internet make in the way modern organisations operate?
5. What are the different types of effects of information systems when used in organisations?
6. What are the main questions about information systems that a manager has to answer?

Research Questions

1. What types of application software are typically used in modern business organisations? Visit some local businesses and find out. Try to visit businesses in different industries such as manufacturing, services and software.
2. While visiting with the local businesses, try to meet with the person in charge of IS, such as the CIO, and ask about the typical decisions he/she has to make.
3. How long does it take to implement information systems, such as a CRM in a large organisation like Tata Motors? Search in library databases for papers on CRM implementation and on the internet for an answer to this question.
4. Find out about the IS used in your college or university. How is this different from the IS used by Tata Motors in the case at the beginning of the chapter.

Key Points

The chapter text is embedded with Key Points, or short summaries of interesting concepts.

KEY POINT

Modern organisations have to sense and respond to information.

Glossary of Key Terms

Key terms and phrases used in the chapter are reviewed at the end. These terms are either technical in nature, or mean something specific, and unusual, in the given context and are highlighted.

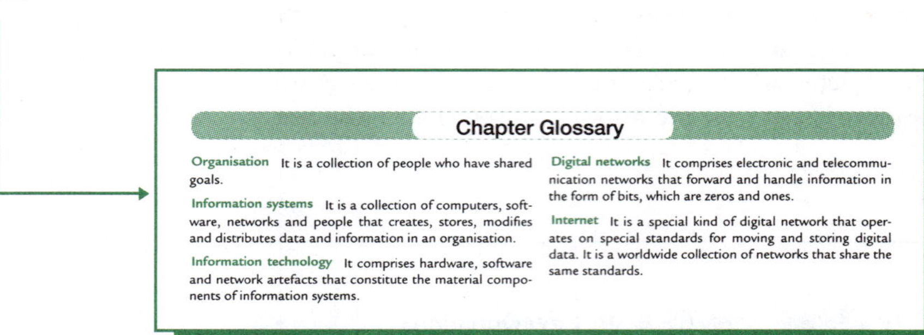

Chapter Glossary

Organisation It is a collection of people who have shared goals.

Information systems It is a collection of computers, software, networks and people that creates, stores, modifies and distributes data and information in an organisation.

Information technology It comprises hardware, software and network artefacts that constitute the material components of information systems.

Digital networks It comprises electronic and telecommunication networks that forward and handle information in the form of bits, which are zeros and ones.

Internet It is a special kind of digital network that operates on special standards for moving and storing digital data. It is a worldwide collection of networks that share the same standards.

Writing Style

The chapters are written in a clear and simple style. Technical jargon is avoided, unless needed, and is appropriately explained when used. Readers are assumed to have some familiarity with common business and management-oriented terms.

Use of Open Source Tools

The draft of this entire text was written with open source tools. The main chapters were written with Open Office and, later, with Libre Office. Figures and drawings were created with Dia and GIMP. The laptop on which the draft was written ran the Ubuntu operating system.

This book consists of 16 chapters. These chapters are organised under three broad themes – MIS and Organisations, Fundamentals of IT, and Social Aspects of IS. In the following tables, the chapters and their contents are outlined under each theme.

Theme 1: MIS and Organisations	
Chapter 1: Organisations and Information Systems	This chapter introduces the concepts of IS and organisations. It dwells on the interactions between people and systems, and the management challenges this poses.
Chapter 2: IT and Innovation	This chapter examines the key drivers of innovation, within IT and in organisations that use and deploy IT. It explores the implications of these innovations and how to manage the constant changes.
Chapter 3: Concepts of Management Information Systems	Beginning with the basic concepts of data and information, this chapter leads on to the different types of MIS and the types of decisions that are supported by these systems.
Chapter 4: IT Strategy and Digital Goods	Businesses exist in a competitive environment and this chapter discusses how IS is used to compete effectively. All organisations have to deal with digital goods, in some form, whose properties are discussed.
Chapter 5: Electronic Commerce, Electronic Business, Electronic Governance	E-commerce is based on the technology of the Internet. This chapter shows the various ways in which e-commerce is conducted, and the manner in which this technology has impacted businesses and governance.
Chapter 6: Managing Information Systems	This chapter discusses the challenges of managing IS in organisations. It outlines the role of the CIO, how to manage vendors, and how IT governance can be set up.
Chapter 7: Ethical and Social Issues	This chapter covers ethical and social issues arising out the use of IS; issues of privacy, power of systems professionals, workplace monitoring, de-skilling and politics are discussed.
Chapter 8: Managing Green IT and Smart Cities	Green IT examines how organisations use IT for green practices and how IT can be designed to reduce energy consumption. Smart cities leverage IT to manage traffic, improve resource management, improve governance and follow green practices.

Theme 2: Fundamentals of IT	
Chapter 9: Information Technology Infrastructure and Choices	The constituents of the IT infrastructure – hardware, software, networks and services – are discussed. Modern solutions such as virtualisation and cloud computing are also highlighted.
Chapter 10: Cloud Computing and Internet-of-Things	This chapter examines Cloud computing, its basic advantages to organisations, its types and some underlying technologies. Internet-of-Things is a key application of cloud computing that impacts businesses. The chapter covers key concepts and how IoT can be managed.
Chapter 11: Networking and Telecommunication	Beginning with the concept of a packet, this chapter discusses the basic structure, services and protocols that constitute the Internet.
Chapter 12: Information Systems Security and Control	This chapter considers the security threats to an organisation and the technology for countering them. It discusses the challenges of managing security.
Chapter 13: Information Systems Development and Project Management	This chapter discusses some techniques of systems development and the challenges of managing the entire development process.
Chapter 14: Managing Data Resources	Data management challenges are discussed, along with an understanding of the modern database environment – its design, creation and use. Data warehouses are discussed.
Chapter 15: Business Process Integration and Enterprise Systems	The chapter begins with a discussion of complex business processes, and then shows how these can be implemented in Enterprise systems, including SCM and CRM systems.
Chapter 16: Decision Support Systems	This chapter outlines the technologies of decision support, business intelligence, analytics and the challenges of knowledge management.
Chapter 17: Artificial Intelligence	This chapter describes the origins and key concepts of AI. It discusses various techniques and methods used in AI, including several methods in machine learning. It explores the challenges of managing AI.

Theme 3: Social Aspects of IS	
Chapter 18: ICT for Development and E-Governance	Deployment of ICT across regions leads to development of the population. This chapter discusses this issue, along the issues of use of ICT by government to deliver services.
Chapter 19: The Society of the Internet	Social spaces on the Internet have grown on the basis of technologies such as search and wikis. This chapter discusses these technologies and the impact of these networks of people on society and organisations.
Chapter 20: Open Source Software	This chapter discusses the phenomenon of open source software – how it is built, why, and how organisations and individuals can benefit from using it.

ABOUT THE AUTHOR

Dr. Rahul De is the *Hewlett-Packard Chair Professor* of Information Systems at the Indian Institute of Management Bangalore (IIMB).

He has a B.Tech. from IIT Delhi, and an MBA from the Faculty of Management Studies, University of Delhi. He went on to join the doctoral program of the Katz Graduate School of Business, of the University of Pittsburgh, and obtained his PhD from there in 1993. His doctoral research was in applied Artificial Intelligence.

Since 1990, he has taught MIS and courses on related topics in the MIS field (such as Databases, Analytics, Artificial Intelligence, and ICT for Development) in various universities in the United States, India, Spain, France, Sweden and Norway. Prior to joining IIMB, he was an Associate Professor in Rider University in New Jersey, USA.

Dr. De's research interests span many areas of MIS and include e-governance, ICT for development, impact of open source software, and applied Artificial Intelligence. He has published over 70 articles in international journals, refereed conference proceedings and as chapters in books. He has co-authored three edited volumes. He collaborates with scholars and research groups from several countries around the world, including from Singapore, Sweden, Spain, the UK, USA, Brazil and Philippines. He has received several international awards and recognition for his research and teaching activities. These include:

1. *Best Professor in Information Systems* award at the Asia's Best B-School Awards ceremony in Suntec City, Singapore, in July 2010.
2. *Outstanding Paper Award* for a paper presented at the EGOV 2009 Conference in Linz, Austria, in September 2009.
3. *Rene Wagenaar Outstanding Paper Award* for a paper presented at the EGOV 2007 Conference, in Regensburg, Germany, in September 2007.

He serves on the Editorial Board of *Information & Management and Government Information Quarterly* journals, which are MIS journal. He also serves on the programme committees of several international conferences related to the MIS field. He was a member of the Board of Governors, IIMB, and currently serves on the Boards of the Institute for Development and Research in Banking Technology (IDRBT) and sflc.in.

TABLE OF CONTENTS

Preface to the Second Edition vii
Preface to the First Edition viii
About the Book ix
Acknowledgements x
Teaching with this Book xi
Special Features of the Book xii
Organisation of the Book xvii
About the Author xix
List of Figures xxxiii
List of Tables xxxix

PART I MIS AND ORGANISATIONS 1

Chapter 1 Organisations and Information Systems 3

Case Study: Information Systems at Tata Motors 5

1.1 Modern Organisation 7
- 1.1.1 IT-Enabled Organisation 7
- 1.1.2 Networked Organisation 7
- 1.1.3 Dispersed Organisation 8
- 1.1.4 Knowledge Organisation 8

1.2 Information Systems in Organisations 8
- 1.2.1 What are Information Systems? 8

1.3 Brief History of Computing 9
- 1.3.1 ENIAC: Way to Commercial Computers 9
- 1.3.2 Advent of Artificial Intelligence 10
- 1.3.3 Advent of Personal Computing 10
- 1.3.4 Free Software Movement 10
- 1.3.5 Advent of the Internet 11

1.4 The Role of the Internet 11
- 1.4.1 Internet and Web: They are Different 11
- 1.4.2 The Internet Changes Everything! 12

1.5 Managing in the Internet Era 13

1.6 Managing Information Systems in Organisations 13
- 1.6.1 The IT Interaction Model 13

1.7 Challenges for the Manager 18
- 1.7.1 What Information Systems to Build? 19
- 1.7.2 How Much to Spend on Information Systems? 19
- 1.7.3 What Level of Capabilities Should be Created with Information Systems? 19
- 1.7.4 How Fast and Accurate Should the Services Be? 20
- 1.7.5 What Security Levels are Required? 20
- 1.7.6 What IS Functions Should be on the Cloud? 20
- 1.7.7 What is the Technology Road Map for the Organisation? 21

Chapter Glossary 21
Review Questions 22
Research Questions 22
Further Reading 22

Chapter 2 IT and Innovation 23

Case Study: Ola Cabs 25

2.1 Innovation Theory 27
2.1.1 Moore's Law 27
2.1.2 Disruptive Innovation 28
2.1.3 Creative Destruction 28
2.1.4 Diffusion of Innovation 29
2.2 Innovation Impact 30
2.2.1 Innovation and Competition 30
2.2.2 Innovation Waves 31
2.3 Types of Business Innovations with IT 33
2.4 Management Issues: Challenges for Managers 35
Chapter Glossary 36
Review Questions 36
Research Questions 36
Further Reading 37

Chapter 3 Concepts of Management Information Systems 39

Case Study: Information Systems in the Indian Railways 41

3.1 Data and Information 43
3.1.1 Measuring Data 43
3.2 Information as a Resource 44
3.3 Information in Organisational Functions 46
3.4 Types of Information Technology 47
3.5 Types of Information Systems 48
3.5.1 Transaction Processing Systems 48
3.5.2 Management Information Systems 49
3.6 Decision Making with MIS 52
3.6.1 Tactical Decisions 52
3.6.2 Operational Decisions 52
3.6.3 Strategic Decisions 54
3.7 Communication in Organisations 56
3.7.1 Types of Communication 56
3.7.2 Examples of Communications in Organisations 57
3.7.3 Decision Making with Communication Technology 58
Chapter Glossary 58
Review Questions 59
Research Questions 59
Further Reading 59

Chapter 4 IT Strategy and Digital Goods 61

Case Study: Flipkart.com 63

4.1 The Competitive Environment of Business 65
4.1.1 Partnering for Mutual Benefit 65
4.1.2 Bargaining Power of Suppliers 66
4.1.3 Bargaining Power of Buyers and Customers 67
4.1.4 Barriers to Entry 68
4.1.5 Threat of Substitutes 68
4.1.6 Industry Regulations 69

4.2 Using IT for Competing 69
4.2.1 Competing on Low Cost 69
4.2.2 Competing on Differentiation 70
4.3 Information Goods 71
4.3.1 Properties of Information Goods 71
4.3.2 Technology Lock-in and Switching Costs 72
4.3.3 Network Externalities 73
4.3.4 Positive Feedback 74
4.3.5 Tippy Markets 75
4.4 Information Systems and Competitive Strategy 75
4.4.1 The Value Chain 77
4.4.2 Information Systems for Value Chain Activities 78
Chapter Glossary 79
Review Questions 79
Research Questions 80
Further Reading 80

Chapter 5 Electronic Commerce, Electronic Business, Electronic Governance 81

Case Study: mJunction 83

5.1 E-Commerce Technology 84
5.1.1 The Dotcom Boom and Bust 84
5.2 HTML and Email 85
5.2.1 Email 86
5.2.2 Networks: A Brief Introduction 88
5.2.3 Electronic Data Interchange (EDI) 89
5.2.4 Online Payment Technology 90
5.2.5 Mobile Commerce 96
5.3 Doing Business over the Internet 96
5.3.1 E-Commerce 96
5.3.2 Portals 97
5.3.3 Search Engines 97
5.3.4 Direct Selling 98
5.3.5 Auctions 100
5.3.6 Aggregators 100
5.4 E-Business 101
5.5 E-Governance 102
5.5.1 Services 103
5.5.2 Advantages of E-Governance 103
Chapter Glossary 104
Review Questions 104
Research Questions 104
Further Reading 104

Chapter 6 Managing Information Systems 105

Case Study: IT at ICICI Bank 107

6.1 Challenges of Managing the IT Function 109
6.1.1 Modern IT Environment 109
6.1.2 Centralisation versus Decentralisation 110
6.1.3 IT Security 114
6.1.4 Technology Selection 115

6.2 Vendor Management 116
6.2.1 Vendor Selection 116
6.2.2 Vendor Contracts and Service Levels 116
6.2.3 Ongoing Relationship Management 117
6.2.4 Vendor Retention or Termination 117
6.3 The Role of the CIO 118
6.3.1 Information Systems Plan 118
6.3.2 Vendor Coordination 119
6.3.3 Technology Updates 119
6.3.4 Return on Investment of Technology 119
6.4 IT Governance 120
Chapter Glossary 123
Review Questions 124
Research Questions 124
Further Reading 124

Chapter 7 Ethical and Social Issues 125

Case Study: Video Surveillance at Jindal Steel 127

7.1 Ethical Issues 128
7.1.1 Privacy 128
7.1.2 Workplace Monitoring 131
7.1.3 Power over Users 133
7.2 Social Issues 135
7.2.1 Workplace Behaviour and Health 135
7.2.2 De-Skilling and Alienation 138
7.2.3 Telecommuting 139
7.2.4 E-Waste 140
7.3 Dark Side of IT 142
7.3.1 Technostress 142
7.3.2 Misuse of IT 143
7.3.3 Impact of Technostress 143
Chapter Glossary 144
Review Questions 145
Research Questions 145
Further Reading 145

Chapter 8 Managing Green IT and Smart Cities 147

Case Study: Aircel 149

8.1 Introduction: The Green Imperative 151
8.2 Greenhouse Gases and Global Warming 151
8.3 Carbon Footprint 152
8.4 What is Green IT? 153
8.5 Green Practices in Hardware Design and Manufacture 153
8.6 Green Practices in Software Design 154
8.6.1 Data Efficiency 154
8.6.2 Context-Aware Design 155
8.7 Green Practices in IT Use 155
8.8 IT for Green Practices 156
8.9 Monitoring Value Chain Activities 156
8.10 Smart Cities 157

8.10.1 Historical Origins 157
8.10.2 Facilities of Smart Cities 158
8.10.3 Smart Environment 161
8.10.4 Smart Buildings 163
8.10.5 Smart Living 164
8.10.6 Smart Governance 165
8.11 Management Issues: Challenges for Managers 165
Chapter Glossary 166
Review Questions 166
Research Questions 167
Further Reading 167

PART II FUNDAMENTALS OF IT 169

Chapter 9 Information Technology Infrastructure and Choices 171

Case Study: IT Infrastructure Virtualisation at Tribhovandas Bhimji Zaveri 173

9.1 What is the IT Infrastructure? 175
9.2 IT Infrastructure Decisions 176
9.2.1 IT Infrastructure Questions: Business Needs 176
9.2.2 IT Infrastructure Questions: Technology Issues 176
9.2.3 The Technology Hype Cycle 177
9.3 Infrastructure Components 178
9.3.1 Hardware 178
9.3.2 Software 186
9.4 Networks 192
9.5 Solutions 192
9.5.1 Virtualisation 193
9.5.2 Enterprise Systems 194
9.5.3 IT Outsourcing 194
Chapter Glossary 196
Review Questions 197
Research Questions 197
Further Reading 198

Chapter 10 Cloud Computing and Internet-of-Things 199

Case Study: IDOS Accounting Software on the Cloud 201

10.1 Cloud Computing 203
10.1.1 What is Cloud Computing? 203
10.1.2 Advantages and Features of Cloud Computing 204
10.1.3 Types of Cloud Infrastructure 207
10.1.4 Cloud Service Models 208
10.1.5 Challenges of Migrating to the Cloud 210
10.1.6 Cloud Technologies 211
10.1.7 Economic Rationale for Cloud Computing 213
10.2 Internet-of-Things 213
10.2.1 What is Internet-of-Things? 213
10.2.2 Examples of IoT 215
10.2.3 Managing IoT Systems 215

10.2.4 Sensors and Actuators 216
10.2.5 IoT Architecture 217
10.3 Challenges of Cloud Computing and IoT 219
Chapter Glossary 220
Review Questions 220
Research Questions 221
Further Reading 221

Chapter 11 Networking and Telecommunication 223

Case Study: AirJaldi 225

11.1 Life of a Packet 227
11.2 Structure of the Network 228
11.2.1 Networks in the Organisation 228
11.2.2 Network Components 231
11.2.3 The Internet 234
11.2.4 What Has to be Managed? 236
11.3 Network Services and Layers 238
11.3.1 Connection-Oriented Services 238
11.3.2 Connectionless Services 238
11.3.3 Protocols 238
11.3.4 Layers 241
11.3.5 Ethernet Topologies 242
Chapter Glossary 243
Review Questions 244
Research Questions 244
Further Reading 245

Chapter 12 Information Systems Security and Control 247

Case Study: The Stuxnet Worm 249

12.1 Threats to the Organisation 251
12.1.1 Malware 251
12.1.2 Cracking and Espionage 253
12.1.3 Phishing and Identity Theft 254
12.1.4 Denial-of-Service Attack 255
12.2 Technologies for Handling Security 257
12.2.1 Encryption 257
12.2.2 Public-Key Cryptography 258
12.2.3 Firewall 260
12.2.4 Virtual Private Network 261
12.2.5 Wireless Technology 262
12.3 Managing Security 265
12.3.1 Securing the Network 265
12.3.2 Securing the Client 266
12.3.3 Creating a Secure Environment 267
12.3.4 Security Audit and Risk Assessment 268
12.3.5 Disaster Recovery Planning 269
Chapter Glossary 269
Review Questions 270
Research Questions 270
Further Reading 271

Chapter 13 Information Systems Development and Project Management 273

Case Study: AMIS for Farmers in Bangladesh 275

13.1 Analysis of Business Processes 277
13.1.1 What is a Business Process? 277
13.1.2 The Business Analyst 277
13.1.3 Analysis Tools 277
13.1.4 Data Flow Diagrams 279
13.1.5 Use Cases 282
13.2 Life Cycle Models 284
13.2.1 Waterfall Model 285
13.2.2 The Waterfall Model in Perspective 289
13.2.3 Alternatives to the Waterfall Model 290
13.2.4 Agile Methods 292
13.3 Software Project Management 295
13.3.1 Top Management Support 295
13.3.2 Team Composition 295
13.3.3 Vendor Selection 296
13.3.4 Project Estimation 296
13.3.5 Function Point Analysis 297
Chapter Glossary 298
Review Questions 299
Research Questions 299
Further Reading 299

Chapter 14 Managing Data Resources 301

Case Study: Unique Identification Number in India 303

14.1 The Need for Data Management 305
14.1.1 History of Data Use 305
14.2 Challenge of Data Management 305
14.2.1 Data Independence 305
14.2.2 Reduced Data Redundancy 306
14.2.3 Data Consistency 306
14.2.4 Data Access 306
14.2.5 Data Administration 306
14.2.6 Managing Concurrency 306
14.2.7 Managing Security 306
14.2.8 Recovery from Crashes 307
14.2.9 Application Development 307
14.3 Database Concepts 307
14.3.1 Fields, Records and Files 307
14.3.2 Basic Architecture 308
14.4 Database Design 311
14.4.1 Elements of Databases 312
14.4.2 SQL 320
14.4.3 Commercial DBMS 321
14.4.4 E-R Diagrams 322
14.4.5 Normalisation 325
14.5 Data Warehouses 326
14.5.1 Data Mining Uses 327

14.6 Big Data 328
14.6.1 Volume 329
14.6.2 Velocity 329
14.6.3 Variety 330
14.6.4 Veracity 330
Chapter Glossary 331
Review Questions 332
Research Questions 332
Further Reading 332

Chapter 15 Business Process Integration and Enterprise Systems 333

Case Study: ERP via the Cloud at Oxford Book Store 335

15.1 Business Process Integration 337
15.1.1 Business Processes 337
15.1.2 Example of a Complex Process 338
15.2 Motivation for Enterprise Systems 340
15.3 Enterprise Resource Planning Systems 342
15.3.1 Finance and Accounting Module 343
15.3.2 Human Resource Management Module 344
15.3.3 Manufacturing and Operations Module 344
15.3.4 Sales and Marketing Module 344
15.4 Supply Chain Management Systems 345
15.5 Customer Relationship Management Systems 348
15.6 Challenges of Enterprise Systems Implementations 350
15.6.1 Managing the Implementation 350
15.7 International Information Systems 352
15.7.1 Outsourcing and Off-Shoring 353
Chapter Glossary 355
Review Questions 355
Research Questions 356
Further Reading 356

Chapter 16 Decision Support Systems 357

Case Study: Revenue Optimisation at Taj Hotels 359

16.1 Decision Support Systems 361
16.1.1 MIS and DSS 362
16.1.2 Decision Making 362
16.1.3 Types of Decisions 363
16.2 Components of a DSS 364
16.2.1 The Database 364
16.2.2 The Model Base 364
16.2.3 The User Interface 365
16.2.4 History of DSS 365
16.3 Analytics and Business Intelligence 367
16.3.1 Business Intelligence Techniques 368
16.4 Knowledge Management 373
16.4.1 Knowledge Life Cycle 374
16.4.2 Strategies for Knowledge Management 375
16.4.3 Technologies for Knowledge Management 377

Chapter Glossary 379
Review Questions 379
Research Questions 380
Case Question 380
Further Reading 380

Chapter 17 Artificial Intelligence 381

Case Study: IBM's Watson 383

17.1 Introduction and History of AI 385
17.2 The Turing Test 386
17.3 Representation and Search 387
17.3.1 Example of Representation and Search 387
17.3.2 Breadth-First and Depth-First Search 390
17.3.3 Planning Systems 391
17.3.4 General Problem Solving 392
17.4 Machine Learning 392
17.4.1 Neural Networks 392
17.4.2 Induction Learning 395
17.4.3 Bayesian Learning 397
17.4.4 Learning from Analogies 398
17.4.5 Genetic Algorithms 399
17.4.6 Reinforcement Learning 399
17.4.7 Limitations of AI and Machine Learning 400
17.5 Implications for Managers 401
Chapter Glossary 401
Review Questions 402
Research Questions 402
Further Reading 402

PART III SOCIAL ASPECTS OF IS 405

Chapter 18 ICT for Development and E-Governance 407

Case Study: The Bhoomi Land Records System of Karnataka 409

18.1 ICT for Development 411
18.1.1 What is Development? 411
18.1.2 The Premise of ICT for Development 412
18.1.3 The Digital Divide 412
18.1.4 The Challenges of Remote Areas 413
18.2 Types of ICT Interventions 413
18.2.1 Informational 413
18.2.2 Transactional 414
18.2.3 Political 414
18.2.4 Educational 414
18.2.5 Sustenance 415
18.3 Examples of ICT for Development Projects 415
18.3.1 Radio Sangham 415
18.3.2 Video Volunteers 416
18.3.3 The e-Tuktuk Project 417

18.4 E-Governance Concepts 417
18.4.1 Stages of E-Governance 418
18.4.2 Stakeholders 419
18.4.3 Economic Assessment 419
18.4.4 Developmental Assessment 419
18.4.5 Implementation Challenges 420
18.5 E-Government 423
18.6 E-Participation 423
Chapter Glossary 425
Review Questions 425
Research Questions 425
Further Reading 426

Chapter 19 The Society of the Internet 427

Case Study: Social Media in Political Uprising 429

19.1 Social Dynamics of the Internet 431
19.2 Services of the Internet 431
19.2.1 Search 431
19.2.2 Blogs 433
19.2.3 Social Networks 433
19.2.4 Peer-to-Peer Sharing 434
19.2.5 Streaming Sites 435
19.2.6 Virtual Worlds 436
19.3 Technology of the Internet 437
19.3.1 Web Pages 437
19.3.2 Wiki 437
19.3.3 Twitter 439
19.3.4 Rating 439
19.3.5 Tagging/Folksonomies 440
19.3.6 Mashups 440
19.4 Social Issues 440
19.4.1 Identity 440
19.4.2 Privacy 441
19.4.3 Media Impact 441
19.4.4 Collaboration 442
19.4.5 Emergence of Order 443
19.5 Social Networks in the Enterprise 443
Chapter Glossary 444
Review Questions 444
Research Questions 445
Further Reading 445

Chapter 20 Open Source Software 447

Case Study: JustDial and Open Source 449

20.1 The Concept of Open Source Software 451
20.1.1 Creation of Proprietary Software 451
20.1.2 Creation of Open Source Software 451
20.1.3 Who Creates Open Source Software and Why? 452
20.1.4 History of Free and Open Source Software 453
20.1.5 Debate Around Open Source Software 454
20.1.6 Popular Packages 455

20.2 Open Source Licences 458
20.2.1 GNU General Public Licence (GPL) 458
20.2.2 BSD Licence 459
20.2.3 Apache Licence 459
20.3 Open Source in Business and Government 459
20.3.1 Open Source in Business 459
20.3.2 Open Source in Government 461
20.4 Open Data Standards and the Open Community 461
20.4.1 Open Data Standards 461
20.4.2 The Open Community 463
Chapter Glossary 464
Review Questions 465
Research Questions 465
Further Reading 465

Appendix A 467

Appendix B 503

Index 509

LIST OF FIGURES

Chapter 1

Figure 1.1 Exchange of information between Tata Motors (TM) and its parts vendor. The diagram only shows information flows and not the flows of physical goods. 6
Figure 1.2 The evolution of computing over the decades. 11
Figure 1.3 Growth of internet users from 1993 to 2014, in millions of users. 12
Figure 1.4 The IT interaction model. 14
Figure 1.5 The hierarchy and matrix organisational structures. 17

Chapter 2

Figure 2.1 Number of transistors included on different generations of chips made by Intel Corporation. 27
Figure 2.2 Rogers' Model of Diffusion of Innovation. 29
Figure 2.3 Market share held by the top 20 US firms in low and high IT industries in the period 1965–2005. 31
Figure 2.4 The innovation wave complex. 32

Chapter 3

Figure 3.1 Increase in passenger traffic for the Indian Railways, from 1950 to 2014 (in millions). 41
Figure 3.2 Data stored in computer memory. Each cell contains a 1 or a 0. 43
Figure 3.3 Percent of tickets sales in a 12-h period (simulated numbers). 45
Figure 3.4 Hierarchy structure of Indian Railways. This is a simplified view of the real hierarchy. 46
Figure 3.5 Components of modern information technology infrastructure in an organisation. 48
Figure 3.6 A transaction performed on an automated teller machine (ATM). The right column shows the data used in this transaction. 49
Figure 3.7 A screenshot of an ESS (simulated). 51
Figure 3.8 Travelling salesman problem. The figure shows the distances between seven cities in India. 53
Figure 3.9 (a) Synchronous and (b) asynchronous communication modes. 57

Chapter 4

Figure 4.1 Competitive environment of business in the automobile industry. 65
Figure 4.2 Bargaining power of a firm vis-à-vis its utility supplier. 67
Figure 4.3 E-commerce is a substitute for traditional commerce. In the figure, the wholesaler and retailer are eliminated. 69
Figure 4.4 Various personal computer platforms consisting of different hardware, operating system and software applications. 72
Figure 4.5 Switching costs incurred while switching from a Windows-Intel platform to a Linux-Intel platform. 73
Figure 4.6 (a) Positive feedback influencing users of Facebook. (b) The S curve of growth of users. 74
Figure 4.7 Production of Betamax versus VHS players. 75
Figure 4.8 Porters' value chain with primary and support or secondary activities. 77
Figure 4.9 Examples of information systems used to support activities of the value chain. 79

Chapter 5

Figure 5.1 The dotcom boom–dotcom bust period is depicted through fluctuation in the prices of IT stocks in the BSE from February 1999 through October 2004. Early in 2000, the sensex peaked, and then crashed, sinking to a low in 2001, after which it climbed again. The figure shows the closing value of the index of IT stocks in the Sensex. 85

Figure 5.2 The original email facility simply copied a file, the email message, from the sender's account to the receiver's account. 87

Figure 5.3 Email sent from one computer on a network to another on a different network. 87

Figure 5.4 Intranets connect computers within an organisation. Extranets link organisations together. Each organisation on its own connects with the internet. 89

Figure 5.5 The first page of the Indian Railways ticket booking website. 91

Figure 5.6 This page of the Indian Railways ticket booking website requests confirmation of travel destination and date. 92

Figure 5.7 This page of the Indian Railways ticket booking website displays the availability of reserved seats on different dates. 93

Figure 5.8 The form on the Indian Railways ticket booking website for entering details about the passengers. 94

Figure 5.9 This page of the Indian Railways ticket booking website displays the various online payment options available. 95

Figure 5.10 Various types of e-commerce - between businesses, government departments and citizens or consumers. 99

Chapter 6

Figure 6.1 Effects of introducing IT in a firm. 109

Figure 6.2 Centralised versus decentralised IT management. 111

Figure 6.3 Criteria for selecting information technology in an organisation. 115

Figure 6.4 The IT governance at most firms and at top performing firms. Shaded cells indicate the decision rights of the archetypes. 123

Chapter 7

Figure 7.1 The octagonal Panopticon. Along the periphery of the structure are the rooms. Each room opens towards the centre and can be fully observed from the observation tower. A room at the tower top is covered with see-through mirrors which make it impossible for the room occupants to verify whether there are observers in the tower. 132

Figure 7.2 Exercise of power by systems professionals. 134

Figure 7.3 Awareness of power exercise by users and systems professionals. 135

Figure 7.4 Resistance to systems. 136

Figure 7.5 Per capita annual paper consumption (in kilogram) since 1971, worldwide and in India. 138

Figure 7.6 E-waste receiving cities in India and China. 141

Chapter 8

Figure 8.1 The increase in the quantity of carbon dioxide present in the atmosphere as measured in Hawaii, USA. The measure is parts of carbon dioxide per million by volume of atmosphere. The data shows the average across all months in the years 1958–2008. 152

Figure 8.2 Diversion of traffic before a busy intersection. Traffic is diverted from intersection A, to prevent a buildup at B. 160

Figure 8.3 A smart building contains sensors to collect data on and control lighting, heating, ventilation, personnel movement and occupation within the building. It has facilities for energy generation - solar, wind and electrical energy - in the basement and on the rooftop. The building has sensors for parking, indicating occupancy levels of parking. 164

Chapter 9

Figure 9.1 Gartner's hype cycle — an illustration with examples drawn from the year 2017. 177

Figure 9.2 Computer architecture. 179
Figure 9.3 The machine cycle. 179
Figure 9.4 Trends in desktop and laptop sales in India 2004–2015, in lakhs of units (one lakh = one hundred thousand). 181
Figure 9.5 Trends in desktop, laptop and tablet sales worldwide 2010–2015, in millions of units. 182
Figure 9.6 Images of a (a) floppy disk, (b) compact disk, (c) flash memory drive and (d) tablet PC. 184
Figure 9.7 (a) iPad and (b) Simputer. 185
Figure 9.8 The operating system loads and unloads tasks in the main memory (RAM) and manages them. 186
Figure 9.9 Use of virtualisation software allows many CPUs to be used together to increase capacity and improve services. 193

Chapter 10

Figure 10.1 Hosted infrastructure. Here the organisation owns and maintains its own infrastructure of servers and draws on some web-based services from the internet. 203
Figure 10.2 Cloud infrastructure: Here an organisation draws on server and storage resources from the cloud and maintains a minimal infrastructure internally. 204
Figure 10.3 Software defined networking. 212
Figure 10.4 Containers reduce the complexity of virtualisation systems. 212
Figure 10.5 IT capacity creation over time versus capacity expansion with the cloud. 213
Figure 10.6 The Internet-of-Things consists of things, which are sensors and actuators, data from the things, software to analyse the data and the internet. 214
Figure 10.7 Four layers of the IoT architecture. 218

Chapter 11

Figure 11.1 Path of packets from source to destination. A packet travels through many devices in the organisation in which it originates before moving to the internet. 228
Figure 11.2 Packet switching versus circuit switching. 229
Figure 11.3 LAN versus WAN connections. 231
Figure 11.4 LAN twisted pair cable. 232
Figure 11.5 Hubs and switches connected to the router. 233
Figure 11.6 A router connects the organisation to the internet. 234
Figure 11.7 Internet service providers (ISPs) at different tiers. 235
Figure 11.8 Example of a protocol for communication between two web servers. 239
Figure 11.9 Star topology. All devices on the network are connected to a central hub. 243
Figure 11.10 The bus topology. 243

Chapter 12

Figure 12.1 Image of the real website of the Indian Income Tax Department. 255
Figure 12.2 Image of the fake website of the Indian Income Tax Department (as of June 2011). 255
Figure 12.3 Denial-of-service attack. 256
Figure 12.4 Distributed DoS attack. 256
Figure 12.5 Examples of encryption of English alphabetic characters. 258
Figure 12.6 Sending a message with a public-key encryption. 258
Figure 12.7 The problem of impersonation with public-key encryption. 259
Figure 12.8 Authentication with public-key encryption. 260
Figure 12.9 Firewall in a typical organisation. 260
Figure 12.10 Wireless mesh networking. 263
Figure 12.11 Typical layout for a demilitarised zone (DMZ). 265

Chapter 13

Figure 13.1 Example of activity flow diagram. 278
Figure 13.2 Flow chart symbols. 278
Figure 13.3 Example of flowchart. 279
Figure 13.4 Elements of the data flow diagram. 280
Figure 13.5 Example of data flow diagram. 280
Figure 13.6 Course Registration System - data flow diagram. 282
Figure 13.7 Large organisation hardware/software cost trends. 284
Figure 13.8 The Waterfall Model. 285
Figure 13.9 The eclipse case tool. 287
Figure 13.10 Cost to correct errors detected at different phases of life cycle. 290
Figure 13.11 Rapid prototyping. 291
Figure 13.12 The spiral model of software development. 291
Figure 13.13 The scrum process. 294

Chapter 14

Figure 14.1 The basic elements of a database - fields; records and files. 308
Figure 14.2 Client-server architecture of a database. 309
Figure 14.3 Three-tier database architecture. 310
Figure 14.4 Distributed databases with homogeneous and heterogeneous architectures. 310
Figure 14.5 The opening screen of the base DBMS showing the 'Classic Models' database. 311
Figure 14.6 The design view of the customers table. 313
Figure 14.7 Form for entering data in the customers table. 314
Figure 14.8 Form for changing data in some fields of the customers table. 315
Figure 14.9 Design of query for identifying customers from finland in the customers table. 316
Figure 14.10 Results of running the query about customers from finland on the customers table. 317
Figure 14.11 Views of data using queries. 317
Figure 14.12 Query that joins two tables 'Customers' and 'Orders' to select those customers whose orders have not been shipped. The results of the query are also shown. 318
Figure 14.13 Schema for classic Models database. The numbers of the relations indicate cardinality (covered later). 319
Figure 14.14 A report fragment showing 'Orders not Shipped'. 319
Figure 14.15 Data dictionary for the customers table. 320
Figure 14.16 Customers entity with attributes. 323
Figure 14.17 E-R diagram showing relationship of the Student entity with the Course entity. The relationship is 'takes'. The cardinality shows that students can take 0-6 courses, while each course can be taken by 0-75 students. 324
Figure 14.18 Different types of relationships between entities. 324
Figure 14.19 Wordle cloud for text from part III of the constitution of India pertaining to fundamental rights. 329

Chapter 15

Figure 15.1 Example of complex process of an online book order and execution involving many departments and two external organisations. 340
Figure 15.2 Motivation for enterprise systems. 341
Figure 15.3 Important modules of an ERP package supported by the central database. 342
Figure 15.4 Depiction of SAP components that support business functions and processes that cut across departments and organisations. SAP ERP and SCM packages are shown. 343

Figure 15.5 A supply chain showing Tier-1 and Tier-2 upstream and downstream partners. Upstream and downstream partners are with reference to the client organisation. 345
Figure 15.6 Depiction of the Bullwhip effect. Small spike in demand at the retailer results in very high increase in inventories at the end of the supply chain. 347
Figure 15.7 Issues having a bearing on the successful implementation of an enterprise system. 350
Figure 15.8 Differences between multinational and transnational organisations. 352

Chapter 16

Figure 16.1 Example of DSS inputs and outputs for decision making at the shop floor of a manufacturing facility. 361
Figure 16.2 Phases of problem solving in the Intelligence-Design-Choice Model. 362
Figure 16.3 Components of a DSS: The database, the model base and the user interface. 364
Figure 16.4 The neural network for loan processing problem. The input layer consists of seven nodes. The output layer consists of one node. The inner layers of nodes are called the hidden layers. 369
Figure 16.5 The neural network for stock price prediction. The network consists of five input nodes and one output node. 370
Figure 16.6 The decision tree for loan approval. 371
Figure 16.7 A simpler decision tree for a loan approval process. 371
Figure 16.8 Bubble chart of populations of different states of India. 372
Figure 16.9 Value of knowledge. 374

Chapter 17

Figure 17.1 Arrangement for Turing test. 386
Figure 17.2 The farmer's problem. 387
Figure 17.3 First 4 states of farmer's problem. 388
Figure 17.4 States (5) and (6), reached from (4). 388
Figure 17.5 States (7) and (8), reached from (6). 389
Figure 17.6 States (9), (10) and (11) reached from (7); and states (12), (13) and (14) reached from (8). 389
Figure 17.7 States (15) through (20). 389
Figure 17.8 States (21) through (24). State (24) is the goal state. 390
Figure 17.9 A neuron or node calculates the weighted sum of the inputs and passes it to a transfer function. 393
Figure 17.10 The three layers of a neural network. 393
Figure 17.11 Decision tree for loan granting problem. 396
Figure 17.12 The problem of stacking blocks. 400

Chapter 18

Figure 18.1 Stages of e-governance evolution. 418

Chapter 19

Figure 19.1 Google's Page Rank Method. Page B has the highest relative rank (38) as it has the highest number of pages pointing to it. Page C has only one page linking to it, which is Page B, but as Page B has a high rank, so Page C also has a high rank. 432
Figure 19.2 Growth in the number of Facebook users in (millions). 434
Figure 19.3 Image of a galaxy classified on Galaxy Zoo. The grey object in the bottom is an unclassified element that prompted further research. 442

Chapter 20

Figure 20.1	Costs of owning open source versus proprietary software.	455
Figure 20.2	Part of the message sent out by Linus Torvalds calling for participation in the Linux project.	456
Figure 20.3	Image of a Linux desktop.	457
Figure 20.4	Dual-licencing business model for open source software.	460

Chapter 3

Table 3.1 Important Facts about the Indian Railways (2007) 41
Table 3.2 Measures of Computer Memory Capacity 44
Table 3.3 Data Regarding Ticket Purchase Transaction 45
Table 3.4 Kinds of Decisions, Their Time and Horizon, and the Employees Who Make Such Decisions 55

Chapter 4

Table 4.1 Use of IS to Support Competitive Strategy 76

Chapter 5

Table 5.1 Some Statistics on Email Usage 88

Chapter 6

Table 6.1 Change in Location of Banking Transactions over 4 Years for ICICI Bank 108
Table 6.2 Downtime for Different Levels of Service 117
Table 6.3 Five Categories of Decisions on IT Governance 121
Table 6.4 Decisions Rights by Governance Archetypes in All Firms 122
Table 6.5 Decisions Rights by Governance Archetypes in Top Performing Firms 123

Chapter 7

Table 7.1 Health Effects of Some E-Waste Pollutants 140

Chapter 8

Table 8.1 Power Consumption by a Hard Disk Drive in Different States 154
Table 8.2 Steps to Reduce Power Consumption in Laptop and Desktop Computers 155
Table 8.3 Growth of Population in Six Major Cities in India, in the Decade 2001–11 158

Chapter 9

Table 9.1 Computer CPU Components and Their Meanings 180

Chapter 10

Table 10.1 Comparison of Three Kinds of Cloud Services – IaaS, PaaS and SaaS 210
Table 10.2 Different Kinds of Sensors and Their Uses 216
Table 10.3 Types of Actuators and Their Uses 217

Chapter 11

Table 11.1 Network Layers and Their Functions 242

Chapter 12

Table 12.1 Economic Losses Incurred from Cybercrime across the World 251
Table 12.2 Examples of Keys, and How the Plaintext Is Converted to Ciphertext 257
Table 12.3 Example of a Fair Use Policy Statement at a University (a Hypothetical University) 268

Chapter 13

Table 13.1 Example of a Use Case 283

Chapter 14

Table 14.1 Two Records of a Student File 308
Table 14.2 Features of Commercial DBMS 321

LIST OF TABLES

Table 14.3 Types of Cardinality for Relationships between Entities 324
Table 14.4 Data for an invoice 325
Table 14.5 Data Converted to 1NF 325
Table 14.6 Velocity of Data from Different Sources. Data pertain to 2016 unless otherwise noted 329

Chapter 15

Table 15.1 Manual and Online Processes of Buying a Cinema Ticket 338

Chapter 16

Table 16.1 Differences between MIS and DSS 362
Table 16.2 Customer payment data 366
Table 16.3 Pivot Table Showing Individual Customer Payments 366

Chapter 17

Table 17.1 Sample Values for Weights and Data Inputs 393
Table 17.2 Sample Weights and Data for Training a Neural Network 394
Table 17.3 Data on Bank Loan Granted in 14 Different Cases 396
Table 17.4 Case Examples for Bank Loan Grants 398

Chapter 18

Table 18.1 Comparison of Per Capita Income and ICT Penetration in Four Countries 412

Chapter 19

Table 19.1 Details about Wikipedia, as of December 2017 438
Table 19.2 Number of Wikipedia Articles in Major Indian languages by December 2017 439

Part I

MIS AND ORGANISATIONS

Chapter 1 Organisations and Information Systems

Chapter 2 IT and Innovation

Chapter 3 Concepts of Management Information Systems

Chapter 4 IT Strategy and Digital Goods

Chapter 5 Electronic Commerce, Electronic Business, Electronic Governance

Chapter 6 Managing Information Systems

Chapter 7 Ethical and Social Issues

Chapter 8 Managing Green IT and Smart Cities

CHAPTER 1

Organisations and Information Systems

Learning Objectives

After completing this chapter, you will be able to:

- Get an overview of the modern organisation
- Understand information systems in organisations
- Learn to manage information systems in organisations

This first chapter introduces basic concepts of the subject. The organisation is defined as a collection of actors engaged in interactions that serve a common broader goal. An essential component of this organisation is its information systems (IS) that bind the organisation internally as well as enables its interactions with the outside world through the internet. Information systems originated with the invention of computers, software and networks. Various kinds of specialised computers and software have evolved that help organisations with different tasks. The advent of the internet has especially changed the way organisations operate and how they have to be managed.

Information systems in an organisation have to be understood as artefacts that interact with the people of the organisation. Their presence has both short-term and long-term consequences, and these effects are moderated by the culture and processes within the organisation. The modern manager has to make many decisions regarding IS, such as determining what services to provide, how much to spend and how to secure the systems.

Each chapter in the book will contain a mind map to show the chapter topics. The figure not only depicts the central ideas but also highlights questions covered in this chapter. A mind map is a diagram with bubbles linked with lines. The bubbles contain the concepts and the lines show how the concepts are related to each other.

MIND MAP OF CHAPTER TOPICS

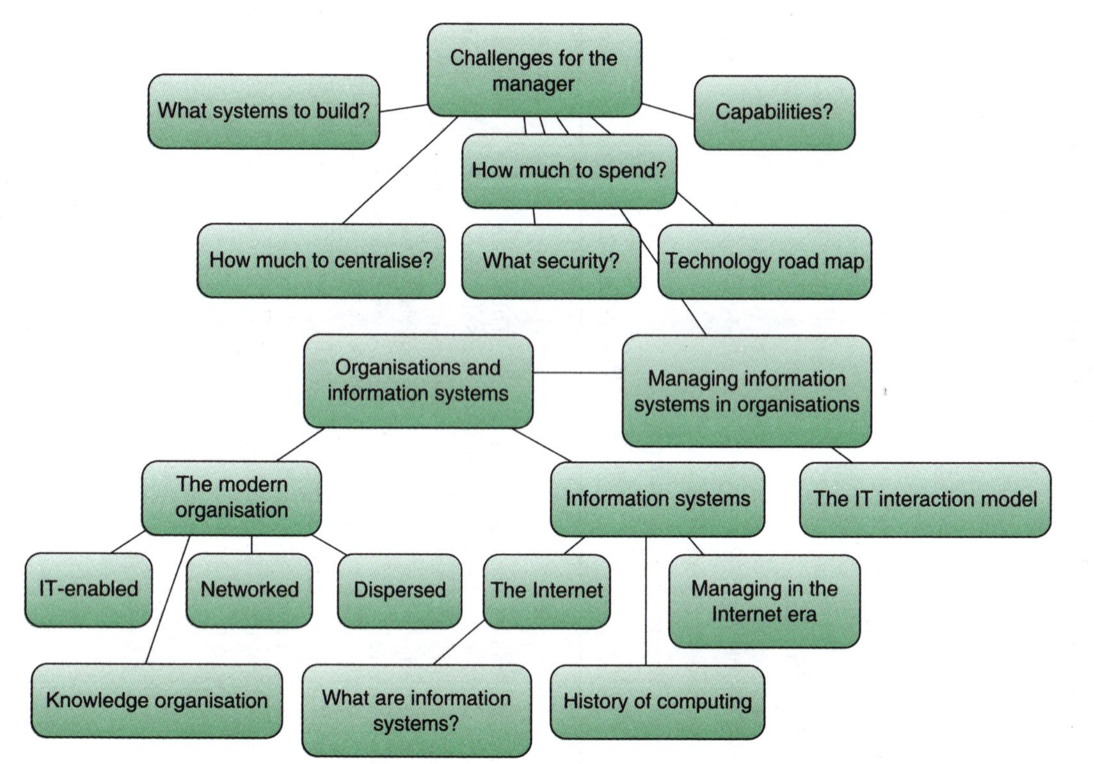

Tata Motors is one of India's largest automobile manufacturers. They make a range of automobiles including commercial trucks, passenger cars, utility vehicles, commercial passenger cars and defence vehicles. In the financial year 2008–2009, they had consolidated revenues of Rs 709 billion (about USD 16 billion). The company manufactures its automobiles in several plants located in Pune and five other towns in India. It markets its products not only in India and the Indian subcontinent, but also across the world in Europe, Africa, and North and South America, and East Asia.

Tata Motors gained worldwide prominence when, in 2009, it launched the Tata Nano, the lowest cost passenger car in the world. The firm had to face considerable challenges in the launch of the Nano, as there was political opposition to the physical site they had chosen. There was also a lot of media attention on the potential success of the car. The Nano was launched on schedule and in accordance with the planned cost targets.

Tata Motors relies extensively on an infrastructure of advanced information systems (IS) to run its business. This infrastructure consists of many computers, a network connecting all the computers, and complex software that stores and processes data. The IS act as a digital nervous system that transmits information across the various offices and branches of the firm, connecting its suppliers, shop-floor workers, managers, retailers and customers. It informs the employees about the activities of the firm, keeps track of material used and needed, accounts for money spent and money received, reports about customer purchases and relays data about service needs to various parties.

The IS at Tata Motors enable managers to view their business and operations in a comprehensive manner and to take decisions accordingly. This is made possible by specific IS capabilities and functions.

Tata Motors has a large network of vendors and suppliers who supply the components that are used to assemble the automobiles. Typically, the firm has over 2000 vendors at any time. These vendors receiving information about component needs at the production facility have to be informed of specific deliveries, have to be paid, and have to be informed about parts delivered, among other things. Vendors too have to inform Tata Motors about their supply position, their deliveries, payments received, balance due, etc. An IS at Tata Motors, referred to as the supply chain management system, is used to both receive and send information to the vendors and keep track of all these exchanges. This system is quite beneficial to Tata Motors as it has increased efficiencies as compared to the manual method by which the same tasks were performed earlier. For example, the time required to pay vendors has reduced from 48 to 24 h with the help of the system. An example of a typical transaction in the supply chain management system is outlined below.

Consider a situation in which Tata Motors has to manufacture about 100 passenger cars of a particular model in a two-week period. For this it has to obtain a part, say door handles, from a vendor. The steps required to complete this acquisition consist of several transactions, each of which is a step in the total assembly process. Broadly, these steps are:

1. The company informs its production schedule for the particular passenger car to the supplier. This will be in the form of a production plan that states how many parts will be required on any given day in a two-week period, the inventories that have to be maintained and the deadlines by which the parts have to be received.
2. The supplier will use this information to evaluate their own inventory. If they already have some parts that they can despatch, they will inform Tata Motors accordingly. If they have to manufacture a part, which will require time, then they may inform the client of their own schedule of manufacture so that Tata Motors is aware of their schedules. The details entered by the supplier in the system will automatically be reflected in Tata Motors' internal reports.
3. The supplier despatches a truck with a portion of the required parts. The information related to the time of despatch, the number of parts being sent, the identity of the truck, and the details of the documents carried by the truck (such as the shipping invoice) are entered into the system.

4. When the truck arrives at the Tata Motors plant, the supplies are checked and this information is recorded in the system. The supplier is informed of the receipt of goods.
5. The parts are moved to the shop floor and checked for quality. Once the quality check is completed, the parts are stored in the inventory at Tata Motors and the records are updated to show the new levels. The system also generates a message for the accounting system to pay the vendor.
6. The payment system checks the amount of payment to be made and informs a local bank to make the payment. This payment is done automatically and the account of the vendor is credited with the amount. Manual checking is only done if there is a surplus or deficit with the account of the vendor and an alteration in the payment account is required.

The exchange of information between Tata Motors and one of its vendors concerning parts supply is depicted in Fig. 1.1.

For Tata Motors the IS not only enables the flow of information between the firm and its vendors, it also enables all the firm's activities to flow smoothly. Information required *for* the activities and *about* the activities is managed by the IS.

Tata Motors also uses an IS to manage its marketing channel. The firm has an extensive network of over 2000 dealer partners in India and abroad, and in 2009 had about 30,000 computers connected to their system. The dealers sell and service Tata Motors automobiles. Dealers report about orders, sales, payments, deliveries, service requests and other data about their business to Tata Motors through the IS. Tata Motors has to inform dealers about delivery of vehicles, shipping notices, amounts received and amounts billed through the system.

Information from the dealers about demand for products helps Tata Motors plan its production schedule. The information systems give precise information about what products are demanded, and where and when they have to be delivered. This information helps the firm understand its market better, plan for advertising and promotion campaigns, and see patterns of demand over the years. The system also helps the firm design its cars as they are able to learn about customer preferences for features, such as the seating styles preferred, engine capacities preferred, colours preferred, etc. Tata Motors can use such information to design its cars according to market needs and also design its promotion campaigns.

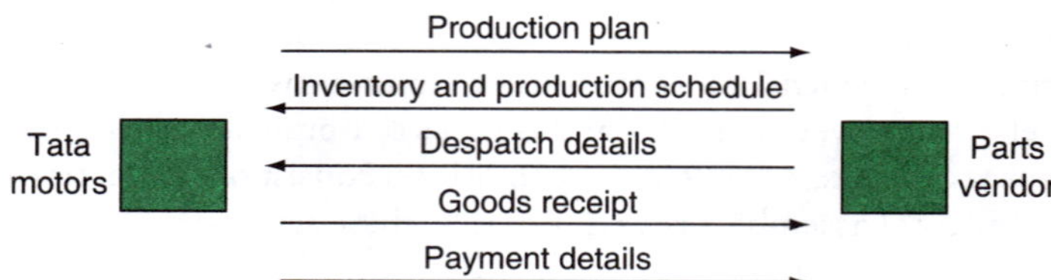

FIGURE 1.1 Exchange of information between Tata Motors (TM) and its parts vendor. The diagram only shows information flows and not the flows of physical goods.

1.1 MODERN ORGANISATION

The world today consists of many *organisations* that have collections of people with shared goals. Examples of organisations are private companies that have a goal of making and selling some product or a department in a government office that has some specific goals to fulfil. The organisation is given a name and usually has a physical location by which it is identified. The most important aspect of the organisation is that it has within its fold members, that is, people who are engaged in activities that are meant to serve the organisation's purpose.

Organisations have many purposes, ranging from making profits by commercial activities to providing information to citizens about their elected representatives and to enabling millions of commuters use the rail services in India. Tata Motors of India, for example, is a commercial organisation that makes cars, trucks and other automobiles. The company employs 23,000 people in various parts of the world. Although these employees would be engaged in various activities as part of their work, as a goal they work towards building and selling automobiles. The Association for Democratic Reforms, based in New Delhi, is a non-governmental organisation (NGO) that informs citizens about candidates who are either contesting elections or have been elected from different constituencies of India. The goal of this small organisation is to inform citizens about the criminal, financial and educational backgrounds of candidates they are about to vote for. Their objective is to strengthen democracy by informing citizens. The Indian Railways is a government organisation that manages the massive Indian railway system consisting of over 9000 trains that ferry 20 million passengers daily. The passengers may alight at any of 7000 railway stations and may traverse any distance of over 64,000 km of railway routes. The Indian Railways also ferries over 2 million tonnes of freight daily. This massive operation is managed by a number of information systems (IS) that help the Indian Railways achieve its goals of servicing its commuters and commercial clients.

KEY POINT

Organisations are a collection of people with shared goals — whether to sell cars or to manage trains.

The following sections discuss some essential features of modern organisations.

1.1.1 IT-Enabled Organisation

The organisations discussed above are modern in the sense that they have built into their structure the elements of information technology (IT) that enable them to function in a manner appropriate to the demands of the environment. This is a fundamental difference between a modern organisation and its older, pre-modern incarnation. Tata Motors, for instance, upon its initiation in 1945 would also have put in place built-in mechanisms to respond to its environment and to function in a manner appropriate to that time. However, what distinguishes Tata Motors' functioning then and now is the difference in the current use of IT to shape its functioning and responsiveness.

1.1.2 Networked Organisation

Modern organisations function in a world of *digital networks* in addition to the physical world that was the same for the old organisations. The organisations are linked as nodes on the network where they receive and transmit information. Remaining on the network requires *sensing* and *responding* to this flow of information. The digital network consists of the internet and telecommunication networks that rely on digits (ones and zeros) to carry information across large distances. Sensing the world means frequent monitoring of the news and information that becomes available. This information is in the form of text, audio or video. Organisations such as Tata Motors have to constantly monitor their digital environment to learn about the markets, their competition, their partners and the business they operate in.

Responding to the digital information available to organisations is also a modern challenge. Information is widely available instantly and in multiple forms. Responding means taking those actions that will move the organisation towards its goals. The response could be in the form of further transfer of information on the digital networks, say, by issuing messages or by taking action in the physical world. Responses are shaped by the context of the situation that the organisation operates in and by the nature of the sensed information. For example, when

KEY POINT

Modern organisations have to sense and respond to information.

Tata Motors launched its widely popular Nano car, it anticipated a huge demand for information from its website by prospective customers. Therefore, it designed the site in such a manner that it could handle the rush adequately.

1.1.3 Dispersed Organisation

Another key aspect of many large modern organisations is that they are highly dispersed. Tata Motors, for instance, has operations in many cities in India and in other parts of the world. The companies disperse their operations to best meet customer needs or to locate functions where the resources such as skilled labour or raw materials are available.

Multinational organisations are well known to seek out new destinations for their operations and also new markets. They are able to do this owing to laws and facilities that are created by host nations, as it benefits their economy. The challenge for multinational organisations is to fully use the opportunities thus created and manage work and organisational issues in a new environment.

1.1.4 Knowledge Organisation

Modern organisations rely on *knowledge workers* to a much larger extent than older organisations. These workers differ from blue-collar workers as their work responsibilities involve accessing and dealing with knowledge about the work and the environment, as opposed to repetitive manual labour related to production. Knowledge workers enjoy greater autonomy in their work and the variety of work they have to perform. Consequently, they are better educated and more informed about the business they are working in.

A major function of modern organisations is to process information. They create information about goods and services, accumulate it within the organisation and use it to achieve their goals. Information is like a glue that binds the organisation and its functions together. For commercial organisations, it is a key component for competing in the market. Information is stored, processed and converted into forms that make it an integral part of an organisation. This is referred to as the organisation's knowledge base. Knowledge stored and accessed in this manner enables the organisation to drive action and shape its own understanding of the world.

1.2 INFORMATION SYSTEMS IN ORGANISATIONS

1.2.1 What are Information Systems?

Information systems are collections of computers, networks, software and people who create, store, modify, and distribute data and information in any organisation. Computers and information technology (IT) are key ingredients of modern information systems (IS). Information technology includes computing devices such as personal computers, notebook computers, personal digital assistants, mobile phones and various types of networks that allow the computing devices to connect and to communicate.

Let us distinguish between information technology (IT) and information systems (IS). IT is understood as the artefacts such as computing devices, software and network devices that constitute the material aspects of IS. However, information systems are constituted by the artefacts of technology as well as the people and organisations that use them.

This distinction between IT and IS is important and has to be emphasised. IT is what people buy and configure and use, whereas IS is the manner in which we understand, conceptually, the use of IT in organisations and by people. Here is an example to understand the difference. Any organisation may buy IT components such as printers that are provided to offices for their printing needs. The printer itself is an artefact of IT, which is a tangible object or a tool. Its function is well defined and limited: it has to print text or images on paper in a manner defined by the user of the printer.

In this example, printer is part of the IS of the organisation and plays a role in preparing reports and memos. It becomes relevant and useful for the organisation when it prints properly and in the manner required by the users (and becomes a problem when it cannot print due to some malfunction). In other words, the role and relevance of the printer are determined by the needs of the organisation, the people who are using the IS and the purpose for which they are using it. In this larger context, the printer is a component of the IS of the organisation and helps to serve its goals.

1.3 BRIEF HISTORY OF COMPUTING

Computers or general purpose computing devices were invented in the middle of the 20th century, but the ideas they are based on evolved a century earlier. Charles Babbage, a renowned British mathematician, first conceived the idea of a computing device in the 1820s when he was confronted with the problem of errors creeping into navigation charts at the time of their writing. In those days this work was done by clerks who used manual methods of pencils, rough paper and slide rules to make navigation charts used by sailors. These charts required extensive numerical computations. Each chart had to be created individually and owing to the tedious nature of the work was prone to errors. The clerks who performed the calculations were known as 'computers'.

Babbage designed a mechanical device that could be moved by pulleys and gears and could be used to make computations. This device was known as the *Difference Engine*. He tried to construct the Difference Engine but never succeeded in doing so. He also designed an advanced version of this engine, which he called the *Analytical Engine*, in which instructions could be given by punched cards. Ada Lovelace, who was a colleague of Babbage and also a mathematician, conceived of a method of writing a series of punched cards for the Analytical Engine that could perform complex calculations. Babbage is thus credited with inventing the idea of a computing device and Lovelace with inventing the idea of programming.

1.3.1 ENIAC: Way to Commercial Computers

The first versions of modern-day computers were built in the 1940s, almost a hundred years after Babbage's first designs. One of the earliest computers was built by Konrad Zuse, an engineer working in Germany during World War II and was based on electrical relay switches. Owing to the war this invention could not be publicised to the world. Another computer was developed by the UK under the guidance of mathematician Alan Turing, also during the war. This computer consisted of both electrical and mechanical parts and was used to compute numbers quickly, mainly to break secret codes used by rival military operations.

World War II was also the period in which two other, independent, efforts to build computers were attempted in the USA. The first was by some independent researchers at the Iowa State University who created the first electronic and digital computer called the *Atanasoff-Berry computer*. This project did not receive much attention at that time. In contrast, a computer called *Electronic Numerical Integrator and Computer* (ENIAC), built by John Mauchly and Presper Eckert in the University of Pennsylvania also during World War II received much more attention and media coverage. This computer consisted entirely of electronic components and differed from the earlier efforts because it was 'general purpose' in nature. The term general purpose means that the instructions required to run the computer were neither specified in advance nor built into the computer, but, could be specified later, so different sets of instructions could be given. This property of the ENIAC made it different from the computers built earlier.

The success of the ENIAC and the lessons learned from it led to the commercial development of computers in the USA. In the 1950s companies such as Honeywell and IBM produced the first commercial computers that they sold to a number of government departments and businesses. These computers were physically large and were maintained in separate rooms of offices. They required specially trained engineers and operators who could program them and also help manage the large amounts of data that was being created and stored. In Europe too, and particularly in the UK, commercial computers were manufactured and sold to governments and businesses.

Research and development of computers and IT was widespread and rapid at this stage. University departments, commercial research departments and government laboratories were created in many countries around the world with massive funding for development of computing technology. Computing hardware was separated from the instructions that were required to run it and a separate stream of research in software evolved. Software was further specialised into systems software and application software. The systems software mainly ran the hardware and its different components and the application software was used for organisational purposes. Software was also created in computer languages, a restricted set of words, which could be translated into a code that the hardware could understand. These computer languages evolved from low-level to high-level languages capable of many and diverse functions.

In the 1960s there evolved a set of technologies that could allow computers to connect to each other. These technologies were a set of hardware and software devices that could allow data interchange between computers. A set of standards were developed to enable sharing of data and messages between computers thus facilitating the formation of computer networks. The first of these was the ALOHA network set up in the University of Hawaii in 1970.

KEY POINT

The first general – purpose computer was known as the ENIAC.

Computers and computing technology began to spread around the world. These were first adopted by wealthy, industrialised nations but others followed soon. Military agencies and government departments were some of the first to buy and adopt these technologies for their own use. In India, the first computer was obtained by the Indian Statistical Institute in Kolkata in 1956 (the computer was obtained from the Union of Soviet Socialist Republics). This computer was used for research in computing as well as for solving computing problems for the Atomic Energy Commission and the National Sample Survey of India.

1.3.2 Advent of Artificial Intelligence

Research in the field of Artificial Intelligence began in 1956 in the USA. This field dealt with building computers and writing software that could emulate human capabilities in problem solving. The field gained popularity and attracted a large number of researchers. It also initiated a sister field of Robotics, whose main goal was to build human or animal-like devices called *robots* that could move about independently. The researchers in these disciplines examined the prospects of keeping information about the world within computer memory that could then be used to generate useful conclusions.

1.3.3 Advent of Personal Computing

Over several decades the size of the computing hardware decreased significantly, and by the 1980s personal computers were available for individuals to purchase. These were not only small that they could be kept on a desk, but were also cheap enough to buy. The technology to make these computers was standardised and distributed, giving rise to an entire industry around the world that manufactured these personal computers.

The software used on personal computers also became a product that could be made and sold for commercial gain and soon became an industry. Several firms provided system and application software for personal computers that were now widely used by both individuals and businesses. Software was no more automatically bundled with the hardware as used to be the case before.

KEY POINT

The Free Software movement initiated by Stallman advocated free usage, modification and sharing of software.

1.3.4 Free Software Movement

The 1980s also saw the emergence of the Free Software movement that insisted that software should be available to all who wanted it and could use it on their personal computers. This movement was initiated by Richard Stallman, a researcher in the USA. The free software movement was opposed to the idea of locking software in licences that prevented its widespread usage by everyone and keeping secret the source of the software by the companies selling it.

The movement advocated free sharing, usage and modification of software. The movement enthusiasts created a large amount of software that they made publicly available to all who were interested.

1.3.5 Advent of the Internet

The proliferation of personal computers in organisations also created the need for networks and these too grew in scale and sophistication. Data networks were increasingly becoming popular. Many universities, governments defence departments and commercial organisations were linked by data networks based on a standard known as the Internet Protocol (IP). In France, the Minitel network was quite popular in the 1980s, which provided text on prices, ticket purchases and news. By the late 1980s, local area networks in organisations were widely used and were found to be so useful that an entire new industry emerged with companies going into the production of computer networking equipment.

In 1990, Tim Berners-Lee, a British scientist, designed and implemented the Hypertext Transfer Protocol (HTTP), which was to become the basis for what is now called the *World Wide Web*. This protocol allowed individuals to easily access data on computers in any part of the world just with the address of the page that contained the required information. After the original protocol was invented, there was rapid improvement and the Web came up with many services, such as transfer of images and video. The internet was opened for commercial access in 1993 and the Web began to grow tremendously. Individuals and organisations from around the world began to create data for the Web and create a unique identity for themselves. The 2000 saw the growth of *social networking* sites on the Web, such as Orkut and Facebook that enabled millions of users to link to their friends and family through the Web. The Web presented a new and almost ubiquitous interface for people and organisations to interact. This had profound implications for businesses, governments and other organisations (see Fig. 1.2).

KEY POINT

The Hypertext Transfer Protocol (HTTP) designed by Tim Berners-Lee became the basis of the internet.

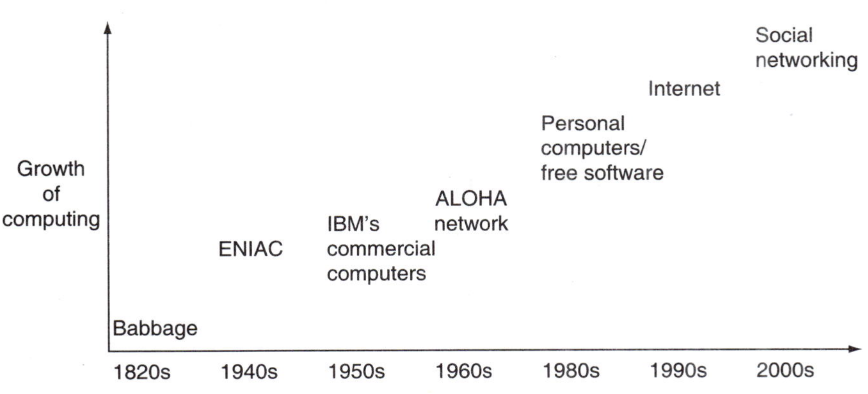

FIGURE 1.2 | The evolution of computing over the decades.

1.4 THE ROLE OF THE INTERNET

1.4.1 Internet and Web: They are Different

The *Internet* is a massive network of networks. It is a networking infrastructure that connects millions of computers together globally. All computers connected to the internet can communicate with each other. Information travels over the internet via a variety of languages known as *protocols*.

The *World Wide Web*, or simply Web, is a way of accessing information over the internet. It is an information-sharing model that is built on top of the internet. A browser (e.g., Mozilla Firefox) is a program that shows us the Web. The Web uses the HTTP, one of the languages spoken over the internet, to transmit data. The Web is a huge collection of documents or pages of information connected to each other around the globe. These pages, called web pages, contain hyperlinks usually called links. Each link points to another web page that can be accessed by clicking its link. There are over 40 billion public web pages on the Web today.

1.4.2 The Internet Changes Everything!

The World Wide Web was designed to provide public access to data. Its design enabled people to provide access to their own data and also be in a position to see what others have provided. Using a software called the browser, anybody with a connection to the internet could see data provided by others and also create pages of data that others could view. The Web created a new and easy-to-use data-sharing medium.

In its modern form, the internet consists of a number of services, including the Web, which allows exchange and sharing of data. For example, one of the most popular forms of data exchange on the internet is email. The phrase 'email' is derived by joining the words *electronic* and *mail*. Practically, everybody who uses the internet today uses email in some form or the other. Email allows anybody on the internet to send a message to anybody else provided the sender knows the address of the receiver. Like other services provided on the internet, the email sender can send a message as plain text or as special data in the form of audio or video.

Free email was one of the earliest popular applications on the Web. Companies such as Hotmail and Yahoo! created free email services that permitted anybody to have an email account with them. This enabled the individual to have an email address, a particular electronic location to which a message could be sent. These services were so popular that the companies that provided them became as popular as traditional media sources, such as radio and television. The companies could attract a large number of users to make it possible for them to create advertising space and charge revenues for it (as was the case with radio and television).

The Web soon became the medium through which organisations could reach out to a vast population of people across the globe. New ways of doing business were now possible. New ways of providing information and services were also possible. Electronic commerce (also called e-commerce) became an important aspect of business organisations, as they sought new means of providing both services and goods to their customers.

Today the internet is a vast network of computers and other computing devices that is continuously evolving and growing. In December 2008, there were about 188 million sites on the Web as compared to about 18 million in 2000. In 2008, there were 1.56 billion people around the globe who were using the internet whereas in 2014 the number was 2.92 billion (according to source, www.internetlivestats.com). The source states that the number of internet users in 2000 was 0.41 billion; thus, the internet users have increased more than seven times in 14 years (see Fig. 1.3).

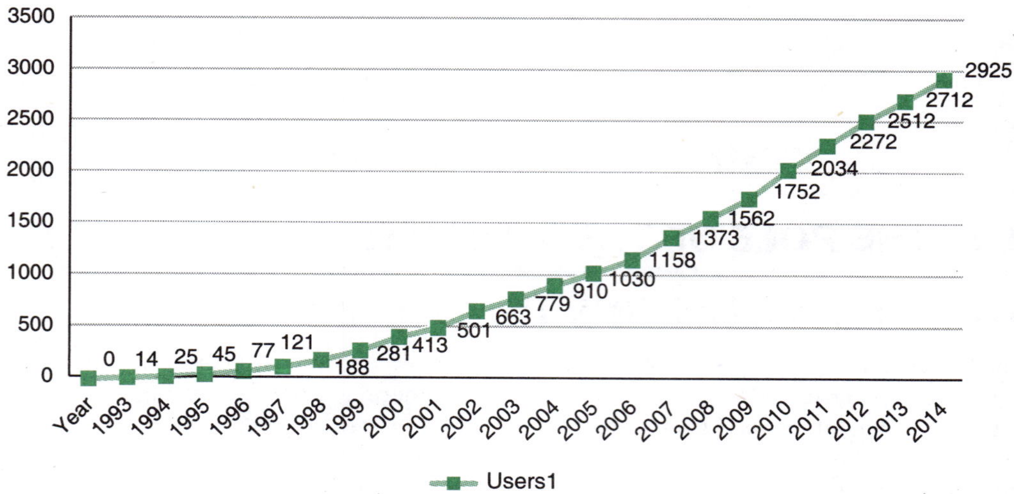

FIGURE 1.3 | Growth of internet users from 1993 to 2014, in millions of users.

Source of data: http://www.internetlivestats.com/internet-users/#trend

Users connect to the internet through their computers and also through their mobile devices such as smartphones and tablets. Besides, human users, independent devices are also connected to the internet. Many homes, cars, cameras and sensors are connected to the internet. Temperature, pressure and air particle sensors in cities are connected to the internet. These devices are used to monitor atmospheric and environmental conditions. This arrangement of connecting devices to the internet is known as the Internet-of-Things (IoT). According to Juniper Research (www.juniperresearch.com, accessed in May 2016), there were 13.4 billion devices connected to the internet in 2016. This figure is likely to reach about 38 billion by 2020.

Along with the growth in the sheer size and usage of the internet, the scale and variety of services has also grown. The Web provides a vast range of services from simple information searches to complex transactions, many of which are now done through smartphones. Many of these services will be covered in later chapters of the book.

1.5 MANAGING IN THE INTERNET ERA

The Web is a vast store of data and information. One challenge for organisations is to have a clear set of practices to frequently find and use the data relevant and useful for them. A large amount of data may be useful, but it can only be so if the data does not overwhelm the seeker. With the current availability of data on the Web, it is easy for the most important data to be buried in some inaccessible manner.

The internet's services, such as email, the Web, data transfer capabilities, online audio and video communication, enable organisations to connect with the world both to learn about the world and also to make themselves be known. It is necessary for organisations to create a *presence* on the internet, which is usually in the form of a site on the Web. Organisations also create Apps that run on smart mobile phones, and give exclusive access to information and services of the organisation to the user. Further, organisations also create a presence on social media sites, such as Facebook.

Many application services are now available over the internet. Earlier these applications used to reside on the internal IS of organisations. Applications that could be used to store data, process it in specific ways and share it with partners outside the organisation are all possible through the Web and internet-based applications. These services are now referred to as Cloud Computing. These external services are usually cheaper and more convenient to access than the older methods and organisations have to decide whether to adopt these services or not.

Though the internet has opened up a world of data and services for organisations, it has also given rise to security threats. Organisations around the world are wary of the many ways in which they could be made vulnerable and harm could be caused to them. The services of the internet have been used to attack the online presence of organisations and use devious means to enter internal networks, impersonate people, steal data or money and release harmful software such as viruses. All organisations have to formulate policies and plans for dealing with such security threats.

KEY POINT

The internet provides access to data and key services, though it also poses security challenges.

1.6 MANAGING INFORMATION SYSTEMS IN ORGANISATIONS

1.6.1 The IT Interaction Model

Managing IS in organisations is a highly challenging and complex task. One reason for this complexity is that neither organisations nor the IS they use remain static over time – both change continuously, and it is the job of management to ensure that the systems remain useful and relevant for their organisational goals at all times. Organisations change to respond to the needs of the business and economic environment in which they thrive. They may have to change their services, their products, their internal structure and the manner in which they do their business

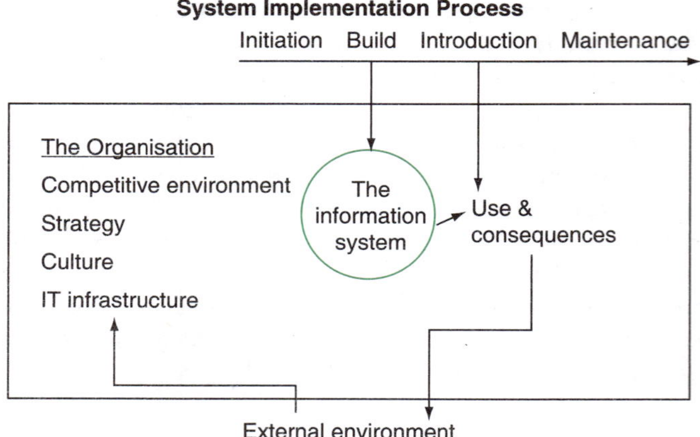

FIGURE 1.4 | The IT interaction model.

to meet the challenges of the environment. Organisations also change as their employees gain more experience and learn and adjust to their work environment. The employees change the manner in which they work, including the manner in which they work with IS, and with this they change the way processes within organisations are carried out.

One way to understand IS and organisations is to see how these two entities interact. When organisations introduce new IS they expect certain changes to happen (see Fig. 1.4). These changes are related to the functions that IS are supposed to perform. For example, if the IS are supposed to process the monthly payroll for employees, then it is quite possible that the organisation has implemented this IS to increase the speed at which the payroll is processed and also the accuracy of the calculations. These are positive changes the organisation wants as it has spent time and money in implementing this new IS.

If the changes the organisation expects are realised then this may turn out to be a positive outcome for it. For a commercial organisation, this may lead to increased profits, which is the very goal of the organisation. The new IS could also lead to better employee satisfaction and an improved ability to manage employee benefits and remuneration. These outcomes are what the organisation would have planned for and would welcome them. However, it is also possible that these benefits are *not* realised. It is possible that the IS may not perform as expected and there is not much improvement either in the organisation's profits or in employee's satisfaction. This possibility could arise if the implementation of the system was not according to the needs of the organisation or it was implemented in a faulty manner and had many problems in delivering its desired results. Or it could be that even though the system was implemented properly, there were employees in the organisation who were opposed to its implementation and did not want to use it in the intended manner. Such situations are known to happen and are often referred to as resistance to change in organisation.

Caselet ID Fresh Foods

ID Fresh Foods is a firm that sells ready-to-cook ingredients for making traditional Indian foods. Their business proposition is to market ingredients that can be cooked easily for freshly made meals. For example, one of their earliest products was batter for idlis and dosas that could be taken from a packet and cooked on a stove or steamed. Their batter retained its freshness and enabled users to prepare fresh meals without the labour of preparing the ingredients. Starting out in 2005, ID Fresh was able to establish a presence and reputation in the Bangalore market, from which they grew and by late 2017 had a presence in many cities in India and abroad. ID's business model is based on preparing ingredients in a factory, shipping them to retail outlets and encouraging customers to purchase the packaged commodities within a specified period. ID maintains a strict control over when its packages reach the retail outlet and how long they stay there. To retain freshness, they had their delivery agents remove older packages and replace them with fresh ones. This adherence to strict quality control grew their reputation and their business.

One of the challenges ID faced was that of store returns - packets that were not sold within a given period (three days for some products) were picked up by their delivery personnel and returned. This was waste and stood at about 22% for their idli batter product. ID used information systems to track the production amounts, the delivery amounts on each truck and van, total sales and cash, and were able to close their books on a daily basis. However, they did not have visibility on delivery and returns data on a real-time basis. For this purpose, ID developed a mobile-based application that enabled delivery personnel to record the number of packets delivered to each store, the packets on display, the packets that were collected for pick up and when they were returned. This information gave ID insights on the demand at a granular level and helped them to manage their inventories and delivery cycle better. Using this new system they were able to reduce the returns to about 2%. The system also helped them plan for their daily manufacturing better as they had store-level and delivery schedule level data with high accuracy. ID could not reduce the returns further, as the causes for these had to do with storage and display problems and not delivery.

As ID grew and established its business in other cities, it relied on this system of collecting data at a granular level and using it to manage their delivery and production cycles. Wastage and returns would be high initially, but as they understood the market better with the available data, this wastage reduced and the efficiency, and profitability, improved.

1.6.1.1 First-Order and Second-Order Effects

The outcome of the implementation of a new IS could be positive or not, and this will depend on the situation at the organisation. The outcomes that arise as a direct consequence of the introduction of an IS are known as *first-order effects*. They are usually visible in organisations in the form of increased speed of processing of data or increased volume of processing and these are what any organisation would have intended to gain from the IS that it has implemented. The first-order effects can be positive or negative depending on how the organisation adapts to the new system. In the case of KRCL, for example, the first-order effects are visible in the increased efficiency of moving files, where users moved over 20,000 files in a few months, a number that was much lower using the manual method.

The increased use of the IS could lead to further changes in the organisation, not all of which may have been anticipated. In the payroll system example, with the increased use the organisation may find that its hiring, transfer and promotion processes are easier to manage, and further it is able to create new and innovative incentive schemes to motivate its employees. This may improve its ability over time to retain and attract better employees, which would further lead to the organisation's standing in the market and improve its overall profitability. Such effects would not be immediately visible as they may require years to become visible or measurable. These outcomes are known as *second-order effects*.

In the case of KRCL, the second-order effects arose from the management's ability to see how and when files moved, and make institutional changes accordingly.

When any particular firm in a competitive industry implements an IS for a particular application and realises benefits from it, it is quite likely that its competitors will follow its example. This is likely because the competing firms would not want to lose out on an advantage that their competitor has, which could result in losing their market share and profits in future. This competitive pressure may force all firms in the industry to adopt such an IS to retain their competitive position. As adoption of the IS grows in the industry as a whole, it presents opportunities for industry bodies or other agencies to use these facilities. For example, if a payroll system is used by all firms in an industry located in a given city, the city government may be able to provide special incentives to the employees of these firms to adopt certain practices, such as car pooling

KEY POINT

Implementation of IS leads to first-order, second-order and third-order effects that are visible over time.

to reduce city traffic congestion. The city government could obtain data about where employees live and where they usually work from the IS used by the organisations. Such large-scale consequences of implementing systems are called *third-order effects*.

1.6.1.2 Effects of Competition and Organisational Traits

Whether an IS is successful and is able to meet its intended effects is largely dependent on the organisation it is being implemented in and on the competitive environment, culture, structure, the processes the organisation follows and the IT infrastructure already in place in the organisation.

The *competitive environment* is the competition that the firm faces in the market in which it operates. Often the decision for adopting an IS is based on what competitors are doing and how one can keep up or get ahead of the competition. In the late 1990s many firms across the world adopted e-commerce because that was the means by which they could remain competitive in a rapidly changing environment.

Information systems are often driven by a particular *competitive strategy* that a firm adopts. Firms can often compete by being the lowest cost provider of a good or service. This is a conscious strategy of the firm and they use it to gain market share from their competitors. In such a situation, IS are often used to further strengthen their competitive position by reducing the cost of their product compared to that of others in the industry.

The *culture* or *work culture* of any organisation is understood as the shared set of values and beliefs within the organisation. The work culture of the organisation shapes the manner in which the IS are both implemented and used and determine what the eventual outcomes of the systems will be. For example, many organisations maintain a competitive culture, where even for internal tasks different groups and departments are expected to compete for assignment. This creates a strong competitive culture within the organisation. Other organisations may follow a different approach, where departments cooperate in team building to tackle the task assignment.

The implementation of IS in an organisation with a competitive culture will have different implications than one in which a cooperative culture exists. In the former, departments or divisions may demand autonomy in using the IS to help them compete better, whereas in the latter a shared, possibly central IS would be welcome.

1.6.1.3 Effects of Organisational Structure

The structure of an organisation is the manner in which employees are constituted or grouped within the organisation. Many government departments, for instance, are structured as a *hierarchy* where the highest level person has the greatest authority and those reporting to that person are delegated responsibility and authority. For example, in a government department the person at the top of the hierarchy would be a Minister and reporting to him/her would be Secretaries. Below the Secretaries would be Joint Secretaries and so on, down to the lowest level consisting of office workers. Along with authority, the functions of different people in the hierarchy would also be different, and these functional differences are used to create divisions, departments and groups within the larger department.

Moreover, many modern organisations use a *matrix structure* where strict hierarchies are not present (see Fig. 1.5). Employees are assigned to groups based on projects and tasks they are working on and a reporting structure is established within the group for the duration of the project. As the project terminates, the employees are reassigned to other groups and divisions within the organisation.

For information systems to be successful they have to support the existing structure in the organisation. For example, many government departments have implemented *workflow systems* that enable documents to proceed from person-to-person within a department. These documents may need modification or approvals, and so they are moved among personnel who may make changes to them or simply approve their content. The workflow systems move the documents among pre-specified people in the department, according to the structure present in the department. The last person whose approval is usually required for the processing to be

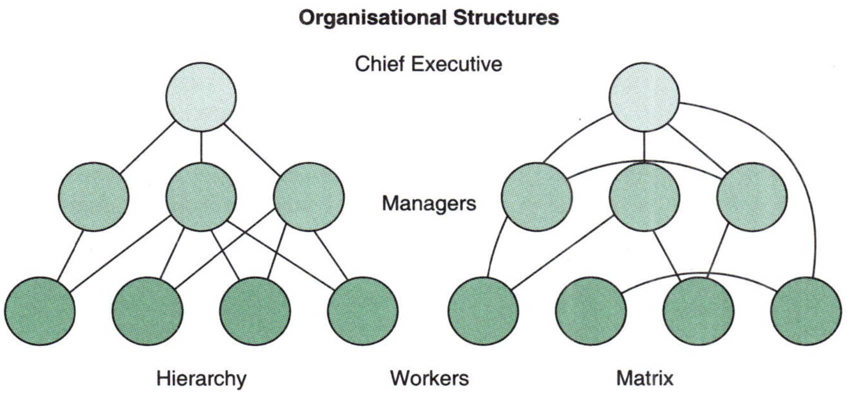

Organisational Structures

Chief Executive

Managers

Hierarchy Workers Matrix

FIGURE 1.5 | The hierarchy and matrix organisational structures.

complete may be the Minister, and so the system will move the document to the Minister's location only towards the end. The system thus maintains the authority hierarchy of the organisation.

1.6.1.4 Support for Organisational Processes

Some organisations use information systems to change or challenge the existing hierarchy in place. Workflow systems may alter the manner in which employees receive and process documents, thus helping to introduce efficiencies in the process.

All organisations have internal processes in place to get routine work done. A process is a set of steps required to accomplish a task. For example, many organisations that discharge a marketing function have processes by which they receive and record an order. When an order is received from a customer or placed by a customer, the organisation may record the time and date at which it has received, the kind and number of goods ordered, the person who has initiated the order and the department within the organisation, which has to deal with servicing the order. This process is followed for all orders received.

Organisations create and use processes for all the functions that they perform, such as materials procurement, manufacturing, storage, distribution, marketing, service, etc. Process steps are carefully designed to achieve the goals of a function. The challenge that most managers face is that of having efficient processes that enable them to achieve their goals in the best possible manner.

Information systems (IS) are widely used in organisations to support processes. In the early years of IS use in organisations, the most that IS did was to *automate* many manual processes. For example, the processes related to keeping accounts in an organisation were implemented using a software. This enabled the people in the accounting department to simply enter the correct data and the system would do the needed calculations. Furthermore, the system could also produce reports on various aspects of the accounts, such as balance statements or cost statements, whenever they were needed.

Today modern organisations use IS both to automate existing processes and to add or eliminate processes that will lead to improved overall functioning. Some IS are available for purchase that have pre-built processes and that can be suitably used by organisations. The challenge is to ensure that processes in the purchased IS suit the needs of the organisation.

It is quite likely that when a new system is introduced in an organisation, it has to blend with an already existing IT infrastructure of the organisation. The IT infrastructure consists of the existing hardware, software and network technologies that are being used by the organisation. The infrastructure also includes the set of policies and practices that the organisation follows while using its IT infrastructure. The new IS have to be designed and implemented in such a manner that it functions within the existing IT infrastructure. For example, if an organisation chooses to introduce a new *customer relationship management* (CRM) system, it has to consider how this system will fit with its existing systems. CRM systems are used widely to maintain details about customers, like their interactions with the organisation, their purchasing and payment details, their service needs and other similar details. These systems help in managing customers as all the information related to customers is maintained at a single place. Such systems are very complex and need a careful analysis before they are introduced. They would have to work with existing systems such as financial systems, marketing and sales systems, e-commerce systems, email system and many others. The manner in which the data in these systems is stored and used has to match that of the new system, and the manner in which the new system would use and modify the data in the existing *legacy* systems also has to be carefully designed.

1.6.1.5 Choosing and Implementing Information Systems

The task of building and implementing information systems (IS) is a difficult and complex one. One of the first decisions organisations have to make is whether to buy the IS from a vendor or whether to build the IS in-house. For many organisations the second choice does not exist as they do not have an in-house team of IS professionals who can build a software. They have to rely on vendors who can take an existing system product from the market and implement it directly or implement it with some modifications to suit the organisation.

The IS implementation process begins with an initiation, or the recognition of a need for an IS. This need arises in the context of a specific problem faced by the organisation or a need to address a future problem. The expressed need is usually based on the competitive position of the organisation, its current structure and culture as well as its current IT infrastructure. For example, an organisation may consider implementing a CRM system because a close competitor has implemented one. The organisation would have to weigh the implications of getting a CRM system in the context of its culture, structure, current processes and infrastructure.

If the initial need is validated, then this is followed by a detailed process of analysis, where the organisation closely examines the specifics of what it could do with such a system, the cost implications and the effects that the system could provide. This is followed by a detailed assessment of how the system can be integrated with the current systems already in use, what new training is required and how processes within the organisation have to be changed to take advantage of the new system. The system is then procured and modified for the needs identified. The next step is to introduce the system to the organisation's users through training. If there are problems with the new system, as there would invariably be, these are remedied. The system is then slowly integrated with the routine functions of the organisation.

KEY POINT

Success of an IS implementation will depend on the competitive environment, the strategy the organisation adopts, the culture within the organisation and the structure of the organisation.

As the new IS are integrated into processes of the organisation, it must invariably undergo changes in its structure, culture and functioning. As the IS are adopted by the people in the organisation it begins to have first-order effects, that is, changes in the manner and scope of doing work, and these effects prompt people to imagine how they could further modify the system to better suit their needs. They adjust to the new system along with creating space for more systems.

Information systems and organisations interact in a manner that is dynamic and evolving. It is imperative for managers in organisations to understand the nature of this interaction and prepare to manage in a changing and emerging context.

1.7 CHALLENGES FOR THE MANAGER

A manager who has to manage an organisation's information systems (IS) faces many challenges. These challenges have to do with the rapid changes that the technology environment faces as well as the myriad issues a modern organisation faces. Managing in a changing and dynamic environment means taking decisions and dealing with issues keeping in mind both the needs of the moment and the issues that will arise in the future.

The issues faced by a modern manager who has to deal with IS are posed as a series of questions below. The perspective from which these questions are posed is that of a *Chief Information Officer* (CIO) of an organisation. A CIO is typically the person in any organisation who has the responsibility of deploying and maintaining IS. This is an executive-level job where the person takes decisions related to IS throughout the organisation and partners with other executives to ensure that the organisation's goals are met with the help of IS. The CIO is invested with all the responsibilities of high-level executives that include managing all IT personnel in the organisation.

1.7.1 What Information Systems to Build?

This questions addresses the fundamental need for an information systems (IS) in the organisation. IS serve many purposes and objectives and the manager has to determine which need in the organisation has to be addressed. Identifying and prioritising the need is the first task in answering this question. For example, a firm may want to monitor its sales activities in an ongoing manner. The manager has to decide whether the need can indeed be fulfilled by a new IS and, if so, whether the IS should be built.

A complication that arises here is that there could be many different types of IS that address a given need. For instance, there are many types of systems that can keep track of and provide information on sales activities. The challenge for the manager is in determining which system best suits the firm's needs. If the system can be purchased from the market, and there are many vendors who can provide one, then the challenge is to determine which will best suit the firm given its resources. If, however, the firm has an internal IS department then it may choose to build the system on its own.

At a third level, the need for an IS is determined by competitive and organisational considerations. For instance, if close competitors have acquired a sales management system and are deriving significant benefits from it, then it is important for the firm to respond appropriately. Furthermore, the manager has to examine the existing culture, structure and infrastructure of the firm to understand if the new system will fit and in what manner it has to be acquired or introduced.

1.7.2 How Much to Spend on Information Systems?

When the need for an information systems (IS) is clear, the next important decision is how much to spend on the system. Systems available in the market will have different prices and capabilities, and systems built in-house by the firm will have their own internal cost estimation. The manager has to decide how much money has to be allocated for the system and in what manner. This is usually referred to as a budgeting decision.

One answer to this question is obtained by considering how much competitors are spending on similar systems. This information may be available from industry reports or from publicly available financial information. The competitors, who are of the same size and structure and who have built a successful IS with the same capabilities, will provide an indication of how much money to budget for the system. Another answer is obtained from estimating the strategic importance of the system. This answer is computed by gauging the future income the system will provide after it is implemented and then computing a return on investment (ROI). Managers often decide on the worth of an investment by assessing if the ROI is appropriate.

1.7.3 What Level of Capabilities Should be Created with Information Systems?

Managers have to decide the extent of the information systems (IS) they are envisaging. For instance, the questions to be considered for sales of IS are:

1. Should the system support the entire sales and marketing team of the firm or should it support a particular department's activities?
2. Should the system include collecting data from and providing reports to primary sales partners such as distributors and retailers?
3. Should the system be available through the internet or should it be made available through an internal organisational network?

These questions entail clearly identifying the needs and priorities of the system (as was done in the first question) and weighing these against the budgets available. Managers have to decide against providing excessive capabilities that are not important and will not be used. Also, managers have to keep in mind the issue of scalability. The system will be used initially with certain capabilities, however, as users grow comfortable with the system, they will demand more from the system.

A related decision is whether certain requirements for computing should be outsourced. Outsourcing a function means asking a vendor, another company that has expertise in performing that function, to do the job. The outsourcing vendor may provide employees who work on the firm's site to do the job or they may work from outside the firm (using network connections to do their work). Outsourcing is an important decision that is covered in detail later.

1.7.4 How Fast and Accurate Should the Services Be?

Many information systems are designed to provide timely and accurate information. However, employees in many organisations now feel that they are being flooded with information, much of it that they don't need. Moreover, the information may not be needed immediately, and could have been provided sometime later also. Managers in many organisations have to consider issues of trade-offs between speed and accuracy of information. The focus has to be on the information needed for decision making, which is usually much less than what managers are flooded with.

Typically, information related to costs, sales, cash flow, payables and inventory levels have to be accurate and timely. This information has to provided in a timely manner to those who have to see this information to make decisions. Information related to market share, competitor information, customer news, supplier news, employee satisfaction are typically not needed immediately, also not with much great accuracy. If the information in these latter categories is not entirely accurate, and is based on rumours and unconfirmed reports, it is usually acceptable to managers, as they don't really expect this information to be accurate.

Researchers have also found that the type of information valued the by managers varies by the conditions of the economy. For example, in an economy in which the firm is doing well, managers value information related to employee satisfaction and market share over other information. However, if the firm is not doing well in the given economy, then managers value information related to budgets and costs, receivables, cash flows and productivity over others.

1.7.5 What Security Levels are Required?

Modern information systems (IS) infrastructures are constantly under threats from internal and external sources. Internal threats arise from employees stealing data or fudging accounts or misusing the systems in some way. External threats arise from computer viruses that enter through the internet services and disrupt the functioning of systems within the organisation. There are many other kinds of external threats that arise from malicious persons wanting to do damage to the organisation.

An important decision for managers is to ensure an adequate level of safety and security for their IS. Excessive security measures are difficult to work with for most users, as they have to maintain many security-related practices on a regular basis while working with the systems. High security levels are also expensive to maintain. Thus, extensive security is not practical unless the situation demands its implementation. Lax security, on the other hand, leads to problems of data theft, viruses, etc. as discussed above. The best security level has to be an organisation-wide decision that brings in the security the organisation is most comfortable with.

1.7.6 What IS Functions Should be on the Cloud?

Cloud computing presents a new and innovative possibility for organisations to move their computing needs to an environment that is different from the traditional one. Cloud computing lets organisations rent facilities from providers and host their computing needs on this facility that is accessed through the internet. The main advantage of Cloud computing for organisations is that they do not have to manage the facilities and infrastructure, and yet use all the features of the IS. For example, many firms have started using Zoho Office (zoho.com) an office suite consisting of a word processor, a spreadsheet, a presentation package, an email software, and many other tools used in offices, through the Cloud. Users simply have to pay a regular charge, on a monthly basis, to use all these software packages, without having to buy hardware and software licences of their own. All employees of the firm that rents such a Cloud facility can access these tools from their devices, such as laptops, mobile phones and tablets, through the internet.

The main decision that managers have to make with regard to the adoption of Cloud computing is that of selecting the functions to move to the Cloud. Some of the challenges that the Cloud presents are those of security, reliable access to the internet, and inter-operability. Managers have to be careful about the security arrangements while moving any functions to the Cloud. Since the facilities are not under their control they may not be entirely sure of the security of their data. Also, if firms move functions to the Cloud that are critical in nature, they will have to ensure reliable access to the internet. Sometimes firms may choose to keep core functions of the organisation hosted on computers on their own premises rather than place them on the Cloud, owing to security and reliable access reasons.

1.7.7 What Is the Technology Road Map for the Organisation?

With information technology growing at a tremendous pace, there is a constant challenge that managers face – the challenge of ensuring that their IS remain current, relevant and useful. For this purpose all managers have to create a technology road map for their organisation. This road map is like a plan for the evolution of the IS in the organisation. The road map considers the current infrastructure as the starting point and shows how the technology is expected to evolve and change in the future and how the organisation will respond to those changes. The road map includes the organisation's strategic goals and plans and creates a technology plan that will support the former.

The technology road map decision includes answering the following example questions:

1. What is the horizon for desktop computers and what will replace them?
2. Which proprietary software in the organisation should be replaced by free and open source software?
3. How should the current enterprise applications be upgraded and expanded?
4. Which of the current networking components being used in the organisation are going to phase out (i.e., they will not benefit from any more development)?
5. What will be the future requirements for networking and telecommunications and how should infrastructure be created?

Chapter Glossary

Organisation It is a collection of people who have shared goals.

Information systems It is a collection of computers, software, networks and people that creates, stores, modifies and distributes data and information in an organisation.

Information technology It comprises hardware, software and network artefacts that constitute the material components of information systems.

Digital networks It comprises electronic and telecommunication networks that forward and handle information in the form of bits, which are zeros and ones.

Internet It is a special kind of digital network that operates on special standards for moving and storing digital data. It is a worldwide collection of networks that share the same standards.

First-order effects These are the immediate (direct) consequences that arise from the introduction of information systems in organisations.

Second-order effects These are the indirect and more long-term consequences that arise from introducing information systems in organisations.

Competitive environment The competitive environment of a commercial firm is the set of buyers, sellers, and rival firms that operate in the market environment of the firm. The firm has to obtain its resources and also sell its products against its rivals to survive in such an environment.

Competitive strategy The competitive strategy of a firm is the set of long-term measures that the firm takes to survive in the competitive environment.

Culture of an organisation The culture of an organisation is a shared set of values and beliefs within the organisation.

Review Questions

1. What are the basic features of a modern organisation?
2. How are information systems (IS) and information technology (IT) different?
3. How did information systems evolve?
4. What difference does the internet make in the way modern organisations operate?
5. What are the different types of effects of information systems when used in organisations?
6. What are the main questions about information systems that a manager has to answer?

Research Questions

1. What types of application software are typically used in modern business organisations? Visit some local businesses and find out. Try to visit businesses in different industries such as manufacturing, services and software.
2. While visiting with the local businesses, try to meet with the person in charge of IS, such as the CIO, and ask about the typical decisions he/she has to make.
3. How long does it take to implement information systems, such as a CRM in a large organisation like Tata Motors? Search in library databases for papers on CRM implementation and on the internet for an answer to this question.
4. Find out about the IS used in your college or university. How is this different from the IS used by Tata Motors in the case at the beginning of the chapter.

Further Reading

1. Tata Motors Company profile is available at: http://www.tatamotors.com/our_world/profile.php (accessed on 18 December 2008).
2. Srivastava, S.C., Mathur, S.S. and Thompson, T.S.H. (2007) Modernization of passenger reservation system: Indian Railways' dilemma, *Journal of Information Technology*, **22**, 432–439.
3. Relationship integration is critical, *Network Magazine*, July 2006. The article is available at: http://www.networkmagazineindia.com/200607/heartofthematter01.shtml (accessed on June 2009).
4. India's first computer is 'lost', *The Times of India*, 2006. The article is available at: http://timesofindia.indiatimes.com/articleshow/msid-1473117, flstry-1.cms (accessed on June 2009).
5. More information on Netcraft is available at: http://news.netcraft.com
6. More information on Internet World Stats is available at: http://www.internetworldstats.com/stats.htm (accessed on December 2010).
7. Silver, M., Markus, L., and Beath, C. (1995) The Information Technology Interaction Model: A foundation for the MBA core course, *MIS Quarterly*, 361–390.
8. Davenport, T.H. and Snabe, J.H. (2011) How Fast and Flexible Do You Want Your Information, Really?, *Sloan Management Review,* 57–62.

CHAPTER 2

IT and Innovation

Learning Objectives

After completing this chapter, you will be able to:

- Know what are the main drivers of innovation in IT
- Understand how innovations spread
- Understand impact of firms innovating with IT
- Get an overview of some recent innovations driven by IT

Moore's law predicts the growth of faster, more complex and cheaper computers. This prediction has driven massive developments in IT that have led to disruptive innovations in business, and also to the growth of new industries.

New ideas diffuse through the population over time with sets of people who are innovators and early adopters, as predicted by Rogers' model of innovation diffusion. They influence the subsequent spread of the idea.

Data shows that firms that adopt new ideas and innovate with IT are competitively better off than others. They are able to garner better market share; however, they may also suffer from quick changes in their industry rankings and their market share.

Innovations in IT have to be understood as waves of ideas, and have to be carefully monitored before they are adopted. This view enables managers to understand how much an innovation has gained traction and when it has matured.

New business models and products focus on providing value to customers through new ways of doing business, including personalisation, experimentation, smart technologies, crowd sourcing and natural language interfaces. These innovation also lead to management challenges of downward pressure on prices of goods and services, finding talent for creating technology solutions, taking risks and integrating with offline models.

MIND MAP OF CHAPTER TOPICS

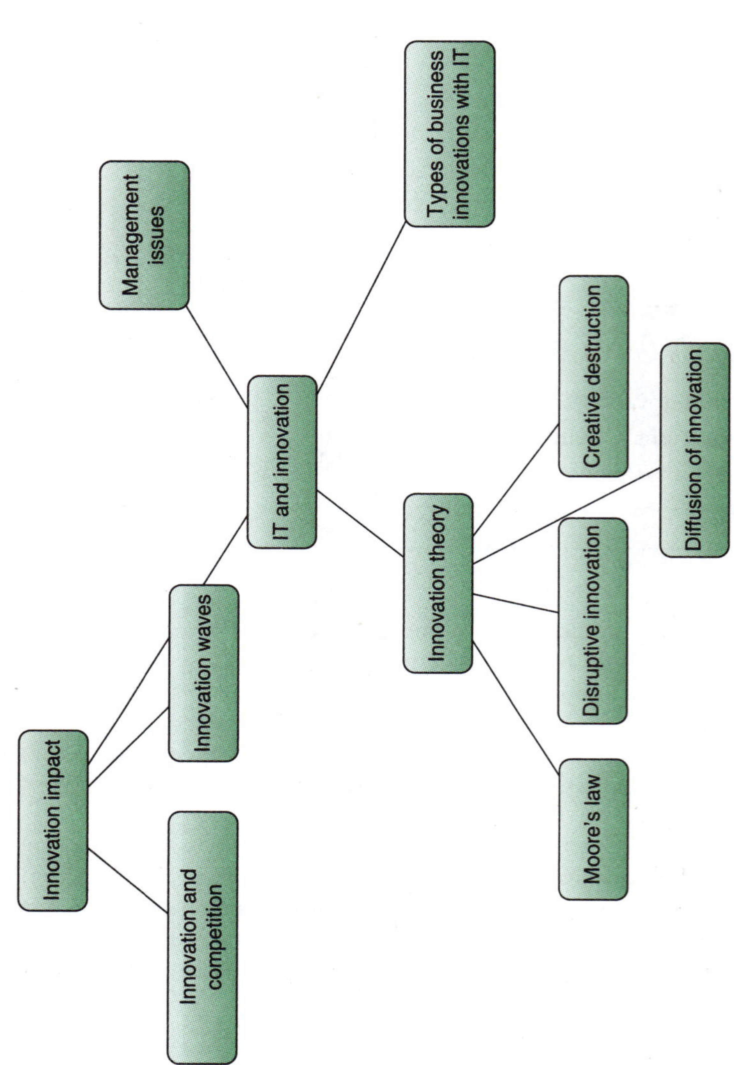

CASE STUDY: OLA CABS

Ola Cabs is an example of a firm that has innovated with technology to enter a highly competitive environment and make a difference. Ola enables users to hail or call taxis with their smartphones. The advantage that the technology used by Ola provides is of knowing exactly where the customer/user is located, using the location services available within smartphones, and notifying available cabs in the vicinity of this request. One of the many cab drivers who receive this notification from the central Ola system can respond to the customer by accepting the request and then drive to the customer's location to pick him or her up. Once the customer is in the cab, s/he can mention the destination to the driver or type it into the phone, and at the end of the ride the app computes the fare and informs both the driver and the customer. The customer can then pay cash to the driver, or allow the amount to be deducted from an online payment account.

The Ola service was started by entrepreneurs in the city of Mumbai in 2010. The state of public transport in Mumbai, and in other large metropolitan cities in India, at that time was not satisfactory. Mumbai had suburban metro trains, hail taxis and auto-rickshaws, and buses, already plying in large numbers. However, commuters and ordinary users suffered immense problems – trains were heavily over-crowded, as were buses at peak times, and autos and taxis were not available reliably. Further, many auto and taxi drivers forced customers to pay extra on arbitrary grounds.

When Ola launched, it promised customers easy availability at their location and within a reasonable period of time (initially, within 20 minutes) and also promised fair pricing based on the distance travelled. This was a very attractive proposition for consumers, and the management too realised that convenience and fair price were the two key attractions of their online taxi service model. Along with GPS-based (GPS is the global positioning system used by many services on smartphones, to exactly locate the position of the user on a map) location identification, they also introduced analytics to identify those locations that had peak demand during different times of the day. They could then allocate more taxis to those locations.

Ola also used technology to have a different business model than their competitors. There were other radio taxi aggregators, like Meru or Savaari, whom customers could call to their location and who provided a fair and distance-based fare system. However, these firms owned their own fleet of taxis and also hired a large pool of drivers. The challenge for this kind of business model was that these firms could not scale rapidly, as they needed heavy capital inputs to buy or lease a large number of taxis. Ola, on the other hand, did not own any of the taxis and neither did they hire the drivers as employees. Ola enlisted drivers on their system who came with their own taxi cars, and hence Ola did not require capital to buy the taxis, and further, the drivers were paid only on the basis of the trips they made and the billing they incurred. Ola did not have to hire the drivers as employees who had to be paid a regular wage. This system also ensured that the drivers maintained their own vehicles and saved Ola the costs of managing the fleet.

Ola's service is similar to the giant ride-hailing service started in the USA, called Uber, which is also known as one of the most valued start-ups in the world. When Ola started, Uber had still not entered the Indian market, but they soon did. Uber started operations in India in 2013 and became the chief rival for Ola. Ola's founders realised that they had to respond to this competition that had access to immense capital resources, and had a strong reputation in foreign markets. They responded by tailoring their system to Indian conditions and for special and unusual needs of Indian commuters. They used their technology platform for all these innovations.

Ola realised that English is spoken by a minority of people in India (in 2016, only about 10% of Indians could write or speak in English), and so it enabled its services in eight other languages. Uber's app could only be used by English-knowing customers.

Ola realised that using only cars as taxis would remain a restriction in Indian markets, owing to the costs involved in buying cars (that the drivers had to buy) and also owing to the higher fares that had to be subsequently charged. Ola enabled its platform to accommodate other forms of vehicles also, and extend the service to auto-rickshaws and also motocycle taxis. These vehicles could charge lower fares as they had lower operating costs. Subsequently, Ola started offering a range of cars in its fleet, including luxury cars, 'micro' taxis and ride-sharing taxis, all at different price points.

Possibly one of Ola's most innovative moves was to help stranded citizens of flood-affected Chennai in late 2015. In November 2015, Chennai, one of the largest cities in India, was flooded by heavy rains. Entire roads were completely submerged, as were entire residential areas. People had to be ferried out of their houses on boats. Ola used its technology platform to allow citizens to call for boats if they were in a flooded region. The app was upgraded to include an option to have a boat sent to the place from where the call was made. Those stranded in waterlogged areas were sent either a boat, a trawler or an inflatable raft with either a professional rower or a fisherman who carried them out to a safe area. Food and water was also distributed by Ola rowers and boatsmen.

Ola also allowed commuters to pay with cash. Ola realised early on that few Indians have credit cards, and so it allowed customers to pay cash at the end of the trip. The fare was displayed on the smartphone of the driver and was also sent as an SMS message to the customer. There was no basis for disagreement and customers could pay cash. Ola later also allowed customers to create a digital 'wallet' that let them store money in advance, using a credit card, that could be used to pay at the completion of a trip.

In August 2016, Ola had a presence in 102 cities in India and had enrolled 450,000 cabs. It enabled more than one million rides per day. Its closest rival was Uber that had gained a presence in the large metropolitan areas in India. Uber had also customised its offering in six Indian languages. Other players, such as Meru Cabs and Savaari, had lost market share but had retained segments of the market, such as airport drop-off and pick-up trips. With the massive demand for public transport, the competition between these technology-enabled taxi hailing services was likely to grow.

Sources:

http://www.business-standard.com/article/technology/technology-is-core-for-olacabs-112082600001_1.html

http://www.cio.in/cio-tv/how-ola-cabs-integrates-technology-city-transportation-users-and-drivers

http://timesofindia.indiatimes.com/tech/tech-news/Ola-launches-boat-service-in-flood-affected-Chennai/articleshow/49816195.cms

http://www.bloomberg.com/news/articles/2016-06-15/uber-finds-passage-to-india-blocked-by-30-year-old-ola-founder

2.1 INNOVATION THEORY

2.1.1 Moore's Law

In 1965, Gordon Moore, a scientist who worked with electronics and was also the founder of the chip-making firm Intel Corporation, made a prediction about the growth and complexity of electronic components. He predicted that the growth of semiconductors (electronic components such as diodes, resistors and transistors, are made with 'semiconducting material' and are referred to as semiconductors) would be steady for many decades. Known as Moore's law, the prediction was that the number of transistors packed into integrated circuits would double almost every two years. The integrated circuit is the basic building block of computers and other components such as memory units and sensors. The law was found to be effective in its predictions and the number of transistors indeed doubled on the integrated circuit, which later became a computer chip. This law then became the basis for predicting the growth of the industry and also for setting targets for research and development.

The consequence of Moore's law is a tremendous growth in the power and capacity of the basic computing hardware that drives innovation. Transistors constitute the elementary circuit elements of the chip. When the number of transistors doubled every two years, this meant that in the same space on the board, where the circuit was being assembled, the number of elements doubled. This implied that the computing capabilities of the circuit also increased. It is important to note that not only did the number of transistors increase, their efficiency in terms of speed and energy usage also improved, and also their costs reduced. The difference between the first chip built by Intel in 1971, called the 4004, and their fifth generation Core i5 processor built in 2015 (see Fig. 2.1) is dramatic: the Core i5 is 3,500 times faster; 90,000 times more energy efficient; and 60,000 times cheaper.

Increased number of transistors in the same space implies that the computer chip or chips can accomplish more specialised tasks. A modern chip, such as the Snapdragon 820, made by Qualcomm, uses several million transistors. This chip is used to make smartphones and consists of modules that handle different functions. For instance, the Snapdragon has different modules for managing the radio signals, the camera, the on-screen graphics, the sensors, the location information and so on. These specialised components work with the central unit to deliver high

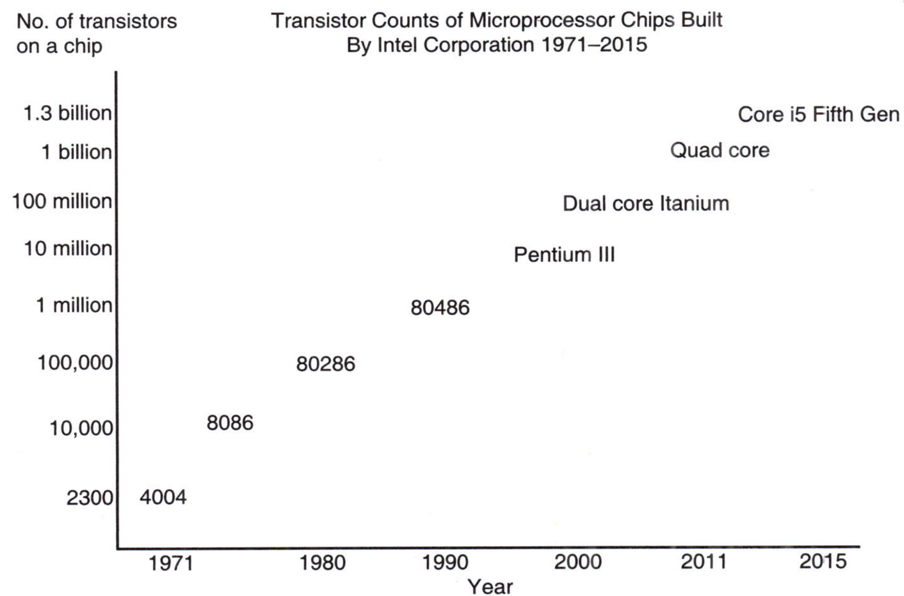

FIGURE 2.1 | Number of transistors included on different generations of chips made by Intel Corporation.

speed functionality in a small size and with a low power consumption, both of which are needed on a smartphone.

The immense sophistication of modern integrated circuits that are showing up in all manner of devices is driven by the predictions of Moore's law. This has led to tremendous innovation with IT. The virtuous cycle of reduced size, reduced power, and reduced costs has led to more sophisticated devices being invented and built. The massive surge in mobile phones, for instance, is driven by low cost chips that enable sophisticated computing. This innovation is spreading to telecommunications devices, sensors for heat, light, pressure, movement and gravity, and has led to development of low-cost computers used in cars, homes, buildings, clothes, household devices, toys, and so on. The internet-of-things (IoT) is a growing phenomenon with embedded devices that can connect and communicate with each other.

Consequences of these massive innovations have been both disruptive and creative for businesses.

2.1.2 Disruptive Innovation

The idea of disruptive innovation was developed by Clayton Christensen in 1997. Christensen observed that there are many products, particularly in IT, that enter the market as cheap goods with lower performance than established products in the same segment. These products have fewer features and do not perform as well as the existing products; however, they are cheaper and provide the right set of features for those in that segment. Over time, though, these technologies improve and begin to threaten and move into the markets of their established rivals. The established products are unable to compete or do not choose to compete, as they cannot reap profits from lower prices. Soon they are eliminated from the market by the disruptive product.

An example of this is digital cameras that were introduced in world markets in the mid-1990s. These cameras were often cheaper than their film-based, analog competitors. Many of the analog camera makers could not adapt and offer digital models (though many did adapt later). The digital cameras grew in features and sophistications and soon outgrew the analog cameras. By 2015, analog cameras were almost entirely absent from markets worldwide. One of the most famous analog film producing firms, Kodak, went bankrupt in 2012, after having dominated the analog films and photography business for almost a century.

2.1.3 Creative Destruction

Innovative change in the economy is often referred to as 'creative destruction.' This term also refers to the new situations brought forth by changes in the economy and political landscape where entire businesses and industries disappear to make way for newer businesses and models. This concept is attributed to the German economist Joseph Schumpeter who coined this phrase, drawing on the works of Karl Marx, to explain the constant change and chaos in capitalist industrial societies. Referring to the 'gale force of creative destruction', Schumpeter stated that the competition in markets and between countries impelled business creators to constantly innovate and bring forth new products and services that would eventually crush existing products, services, and ways of doing business.

Information technology is said to lead to creative destruction in the modern world, where new innovations, such as the digital camera, almost completely eliminated the analog camera and film industry. Web service firms like Netflix.com or Hotstar.com, that directly stream movies and television shows to people's homes, may eventually completely eliminate film screening halls and the concept of broadcast television. Netflix is an example of a technology that leads to creative destruction - something is destroyed as something new is created. The case example of Ola is a depiction of a technology innovation that is both disruptive and possibly destructive. Ola's model of hailing public transport challenges the existing and dominant methods of waving and hailing taxis or auto-rickshaws on streets. Many cities around the world have contemplated banning services like Uber as they are a strong challenge to the existing players.

2.1.4 Diffusion of Innovation

It is widely recognised that the spread of innovations, such as new ideas or products, happens in society over time, through communication from person to person. Research shows that when an idea is first introduced in a social system, it spreads through creation and sharing of information about the innovation between members of the system. The information that is shared is about the new idea, which carries with it some uncertainty. This uncertainty then leads to those receiving and sharing the idea being convinced by it or not, and taking up the idea or not.

For example, when Ola was first introduced in the city of Bangalore, not many people had heard of it and did not want to try it out. Soon some tried the app and booked a cab and liked their experience. Some tried the service and did not like the experience. There were many who liked the service and then talked to their friends and family about it. This began to spread the word and many more people started to download the app and try the service. Newspapers and television news reporters interviewed customers of Ola users and did news reports, thus further spreading the information about the service. Soon, many people had tried the service and their influence made others try it also, leading to a huge surge in Ola's popularity and demand.

The theory of diffusion of innovations, as proposed by Rogers (1983), states that there are four elements that enable the process of diffusion. These are:

1. An innovation – a new idea.
2. Communication channels – which are the media or means by which the information about the new idea is shared by people.
3. Time – the period over which the innovative idea spreads.
4. A social system – which is a combination of elements in a society that encourages or inhibits the innovation.

New ideas, new ways of doing things, or new products are all spread through diffusion in the social system. All new ideas that emerge from labs or businesses, or even from government departments, spread through the diffusion model that Rogers framed. The example of Ola is mentioned above. Other examples include the spread of email usage amongst people across the world in the early 1990s; the spread of enterprise systems by organisations; the use of social media by people; and so on. The spread and use of the internet itself is an example of the diffusion of innovation.

KEY POINT

Spread of new ideas happens over time with the sharing of information within a social system.

Innovation is often first adopted by the *Innovators*, as described by Rogers' model (see Fig. 2.2). Innovators are usually active information seekers, have a relatively good network of friends and acquaintances, and are usually able to adjust to the uncertainty of the new idea. They keep themselves aware of the latest technologies and ideas, and are able to take the risk of trying out the new idea for themselves. For instance, the innovators in Mumbai would have been the first to try out Ola when it was launched in 2010. Innovators may also have the necessary financial

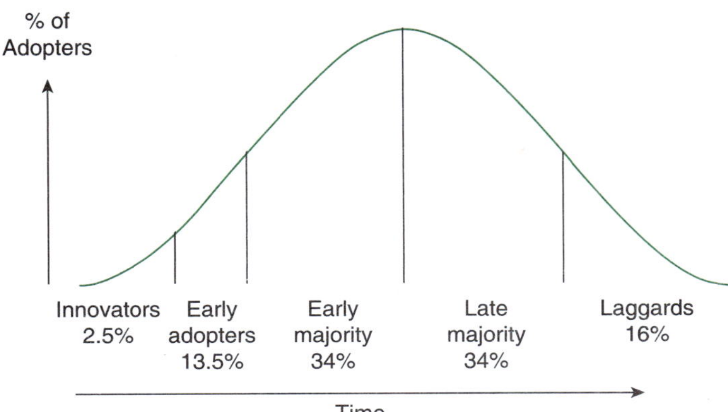

FIGURE 2.2 | Rogers' Model of Diffusion of Innovation.

resources to take a risk and suffer a loss. Innovators are a tiny minority of the population and consist of about 2.5% of the total.

As time progresses and more people come to know about the innovation, another set of people, called *Early Adopters*, begin to adopt the new idea or technology. This set consists of people who have a relatively high social standing in the community, are usually financially secure, but they are more careful with their selection than the innovators. Early adopters influence the thinking of their peers and are important for the ideas to spread. For Ola, the early adopters were the educated, middle-class in Mumbai and Bangalore, who saw the value that Ola provided and stepped forward to try out the new service. Early adopters consist of about 13.5% of the total population of adopters of the innovation.

If the message conveyed by the early adopters succeeds, a huge mass of people usually follow and take up the innovation. Known as the *Early Majority*, this group takes a long time to learn about and take interest in the innovation. They are influenced by the prior groups that have adopted the innovation, but they are not influencers or opinion leaders themselves. This group constitutes 34% of the total. Following the early majority are the *Late Majority*, who constitute 34% of the population of adopters. The late majority are invariably skeptical of the innovation, are hard to convince, and do not influence others. However, they are influenced by the early adopters and the early majority of adopters. This group may not be financially strong.

Finally, the *Laggards* constitute the last group that takes up the innovation. This is the most conservative group and with the least inclination to change. They do not have any social influence and are usually low on financial and social status. They constitute 16% of the total population.

The key implication of Rogers' model for managers who want to ensure an innovation is adopted, is that the innovators and the early adopters are the most important groups to focus on. These two groups consist of risk takers and also influencers, who will try out the new idea and then, if they find it useful or valuable, pass on the message to others in the population. Managers must also keep in mind that, over time, the spread and influence of the innovation has to be sustained such that the early majority is brought into the group of adopters. Once this group is included, almost half the total population is in the adoptive category.

2.2 INNOVATION IMPACT

2.2.1 Innovation and Competition

Research shows that to remain competitive, commercial firms have to innovate with IT and have to develop new ways of doing business that is superior to that of the competition. Two researchers, Brynjolfsson and McAfee, in a study published in 2008, showed that of all US companies in the period 1960 to 2005, the ones that gained the greatest competitive advantage did so on the basis of use of IT. This phenomena was particularly sharp after the mid-1990s since it was at that time that companies started using IT extensively, along with the presence of the commercial internet, and did so for strategic reasons. Competitive advantage here implies that firms are able to take market share away from rivals, and are thus able to achieve higher growth and better profits.

The study found that there are broadly two categories of IT users – those who use IT in their business heavily and those who use it lightly. These are classified as high and low IT using industries. Industries with high IT usage means that most companies in those industries are heavy IT users. Similarly, there are industries in which most firms are low IT users. When these industries are compared, with regards to the market share of the individual firms, some sharp results emerge.

One of the key findings is that post-1995, the market share of the top firms in the high IT industries began to increase. Figure 2.3 shows the market share of the top 20 largest firms in an industry, in the USA, and how that share changed in the period 1965–2005. One clear observation is that market share of the top 20 firms declined for about four decades. In 1995, the market share started increasing but more sharply for firms in high IT industries than in low IT industries. Brynjolfsson and Mcafee explain that since the mid-1990s, firms started investing

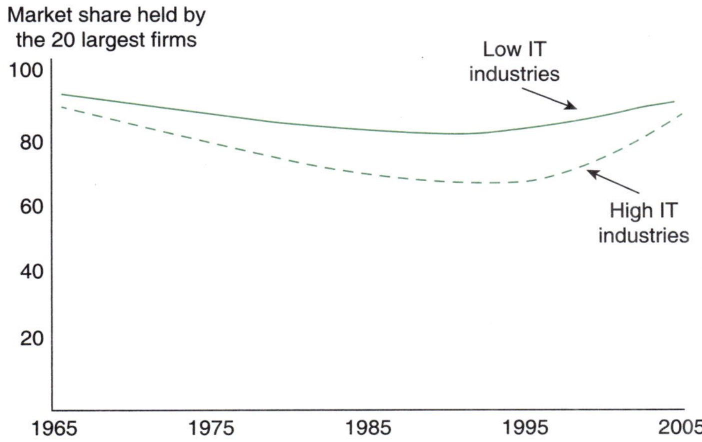

FIGURE 2.3 | Market share held by the top 20 US firms in low and high IT industries in the period 1965–2005.

in and using enterprise software such as enterprise resource planning (ERP) systems, customer relationship management systems (CRM), and other such systems that enabled firms to have consistent, standard, and uniform processes across the organisation, thus leading to massive gains in efficiency. Those efficiency gains led to better customer satisfaction, lower costs, and then increased market share.

Another finding of the study was that industries with high IT investments tended to show 'turbulence.' This means that firms that had a high ranking in terms of market share, could, in the following year, drop significantly. The competition for customers was strong and no one firm could remain dominant for long.

This phenomenon is observed in the mobile phone industry, which is a high IT user industry, where once dominant players like Nokia or Blackberry lost significant market share rapidly, within a space of a few months since the launch of powerful rivals.

The study also showed that there was a large difference in the profitability of firms that were winners (had a high percentage of the market share) and losers (had a low percentage of the market share) in the high IT industries. Even though all firms were investing heavily in IT, those in this segment, those who were winning were taking away more market share from their rivals. These are also called *winner-take-all* markets. Examples of winner-take-all markets are found, among other examples, in social networking sites, where winning players like Facebook tend to wipe out rivals like Orkut and Second Life. In the early part of the decade of the 2000s, Facebook was a mere start-up with a small but growing following. Social networking sites like Orkut, Second Life, and blog sites were dominant. These were all in the high IT investment industry. By late 2000s, Facebook all but wiped out Orkut (which shut down in 2014) and the virtual reality social networking site Second Life.

The dynamics of turbulence in markets and the phenomenon of winner-take-all competition arises from the widespread use of IT in these industries. These are third-order effects of IT, where rearrangements of entire industries results from the deep impact of IT. This phenomena is also in the nature of creative destruction within business firms, as predicted by Schumpeter.

2.2.2 Innovation Waves

With the massive scale and pace of innovations in IT, one challenge managers face is that of deciding which of the innovations are sound and can be investigated further, versus innovations that are a flash and may disappear. Managers could perhaps take a conservative approach and wait for innovations to be absorbed by the market, and be the late majority for adoption; however, this strategy is fraught with the risk of being too late and being a follower rather than a leader. Another problem is that many IT innovations tend to be oversold and confuse managers as to their true worth. Or managers could become innovators or early adopters and seek to gain

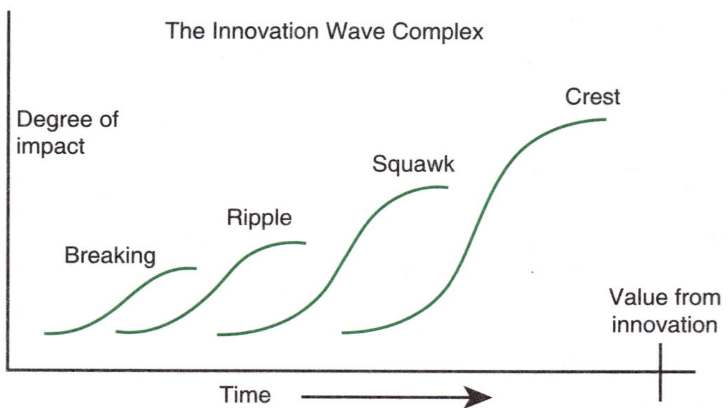

FIGURE 2.4 | The innovation wave complex.

competitive advantage from their strategy. This section explores the challenges associated with considering new and innovative IT products.

Innovations spread in a distinct manner, as explained by Rogers' model. However, there are many added complexities in the diffusion process for IT innovations. One way to understand innovations in IT is to think of them as waves in the ocean – an idea breaks the surface, sends out ripples, causes a swell, builds up, and then subsides (see Fig. 2.4).

Innovation researchers describe the first appearance of an idea as that of *breaking the surface*. In the IT world this would be a new software or hardware or a combination of both that enables something new. Somebody, somewhere tries this new software or hardware and finds it to be useful. The news of this finding is recorded. If the IT innovation was not that useful, it would die down, nobody would talk about it. For example, the idea of cloud computing first originated in the early 2000s, when one or two firms tried it out and found it to be useful. The idea was a good one and the innovators who adopted it helped to show that it was useful.

KEY POINT

Once an idea breaks the surface, the innovators articulate an organising vision for the community.

Once the idea breaks the surface, the innovators backing the innovation then try to 'cause a ripple.' This is usually in the form of an articulated *organising vision* – which is a focal idea or a key idea for the community (usually of users). This focal idea describes or illustrates the vision in a succinct manner, enabling others to understand it. The ripple can be sent out by commentators outside the firm, such as industry analysts or journalists, who write about the innovation, about how it is being used, and how the community could benefit from it. For example, in the early 1990s, some analysts from Gartner, which is a well-known technology analysis firm, sent out ripples about enterprise resource planning (ERP) systems, which later became widely popular. The organising vision they articulated was that of a single system addressing the needs of all the departments and functions of an organisation, which could address the problems associated with many systems.

Once the ripples have gone out, the innovators have to 'cause a squawk.' This involves informing a larger community of analysts, consultants, commentators and journalists about the innovation. Users are typically deluged with IT news and advertisements and are unable to decide whether this new thing is different and better. The community of commentators help to filter out all but the most interesting innovations. For example, online magazines such as Digit (Digit.in) and Wired (Wired.com) write and inform readers about the new innovations that are gaining momentum. Further, there are many conferences such as Interop (interop.com) and Techmentor (tecnmentorevents.com) that enable innovations to be viewed by the public. These magazines and events allow the innovation to be seen and read about by a wider audience; also, the selection of these innovations assures readers that they are of value.

For innovators, the step after causing a squawk is that of 'building a swell.' Here the main goal is to ensure that many clients and customers adopt the innovation and create the band-wagon effects that further influence others, the late majority, and encourages them to take an interest. As more attention is given to the innovation, it leads to positive reinforcements and attracts more attention. It is ideal if the innovation becomes a fad, a management fashion that attracts a lot of attention and draws many more adopters. For example, by the 2010s the idea of using Cloud technologies became a management fad and many organisations were considering its adoption simply because it was so popular.

With many adopters now using the innovation, the innovators move to 'ride the crest.' At this phase they try to involve other players to build complementary products and services that support the innovation; they try to create an *eco-system* around their product. Innovators also seek new market segments that can adopt the product. The most important thing to keep in mind about innovation waves is that the commercial value that can be realised from the innovation comes long after the innovators broke the surface and sent out ripples. Long after the innovation has been widely adopted will it turn 'valuable,' that is, the revenues will be large enough to justify the investments this far. Even users and adopters of new innovations will find that value from the adoption is realised much after they first heard of the innovation and moved to adopt it. For example, the investments in enterprise systems paid off much after the initial buzz about ERP had died down.

Caselet Blockchain Technology

Blockchain is a new, and highly disruptive, technology that has emerged since 2008. Its first major application was a digital currency known as Bitcoin. Blockchain technology was used within bitcoins to maintain a highly encrypted and reliable ledger of the currency, which was generated by a crowd of users who used their computers to allow entries on the ledger to be updated. Bitcoin was immediately successful as a payment mechanism, as it was not tied to any bank or central authority. However, the technology underlying bitcoins, blockchains, became more prominent as a mechanism to create a distributed and highly secure ledger for maintaining accounts of transactions.

The basic idea of Blockchain technology is that a vast public ledger is maintained collectively by all the users of the system. This ledger is tamper-proof in the sense that if a transaction is recorded it cannot be changed or tampered in any way. Further, the ledger is entirely transparent, and any user can verify at any time whether a transaction has been recorded or not. For example, if the blockchain ledger is being used by some users to transact in money, whenever anyone gives or receives money, this transaction is recorded in the ledger. There is no central authority needed to verify whether this transaction occurred; the moment it occurs it is reflected in the ledger. Further, since the ledger is distributed and a version of it is held by all the users, tampering is prevented as all versions would have to be changed also.

The potential uses of this technology are many. One possible application of this is in distributing artistic works, like songs or books, directly from songwriters and authors to buyers, without intermediaries. The blockchain enables the artists to create 'executable contracts' that allow the buyer to receive the song or book the moment the payment is made, with authentication, and without any scope of piracy. Such an arrangement removes the traditional intermediary, the publishers of songs and books and the retailers from the picture. Artists can sell their works directly to the buyers. Another possible application is being explored by banks, who are setting up blockchain ledgers for lending money to customers and also recording payments through the system. This is being extended to give credit, as opposed to using credit cards, with the transactions and credit history being maintained in the ledger.

The potential for the use of the technology are being explored by a wide variety of business firms and governments. The idea of having a technology enable accountability in a distributed and transparent manner is attractive and many are keen to explore the possibilities.

2.3 TYPES OF BUSINESS INNOVATIONS WITH IT

Digital innovations are of many types: some are products that are made by firms that compete against existing, pre-digital products; others are process innovations that are innovations made by firms to change some internal way of doing business using digital technology. Another innovation category is that of business models, which implies a way of delivering value to customers that is different and digitally based.

Innovating with products implies building or creating new digital products, whether as apps or software for laptops and servers, or new hardware such as wearable devices. The focus here is on the firm making these devices or technologies and on the decisions managers in these firms have to make to ensure the innovation succeeds in the market.

When firms innovate with processes, they use digital technologies to do things in newer and better ways. The innovations may be to reach new markets, serve customers better, provide new services to customers or to reduce costs of certain processes. The focus is on the users of IT and the manner in which they innovate.

KEY POINT

New business models focus on providing value to customers through different ways of doing business.

New business models may include new products and new processes, where the focus is on providing value to customers that is different from the existing way of doing business. For example, the Ola taxi aggregator provides a new business model in terms of how it allows users to call and book taxis. Although radio taxis and hail taxis have existed in India before, Ola's value proposition is in enabling customers to call taxis from wherever they are located, at the moment they need the taxi, with a simple interface. The other innovation Ola introduced was that of allowing independent taxi owners to join the Ola service, thus increasing the fleet of taxis rapidly. Ola provided value to customers on the demand side and also improved its services for its drivers on the supply side. Thus, Ola presented a new and innovative business model to generate revenues.

Examples of digital innovations in recent times are many and are also growing at a massive speed. In addition to the examples mentioned, some types of business innovations using IT are highlighted below.

1. **Industry transformation:** Digital imaging and photography products have completely disrupted the analog photography industry. Online video content distributors like Netflix, Hotstar and YouTube are in the process of disrupting the television and commercial movie distribution industry.
2. **Diversity and variety:** Digital products and services introduce immense diversity and competition to existing markets – e-commerce firms like Flipkart.com and Makemytrip.com have changed the nature of competition in the retail and travel industries.
3. **Personalisation:** One of the most significant advantages of digital products and services is that they can be tailored to the needs of individual users. For example, e-commerce sites like Flipkart offer recommendations on products based on past purchases. Information systems within organisations are often customised for users through special screens and menus.
4. **Experimentation:** Sites that offer digital goods run live experiments with customers to elicit tastes and preferences. For example, e-commerce sites run different ads for different sets of customers to understand how they respond, and thus learn about their preferences.
5. **Plug-and-play innovations:** In the digital space many firms are able to position themselves alongside existing players by adding a service or product over a platform. For example, the firm InMobi.com provides a service that places advertisements from their clients (the seller) with their buyers, based on their location and profile. InMobi does this in partnership with the goods seller and the platform provider; it provides its service on top of the existing platform, such as Android, without having to build the platform.
6. **New marketing opportunities:** Many digital services now act as vehicles for marketing. Ads are shown to consumers as they use freely downloaded apps.
7. **Use of smart technologies:** New products and devices, such as smart watches and fitness bands, enable collection of data on user behaviour and lifestyle thus enabling newer products to be designed. Devices installed in homes and buildings relay information about usage that leads to new products and services, and also to privacy concerns.
8. **Natural language interfaces:** Services like Siri and Google now allow users to talk and give instructions or take notes on devices. These facilities of voice-based services are now being extended to other devices and applications.

9. **Analytics:** Data is captured at a massive scale on users and their behaviour, and this is used to innovate on new products and services. For example, massive open online courses (MOOC) sites, like edX.org, collect data on how students take the courses, which videos they watch, for how long they watch the video, how many times do they return to the video, how long do they spend on the assignments, what posts they make in the discussion forums and on comment sites, and so on. This data is analysed to understand how students enrolled in courses behave while on the site or app, and how the offerings can be re-designed to suit student needs.
10. **Crowd sourcing:** Massive IT platforms enable firms to draw innovative ideas from their customers, other interested people, and from the public at large. The Indian firm Wishberry.com sources funds from people to support artistic and creative projects. Wishberry enables artistes to describe and list their projects, for making films, or writing novels, or creating dance routines, on the site and then visitors are invited to provide funds. These funds are philanthropic in nature and no returns are given, except some tickets or invitations to the event. Such crowd sourcing sites allow firms, individuals, or groups to source ideas, money, and support from masses of people, thus bypassing traditional agents, contracting firms, and even government departments.

2.4 MANAGEMENT ISSUES: CHALLENGES FOR MANAGERS

With the advent of massive innovation in IT and the transformations that they are bringing about, many management challenges emerge. These are issues that modern managers face and have become particularly important with the growth of innovations.

1. **Prices and margins:** The competition in the digital space has increased tremendously, with the result that prices of commodities and services are getting lowered. The 'price wars' between e-commerce firms in India is well known, where, in certain periods, goods are discounted heavily, and this forces competitors to lower prices also. The emergence of Ola cabs too forced its competition, other taxi aggregator firms and independent taxi owners, to lower prices to remain competitive with Ola. Managers have to remain alert to price competition and respond adequately; however, sustained price wars lead to reduced profits and a lower ability to invest further and innovate.
2. **Talent shortage:** Many firms are finding that recruiting the right employees with the necessary skills is a challenge. Products require skills in new and cutting edge technologies, like date science and artificial intelligence, that are lacking in the workforce at large. The challenge for managers is to find and recruit personnel with the adequate skills, enable the existing workforce to acquire new skills, and also retain skilled employees who will be in demand in other firms.
3. **Global presence:** Digital technologies like cloud computing enable firms to offer services and products across national boundaries. Storage of data, for example, is subject to the laws of the nation in which the storage servers are physically located. This presents challenges to manager to navigate laws in many countries and regions.
4. **Risk-taking abilities:** Innovation in IT is driving change so rapidly that managers have to take risks with building and sustaining innovations. The option of doing nothing, or waiting for the innovation to stabilise, risks losing out to competition. Also, taking action too early risks taking the wrong choice before the technology has matured. Managers have to consider technology mindfully and ensure they have a deep understanding of the choices they are facing.
5. **Integration of online and offline models:** With the digital innovations growing, it is imperative that managers who are responsible for offline and traditional businesses, actively consider the digital challenge and include that in their offerings. Competitors to Ola, such as Meru cabs, who relied on an offline model, have built an online presence and integrated

their business with modern technologies, such as apps and websites. On the other hand, business that emerged from the digital space, such as e-commerce firms, have begun to build offline stores that complete their presence in the physical space also. Managers will have to seek greater integration between online and offline presence in future.

Chapter Glossary

Semiconductors Electronic components such as transistors, diodes and resistors are made with this material. These materials allow electricity to pass more easily in one direction than the other, are sensitive to changes in light and heat, and also have variable resistance. These properties make them useful for use in computer chips and other components.

Transistor This is an electronic component made with semiconducting material that behaves like a switch, allowing electric current to pass or not pass. This is a key component of all computer chips.

Disruptive innovation Situation where cheap products with lesser functionality challenge existing products, and eventually beat the latter by gaining market share.

Creative destruction A phrase to describe the phenomenon of new businesses emerging while destroying and eliminating earlier businesses.

Diffusion The spread of an idea across a population from an origin, over time.

Innovation A new idea, product, or service that has an economic value and leads to new business opportunities.

Innovators Those who invent new ideas, products, or services. In Rogers' model innovators are the early adopters of ideas.

Turbulence in markets Sudden and unpredictable changes in the market position of firms in terms of market share and value.

Business ecosystem A network of businesses that are dependent on each other for resources and business opportunities.

Review Questions

1. What is Moore's law and how has it shaped the progress of the IT industry?
2. How is a disruptive innovation different from a normal innovation? Why are the former important?
3. What is creative destruction?
4. How do ideas and innovations diffuse through a population over time?
5. What is the main difference between firms that are heavy users of IT and firms that are low users of IT?
6. What is an organising vision for an innovation?
7. What is the innovation wave complex and what phenomenon does it explain?
8. Why is Blockchain technology considered to be so promising?
9. Identify a few business innovations with IT that have appeared recently.
10. What are the key management issues for managing innovations with IT?

Research Questions

1. Given that Ola Cabs has garnered a fair share of the market, is it possible that they will have many more competitors to deal with in future? Do research to find out the new innovations that threaten Ola's market.
2. Moore's law has limits: the size of semiconductors cannot be reduced beyond a certain point. What is that point? Find out how for the size of the components on chips can be reduced.
3. Rogers' model explains many diffusion phenomena. Research one phenomena, such as the spread of a game or an app, and examine who were the innovators, the early adopters, and those in the other categories of the model.
4. Consider the example of one technology innovation, such as the mobile phone or the laptop, and see how the growth and spread of the innovation followed the wave complex.

Further Reading

1. Christensen, C. (2013). *The Innovator's Dilemma: When New Technologies cause Great Firms to Fail*. Harvard Business Review Press.
2. Rogers, E. M. (2010). *Diffusion of Innovations*. Simon and Schuster.
3. Swanson, E. B. (2012). The Managers guide to IT innovation waves. *MIT Sloan Management Review*, *53*(2), 75.
4. Weill, P., & Woerner, S. L. (2015). Thriving in an increasingly digital ecosystem. *MIT Sloan Management Review*, *56*(4), 27.
5. Kane, G. C., Palmer, D., Phillips, A. N., Kiron, D., & Buckley, N. (2015). Strategy, not technology, drives digital transformation. *MIT Sloan Management Review and Deloitte University Press*.
6. McAfee, A., & Brynjolfsson, E. (2008). Investing in the IT that makes a competitive difference. *Harvard Business Review*, *86*(7/8), 98.
7. Tapscott, D., & Tapscott, A. (2016). The impact of the blockchain goes beyond financial services. *Harvard Business Review*.
8. http://www.computerworld.com.au/article/606253/understanding-blockchain-hype-why-much-it-nothing-more-than-snake-oil-spin/ (Accessed in October 2016.)
9. http://www.nytimes.com/2015/05/13/opinion/thomas-friedman-moores-law-turns-50.html?_r=0 (Accessed in June 2016.)
10. http://iq.intel.com/5th-generation-intel-core-processors-make-waves-ces-2015/ (Accessed in October 2016.)

CHAPTER 3

Concepts of Management Information Systems

LEARNING OBJECTIVES

After completing this chapter, you will be able to:

- Learn to differentiate between data and information
- Understand information as a resource
- Get an overview of the role of information in organisational functions
- Learn about the types of MIS
- Understand decision making with MIS
- Get an overview of communication in organisations

Data is a raw collection of facts and information is processed data. These are the key resources that have to be managed in organisations. Data is collected and used in all major functions of an organisation, and the information resources thus created are used across the organisation. Any organisation uses three types of information systems:

1. Those that are for individual users.
2. Those meant for people working in groups.
3. Those meant for the entire organisation.

Information systems are also viewed as transaction processing systems that enable the basic processes of the organisation, or as management information systems (MIS) that enable managers to have a high-level comprehensive view of the processes and functions in the organisation. These systems help employees and managers make decisions. Decisions are either for the short term, meant for immediate action, or for the medium term where the impacts of decisions are felt over days or weeks, or for the long term where impacts are experienced over weeks and months. Systems are designed specifically for all types of decision-making situations.

Information systems are also used extensively for communication within organisations. There are many forms and types of communication that enable the modern organisation to function effectively.

MIND MAP OF CHAPTER TOPICS

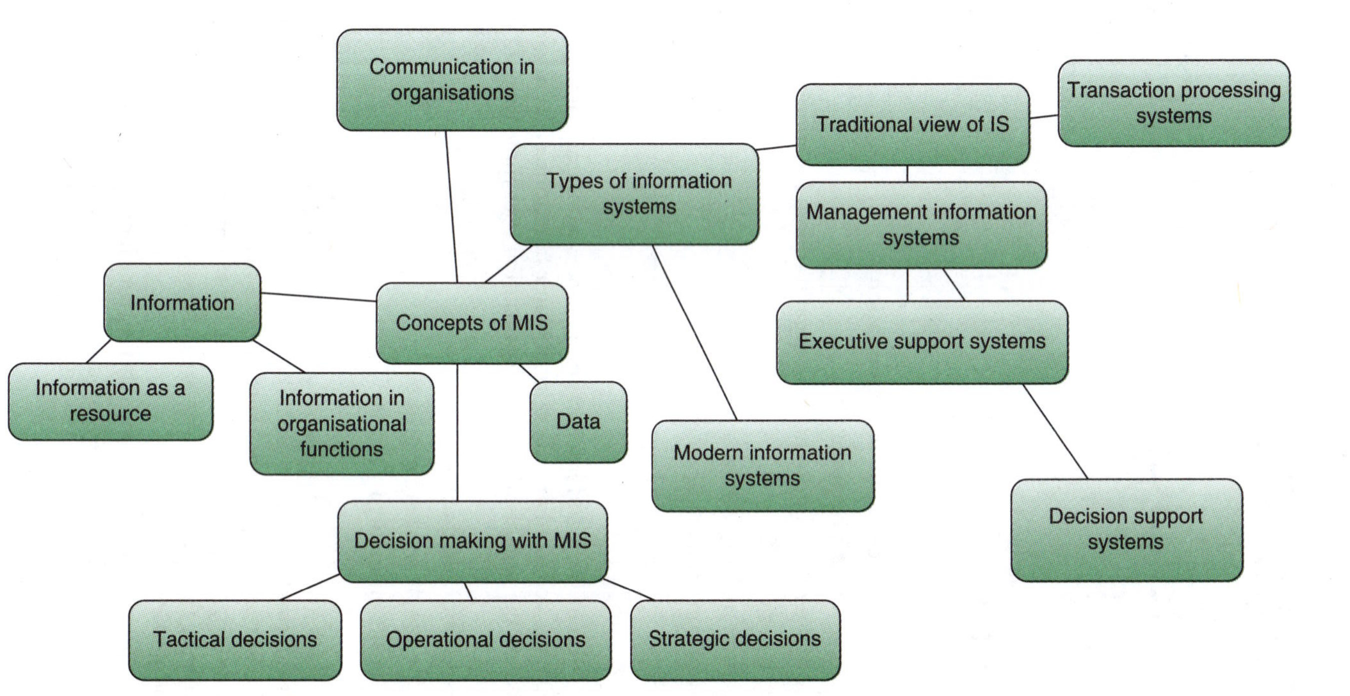

The Indian Railways was started in 1853 when the first track was laid over a distance of 34 km, and passenger trains started plying on it. About 150 years later, that is, by 2008, the Indian Railways had the fourth largest network of rail tracks in the world, standing at about 67,000 km. These tracks connect about 7000 stations, all over the country. The Indian Railways not only moves passengers, almost 22 million of them daily, but also moves a very large amount of freight, and is also considered to be the business and industrial lifeline of the country. Some facts about the scale of operations at the Indian Railways (IR) are presented in Table 3.1.

Over the years the IR has faced challenges of a growing passenger base, increased competition from improved roadways and increasing air services, and a growing demand for efficient and increased movement of freight. The growth in passenger traffic is depicted in Fig. 3.1.

Table 3.1 | Important Facts about the Indian Railways (2007)

Total length of rail tracks	67,312 km
Total number of railway stations	7112
Total number of passengers carried daily	22 million
Total amount of freight carried annually	1.1 billion tonnes
Total number of employees	1.37 million
Total number of wagons and coaches	311,659
Total number of locomotives	10,499
Total number of passenger trains	12,617

To manage immense requirements of passengers and freight customers, the IR has created a number of information systems for handling various tasks such as passenger ticket reservation and sale, management of staff and freight management. Each of these systems is briefly described below.

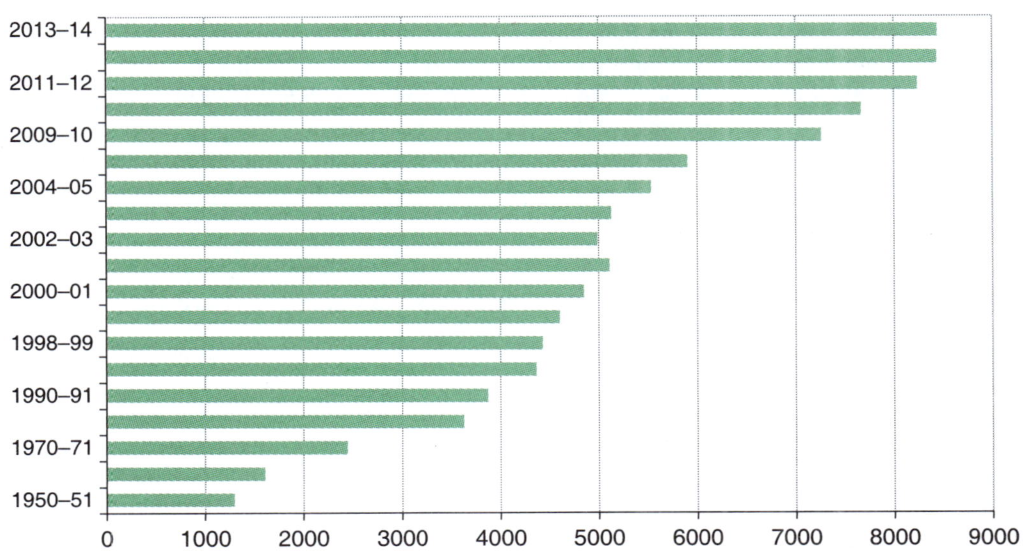

FIGURE 3.1 | Increase in passenger traffic for the Indian Railways, from 1950 to 2014 (in millions).

Passenger Reservation System

This system is the most important for the IR as it allows millions of customers to see the reservation status on different trains in real time and book tickets. The passenger reservation system was first implemented in the mid-1980s. Initially, it was implemented in only a few major stations and covered only a few trains, only for certain classes of reserved tickets. As the demand for the system grew and as competition for the railways services increased, the management decided to increase the scope of the system to allow more passengers and trains to be available through the system. The system currently is accessible through the internet where passengers can check the current position on any train, make a reservation from origin to destination anywhere in India, pay for the ticket with any of several means including with a credit card, and use a printout of the ticket to board a train. The system also allows tickets to be delivered to customers' homes if they so desire. Furthermore, using the system, the customers can change or cancel their booking, and their money is refunded.

A typical transaction on the reservation system takes only a few minutes. Computer kiosk operators permit users to access the system from practically anywhere in India to book tickets on any train. Currently, the system also sells unreserved tickets on most trains.

Freight Operation Information System (FOIS)

The Indian Railways operates over 200,000 wagons or rakes to move millions of tonnes of freight. This operation has to be managed carefully to ensure that the rakes are available where they are needed to load freight, and, once used, are sent to another destination. When the rakes remain unused, they are a cost on the system, especially when they could have been used elsewhere. The IR wanted to manage its freight operations in such a manner that they could have a quick and real-time update on where the freight trains are, how many rakes are being used, how many are idle, where they are located and where they are needed. For this purpose they built the FOIS that allows them to see in real time where the goods trains are, where they are headed and how much goods they are carrying. Once equipped with this information, the IR can inform their clients about the exact arrival times for their goods or when their shipments can be loaded. The FOIS also helps the IR allocate rakes efficiently, ensuring they are used to their full capacity.

Crew Management System (CMS)

This system involves monitoring the activities of over 55,000 crew members across locations in India. The system allows the management to know where the crew are located, when they arrived there and how long they have waited. The system also has details about the crew payment schedule, their experience with different locomotives, their duty allocation and their training schedule among other information. The crew input their details using various terminals at over 140 locations, and this data is aggregated to form the reports. The system operates in real time round the clock and round the year. It is a very successful system and is crucial for the IR to manage their trains and crew.

Integrated Coaching Management System (ICMS)

This enables the IR authorities to view in real-time manner where each passenger train is located at any time. Data about the movement and location of trains is monitored on a screen. The ICMS is particularly useful for scheduling trains' movement near bottlenecks such as bridges and heavy traffic zones. Traffic managers can delay or speed up trains near these bottlenecks so that the overall traffic movement is smooth. With the ICMS, the IR is able to improve the train arrival time accuracy by 10–15% in a zone where it has to manage over 400 passenger trains. The system also includes a module to manage freight trains whose traffic also contributes to congestion.

3.1 DATA AND INFORMATION

Data is a raw collection of facts. The word raw indicates that the facts have not been processed in any way. When processed, data is called information.

For example, consider the act of booking a ticket on the Indian Railways (IR) website. Let us assume that you have already picked your source station, the place where you will start your journey, and the target station, where you want to go. Let us further assume that you have provided the following data: Your name, your age, the date on which you are travelling and the number of persons travelling with you. With this data, which is entered in the specially marked *fields* on the IR website, the IR system is able to process the request for a ticket. It looks at the availability of trains, seats and reservations and provides information to you about:

1. The seats available.
2. The days and trains on which these are available.
3. The cost of the tickets.

In this case, we see that the raw data you provide about your travel details is used by the system to provide *information* regarding ticket availability and prices. This information is based on the processing done on the raw facts provided.

Data and information are often used interchangeably, as information can be treated as raw data that is used for further processing. For example, the details regarding your confirmed booking may now be rearranged in the system as data about reserved seats, the train on which booking is done, the details of payment made, etc. This data is used to produce information about the availability of trains and seats, revenues collected from ticket sales and prepare passenger lists.

The raw data and the information produced from it are stored in software programs called *databases* in the internal storage of organisations. Databases help store, retrieve, protect and manage the data and information. Most organisations, like the Indian Railways, have vast stores of information that they retain in their databases. This information forms the basis for managing the organisation.

KEY POINT

Data is a raw collection of facts, whereas information in processed data. Data and information are stored in databases.

3.1.1 Measuring Data

Data is stored in computers as 1s and 0s. All data is stored in this manner. It is also transmitted as 1s and 0s. A typical memory space in a computer would look like the strip shown in Fig. 3.2.

The slots in the strip shown in the figure are memory spaces that contain *binary digits* or *bits*. Bits are the basic data that computers work with and store. Bits are stored in various kinds of memory - random access memory (RAM), secondary memory or the hard disk, or a flash memory stick.

Bits were originally aggregated in sets of 8 bytes. Much of the original development of computers was done with 8-bit bytes. Later, byte sizes were changed to 16- and 32-bit bytes (and also 64-bit now), but the memory storage is still referred to by the 8-bit byte units.

Memory capacities are designated in kilobytes, megabytes or gigabytes. Strictly speaking, a kilobyte is 1024 bytes. It is not 1000 bytes as the name would suggest. Computer equipment manufacturers often use the term kilobytes to imply 1024 bytes of storage space. Measures of higher memory capacities are given in Table 3.2. It is quite common nowadays for organisations to have access to storage capacities of many petabytes on their premises or on Cloud.

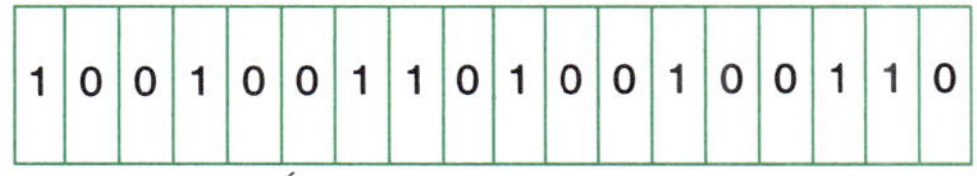

FIGURE 3.2 | Data stored in computer memory. Each cell contains a 1 or a 0.

Table 3.2 | Measures of Computer Memory Capacity

Memory Size Term	Actual Size in Bytes
1 Kilobyte (KB)	1024 bytes
1 Megabyte (MB)	$(1024)^2$ bytes
1 Gigabyte (GB)	$(1024)^3$ bytes
1 Terabyte (TB)	$(1024)^4$ bytes
1 Petabyte (PB)	$(1024)^5$ bytes
1 Exabyte (EB)	$(1024)^6$ bytes

3.2 INFORMATION AS A RESOURCE

It is well known that commercial firms use three principal resources to carry out their business – money (or capital), labour and materials. These resources may be specific to a particular activity or task; for example, some machines are used for only one task in any firm, such as for stamping metal sheets of one size. Resources can also be used generally, as money can be used for many things, and some machines, like lathes, can do many things. For commercial firms, each unit of resource is said to contribute to produce some output. The economic productivity of a firm is measured by the units of output (which may be seen as cars made or passengers serviced) that are produced per unit of input resources such as money.

Information too is a resource for an organisation. Like money or labour, information is used in many tasks and activities to produce the output of the organisation. Also, like other resources, it has to be carefully managed. Treating information as a resource allows us to ask in what way does this resource contribute to the functioning of the organisation and also what is its value for the organisation? This clarifies what the role of information is in the organisation's context and how and why it has to be managed.

In the previous section we saw that processed data is information. When organisations collect data and process it for doing their normal work, as we saw in the example of buying a ticket from the Indian Railways, they create large stores of information. These information stores are a byproduct of the processes that an organisation performs, and they are resident in various forms in the organisation's databases. As such, one could argue, these byproducts do not have much value for the organisation, other than for accounting purposes, after the work is done, and the organisation will have no need for this information again. By this argument, then, the information could simply be stored in some compressed form, called *archiving*, or it could be gotten rid of altogether. However, most modern organisations do not agree to this argument – they treat information as a valuable asset that has to be managed and used for different purposes. The information can be used for decision making and for planning about future activities. An example will make this aspect clear.

Consider the information collected by the Indian Railways while it sells tickets for its many trains. Data about the particulars of the passengers and their journey is stored in the databases. However, along with this data, other details can also be collected, such as the time and date of ticket purchase, the number of choices considered, the manner of payment, the time required for the transaction, whether an agent did the booking or it was done by the passenger, etc. Table 3.3 lists this information with regard to ticket purchase transaction.

This information collected during ticket purchase transactions can then be used by the Railways management to answer the following questions:

1. At what time of the day do most passengers buy tickets online?
2. At what time of the year do ticket sales increase and peak (or decrease)?

Table 3.3 | Data Regarding Ticket Purchase Transaction

Data Items
Time of ticket purchase
Date of ticket purchase
Duration of transaction
Whether Agent used (who was the Agent)
Number of alternatives considered

3. How many choices do passengers usually consider before buying a ticket?
4. Do passengers usually rely on the services of an agent to buy tickets?

Among the above questions, the first one can be answered by analysing the ticket sales data along with the time of purchase. If the time units in a day are broken up into 'buckets' of 1 h each, the number of ticket sales in each hour can be computed easily (see Fig. 3.3). When managers know the load on the ticket sales at different times of the day, they can plan for additional resources that may be required, whether for staffing, for additional data storage and backup or for additional network resources.

The answers to all the questions will help IR managers decide on the nature and type of services that can be provided by the system in future, manage train schedules and manage the ticket sales process. The information thus stored in the databases is resources that enable the organisation function better.

The example above shows the information resources are assets created by an organisation. These assets are specific to the organisation, in our example, and have value in managing the organisation. Sometimes information assets could be of value not only for the one that created them but also to other organisations. In such a case, the organisation that owns the data could share or sell the assets for furthering its goals.

KEY POINT

Information is an organisational resource like money, labour and materials.

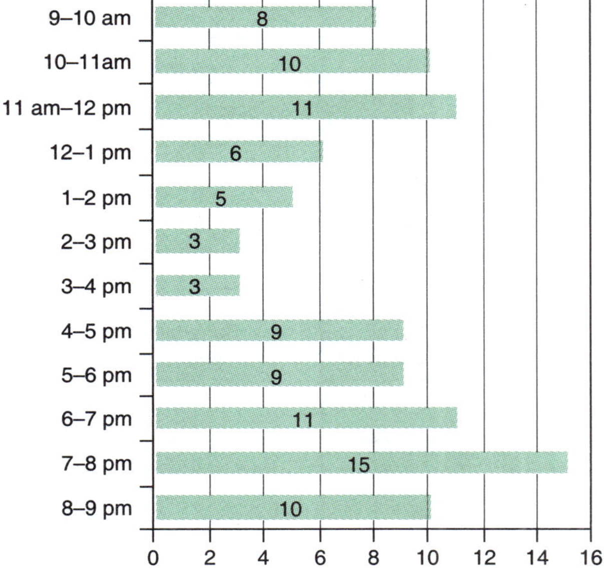

FIGURE 3.3 | Percent of tickets sales in a 12-h period (simulated numbers).

3.3 INFORMATION IN ORGANISATIONAL FUNCTIONS

Any organisation works by dividing up the tasks that it has to perform among its various departments or functions. Typical functions in any organisation include accounting (and finance), marketing, operations, human resource management and information systems management. These functions may have their own staffing and reporting relationships. The break-up and structure of the functions within an organisation depend on the kind of work the organisation is engaged in and also on its size and age.

Personnel involved in functions and working in departments in any organisation are placed in a hierarchy. A typical hierarchy is considered similar to an inverted tree with the top management at the tip. Below the top level are the middle managers who head functions or departments. At the bottom of the hierarchy are the workers, sales personnel, office staff and others who report to the managers (see Fig. 3.4).

In the modern organisation, information, data and information systems are used extensively within and across organisational functions. Consider, for example, the *accounting* function within any organisation. The main task of this function is to manage and control the most important resource the organisation uses, which is money. A typical accounting department maintains accounts or books or ledgers on the various activities of the organisation. So it will maintain accounts on material acquisition, material usage, wage payments, vendor payables and receivables, operations expenses, transportation expenses, sales receipts, etc. The data from these activities is collected from different departments, offices and functions and is stored in a database of some accounting software.

Through the accounting function, data is used to create information about money, its use and its flow within the organisation. Managers are able to assess where more money is required, which activities need attention, how much money is needed for an activity, what tax payments are required, etc. The information is used to prepare *reports* about various aspects of the organisation. Data and information then become the resources that provide a perspective through the accounting function to the entire organisation.

Data created and used by the different members of the function vary by the level at which they are located and the functions and responsibilities they need to discharge. For example, the

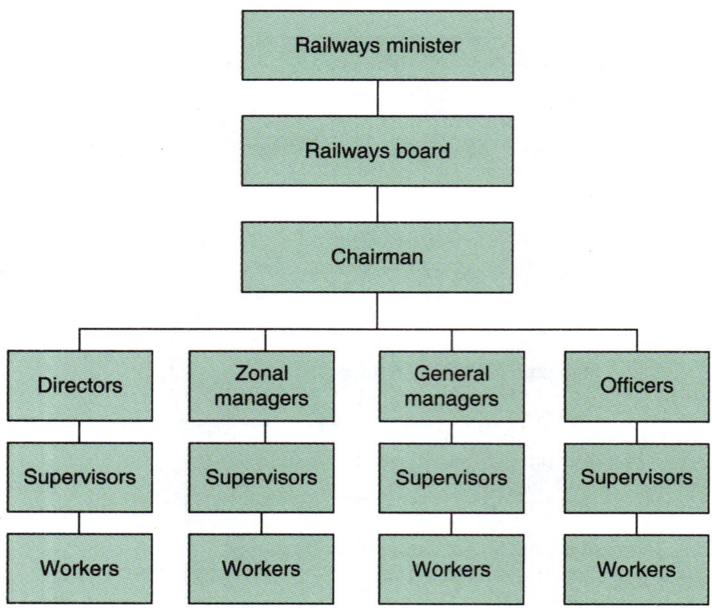

FIGURE 3.4 | Hierarchy structure of Indian Railways. This is a simplified view of the real hierarchy.

marketing function of an industrial manufacturing firm provides laptops to its marketing executives who visit potential and existing customers. When they make a visit to a potential customer, they record data about the customer's address and contact numbers, the customer's specific needs, the customer's intention to buy the product, the customer's time horizon for the purchase and so on. This information is then used by the marketing manager to decide on:

1. What kind of product to pitch to the customer.
2. When to make another contact.
3. Whether to make a special offer.

The information created and used by the field marketing executive is different from that used and created by the manager.

In a modern manufacturing facility, information assists in managing the *operations* function. An assembly line worker in an automobile assembly unit uses information technology to determine what components to use, test the assembly, record the number and type of components used, inform the inventory department of material consumption and read the total production demand for the shift, etc. The worker creates data that is entered into the information systems and this acts as a record of the production process. The worker also reads current information from the systems to do his/her work. Managers and supervisors at the plant use the information in the systems to determine production targets, assess production levels and report on inventories, working capital and other resources. Workers and managers use the same systems but see and use different aspects.

In the *human resources* function of a firm, employees enter data about their attendance, their days of leave, the functions they perform, the projects they are assigned to, the persons they report to and work with, and their travel on work, etc. Managers use the data, available in the human resources function, to determine how to staff their projects and which personnel to send for specific training, and to monitor the performance of the employees for promotions and transfers.

KEY POINT

Different departments access data and information from the systems according to their varying needs.

3.4 TYPES OF INFORMATION TECHNOLOGY

Historically, information systems were created for specific functions in the organisation and for particular levels of personnel in the hierarchy. Systems for accounting, operations, marketing and other functions were largely designed, built and maintained independently with little sharing of data among them. Each system supported the function for which it was designed. It was in this function that the data for the systems originated and the information and reports originating from the systems were used by personnel in that function.

Modern information systems are designed largely to support individuals, groups or enterprise functions. This view of the systems is derived largely from the perspective of the modern information technology infrastructure that is being used. Figure 3.5 depicts the components of a modern information technology infrastructure. The functional information technology component consists of applications that are used by individual users within a function for their own work. These applications could be word processors, spreadsheets, computer-aided design software or others that help individuals to do their work. These systems need not rely on other systems in the organisation except perhaps to retrieve or send data. These are highly valuable to the user who is able to function with them.

The network information technology enables individuals within functions to communicate with others to collaborate in groups. The individuals can communicate with others within the organisation or outside in the organisation's economic environment. Applications such as email, blogs, wikis, etc. enable such groups to function and work. The groups may use the network infomation systems to communicate with each other, share documents, share knowledge, decide and plan for meetings using a common calendar, jointly solve problems, etc. The systems are based on the network infrastructure of the firm. The groups can be formed spontaneously and need to be fixed in advance; they may also merge with others or collapse as and when desired. The network information technology allows patterns of work to 'emerge'.

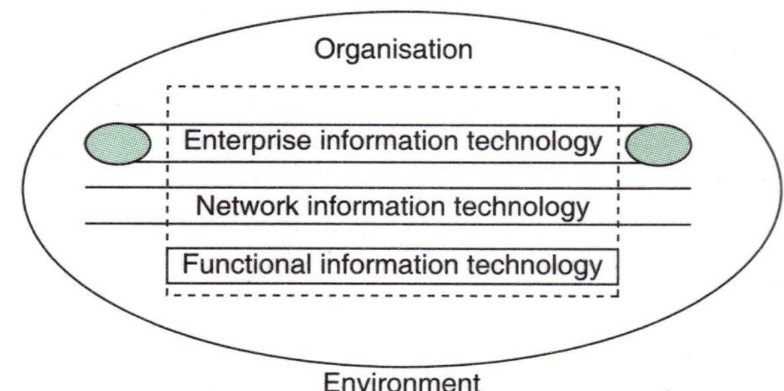

FIGURE 3.5 | Components of modern information technology infrastructure in an organisation.

KEY POINT

Modern information systems in organisations enable individuals to do their own work, help groups to communicate, and enable organisation members to share data and processes.

The enterprise information technology is used to support activities of individuals, groups and entire functions across the organisation. The enterprise systems rely on data entered by various individuals in different functions. The data is shared across the organisation and serves to inform different people about all the ongoing activities. For example, the accounts department may use the data input by marketing, production, sales and inventory functions to determine the asset, credit, payment and other balance details to create a consolidated balance sheet of the organisation on a monthly basis. The enterprise systems are designed for the processes in the organisation and are very efficient in moving information. However, they do not permit much flexibility to individuals to change processes or communication patterns. Such systems also interact with outside partners, either vendors or channel sellers.

We will now discuss the historical view of information systems within the organisation.

3.5 TYPES OF INFORMATION SYSTEMS

3.5.1 Transaction Processing Systems

A transaction is any activity of the organisation that generates information. For example, the activities related to buying a ticket from the Indian Railways generates many transactions, each of which produces information that is recorded by the systems. Some transactions involve exchange of goods or services while others may be purely informational. A transaction processing system records all the transactions as they happen. In this sense, such systems are considered to be online systems.

When users initiate transactions, the systems respond in a pre-specified manner, such as asking the user to fill in information about themselves. Most systems are designed to serve many users simultaneously. They are also designed to respond quickly and in a manner that makes the systems appear 'live' to the user.

Most transaction processing systems present carefully designed interfaces to the user that guide the transactions. A transaction processing system helps the user during a transaction by changing screens and the information on the screen. This requires the systems to provide information that is relevant for the situation. The exchange of information is highly sensitive to the context that is desired by the user. Modern transaction systems allow users to change the information input by them and backtrack to earlier parts of the transaction stream.

KEY POINT

Transaction processing systems store and manipulate data pertaining to activities in the organisation.

Transaction data is recorded as the transaction proceeds. This data is transferred into large databases that become a resource that the organisation can use. For very large e-commerce systems, like that of the Indian Railways, the data may be recorded and stored in databases located at many sites.

Transaction processing systems enable the day-to-day functioning of the enterprise. Activities ranging from procuring materials to receiving payments to shipping goods out to warehouses are all recorded by these systems. The systems thus preserve a digital record of the functioning of the enterprise.

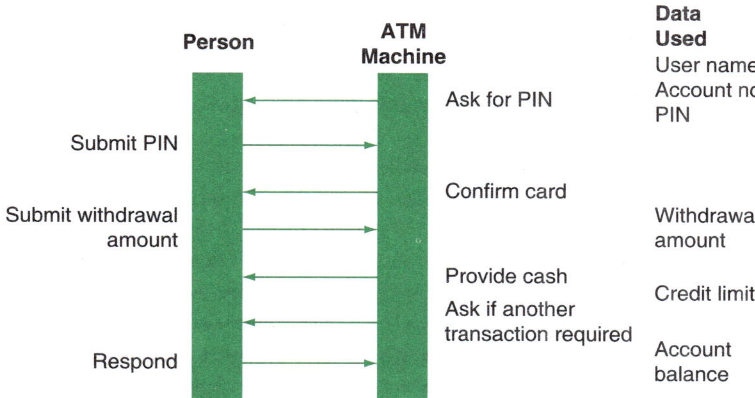

FIGURE 3.6 A transaction performed on an automated teller machine (ATM). The right column shows the data used in this transaction.

An example of a transaction is depicted in Fig. 3.6. This transaction involves a person withdrawing money from an automated teller machine (ATM). The column on the right-hand side of the figure shows the data used for the transaction. Some of the data is provided directly by the person's ATM card and some is obtained by the system from the database belonging to the bank that owns the ATM.

3.5.2 Management Information Systems

Management information systems (MIS) process the information generated by the transaction processing systems of an organisation and create reports for use by the management. A typical MIS report may consist of the following information that depicts various activities of the organisation:

1. A report on the average daily sales of the organisation with details for each product and each region.
2. The daily production of goods.
3. The seasonal sales of the organisation with regard to each region and product.
4. The cash balances for each division, with details of inflows and outflows for the week.
5. A report on personnel and project assignments and the number of hours logged in by each person for the month and for the week.
6. A report on printing and paper charges across the organisation for the year, with details related to divisions and seasons.

MIS help the management sense the organisation by seeing and reviewing all the activities as well as take decisions regarding future activities. Sensing the organisation may be done in real time, with data updates provided on screens for managers to see. These data may pertain to production, sales, financial activity or network traffic activity. The information is aggregated according to the needs of individual managers to monitor their domain of responsibility. Sensing may also involve accessing and viewing data outside the organisation, such as economic activity, industry trends, market data or competitor activity. Such information may be purchased from other sources and then aggregated with the organisation's data to see a comprehensive picture.

Sensing and monitoring of the organisation may be done in *real time* or in *batch* mode. Real-time monitoring involves presenting aggregated data as soon as it is created. For example, many firms view market activity on their investments or the prices of their stocks in real time. This information is collected as soon as there are changes in the market prices; it is aggregated with existing data and depicted in a chart. For this purpose, the information systems of the firm have

KEY POINT

Real-time processing of data is done as soon as the data is available.

to be networked and connected with the data source. Real-time data can also be provided on internal activities of production, sales, cash flows or network traffic, etc. This data is collected and processed as soon as a transaction happens, and then displayed in an appropriate form.

KEY POINT

Batch mode processing of data is done after data is collected and aggregated up to a certain level.

Batch mode monitoring involves showing data and information in an aggregated form after a period of time. For example, managers may want to see data on sales only on a daily basis and in an appropriate format. The data on the sales for a day is collected and then summarised and processed in the manner desired. Information depicted in the batch mode is usually more comprehensive and provides a better analysis.

Reports prepared in the batch mode allow managers to *drill down* to details. The drill-down procedure, if it is on the computer, allows managers to click on a point on the screen where details are required, and this takes them to another screen where the relevant details are provided. For example, if a manager is seeing the aggregate data on sales for the month, he/she could click on the data for a particular product and see the sales for it on a weekly basis. If the report is given as a printed document, which makes it impossible for the manager to click on any detail, then drill-down details are printed out and provided with the report.

KEY POINT

Drill-down procedures involve seeking greater detail in the data presented.

When MIS reports are available, these can be used for decision making. Often reports are tailored for specific decisions. For example, managers often have to decide on how much money to borrow from a bank, for the week, which has to be used as *working capital*. Their decision is based on how much cash the organisation has currently in its accounts and how much will be required for the week. MIS reports can be designed to inform the manager of the exact amount of cash available at any time and the current production and sales activity levels for which working capital is required. With the current data on balances and activities available in a single convenient report, the manager finds it convenient to take a quick decision on how much to borrow from the bank. Advances in information systems now permit the manager to automate the decision, wherein the systems also suggest how much to borrow to the manager based on the past experiences of the organisation.

Tailoring MIS reports to assist the manager with his/her decisions requires finding out about the manager's decision-making tasks and the manner in which he/she goes about them. As MIS are built on top of the transaction processing data, they can be configured to reflect the needs of the manager. Building MIS thus involves collecting the manager's requirements and then designing systems that will help with his/her decision-making activities.

3.5.2.1 MIS at Different Levels

The needs of managers at various levels in the organisation are different. Some need information that is real time and detailed while others need information that is aggregated and covers a long period of time.

Those at the highest level of any organisation, such as Managing Directors and Chief Executives, usually need information that is aggregated, enables drilling-down, summarises all activities and provides details about the industry at large. MIS that provide reports for executives at this level are often called *executive support systems* (ESS). An example of a typical screen of an ESS is shown in Fig. 3.7. Some examples of information provided by such systems are:

1. A report on sales forecasts for all products, plotted against the forecasts for the entire industry.
2. A summary of cash balances for all divisions for the year, the month and the week, with an ability to drill down to details for all divisions.
3. A summary of completion of all projects, with details of work remaining, estimated overruns on time and cost with comparison figures of projects in the past.

KEY POINT

Executive support systems assist top-level executives in making decisions.

Executive support systems are usually highly visual in nature with graphs, charts and diagrams used to convey most of the information. While designing these systems, it is imperative for the designers to understand the style of functioning of the executive. ESS are usually linked to other MIS and transaction processing systems and databases that provide industry data.

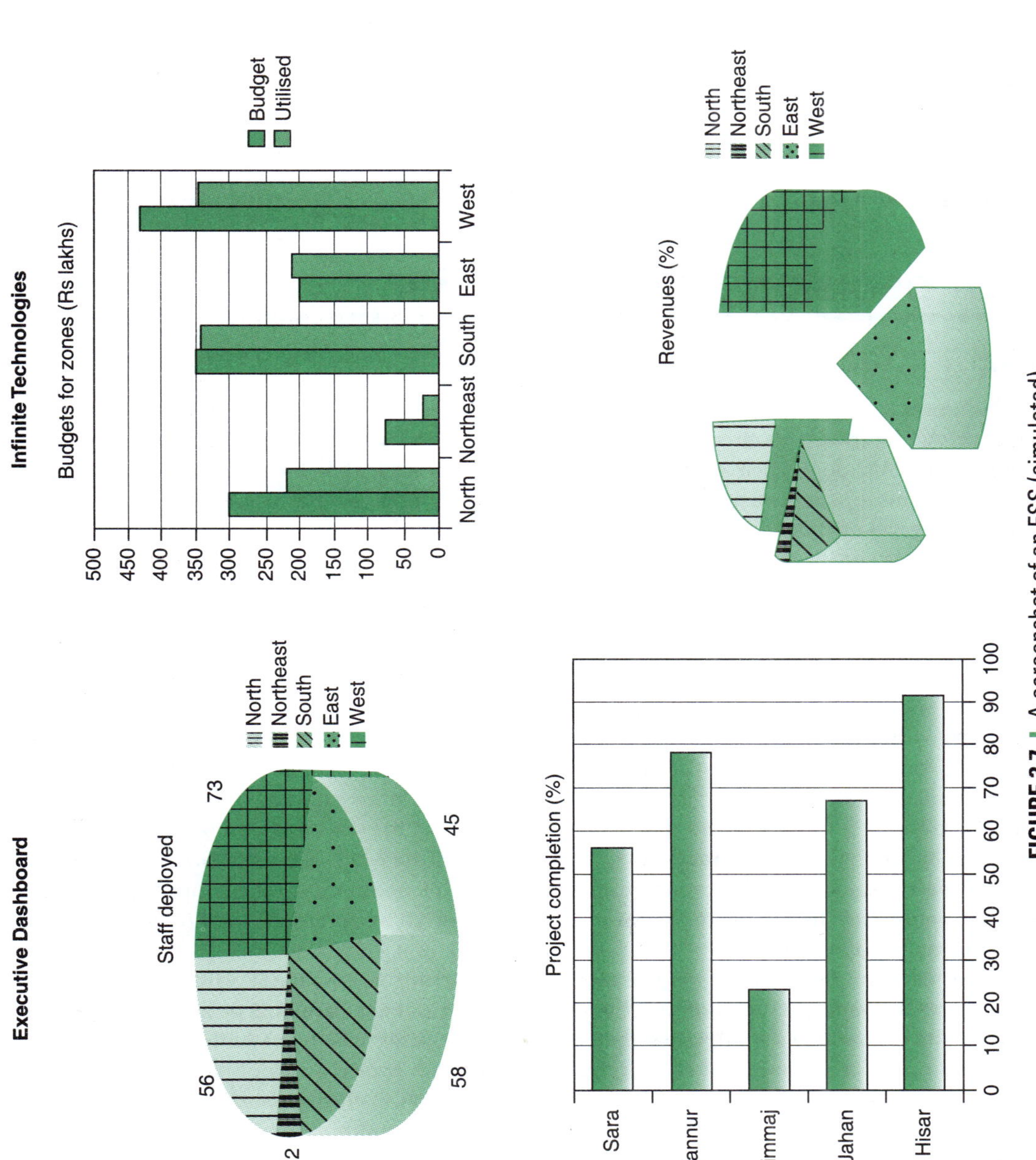

FIGURE 3.7 | A screenshot of an ESS (simulated).

Managers in the organisation, who report to the executives, use MIS and require reports, examples of which have been provided above. The systems used by managers are usually categorised as either MIS or *Decision Support Systems*. The latter use scientific models of decision making to help managers in the specific tasks of making decisions based on available data.

Another class of employees, similar to managers but not directly involved with decision making, are the specialised knowledge workers such as designers, planners and analysts. They use transaction data and other data related to the industry and economy to make strategic-level plans and do analysis for the organisation. They too use sophisticated models of analysis and produce reports that assist executives and managers with their decision making. For example, strategic planners may consult the industry and economy data and compare this with internal sales data to predict which products of the organisation will have a better chance of success in the competitive environment. Models such as time series analysis and forecasting may be used to arrive at such analysis.

3.6 DECISION MAKING WITH MIS

3.6.1 Tactical Decisions

KEY POINT

Tactical decisions are made by employees regarding minute, everyday matters, to get their work done.

An important task of all employees within the organisation is to make decisions about various things. At the lowest level of the organisation, the workers have to decide how to go about their work. Although their work is usually quite structured, they have to make choices and evaluate consequences, using the given details. For example, a sales person may have a fixed route to travel to meet several clients during the day, but he still has to decide the manner in which to proceed given the actual conditions on the ground and also how many appointments he already has and how many are pending. These are called *tactical* decisions. The sales person has clear objectives to attain and has to make minute, low-level decisions to achieve those objectives.

Consider another example of a shop-floor assembly line worker. In a typical manufacturing assembly line, say in a factory that makes automobiles, the worker is given a fixed set of jobs to do. The worker is provided the equipment and the material required to do the job and is given a timeline for completing the work. The worker also has to attend to other constraints that involve communicating with the supervisor; adhering to company rules regarding safety, security, health and interacting with co-workers. The worker who is doing the job of assembly within such constraints has to make minute, tactical decisions regarding the work, like selection of tools, setting up of tools, use of material resources, information to be entered into the shop-floor information systems, and the timing and content of information to be communicated to upstream and downstream workers, etc.

Another example is that of a nurse attending to patients in a hospital ward. A typical nurse has to make many decisions during the day regarding patient care and providing support to physicians. The nurse's main tasks may be outlined clearly, which may include attending to patients on a fixed number of beds, providing them with timely doses of medication, recording the medication and nutrition given to the patient in the information systems, assisting the physician with check-ups and diagnosis, and ensuring the health care provided is according to the quality norms specified by the hospital. The nurse's decisions will revolve around all these activities - which jobs to prioritise, when an emergency occurs how to proceed with the activities, what information to convey to managers and attending doctors and how to coordinate activities with other nurses.

3.6.2 Operational Decisions

Decisions made by managers that have a medium-term scope are often called *operational decisions*. These decisions are based on aggregate data and impact the activities for the medium term that could range from the next few months to the next few quarters.

Operational decisions are often supported by decision support systems that use specialised models to provide detailed and carefully analysed solutions to decision problems. The following examples show the types of operational decisions supported by decision support systems:

1. Operations managers can decide on inventory levels to be maintained to meet the production targets for the firm and also control the amount of working capital locked into inventory. Decision support tools allow managers to use mathematical models that rely on current and past inventory and production levels to predict, quite precisely, the quantities of materials to be in inventory.
2. Finance managers can use decision support tools to arrive at the best allocations for investment in various types of market opportunities. Finance managers have to balance the available liquidity against the market risk of investment and the best returns possible. The tools help answer the question of how much to invest in what and also the possible scenarios that might result from the decisions.
3. Software project managers have to make decisions regarding: (a) How well projects are progressing, (b) whether they will complete on time, (c) whether they will be completed within the allocated budget and (d) whether the projects will meet the objectives of the customers. Project managers control the number of people on a project, the money allocated to the project, and the deliverables of the project. Decision support tools help them visualise and estimate, using past data on the current and similar projects, how the projects will fare.
4. Decision support tools are used in the strategy function of various organisations. The tools enable managers to visualise future trends in the economy, competitor's responses and industry trends. The tools can also help in simulating the impacts of strategies formulated by the organisation. For example, the impact of introducing new products in a market with many competitors can be simulated in a computer program that shows how the products will fare under different price scenarios.
5. Marketing managers can use decision support tools to find the most cost-effective routes for the sales persons to cover the market. Travel entails costs and hence managers want to follow the least cost routes that also allow sales personnel to meet all their customers. This decision is often complicated with customers making sudden calls on the salesperson, or weather or traffic conditions not permitting some routes.

3.6.2.1 The Travelling Salesman Problem

The travelling salesman problem is an example of an operational decision. The problem is depicted in Fig. 3.8. The salesman has to cover all the cities in one tour at the lowest possible cost.

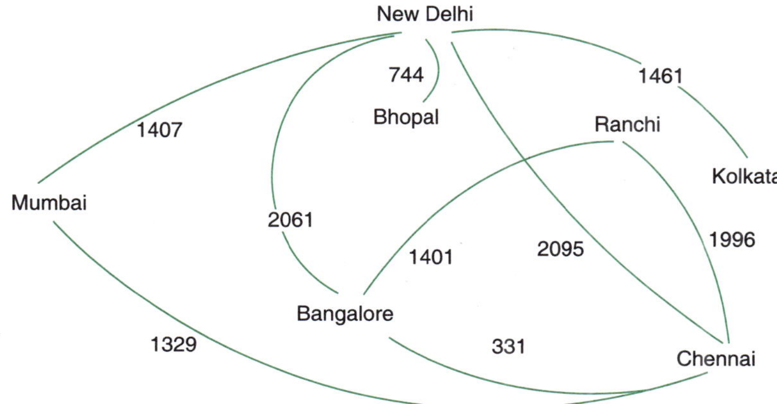

FIGURE 3.8 Travelling salesman problem. The figure shows the distances between seven cities in India.

The salesman can start from Bangalore and then follow any sequence, such as Chennai-Mumbai-Bhopal-New Delhi-Kolkata-Ranchi or Kolkata-Ranchi-New Delhi-Mumbai-Bhopal-Chennai. If all the combinations of cities are counted, there are 720 ways in which the salesman can cover all the cities after starting from Bangalore. Each of these is called a tour. For the lowest cost tour the salesman would have to calculate the distance covered for each possible tour and take the shortest one.

If the salesman starts the tour from any of the other six cities, the problem increases to 5040 possible tours! It is very difficult to compute the lowest cost for such a large number of tours. Hence it is a wise step to rely on a decision support system that can do the job efficiently.

The travelling salesman problem is a very well known and well-researched problem. When the number of cities increases to about 20, the possible tours increase to more than 2×10^{18} tours which are about 2 million trillion tours! Such a large number of calculations become hard to complete, even for computers.

3.6.2.2 Control and Planning

Supervisors, managers and knowledge workers have to make decisions that are more long term in nature and are far removed from the hour-to-hour and day-to-day activities of the firm. Managers and supervisors need information for control and planning. *Control* implies monitoring activities against given objectives, and taking action relevant to the situation. To exercise control, managers need summary information that shows how the activities of the organisation have progressed and how close they are to the given objectives. For example, managers in charge of marketing of a product have to see:

1. How much the sales have been as compared to the targets.
2. Which regions have either exceeded or fallen behind the targets.
3. Which schemes for marketing are most successful.
4. How the sales personnel have fared against their targets.
5. What is the nature of comments from customers, etc.

When these information are provided on monthly or quarterly basis, managers can take decisions that change the course of activities for the next time period. They could, for example, provide more personnel to a region that is slacking in sales, increase incentive schemes in another place, launch advertising campaigns, modify budgets of personnel, etc. to achieve their targets. Controlling of activities is thus guided by the information available.

Planning is another activity that managers undertake. Planning involves forecasting situations in the future and arranging for activities that will address them. For example, for the marketing manager, planning may involve setting up marketing incentive schemes to boost slack in sales, or redeploy sales personnel in a region, or send personnel to special training programmes and so on. Planning thus involves envisaging a set of activities for the future.

Control and planning are intertwined decisions that managers often have to take. For example, for a manager of the finance function, the job will involve monitoring the finances of the organisation that will include borrowing, lending, monitoring of current assets and liabilities and investing in stocks, bonds, futures, funds, etc. The manager has to control all these accounts by changing allocations and positions so that they are in line with the organisation's objectives of financial performance, and also plan for the future based on the current activities of the organisation. So, if the organisation is growing in terms of revenues and there are likely to be accumulated surpluses, the finance manager will have to decide how to invest the surplus to obtain proper returns.

3.6.3 Strategic Decisions

Another set of decisions made by top managers of an organisation are termed as *strategic decisions*. These are long term in scope and have a long time horizon of years. By nature, these decisions impact the very manner in which the organisation does its work. Strategic decisions are related to the *vision* and *mission* of the organisation – the decisions determine how the organisation will realise what it was created for originally and what it strives to achieve eventually. Information systems such as executive information systems are used for making strategic decisions. Some examples are as follows:

1. For a firm manufacturing pharmaceuticals, strategic decisions will revolve around what markets to enter, what type of population segments to target and how to survive the competition. Information systems can provide data and inputs on the current operations of the organisation, the market response of various segments, and industry data on the competition. These can be used with models that forecast trends of pharmaceutical sales, show potential changes in market segments, highlight potential untapped and niche areas and help in predicting economic factors that will affect the organisation.
2. For a government department, such as the revenue department of a state in India, the strategic decisions will include deciding on how to reach out to all revenue segments in the population, how to provide government services in an efficient manner and how to enhance services that improve revenue intake. Information systems support tools can be used to understand the demographics of the revenue population, the segments that are most underserved, and identify trends in revenue collection.
3. The Indian Railways uses information on ticket and freight transport sales to decide on which routes to further enhance its services and in which regions to start train services. The strategic decisions involve long-term infrastructure growth and planning for future demand for services.

A summary of the three kinds of decisions that are supported by MIS is shown in Table 3.4.

Table 3.4 Kinds of Decisions, Their Time and Horizon, and the Employees Who Make Such Decisions

Type of Employee	Type of Decision	Time Duration of Decision
Executives	Strategic	Months, years; long term
Supervisors, managers, knowledge workers	Operational	Days, weeks, months; medium term
Workers, nurses, drivers	Tactical	Hours, immediate; short term

Caselet ABC Bank

ABC Bank is one of India's oldest banks, having being established in 1906, in a town in the state of Karnataka in India. It has had a remarkable history within the segment known as Public Sector Banks (PSBs) in India. Though considered to be conservative in their approach, several PSBs, like ABC, have stood out for their innovations with IT. ABC's achievements include having a massive network of over 9000 ATMs in both rural and urban centres in India; it was one of the earliest to issue credit cards to farmers; and it was also one of the first to launch a subsidiary for IT consultancy.

In the current scenario, ABC has a large number of integrated IT systems that provide it with real-time and batch mode periodic data. This data is aggregated into reports and are used for decision making at many levels of the organisation. At the heart of the bank's IT infrastructure is the core banking solution – a customised package it obtained from Oracle corporation, known as Flexcube. This core package contains all the processes that the bank needs for all its main operations. The reports obtained from this package are used by the top management for planning, control and strategic decisions.

The bank's systems also use inter-back transfer services such as real-time gross transfer (RTGS) and National Electronic Funds Transfer (NEFT). These services achieve the same purpose, that of transferring funds from one bank to another; however, the first achieves this on a real-time basis where NEFT works on a batch mode. In the latter case, the request for transfer is recorded, and at the end of the hour, the entire set of requested transfers is executed.

The IT system also includes a sophisticated ATM switch, a software that manages the transfer and accounting of funds across ATMs and the branches. This switch allows users to see their current balance, make a withdrawal, make a deposit, ask for a transfer of funds, amongst other services. The information accumulated through the switch is useful for tactical and operational decisions by the bank regarding cash availability and refilling at ATMs, the extent of customer usage and the demand for cash withdrawals.

The bank has recently implemented a data warehousing and analysis software that provides a detailed dashboard of the bank's activities to the senior management. With this tool, management can have a consistent and uniform view of the activities of the bank, explicitly include risk calculations in making decisions, derive insights about different policy initiatives and their impact. The tool also provides simulations of possible scenarios and future situations that management can use to assess their strategic decisions.

3.7 COMMUNICATION IN ORGANISATIONS

An important role of the information systems infrastructure in organisations stems from their ability to facilitate communications. Communications can occur through any form - data, voice or video. Data communication are associated with a wide variety of forms:

1. Data as short text messages.
2. Data as email messages.
3. Data as entire documents.
4. Data as structured files.

Communication networks form the core of the information technology architecture of any modern organisation. As organisations grow across regions and countries, and partner with other organisations for doing their work, their needs for communication grow.

Communication is critical for transactions, decision making and for strategic collaborations.

3.7.1 Types of Communication

There are many types of communication that can be effected with digital networks in organisations. These are described below.

1. **Synchronous communication:** This happens when two or more parties communicate simultaneously. For example, a phone conversation between two people or a chat session on the internet between two people is an example of synchronous communication. Both parties can send and receive messages at the same time.
2. **Asynchronous communication:** This happens when two or more parties communicate but not simultaneously. They may send messages to each other, to which they may respond at a later point in time. For example, email works in the asynchronous mode, where a person sends a message to another person who responds to the message later. Chat messages, not during a chat session, exchanged between persons also come in the asynchronous mode category. Figure 3.9 shows the difference between synchronous and synchronous communication.
3. **Simplex communication:** This happens when the communication is possible only in one direction. Radio receivers are examples of simplex devices that can only receive signals, but

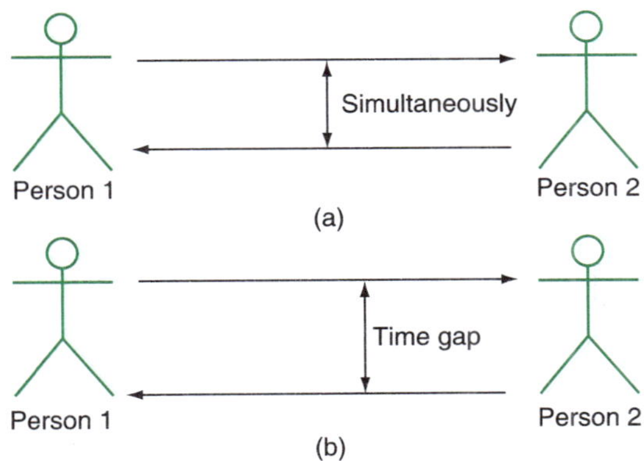

FIGURE 3.9 | (a) Synchronous and (b) asynchronous communication modes.

they cannot transmit any signals. Online streaming services, for video or audio, operate in a simplex manner.

4. **Half-duplex communication:** This happens when two persons communicate with each other, but not at the same time. For example, radio transmitter receivers can only send or receive signals at any one time. Email communication is essentially half-duplex in nature.
5. **Duplex communication:** This happens when two persons can communicate with each other while sending and receiving signals at the same time. All phone networks are duplex in nature.

3.7.2 Examples of Communications in Organisations

Sales personnel who have to travel a lot to meet their customers carry various communication devices. Mobile phones allow them to send short messages to potential visit sites and also allow them to call the clients. Smart mobile phones also allow them to connect to corporate systems such as a customer relationship management system to see the status of the client – whether the client has responded to a query, has had any earlier transactions, etc. The sales person may also have a laptop computer on which he/she carries data and programs that will allow him/her to connect to the organisation's central servers and read and write data about the client. The connection could be made using wireless network cards or locally available internet facilities.

Many hospitals now provide hand-held computers to doctors, who, on their visits to patients in various wards in the hospital, enter data about their visits either by typing it in or by recording a voice message. Once in their office, they are able to conveniently transmit the data to a desk-top computer or to a server through wireless networks. The hand-held devices are also used to request specific services such as equipment or medication or nursing assistance.

The Ola taxi service in Bangalore uses the Global Positioning System (GPS), a service that pin-points the exact location of its taxis carrying GPS devices, to identify where any taxi in their fleet is located. When any customer calls in for a service, the system identifies the customer's location, and finds the nearest available taxi that can be sent to him/her. The GPS is located in taxis and beam across information about its location to the central server of the taxi service. The taxi service also uses the data from GPS information to assess the demand for their taxis across the city.

GPS is also used by bus services in many cities in the world, including in India. The GPS devices in the buses send information about the location and speed of each bus to a central server, which then uses the information to communicate to the commuters at various bus stops along the route on how much time will elapse before the next bus arrives. The commuters waiting at bus stops can then use the information to either wait for the bus or use alternate means of transport.

Smart mobile phones enable users to receive email and other messages on their mobile phones. As the owner of the service receives an email message, say in his office mailing address, the email software 'pushes' the email message out to the mobile phone device. The person using the service receives the email instantly and can also read it and reply to it using the phone. Users of smartphones stay constantly in touch with their colleagues and collaborators using such instant messaging services.

3.7.3 Decision Making with Communication Technology

Communication is at the heart of the functioning of most modern organisations. Messages sent and received from devices to people, from people to people and from device to device are sent across in various formats and channels, some of which have just been described.

Decision making is supported by communication networks which aid in data and information collection and dissemination of decisions. Some examples of decisions aided by communication networks are as follows:

1. A large automobile fuel retailer in the USA has a network of thousands of stations across the country. Since fuel prices fluctuate quite often and there is strong competition from rival retailers, it is quite important that changes in prices are communicated quickly to all the retailers. The pricing of fuel is done at the headquarters of the firm, which collects data on pricing from across the country and determines prices for each region. Prices of fuel at every station are sent out as messages at the end of each 24-h cycle on the computer networks. The headquarters message out the new price information at night so that retailers can change the price information on the fuel pumps as well as on the large hoardings that display the prices. Decision making here is tactical in nature, as prices are changed by the headquarters but reflect the competitive needs of the local fuel station. The information used to make the decision sent across on a daily basis and reflects the current situation accurately.
2. A bank in Mumbai uses radio-frequency identification (RFID) tags to identify customers who enter its offices. These RFID tags are placed on cards given to customers who carry them in their wallets. As a customer enters the bank, the RFID tag is identified and information regarding the customer is made available to the bank employees. Someone then approaches the customer immediately, addressing them by their name, and takes them aside to help them. This service is only provided to special, high-value customers. The message regarding the customer is of strategic value to the bank and helps it improve its service quality and also retain customers.

The communication requirements of employees within organisations have grown immensely with the advent of electronic wired and wireless networks. Along with this have emerged a number of technologies that meet these communication needs. A typical employee of a modern corporation will often have more than one communication device on him at any one point of time, which will include the mobile phone and a laptop computer with wireless or wired connectivity. Such high levels of connectivity also lead to an overload of communication information. Organisations are currently evolving means by which such overload is minimised and only relevant and useful communications are presented to the user.

Chapter Glossary

Data A raw collection of facts maintained in unprocessed form.

Information Processed data is information. The word *information* has many meanings and connotations in the English language, such as pattern, sensory input, stimulus, meaning, knowledge and also data. In computing literature, it is also used interchangeably with data. For this book, information is understood as data that has been transformed (or processed) in some manner.

Database A repository of data. A database is a software application that allows storing, retrieving, updating and displaying data.

Field A marked place in a database where data is stored.

Archiving Storing large quantities of data in compressed format, which reduces the size of the data set while preserving its content.

Transactions Activities engaged in by an organisation and its employees that involve processing of information.

Real-time processing Processing of data and information done simultaneously with the execution of a transaction.

Batch processing Processing of data after the transaction has been completed. All the data is stored and then processed later.

Tactical decisions Decisions that have a short-term impact and are taken by workers and operators.

Operational decisions Decisions that have a medium-term impact and are taken by managers and supervisors.

Control Monitoring organisational activities to see whether they are helpful in achieving given objectives.

Planning Forecasting situations in the future and planning actions to achieve certain goals.

Strategic decisions Decisions taken by high-level executives that have a long-term impact.

Review Questions

1. What is the main difference between data and information? Give some examples.
2. Why is information considered to be a resource for organisations?
3. How is information used and processed in the accounting and operations functions of an organisation?
4. Give examples of the three fundamentals types of information technology used in organisations?
5. Give a detailed set of transactions for purchasing an airline ticket. How are these different from buying a railways ticket as outlined in the text?
6. How are management information systems different from transaction processing systems?
7. How are the three decision-making levels different? Give examples of each.

Research Questions

1. What was the manual system of buying railway tickets? How is the computerised system different?
2. Read the travelling salesman problem described in Section 3.6.2.1 and identify the costs in terms of distance travelled of three different tours starting from Bangalore and covering all the cities.
3. Identify examples of tactical, operational and strategic decisions from your own work and life. By what criteria will you able to separate them into the three categories.
4. Visit a small or medium commercial enterprise in your neighbourhood and explore what kind of transaction processing systems and MIS they have.

Further Reading

1. Srivastava, S.C., Mathur, S. and Thompson, T.S.H. (2007) Modernization of passenger reservation system: Indian Railways' dilemma, *Journal of Information Technology*, **22**, 432–439.
2. *Annual Report 2008–09*, Indian Railways Catering and Tourism Corporation Ltd.
3. Jena, C. (2007) Indian Railways Gets Freight Operation Information System.The article is available at: http://biztech2.in.com/india/casestudies/software/indian-railways-gets-freight-operation-information-system/1492/0 (accessed on June 2009).

CHAPTER 4

IT Strategy and Digital Goods

Learning Objectives

After completing this chapter, you will be able to:

- Get an idea of the competitive environment of business
- Learn about information goods
- Understand Information systems and competitive strategy

Businesses exist in a competitive environment where they have to compete with rival firms for market share, and form partnerships with others to survive. Partnerships are formed when the benefits of the relationship outweigh the costs. Businesses have to sustain the bargaining power of suppliers and customers to remain competitive. Furthermore, they have to create barriers to entry for new firms and compete with those with substitute products. They may compete as low-cost players or as differentiators. Businesses also have to compete within the ambit of industry regulations.

Information systems enable businesses, in many ways, to compete as strong players. Businesses also rely on information systems to sustain many activities in their value chain.

With the widespread availability of electronic networks, businesses have to manage information and digital goods. These too change the nature of competition. Digital goods have low costs of reproduction, can have many versions and usually have to be experienced or used to know their value. Furthermore, many digital products and services have lock-in and switching costs. Digital goods display network externalities, and their usage is often influenced by positive feedback.

MIND MAP OF CHAPTER TOPICS

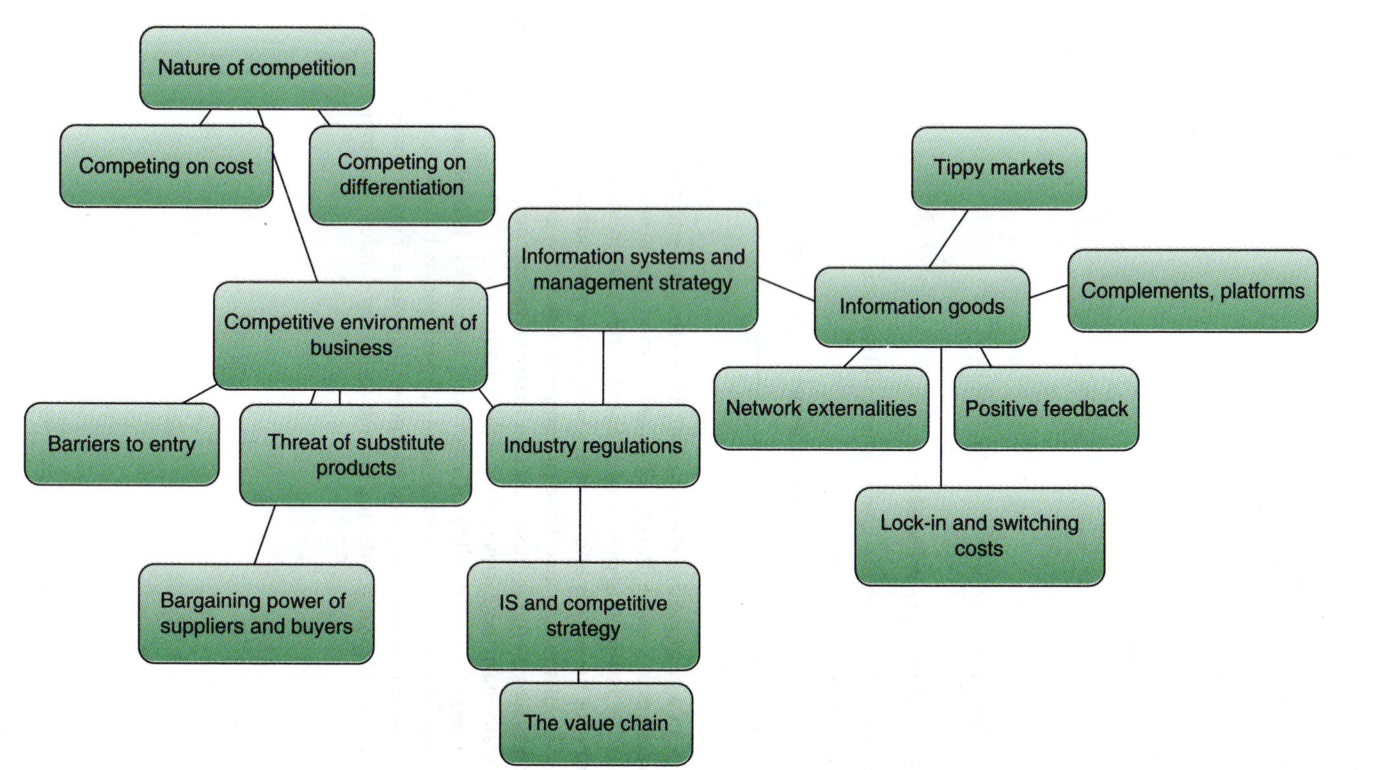

Flipkart is a Bangalore-based firm that operates in the e-commerce domain. It was set up in September 2007 as an online book retailing venture with the objective of making books accessible to customers anywhere in India, at competitive prices, through excellent customer service and prompt delivery. The co-founders of Flipkart, Sachin Bansal and Binny Bansal, are both engineering graduates. They decided to start Flipkart after having worked at Amazon India.

The e-commerce sector is highly competitive in India, but it offers immense growth potential. The entire market for e-commerce is growing quite rapidly with advantages for consumers of doorstep delivery, 24-h shopping experience, and a highly efficient market experience. When the Bansals started their venture, there were no reputed online book stores for the Indian customer. With the success of book sales, Flipkart soon started offering other products on its site, and today is one of the best-known e-commerce sites in India. There is fierce competition in the e-commerce segment with many strong players, such as Amazon.in and Snapdeal.com; however, Flipkart has retained its market share and dominance.

The experience of buying a product, say a book, at the Flipkart website is similar to doing transactions on other online stores. Upon arriving at the site, a customer is presented with an array of options for purchase. In 2016, Flipkart offered seven broad categories to choose from – electronics, appliances, furniture, books, and products specific to men, women, and children (such as clothes or toys). When the books menu is selected, the site shows books that are currently popular or have been just released. The customer can search for a book by typing in the title or the name of the author in a search text box. The result of the search displays a number of books with similar titles or books by the same author. The customer can also browse the website by subject and see a list of books on a particular subject. If the customer decides to buy a book then he/she can select the particular book and move it to a 'shopping cart' application. This software application then allows the customer to specify his/her address for book delivery, the manner by which the payment has to be made, and how the delivery should be made. Upon submitting the order, an email message and an SMS message is sent to the customer to confirm the order. Subsequently, the site sends out messages informing the customer of when the order is dispatched and when it will be delivered.

Once the online order is placed, the book is taken out of the Flipkart inventory, maintained at its offices and shipped to the customer. In case the ordered book is not available with Flipkart, it is purchased from a supplier and shipped immediately. Flipkart currently has partnerships with many courier companies, and also owns a shipping firm, called Ekart. It also uses the Indian Post services to reach areas which are beyond the reach of courier companies. In this way it can maintain a prompt delivery service, which is a competitive need of the company.

When the firm started out, it was hard to earn the customer's trust as most people in India were more comfortable with the conventional method of browsing and buying books in a book store. Moreover, people were sceptical of the idea of online payments. To address this issue, Flipkart started a 'cash on delivery' service in many cities, which included the metros and tier-one cities. Under this service, the customer would pay the courier the book price in cash, only upon receiving the book. Customers felt more comfortable with this payment method, and Flipkart gained their trust that was of great importance to it. This also helped the firm increase the number of target customers, as book buyers, such as students who did not have credit or debit cards for online payment, could also avail of its service. This was a key differentiator for Flipkart, gave it a lot of positive feedback and helped to bring in more customers.

Flipkart offers a strong customer care service (where products may be returned free of charge if they are defective or not as advertised), free and on-time delivery, a user-friendly website that is easy to browse, a large stock of products, discounts on most items and an easy and reliable payment service. Flipkart partners with local vendors who maintain an updated inventory. Additionally, it has tie-ups with many local and international suppliers that enable it to sell a wide assortment of goods. For instance, it has exclusive sales arrangements with some mobile phone manufacturers (such as Lenovo), to offer their phones on Flipkart's site alone.

One of Flipkart's most successful features is the rating and review system it provides for customers to give their opinion on products. For every product purchased from the site, customers can rate the product using a 5-star system and also write a review about their experience of the product and why they gave it the star-rating. This helps other customers make their decisions as to the value of the goods they are buying, what are its strengths, and its weaknesses. Some customers go to great lengths to write their reviews, giving details about the product that often exceeds that given in the main product description by the seller. Those reading the reviews are also in a position to give a 'thumbs up' or a 'thumbs down' to the review, saying how helpful it was, thus giving feedback to the reviewers for their work. This feature is so successful that some products attract hundreds of reviewers.

As Flipkart does not have an offline presence, it need not spend on infrastructure facilities for display counters, shop assistants and rental costs, thus cutting down its expenses. The company's expenses are limited to maintaining the websites, paying the suppliers, cost of packaging and delivery, and salaries of the people working at its office. In 2015, Flipkart had about 35,000 employees.

One challenge Flipkart faces is that online shopping is popular only with the young, urban class that is technology savvy. The company's system is also dependent largely on the efficiency of the courier companies as only they can ensure on-time delivery. Although Flipkart does face a threat from other, more established e-commerce sites, such as Amazon.in and Snapdeal, it has maintained a consistent and growing presence in its customer segment.

Flipkart has grown its product and service offerings with acquisitions of other, and rival firms. In a move in 2014, it acquired the online fashion and apparel firm Myntra.com. Online apparels were a strong and growing segment in the e-commerce space where Flipkart did not have a presence and this acquisition helped it enter that segment also. Apparels are highly profitable and also drive a lot of customers to visit the site.

Flipkart has grown significantly over the years and is one of the few 'unicorns' from India. Unicorns are start-up firms with more than a billion dollar valuation. Flipkart has achieved this with a strong following from its customers, a highly successful website and mobile app, that make it very easy to search for products and make sales, and strong strategic focus in buying and acquiring firms that are complements to its business growth. By 2016, Flipkart had revenues of about USD 1.5 billion.

4.1 THE COMPETITIVE ENVIRONMENT OF BUSINESS

All businesses exist in a competitive environment. This means that all firms have rivals in the industry in which they operate. The rival firms can potentially take business away from each other. For example, there are many firms making cars including small cars in India, such as Tata Motors, Maruti Suzuki and Hyundai Motors India. A consumer looking for a small car can buy one from any of these firms. These firms are thus competitors in the small car market.

The firms not only compete for buyers of their products but also compete to get the best vendors for buying components. Large automobile firms buy most of their components which they then assemble into cars. Therefore, they have to find the best vendors to fulfil their component requirements. For an automobile firm, selecting and holding onto the best vendors are important as there are few vendors who have the skills and capabilities to provide different kinds of specialised components. The firm has to ensure that its vendors prefer to do business with it and also remain healthy financially by making suitable profits. Else they would be lured away by the competitors. So in the competitive environment of the automobile industry firms have to compete with each other and also maintain relations with their vendors and partners (see Fig. 4.1).

KEY POINT

Commercial firms face competition for their products and also retaining their partners.

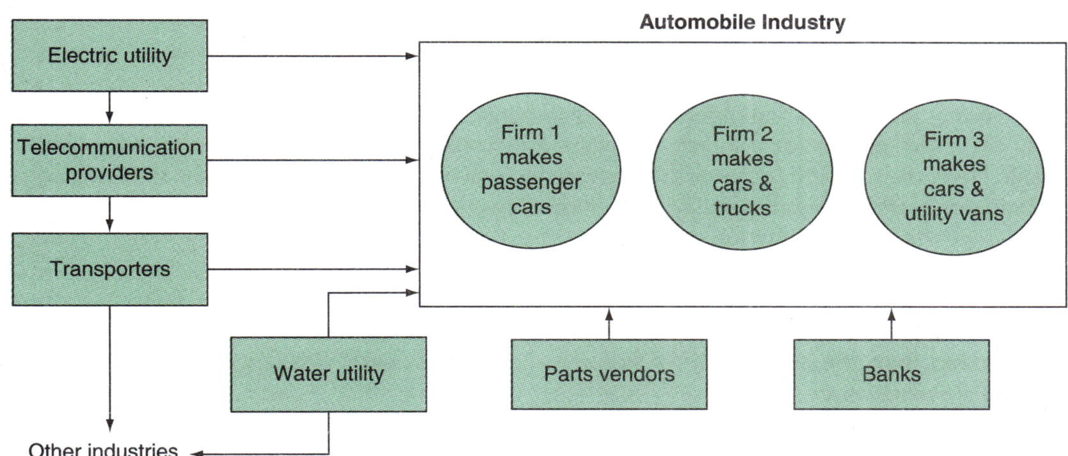

FIGURE 4.1 | Competitive environment of business in the automobile industry.

4.1.1 Partnering for Mutual Benefit

To function in a sustained manner, individual firms have to partner with others for a variety of reasons. These partners may provide essential infrastructure such as electricity, water, transportation and communication, or may provide goods and raw materials, or may help market finished goods and services. For example, a manufacturing firm may need to partner with an electric utility that would fulfil its energy requirements. By putting this partnership in place, the manufacturing firm hands over its responsibility of maintaining steady electricity supply to the utility. The benefit accruing from this partnership to the manufacturing firm is that it does not have to build internal employee skills to create and maintain power generation. With one function less to manage, the manufacturing firm would be able to devote focused attention to other important aspects of its competitive environment. The utility firm, on the other hand, may generate enough power to supply to various firms in the region, thus enjoying benefits of scale and a wide market. This would enable the utility firm to specialise in power generation by building up internal skills without bothering about its potential market. Thus, partnering to provide services is beneficial to both parties.

KEY POINT

Partnering helps firms to have access to functions they don't have internally.

Another example of beneficial partnership is that of a firm with a bank. The bank is able to provide credit, investment opportunities and cash management services to the firm. This can be a very close partnership where the firm draws credit or cash from the bank, with return payments, at a very high frequency – several times an hour – and at a high scale. The bank has the resources and the infrastructure to provide the services needed by the firm, and profits from the service fees it levies. On the other hand, the firm benefits from having access to high-quality banking services without having to maintain and manage internal resources.

The above examples show that partnerships between organisations are mutually beneficial, but they also imply a strong degree of trust and reliability on the partners. Partnering organisations have to prove that they can deliver on the promises made while creating the partnership. If there is a breach in the promises of services or goods delivery then the partnership is jeopardised.

KEY POINT

The core competence of a firm is the skill or set of skills that it uses to run its business in a unique manner.

One benefit of creating partnerships is that it allows firms to focus on their *core competence*. A core competence is a specific skill or set of skills for making a product or doing business in a unique manner. For example, Flipkart's core competence is in being able to run and maintain a website through which they can sell books and other goods. They have deep know-how of creating and maintaining their website, which distinguishes them from their competitors and enables them to run their business. They rely on partners for other tasks that their business needs – such as banking and delivery of the books. By partnering with the shipping firms, Flipkart can rely on the core competence of its partners, which is of managing shipping logistics.

Partnerships are possible when the cost of doing business or making partnerships is low. In the firm–bank partnership example, the firm has the option of creating a strong finance and accounting department that takes on the role of the bank. It can do this with some effort, as many firms do, and make the function as efficient as handled by a bank. However, the firm will have to incur costs to do this internally – on hiring and training employees in finance and accounting, on maintaining offices for the personnel, on setting aside capital for the function, etc. The other option for the firm, as in the above example, is to have a partnership with a bank. Here, the decision to go for the partnership would be largely based on the cost criterion: Whether the service fees charged by the bank are lower than the expenditure incurred by the firm in running the banking function internally. Seeing a cost advantage in partnering with the bank, the firm would go for the partnership.

KEY POINT

Transaction costs are the costs of creating and maintaining partnerships with partner organisations.

The costs incurred on running a function through partnership are called *transaction costs*. When firms find that they have to incur lower transaction costs in running a function through partnership than the expenditure of keeping the function within the organisation then they choose a partnership.

For modern business environments, transaction costs are lowered by the use of information systems. These systems connect the partnering organisations by allowing convenient and speedy transfer of information across their boundaries. For each transfer of cash from the bank to the firm, only a few messages have to be exchanged across their information networks. In the example of the firm, electricity utility partnership, information systems allow the partnering organisations to coordinate their activities related to production and consumption of electricity through joint networks.

4.1.2 Bargaining Power of Suppliers

The competitive position of a commercial firm that enables it to serve its customers and be successful in the market is determined by a set of 'forces'. These forces are based on its competitive relationship with its suppliers, customers, rivals and substitute products. This theory about the competitive forces was first propounded by a famous economist Michael E. Porter and is known as Porter's Competitive Forces Model.

For a given firm, all the partners that it works with to obtain resources are its suppliers. All suppliers have a certain bargaining power. This power is their ability to influence decisions regarding the partnership commitments of goods, services and prices. If the supplier has strong bargaining power then the firm is in a weak competitive position. This can happen when the supplier has many other clients from which it draws its business, whereas the firm is dependent on the supplier for its own functioning. For example, a manufacturing firm has only one power

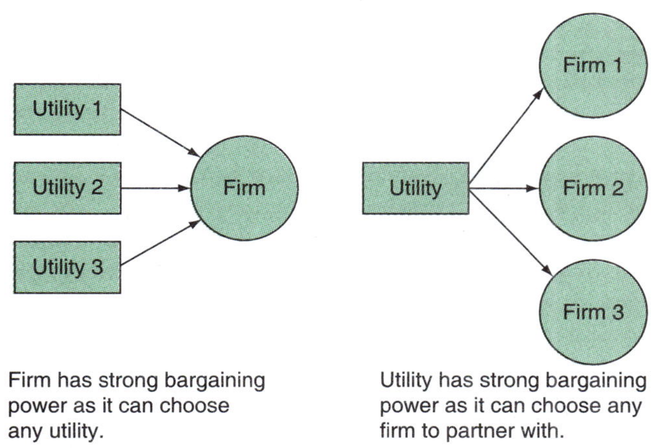

FIGURE 4.2 | Bargaining power of a firm vis-à-vis its utility supplier.

utility to rely on whereas the power utility has many customers to sell its power to. In this case, the firm is in a weak bargaining position (see Fig. 4.2). But, if the manufacturing firm has many electricity suppliers to choose from, and it also has its own internal power generation unit, then it can bargain strongly with any electricity supplier as it is not dependent on a particular supplier.

For many firms, the best competitive strategy is to partner with many vendors to maintain a strong bargaining power relationship. Information systems have the ability to reduce transaction costs and help form partnerships that enable firms to improve their bargaining power with vendors. These systems are particularly useful in this competitive manner when they are tailored to suit the needs of the vendor organisations. For example, a direct digital connection for transfer of data between a firm and its vendor, such as a bank that helps specific aspects of business between the two organisations, such as immediate cash transfers and electronic deposits, is likely to be a better option for the competitive positions of both organisations. Creating a direct digital connection between organisations is expensive, so when the firm and the bank choose to invest in such a connection they will be careful in making the choice. For the firm it will ensure that its costs of operating with the bank are very low, whereas for the bank it will ensure that the firm will not easily go off to seek alternative banks to partner with.

KEY POINT

Information systems help to form partnerships that help firms improve their bargaining power.

4.1.3 Bargaining Power of Buyers and Customers

Buyers, who buy the services or goods of a firm, also have a bargaining power. They can bargain, among other things, over prices and delivery schedules. They can seek other firms who have better prices or delivery schedules and thus bargain with the firm on these issues. Firms operating in a highly competitive market have to make attempts to improve their bargaining power over buyers.

One way to improve the firm's bargaining power is by ensuring a superior product or service that buyers feel compelled to buy in preference to competing products. Another way is to offer *complementary* products or services that attract buyers to the firm's product. For example, some automobile firms improve their bargaining power over car buyers by offering high-quality car servicing than their competitors. Here servicing of the car over its lifetime is an added benefit, or a complementary benefit, which enhances the car's value for the buyers and hence they prefer it over the competition.

Information systems assist sellers to reduce the bargaining power of buyers by various means: by creating exclusive online channels by which buyers can buy, thus keeping out competition; they can reduce costs by using information systems; and they can offer faster and more efficient service than their competitors.

4.1.4 Barriers to Entry

One way to stay competitive is to prevent new players from entering the competition. All firms thus have to erect barriers to entry for new competition. However, this cannot be done physically, as such a thing would be considered illegal and against fair competition in most nations. Therefore, it has to be done by adopting certain policies that make it very difficult for new entrants to tap the market. For example, many biotechnology firms, which invent and manufacture drugs, take *patents* on them. A drug patent is a right granted by the government to ensure that the firm owning the patent is the only one with the legal mandate to make the drug. Other, rival, firms wanting to make the same drug can only do so by paying a royalty fee to the patent-owning firm. This drives up the costs for the rival firms trying to compete for the same product, hence putting them at a disadvantage. A patent, thus, becomes an entry barrier for rival firms.

Another example of entry barrier is creating strong links with buyers, based on long-term contracts or other means. Firms providing services, such as computer facilities management, may be able to draw up a long-term contract that lasts several years in which they become the sole services vendor for the client firm. Other competing firms will have to wait out the contract before being able to approach the buyer again.

Information systems assist in creating entry barriers for competitors by allowing formation of partnerships. Highly specialised information systems facilitate these partnerships by linking together partnering firms across regions and countries. For example, Deutsche Post DHL is a logistics firm operating internationally and has created distributed information systems that link its partners together in a global network. The firm's main line of business is to transport packages from destinations all over the world to any location. For this purpose, the firm relies on its partners in different countries who carry its packages to remote locations. The firm's information systems track the packages on the way to their destinations and provide real-time information about their location till their delivery. The partners of the international logistics firm also link with the same system through their own systems to do the business smoothly. Competitors of the Deutsche Post DHL cannot enter its various markets easily as they will also have to create similar links with the local carriers, which is very difficult and expensive.

KEY POINT

Patents and long-term contracts create barriers to entry for rival firms.

4.1.5 Threat of Substitutes

One of the biggest threats to a business is a substitute product or service. A substitute product is a type of product that is very different from the original but serves the same function as the original and acts as a replacement. For example, the compact disc (CD) for carrying music was a substitute for the cassette and the long-playing record. When CDs entered the market, they were able to offer a better value product to music lovers as they stored more music in better quality than the cassettes. Although cassette manufacturers could compete with each other, they had no answer to the CD which was a better substitute product that could entirely replace the cassette.

Substitute services, similar to substitute products, present a viable alternative and a replacement for an existing service. For example, ATM machines provided by banks are a substitute for the services provided by a human teller at a bank branch.

Substitute products and services can create entirely new markets. For example, mobile phones emerged and became popular in India as a better substitute for landline phones. Those who owned landline phones shifted to mobile phones. However, a large section of the population that did not own landline phones was able to buy and use mobile phones. The mobile phones were easy to acquire and use as opposed to landlines. Besides, mobile networks succeeded in covering much larger areas than the landline networks, hence they could tap a large latent telephone market.

Information technology provides powerful opportunities to create and sustain substitute products and services, and also create new markets in the process. The entire e-commerce market came into existence only because of information technology - communication networks, the internet, personal and office computers, and browser software. E-commerce has created a substitute channel for traditional channels consisting of wholesalers and retailers (see Fig. 4.3).

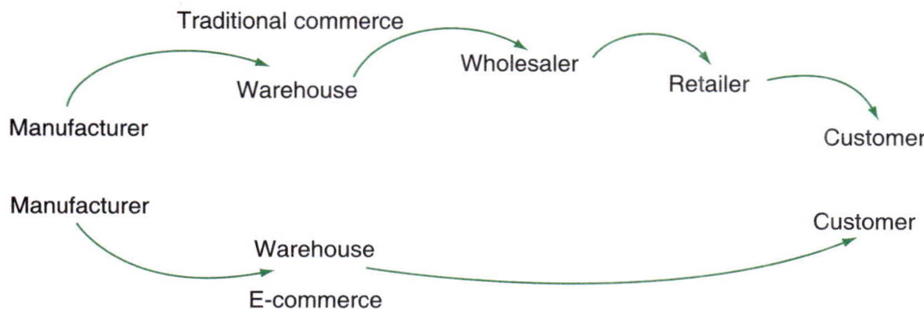

FIGURE 4.3 | E-commerce is a substitute for traditional commerce. In the figure, the wholesaler and retailer are eliminated.

Book sellers such as Flipkart do not sell by the traditional method at all. They sell only via the internet. They do not maintain stores for selling products directly to customers. All their sales are through their online shopping. Their online store is a substitute for the physical store.

E-commerce has enabled a large number of commercial firms to place their business and services on the internet. Substitutes for many kinds of businesses have sprung up, such as online auctions and online banking. What is more, information technology has also helped create businesses that did not exist before. Online search is one example of a new business. Search engines did not have a physical counterpart other than telephone directories and yellow pages directories. These physical directories with their limited capabilities just cannot match the range and scope of services that a search engine like Google offers.

4.1.6 Industry Regulations

Regulations and laws implemented by nations have a strong bearing on the nature of the business environment. These laws determine the manner in which firms can compete and the type of products and services that can exist in the market. Nations enact laws regarding business and industry to enhance their industrial growth and to protect their citizens. So laws exist to control and direct the businesses operating within the boundary of a nation. Furthermore, laws also control the manner in which foreign businesses and organisations can operate within a country.

Like other technologies, information technology too is subject to regulations in most countries. These regulations pertain to issues such as the use of radio frequencies for communication, the availability of high-end computing devices, the level of taxation to be applied to certain products and thus making them more or less competitive, the levels of security to be maintained, and the audit procedures a firm has to follow.

India is well known for its software services firms. These firms have thrived in an environment where favourable laws helped them by providing reduced or delayed taxation levels, in hiring and training of personnel, and facilitating easy movement of their employees internationally. These firms have consolidated their competitive position worldwide thanks to the Indian regulations that favoured them. However, such is not the case for other industries. For instance, some firms in the IT hardware sector find that laws for import of hardware components are not suitable for competing with foreign players. Import of hardware is not easy owing to regulations governing duties, taxes, security checking and customs.

KEY POINT

Laws of a motion determine whether it is easy or hard to do business in the nation.

4.2 USING IT FOR COMPETING

4.2.1 Competing on Low Cost

Providing low-cost substitutes for rival products is one of the proven ways to compete. Firms offer low-cost products or services to draw away customers from their competitors and establish their presence. There are many examples of this kind of competition – the large American retail chain, Walmart, is a low-cost supplier of all kinds of consumer goods. It has created a strong competitive advantage by providing cheaper goods, of a certain quality, than its rivals. Similarly, many airlines in India are competing on the basis of low fares as compared to their competitors. They provide cheaper fares with less facilities on-board and attract those customers who are price conscious.

Information systems help firms in reducing costs of operations, which then helps them gain a low-cost competitive position. Many businesses have used information systems and the internet to reduce their operating expenses and gain the ability to offer lower prices to consumers. For example, the online brokerage firm Schwab created an entirely new business model by offering individual traders the ability to trade in stocks at a very low price by using online trading facilities. The firm, based in the USA, is one of the first in the world to offer such an option. When it entered the market, the typical cost to trade stocks was close to USD 800, but Schwab introduced an alternative in which investors could trade at USD 30 per trade. This low-cost alternative was possible only because of the investments that Schwab made to use the internet for permitting online stock trading.

Here another relevant example is of mobile telephony in India. In 2016, India had over 1 billion users of mobile phone services and one of the lowest phone tariffs in the world. The Indian cellular and mobile phone providers, such as Airtel, Vodafone and Bharat Sanchar Nigam Ltd (BSNL), provide mobile phone services at rates that are among the lowest in the world. When mobile phones were introduced in India, the call tariffs for landline phones were quite high. The mobile service firms used information technology to introduce low-cost services that could be scaled up quite rapidly. These firms use information technology for billing and keeping track of calls for prepaid users, thus reducing the costs associated with charging calls, billing and accounting.

4.2.2 Competing on Differentiation

Some firms compete by differentiating their product from that of their rivals. This happens in a strongly competitive market where there are many players and the ability to stand out makes a difference. Firms that compete in this manner may actually take a high-price, high-quality stance that clearly identifies them as different from the others. For example, the MacIntosh brand of personal computers, since its inception, is known to be different and pricier than its rivals. MacIntosh has clearly branded itself as being different from the Windows Intel-based personal computers and others in the market. It stood out for its higher quality of software and hardware, its higher price and the respect of users it commanded.

The idea of differentiation is that of creating a distinct identity, a brand, which separates out the competition. For example, the United Parcel Service (UPS) firm of the USA, which is in the business of delivering parcels and letters across the world, came up with the idea of information systems that would track parcels. It wanted to differentiate itself from the strong competition in the logistics business. So it put in place a system that would track each parcel from its source to its destination and the operators could constantly monitor the parcel's position, and address any problem that could arise. This system also allowed customers to see where their parcel was located and how much time they had to wait before it reached them. This service was unique when it was launched by UPS and became a landmark system; it clearly differentiated UPS from its competitors.

KEY POINT

Differentiation means creating a distinct identity for a product to separate it from the competition.

Another important example of differentiation is of the Amazon.com company of the USA that is best known as an e-commerce pioneer. When Amazon started its operations in the mid-1990s, books were sold only in book stores. Amazon created an online book store in which customers could browse and buy books from their homes, and the purchased books were shipped to them. This model was so unique that it became very successful and Amazon became one of the leading firms in the book-selling business. Subsequently, Amazon added many products to its online e-commerce site, including consumer goods and electronics. Amazon continues to differentiate itself from other online and physical retailers by offering information-systems-based services such as recommendations, individualised updates and user reviews.

The Flipkart case at the beginning of this chapter details the manner in which this firm replicated Amazon.com's success in the Indian market.

4.3 INFORMATION GOODS

With the widespread availability of computers, networks, mobile phones and access to the internet, *information goods* are now widely used. One form of information goods is digital products that can be distributed over digital networks and consumed over digital devices. For example, MP3 music files are information goods that are sold and distributed over the internet. Music was earlier sold on vinyl discs or cassette tapes on which music was recorded in analog format. The analog format differs from the digital format in the sense that the latter consists entirely of electronic 0s and 1s, whereas the former consists of continuous electrical signals. In both cases the music is stored, retrieved and transmitted in the analog or digital manner. In case of digital goods, it is far easier to store and transmit them as compared to analog goods. It is possible to send a song, in the digital MP3 format, simply as a file attachment with an email whereas this is not possible with an analog song.

There are many examples of digital goods. Companies such as Amazon.com are selling digital versions of books over their site. These digital books can be read on special readers that display the pages on a screen. Cricket scores are also digital goods that are distributed over mobile phones, internet sites and on email messages. News, stock prices, airline tickets, etc. are all sold or accessed over the internet in digital form and are all digital goods.

4.3.1 Properties of Information Goods

Information goods have certain properties that make them distinct from physical goods. Information goods are typically expensive to produce but very cheap to reproduce. For example, the original cost of producing a music track by a professional band may run into millions of rupees. However, once the digital version of the track is available, it can be reproduced or copied for almost no cost or at a very low cost.

KEY POINT

Information goods are typically expensive to produce but cheap to reproduce.

To broadcast cricket scores in India, the mobile phone companies have to pay a high upfront fee to the cricket match organisers. Once the scores are purchased and sent out on SMS networks, as is the case for many international cricket matches in India, the cost of reproducing the message across the network is very low.

It is widely believed that owing to the spread of MP3 music files across the internet, the music industry as a whole has been deeply affected. Many new businesses have evolved that directly sell music files off the internet; the most famous example of this is the iTunes store that sells music files for the Apple music players. Many bands and music groups have also started selling and distributing their songs directly over the internet.

Many argue that the life of the physical, paper-based book is about to decline with the advent of the digital book readers. Book buyers can now buy books directly over the internet and have them instantly available on their digital readers. The digital readers have massive capacities; one such device can store thousands of books. Besides, some of them provide access through wireless networks to a huge library of free and paid books that the readers can access instantly.

KEY POINT

The capacity for devices to store digital goods is very high.

Another property of digital goods is that they can be converted into *versions* quite easily. A version of a good is a form that is different from the original, yet of the same nature. For example, physical books are typically released in the market as cloth-bound books that are more expensive; and a few months later the same book is released in a paper-bound version. The content of both the books is exactly the same except that the expensive version has a better quality of binding and better printing; and the cheaper version usually has smaller print and the paper is of lower quality. The main difference in the two is that one is released earlier and one later. Those customers who are keen to read the book early pay a higher price for the cloth-bound book.

KEY POINT

It is easy to make versions, or variants, of digital goods.

Information goods that have a time value can be versioned quite easily using information technology. For example, cricket scores that are sent out on SMS have a small price. However, the same scores can be obtained a few minutes later in an online form for free. Many providers of free stock quotes still give a delayed version, whereas the real-time quote is available for a small fee.

Many software makers give away a free version of their software for users to sample, and keep a priced version for sale. This addresses another property of digital goods – many information goods are *experience goods*. This implies that the true value of the goods is evident only after they have been experienced. For example, the value of a magazine article or a book can only be realised after it has been read. This is true for all magazine articles and all books. Even the value of weekly magazines, which arrive every week, can only be gauged when they have been read. This is a strong contrast to consumables such as a soft drink whose value is known after consuming it only once. Owing to the property of experience, sellers of information goods often find it useful to allow customers to sample the goods, often through a free download of a lesser quality version. Many websites allow visitors to hear portions of a music track or see clips of videos to allow them to experience the goods and make a choice about purchasing them.

KEY POINT

Experience goods are those whose value is known only after they are sampled.

4.3.2 Technology Lock-in and Switching Costs

Information technology is the medium by which information goods are carried. Information technology allows the goods to be distributed, managed and made available in a form that is convenient for users. In this sense, technology is the essential platform from which information goods can be obtained.

A *technology platform* is a combination of hardware, software and networks which create the environment through which information goods are created, stored, retrieved and reproduced. The choice of the technology platform is important as it determines the nature of the goods and the manner in which they can be distributed. The most well-known example of a technology platform is that of Windows and Intel. Worldwide personal computer users opt for this platform that consists of computers made with Intel microchips and the Windows software that runs on these microchips is made by the Microsoft Corporation. Although now there are other competitors who make both hardware and software for this platform, Intel or Microsoft is still dominant. For example, the AMD Corporation makes chips that compete with Intel's chips, but AMD chips too run with the Windows software. Similarly, Linux is an operating system that rivals Windows, but it runs on Intels chips. Other examples include the Android operating system, which is a version of Linux, that runs on many hardware devices; such as tablets and phones. Examples of different platforms are shown in Fig. 4.4.

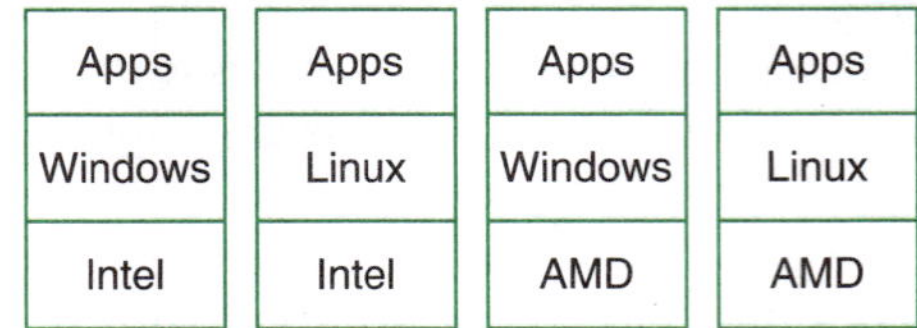

FIGURE 4.4 | Various personal computer platforms consisting of different hardware, operating system and software applications.

When a particular platform is selected, it becomes the basis for creating both data and software. A large number of users use the data and software, without using alternatives. This leads to *lock-in* to the platform. Lock-in occurs because users have created many files of data, and also have got used to how the software works. Users create shortcuts and workarounds for the work they do with the software, and are then reluctant to change to anything else, as all their efforts would go waste. Lock-in is caused by these habits and data formats that force users to stay with the same platform.

KEY POINT

Lock-in is the phenomenon of being attached to a particular platform, software or data.

Lock-in can result from other causes too. Sometimes lock-in results from contractual causes, where an organisation signs off on a long-term contract to use a particular platform. This is usually done to avail a strong commercial benefit. Lock-in also results from purchasing durable goods such as hardware. When money is invested in hardware, it is difficult to move away from it unless the investment is recovered; till then the hardware has to stay in use. Lock-in may also result from legal reasons, where certain laws protecting consumer rights prevent organisations

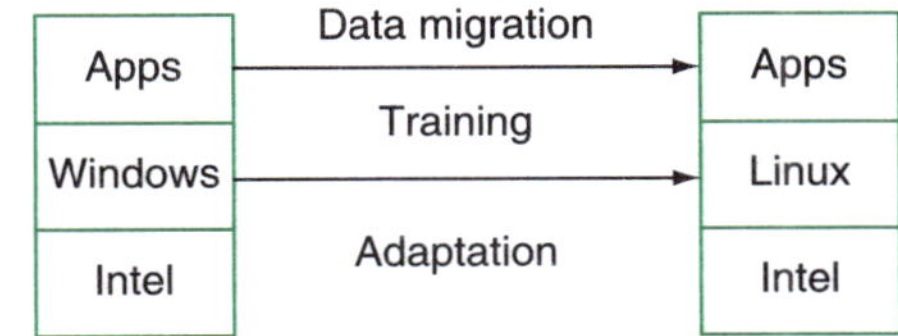

FIGURE 4.5 | Switching costs incurred while switching from a Windows-Intel platform to a Linux-Intel platform.

from changing the data or platforms they work with. In a similar manner, lock-in also results from the databases or information stores that organisations build and rely on. These databases are in formats and standards that are, usually, only accessible in the platform on which they were created.

Lock-in can be overcome by incurring *switching* costs. Switching costs are faced by organisations or individuals who have to move away from a particular platform and start using a new one. For example, users who have worked with and are comfortable with the Windows operating system and want to move to the Linux operating system, face switching costs (see Fig. 4.5). Users will have to learn how to use the new system, which may require training, migrating their existing files to the new system, migrating their applications to the new system or find substitutes, and migrating their peripheral equipment, like drives and cameras, over to the new system. Costs are incurred if employee time is spent on doing these tasks, vendors have to be hired to do these and new applications have to be purchased.

KEY POINT

Switching cost is the price paid to move away from a Lock-in.

4.3.3 Network Externalities

Technology use is often common to entire organisations and to many people within the organisation and outside. When a group of people use the same technology then each member of the group benefits from the common use of the same technology. This benefit is referred to as *network externality*.

Consider, for example, a word processing application. This application is used by people to create documents and files with data. When users create such documents, they do so with a view to share the data and files with others. If others, within an organisation, are also using the same type of word processor then they can read and modify the data too. In this case, for a user in the organisation, it is convenient to share data and files with a large number of fellow staffers. If the fellow staffers are not using the same application, then the user who created the document will have to create it in a format that can be seen and modified by others. This presents an inconvenience to the user. The situation becomes more complicated when different types of word processor applications are being used in the organisation. Now the challenge before the user is to create many versions of the same data and document so that others can use and modify the files in their respective word processor applications.

Network externalities are stronger for devices that are network-based such as mobile phones, fax machines and computers. When fax machines, for instance, were invented and introduced in 1848 for the first time, not many people or organisations had them and could use them. The technology was advanced and digital fax machines were made available in the 1970s. These machines were more convenient to use and were cheaper. Consumers started buying them and using them as there were now more places to send faxes to as opposed to the earlier times when few people had fax machines. The value of having a fax machine increased, and continued to increase as more people started buying and using fax machines. A similar argument holds for mobile phones too. As more and more people in our social network, friends, family and acquaintances use mobile phones, the value of our using such phones also increases.

KEY POINT

A network externality is usually a benefit that accrue to a user when others join the network.

An important distinction has to be pointed out here. As more and more people known to us start using mobile phones, our *value* of using the network increases but our *costs* of using remain the same. In our example of using a word processor for creating files, our costs associated with using the word processor remain the same regardless of how many others are using it; however, our value of using it is far higher if many others are using it. The value is a benefit that is derived from using the software, whereas the cost is the price paid for using it.

4.3.4 Positive Feedback

In a situation where there is a benefit for individual users when many others start using a network technology, the benefit from using the network acts as a boost for all the users. For example, when people start using email that allows them to send messages and documents to many others, they realise the benefit or value of the network and then are encouraged to use it even more. When they use the email network more often, others are further encouraged too, and the usage of the technology grows. This is positive feedback.

KEY POINT

Positive feedback is the news about the benefits of joining a network that people receive.

Positive feedback has been observed in many technologies that have network externalities. The growth in users of a network technology that has positive feedback follows an S-shaped curve, as shown in Fig. 4.6.

At the initial stages of introducing a technology, there are few users and they realise less value from their use as there are very few other users. When the usage grows, over a period of time, the value to individual users grows and this fires greater positive feedback. At a certain point, a critical mass of users is reached, where the positive feedback is so strong that many other users now start to join the network quickly. The curve rises sharply at this time. The number of users finds a saturation point at which time the curve levels off.

The S-shaped curve of positive feedback depicts the phenomenon explained above. However, there are some issues that are pertinent. The flat part of the curve, where users are still adding to the network and the critical mass has not been reached, may last for a long time. For example, the fax machine was at the flat part of the curve for over a hundred years before it reached critical mass and lots of organisations started buying and using fax machines.

The effect of positive feedback is strongly evident in social networking sites such as Facebook. When people join the site and become users of Facebook, they may like the experience. This prompts them to encourage their friends, family and colleagues to join too. Potential users find that it is easy to join a networking site like Facebook. This encourages new users to join and the cycle continues. As more users join the network, the value that each derives is increased and thus their enjoyment too increases.

The opposite of positive feedback is negative feedback. In the above example, if the new users find that they do not like the social networking site then they will not encourage others to join. This will cause negative feedback which will not allow the network to grow.

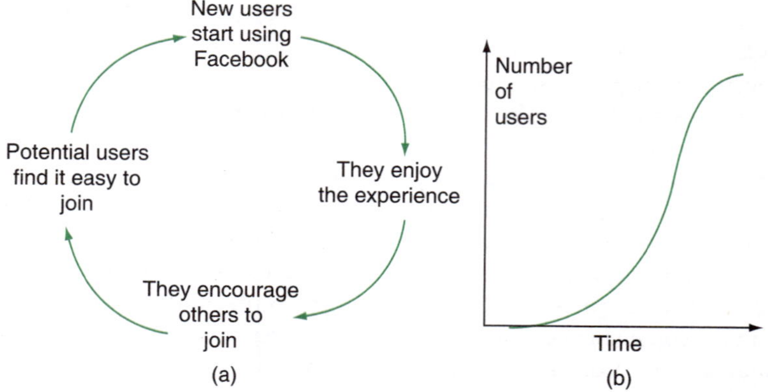

FIGURE 4.6 (a) Positive feedback influencing users of Facebook. (b) The S curve of growth of users.

4.3.5 Tippy Markets

The combination of network externalities and positive feedback leads to tippy markets. A tippy market results when there are two or more products competing in the market, and in the eventual outcome only one survives. Each product is tippy in the sense that it could either succeed or fail, and with the effects of positive feedback only one succeeds and the others fail.

The competition between the two video recording standards, VHS and Betamax, is an example of a tippy market resulting from network externalities and positive feedback. Betamax was introduced as a video tape recording technology in 1975. It allowed users to tape-record television programmes and also enabled recording studios to pre-record and sell tapes of television programmes and films. VHS was a similar and competing technology that was introduced later. For both formats, users had to buy tape recorders and playback units that could play the format. If users committed to one, then they could not use the tapes made in the other format. The network effects resulted from many users selecting one technology and then the market for pre-recorded tapes growing for it. In the competition, the VHS format won out as the number of its users grew, the number of manufacturers making and selling the recorder players for VHS grew, which resulted in positive feedback, and drew more customers to VHS. Finally, the market tipped for VHS, and the Betamax format lost out entirely and its recorder players went out of the market (see Fig. 4.7). Ironically, many users considered Betamax a superior format than VHS.

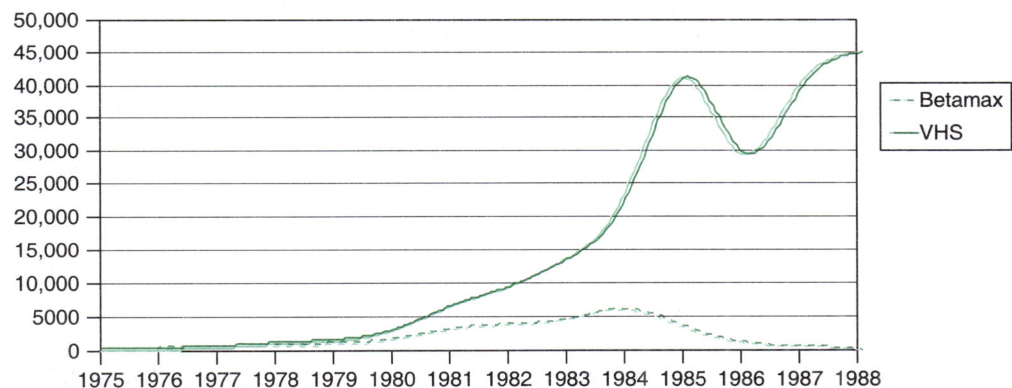

FIGURE 4.7 | Production of Betamax versus VHS players.

4.4 INFORMATION SYSTEMS AND COMPETITIVE STRATEGY

The promise of information systems is that they enable the competitive strategy of commercial firms. The competitive strategy of a commercial firm is its long-term competitive position, such as of being a low-cost player or a differentiator, which the firm adopts. A firm's strategy is the set of activities it engages in as part of its long-term competitive goals. Strategies lead to operational goals and to tactics that the firm undertakes.

Long-term goals are of value to non-commercial organisations too. For example, government departments may adopt a goal of reaching out to all citizens to provide services, for which they can evolve a strategy based on information systems. Government departments do not face competition as such, and their main concerns are of service delivery and efficiency.

Examples of how information systems help firms implement their competitive strategy were discussed above. Some of the specific strategies are summarised in Table 4.1.

Table 4.1 | Use of IS to Support Competitive Strategy

Competitive Strategy	Use of Information Systems	Example
Create barriers to entry for competition	To create barriers to entry of new competition, firms may lock-in existing customers with loyalty programmes and free-access accounts created with information systems. Data from such loyalty programmes can also be used to identify customer tastes and patterns of buying to further provide them with goods and services.	Yatra.com is an online travel portal that enables customers to buy airline and railway tickets from its site. It maintains a loyalty programme by providing discount coupons to customers who purchase frequently.
Reduce bargaining power of suppliers	The bargaining power of suppliers is reduced by creating customised logistics channels with suppliers that enables an exclusive access, thus increasing costs for suppliers if they want to seek other customers.	Deutsche Post DHL has information systems to link all its partners in its logistics chain. This not only creates barriers to entry to competition, but also prevents its suppliers from seeking other partners.
Reduce bargaining power of buyers	The bargaining power of buyers is reduced by providing low-cost, bundled services from a single source that is highly customised to their needs. They would not be prone to seek alternative sources if a sufficient lock-in is created.	By creating an online facility for buying tickets, the Indian Railways has reduced the need for its customers to seek alternatives.
Provide low cost products	Transactions costs are reduced by having information systems that increase the volume and speed of transactions. When scaled up, this gives a significant competitive advantage.	The ICICI Bank initiated a network of automated teller machines (ATMs) across India to reduce costs of banking for clients. Clients could access their accounts any time and easily.
Provide niche products.	A differentiation strategy is possible by reaching out to new markets and customers using the internet. Information systems help customise offerings and also provide high efficiency levels for implementing the strategy.	The United Parcel Service (UPS) created a special information systems that kept track of parcels as they were shipped. This was a unique offering, differentiating it from its rivals.

Caselet Kindle e-Reader

Amazon.com, the US-based e-commerce giant launched a device for reading books called the Kindle in 2007. The idea behind the e-reader was to allow users to buy digital versions of books from the online Amazon.com store and read them on the device. Kindle was designed with a special non-reflective screen that displayed 'e-ink', a type of display that required very little power to render pages; this ensured that a single charge of the battery on the device would last for days if not weeks. Users could download and read books, magazines and articles on the device.

The Kindle reader has many advantages over traditional books. The user can browse the online catalogue of books through the reader without having to visit a store. The user can then purchase the book online and have it delivered instantly to the device, through an internet connection, regardless of where the user was physically located. The original Kindle could store hundreds of books and later versions could store thousands. Books could be read in any order, and the reader automatically bookmarked the page. Later versions of the device could also read aloud the text.

The Kindly became immensely successful and later Amazon advanced the software so it could be used to read books on other devices, such as smartphones and tablets. This enabled users to read their books on any device, their phone or their laptop, as the file could be accessed on all of them through a common account.

The success of the Kindle led to a huge shift in people's reading habits, and many shifted from reading paper-based books only to e-books also. In 2016, Amazon had listed over 4.3 million e-books on its online store. Earlier, in 2011, Amazon had announced that it was outselling e-books to paper books through its online store.

The device has become so popular that many libraries around the world are now enabling their patrons to borrow e-books to read on their Kindles. On the other hand, the huge surge in e-books has helped to wipe out traditional bookstores. In the US and in Western European countries, and also in India, many bookstores have seen decline in sales and have either closed down or have reduced their stocks significantly.

4.4.1 The Value Chain

Analysis of competitive strategy is often based on the Value Chain Model, originally proposed by Michael E. Porter. In this model, it is assumed that to meet its goals, an organisation carries out its functions in a series of activities that add value to the final product the organisation makes or sells. These activities consist of primary and support or secondary activities. The primary activities directly add value to the organisation's product and the secondary activities assist the primary activities. Figure 4.8 depicts the primary and secondary activities normally associated with the value chain analysis. The primary activities consist of inbound logistics, production, outbound logistics, sales and marketing and maintenance. The support or secondary activities consist of infrastructure management, human resource management, research and development, and procurement.

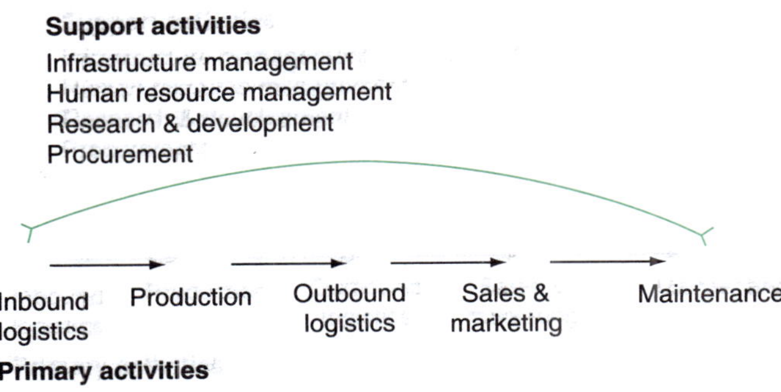

FIGURE 4.8 | Porters' value chain with primary and support or secondary activities.

4.4.1.1 Primary Activities

Inbound logistics is a primary activity in the value chain. This activity entails managing the resources that are brought to the firm from outside, such as raw materials and working capital. When materials are obtained and managed by the firm, they add value to the firm's overall output. In a manufacturing firm, input raw materials are stored at selected bins, and parts are also stored in a manner that they can be easily assembled during production. For a services organisation, like a hospital, inbound materials include medicines and surgical and clinical equipment needed by the doctors and nurses to do their work.

Production is the act of converting input materials into the finished product. In manufacturing, this is the final product such as an automobile or some other commodity the firm manufactures. For a hospital, the production is in the form of services delivered through patient care or surgery. The production activities usually add the highest value for the organisation.

Outbound logistics refer to the movement of the firm's products to various warehouses and dealer locations to sell in the market. Managing this activity requires coordinating the movement of finished goods to locations where they are demanded and can be stored. For services organisations, like a hospital, outbound activities include billing and transfer of patients as also disposal of waste materials.

Sales and marketing refer to all those activities that the firm undertakes to inform its customers of its product and bring it to them for the final sale. This activity includes advertising, branding and publicity for the product. For other organisations, such as government departments and hospitals, this activity involves informing citizens about their activities and how their services can be availed of.

Maintenance activities include servicing the needs of the customers after a sale has been made. For manufacturing firms this may include servicing goods in case of breakdown, supplying parts for replacement and training client personnel. Maintenance activities add a lot of value as contracts for maintenance constitute a strong revenue stream for many firms. For services organisations, like a hospital, maintenance implies keeping in touch with patients and ensuring they follow the prescribed medical or lifestyle regimen.

4.4.1.2 *Support Activities*

Infrastructure management involves managing all the facilities, such as buildings, electricity and water, of the firm to enable it to function properly. Human resource management involves the recruitment, training and development of personnel of the organisation. Some organisations also engage in research and development, and this activity examines ways by which operations can be made more efficient, or newer and better products and services can be launched. Procurement involves searching for and acquiring resources efficiently. Each of these activities enables the primary functions and does not directly contribute to value addition.

4.4.2 Information Systems for Value Chain Activities

Information systems are used to support and enhance all the primary activities. Special systems have been developed as products that either support one or more of the activities. The supply chain management (SCM) system assists in inbound logistics. It enables direct electronic links with vendors to manage the entire delivery process. Enterprise resource planning (ERP) and production planning systems are widely popular for manufacturing and services organisations. These systems focus on the production activity as well as support activities such as human resource management and procurement (see Fig. 4.9). The customer relationship management (CRM) systems help organisations with their sales and marketing activities by managing the entire history of contact with customers and channel partners.

From the perspective of competitive strategy, organisations have to decide which systems to use to maximise the value that can be obtained from them. For example, the Dell Corporation, a famous manufacturer of personal computers and laptops, introduced information systems for inbound logistics, where each of its vendors delivered parts as and when needed. This resulted in Dell doing away with inventory maintenance at its premises. Dell was also a pioneer in using its online website to collect direct orders from customers, and these were translated directly into its production targets. Dell was able to outpace its competitors by drastically reducing costs of operations and hence providing cheaper products, thus gaining considerable market share.

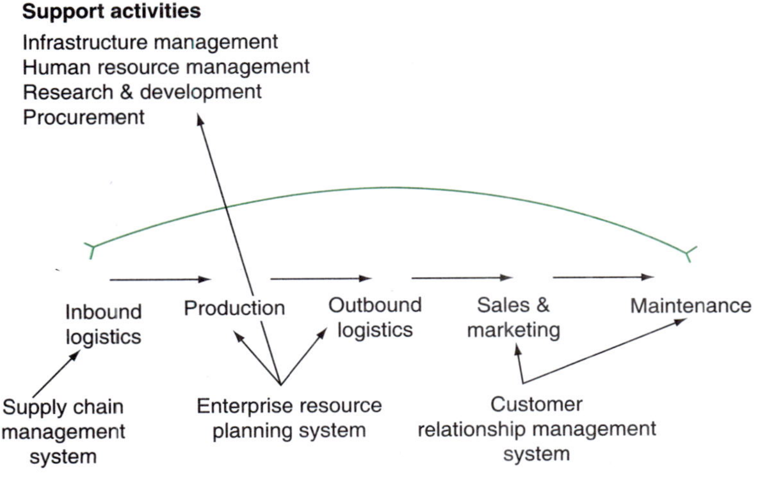

FIGURE 4.9 | Examples of information systems used to support activities of the value chain.

Chapter Glossary

Transaction costs The costs incurred for doing business with partners, such as costs for searching, contracting and communicating with them.

Bargaining power The ability to negotiate with business partners on the terms of business such as prices, dates and deliverables.

Complementary products Products or services that work with or support the main product or service sold by a firm. These products enhance the value of the main product.

Substitute products Competing products that are of a different nature but do the same job.

Information goods Goods whose main content is information such as music, scores, video or news. Many digital products are information goods.

Versions A form of an existing product that is different but of the same nature and contains same information.

Experience goods Goods whose value is evident only when the user gains direct knowledge of them by sensing them in some manner.

Technology platform The combination of hardware, operating system and application software that is available on most computers.

Lock-in When an information product is acquired by a user and used for some time, the user is restricted from giving up on the product owing to reasons of habit, cost or some benefit.

Switching cost The cost incurred by a user to move away from an information product to which he/she is locked-in.

Network externality An additional benefit (or cost) of being part of a network, which may not have been foreseen.

Positive feedback Evaluative information obtained about using a product or service that encourages more users to select the product or service.

Review Questions

1. Describe in your own words the competitive environment of the textile industry? Who are some of the main players? Who are the material providers? Who are the key vendors?
2. Analyse the bargaining power of the courier firms versus Flipkart. Who has an edge – Flipkart or the courier firms?
3. What is a substitute product for automobiles?
4. Explain the concept of a barrier to entry using the Flipkart case.
5. What is the difference between competing on cost versus competing on differentiation?
6. Give three examples of versions of software products that you are aware of ?

7. Why is a fiction novel an example of an experience good?
8. What is the difference between the cost and value of being on a mobile network?
9. Explain the value chain for making a passenger car.

Research Questions

1. What are the Indian laws regarding application of sales tax for e-commerce firms?
2. Examine all the software applications that you use? What is the nature of your lock-in to them?
3. Visit a neighbouring business and talk to the owner or manager to find out the following – the bargaining power of suppliers, the bargaining power of customers, the threat of substitutes and how the business has created barriers to entry to competition.
4. For the business you are studying, in the previous question, identify if there is any use of IT for gaining competitive advantage.

Further Reading

1. More information about Flipkart is available at: http://www.linkedin.com/companies/flipkart.com (accessed on 28 May 2010).
2. Interview with Sachin Bansal is available at: http://bookshopblog.com/2010/05/24/an-interview-with-sachin-bansal/ (accessed on 28 May 2010).
3. Interview with Binny Bansal is available at http://www.startupdunia.com/interview/interview-with-flipkart-founder-binny-bansal-776 (accessed on 28 May 2010).
4. http://blog.flipkart.com/ (accessed on 28 May 28 2010).
5. Shapiro, C. and Varian, H. (1999) *Information Rules: A Strategic Guide to the Network Economy,* Harvard Business School Press, MA, USA.
6. Website of Deutsche Post DHL can be visited at: http://www.dp-dhl.com/en.html (accessed on December 2010).
7. Porter, M.E. (1980) *Competitive Strategy,* Free Press, New York. USA.

CHAPTER 5

Electronic Commerce, Electronic Business, Electronic Governance

Learning Objectives

After completing this chapter, you will be able to:

- Understand e-commerce technology
- Learn doing business over the internet
- Get an overview of electronic governance

Electronic commerce (E-commerce) is an innovation that has created immense excitement among entrepreneurs and investors around the world. It is based on the basic technology of the internet, where pages are created in a specific language, and messages are exchanged across computers by means of email. With the success of the internet, advanced technologies have evolved that include direct digital data transfer between businesses, payment through websites and payment through mobile phones. Various models of doing business too have evolved. Portals are entry points for moving across the internet, for searching information, and also for direct sales to customers. Search engines, having grown as an independent business, have developed methods by which users can easily find what they want. Auctions sites have used the massive presence of sellers and buyers to enable large-scale online trading of goods. Aggregators have brought together large volume buyers and sellers through the internet. Electronic governance (e-governance) too has evolved in many countries, where governments use the internet to bring information and services to citizens.

MIND MAP OF CHAPTER TOPICS

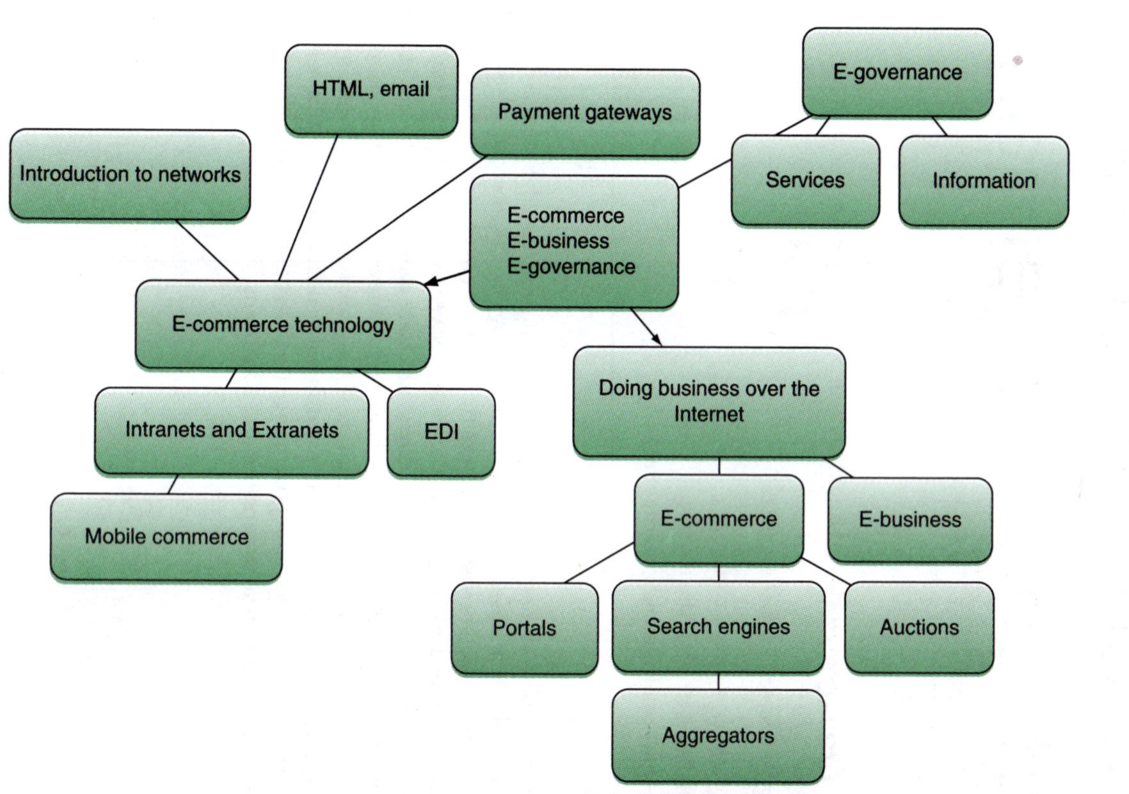

Metaljunction (mJunction) is one of the largest e-commerce firms in India. mJunction was started by two very large industrial steel production houses in India – the Steel Authority of India (SAIL) and Tata Steel. The initial goal of the steel giants behind the mJunction idea was to sell steel to industrial consumers through a common website. However, the idea grew into new dimensions, and today mJunction deals with metals and minerals, steel, auto components, coal, books, equipment and other products. They allow buyers and sellers of all these industrial products to list their needs and offerings on mJunction. In this manner, mJunction has grown tremendously and is currently one of the largest e-commerce sites in India, and the largest steel-selling site in the world.

As stated earlier, mJunction started out as a site for selling raw steel (it was called 'metaljunction' then). At that time steel was sold manually in India. Producers made steel of various types and qualities that were stocked in their manufacturing plants to be picked up by dealers and wholesale merchants. Pricing was ad hoc and often subject to stiff bargaining as manufacturers were keen to reduce inventories and offload their products. Merchants purchased steel at prices much lower than their fair value thus realising huge profits.

When Tata Steel and SAIL decided to create an online site for selling steel, their goal was to regularise the market to increase sale volumes and realise better prices for their products. They started hesitantly in times of the infamous *dotcom bust* when many e-commerce ventures had failed, without being sure of the outcome of their venture. However, they were able to enrol other steel manufacturers rapidly. Though Tata Steel is a public firm, with the shares held by the Tata family and a large number of shareholders, most other large steel producers are government-owned firms. So mJunction was an unusual collaboration where the partners saw the value in such a venture to streamline their channels for selling steel. mJunction's first-order effect was to allow a largely dispersed and fragmented market, consisting of product makers spread all over India and abroad, to go to one place to find products and discover prices. Response time for orders, payments and delivery was cut down dramatically along with uncertainties in shipments. mJunction also introduced auctions that further allowed the sellers to realise better prices for their stock.

After their success with steel, mJunction decided to branch out to other commodities, and selected coal. Coal sales in India, at that point, were mired in corruption, red tape and large-scale mafia involvement. Coal producers, like the government-owned Coal India, mined coal and then left the distribution to the largely criminal-controlled dealers and distributors. mJunction created 'coaljunction' as an e-commerce site for selling coal and its various products to buyers across India. Here too auctions were introduced to allow users to bid for different kinds and lot sizes of coal for bulk purchases. Coal sales through the site were very successful with many buyers and sellers switching their sale and acquisition functions to this site.

Following the success of steel and coal, mJunction diversified into automobiles for industrial customers. Here customers could buy used and new vehicles for use in a fleet or commercially. After its foray into the automobile business, mJunction moved into financing, procurement and asset sales.

Initially, all these businesses were targeted at corporate customers, not individual customers. Each customer had to register with mJunction, proving their business and financial credentials to be admitted to the site. Once admitted, members could buy or sell products with their financial transactions handled directly by the site. Recently, mJunction has diversified to consumer-oriented e-commerce, with their site called 'straightline.in' that sells a whole range of consumer products. They have also added other business transaction portals such as 'buyjunction' (for sale and purchase on non-core assets) and 'valuejunction' (which focuses on sales of stressed or idle assets).

mJunction's business model is based on transaction revenues. They charge clients a fee for each transaction enabled by the site. Since the transactions are usually in very large quantities, the rupee volume of transactions grew rapidly. In 2009, mJunction transacted business worth about Rs 650 billion (about USD 14 billion), having grown at more than 100% in revenues annually for many years. By 2015, mJunction had transaction volumes of Rs. 4.2 trillion (about USD 60 billion).

5.1 E-COMMERCE TECHNOLOGY

Electronic commerce or e-commerce in the modern world defines a powerful means of doing business. The origins of the word e-commerce are in the early days of the commercial internet, in the early 1990s, when businesses started extending their market reach using the new electronic medium. Initial transactions included providing information, taking orders and sending out information goods; and for these purposes the internet proved to be a convenient means. These activities indicated that there is an immense potential that could be realised by using e-commerce technology.

There was massive growth of e-commerce around the world as the technology became available to all, and also, as it evolved over time. From simple information provision, the technology grew to support complex exchange of goods and payments. A whole new industry evolved that built its business on electronic networks and the facilities it provided. The famous *dotcom boom* of the late 1990s is symbolic of the hope that businesses placed on electronic networks. Hundreds of firms started out with different ideas to show how internet technologies could be used to provide new goods and services. They improvised on the technology, created new technologies and invented processes by which business could be done. Some business models completely undermined the existing models, whereas others complemented the existing ones.

5.1.1 The Dotcom Boom and Bust

When the internet was opened for commercial use in 1993 in the USA, it resulted in a huge upsurge of business ideas and models for using the new medium. Many entrepreneurs started building websites that offered new propositions for both consumers and businesses. Many *venture capitalists*, those who provide investment money to new businesses, came forward and a huge number of new *startups* were funded. Between the years 1995 and 2000, in the USA, hundreds of new startups were funded and began operations on the internet. These firms usually had a name called x.com, where x was some name followed by the .com suffix. This gave rise to the term the *dotcom boom*.

KEY POINT

Initial excitement about the potential of the internet gave rise to the dotcom boom, which led to experimenting with e-commerce.

The dotcom boom was not restricted to the USA as firms in other parts of the world, including India, started out with new and innovative business ideas. One common theme running through these startups was the belief in network effects. Most of them believed that they simply had to get a site going that could attract a lot of visitors who wanted to use or see what the site had to offer. Then as the pool of visitors increased, the value of the site would also increase, as now the site developers could charge money from advertisers and other sponsors of the content on the site. The money obtained from venture capitalists thus was used for massive advertising and publicity campaigns in other media to attract customers. This created a lot of visibility for the firms, and consequently they became well known. Many used this opportunity to launch their stocks for the public to buy so as to raise capital. A significant number of these launches were very successful, making the owners instant millionaires. This garnered further publicity, leading to more public launches of stocks of these new firms. Overall stock prices in the USA and India rose dramatically for these dotcom firms, giving rise to the term 'bubble'.

The net effect of this bubble was that many firms that hardly had any secure revenues were priced very handsomely in the stock market. Many individual investors started playing on the stock markets, further pushing the stock prices.

In the year 2000, the market crashed. Many large investors realised that the dotcom firms were overpriced and started selling their stocks. This led to an overall crash in the stock prices in the market. Many firms that had sky-high valuations went bankrupt overnight, and others lost a lot of value on their shares. This is referred to as the 'bust' of the dotcom bubble. In India too there was an overall crash of the stock markets, especially of the dotcom startups (see Fig. 5.1).

The idea of doing work over the internet and doing transactions online caught on in other areas also – notably with governments and in the social space. Governments started creating websites to provide information to citizens, and later also allowed transactions such as downloading of forms, filling of forms, paying dues, sending notices, etc. For governments around the

FIGURE 5.1 The dotcom boom–dotcom bust period is depicted through fluctuation in the prices of IT stocks in the BSE from February 1999 through October 2004. Early in 2000, the sensex peaked, and then crashed, sinking to a low in 2001, after which it climbed again. The figure shows the closing value of the index of IT stocks in the Sensex.

world, the idea of providing universal access to the internet to all citizens became a priority and many countries followed up with massive investments in electronic infrastructure.

Many citizens' groups and non-governmental organisations (NGOs) too saw the potential of the internet and started using it for communication, coordination and transactions. Citizens formed communities with like-minded interests that linked up and shared information via the internet. Many groups organised civil action around political issues by using the facilities of the internet such as email and websites. NGOs used the e-commerce facilities extensively to support developmental activities such as education, health care, skills training and employment generation. Also, they have created extensive portals and other e-commerce resources for their members, stakeholders and partners.

This chapter explores these developments in business, government and society in greater detail. The following section first gives an overview of the technologies underlying e-commerce. These technologies are at a higher level of the technology hierarchy, something that will be described in a later chapter, and enable many of the e-commerce applications. Later sections discuss e-business, e-commerce and e-governance.

5.2 HTML AND EMAIL

The principal driver for the commercial growth of the internet is the World Wide Web. The Web is a technology that permits linking of data files over the internet. The files could be pure text, or multimedia files such as video or music. The files are linked together by a technology known as the Hypertext Markup Language (HTML). HTML is not a computer language in the same sense as C or Java is; it is a markup language, with a limited set of functions as compared to other computer languages. HTML was created by the physicist Tim Berners-Lee in 1989 as a way to create a network of documents related to physics research. Berners-Lee is widely considered to be the inventor of the World Wide Web.

The idea of hypertext is to link files to each other through words or other related associations. The Web has many pages dedicated to the discussion of, for example, dogs. Each page is created by an author who has an interest in the subject. This author can create a link to another page on the Web that also discusses dogs. The link is called a hyperlink because the pages that are linked together are not on the same computer but on different computers on the internet. The job of the hyperlink is to mark the exact position of a page, at which address and on which server it exists, so that the reader interested in this page can go to it.

To see an example of the HTML script, start up the Mozilla Firefox browser on any computer (any other browser can also be used). Under the View menu select the Page Source option. This will pop up another browser window that shows the HTML source for the page you are viewing. The script consists of tags that begin and end with the '<' and '>' symbols. For example,

```
<title> .... </title>
```

The tags are special commands in the markup language that indicate to the browser how to process the material contained within them. The text contained within the tags mentioned above will be shown as a title, which means it will have a certain size and shape to differentiate it from the other text on the page.

Links to other pages in HTML are marked with the `href` tag. This tag tells the browser to search for and retrieve this page. The content of the tag is an entire valid page address on the internet. For example,

```
<a href= "http://www.google.com"> Google </a>
```

This tag example shows a link to the Web search engine site Google. The internet address for Google is in quotes, and this is not visible on the page as shown by the browser. The browser shows instead the text 'Google' to indicate the name of the link that can be clicked. When a user clicks on the link, the browser initiates a request to the server that hosts the page www.google.com, and if the server responds then this new page is displayed by the browser.

HTML has many tags that correspond to the structure of the document (such as a title or heading), the presentation of the text (such as the font type and size) and tags that create links. Furthermore, data tags provide ways to link to files of different data types such as image, or audio or video files.

Later, languages such as XML (Extensible Markup Language) became popular and were developed extensively. XML, unlike HTML, allows the creation of unique tags that are specific to an application. This allows programmers to create a wide variety of data exchange formats that can be used for efficient transfer of data across the internet. For instance, the entire HTML specification can be created in XML along with many other languages.

KEY POINT

HTML is a core technology by which Web pages are created.

By 2015, the development of Web pages relied extensively on HTML, and two other languages that allowed rich, interactive pages to be created. These languages are Cascading Style Sheets (CSS) which is a language for the presentation of Web pages, and JavaScript, which allows interactivity and complex logic to be embedded in Web pages. For an example of how – HTML, CSS and JavaScript are used, see the source page of www.mjunction.in.

5.2.1 Email

Email was one of the first popular applications to be provided on the internet. It precedes the Web, and was first available in the mid-1960s within university departments in the USA. Initially, email was a facility that allowed people sharing a mainframe computer to send messages as files to each other. Each user owned an *account*, which was a named file storage area that only the user had access to, and messages could be sent to the account. The underlying processes for sending and receiving messages were determined by a computer *protocol* (a communication specification that is common to all computers, and is an accepted norm). The email software then simply copied the file from the sender's account to the receiver's account (see Fig. 5.2).

As the internet grew and large networks of computers appeared, it became possible to send messages to computers across networks. The idea of addressing with the @ symbol was introduced in 1971 by Ray Tomlinson in the USA. The text following the @ symbol specified the location address of the computer on the network where the email could be sent. The text before the @ symbol specified the name of the account to which the email could be sent. One of the earliest protocols that was used for the purpose of sending emails across computers on a network was called the SMTP (Simple Mail Transfer Protocol) that specified the manner in which the email message had to be formatted, such as the *From* address line, the *To* address line, the *Subject* address line and the message body (see Fig. 5.3). Only text messages were permitted by

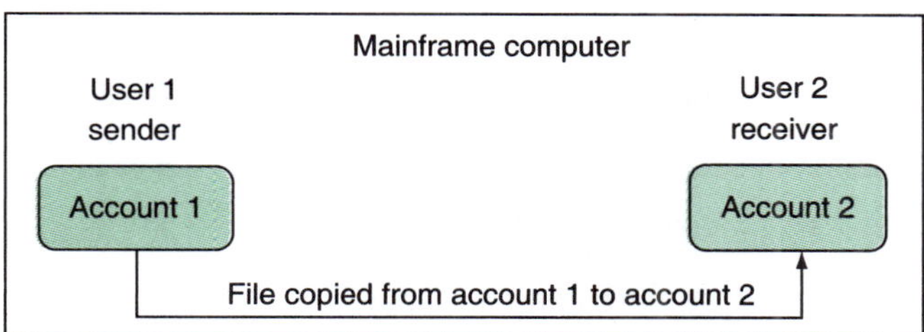

FIGURE 5.2 The original email facility simply copied a file, the email message, from the sender's account to the receiver's account.

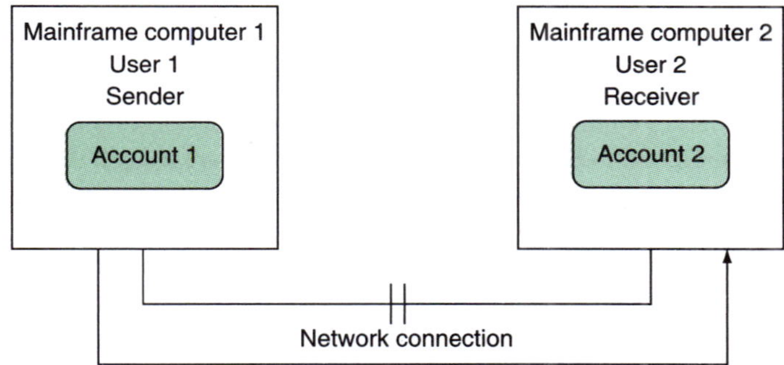

FIGURE 5.3 Email sent from one computer on a network to another on a different network.

the early protocols, but the modern email protocols allow many types of attachments such as multimedia files.

Email is an asynchronous communication technology. It allows users to communicate while they are not simultaneously present. For instance, User 1 can send an email message to User 2 any time, whether User 2 is accessing the email message at that time or not. The message from User 1 stays in User 2's mailbox, which is a storage facility for emails. User 2 can read the email at a later date. The asynchronous communication property of email is very important as it permits extensive sharing of messages without the active presence of the recipient.

Another important property of email is that it allows the message to be directed at an identified individual. The message will be available to the target recipient only, and this forms a kind of identity and security. When organisations started using email, this feature proved very useful as messages could be directed and sent very quickly. Currently, this property is used to verify the identity of individuals through a confirming message sent to an email address by banks, ticket booking sites, tax payment sites, etc.

Email identifies the sender, the institution from which the sender originates the message, and the time at which it originated. This information is useful within organisations to establish a network of persons who need to work together, without physical meetings, and who need to be sure of each other's identity.

Initially, before the popularity of the Web, email was available to a few organisations such as businesses, government departments and educational institutions. After the launch of the public Web, email was made available to the public at large with popular services such as Hotmail and Yahoo Mail. These services were available to users on the Web, and could be accessed through a browser. They were free services, where users could get an account by just signing up. After its launch in 1996, Hotmail became very popular and had about 8.5 million subscribers by the end of 1997. Dozens of free email services sprang up on the Web and millions of users around

Table 5.1 | Some Statistics on Email Usage

Number of emails sent out in 2009	90 trillion
Number of email users worldwide in 2009	1.4 billion
Number of internet users worldwide in 2009	1.73 billion
Percentage of emails that were spam	81%

Source: www.royalpingdom.com (accessed on October 2010).

the world could access an email account from which they could send and receive messages. This phenomenon made email an important ingredient of e-commerce.

Currently, services such as Gmail and Yahoo Mail constitute an important email access point for millions of people around the globe. Although most institutions have their own email services, and provide users with institution-specific email identities (called email IDs), the free services are still popular. Many small and medium enterprises in developing countries use Gmail as their organisational email. Table 5.1 presents some data on email usage. This data is for the year 2010. Email usage grew. Significantly since them and, according to the Radicati Group, stood at about 205 billion emails per day in 2015, sent out by 2.5 billion users.

Email groups and lists are quite popular too, and attract users who have shared interests. These groups follow a practice of broadcasting messages to their users on a regular basis, usually daily, and users can also post their own messages. Some email groups are *moderated*, which means that their content is controlled and what is broadcast is edited by someone. Many websites now have subscription services where users can list their email IDs for the website to send them regular emails.

The downside of the popularity of email is the problems of *spam* and *viruses*. Spam is unsolicited email that is sent out by persons who are unknown to the recipients. Spam is mainly generated for marketing purposes – to sell products and services. Spam is also sent out as a lure to attract users to illegal and contraband goods. Some organisations estimate that spam now constitutes a bulk of all emails sent out. Most email services provide spam filters that help filter out email that appears to be spam. These filters are not always reliable and often regular email is classified as spam or spam email is allowed to go through as regular email.

Sending out viruses is another scourge of using email. Viruses are malicious computer programs that secretly enter computers and destroy or otherwise adversely affect files and programs. Despite the problems of spam and viruses, email usage firmly remains as the basis for e-commerce transactions. When users create accounts on e-commerce sites, when they place — orders, when they seek responses to queries about their orders, they invariably have to use email accounts. Most e-commerce sites do not even allow users to register without an email account.

5.2.2 Networks: A Brief Introduction

HTML and email are the services that are provided over the internet. Networks constitute another important component of the internet. Before delving into other technologies important for e-commerce, it is useful to examine the nature of the networks that organisations are using and what is essential for e-commerce and e-governance to flourish.

The internet is termed as a network of networks. The internet, at the technological level, is a collection of networks connected together by common, shared standards of communication. These common standards are the backbone on which the internet is built. The standards specify the manner in which data and messages can be passed between the different parts of the network. They also ensure a certain level of reliability for sharing of messages as also security of the networks. As these are open standards, they have been adopted for a variety of networks and devices that enable the networks.

Most organisations create networks within their establishment, either within a geographic location, like a campus or across many locations. These networks are private and are designed

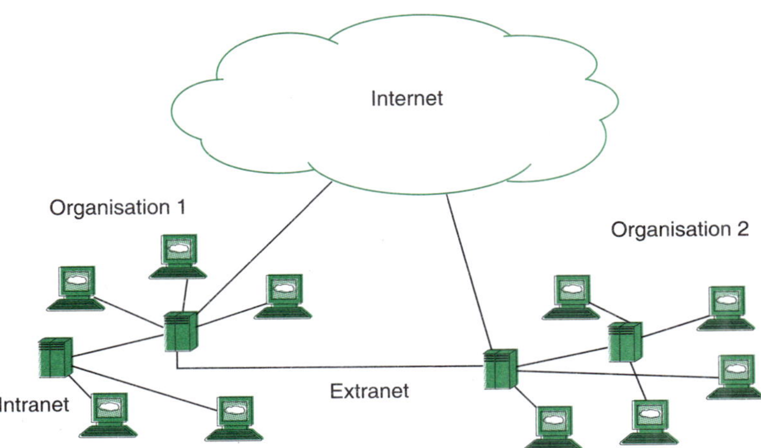

FIGURE 5.4 Intranets connect computers within an organisation. Extranets link organisations together. Each organisation on its own connects with the internet.

for internal use by the organisation's members. Such networks are called *Intranets*. Intranets are built on the same common standards of data sharing that are used across the internet. Messages are created and passed across an Intranet in the same manner as across the internet (see Fig. 5.4). Intranets thus allow the organisation to use the same set of application tools for internal communication as it would with the external world.

When an Intranet is built in a single geographic location, or campus, it is built on a *local area network* (LAN) that consists of hardware and cables that are suitable for a local setting. If the organisation has many offices, maybe within the country or across many countries, then the organisation has to use the features of the internet to create its Intranet. A technology called the *virtual private network* (VPN) is used for this purpose. This technology allows the organisations to create a private network across the public internet.

Organisations also create *Extranets*, or networks that link them to their partners and collaborators. Extranets too use the common and shared standards for data communication and allow organisations that are linked to use the same tools both for their internal and external communication. Extranets are a convenient and powerful means by using which organisations can set up links for purposes of commerce. Typical exchanges of data and documents over Extranets include invoices, purchase orders, shipping notices, receipts and other related documents.

5.2.3 Electronic Data Interchange (EDI)

Before the growth of the common standards for the internet and the growth of Extranets, firms exchanged data electronically through private networks. This process was called electronic data interchange (EDI). The EDI standards were initiated in the 1960s in the USA and Europe to allow transportation firms to exchange data across national boundaries. Later, many trade bodies evolved further standards for exchange of commerce-related data. EDI standards are not similar to the data standards used by the internet; they are based on different, often proprietary, standards that are used only by the partner organisations.

5.2.3.1 An EDI Example

When banks first introduced automated teller machines, or ATMs, the idea was to have a cash dispersal unit that could look up a customer's account maintained at the bank and determine whether the cash request could be met or not. The ATMs had to be connected to the bank's computers to look up the necessary information. Thus, when a customer initiated a session at an ATM, the ATM exchanged data with the bank using an EDI standard. The advantage of the

EDI was that it provided a very quick means of exchanging data; it was secure and instantly updated records at the bank.

The EDI standards of communication are still used by many institutions. These standards provide a continuity with older methods of communication and also a certain measure of security as the standards are not well known.

5.2.4 Online Payment Technology

One of the biggest challenges posed to e-commerce has been the issue of payments. In a typical commercial transaction conducted manually, a customer is able to pay cash for a purchased item or pay by credit card. If it is by credit card, this transaction is verified by a service to ensure that the card is valid, and then the transaction is posted. The seller can also verify the authenticity of the buyer by seeing an identity card.

Online payment technologies address the issue of managing transactions in a secure and efficient manner. Establishing the identity of the buyer is one of the first problems that the payment technologies face. Once the identity is established, the next challenge is to have an easy process by which the payment can be made without the intervention of too many intermediaries and also at a reasonable cost. Once a payment has been secured, the remaining problem is that of chargebacks, that is cancellation, for some reason, of the transaction and a subsequent reversal of the payment.

The service called Paypal is a USA-based payment service agency that acts like an intermediary. In a typical Paypal transaction, both sellers and buyers have an account with Paypal. When a buyer agrees to buy a good online, he/she is in a position to simply send an email from his/her Paypal account to the seller, stating the amount that is to be paid. Paypal accesses either the buyer's credit card account or the buyer's bank account and debits the payment amount from there. The permission for doing this is granted by the buyer at the time of creating the Paypal account. The amount is then credited to the seller's Paypal account.

Paypal is not a bank by itself, but has the capabilities of one. Its main advantage over traditional banks is that it allows the buyers and sellers to interact via a simple email. It provides the security of identifying the buyer and seller through prior arrangements of creating the accounts. Creating an account with Paypal requires having an email ID, a credit card or a bank account and sufficient credit availability.

Most e-commerce sites rely directly on credit cards. The Indian Railways ticketing service accepts a number of credit cards from Indian banks to complete a transaction. To buy a ticket with the Indian Railways, customers specify what ticket they want, have to provide details of their credit card, such as the number and the verification code. They also have to provide their home address as would be recognised by the credit issuing bank (see Figs. 5.5–5.9). After this the Railways website redirects the information to the credit card issuing bank, which verifies the card number against the address information. Some banks also ask for a password from the customer to further establish if he/she is the real owner of the credit card. Once the transaction is approved, the Railways site charges the amount to the credit card and completes the ticket purchase process. For chargebacks, the Railways uses the same information to reverse the sale and refund the amount.

A third kind of service that has evolved in countries such as India, where many people do not have bank accounts or credit cards, is the use of cash cards. Services such as the ITZ Cash Card allow customers to pay cash and buy a card that can be used for online transactions. During an online transaction such as buying a Railway ticket, the customer can enter the cash card number and the Railways service deducts the relevant amount from the card. This is done by accessing the account on the cash card as maintained by ITZ and updating the value. Cash cards do not identify the user; they only help provide a secure and quick transaction. Cash cards are widely available in retail outlets and are sold to customers with an identity proof.

The fourth type of service related to cash cards is that of digital wallets. These are similar to cash cards, in the sense that users can load cash into them and then spend it later. Paytm (paytm.com) is one such service in India that allows payments to be made through an app on a smartphone. The customer can purchase some good online and then select Paytm as the

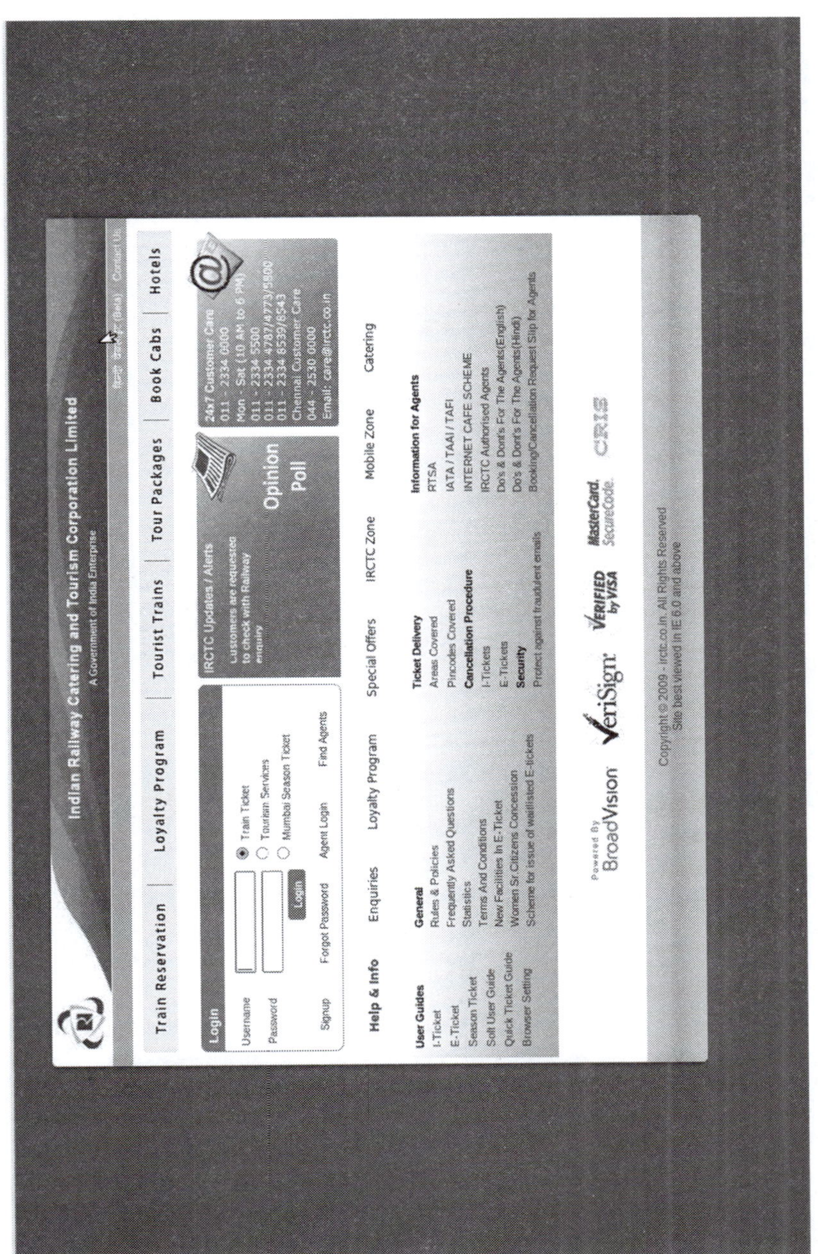

FIGURE 5.5 | The first page of the Indian Railways ticket booking website.
Source: irctc.co.in

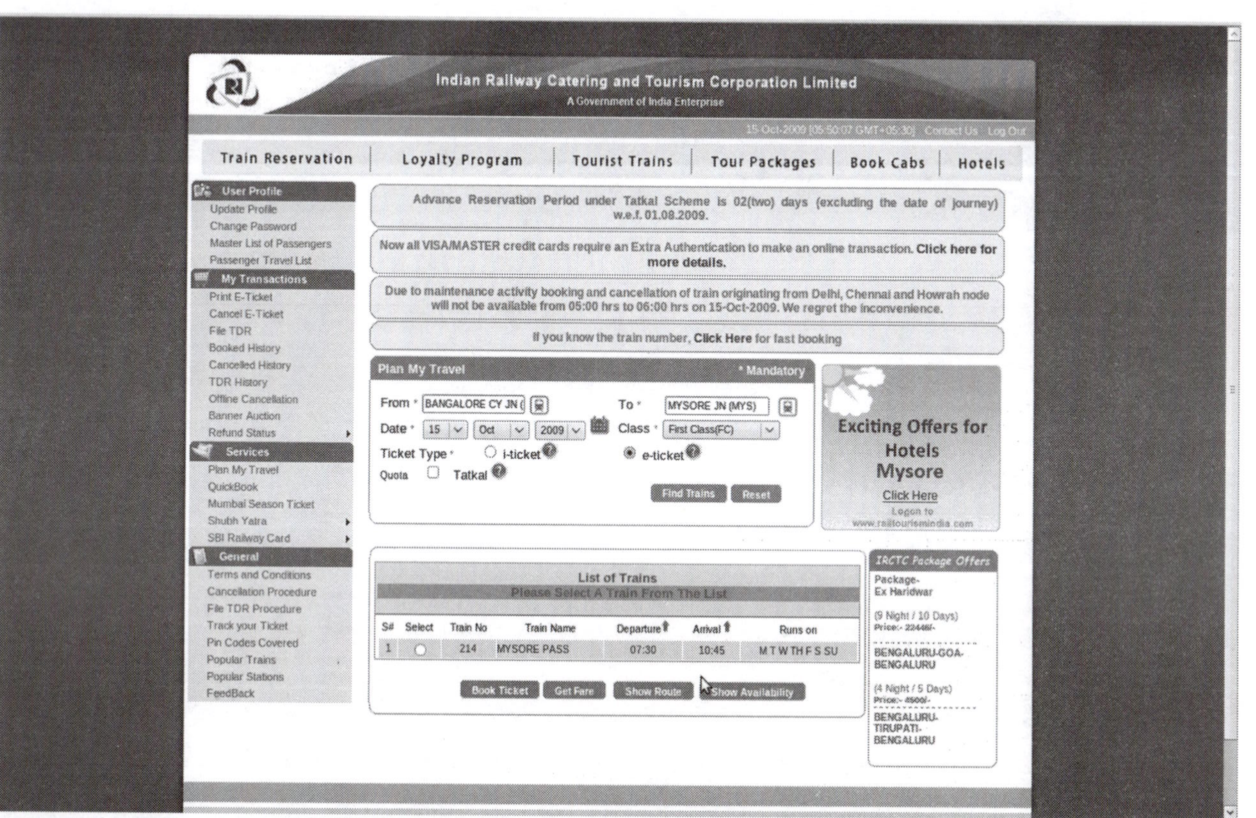

FIGURE 5.6 | This page of the Indian Railways ticket booking website requests confirmation of travel destination and date.

Source: irctc.co.in

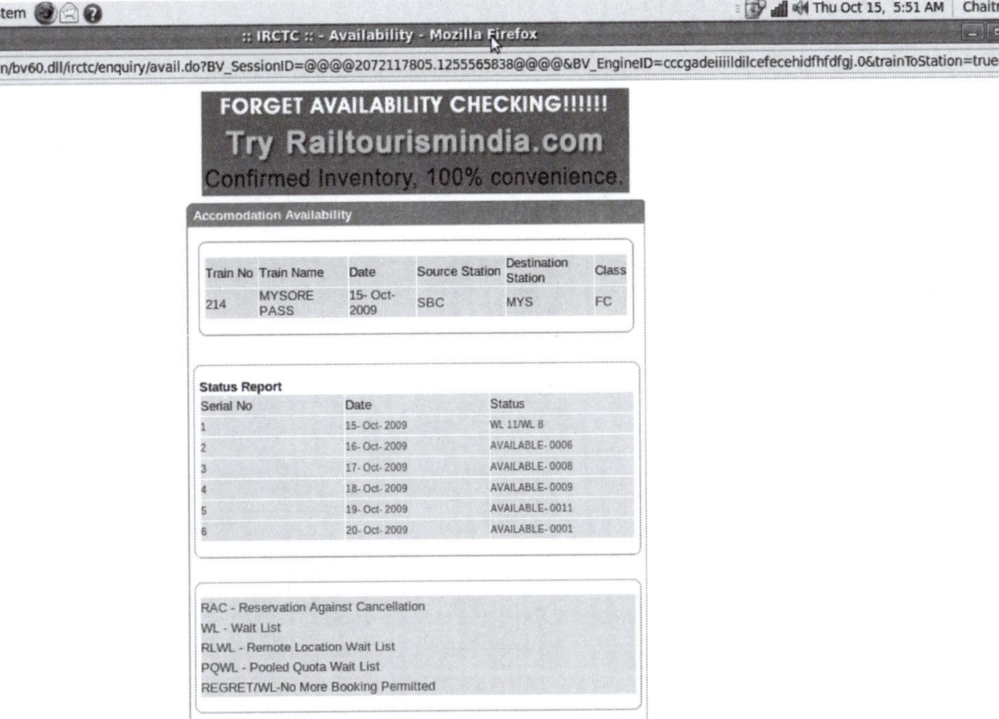

FIGURE 5.7 This page of the Indian Railways ticket booking website displays the availability of reserved seats on different dates.

Source: irctc.co.in

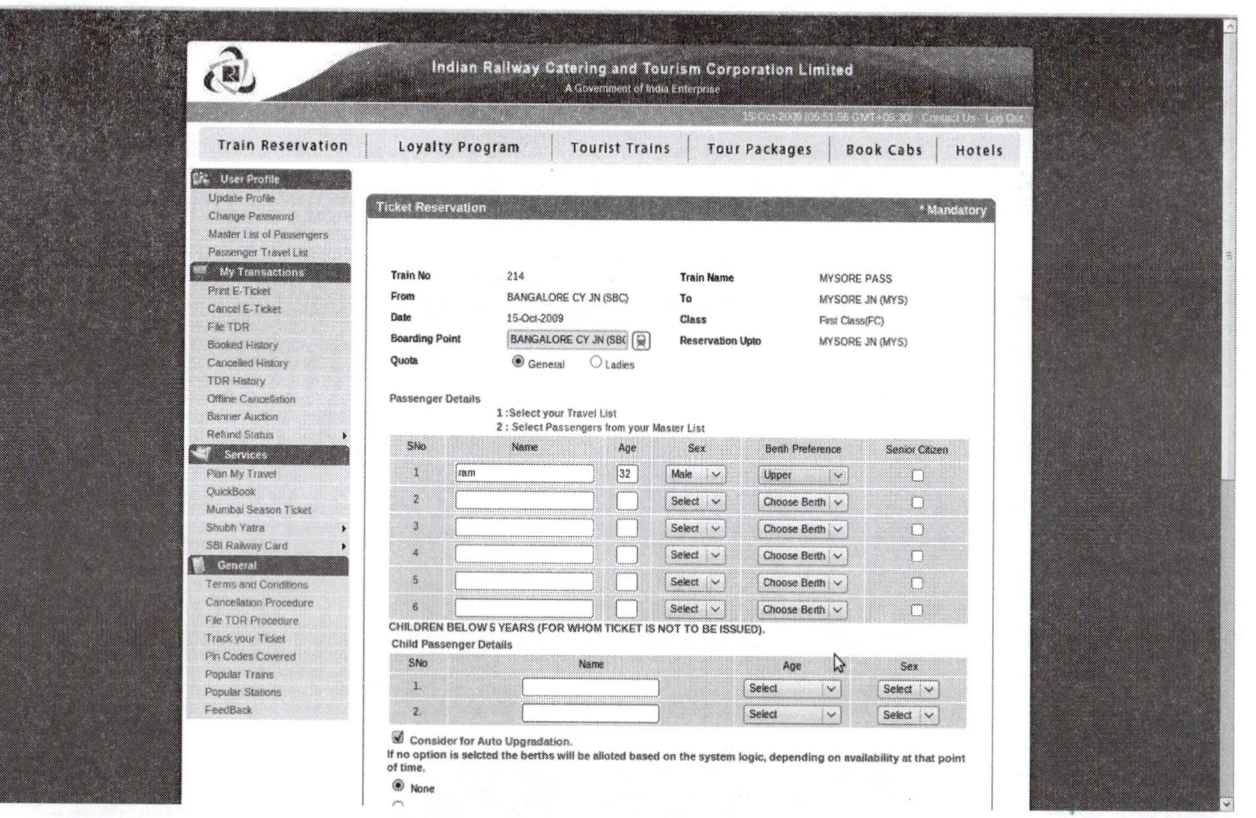

FIGURE 5.8 | The form on the Indian Railways ticket booking website for entering details about the passengers.
Source: irctc.co.in

https://www.irctc.co.in/cgi-bin/bv60.dll/irctc/booking/listbanks.do?fare=240&totapoints=NaN&BV_SessionID=@@@@2072117805.1255565838@@@@&BV_EngineID=cccgadeli

Select your bank for making payment. On completion of payment procedure, you will automatically come to IRCTC site and proceed with the booking confirmation. **Click Here** For Transaction Charges

All VISA Debit cards (If enabled by card issuer) can also be used for booking tickets through any of the credit card Payment Gateways (ICICI PG, HDFC PG, CITI PG, AXIS PG). **Click Here** For List of Banks

Payment by Credit Cards and Debit Cards (If enabled by card Issuer):		
ICICI PG	HDFC PG	AXIS PG
CITI PG	American Express	
Payment by Credit Cards EMI Option:		
CITI Bank EMI		
Payment through Net Banking facility		
ICICI Bank	HDFC Bank	AXIS Bank
ABN Amro Bank	IDBI Bank	SBI - Internet Banking
Punjab National Bank	Federal Bank	Syndicate Bank
Indusind Bank	Karnataka Bank	Oriental Bank Of Commerce
Corporation Bank	Bank Of India	Rajasthan Bank
Indian Bank	SBI Associate Bank's	Union Bank Of India
Bank of Baroda		
Payment through ATM cum Debit Card		
CITI Bank	SBI ATM-cum-Debit Card	Punjab National Bank
Andhra Bank	Indian Bank	Canara Bank
Payment by Cash Cards:		
ITZ Cash Card	Done Cash Card	I Cash Card

FIGURE 5.9 This page of the Indian Railways ticket booking website displays the various online payment options available.

Source: irctc.co.in

payment agency. Paytm then authenticates the buyer, through the mobile phone number or account name, and makes payment from the wallet. Paytm is widely used by taxi-hailing service Uber, which is a competitor to Ola cabs.

A fifth kind of service is provided by banks. Banks have created a net-banking service in which they allow their customers to create accounts. During an online transaction, at the stage of payment, the customers can point to and provide the details of their net-banking service to the seller who can subsequently charge the bank for the sale amount. This service is possible if the seller permits it, and has a prior arrangement with the customer's bank for such a service. Usually large organisations, such as the Indian Railways or airlines, enter into arrangements with banks for utilising the net-banking service. In this service, the convenience for the seller is of knowing that the customer's identity is authenticated and also that the transaction will get completed smoothly. Chargebacks can be handled easily as the seller can simply reverse the charges to the bank. Banks also rely on services such as NEFT (National Electronic Funds Transfer) and RTGS (Real-time Gross Settlement) for inter-bank account to account transfers. These services enable a customer to make a payment directly to a seller's account.

KEY POINT

E-commerce relies on electronic methods of transfer of money from buyers to sellers, such as via email (Paypal), via credit cards, via cash cards (ITZ cash), via wallets (Paytm), and by net-banking.

5.2.5 Mobile Commerce

With the widespread availability and use of smartphones, e-commerce firms have increasingly made their presence in apps. Firms such as Flipkart, Amazon.in, Snapdeal.com and others have created apps on smartphones that allow customers to search for products, select them, make payments, and complete the purchase directly through the mobile phone. These services make the process of purchasing very easy and convenient.

Mobile commerce in India has increased significantly with the spread of smartphones. According to the internet and Mobile Association of India (IAMAI), the number of users accessing the internet through smartphones was about 370 million in India, which constitutes about 80% of the total number of internet users in India. This massive growth in access through smartphones has prompted a massive growth in the number of e-commerce startups that are offering different services mainly through apps on smartphones. Examples in India include Swiggy.com (for restaurant food delivery), Stayzilla.com (for homestays) and Bigbasket.com (for groceries purchase and delivery).

5.3 DOING BUSINESS OVER THE INTERNET

The internet presents a unique and unusual channel for business as compared to older methods. It has several properties that make it very different from the ways of doing business in the past - the internet permits almost instant communication; messages sent in by email arrive at destinations across the globe in a matter of seconds; people can chat or talk online simultaneously while being located in different countries; images and sounds and video can be shared and broadcast instantly; the cost of sending messages is much lower than by physical means and it is possible to search vast quantities of information on the internet, something that was practically impossible in the manual methods of information exchange. These are some of the unique facilities of the internet that organisations across the world have built upon to create entirely new ways of doing work and business. This section outlines some of the ways in which organisations have innovated with the new technologies.

5.3.1 E-Commerce

Electronic commerce, or e-commerce, for short is a phrase that was coined to designate businesses that were created to use the internet technologies as a basis for transactions. The first few prominent e-commerce firms used the technologies such as HTML and email to set up businesses. The business model that they used relied on interactions with consumers and collaborators principally via these technologies. The immense success of this business model led to more innovation and newer technologies being invented.

5.3.2 Portals

Web portals were one of the first e-commerce businesses to arrive after the commercial launch of the World Wide Web. A portal is a single site that contains links to and information about other sites. A portal is designed as a starting point, an entry point to the Web, where links to other sites are collected under appropriate headings, which guide users towards their interests. Portals also include search facilities where users can seek out links to sites of their interest.

One of the first portals to gain popularity and be commercially viable is Yahoo! This portal was started in 1994 by two students who were interested in listing all the sites they liked on a single page in appropriate categories. Initially, Yahoo! provided links to other pages and a search facility. As a portal, Yahoo! enabled users to go to one place as their starting pointing for browsing the Web. And, as a strategy to popularise this practice, Yahoo! encouraged users to make it their homepage (a homepage is the first page that shows up when a browser is started). After its launch, Yahoo! was immensely popular and drew thousands of visitors to its site and associated links daily. The popularity of Yahoo! among users can be gauged from the fact that throughout its history it has remained one of the top five most visited sites on the internet (according to data available on www.Alexa.com, a site that computes ranks of websites based on the viewer traffic the site receives).

Yahoo! became a successful business by placing advertisements on its web pages. As it had a large viewership, it followed the business model of large media firms of charging for advertisements with rates varying on size and placement of the messages. Yahoo! was very successful as a commercial firm, and had a successful launch of its public offering of shares during the height of the dotcom boom. With the available capital, it created a host of other e-commerce services such as a very popular free email service, news feeds related to stocks, sports, movies, a travel site, listing services for commercial establishments (yellow pages), etc.

Other portal sites also sprang up that provided aggregations of web pages that had a common theme such as travel, sports, finance, entertainment, etc. Specialised portals were also created for individual organisations that would allow their employees and partners to have a single place to find information that would be of interest to them.

Portals are often differentiated from other e-commerce sites on the basis of being 'pure-play' internet sites that rely mainly on providing directed and valuable information. They usually do not have a facility for commercial transactions involving exchange of goods or money. Many do not have a payment gateway for monetary transactions. However, these categories are changing rapidly with the evolution of technology, and portals too are seeking out new avenues of e-commerce.

KEY POINT

A portal is a website that acts as a gateway to other sites on the internet.

5.3.3 Search Engines

The World Wide Web has grown from a few thousand pages in 1993 to about 200 million pages in 1999 to estimates ranging from 1 billion sites in 2016 (according to www.internetlivestates.com), where each site may contain thousands of web pages. This immense growth has followed from the deep penetration of the internet technology in all parts of the globe. The challenge that faces common users as well as large corporations that want to leverage the Web for their business is that of having a coherent way of organising the Web for users. Search engines provide one answer.

Search engines are special programs built upon HTML to search information and data within web pages and categorise them. The main challenge is in understanding the context of the pages and categorising them appropriately. Early search engines that searched through and categorised web pages relied on using word counts for assigning weights. For example, if the user is searching for the word 'penguin' with the intention of finding out about the bird by that name; and suppose there are a few pages that discuss penguins, their habitat, their eating habits, etc. and use the word 'penguin' very often, then these pages would be picked up as important by the search engine. It would list the page with the largest count of the word 'penguin' first, followed by other pages with lesser counts. The assumption of the search is that the most relevant page will have the highest occurrence of the word or phrase being searched. A cursory examination

KEY POINT

The task of Web search engines is to find the post relevant Web page for the search query.

of this assumption will reveal that this need not be the case. A page on, say, the mating habits of penguins may not use the word 'penguin' very often; it may use other words to describe the behaviour.

Using the word-counting method for search, the earliest search engines 'crawled' the Web to find and index all pages. Crawling the Web entailed looking up pages and the links contained therein and tracing out all possible pages linked there. With this method, it was assumed that all possible web pages could be tracked and indexed. Very large servers were required to store the indexes thus created, and the servers had to be very fast to respond to the millions of queries that required looking up the index to find the relevant pages.

Google created a search engine in the late 1990s that overcame some of the problems of ranking pages by word counts. It used a method that looked at links to a page as a measure of its worth rather than word counts. For example, for a search on 'penguins' if there are, say, two pages found by the engine, the ranking is based on how many other pages link to these pages for the subject concerned. In doing so, Google's method explicitly places more weight on the value others give to the page, possibly after reading it, than a mere word count would provide.

KEY POINT

Google's search engine ranked pages by seeing how many other pages linked to them.

Google's search method proved immensely useful as it became one of the most used websites on the internet. It indexes close to a trillion pages (according to one estimate) on its servers, which are spread out across the globe. Google is also a commercial firm that gains revenues from advertisements placed on its site. It evolved a special model of obtaining advertisement revenues by charging differently for different types of usage and viewing.

Media firms usually charge revenues for advertisements placed on their media, print or television or online pages, based on the extent of viewership. Media that have a larger number of viewers or readers can charge a higher price for the same advertisement than another media with a lower number of viewers. Google took this model of revenue generation from advertising further. It leveraged the convenience and power of IT significantly.

1. Google enables clients to place their advertisement content on the sites easily, through a convenient interface. Clients do this through a form on Google's site. Once the material is uploaded it can be on display in minutes.
2. Google created a charge scheme by which clients pay only on the actual number of 'click throughs' for their advertisement, rather than on a fixed charge basis. Google tracks the number of times viewers click on the displayed advertisement and charge their clients accordingly. This is a remarkably different payment scheme, as clients pay according to the number of viewers who actually select their advertisement, as opposed to the number who saw it on display.
3. Google places the advertisements in a context-sensitive manner. When customers write words into Google's search box, these words reveal their need for information, and become the context for advertisements. For example, a search for the term 'penguins' on Google shows many pages about the bird, but no related advertisements. However, a search for 'penguins cruise' displays number of pages listing cruises to the South Pole to see penguins, and this page on Google also shows advertisements from commercial firms that organise cruises.
4. Google records the click-throughs of all its viewers and researches this information to understand why certain keywords are relevant in some contexts and not others. For instance, a viewer who is searching for cruises and nature travel on Google, may be more likely to be interested in a cruise to the South Pole, than one who has visited many pages regarding penguins and other creatures of the South Pole. The first one is more interested in travel and may respond to an advertisement for such, whereas the latter is most likely only interested in reading about fauna.

5.3.4 Direct Selling

Traditionally, goods are sold through a retailer where customers arrive at the premises, observe and examine the goods they are interested in, ask questions to the seller, if necessary, and then make the purchase. The goods are brought to the retail outlet through intermediaries such as wholesalers and distributors. When a customer leaves with the goods, he/she does not directly interact with either the manufacturer of the goods or the intermediaries. When goods are sold through a website, manufacturers can directly connect with customers without the need of intermediaries. This latter model is what Amazon.com adopted when it created a website that listed books with detailed information and user ratings about them, and allowed customers to directly buy them off the website. Customers paid mainly with credit cards and the books were shipped to them via mail or by courier. Amazon.com had made an arrangement with one of the largest distributors of books in North America to list their entire database of books on its website, thus giving it one of the largest possible collections of any book store.

Amazon.com went into direct competition with book stores that kept book stocks physically on shelves, which customers bought directly. The advantages it highlighted were those of convenience, having a larger choice and the ability to search easily. On Amazon.com's website the customer can browse books by subject or by author, or simply search for all books on a particular topic or by an author. This is not easily done in traditional book stores and was a significant competitive advantage for Amazon.com.

Amazon.com realised revenues from the commissions available from the sale of books. It was hugely successful and prompted a number of rivals to also launch their own sites. A book store chain in the USA, called Barnes and Noble, also launched a website with books from its collections. This is an example of what is called a 'click-and-mortar' e-commerce firm that offers customers choices of buying online as well as physically from a book store.

Direct selling is very popular on the Web with almost all kinds of goods and services being available online. Most manufacturers have created websites and sell directly from the sites as well as through their regular channel. Goods range from books, music, consumer durables, medicines, automobiles to even real estate and airplanes. E-commerce revenues in a developing country like India are also growing, at a very rapid pace, led by firms such as Flipkart, Snapdeal, Shopclues and others.

Direct selling to consumers is often referred to as business to consumer (B2C) and commerce between businesses is referred to as business to business (B2B). mJunction is a B2B e-commerce firm. These relations are distinguished from other types of business or relations (see Fig. 5.10). B2G are direct transactions between businesses and government departments, whereas government to government (G2G) are transactions between government departments. Transactions between government departments and citizens are referred to as government to citizen (G2C), and this is usually referred to as e-governance. Transactions between customers or citizens are called C2C.

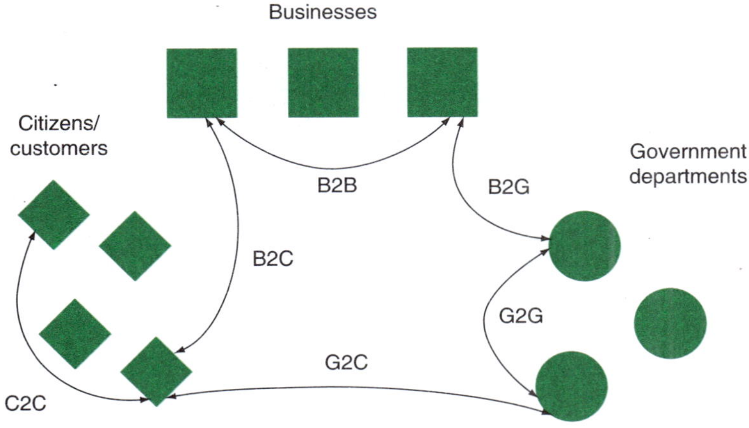

FIGURE 5.10 Various types of e-commerce – between businesses, government departments and citizens or consumers.

5.3.5 Auctions

Another very successful e-commerce business is that of auctions. A typical auction is an aggregation of many buyers and sellers, where the sellers provide the items for sale and buyers price them according to some principles. For instance, one method of pricing is by bidding. Buyers bid prices for a particular product and the product is sold to the highest bidder. In this method, bidding increases the value of the product, and it is usually the last bidder that wins the auction.

In an auction, both buyers and sellers benefit if their numbers are high. If there are many buyers but few sellers, the sellers will have an advantage as the price will tend to be high than that in a situation where there are many sellers. If there are many sellers and few buyers then this is a disadvantage for sellers as prices will remain low.

Online auctions, held through websites, overcome the problem of few buyers or sellers. Anyone can access an online auction, either as a seller or as a buyer. One of the most successful online auctions sites is eBay, which is an example of a C2C e-commerce site. eBay's website allows anyone to list products that they want auctioned. When sellers list their products, they fill out a form on eBay that allows them to describe the product, provide a picture of it and also specify a base price that they want for it. After the form filling, the product is listed on eBay's site and bidding by buyers is permitted for a fixed period of time, usually 1 week. Bidding brings up the price, and at the close of the bidding period, the bid of the highest bidder is accepted and he/she is declared the winner. The buyer and the seller then exchange money and goods independent of eBay.

After the auction, eBay permits buyers and sellers to rate each other. This rating is publicly declared and forms a basis for building reputations of buyers and sellers. Sellers with high ratings are able to attract more and higher bids for their products.

KEY POINT

Online auction sites are successful because they can attract a large number of buyers and also a large number of sellers.

Auction sites are subject to strong network effects. Successful auction sites attract more and more buyers and sellers, who are then weaned away from other auction sites. eBay's success forced many other auction sites to shutdown. Recently, an auction site run by Yahoo! had to shutdown as it could not attract enough visitors.

eBay collects revenues as a percentage of the sale value of an article listed on its site. This value is usually quite low and permits sellers to list items at very low initial prices (sometimes $0.01 or Rs 0.4). Auction sites now also allow sellers to present a direct buy price. In this selling, the buyer does not have to go through a bidding process and can buy the product at the stated, higher price.

5.3.6 Aggregators

E-commerce is also used extensively by businesses to transact with each other. These are called B2B e-commerce transactions. B2B e-commerce differs from B2C e-commerce in several ways, some of which are listed below.

1. B2C transactions are ad hoc in nature with one seller, like Amazon.com, selling to customers in a single transaction. B2B transactions involve many buyers and many sellers in the market who establish long-term purchasing contracts.
2. The value of transactions in B2C is low as compared those in B2B markets. The latter may involve millions of rupees for a single transaction.
3. The delivery schedule and timing of goods purchased is of critical importance in B2B e-commerce. Firms use these marketplaces to manage their supply chains and hence require a high degree of commitment in terms of delivery.
4. As opposed to B2C, B2B markets do not have fixed prices and may involve auctions of goods.

In B2B markets, buyers and sellers may place their requirements and products on a single website that manages the bidding and sale process. These websites are called aggregators (or hubs).

Most aggregator sites deal with industrial products such as automobile parts, medical equipment, electronic components, industrial chemicals, etc. mJunction mentioned in the Case Study at the beginning of the chapter is a typical example of a B2B aggregator.

Caselet Alibaba.com

Alibaba.com is a China-based company that is considered to be one of the largest e-commerce firms in the world. It was started in 1999 as a B2B portal, much like mJunction; however, it soon diversified into B2C, C2C markets and then into many more businesses. The original firm, Alibaba.com, was started as a portal to enable small and medium enterprises to conduct trade. These firms could list themselves on the site and offer their goods and services to other firms. Firms were authenticated by Alibaba to ensure that they were genuine and had reliable products to offer. The site also allowed the transacting firms to chat with each other on forums. The site allowed firms to transact commercially through a secure and trustworthy method, and collected a small revenue from the business that was transacted.

After the initial success of Alibaba.com as a B2B portal, the firm then created the C2C portal called Taobao. This site enabled thousands of sellers to list their products and sell directly to buyers, much like e-commerce firms such as eBay.com. Taobao also enabled auctions on its site, where sellers could ask for bids for products along with direct payments. This feature attracted millions of sellers and buyers on the site, further boosting the network effects that led to its success. One challenge that the firm faced was that of online payments; customers in China, at that time, did not trust the online sellers to send them quality products. To solve this problem, Taobao set up an online payment firm, called Alipay, that enabled customers to put money in an escrow account with the provision that they could release the money if they found the product to be suitable. This solved the problem of trust and customers took to online selling and purchasing with enthusiasm. Within two years Alipay was so successful that it was spun off as a separate firm that could be used for payments for many different kinds of services, not just for purchases from Taobao.

Taobao's success also led to the formation of a B2C firm called Taobao Mall (Tmall.com) that allowed thousands of vendors to sell directly to customers. This site too relied on Alipay to enable payments. Taobao's success was largely driven by Chinese customers who relied on banks that cooperated with Alipay. In 2010, Alibaba launched a portal called AliExpress.com that allowed buyers from anywhere in the world to make purchases. The portal allowed additional payment options, along with Alipay, such as international credit card services to enable payments. Alipay too expanded its offerings to cater to international customers and provided accounts in many other currencies. AliExpress provided international shipping and customs clearance services for a nominal fee.

Taobao has some of the highest consumer traffic in all e-commerce sites in the world. In 2016, it listed more than a billion products on its site and accounted for about 80% of online sales in China. Alibaba's success was so well known that when it applied for a stock market listing in the US in 2014, its initial public offering valuation was the highest ever (at about 25 billion USD) recorded for an initial offering. The firm continues to grow and expand into newer markets.

5.4 E-BUSINESS

E-business refers to the manner in which modern commercial organisations create information links and conduct business. In contrast to the purpose of e-commerce which is to conduct commercial transactions with customers through buying, selling, auctions and searching, the purpose of e-business is to enhance the internal functioning of organisations by using the facilities of the internet. E-business enables firms to maintain a rich information interchange with their partners, collaborators and suppliers. E-business relies on either the open HTML standard or on proprietary standards for data exchange.

The main economic benefit of e-business is reduced transaction costs. To collaborate with their counterparts, firms have to maintain an infrastructure for communication, including shared understanding of documents and messages exchanged. In the past, while exchanging information manually, firms sent messages or letters to partner firms prescribing the nature and process of the transaction they were engaged in. If there were complications in the transfer of messages or errors in messages then these would increase the cost of the transaction, as more time and effort would be required to rectify the problem.

KEY POINT

E-business enables businesses to have a smoother and more cost-effective method of information flow with their partners.

With an e-business infrastructure, transaction costs arising out of message delivery complications are reduced. Information can be exchanged in a rich and detailed manner within the organisation and with outside partners. The exchange is faster and more accurate. If there are errors in the message then these can be rectified faster. Typical messages that are exchanged include work reports, invoices, credit notes, account balances and delivery schedules. E-business thus resembles the internal MIS of any organisation, with the difference that the data and information are being shared with partners outside the firm, and the infrastructure is based on the HTML.

Another reason why transaction costs are reduced in e-business is the increased security. Messages on an e-business platform can be sent across in a secure manner without the knowledge of the outside world of when, what and how messages are being transferred. Also, internal security measures can be strengthened to the required levels without the worry of cumbersome procedures affecting transactions, and employees can be trained to use them.

E-business infrastructures have made the biggest difference to large multinational businesses that work with a large number of partners in different countries, working in different time zones and in different languages. For example, large multinational banks operate round the clock with data and information regarding millions of transactions being transmitted around the globe. The e-business infrastructure allows the banks to reach out to diverse markets and to create complex business processes that can respond adequately to the needs of the local and global environments simultaneously.

Supply chains for large organisation are a fine example of coordinating complex activities worldwide. A supply chain is a set of firms that are involved in providing components to manufacturing firms. Firms are linked to each other in a chain – *upstream* firms provide components to *downstream* firms in the chain. The advantages of such chains are that both suppliers and buyers can rely on a number of players that provide them with goods or markets, and help reduce their risks of doing business, as also improve quality and provide better prices.

E-supply chains are now widely used by multinational organisations. Using an e-business infrastructure, a large multinational manufacturing firm can source components and products and market them worldwide. For example, Cisco Systems, a very large producer of networking equipment, is based in the USA but has a supply chain that extends to many parts of the world. Cisco has created an e-business infrastructure that enables component producers to receive orders and deliver parts to its various component and product manufacturing units in Malaysia, Singapore and Mexico among others. All designs, component information and information about parts production and movement are managed across this infrastructure. Every order placed with Cisco is routed through this supply chain, manufactured at some remote facility, and then packaged and shipped to the customer directly.

5.5 E-GOVERNANCE

E-governance refers to the use of e-commerce and e-business technologies by governments and their departments to conduct their own business. E-governance also enables transactions to be conducted across an electronic network where the basic infrastructure is the same as that of e-business. E-governance has gained popularity in countries across the world as it enables governments to offer services in an efficient manner, overcoming some of the hurdles posed by earlier manual methods.

In India, e-governance gained popularity with the spread of electronic networks and availability of computing technology within government departments. The initial phase of computing created a set of applications for a department's internal use – for personnel management, accounts, project management and file management among others. Later, some citizen-facing services were set up that allowed citizens to access information and forms on computer terminals maintained at some offices.

5.5.1 Services

Services offered by e-governance are classified as:

1. **Government to business (G2B):** These services enable businesses to interact with government in a smooth and seamless manner. In India, the government provides an online interface to businesses to file their taxes online. This has been made mandatory in many states in India. Each business has to obtain a tax identification number and using this it can file taxes online thus reducing paperwork and delays associated with the former manual mode of tax filing.
2. **Government to citizen (G2C):** These services provide convenience to citizens in fulfilling various needs. For example, the Bhoomi system in the state of Karnataka in India allows farmers to access their land records through a computerised system. The land records provide information on the nature of the land, its ownership, its location, the crops farmed and loans taken against the land. These records are used by farmers to mainly obtain bank loans for farming. The Bhoomi system maintains 20 million land records in its database, and the service is used by almost 800,000 farmers annually.

   Another G2C example is of the eSeva system in Hyderbad city in the state of Andhra Pradesh in India. eSeva enables citizens to pay utility bills conveniently; it provides a single point at which citizens can pay their electricity bills, water bills, road taxes and other taxes required by the city. eSeva is widely popular as it has provided a convenient alternative to citizens who earlier had to travel to the different departments to pay their bills.
3. **Government to government (G2G):** These services are internal to government departments. Currently, in India, there are many data applications that are shared between departments, and there is a common platform on which such sharing can occur. The systems here are not very different from MIS used in commercial firms and as such achieve the same ends. Many of these systems are built on the e-business architectures discussed above.

5.5.2 Advantages of E-Governance

E-governance reduces transaction costs for governments. G2C systems in particular are very helpful to citizens as they save their time, effort and money in getting the services they need. Transaction costs here have to be seen both from the *supply-side* and *demand-side* perspective. The government is the supplier of services for governance. For certain services, it is also a monopoly supplier (which means that only a government department can provide a particular service). For the government, the ability to use electronic networks to reach out to thousands of citizens means reduced costs of physical infrastructure such as buildings and offices, and of personnel required to do the work. The e-governance applications also have the potential of reducing errors committed during processing as compared to manual processing. On the demand side are citizens who benefit from easier access, faster processing, more accurate transactions and possibly lower costs.

The motivations for using e-governance are strong for countries across the world; however, they are different for developing and developed countries. In Denmark, for instance, which is a developed country, e-governance serves to reach out to a population that is small but widely dispersed, and also quite literate and with access to the internet. More importantly, the Denmark government has to do this work with limited staff. In a developing country, like India, staff is plenty, but the problems are more of access and reaching out to a vast population that is not computer literate.

E-governance implementations in developing countries are not without their problems. They are prone to failure owing to lack of use or support from various government changes. They tend to over or underestimate the needs of the population owing to which they end up being very expensive to sustain or unable to meet the needs of the citizens.

Chapter Glossary

Hypertext Pages displayed on the Web that are linked to other pages that can be accessed immediately by clicking on a link.

Hyperlink The technology used to link words and phrases in one file with other files.

Tags Specific characters or marks in web pages that determine how the text or page is displayed and how it behaves.

Email account A protected file space on a computer in which an individual user can receive messages and from which the user can send messages.

Protocol An accepted manner of communication between computers and devices on a network.

Intranets Networks of computers within organisations that follow the protocols of the internet.

Virtual private network A technology that allows organisations to create a private channel of their own over the public internet.

Electronic data interchange A network used by some organisations to link their offices. The protocol used in these networks is different from the internet.

Portal A web page that acts as an entry point to the Web. Portals list pages according to themes and have search facilities.

Search engine A website that allows users to search for pages on the internet.

Auctions Websites that allow sellers and buyers to meet over the internet.

Aggregators Websites that allow institutional buyers and sellers to transact over the internet.

Review Questions

1. Briefly review how web pages are created and linked on the internet.
2. Why did e-commerce become so popular all over the world?
3. Review the underlying mechanism of email. Why did it become the most popular application on the internet?
4. How is Electronic Data Interchange different from the internet?
5. What are the different ways of making online payments?
6. How is a portal different from an aggregator?
7. What is the basic logic of ranking web pages used by Google?
8. Why are auction sites subject to strong network effects?
9. What is e-governance? How is it different from e-commerce?
10. Review the mJunction case. What has been mJunction's strategy to increase its e-commerce revenues?

Research Questions

1. Meet the System Administrator in your organisation or college to estimate the number of emails your institution receives and sends out per day. Try to estimate what fraction of the incoming emails are spam.
2. Search Google for a number of keywords and see whether Google places advertisements on the search results page or not. What kind of search queries result in advertisements being included?
3. Visit an electronic auction site like eBay and find the manner in which buyers and sellers are rated? How can you verify if the ratings are genuine?
4. Visit a few of the e-governance portals created by different government departments in India. Are the sites clear and understandable? Do they provide relevant information? Are you able to navigate them easily?

Further Reading

1. Battelle, J. (2005) *The Search*, Nicholas Brealey Publishing, New York.
2. A busy junction, *Tata Review*, September 2010.
3. Consumer E-Commerce Market in India 2006/07. *Report of the internet and Mobile Association in India*, September 2007.

CHAPTER 6

Managing Information Systems

Learning Objectives

After completing this chapter, you will be able to:

- Learn about the challenges of managing the IT function
- The role of the CIO vendor management
- Understand IT governance

The modern business environment presents challenges to management as it is constantly evolving. Information technology too is evolving and has strong impacts on the nature of business. These impacts are classified as:

1. First-order,
2. second-order and
3. third-order effects.

To manage in such a dynamic environment requires administering and handling IT in such a manner that the desired changes are effected. IT can be managed as a centralised function or in a decentralised manner where the trade-offs are between standards, costs and innovation, and the fit with culture. IT security too poses management challenges; security threats emerge from external or internal sources. Often vendors are required to supply or manage essential IT functions, and managing them carefully is important. The issues involved in vendor management include vendor selection, drawing up the contracts, managing the relationship and deciding on termination or renewal. The role of the Chief Information Officer (CIO) is very important for managing the IT function and also for managing vendors. The CIO also prepares the plan for IT use in the organisation. The decisions regarding IT management are often governed by top management and other stakeholders. There are distinct governance patterns that are followed by top performing firms in their IT management.

MIND MAP OF CHAPTER TOPICS

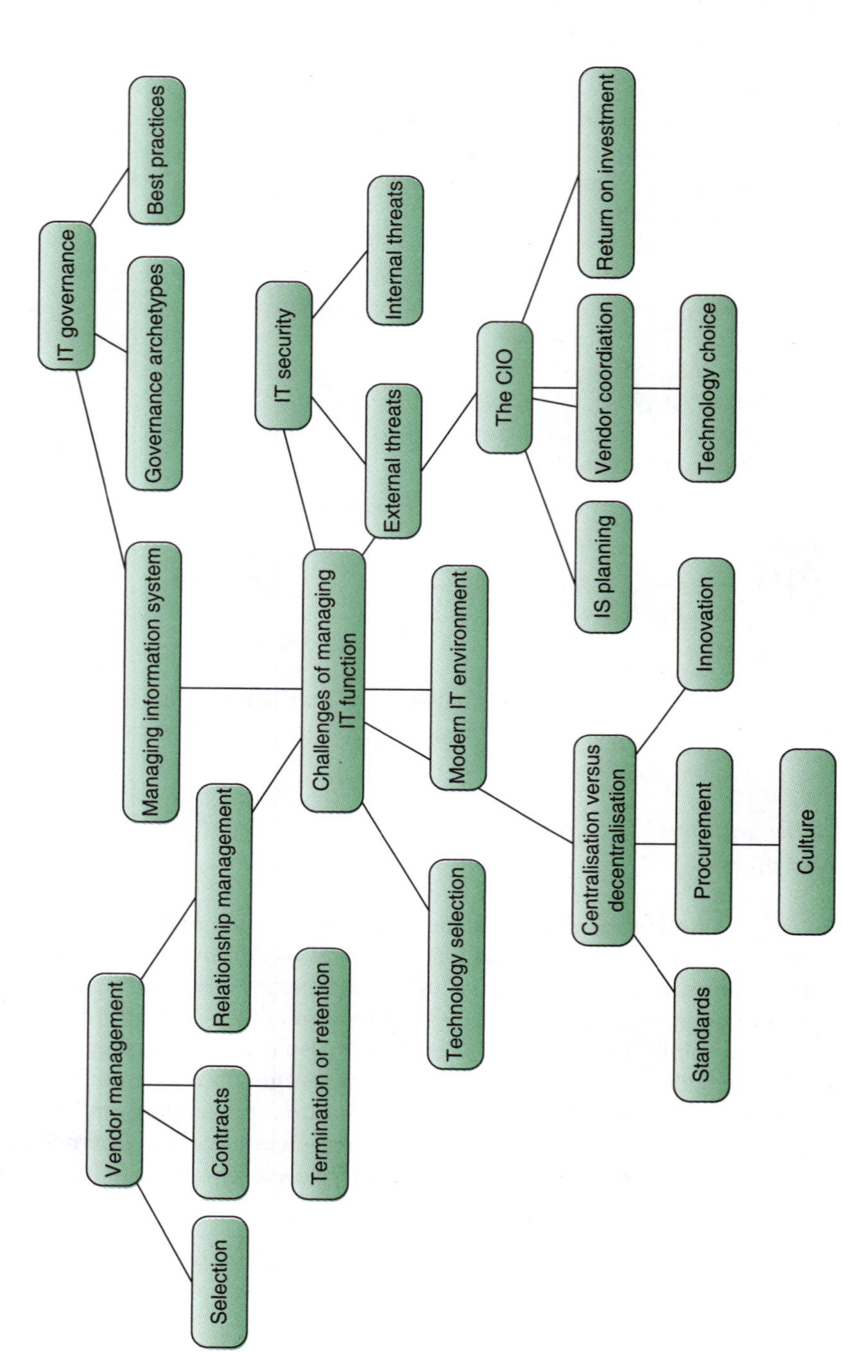

Though ICICI is the second largest bank in India, it is credited with being the pioneer in using information technology (IT) to reshape its business. ICICI Bank was started as a subsidiary of the Industrial Credit and Investment Corporation of India, and later the parent company was merged into ICICI Bank. In 2016, ICICI Bank had about 4400 branches and over 14000 automated teller machines (ATMs) across India. It was the largest Indian private sector bank with assets of over Rs 7.2 trillion (USD 109 billion), and had a presence in over 19 countries. It offered a wide range of banking services—from retail and commercial banking to insurance and microfinance.

When ICICI started out in the 1950s, it was a 'public sector' bank, owned by the government, and its main business was with commercial firms. It was designated as a development bank and was meant to serve only commercial organisations, not individual consumers. When the emphasis of the Indian economy changed in 1991, following large-scale privatisation and liberalisation, ICICI felt the urgency to change too. Its core business clients were not doing very well owing to the increased competition and the changed nature of the liberalised economy. ICICI decided to extend banking services to individual consumers through services such as retail banking, home loans, car loans, etc. It did not have any prior experience of catering to an individual's banking needs nor did it have trained personnel who could work in such markets.

At that time, the mid-1990s, the choice for the CEO of ICICI, K.V. Kamath, was clear - Kamath decided to leverage their 'core competency', that is, their ability to use information technology (IT). Kamath said that he had seen how start-ups in Silicon Valley were using IT to bring new and daring products and services to market in a short span of time. As Kamath said, 'In the late 1990s, garage start-ups in Silicon Valley were taking products from concept to market in 90 days because if they didn't, somebody else would'. (Refer to Ref. #1, Further Reading for more details on an interview with K.V. Kamath of ICICI.) Following a similar strategy, ICICI Bank had started rolling out IT-based banking products such as online trading, online banking and ATMs. At that time only a handful of multinational banks provided online banking services, and there were very few ATMs in the country.

Kamath's plan did not include an information systems department or a CIO. He wanted IT to be 'embedded' in every business and the business head would manage the technology. To control the anarchy that could ensue, Kamath set a small team of relatively young people. They reported directly to him and were responsible for recommending technology solutions and making high-level plans. As their entire business revolved around IT, Kamath felt it was the CEO who had to bear this responsibility. So in the new scheme of things, Kamath took the highest responsibility for the functioning of the technology on his own shoulders.

ICICI Bank adopted an open and decentralised policy where they stayed away from large mainframe computers to which they would have a lock-in, and relied on a smaller, function-based computing architecture. The policy helped them upgrade at a low cost and also remain largely free from long-term commitments. Furthermore, this policy enabled them to reduce costs of technology implementation to a fraction of what their industry rivals had spent on technology.

They faced many challenges at the time of rolling out ATMs across the country. The ATM technology was new, network connectivity was hard to sustain, electricity was not easily available and the machines were located in places where they had to survive harsh weather conditions. In some cases, they provided three levels of redundancy for network connectivity to ATMs through

1. Satellite link,
2. dial-up line and
3. a line leased from a local telecommunications operator.

ICICI Bank had a very fast turnaround time for the rollout, at about three ATM machines per day or about a 1000 a year. Besides the ATM rollout speed, they also wanted 99% uptime for ATMs, so their technology planning and execution had to be of a very high quality.

ICICI Bank relied on outsourcing their technology implementation tasks to vendors. For their 'core banking' application, they selected Infosys Corporation's product Finacle. This application allowed them to integrate almost all their services in one technology solution that could then be scaled according to their needs and growth. This application could manage internet banking, brokerages, insurance, credit cards, SMS alerts and a call centre among many other services. With this solution in place, ICICI Bank was able to process many of its services electronically instead of handling them manually. The increase in both speed and accuracy of such processing allowed them to scale dramatically, adding millions of clients to their customer base annually. As depicted in Table 6.1 between the years 2000 and 2004, the traffic at the ICICI Bank branches declined significantly, whereas the transactions at ATMs, on the internet, and at call centres increased.

Table 6.1 | Change in Location of Banking Transactions over 4 Years for ICICI Bank

Channels	Share of Transactions (March 2000)	Share of Transactions (March 2004)
Branches	94%	25%
ATM	3%	45%
Internet and mobile	2%	21%
Call centres	1%	11%

Source: ICICI bank India, technology-led transformation, Infosys case study, 2005.

ICICI bank has also partnered with other vendors to build key applications. Their emphasis has always been on scale and reliability. With Symantec Corporation, for instance, they insisted on 99.99% availability for the storage server they were acquiring. They also wanted the application to blend well with their existing software and hardware and also be able to scale. They implemented a disaster recovery unit for their operations, which is a site that keeps a backup of all their data in a safe environment that is about 800 km away from their headquarters. This backup unit stores hundreds of gigabytes of data every month on the remote storage facility.

6.1 CHALLENGES OF MANAGING THE IT FUNCTION

6.1.1 Modern IT Environment

The modern IT environment of business presents strong challenges for management. It is a dynamic and changing environment with technology leading dramatic changes in the competitive space and also in the internal functions of organisations. As technology is never constant, the organisations that use the technology to perform their work also have to change and adapt. The constant need to change and adapt implies that managers and users of technology also have to remain alert, learn, and re-skill themselves. Organisations also have to change themselves as they grow or decline in response to the market.

Commentators and researchers say that IT has impacts that can be categorised as first-order, second-order, and third-order impacts. The first-order impacts are those that are felt immediately upon adoption of new technology. IT adoption for organisations typically means that the functions that are computerised can now be performed at a faster rate, leading to processing of larger volumes of data. This increase in volume of processing data also entails greater accuracy of processing. For example, when banks adopted information technology (IT) they could perform a larger number of transactions as the processing was faster, and their transaction efficiency also increased as there were lesser errors in the data that was accumulated.

KEY POINT

First-order effects of introducing IT in organisations are the immediate improvements in speed, volume and accuracy of processing.

The first-order effects are realised first and are usually the initial targets of the IT implementation. Organisations implement IT to achieve efficiencies in processes in terms of both speed and volume. But once the first-order effects are realised, organisations can effect further changes in their internal functions. They can re-order and re-staff the internal functions, and re-engineer the processes that are now outdated. These are called second-order changes.

The second-order changes are introduced because IT makes redundant or irrelevant certain older manual processes. Also, owing to increased speed and efficiency, there is no need for certain manual tasks to be performed, so employees can be re-trained and deployed elsewhere. Sometimes entire departments can be removed, as the work they performed is not needed any more. Such re-engineering leads to structural changes in the organisation, giving a new dimension to its competitive position in the industry it operates in.

KEY POINT

Second-order effects of introducing IT have to do with changes within the organisation, and are visible after some time.

The third-order changes happen when the industry in which the organisation is located also changes owing to the changes brought about by IT (see Fig. 6.1). For example, when banks introduced IT, they changed their internal functioning sufficiently to alter the manner in which they competed. They forced other banks to adopt IT too, leading to all banks and similar institutions adopting IT to offer competing services. With an IT infrastructure in place, the entire banking industry started to offer a larger number of services to customers, not just individual and commercial banking, including services such as financial investments and trading, insurance,

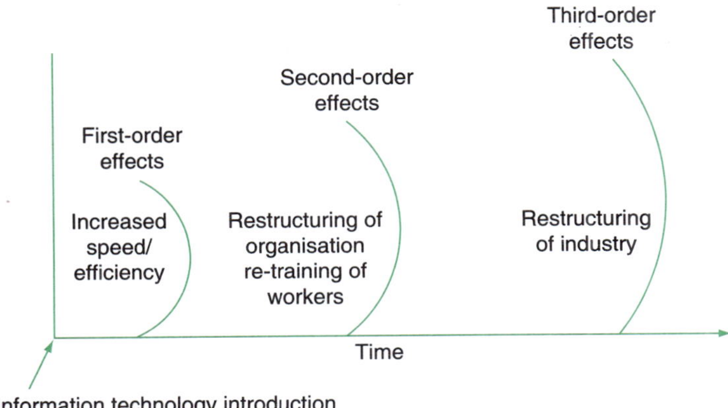

FIGURE 6.1 | Effects of introducing IT in a firm.

loans for more diverse markets, etc. The number of bank branches increased as did the automatic cash dispensing devices. The nature and kind of employees changed, with an emphasis on people with IT skills.

KEY POINT

Third-order effects of introducing IT in organisations are realised much later and have to do with changes in the industry structure.

These effects are visible in all organisations - albeit with different levels. Many government departments in India that have added IT to complement their processes have realised the first-order effects, but few second- and third-order effects owing to the structure of laws and public processes to which they are bound. Some small and medium organisations in India have realised the first- and second-order effects, particularly those that function in the IT and telecommunications industries. Schools, colleges and other educational institutions have also adopted IT to realise the first-order benefits, and some have changed their internal organisation sufficiently to have significant second-order effects.

The important point is that in all modern organisations such changes have to be anticipated and managed according to their goals. This poses an interesting and very challenging problem for IT managers.

6.1.2 Centralisation versus Decentralisation

6.1.2.1 Centralised IT Management

A large multinational commercial firm in India has manufacturing units located across the country and also marketing offices for its engineering products. The firm employs over 5000 persons and has a revenue running into several billion rupees. The firm has leveraged IT for all its functions, including an enterprise system that is at the root of managing all its manufacturing operations. The firm is organised around divisions that manufacture different items. Each division has its own supply chain of vendors, its own manufacturing unit and marketing unit. Sales and distribution, accounts and human resource management functions are shared across divisions.

The firm's IT infrastructure is managed centrally. The enterprise system that is used across the firm mainly helps with accounts, human resource and marketing functions. Divisions maintain their own manufacturing systems and also their own desktop applications. The central IT team coordinates all IT acquisitions, software implementations, maintenance, application requests and all activities related to security, data backup and recovery. The IT department ensures data standards are maintained and all hardware purchases are standardised. Vendor selection is done by the IT department for all divisions. The IT department maintains personnel in all divisions, whereas the coordination is done from the headquarters in Mumbai.

KEY POINT

In centralised IT, all decisions regarding design, purchase, standards of IT are managed from a single department in the organisation.

When requests for applications are sent in from divisions, forwarded by the division heads, then the IT department creates a joint team with the division to understand the problem, the need for IT support, the vendor selection, acquisition of technology and the eventual roll-out of the system. The funding for the project is secured by the central IT department, as the expenses are needed for its continued use and maintenance.

6.1.2.2 Decentralised IT Management

An alternative to the centralised management of IT is the decentralised approach. A large university campus in South India has a decentralised approach to IT management. The university consists of many colleges and departments, spread over a large campus. Each department has a different disciplinary focus and hence varied IT needs. Each department, or cluster of departments, maintains its own IT unit with personnel that support the computers and servers for the department. The funding is available from budgets that the departments allocate to their IT units. All acquisitions are done at the department level and also the use of systems for functions such as accounting, facilities scheduling, etc. The only services managed centrally are the payroll for the entire university and the network connection that is managed by a centrally located router. The individual departments draw their connectivity from the router and then manage their own local networks.

KEY POINT

Decentralised IT implies that decisions related to IT infrastructure are made by various user departments in the organisations.

The university finds this to be a suitable arrangement for managing its IT infrastructure owing to the fact that the departments have very different needs. For example, the civil engineering

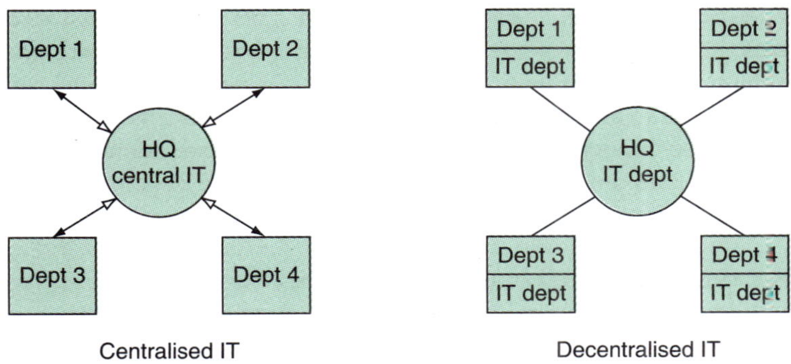

FIGURE 6.2 | Centralised versus decentralised IT management.

department has computing needs which are quite different from those of the communication arts department. Departments manage their own IT by using some shared vendors and IT facilitators, but from their own budgets.

Of the two cases discussed above, it is evident that centralised or decentralised management of IT is a choice that organisations have to exercise (see Fig. 6.2). Either manner of managing IT leads to both advantages and disadvantages. Some of these issues are discussed now.

6.1.2.3 Standardisation

Standardisation is a key issue in the centralised IT management. Standardisation implies that all components, physical and software, which are used to create the IT infrastructure across the organisation are of the same type or follow the same standard. A standard is an externally defined set of parameters to which IT components conform. For example, a cable standard refers to the width, components, capacity, among others, of the cable that is used for carrying data. A standard for data specifies the manner in which the data will be stored and accessed. Standards allow easy interoperability between components and also easy replacement and maintenance. Non-standard components will not work with all the elements of the infrastructure and may not be easy to acquire and procure.

Data standardisation is a key issue in the centralised IT management. When individual departments run their own operations, they create data for their key functions, such as operations, scheduling, accounts and personnel, with formats and on software that is their own. These data may not be in a form that can be shared across the organisation. Data standards imply lock-in to specific software applications, and once such a lock-in sets in, switching costs are very high at later stages.

With centralised IT management standards of all components are enforced. The central IT sets the standards, provides a list of vendors and products that comply with the standards, and has procedures in place to maintain the standard components. For example, the central IT may specify that all laptop computers purchased within the organisation will need to have a certain make and certain parameters. They may also specify the vendors from which these laptops may be purchased and the type of warranties and post-warranty contracts that have to be signed. Furthermore, the central IT may approve all laptop purchases.

With decentralisation, standards are easily loosened. Different departments may want to acquire technology from different vendors and of different types and quality. This gives the departments immense flexibility to choose and fit the technology to their needs and budgets, and also addresses the concerns of the pent-up demand for technology access that employees sometimes express. Employees can participate actively in technology assessment and design, and be assured that their concerns are being met. With a centralised structure, even though employees' concerns are heard and recorded, they may feel left out of the final decision-making process.

KEY POINT

Standards are externally defined parameters about IT. Centralised IT management helps set standards.

Decentralisation propagates multiplicity of standards, or no standards at all. Desktops, laptops, keyboards, mice, monitors, operating systems, application software, email client, etc. may all be different across departments and even within departments. Employees may acquire technology on an ad hoc and as-needed basis without heed to standards and would end up with a panoply of different technologies that would have to be used and maintained.

6.1.2.4 *Vendors*

When vendors are required to support long-term activities, such as managing facilities for the organisation or building an extensive organisation-wide application, then it is usually preferable to have the centralised IT management that manages vendors. These services are usually of high value and high impact and are crucial for the organisation. Therefore, the centralised management can deal with the issues concerning these services and the vendors handling them in a more reliable manner.

Vendors are often viewed as strategic partners who have a stake in the success of their clients. In such situations, vendors invariably look for and demand centralised management and control. Vendor management requires a careful control of the selection process, creating a relationship that has clearly defined roles and responsibilities, identifying how reporting is to occur, specifying the required quality and service levels, and managing the termination process. When many vendors are hired for managing the IT infrastructure, each has to be managed with the same set of considerations. Large vendors, who want to deal with large contracts, often work with the centralised IT management. For example, ICICI Bank relied on Infosys as a Vendor to build and support the core banking infrastructure.

For example, when the State Bank of India (SBI), one of the largest banks in India, and the second-largest in the world with over 10,000 branches, wanted to computerise its core banking operations it had to select the vendor carefully. SBI already had local, decentralised information systems at many of its branches but felt the need for a system that was central and could unify its operations across the country. SBI initiated a call for vendors by asking them to bid as a consortium – where each partner in the consortium would bring its product or special skills to the group. When SBI evaluated the bids it considered issues such as the size of the consortium members and their capacity to deliver on the large scale of the project, the skills and experience of all the partners, and the specifics of the technology they were proposing. SBI eventually selected a consortium led by the Tata Consultancy Services (TCS) that included partners such as Hewlett-Packard and other multinationals, owing to their proven skills in handling such large projects.

Small vendors, on the other hand, prefer to deal with the decentralised IT management, which enables them to interact directly with the end-user of the technology. Small vendors can provide a range of services – from ad hoc support for technology to services on a long-term basis. Managing small vendors requires less paperwork and bureaucracy, but they do bring the risks of unreliability and lack of quality.

6.1.2.5 *Innovation*

Possibly the most important advantage accruing from decentralised IT management is the ability to innovate. When individual users or departments can acquire and manage technology on their own, they are able to address their own needs in the most direct and efficient manner. With the availability of a large pool and variety of high-quality open source software, end-users are often tempted to try out and experiment with new technologies and solutions at their own risk and in their own time. Such innovations often prove to be successful and are then adopted organisation wide.

Centralised IT management can also drive innovation, but this is more organised and slow. It requires a setup of laboratories, experimental software and engineers who are dedicated to working on new solutions. Here, the innovation can be worked on more thoroughly, with a focus on design and testing rigour that would otherwise not be heeded with individual innovation spurts. Centralised IT management can also ensure that the innovation is supported by adequate resources and can also rely on support from departments that would benefit from it. However, users also believe that the bureaucracy and tedious procedures introduced by the centralised IT management chokes innovation and frustrates those employees who are seeking a difference. For example, policies of standardisation will compel individual users to buy only certain kinds of hardware, preventing them from experimenting with other, newer technologies available in the market.

6.1.2.6 *IT Procurement*

Centralised IT management leads to the scale and standardisation that make IT procurement highly beneficial. The centralised management of IT infrastructure brings in advantages of reduced prices and better component matches. With organisations often undertaking bulk purchases of IT components, such as laptops and desktops, and spending millions of rupees in the process, the centralised purchasing can help bring down costs quite significantly. Discounts on bulk purchases can be very significant in controlling costs. The other advantages are that a single vendor can be enlisted to support the purchased products, and spare parts, in case of hardware, can be inventoried and kept in stock for emergency use.

Decentralised procurement, on the other hand, can enable a stronger fit with the end-user's needs. It is often seen that large-scale purchases take so much time to complete that the technology being considered is often overtaken by newer offerings in the market. In such cases, the decentralised purchasing is better as it allows the buyers to act quickly and acquire the product when needed.

6.1.2.7 *Fit with Work Culture*

Many organisations work in a largely decentralised or centralised management culture. In an organisation that is mainly decentralised, the managers and employees of different divisions or departments have autonomy over their work. They decide on most issues themselves and enjoy a work culture that celebrates this autonomy. On the other hand, some organisations thrive on a centralised, hierarchical work culture where most decisions are taken at the top and percolate down (ICICI Bank has such a culture). Decentralised organisations develop their own norms of working, work practices, reporting relationships, partnerships with other firms, employee productivity and growth norms, and divisional performance targets. Centralised organisations rely on organisation-wide norms and practices that are adhered to and enforced through management practice.

The IT infrastructure typically has to support the organisational culture that is present. The possibility of conflict and resistance arises if the IT infrastructure management strategy conflicts with the prevailing work culture. For instance, a centralised IT in a decentralised management culture will result in employees resisting the systems, and some may actually subvert the systems' objectives. On the other hand, a decentralised IT infrastructure in a centralised management culture may be difficult to sustain as it will counter employees' expectations of IT's role.

KEY POINT

IT must support the prevailing work culture of an organisation, whether centralised or decentralised IT often changes the work culture.

Occasionally, some managers have tried to introduce IT to deliberately change the work culture. For example, enterprise systems tend to support a centralised IT management style, as they really cannot function as stand-alone applications in individual departments. Owing to this property of enterprise systems, some managers have brought in such systems to control departments in a strongly decentralised management culture. This is an example of using information systems to orchestrate organisational change.

6.1.2.8 *Career Paths of IT Staff*

For many organisations having internal IT staff is a necessity. The IT staff is responsible for managing and executing the IT functions. For a centralised IT infrastructure, they may work with the centre and be appointed at various divisions according to need. For a decentralised IT infrastructure, the IT staff has to be hired for independent divisions or departments.

Owing to the current emphasis on outsourcing IT services, the career path for most IT staff is not well established. It is seen that in centralised IT management, IT staff have a career path to follow. They can move up the hierarchy either in the divisions or at the centre and have a path they can envisage. However, in a decentralised situation this is difficult, as the roles of the IT staff may often be outsourced to vendors, depending on the needs of the department.

Many organisations have a Chief Information Officer (CIO) as the highest officer responsible for the IT function in the organisation. The CIO is typically part of the top management team and represents the IT function. In such a situation, the career path for IT staff is clearly defined within the IT function. Some organisations also permit IT staff to rotate with other functions, thus allowing them to grow their knowledge and skills within the organisation. This tactic requires a centralised approach to IT management.

6.1.3 IT Security

Possibly one of the most difficult challenges of managing modern IT infrastructures is that of managing security. The threats to the IT infrastructure from harmful software and from internal security violations are very strong. IT managers have to focus quite strongly on this aspect of management. Some estimates say that the cost of managing security is as high as 50% of the total IT budget for some organisations.

6.1.3.1 External Threats

All organisations using IT have to be careful against external threats from harmful software, often called malware, and from humans who are bent on causing harm or playing mischief. Malware consists of software viruses and worms that infect computer systems. Viruses infect operating systems and destroy files or corrupt them in some manner, whereas worms chiefly enter computer networks to capture computers for other criminal activities on the internet. Worms and viruses are countered by security software that searches for them on the computer storage and network connection points. Viruses and worms enter systems through simple devices such as emails and email attachments. Furthermore, they may enter through infected removable storage media such as flash drives that are used on computers in the organisation.

Human threat to organisations arises from people trying to break into the computers and networks of the organisation. These people may be expert programmers who have no more harmful intention than to test their abilities to break into systems, or they may have a desire to steal information and data. Their primary mode of operation is to slip in through network points that are weakly protected and then they test out all nodes in the network that are weak and can be exploited.

Another mode of breaking into a system is called *phishing*. In this process, websites for banking, auctions, e-commerce or education are presented as legitimate sites to lure users to reveal their personal information. This information is invariably used for fraud or theft. For organisations that have sensitive customer information, phishing is used lure employees to reveal their login and password information, which is then used to break into their systems.

6.1.3.2 Internal Threats

Organisations face significant security threats from within too. The entire IT infrastructure enables employees to access vast stores of information, something which was not possible in the manual world. Records, files and entire databases can be accessed easily by anyone, if they are not carefully protected. According to one report, 60–70% of the computer-based crimes in the world are committed by persons inside the organisation.

The internal security threats are of the nature of theft of information, replication of sensitive information such as designs, leaking of information to competitors, deliberate destruction or corruption of data, breaking into other employees' computers, replacement of files with fake files, etc. These threats arise for various reasons, ranging from disgruntled employees to deliberate industrial espionage.

6.1.3.3 Managing Security

Information managers have devised numerous plans and procedures to counter the external and internal security threats. Many of these procedures involve the process of *authentication*, which is identifying the user entering a system. Authentication can be done by a simple process of typing in a password, or by a more complicated process of using biometric information such as fingerprints and retinal scans. Authentication addresses both external and internal threats as it is a process by which certain persons or entities are allowed access and others are not. This filter is what acts as a security device.

Monitoring is another method by which security is enforced. Monitoring involves watching process logs of all activities on computers and networks in the organisation. It also involves physically observing the organisation's activities through video cameras and surveillance equipment.

The security level that an organisation wants to have is grounded in the policies that the organisation draws up. High security entails cumbersome procedures and also loss of privacy. For example, to access any data in the organisation employees have to go through many steps of authentication, thus slowing down the process. Furthermore, they also have to reveal how, when and what they are looking for, which is often a breach of privacy. Low levels of security, on the other hand, entail a free and open environment for employees to work in, which is preferred by many, but this also leads to security breaches and, occasionally, loss of customers and legal problems. The choice of the kind and level of security is thus a matter of management decision.

6.1.4 Technology Selection

With the constant innovation in technology, the challenge to select the most appropriate one for the organisation is based on many criteria. Technology changes are reflected not only in the innovations but also in the scope of what the technology can deliver. Technology selection is driven by many criteria as depicted in Fig. 6.3 and is explained below.

1. **Cost:** The price at which the technology can be acquired.
2. **Scalability:** How far the technology can be scaled to meet the growing needs of an organisation?
3. **Interoperability:** The ease with which the new technology will work with existing technology.
4. **Security:** How secure is the technology with regard to the organisation's activities?
5. **Maturity:** How mature is the technology in its innovation cycle, and has it been tested enough or is it new and carries some risk?
6. **Upgrades:** How will the technology mature further and how well will it integrate with the existing technologies?

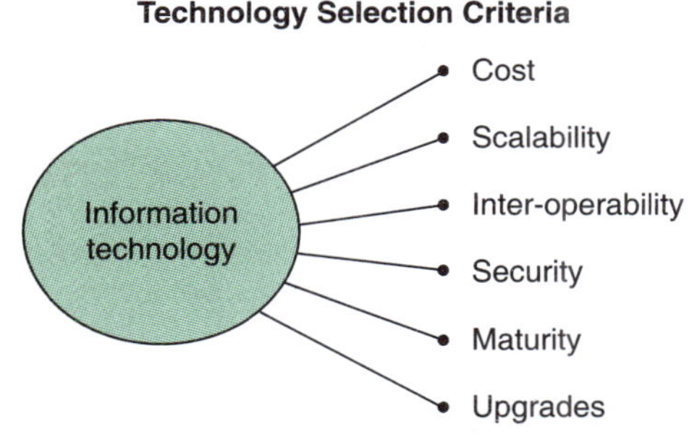

FIGURE 6.3 | Criteria for selecting information technology in an organisation.

On the basis of the above criteria, the choice of technology is driven, very importantly, by the business and processing needs of the organisation. These needs, either for competitive advantage or for comprehensive performance improvement, determine the fit that the technology can achieve with the requirements of the organisation. Needs and requirements are determined by the relevant stakeholders - those who will fund the technology, those who will use it and those who will be affected by it. With such information the technology acquisition is not only initiated but also implemented and used effectively throughout its life cycle.

6.2 VENDOR MANAGEMENT

Organisations that manage their own IT infrastructure, and not outsource it, usually rely on vendors to provide certain services. The services may range from one-time purchases to long-term service contracts. Vendors too may range in size from very small, one-person operations to large multinational firms. Managing vendors is a challenge for all organisations. Some of the issues that arise in vendor management are highlighted below.

6.2.1 Vendor Selection

Vendors are located and identified through different processes. Usually, organisations release advertisements stating their requirements in the popular media, and ask for vendors to respond. In other cases, vendors may be found in online and published listings of industry and commerce associations. Vendors are listed in directories with their contact address and the services they can provide.

After initial screening, vendors are usually requested to bid for a service or project, with technical details and commercial terms. In many cases, vendors visit the clients and make presentations about their capacities and the services they offer. Vendors have to demonstrate that they have requisite skills within their firm to be able to complete the job they are bidding for. They also have to show prior experience in such tasks, and the quality, scale and scope of projects they have undertaken. Client organisations also arrange for site visits to other clients of the vendor to see for themselves the quality of work performed. It is also useful to check for the ratings of the vendors, which are sometimes maintained by industry association and watchdog organisations. If a vendor is found suitable, only then are its technical and commercial bids examined.

A technical bid is a proposal that the vendor prepares regarding the work it plans to do and the manner in which it will go about doing it. It includes all aspects of the technology that will be used - hardware, software, networks, applications, etc. Evaluation of the technical bid by client organisations requires a careful mapping of the requirements document, which was prepared and sent to the vendors before the bidding process, to the technical bid presented by the vendors. All the major issues of technology selection have to be considered here.

KEY POINT

Vendors are selected on the basis of their technical capabilities as well as their cost of services.

Many government organisations have rules specifying that the commercial bid of a vendor can only be opened after its technical bid has been examined. However, for other organisations, there is no such restriction and both bids can be examined together. A best practice that is followed by many is to rule out vendors who do not meet the technical criteria entirely, even though they may have very attractive commercial terms. The focus here is on the merits of the technical service that is to be provided rather than on the price of the service.

6.2.2 Vendor Contracts and Service Levels

Once a vendor is selected, a contract has to be drawn up that specifies clearly the terms of the work that has to be performed, the payment terms, the service levels that have to maintained, etc. The most important aspect, from the point of view of IT management, is that service levels have to be clearly specified. A service level is specified for various types of technologies differently. For instance, if the vendor's job is to maintain servers then the service level may specify the amount of downtime the server is permitted per day, per week or per year. This may be the scheduled downtime when the server is pulled down for maintenance or may be the

Table 6.2 | Downtime for Different Levels of Service

Service Level (Percentage of Uptime)	Downtime per Day	Downtime per Month	Downtime per Year
99%	14.4 min	432 min (7.2 h)	87.6 h (3.65 days)
99.9%	1.44 min	43.2 min	525.6 min (8.76 h)
99.99%	8.6 s	4.32 min	52.56 min
99.999%	0.86 s	26 s	5.26 min

unscheduled downtime resulting from problems. Service levels are often specified in terms of percentages. Table 6.2 shows the percentage levels of service desired and what these levels imply for the amount of downtime that can be permitted.

What Table 6.2 shows is that for any given level of uptime service demanded there is a corresponding amount of time for which the servers can go down, and the rest of the time they have to stay up and running. For example, for an uptime guarantee of 99.9%, the server can be down for about a minute and half per day, about 43 min per month and about 9 h in a year.

Vendors who sign such contracts need to provision for the downtime and ensure that all their maintenance activities are conducted in the downtime allowed to them. The penalties for violation of service level agreements (SLAs) are specified in the contract and tend to be quite steep for high uptime guarantees. Consequently, the price for high uptimes is also very high. As the service guarantees increase, going down the first column of the table, the prices demanded increase non-linearly.

Clients have to carefully evaluate their needs for server uptime and select a service level accordingly. Service levels that are higher than those required lead to wastage of money spent on vendors who provide that level of service. When service levels are lower than those required then there is a risk of downtime that hurts the business.

Typically, banks, e-commerce organisations, financial institutions use 99.999% service levels (these are known as *five nines*). Such institutions must have service presence on a 24-hour-a-day, 7-day-a-week basis (often called the 24 × 7 service). Vendors provide such services by maintaining high redundancy in the infrastructure, which means that they have many more servers than are required so that if some fail, others can take over the work.

6.2.3 Ongoing Relationship Management

Once a vendor has been hired and a service level agreed upon, it is important for the IT management to ensure that a clear plan is in place to manage the ongoing relationship with the vendor. Routine reporting plans have to be established along with the personnel who will have various responsibilities. The client organisation has to identify a person or team that will interact with the vendor, have a point person who will be the first person to contact on breaking issues, and have a clear plan for responding to requests and emergencies.

Once a vendor is hired and begins delivering the service, there are natural changes in the client organisation, which adjusts to best utilise the new service. In such situations, the organisation's new requirements evolve. The individual or team that manages the vendor has to convey accurately the new and evolving requirements to the vendor so that appropriate steps are taken.

6.2.4 Vendor Retention or Termination

At the end of the contract period, vendors may be retained and their contracts extended or their contracts may be terminated. Client organisations have to make an assessment of the adequacy of the service provided by the vendor: Whether the service was up to the standards expected, whether there is a continuing need for a vendor (or can the service be provisioned internally), and whether the relationship has matured and is stable. Termination of the contract is taken up only when this benefits both parties - the vendor and the client.

Many organisations routinely consider rival vendors before renewing the contract with the current vendor. This enables the client organisation to negotiate better prices and service agreements. Furthermore, it helps them to benchmark the performance of their current vendor against services offered in the market.

6.3 THE ROLE OF THE CIO

The CIO is typically the designation of the person who heads the information systems management function in an organisation. The CIO is a part of the top management and is considered at par with the Chief Financial Officer or the Chief Operations Officer. The CIO has the same powers of decision making and authority with regard to managing the IS function as the other chief officers.

The role and responsibilities of the CIO varies in organisations. In some organisations the CIO has a staff of systems engineers, technicians, data entry operators, network engineers and project managers reporting to him/her. These employees may be in a central location, operating out of the organisation's headquarters, or may be attached to various divisions. The CIO manages the roles, jobs, funds and time allocation for the employees. In other organisations, the CIO may have more of a coordinator's role, where MIS managers from different divisions and functions report to him/her. The CIO interfaces the IS function with other functions at the top management level.

The CIO's role is to primarily participate in decision making at the highest levels about the management of the organisation's IT infrastructure. The CIO is the key person responsible for aligning the IT infrastructure with the goals of the organisation. The CIO's most important roles are outlined below.

6.3.1 Information Systems Plan

The information systems plan of an organisation states the precise roles that the IS have to play in supporting the vision and goals of the organisation. This is a high-level statement that outlines the nature of the IT infrastructure, the processes that will be enabled by and supported by the IS, the manner in which business will interact with the IS and the future direction that the IS function will take. This plan is a crucial document that frames the role of the IS function and its precise nature of interaction with the organisation.

The CIO has to create the IS plan for the organisation in consultation with the other officers. Typically, a high-level plan is made once with the involvement of the entire organisation in its creation in terms of giving inputs and stating requirements, and then the plan is revisited on a periodic basis and revised, if needed.

The typical contents of an IS plan are:

1. Specifying the role of IT to support different activities and processes.
2. The manner in which the IT infrastructure will be designed and managed.
3. The specific tasks that will have to be undertaken to manage the IS.
4. The organisational setup of employees and reporting relationships that will be created.
5. The policies that will be followed for the use of the IS.

In addition to the plan, the CIO also creates the policies by which decisions will be taken regarding IS acquisition, use and management. These policies are detailed guidelines on activities related to the sustained use of IS. For example, for IT acquisitions the policies state how the requests will be initiated, who can initiate the request, how will the requirements be drawn, how will vendors be selected, etc. Sometimes checklists are created to guide such processes. The policies also have to specify the security and access guidelines for all the data and information residing in the organisation. Some organisations also create fair-use policies, spelling out what can be done with the IS of the organisation and what cannot be done, where the latter usually refers to illegal downloads, piracy and so on.

6.3.2 Vendor Coordination

The CIO is usually the nodal person who interfaces with large vendors, particularly for the centralised IT management. The CIO is responsible for selecting, contracting and managing the vendor. This high-level interaction enables the vendors to report to and request resources from a person of responsibility. This role also entails careful monitoring of the vendors and producing reports on their activities for the top management.

6.3.3 Technology Updates

The CIO also has to monitor the technical developments happening in the industry. This role requires a certain background in and knowledge of IT and the ability to follow the multiple and varied trends in the industry. CIOs often attend conferences and seminars organised by industry associations to understand the growth path of technologies and firms supporting them. This knowledge is crucial for technology selection and upgradation. The CIO provides the essential link between the needs of the organisation and the technology advances that can help meet those needs.

6.3.4 Return on Investment of Technology

The return on investment (ROI) is a numerical measure of the financial value of an investment. It is usually computed as a percentage. Thus, if an amount of 100 units is spent on an asset, and this asset helps earn 10 units for the organisation, then the return on the investment is said to be 10%.

One part of the CIO's job is to compute whether IT investments have provided a return, and if so, how much is the return. Computing ROI for IT is very difficult, mainly because the improvements brought about by IT are in the processes that are used to sell or make the end product of a commercial organisation, and such improvements are sometimes intangible and hard to measure. IT by itself does not contribute to the revenue generation for commercial firms unless they are themselves in the IT business. ROI is computed by measuring the improvements in processes that enable better productivity and hence better revenues or profits.

The CIO has to ensure that IT investments lead to an adequate return. This involves determining the improvements in processes that are supported by IT, and devising measures of productivity gains. For example, the measures could lead to an increase (or a decrease) in the speed of transactions in a commercial firm, or reductions in the errors introduced in accounting entries. Such measures show the manner in which IT is impacting the firm and hence indirectly point to the improvements in productivity and ROI.

KEY POINT

The ROI from IT investments is obtained by measuring improvements in processes.

Caselet DEF Corporation

DEF Corporation (name changed) is a large multi-national, US-based firm that is in the high-technology engineering industry. It is considered a market leader in its space and has a presence in over 100 countries. It has an office in India, which has over ten thousand employees. The Indian business has grown significantly over the last two decades and the firm now operates almost independently of its parent and handles business in Europe, the Middle East, Africa and India. The India office manages operations such as design, engineering, sales and marketing. The firm has extended its operations to 12 cities in India.

DEF's India business has grown strongly and in order to sustain this, the Board of DEF decided to upgrade its information systems. The systems were intended to support efficiency in operations and also in innovation and growth. The firm's Board settled on some key objectives for the system:

1. It would assist with data storage, to handle the massive amounts of data being generated and also to remain consistent with its sister operations.
2. It would assist with workflows and processes across the organisation.
3. It would assist with faster decision making.

The Board also decided to leverage Cloud infrastructure in the firm, which would help to inter-operate with numerous different kinds of devices being used by the employees and partner organisations. They wanted to go with a web-based centralised architecture to which the existing, legacy, functions could connect. Further, the centralised architecture would also enable vendor-supplied systems, such as an Enterprise Resource Planning (ERP) system, to inter-connect and work seamlessly with the firm's systems.

A key decision that the Board took was to hire and maintain a permanent, in-house IT team that would manage the infrastructure. This was necessary as the firm wanted to scale up its business quickly and wanted all the detailed know-how on its operations and practices to be known by its own employees. These employees could be called upon at short notice help with the extensions of the system and for further design and implementations.

DEF planned to rollout the system, which had many modules, in a few key departments initially. This would provide them with data and insights on how to further improve workflows and data usage. The system was implemented and DEF then undertook a thorough analysis of the processes and workflows by looking closely at wait times for decisions, approval cycles, routing complications and queuing delays. The management was able to identify choke-points and bottlenecks for decision-making and addressed these in later rollouts of the system.

6.4 IT GOVERNANCE

Governance in an organisation specifies the high-level decision-making capacities of individuals and groups that ultimately guide the everyday management of the organisation and its activities. Governance relates rights and responsibilities, control and guidance, and the overall relationship of the organisation with its primary stakeholders. The governance responsibilities and mechanisms situate the organisation and its leadership in the larger economic environment, thus shaping the manner in which the organisation manages its activities both within its own boundaries and with the outside world.

The governance of IT refers to the manner in which the organisation better utilises its IT infrastructure by designing a structure of decision making that outlines roles and responsibilities for various stakeholders. The management of the IT infrastructure is not left to any single department or individual. Rather, it is understood as an activity in which many have a role and a responsibility. The IT governance enrols stakeholders in formulation and implementation of an IT strategy that furthers the organisation's goals. Specifically, the governance mechanism specifies a framework of decision rights and accountabilities that encourage individuals and groups to use the infrastructure effectively.

The IT governance is specified by the rights to make decisions and to give inputs for decisions by individuals and groups. The decision-making domains, or the matters on which decisions have to be taken, are divided into five categories. These are high-level conceptual categories that are defined by the nature and scope of decisions. These five categories are listed in Table 6.3 and explained below.

1. **IT principles:** These are high-level statements and ideas by which the organisation wants to organise and use its IT capabilities. Examples of such principles could be to use IT for lower cost competitive advantage; to use IT for high-speed marketing of products; to use IT to reach a wider customer base; to use IT for efficient and high-quality service; and so on.

Table 6.3 | Five Categories of Decisions on IT Governance

Decisions	Detail
IT Principles	High-level ideas about how to use IT
IT Architecture	Blueprint of hardware, software and networks
IT Services	Functions required throughout the organisation
Business applications	Specific applications required for different departments and functional needs
IT Budgets	Money allocated for spending on IT

Such statements reflect a broad goal or strategy that the organisation wants to achieve without specifying the details of the required IT infrastructure. These decisions guide selection and implementation of IT, and also shape the manner in which the organisation reorders its internal processes to better use IT to achieve its goals.

2. **IT architecture:** These decisions pertain to specific choices for the architecture, such as the kind and size of the database, the networking configuration and topology, the application choices, the hardware configurations, the operating system choices and so on. These decisions specify and constrain the manner in which IT can be deployed and used by the organisation.
3. **IT services:** These are infrastructure services that are used throughout the organisation and support IT functions and activities. Examples of these services are: help desk support, communication services, security services, commercial transaction services and so on. The services in question enable applications to work smoothly, and allow business transactions to proceed.
4. **Business application needs:** These are specific application packages that the organisation may buy, build or integrate from components. Examples of such applications include enterprise resource planning, customer relationship management, supply chain management, e-commerce software and so on. These applications run the main transactions for the business and enable the business to meet its goals.
5. **IT budgets:** These decisions specify how much to spend on IT, whether to allocate money annually or across many years, whether to budget as capital expenses or as operational expenses, whether budgets are to be allocated through departments or centrally, whether the budgets have to be capped, what are the priorities for various projects and how the approvals process has to work.

The five categories of decisions, explained above, are crucial to determine the IT governance of any organisation. The important question here is how and by whom these decisions are best made. Researchers have used political metaphors to explain the decision making that different individuals and groups participate in to address IT governance. These metaphors are referred to as archetypes or models by which decision making is done. The archetypes are as follows:

1. **Business Monarchy:** In this archetype, all the decision-making powers are held by the heads of the organisation, such as the chief executive or the managing director and others at that level. The CIO may be included in the decision making, but the entire control is with the business heads. Here, the business head may be compared to a monarch. A monarch refers to a king or emperor who is the sole ruler of a state.
2. **IT Monarchy:** In this archetype, the decision making is done exclusively by the head of IT in the organisation. The head may be the CIO or a President or Vice President of IT. The head of IT may include others, but all are at a senior level and involved directly with the IT function.
3. **Feudal:** A feudal political state consists of powerful local lords or feuds who serve a state head such as the king. In the feudal archetype, the decision making is done by business,

department or unit heads, and they have the most power for all decision and input rights. In organisations they may have designations such as General Manager, Unit Director, Vice President of Sales and so on. They have independence in their functions, and are directed by the business heads.

4. **Federal:** In this arrangement, the decision making is done jointly by the business heads and the unit heads. This is the model of political decision making in many countries where decisions are made jointly by the head of the nation and the local heads, such as chief ministers or governors of a state. IT heads may be included in the decision making, or may be left out. This is usually considered to be the most democratic form of decision making albeit the most tedious and long winded.
5. **IT Duoply:** In this model the decision making is done jointly by the IT heads and either the business heads or the unit heads, but not both. In the first instance, the IT heads team up with the CEO or managing director to make IT decisions, and in the latter case, the IT heads work with the department or unit heads.
6. **Anarchy:** This is a political term referring to no central or high-level control. In the archetype, the decision making about IT is done by the users at the low levels where there is no higher oversight and control. The users implement IT purely based on their own needs.

In a study of 256 organisations in 23 countries across the world, researcher Peter Weill and his team found distinct patterns of governance. Table 6.4 depicts these differences.

For each decision domain, the number of firms following a particular archetype was counted. The dominant archetype for each decision is reported in Table 6.4. Some decisions were made by more than one archetype. The study found that for IT Principles, the decision making was mainly with the IT Duopoly. The IT Architecture decisions as well as the IT Services decisions were made by the IT Monarchy. Business application needs were decided by a mix of archetypes, the Federal and the IT Duopoly. For IT Budgets, the decision making was done by the Business Monarchy, the Federal and the IT Duopoly archetypes.

The study then went on to separate the top performing firms in the sample from others. The top performers were identified on the basis of their financial performance over a number of years, their use of IT for growth and competitive advantage, and their use of IT for flexibility. The top performing organisations showed a clear difference in their IT governance patterns. Table 6.5 shows how the top performing firms make their decisions.

Table 6.5 clearly shows that the best performing firms follow almost the same governance patterns as the bulk of the firms, with the exception of deciding on business application needs and IT budgeting, where the Federal and IT Duopoly models dominate. When the focus is shifted to firms whose performance is not as high (they are worse than the top performing firms), then the difference is quite stark: the first three decisions, of principles, architecture and services, are all made by the Business Monarchy, the business applications are decided by the Federal archetype and the budgets are decided by the Business Monarchy. There is thus a contrast between the best performing firms and the ones that do not perform as well in terms of their IT governance (see Fig. 6.4).

Table 6.4 | Decisions Rights by Governance Archetypes in All Firms

Decisions	Predominant Decision Rights
IT Principles	IT Duopoly
IT Architecture	IT Monarchy
IT Services	IT Monarchy
Business application needs	Federal and IT Duopoly
IT Budgets	Business Monarchy, Federal and IT Duopoly

Table 6.5 | Decisions Rights by Governance Archetypes in Top Performing Firms

Decisions	Predominant Decision Rights for Top Performing Firms
IT Principles	IT Duopoly
IT Architecture	IT Monarchy
IT Services	IT Monarchy
Business application needs	Federal
IT Budgets	IT Duopoly

For the IT governance to succeed, it is essential that it is actively designed by any organisation. The decision-making process has to be clearly enunciated, and the parties involved have to be aware of their responsibilities for the same. With transparency of the governance process and stability, the governance mechanism should not be changed too often. There is a distinct possibility of having a strong governance mechanism and high utilisation of IT resources.

	IT principles	IT archite-cture	IT services	Business apps	IT budget
Bus monarchy					
IT monarchy		■	■		
Feudal					
Federal				■	
IT duopoly	■				■
Anarchy					

IT Governance at top-performing firms

	IT princi ples	IT archite-cture	IT services	Business apps	IT budget
Bus monarchy	■	■	■		■
IT monarchy					
Feudal					
Federal					
IT duopoly				■	
Anarchy					

IT Governance at firms not at the top

FIGURE 6.4 | The IT governance at most firms and at top performing firms. Shaded cells indicate the decision rights of the archetypes.

Chapter Glossary

Centralised IT Where an organisation's IT infrastructure is located and managed from a central point. All functions and applications are accessed by departments and units from this centre.

Decentralised IT Where an organisation's IT infrastructure is distributed across departments and functional units. Each unit manages IT on its own.

Standard An externally defined set of parameters that specify hardware and software in an organisation.

Interoperability The ability of hardware and software of a certain type – made by a certain manufacturer or according to some standard – to work with another type of hardware or software.

Technical bid The specifications of hardware, software and networks made by a potential vendor to address the needs of an organisation.

Commercial bid The prices specified for a specific technical bid made by a vendor.

Information systems plan A document specifying in a high-level manner how IT will support the activities of the organisation.

Return on investment A technical formula specifying the increase in revenues or other benefits to be realised from an investment.

IT governance A high-level specification of who makes IT decisions in an organisation.

Review Questions

1. How would you characterise the modern business environment? What does it mean for IT choices?
2. What are the first-, second- and third-order effects of information systems when introduced in organisations?
3. Describe the difference between the centralised versus decentralised management of IT.
4. Read the ICICI Bank case. Is the IT management centralised or decentralised? Why did the CEO Kamath choose such a management style?
5. What are the two main categories of IT security threats? Give specific examples of each.
6. What factors influence technology selection?
7. Why is vendor management important? What are the key issues to consider for managing vendors carefully?
8. Why is the CIO important? What are the important tasks the CIO has to perform?
9. What are the various decision rights and responsibilities in IT governance? What are the various archetypes by which various corporations make decisions?
10. For top performing firms, there is a distinct pattern of decision making. Why does this difference exist?

Research Questions

1. Research the IT function in your college or organisation. Is this function run in a centralised or decentralised manner? Are there elements of both types of IT management present?
2. Continuing with the previous question: Find out how many vendors provide services and support to your organisation. Is there a Service Level Agreement that any vendor has to comply with? What is the nature of the contract they have signed?
3. How is IT procurement done in the organisation you have studied? What is the process followed for buying equipment such as laptops, wireless routers, printers and scanners, etc.?
4. The discussion on IT governance uses terms such as monarchy, feudal, federal, duopoly and anarchy. What do these terms mean in the Indian political context? Give an example, from history and from the current political situation, of each term.

Further Reading

1. The CEO as CIO: An interview with K. V. Kamath of ICICI, *McKinsey Quarterly*, 2007.
2. *ICICI Bank India: Technology-led innovation* Case Study Is available at: http://www.infosys.com/finacle (accessed on November 2010).
3. An article 'K. V. Kamath: The entrepreneur that transformed ICICI Bank', 2008 issue is available at: http://www.moneycontrol.com (accessed on November 2010).
4. Weill, P. (2004) Don't just lead, govern: How top-performing firms govern IT, *MIS Quarterly Executive*, 3(1), 1–17.
5. Hunt, R. (2009) Case Study: State Bank of India, World's Largest Centralised Core Processing Implementation. *Report of the Tower Group*.

CHAPTER 7

Ethical and Social Issues

Learning Objectives

After completing this chapter, you will be able to:

- Understand the ethical issues concerning information systems
- Get an overview of social issues concerning information systems

Information systems are pervasive across organisations. When their use confronts existing norms and practices at the organisation, ethical and social issues arise. Ethical issues relate to privacy, workplace monitoring and use of power. Privacy of individuals in modern organisations is often at risk as substantial private data about personal details is resident in the organisation's databases. Furthermore, work-related practices such as sending email and browsing are also visible to the organisation. Workplace monitoring often relies on such data to determine how employees are performing, where they are, how much time they have spent on work, who they have communicated with, etc. Monitoring enforces disciplined behaviour on employees and also protects them from abusive or threatening behaviour. Systems professionals in organisations enjoy a power over information systems users owing to their privileged knowledge and position, and this raises ethical issues about how they influence the decisions of the users.

Politics within organisations and their social aspects are affected by information systems, mainly because they change the basis of power for many employees. They also affect the work practices of employees, creating distinctions based on the educational background and age of the employees. For some employees, this means losing some of their skills and their social links at the office. When employees choose to work from home, as telecommuting employees, such issues arise too. Information systems usage has increased tremendously over the years, and this has created the problem of e-waste that has strong environmental and health consequences.

There is a dark side to IT also, where excessive work pressure leads to technostress and also to misuse of IT assets. Incessant use of IT also leads to digital distraction.

MIND MAP OF CHAPTER TOPICS

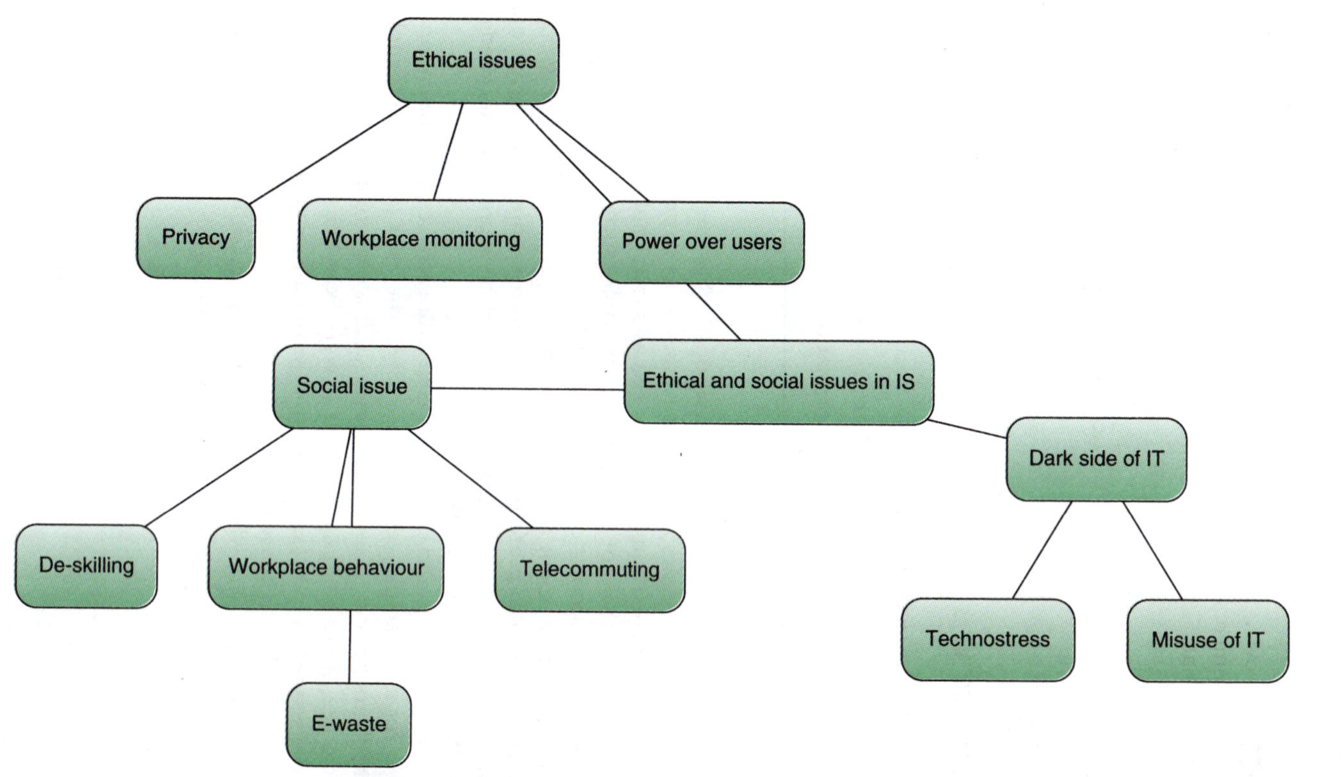

CASE STUDY: VIDEO SURVEILLANCE AT JINDAL STEEL

Jindal Steel and Power Ltd (JSPL) is a large multinational steel producing firm in India. Besides steel, it has business interests in mining, power generation, and oil and gas. Its annual revenue stands at Rs 100 billion (about USD 2 billion), which is growing rapidly. JSPL currently has one of the largest sponge iron manufacturing facilities in the world.

In 2004, JSPL inaugurated the Angul project in Orissa, which is an integrated steel plant and captive power project. The plant was allocated 5000 acres of land near Angul, a region in Orissa, and it began operations to install its facilities there. The project was to be situated on farming and forest land, which had to be acquired and clearances had to be obtained. These proved hard to obtain. However, JSPL was able to work with the local residents to develop the region and obtain environmental and forest clearances for the project.

One of the problems that JSPL faced was that of monitoring activities across their vast estate. The 5000 acres of undeveloped land that they owned did not have any permanent boundaries. One major challenge they faced was how to restrict the unauthorised access of the local population to their estate: they could not really tell whether the people who had come into the estate construction sites were employees and workers or others who had simply walked in. This led to some instances of theft and damage to property.

To address this problem, the management decided to install video surveillance cameras across the site. These cameras, known as closed-circuit television (CCTV) cameras, are used in various commercial establishments such as retail shops, laboratories and office buildings. The cameras feed a video image to a monitor that is maintained at a central facility, which is constantly monitored by security personnel. The cameras can be remotely controlled, and a continuous stream of video data, running 24 h, 7 days a week, can be viewed and recorded.

The IT department at JSPL surveyed the site and carefully selected such positions where they could install a minimal number of cameras to get the most coverage. One challenge was to cover the areas that were not well lit and were a concern at night. Another challenge was to ensure that the cameras were connected to a central server where the video data could be stored. The solution they hit upon was to use wireless networks as the carriers of the data. Wi-Fi hotspots were located across the campus, and all the cameras could transfer their data through the Wi-Fi network. The Wi-Fi hotspots not only allowed connecting to cameras at remote locations but also allowed large volumes of data to be transmitted. The video data was then recorded on specially configured servers where it could reside as a permanent record.

Once the surveillance cameras were installed, the management found that not only did theft and equipment damage reduced but that they could also monitor activities at the project site. Earlier, the top management of JSPL, located in Delhi, had to make many trips to the site to monitor the construction progress. However, now the surveillance cameras enabled them to monitor the entire project from Delhi itself, thus saving them costs of making many trips. Furthermore, they could also monitor the planned progress of the project, as they could now physically view the use of equipment, materials and the work on the site. If any incidents happened at the construction sites, the management now had a video record of them and could decide on who was responsible, avoiding unnecessary finger-pointing that is endemic to any project working on a tight schedule.

The JSPL management found the project of video surveillance highly beneficial. Thanks to it they were able to reduce petty theft and criminal damage to equipment, and also track unknown persons on their premises. Furthermore, they found that the video surveillance could also serve as an effective management tool. Their ability to monitor project personnel and the project progress improved with this tool. They could save costs by not having to travel to the site, and yet receive continuous and real-time updates on the activities at the site. The pressure to perform better increased on project managers and workers as they knew that they were being watched constantly. From being a mere tactical system, the video surveillance unit had become a strategic tool for the management.

7.1 ETHICAL ISSUES

Information systems are used by people in organisations and in society. The use of these systems is guided by the limits imposed by the systems themselves, such as how much connectivity is possible, and also by the norms and codes of conduct that the organisation or the society subscribes to. Sometimes information systems enable capabilities that clash with existing norms, and here issues of ethics and responsibility arise.

KEY POINT

Ethics are moral rules and codes that individuals in a society are expected to follow.

Ethics are publicly accepted rules of behaviour for social engagement. In a larger sense, ethics are the moral rules and codes that individuals in a society follow. These rules are often derived from religion or a community ethos. The dividing line between ethical and unethical behaviour is determined by the community ethos and what is considered, widely, to be acceptable.

Ethics are different from legal issues. What is legal is determined by an explicit set of laws, usually written, in any country. The system of justice in the country decides on the legality or non-legality of actions, issues, rules, etc. Ethics, on the other hand, are not sharply encoded in texts; they are determined by loose codes outlined as conduct rules or ethical guidelines.

7.1.1 Privacy

Privacy is defined as "claim of individuals, groups or institutions to determine for themselves when, how and to what extent information about them is communicated to others." This definition implies that individuals or groups can withdraw themselves from society, by restricting the information about themselves to be made available. This definition includes a notion of society that includes the family or immediate social group, the workplace and the living space or society at large.

This definition of privacy has two implications: one is that of policy, where organisations or governments have to ensure privacy when it is demanded by groups, employees or citizens. The other implication is that privacy has an emotional or psychological content, where individuals or groups may feel they the need to withdraw from society or not have their personal details known.

Information systems are used widely across organisations and they enable data and information to be widely distributed for use. When the data pertains to individuals (relating to their work, personal habits or personal life), and it resides on organisational information systems, the question of privacy that arises here is: whose data is this–of the individual or of the organisation? Owing to the complex nature of information systems and the manner in which data is created, stored and manipulated, the answer to this question is usually difficult.

To answer the question of privacy one has to consider why it is important in the first place. Data and information relating to individuals could be of sensitive nature. Some examples of such kind of data are as follows:

1. Employees who work extensively with computers, log in every morning when they come to work and log out in the evening when they leave. During the working day, every time they leave their desk or are not working on the computer, the system logs their inactivity at work. For example, a United Airlines worker, in the USA, was threatened with job loss on the grounds that she had spent more than the allotted time in the bathroom, making her co-workers take up her work.
2. Medical records detailing illnesses and treatments, hospital visits and medication routines are all stored on organisational databases that contain personnel data. The data is specific to individuals and, for some organisations, also contains details about the individual's family members. In the USA, for example, the medical records of the famous singer Britney Spears were read by employees of a hospital in which she was treated. The employees later leaked the information to the press. Spears took legal action against the hospital, which had to fire several employees.
3. Web surfing activities of individuals are also logged by corporate web servers. Which sites individuals have visited, how long they have been on the site and what kind of material they

have downloaded are also logged. A multinational media firm, for example, threatened to fire an employee based on his visits to Yahoo.com from an office computer. The firm had obtained details about the employee's surfing behaviour from server logs.

4. Security systems in some organisations, which are based on swipe cards or security cards that enable doors and office buildings to be opened or accessed, retain records of all individual movements across buildings and workplaces. Data pertaining to individual movements is available in security logs. In the Vatican, for example, swipes were re-introduced in 2008 to monitor the movement of employees. This was in response to criticism that employees were 'slacking off'. Even though the Pope was not entirely in favour of such monitoring, it was introduced to improve efficiency of staff.
5. Many organisations also check all incoming and outgoing emails of their personnel. The emails are checked for content and attachments. Some organisations either remove emails containing certain keywords, such as expletives, or flag them to warn employees.

With the above information residing in organisational databases, it is possible for organisations or individuals within organisations to access and use or misuse this information. For example, if the medical history of an employee is known to others, it may be used to deny promotions or job opportunities. This is an issue of ethics as many countries discourage discrimination against people who have disabilities or health issues.

The matter becomes complex when the decision is not easy to make. For example, employee J has a health problem for which he/she has received medical treatment that has been reimbursed by his/her firm. Suppose an opportunity opens up in the firm that requires extensive travelling, and this opportunity is something that J desires and feels is important for his/her career. However, the firm's management could take a stand of denying the opportunity to J, based on their knowledge of J's health issues and the problems concerning his/her ability to travel. Or, the management could also inform J of the opportunity and seek his/her opinion on the matter without raising the issue of his/her health. Should the management use J's private data to inform their own decision making? Should they ask J about his/her willingness to avail of the opportunity and not inform J of their knowledge about his/her health?

The important ethical issue here is whether the management should use private data related to an employee for their decision making. The option they have is of asking the employee for his/her opinion, and then not divulge the information. The resolution of this issue varies in different countries. Many courts in the USA, for example, have ruled that an employee's personal information available to an organisation is not necessarily personal and can be used by the management.

Another aspect of privacy is that of maintaining confidentiality of clients and partners of an organisation. It is often the case that the firms who have data on clients sell the data in aggregate form for commercial profit. Some contracts between clients and firms explicitly forbid this. However, many firms exploit weaknesses in contracts to disburse the information. For example, many banks are known to sell information regarding their clients' names, address and telephone numbers to credit card firms that use this information to make marketing calls to customers.

Countries around the world have framed legislation around this issue, mandating that commercial firms must have explicit permission of the users before such information is divulged to others. In a famous case, in 2006, an employee of the Hongkong and Shanghai Banking Corporation (HSBC) was caught trying to sell credit card details of 200,000 customers. He had collected all the data on customer details that he was willing to sell to the highest bidder. Owing to the prevalent laws in the UK, to which country most of the customers belonged, the data dissemination was considered a theft hence the perpetrator was prosecuted.

However, in many cases the law is ambiguous, and individuals and firms are able to dispense various forms of data. The major ethical questions that arise in these situations are:

1. Who has the ownership of the data – the firm or the customer from whom the data is obtained?

2. If a profit is made with the data then should this be shared with the customer?
3. Do customers have any rights to the information that is derived from their data?

The questions of privacy and ownership of data become critical when the government also participates in the collection of data from citizens and also in its use. In India, it is common for government departments to collect data on citizens' details and store them in massive databases. For example, the tax department will have details about individual citizens and their tax histories. Is it legally feasible for the department to share its data with other departments? With the increasing prevalence of e-governance systems, these data stores have increased in both scale and scope. Many countries, including India, have introduced or are in the process of introducing unique identity numbers for all citizens, thus enabling all databases to have a common unique number that can be used to collate records. This is a substantial challenge to the privacy and right to privacy of individuals. The unique identity number project in India has been challenged by many civil society organisations on the grounds that it will violate individual privacy. Till late 2010, India did not have a specific privacy law in place; privacy is granted to individuals as a basic right, the 'right to life and liberty', under Article 21 of the Indian Constitution. Section 72 of the Indian IT Act 2000 also protects privacy by specifying penalties for breach of confidentiality. Owing to the challenge to the unique identity number project, the Indian government has considered introducing a privacy act.

In this context of the individual's privacy, it is worth mentioning that many countries, including India, have also passed the right to information laws that require government departments to open up their internal records and files to citizens who desire to see them. These transparency laws strengthen the democratic process as they allow citizens a view of the internal functioning of the government. However, these laws also tend to infringe the privacy rights of individuals if their data, which is maintained and used by the department, is the subject of a right to information request.

7.1.1.1 Internet Challenges to Privacy

Cookies are small files that are maintained by the browser a user is using to surf the internet. These files keep track of the user's activity to help sites that the user has visited or is working with. For instance, if a user is at an e-commerce site and is selecting and purchasing items, then the cookies help to keep track of what the user wants, help him/her with making the payment, and allow him/her to go back and forth over different pages without losing track of his purchase items. Cookies may be enabled in browsers to help with surfing, or may be actively turned off by users.

Cookies present a threat to privacy, as they reveal the user's surfing behaviour. Many e-commerce sites use cookies to learn what kinds of sites and pages the user has visited, and then target advertisements at him/her. Sometimes cookies also reveal personal details about the user–such as the name, phone number and address of the user.

Several countries, such as the USA, have passed laws banning the use of cookies by agencies that host web pages. Furthermore, the laws also restrict the manner in which cookies can be used.

Spyware are computer programs, pieces of software, which enter and reside on personal computers and monitor user activity. A typical spyware program may enter the computer through email or through the browser, and then it resides on the computer. Spyware are malicious software created to invade the privacy of users and report to their creators details about what software the user has, what sites the user views and how the user uses his/her computer. Spyware typically send out information they have gathered over the internet to their creator.

To counter the privacy and confidentiality violation arising from cookies and spyware, many organisations have formulated strict policies about internet surfing and access. Many commercial firms entirely ban visiting specific sites that use cookies or deploy spyware. Other policies include setting strong privacy controls on the browser and on the routers used to connect to the internet.

7.1.2 Workplace Monitoring

Throughout the history of the industrial revolution, workplace monitoring has remained one of the most contentious and prevalent management practices. This practice is of maintaining a vigil on the workers' activities in an organisation, particularly in a commercial firm, with the objective of ensuring higher productivity. When the workers are monitored in their workplace, they are required to conform to certain work norms, such as how fast or efficiently they work and how they behave with co-workers. And, the objective of workplace monitoring is to discipline them to conform to these norms.

Supervision in factories of the industrial era involved closely watching workers as to how they went about their work, how many units they produced, how they interacted with co-workers, how efficiently they used their time, and other details. The supervisors used the data they collected from their observations to reward workers who performed well and to discipline those who did not perform. Disciplining often involved giving close attention to under-performing workers, providing them detailed instructions, and meting out mild punishments such as threats of termination. In cases where workers did not improve their performance, termination of their services was done based on the evidence of their non-performance collected during the supervision process.

From the management's perspective, monitoring and supervision aim at improving the productivity and hence the earnings and morale of the workers. Supervisors ensure that there is no 'freeloading', that is, in a unit some workers are slack in their work and others have to work harder to meet the goals of the unit. Supervisors are also able to spot the best performers and reward them, thus improving the morale and motivation of the group.

On the other hand, critics of monitoring argue that close supervision leads to a loss of privacy and confidence of the workers. They feel that the supervisors do not trust them enough to let them do their work independently, thus leading to decline in their confidence. If performance has to be measured for individuals and for groups then this can be done by measuring the output of the workers and groups without close monitoring, and this would be less obtrusive. Individuals do not like to be monitored as this affects their personal choices and their ability to function independently.

With the pervasive use of information systems in organisations, the scale and precision of monitoring has increased for certain kinds of tasks. For example, for many 'back office' tasks, where employees of a commercial firm have to talk to and interact with a wide range of customers, information technology is extensively used to enable the employees to have all the relevant information. Credit card issuing agencies have such offices where the credit card customers can call in and have their needs addressed. In such situations, the entire duration of the call is often recorded digitally and stored, and also data and files used to address the customer's needs are digitally recorded. Supervisors then use the data thus collected to evaluate whether the employee spent the optimal amount of time talking to the customer, whether the right data was used and whether the right information was provided to the customer. As the work of the employees involves repetitive, often mechanical, tasks, the management specifies guidelines and norms for them. Employees then have to conform to these norms such as the amount of time taken to respond to the customer, the number of times the customer had to ask questions or call back, etc. And, the information system allows the supervisors to measure this conformance.

KEY POINT

Use of IS in organisations has increased the scale and precision of monitoring of employees.

7.1.2.1 Types of Workplace Monitoring

There are many possible ways in which electronic monitoring can be effected in organisations. Some of these are as follows:

1. Use of digital video cameras for internal monitoring of employees, offices, hallways and buildings. The video footage is stored for later retrieval and viewing.
2. Use of computer network logs to record all use of files, visits to websites, and access to other computer networks and programs.
3. Scanning and storage of all outgoing and incoming emails from and to employees.
4. Use of employee identity cards to monitor physical movement of employees.

5. Access given to outside agencies to obtain personal data on employees, such as credit card statements, bank records, medical records and pharmacy purchases.
6. Access to all files on employees' personal computers and laptops, including removable storage devices.

Often other types of workplace monitoring are also conducted by firms, such as testing for drugs and alcohol. However, these are not dependent on digital technologies and are not considered here.

7.1.2.2 The Information Panopticon

Electronic workplace monitoring is considered by some commentators as the modern equivalent of the Panopticon of the 19th century. The idea of the Panopticon was first conceived by the British economist and philosopher Jeremy Bentham (see Fig. 7.1). Bentham proposed a structure composed of an eight-sided building that had rooms along the periphery with windows that opened towards the centre. The centre had a high columnar structure with a room at the top that was open on all sides. This structure, called a Panopticon, would serve to closely monitor those in the peripheral rooms and also help discipline their behaviour. Bentham had envisaged that structures of this nature could be used to discipline those who needed disciplining, such as workers, jail inmates and students.

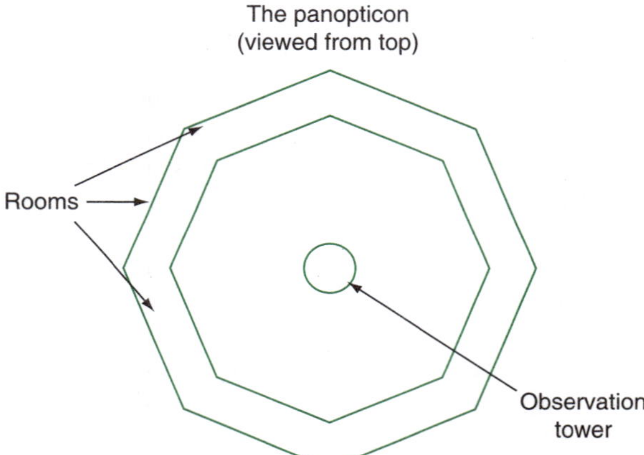

FIGURE 7.1 The octagonal Panopticon. Along the periphery of the structure are the rooms. Each room opens towards the centre and can be fully observed from the observation tower. A room at the tower top is covered with see-through mirrors which make it impossible for the room occupants to verify whether there are observers in the tower.

A major advantage of the Panopticon was that those in the peripheral rooms were usually not in a position to see whether there was anyone in the central tower seeing them, but they always knew that someone could be there. The disciplining was possible, according to Bentham, because the source of power was always present but its presence could not be verified. Thus, some jails were designed to have a similar structure, of an octagon with a tower at the centre, and the room in the central tower covered with see-through mirrors. Here, the prison inmates could always see the tower from their rooms but not know easily if anyone was watching them at that time.

KEY POINT

Information systems in organisations have a Panopticon effect on employees, where they are aware they are being monitored but are not sure.

Monitoring through information systems too has the same effect as that of the Panopticon: those being monitored are always conscious that they can be observed but are never sure that the monitoring is going on. Most users across organisations know that their files, data, activity and web surfing behaviour can be monitored, however, they are never sure of this. When organisations implement rules of conduct, such as those for visiting websites, employees show conformity and discipline because of the Panopticon effect.

7.1.2.3 The Role of Monitoring

The rationale for monitoring draws from the fact that information about activities is useful. For commercial organisations, the security aspect of information is paramount. Information entering the organisation through email and websites represents security threats owing to the massive presence of viruses, worms and other malicious software. Management concerns of privacy are often overridden by the concern for security – all activity related to data and files being brought into the organisation are thus monitored.

Another concern of organisations is that of abusive and threatening software and data that may be brought in from outside and that may harm employees. For example, organisations monitor computers and networks for pornographic or hateful literature or videos that employees will be wary of. These materials are not owned by the organisation but if found on its digital networks, the organisation could face serious charges of discrimination, harassment or abuse from its own employees. Many courts around the world have upheld such charges, and have forced organisations to adopt very stringent monitoring policies.

For example, in a famous case, the Chevron Corporation in the USA had to pay a fine of USD 2.2 million owing to a gender insensitivity case filed by four of its women employees. When the case was filed, in 1992, the women employees alleged that they had been a target of offensive jokes, sexually explicit material and gender discrimination in the firm. Much of the material had been sent to them via email. The court settled the case in their favour and fined Chevron for what was, at that time, one of the highest fines ever levied for a charge of this nature. Subsequent to this, many firms resorted to electronic monitoring of email to prevent occurrences of this nature.

Commercial firms and even government departments use monitoring to restrict the personal use of computers and networks within the premises. Such use not only wastes time of employees but also presents a poor image of the department to the outside world. Firms are also wary of employees using their electronic networks to either work for some other agency during their off hours or provide information about themselves to seek alternative jobs.

For many commercial firms, monitoring is a competitive necessity. There are many examples of employees leaking out company secrets to rivals to the detriment of their own organisations. The employees may do this for monetary gain or to extract revenge on their own organisation for not gaining a promotion or a salary increase. The firms therefore maintain strict control over their employees' computers, desktops and laptops, and monitor all file exchanges. Employees are also not permitted to use removable media such as flash storage drives, and in case they have to, these are carefully monitored during entry and exit.

For the Jindal Steel case given at the beginning of this chapter, the need for monitoring and surveillance was to control unrestricted access and material theft. However, the installed cameras also provided a means to monitor other activities also.

7.1.3 Power over Users

Every organisation that uses information systems also hires information systems professionals who are responsible for ensuring that the systems are managed and run properly. In modern organisations, the role of such professionals has increased considerably owing to the heavy dependence of the organisations on information systems. Due to the important role the systems professionals play, they come to have power over others in the organisation.

An individual is said to have power over a person when the individual can influence the thinking or behaviour of that person. For the information systems professionals, this power is their ability to make IT users listen to and agree to what they say. For example, if a user wants to send an email with an attached file, he/she may ask the systems professional how to do this. The professional may answer that the file can only be attached in a zipped format (a format that allows a file to be compressed to a smaller size). The user may not be persuaded by this answer as he/she knows that files can also be attached in the uncompressed format, provided they are not larger than the size permitted by the email system. However, the user listens to the professional and sends the file in a zipped form.

KEY POINT

IT professionals may exercise power over ordinary users in the organisation.

There is a subtle difference between having power and exercising power. Exercising power implies that the individuals who have power actually enforce it and have their way over the thinking and behaviour of others. The exercise of power is a deliberate act that ensues in a particular situation. Power in an organisation is associated with a position in the hierarchy or with the assumption of superior knowledge. A systems professional is more powerful in some situations owing to his superior knowledge of information technology.

Consider the situation of a project in which specific information systems are being built or used. The context is narrow and technical. In such a situation, systems professionals may exercise power over a user, as in the example of using a zipped file as an attachment, by simply stating a particular technical fact. This technical knowledge, of which the user is not aware, acts to settle a conflict or decide on a course of action. The professional simply states the fact and has his way, which is the exercise of power, without bothering to explain why. Had the professional explained that zipped files take less space and are faster to use, it would have been a rational argument to support his recommendation. However, if this argument is not used, it becomes a *technical* exercise of power (see Fig. 7.2).

A different situation arises when the matter is of a specific technical issue but outside any specific project or usage context. For example, in many organisations there is a policy that all computer and related equipment purchases have to be routed through the IT department or have to be approved by the information systems professionals. The exercise of power is now *structural*, where the systems professionals use their position in the organisation to influence decisions about what to buy, how much to spend, where to buy and so on. The users are bound to listen to the professionals owing to their role in the organisation.

Outside of any issues of fact, such as the use of a system or building a system, the systems professionals often exercise power by affecting the wants and desires of the users. Users who are not familiar with the information systems terminology may not find the exact words or phrases needed to express what they want to do or have done. In such cases, the frameworks, models and terminology used by the professionals shapes the users' expression of their wants. For example, if a user desires to have a file sent from his department, say Stores, to another department, say Accounts, then he/she may express this by saying he/she wants the file 'sent to Accounts'. However, in the systems terminology he/she may be obliged to state his/her requirements as one of the following:

1. Copied into the folder of the Accounts department.
2. Sent to a central folder with access by the Accounts department.
3. Sent as an email attachment to the Accounts department.

When the user chooses any of these alternatives, he/she is giving in to an exercise of power, where the systems professionals are determining his/her wants by restricting the manner in which they can be achieved. The desire that arises in the physical world is now shaped by the digital world to a new form. This is known as a *conceptual* exercise of power.

	Issues of fact	Issues of values
Specific project	Technical	Conceptual
IS policy	Structural	Symbolic

FIGURE 7.2 Exercise of power by systems professionals.

	User is aware	User is unaware
Systems professional is aware	Mutual negotiation	Professional manipulation
Systems professional is unaware	User resistance	Unintended influence

FIGURE 7.3 | Awareness of power exercise by users and systems professionals.

The users' values and beliefs are also affected by the exercise of power by the systems professionals. Values and beliefs about the use of technology, their role in the world of work, their usefulness and their ability to shape human interaction are some of the ideas that may be shaped by a power exercise. For example, many systems professionals now argue that social interaction, through social networks on the internet and within the organisation have increased with widespread use of information systems. However, many social scientists argue that computing and networks have actually reduced social interaction and increased alienation in the workplace. Individuals in organisations interact less with each other, not more, owing to information systems. When individuals believe that computers and networks have increased socialisation, they are succumbing to a power exercise that is *symbolic* in nature.

The power that the systems professionals exercise may be in a context in which the users are aware of it or are not (see Fig. 7.3). Furthermore, it may be the case that even the systems professionals are consciously not aware of the power they are exercising. When both the users and the professionals are aware of the power exercise, this results in a situation where both have negotiated and come up with a solution that is acceptable to both. In a situation where the user is not aware of the power exercise, this results in manipulation by the professional. The user is led into a decision where he/she is not even aware that other possibilities exist. If the professional is unaware of the power exercise, and the user is, then this results in a situation of resistance from the user. The user refuses to be manipulated but the professional believes he/she is not exercising any power. When either party is unaware of the power exercise, a case of unintended influence is likely to result.

KEY POINT

The exercise of power may be over technical issues or even influence values and beliefs.

Both the users and the systems professionals have to be aware and fully cognizant of any power exercise to have the best possible situation for decision making. The ethical issues may arise in situations where either is not aware.

7.2 SOCIAL ISSUES

In the context of information systems, social issues arise when information systems create conditions that are different from existing social conditions or situations. The new situations introduce a novelty that people and organisations have to adjust to and deal with. They may also introduce new ethical concerns and those of legality.

7.2.1 Workplace Behaviour and Health

7.2.1.1 Resistance and Conformity

It is well known that information systems face resistance from users within organisations. Resistance arises from many reasons:

1. A dislike of the technology,
2. malfunctioning of the technology,

3. fear of new work norms or
4. fear of unknown technology among others.

The resistance may manifest itself in the form of denial to use the technology, active sabotaging of the system, feeding in wrong data, misusing the system, physically shutting down or damaging the system or preventing others from using the system.

Researchers have found that the most prominent reason for resisting information systems is not resistance to change or malfunctioning of technology, as is widely believed, but it is resistance to a shift in the power base of individuals. Individuals in organisations derive power from their position in the hierarchy as well as from the information flows they control. Information systems change their hold over information flows and hence their power roles in the organisation, which leads them to resist change. For example, in an organisation the old system of accounting was to manage accounts at the division level and then send these up to the corporate headquarters for resolution and for the organisation's account closing. The accountants at the division level controlled the information and derived power from this activity. A new system was introduced, which only permitted the division-level accountants to enter data but not do their accounts themselves, as this was done directly at the corporate level. The division-level accountants resisted the system. Their power was eroded because their job roles changed, and they could not decide on the division-level accounts. They did not resist the change owing to faulty or difficult technology, nor did they resist change per se. Their resistance was targeted at their reduced power in the organisational hierarchy. Figure 7.4 shows field staff originally reported to a regional manager who sent data to the head office. With the introduction of a system at the regional office, the field staff started reporting their data to the system thus bypassing the regional manager. The manager loses power and resists the system.

KEY POINT

Resistance to information systems arises mainly due to individuals losing their power base in the organisation.

Politics in an organisation has to do with the changing dynamics of power and power relations. When individuals use technology to change their relative power, they are engaging in acts of politics. For example, with the advent of email as the principal form of internal communication in many organisations, employees have resorted to sending emails selectively to establish their power relations. An employee may send out an email to members of his group to call for a meeting, but leave out one crucial member who is a rival in a power play. This is easily enabled by email systems that can blot out the names of multiple recipients thus preventing the group from knowing who has or has not been informed.

Organisational politics is also affected by information systems when their entire design is influenced by some users or groups to give them access to services and data and not to others.

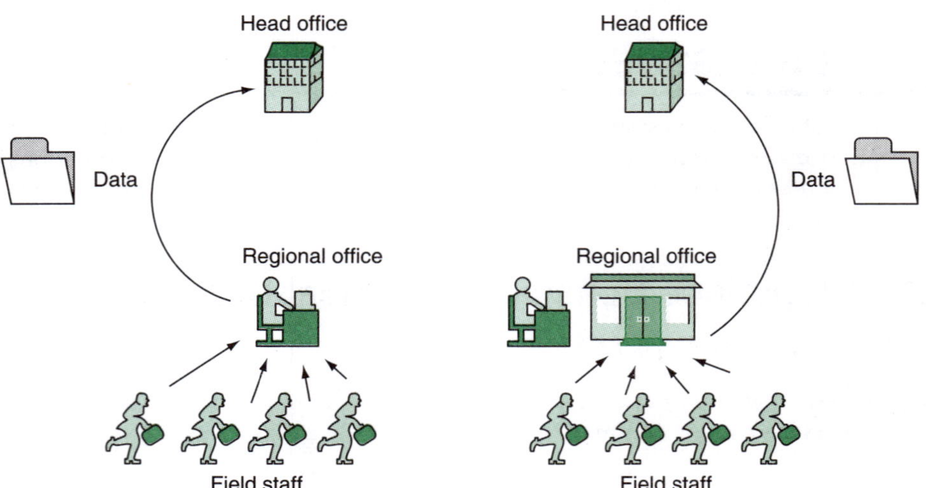

FIGURE 7.4 | Resistance to systems.

For example, in a manufacturing organisation with many divisions, one division was able to influence the design of an enterprise-wide system so that their transaction data was not accessible to the rest of the organisation, whereas they were privy to information about all others. They were able to influence this design on the ground of higher security. This did not sit well with other divisions and they protested the design, bringing the top management in to resolve the issue.

The responsibility and authority structures in the organisation are shaped by information systems. For example, it is well known that use of information systems usually leads to less hierarchical organisations with flatter reporting structures. As compared to the era of purely manual work environments, information systems have effectively reduced an entire level of middle managers and supervisors whose main job was to provide information to the top management on various activities. With automated transaction processing and management information systems, these managers literally had nothing to do and moved out of these roles.

Over the last 50 years, in commercial and public firms across the globe, the increased computerisation has led to the rise of a category of workers known as *knowledge workers*. Knowledge workers work with information technology to search, acquire and interpret information and then use it for planning, decision making and analysis for the organisation. Knowledge workers are typically professionals with advanced college degrees and specialised knowledge of both computers and networking technology, and some domain knowledge such as business, health, manufacturing, services, government administration, etc. This class of workers replaced the older middle managers whose job was simply to create the information needed by the management. Knowledge workers add an extra dimension to that role by interpreting and analysing the information available from information systems.

Currently, knowledge workers in organisations have designations that may be found across the hierarchy and across various divisions and departments. They may be designated as analysts, programmers, program managers, information directors, web managers, etc. Even some managers and executive-level officers perform roles similar to knowledge workers.

Knowledge workers in organisations tend to be younger and more educated than their senior colleagues. With increasing use and teaching of information technology-related subjects in higher education, the workers being employed in modern organisations have a better grasp of information technology and are in a better position to use it to their benefit than their senior colleagues. This has led to a *generational difference* in employees of the same organisation. In India, this phenomenon is particularly visible in government departments where senior employees are usually unaware of or ignorant of information technology, whereas the younger recruits are comfortable with and demand the technology. This generational difference leads to certain problems of acceptance of and resistance to information systems in the departments. Older employees are usually required to give inputs on and also decide on new information systems implementations, and they do so without full knowledge of and trepidation of what they are in for. This has often led to failure of the systems deployment and use.

KEY POINT

Knowledge workers in organisations use IT effectively and integrate it with their everyday work.

7.2.1.2 Changing Work Practices

Information systems in organisations have not only created new kinds of jobs (such as those of knowledge workers, data administrators, web administrators and security analysts) but have also put in place new work practices for all employees. Compared to the older, manual methods of working, modern employees of organisations that use information systems have to do things differently.

1. Employees have to deal with and use more information for their work. This may be in the form of messages, files, data inputs or data manipulation. The variety and volume of information has increased for all employees.
2. Owing to increased monitoring, employees are more careful and disciplined in their workplace. This shows itself in greater productivity and lesser errors in work. Developed countries have far higher productivity gains from using information technology than developing and underdeveloped countries.

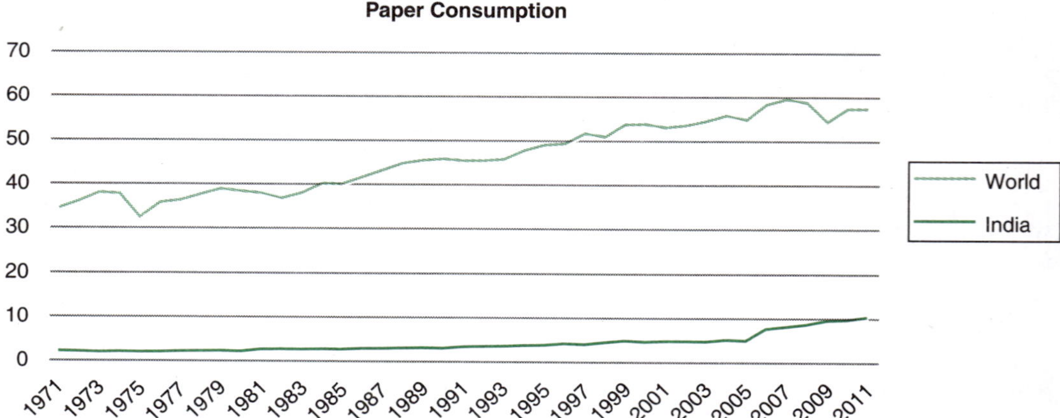

FIGURE 7.5 | Per capita annual paper consumption (in kilogram) since 1971, worldwide and in India.
Source of data: World Resource Institute, earthtrends.wri.org

3. Information systems have increased the volume of work that typical employees do. Owing to their ability to process faster and more efficiently, information systems have forced employees to work faster too. Though information systems have introduced errors and problems of different kinds that have to be resolved, they have overall increased the work-load of most office workers.
4. Information systems have increased paperwork for most offices. Although the promise of computers was that they would reduce paperwork, it is observed worldwide that information systems have increased paperwork in most offices, resulting in massive increases in the sales of printers, copiers and reams of paper (Fig. 7.5). The USA has the highest consumption rate of any country in the world, and accounts for more than 30% of paper consumption worldwide.
5. Workplaces have been rearranged to account for the presence of computers. Offices now consist of cubicles where employees work with their computers, with meeting rooms at the periphery. Cubicles are usually placed in open spaces in which network and electrical wiring can be introduced and maintained easily. They also provide easy access to the computers. These spaces are temperature controlled to ensure smooth functioning of the computers.

Along with changes in the workplace and work practices, information systems have also introduced new health and sickness issues. When employees spend almost all their work time sitting in front of computer screens and using the keyboard and mouse, for years, they suffer from back strain, eye strain, wrist injuries and posture problems. In offices where workspaces are not designed ergonomically, such problems are escalated.

7.2.2 De-Skilling and Alienation

When information systems were first introduced in organisations, it was found that many employees who began working with them lost some of their skills that they used in the manual methods of working. This phenomenon was called *de-skilling* and attracted considerable criticism. An example of de-skilling is as follows:

1. A person who used to manually search and retrieve files had to have skills of reading labels quickly,
2. had to remember where the files were located,

3. had a sense of why the files had been removed and where they could be located,
4. what information certain files had and others did not and
5. how the files had been updated and placed within their location.

These were the details the employee used to conduct his/her job. These were built on a wealth of experience gained while working in the office over a long time. With computerisation of the file system, the employee has to learn a new set of skills, requiring use of the computer to locate the files. This new skill set is far smaller and requires less effort to execute file search than what the employee had to do earlier. There is thus a de-skilling of the employee.

Critics argue that de-skilling affects employees in many ways. Some were so far removed from their earlier jobs that they were not able to function in the new work environment; others felt *alienated* from their workplace, losing their bearings in a workspace that was familiar but now appeared strange. De-skilling also led to job losses for employees who were not able to cope with the new systems of work. Although many organisations took measures to re-train employees and help them acquire new skills, many found the new work less challenging, as it employed less of the skills and knowledge they had acquired over the years.

Alienation also resulted from the employees not interacting with each other as much as before and not doing many such tasks that required meeting and discussing. Working alone for much longer times resulted in their feeling disconnected from the workplace. Alienation created an atmosphere of isolation and disorientation for some workers, with resulting loss in confidence and self-esteem. Information systems had induced these negative feelings in workers who earlier used to feel comfortable in their work environments and worked productively.

7.2.3 Telecommuting

Telecommuting is a way of working where the individual employees do not have to physically come to their place of work. Employees can log into the organisation's computer network from their homes and can access their files and continue work. They can use phones or email or voice-chat facilities to communicate with their co-workers. They can share files, data, information and process instructions over the networks. They can also, if required, have face-to-face meetings with co-workers using video conferencing.

With the availability of high-speed networks in homes, the ability to telecommute has increased. Furthermore, most developing and industrialised cities around the world have problems of commuting, with a lot of time wasted by employees waiting in traffic jams or waiting for public transport. Telecommuting effectively increases time at work because the time used to commute can be used for work, and telecommuting also reduces travel expenses.

Telecommuting has been adopted by many organisations to allow workers to work from home, or away from office, as long as their work is completed according to their goals. Employees have found this to be of value, particularly women employees who have family responsibilities at home, and who can continue to work without having to be physically present in their office. Organisations have evolved various models of telecommuting, including coming in physically on selected days and telecommuting on other days depending on office requirement.

Although telecommuting has many advantages, it has some drawbacks too. Employees who telecommute a lot say that it does alienate them from the workplace as they cannot interact informally with their co-workers; they miss the sense of belonging to a place; they cannot take lunch and coffee breaks with friends; and they cannot participate in unplanned and ad hoc office activities. They often have to work longer hours, as they are at home and they do not want to be seen as 'slacking off'. Many telecommuters also feel that as they are not seen at office by their supervisors and other seniors, they are often overlooked for promotion and career opportunities.

Telecommuting also presents security challenges for the organisation. Since employees may transfer files from the organisation to their remote computers, there is a possibility of data loss or theft or deliberate misuse. Security technologies have now evolved that monitor telecommuting activities vigilantly and prevent misuse and theft.

KEY POINT

Telecommuting relies on IT and networks to allow employees to work from home and not come into office.

7.2.4 E-Waste

Electronic goods such as computers, mobile phones, music players and game devices usually have a short life cycle of a few years after which they are either discarded or traded-in by users. In the case of computers, the recycle rate is about 3–5 years, that is, organisational users upgrade their personal computers or laptops after this period; they either discard or trade-in the old computers. With the tremendous growth and evolution in the computer hardware industry, organisations and individual users are under pressure to acquire and use the latest computers that are invariably faster and have greater capacities than the older ones. The discarded old computers and devices turn into e-waste whose proper disposal poses a huge problem.

E-waste refers to all categories of electronic products that are discarded and have to be treated as waste. A bulk of the products is constructed with materials that are toxic and cause pollution when disposed of, untreated, in nature. Industrialised and developed nations typically treat all types of waste by burying it in huge pits in the ground called landfills. These landfills are created at places away from human habitation, where the pollution created by them will not be harmful to humans. Some waste products, which can be recycled, are separated out. For instance, carbon-based wastes can be reused as fuel. E-waste too is often sent to landfills. However, owing to the massive quantities of waste being generated, landfills too are not a solution.

Developed nations export, legally or illegally, e-waste to underdeveloped or less developed countries, where the waste is recycled or disposed of. Underdeveloped countries take the e-waste thus exported as, it costs them nothing, and then can extract minerals such as copper and iron from the waste and make profits. This process, however, is fraught with problems. In most underdeveloped and developing countries, e-waste disposal is neither an organised activity nor well regulated. Waste disposal is done in an ad hoc and unscientific manner, causing massive environmental pollution. The pollution affects the health of the workers employed by waste disposal agencies. Some examples of these health effects are listed in Table 7.1.

India is among the nations that receive e-waste from developed nations. According to the Centre for Science and Environment (CSE), India imports almost 50,000 tonnes of e-waste illegally. Besides illegal e-waste import, India itself generates e-waste. In 2007, the country generated almost 330,000 tonnes of e-waste. The CSE estimates that hardly 10% of the total e-waste produced and imported is properly recycled; the rest is disposed of by ad hoc means, adding to pollution of a very high order. China is also among the countries that receive e-waste from the developed world. The map, depicted in Fig. 7.6, indicates the major regions in India and China where e-waste is accumulated.

Table 7.1 | Health Effects of Some E-Waste Pollutants

E-Waste Pollutant	Health Effect
Lead in printed circuit boards and monitors	Damage to the central nervous system and brain development of children
Cadmium in electronic components such as resistors	Neural damage and accumulation in organs like liver and kidneys
Mercury in circuit boards and switches	Damage to brain; kills fish and other creatures living in polluted water bodies
Plastics and polyvinyl chloride (PVC) in cables, released as dioxins when burnt	Affects the reproductive system, the immune system and regulatory hormones
Beryllium found in computer motherboards	Carcinogenic – cancer causing, and also causes skin diseases

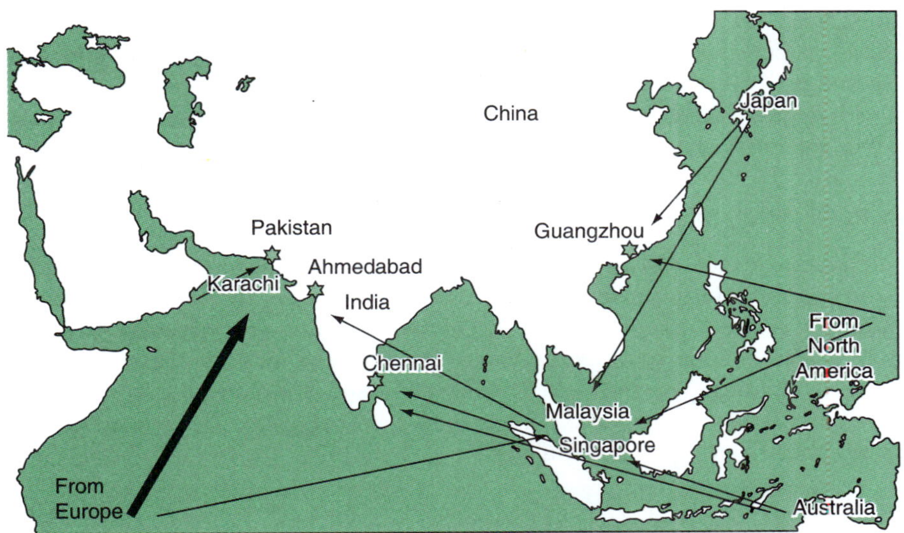

FIGURE 7.6 | E-waste receiving cities in India and China.
Source: UNEP.

In 1992, the Basel Convention was formulated in Europe to regulate e-waste exports. This convention made it mandatory for European countries to recycle as much of their own waste as possible and export only those that could be managed by less developed countries. The convention was not ratified by the USA, which is one of the largest producers of e-waste in the world.

One side-effect of the Basel Convention and its later amendments was that it became very expensive for countries in Europe to dispose of their e-waste in comparison to its export. For example, in the Netherlands, it is four times more expensive to dispose of trash legally than to export it illegally. Following the imposition of controls on exports in Europe, an illegal trade flourished.

7.2.4.1 Managing E-Waste

Many organisations have evolved policies to manage and control e-waste. These procedures are intended to control e-waste internally and as well as reduce the organisation's contribution to global e-waste streams.

Managing Acquisition

Vendors of hardware products often insist that users upgrade their computers and peripheral equipment every 3–5 years to take advantage of the new technologies available. However, firms have found that not all components need to be upgraded, and indeed, with some forethought, have stalled acquisitions by the following methods:

1. Acquire components that are predicted to have a life more than 3–5 years.
2. At the end of the life cycle, move components to less demanding environments where they can be used further.
3. Re-install software on computers that prolongs their useful life (e.g. install special configurations of open source software on old laptops and desktops to enable them to function with new hardware peripherals).
4. Enable users to share resources that are functional and remove unusable ones.

Managing acquisitions requires a careful control of the uses of computing facilities. For example, many e-commerce operations may require high-performance computing that is possible on the latest hardware and software. However, many routine functions can be run on older hardware and also on shared computers. Furthermore, IT managers actively seek out computer processors and peripherals, such as printers, which can be used for longer periods, more than 10 years, with frequent servicing and maintenance. When printers break down and are not serviceable, they are removed and the remaining ones are shared among employees.

Centralised Computing

Many firms have started centralising their computing resources using a technology called *virtualisation*. Using this technology, most of the computing resources of the organisation are consolidated under one central computing environment and users and departments can access these resources through their internal networks. Virtualisation allows older computers to be included in the central computing. This technology reduces e-waste as it requires less number of computers to be purchased as servers, and it also allows older computers to be included in the new configuration, thus extending their useful life.

Use of Renewable and Recyclable Materials

Many computer and device manufacturers have realised the value of using renewable materials and are actively including them in their design. Such materials allow safe disposal after their useful life. Furthermore, manufacturers are also publicising procedures for recycling products in an environment-friendly manner.

7.3 DARK SIDE OF IT

Though IT has powered much economic progress, with the presence and continued growth of the massive IT industry worldwide (which was estimated to be about $2.5 trillion in 2016), there is also a "dark side" of it, much of it resulting from unintended consequences of using IT. In this section we examine three aspects of this dark side - technostress, misuse of IT and the impact of technostress.

7.3.1 Technostress

Technostress refers to the work pressure experienced by employees owing to the increased use of IT. The causes of the increased stress are many.

1. **Multi-tasking:** With increased use of digital technologies for collaboration and sharing, employees find that they have to do many things at the same time. It is quite typical for those working on computers in offices to have multiple screens open on their desktop: they may have to switch from reading and sending emails to responding to messages to working on a spreadsheet to responding to collaborators on a platform like Slack. Working on many tasks or multi-tasking creates technostress, as employees have to change their focus and re-focus on many different tasks at a rapid pace.
2. **Flextime:** Employees often do not follow a 9-to-5 work routine in offices. Flextime refers to having the freedom to start and end work in office at one's convenience. However, owing to IT communications, flextime now means that people access their work from anywhere, at any time. The earlier era of not doing work before 9 am or after 5 pm is not applicable anymore as work can be done all the time. This has enabled co-workers and managers in organisations to assume that employees are available any time, either in or out of office, and hence demand responses to their messages and work requests. This induces technostress in employees as they do not find any time in which to not be responsive to work requests.
3. **Changing Technology:** With the ever-changing technology landscape and push by the technology vendors, employees have to constantly learn new applications and about new devices. New technologies bring new interfaces, new functionalities and new security

measures without much explanation. Employees usually have to figure things out on their own which leads to technostress.

4. **Addiction:** Many employees show symptoms of being addicted to certain technologies. Addiction implies that they are so habituated to using the technology that they suffer trauma if removed from it. Use of email, for instance, is addictive and studies have shown that employees check email while at home, while commuting to work and while on vacation. They are addicted to email as they are unable to stay away from it while not working. Others show addiction symptoms in the use of social media like Facebook and WhatsApp. They use these applications during work, even though many firms have restricted or banned their use at work. These addictions cause technostress.
5. **Digital Distraction:** It refers to a digital event that diverts attention away from the work at hand. Digital events could be notifications on a mobile phone, pop-ups on a computer screen, messages on a system tray, or other visual or aural cues. Digital distraction is possible in the workplace, or outside the workplace, where the distraction happens when people are diverted from their current pre-occupation. Research shows that there are many causes for digital distraction - employees feel compelled to multi-task and respond to all message on the screens; some are addicted to social media sites and are unable to distance themselves; many wear devices, such as smart watches, that force them to sense or feel notifications; and there is a massive overload of information for most people, that is obtained from many different sources. This distraction feeds technostress.

7.3.2 Misuse of IT

Organisations find that employees often misuse IT, whether intentionally or unintentionally. Misuse is understood as using the IT resources in a manner that is contrary to the organisation's policies or the organisation's interests.

1. **Intentional Misuse:** Employees retrieve organisational data and give it away to outsiders, sometimes for monetary gain. Malicious use also includes releasing malware in the organisation's networks. Another intentional misuse is of uncovering confidential data from inside and giving or selling it to rivals.
2. **Naive or Unintentional Misuse:** This category of misuse happens when employees are unaware of the organisation's policies or when they are unaware of the consequences of their actions. One common type of misuse is when employees install software on their organisation's laptops on their own, without asking for permission or informing the IT personnel. This is usually done to improve work efficiency. Such downloads can lead to malware infections and security breaches.

Another common type of unintentional misuse is when employees reveal the organisation's details or particulars to outsiders without the intention of doing harm. For example, employees who have access to personnel records may reveal to outsiders salary information for particular positions and levels without knowing or being conscious of this being against the organisation's policy.

7.3.3 Impact of Technostress

Stress induced by excessive and addictive use of IT leads to loss of productivity of employees and also impacts their ability to be innovative. Employees tend to respond to information impulsively and hurriedly. This leads to uninformed and hasty decisions. It also prevents people from being able to think about what they are doing, which is essential for being creative. Technostress has a negative effect on the well-being and balanced life of employees. This has often led to people leaving their jobs, as they cannot deal with the excessive stress.

Misuse of IT can lead to financial loss - sometimes from lawsuits following use of pirated or illegal software. Some firms have also faced public exposure and reputation loss for misuse of

IT by the employees. Misuse also leads to violation of technical integrity of systems – stemming from malware and unauthorised software. Sometimes employees who are addicted to social media sites land up posting company information publicly or make improper comments on issues that the company is not concerned with.

Caselet Technostress at Amazon.com

In an article that appeared in the New York Times in 2015, the work culture at the famous e-commerce pioneer, Amazon.com, was critiqued. The article described the highly action- and results-oriented culture that thrived on both hard work and strong competition. This culture called for, and employees agreed to, monitoring and measurement of all activities. For example, in Amazon's warehouses, the packers who placed purchased items in packaging for shipment, were monitored to know how many boxes they packed every hour. Employees within offices too were monitored for their performance, mainly based on the success of the project they were working on.

Many employees felt motivated to work continuously, whether at home or on vacation. One employee reported that she worked for four days and nights continuously, without sleep, to achieve her targets. She even employed other workers, from outside the company, to help with her own work and paid them on her own. Another employee reported that even when she went on a vacation to a holiday resort, she used the free wifi available to get work done.

Amazon relies extensively on data and metrics that report on all aspects of employees' work. One employee had requested flextime, with the flexibility to come in early to work and leave early, to attend to her newborn baby. She used to work from home after leaving office. However, her metrics were not up to the mark and her co-workers complained. Owing to the stress of the job she left the company.

The data collected on employees' work and performance was used to decide on promotions and annual reviews. Some employees reported that they were given dozens of pages of data, tables of metrics on their work, and were often asked by their management to explain why certain numbers were at their level. Employees had to be fully familiar with the tables and data and be ready to respond to the queries, without having the option to respond later. This increased work-pressure on them.

The work culture at Amazon encouraged employees to put in 80-hour work weeks, which is double what is considered normal (40 hours per week). This massive amount of work was done voluntarily, as many employees in the article mentioned, and they wanted to participate in the go-to culture that enabled them remain highly competitive and innovative. Other writers have commented that the work culture at Amazon.com is likely to become the norm in other modern firms as well, demanding massive effort and competitiveness from employees, usually at no extra pay, and complete dedication to the firm's values.

Chapter Glossary

Ethics Moral rules and codes of behaviour for social engagement.

Privacy The condition of being secluded from scrutiny by electronic means.

Workplace monitoring To observe or record the behaviour of employees in their place of work through electronic devices.

Panopticon An eight-sided building structure, with rooms along the periphery and a central tower. The structure is designed to ensure that those inside the rooms are always visible to anyone in the tower.

Power Individual power refers to the ability of persons to influence the thinking or behaviour of others.

Knowledge workers Employees of organisations who work extensively with information technology.

De-skilling Loss of some manual skills of employees, as they start using information technology in their workplace.

Alienation The sense of loss within the workplace or community, resulting in isolation and disaffection, which is created by information technology.

Telecommuting Working from home using a telecommunication link to the office.

E-waste Discarded electronic components or devices.

Technostress Work pressure experienced by employees due to the increased and pervasive use of IT.

Digital distraction Digital events that divert attention of people from the work at hand.

Review Questions

1. Give two reasons why privacy is important for individuals in organisations?
2. How is privacy being affected by information technology in modern organisations?
3. How does workplace monitoring affect workers?
4. What is the concept of the Information Panopticon? Do you see examples of it in modern organisations?
5. What are the different kinds of power that systems professionals exert over users?
6. Why do individuals resist the introduction of information systems in organisations?
7. Why is generational difference an issue in organisations that use information systems?
8. What are some of the changes in work practices introduced by information technology?
9. What is de-skilling? How is it introduced by information technology?
10. What are the advantages and disadvantages of telecommuting?
11. What is e-waste? Why is it a problem?
12. How can e-waste be managed in organisations?
13. What is technostress and how is it caused?
14. What constitutes misuse of IT?

Research Questions

1. Read the case at the beginning of the chapter and identify what was the original intention of video surveillance at JSPL. What was the surveillance later used for? Using the theory in the chapter, identify three monitoring and privacy issues.
2. Explore examples of privacy loss in organisations due to information technology. Are these seen as problems by the employees? Is privacy loss considered a problem created by the employers?
3. Explore in your region how many organisations are aware of the problem of e-waste? If they are then what are they doing about it?
4. Have you ever been subjected to an exercise of power, as depicted in Fig. 7.2? What was your experience? Search the internet for descriptions of other incidents like the one you have experienced.
5. Find employees of organisations who may have experienced technostress, through excessive use of IT. Are they addicted to any sites? Do they experience digital distraction? How are they coping with this technostress?

Further Reading

1. Pasha, A. (2010) Wi-fi video surveillance system for overseeing projects, *Express Computer*.
2. Rosenthal, E. (2009) Smuggling Europe's waste to poorer countries. *The New York Times*.
3. The e-waste industry in India: CSE exposes what lies beneath. To know more about the article, visit Press release on Centre for Science and Environment website at: http://www.cseindia.org (accessed on November 2010).
4. Markus, M.L. and Bjorn-Anderson, N. (1987) Power over users: Its exercise by systems professionals, *Communications of the Association for Computing Machinery*, **30**(6), 498–504.
5. An article *Spears hospital to punish staff* in BBC News, 16 March 2008 is available at: http://news.bbc.co.uk/2/hi/entertainment/7299510.stm (accessed on November 2010).
6. Tarafdar, M., Darey, J., Turel, O., & Gupta, A. (2015), The Dark side of Information Technology. *MIT Sloan Management Review*, **56**(2), 61.
7. Agrawal, P., Sahana, H.S. and De, R. (2017), Digital distraction, in *Proceedings of the 10th International Conference*

on Theory and Practice of Electronic Governance, New Delhi, pp. 191–194.

8. Duffy, M. (2008) Vatican monitoring workplace slackers, introduces swipe cards for staff, *Digital Journal*. The article is available at: http://digitaljournal.com/article/262051 (accessed on November 2010).
9. Crampton, S.M. (2001) Employee monitoring: Privacy in the workplace, *all Business*. The article is available at: http://www.allbusiness.com/human-resources/workplace-health-safety/699768-1.html (accessed on November 2010).
10. Lewin, T. (1995) Chevron settles sexual harrassment charges, *The New York Times*. The article is available at: http://www.nytimes.com/1995/02/22/us/chevron-settles-sexual-harassment-charges.html (accessed on November 2010).

CHAPTER 8

Managing Green IT and Smart Cities

Learning Objectives

After completing this chapter, you will be able to:

- Understand the meaning and importance of Green IT
- Understand the concepts of Greenhouse gases, global warming and carbon footprint
- Learn how IT systems can be designed to be green
- Learn about some ways in which green IT practices can be followed in organisations
- Get an understanding of smart cities
- Understand what types of sensing and measuring is done for managing smart cities
- Learn how traffic, the environment, buildings, living and governance are managed in smart cities

There is a growing and urgent need to control the environmental consequences of industrialisation and the growing use of IT. Greenhouse gases lead to global warming and potential environmental destruction. IT has two roles in green practices - in the use and making of IT artefacts, and in the use of IT for greening. Green practices are followed both for hardware and software design, to reduce energy and resource consumption. Use of IT in organisations can also follow green practices. IT can be used in the entire value chain of activities in firms to monitor and control greening.

Smart cities are defined as urban areas that use ICT to improve living conditions of citizens. Historically urban areas have grown with increasing industrialisation, leading to population growth and increased demand for resources. The facilities of smart cities include sensing and measuring of various parameters, such as traffic density, air quality, water quality, land use, and so on. The sensed data is used for facilities such as smart transportation – managing traffic congestion; smart environment – managing water, controlling pollution, and managing energy; smart buildings – controlling the energy and resources in buildings; smart living – enabling citizens to participate in collecting data and providing information on the living spaces; and smart governance – where governments draw on citizens for providing data and information on services.

MIND MAP OF CHAPTER TOPICS

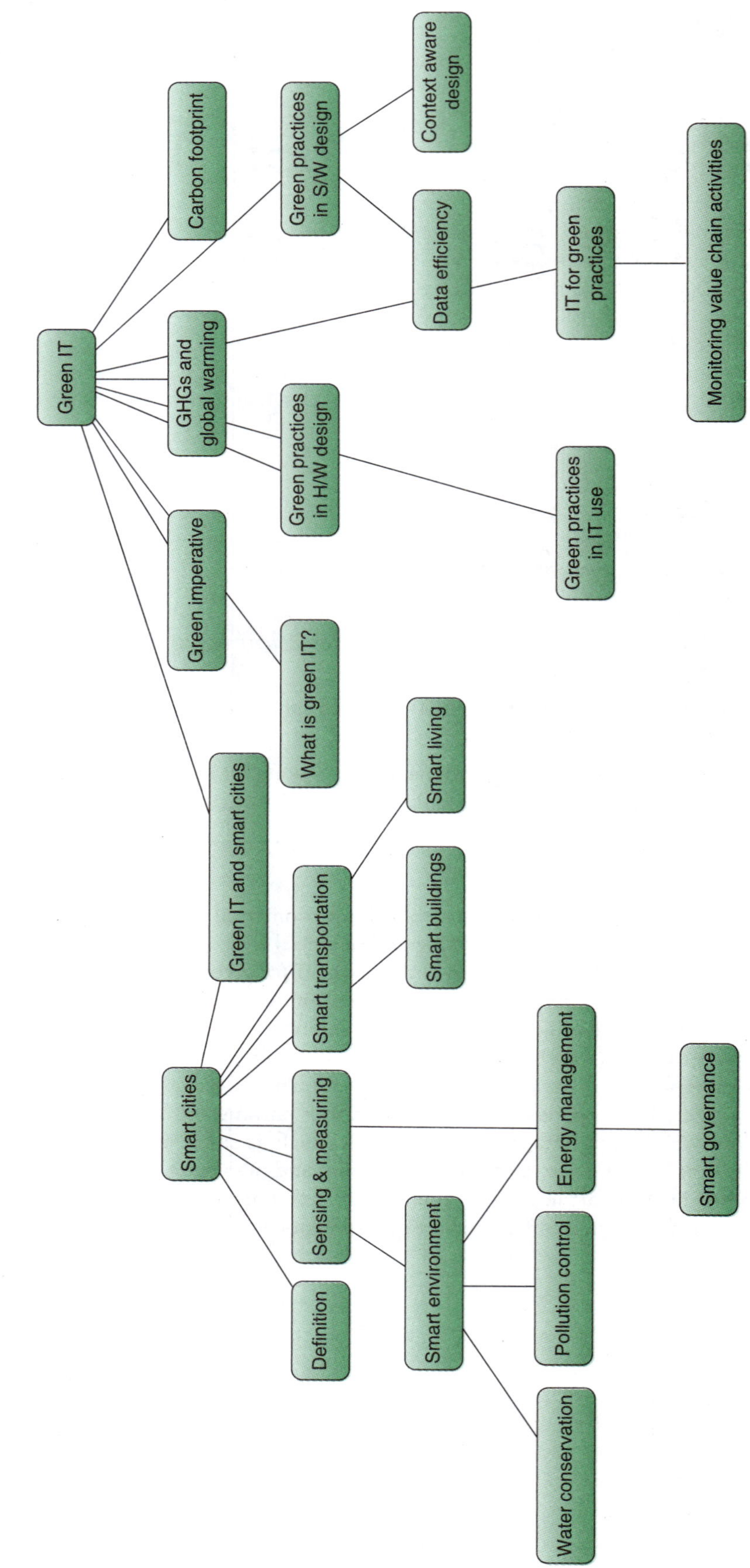

The telecommunication industry in India stood at Rs 2346 billion (USD 39.1 billion) in June 2014. This represented the combined income of more than a dozen firms that provided wired and wireless phone access across India. This is a highly competitive industry where firms had to compete against each other to gain market share and also had to ensure that they constantly sought and enlisted new subscribers in new markets.

Aircel was one of the telecommunication firms that provided wired and wireless, or mobile, access to consumers in many states in India. It operated in 18 "circles" that covered regions across more than 15 states. Headquartered in Chennai, Aircel had about 7% of the of the market share amongst mobile phone service providers in India. These service providers operated mainly in the GSM and CDMA protocols. With this market share, Aircel was ranked seventh in India. In 2016, Aircel merged with a competitor, though it continued to retain its identity.

Since the late 2000s, Aircel had added many services to its portfolio, including - 2G and 3G services, broadband wireless access, Long Term Evolution (LTE), also known as 4G, and also value-added services such as virtual private networks. Aircel had driven this innovation in service and product offerings by forming partnerships both for accessing capital and new technologies.

As Aircel grew its customer base across many geographic regions it felt the need to consolidate its data centres. Aircel had grown in a decentralised manner, where different circles had their own database applications and datacentres, with the consequence that there were problems of inter-operability between them. Since each data centre maintained its own policies, there was no common policy through which data could be accessed and maintained. Further, consolidation to a common data centre would help create redundant capacity that could help with its expansion plans.

A common data centre entails creating a massive computing and data storage facility that can host petabytes of data and also respond to millions of data transactions per day. Whenever any of the millions of customers of Aircel made a phone call, the wireless networks switched the call to the destination location to enable the connection, and data about the call - when it was made, to whom it was made, from where, for what duration, etc. - were recorded. Thus each call created a record that was stored in a database. The data centre stored and processed all the transaction data, keeping track of each customer's plan (the voice and data contract the customer had), the transaction costs, the usage levels and other information that went into creating the bill that the customer had to pay. Data centres had to operate in real-time to record and track all transactions and had to ensure that they remained available 24 × 7, every day of the year.

Data centres are important facilities for the telecommunications firms, as their entire business rests on them. A typical data centre will have thousands of items of networking equipment, storage disks, digital displays, CPUs, racks and cables. The equipment is closely arranged, in rows and stacks, to conserve space and to have convenient cable connections. Such dense arrangements cause the rooms to heat up as there are many servers and computers located together. The electric consumption of such centres is massive, often compared to the electricity consumption of a small city. Electricity is used for both running the computing equipment as well as for air-conditioners and coolers. The electricity supply has to be reliable, with adequate backup available if any of the power sources fail.

Data centres are often designed to conform to international standards. One set of standards is provided by the Uptime Institute (uptimeinstitute.com) of the USA. This institute rates data centres from Tier 1 to Tier 4. These ratings are based on the availability or uptime guarantees of the centres. For instance, Tier 4 centres guarantee 99.95% uptime, thus stating that they will not be available for only about 26 minutes in a year. Higher ratings attract customers who want guarantees of availability at higher prices. Higher ratings also mean that the data centres have to ensure backup power is adequately available, which uses higher energy.

At a rough estimate, about 60% of a data centre's energy requirements are for cooling. It was thus imperative that Aircel designs and constructs the data centre in a manner that would reduce its energy costs, and also help it create an image of being socially responsible. Aircel adopted a number of measures to reduce its energy consumption, and some of these are as follows.

At the data centre, Aircel built an innovative earth air tunnel (EAT) system to provide cool air for the air-conditioning unit (which is needed to control the temperature within server rooms that tend to heat up). This system consists of four 60-metre pipes buried about 5 metres below the ground through which air is pulled out for cooling the air-conditioning units. Since the temperature below the ground is invariably cooler than the air temperature at the surface, the cool air reduces both the water and electricity needed to cool the room. Since the data centre was located in Gurgaon, where surface temperatures during the summer months could hover around 40 degrees centigrade, and sometimes exceed 45 degrees, the contrast of 26 degrees centigrade for the air in the EAT system helped greatly.

The building to host the 50,000 square foot data centre was designed to have rain-water harvesting. Rain water was directed from the roof to underground percolation pits. Since the Gurgaon region receives over 500 mm of rainfall in a year, the rain-water harvesting system could receive about 500 kilolitres of water. This water was then used as a cooling system that also helped to reduce the air-conditioning load on the centre.

The designers used light-emitting diode (LED) lighting to reduce the energy consumption further. Such lighting uses less energy than filament-based lamps or compact-fluorescent lamps (CFL) to produce the same amount of visible light. Further, sensors were built in the building that would enable the lights to be switched on only when there were people present in the room or region. The design also included solar water heaters on the roof of the building, to ensure that energy for heating water was also kept to a minimum.

Once completed the data centre allowed Aircel to rapidly deploy its services to its various regions. According to the CIO, Ravinder Jain, they enabled 8 circles to start using the data centre services in less than 2 months. They relied on a service-oriented-architecture concept, where the peripheral regions could access services from the central data centre on an as-needed basis and over digital networks. Aircel was also able to reduce the total carbon emissions from its centers by 400 tons per year. In addition, owing to rain-water harvesting it was able to save 500 kilolitres of water and re-charge groundwater.

Aircel won recognition and awards for its green IT initiative. It also created a highly efficient and scalable data centre that it planned to replicate in other regions to meet its growing market demand.

Sources:

http://www.ibef.org/industry/telecommunications.aspx (Viewed on 22-8-2014)
http://www.wipro.com/Documents/CaseStudyforaircellpage.pdf

8.1 INTRODUCTION: THE GREEN IMPERATIVE

Usage of computers and networking technology requires energy to both make the devices and run them. As computer technology use in business, government and society has grown, so has the consumption of energy. Energy consumption usually entails burning fossil fuels that add to greenhouse gases in the atmosphere, most notably carbon dioxide. It is estimated that information technology contributes almost 2–2.5% of carbon dioxide emissions across the globe. Manufacturing of computer equipment, and its subsequent disposal at the end of its useful life cycle, also entails use and disposal of hazardous materials that lead to environmental pollution.

Governments have recognised the threat of unrestrained and uncontrolled carbon emissions and have formed guidelines to control emissions and pollution. The Kyoto Protocol, established in 1997 by the United Nations, recommended stringent guidelines on restraining carbon emissions by certain developed countries that had agreed to implement the protocol. Though not binding on developing countries, such as India, the protocol helped influence thinking on improving energy efficiency, reducing deforestation and seeking alternative energy sources. Though the term of the Kyoto Protocol has expired, an extension, known as the Doha Amendment, to the Kyoto Protocol has been proposed.

Such initiatives have encouraged green practices in all sectors of the economy, including information technology. Many firms have taken steps to understand their energy consumption patterns, with regard to their IT usage, and have implemented steps to "go green." There are economic advantages of going green, in addition to those of acting responsibly. In the realm of information technology, going green means using technology in an environment friendly manner and also using IT to manage carbon emissions. These ideas are discussed in the sections below.

KEY POINT

There is a growing need to control carbon emissions, including while using IT.

8.2 GREENHOUSE GASES AND GLOBAL WARMING

Greenhouse gases (GHGs) are gases such as carbon dioxide and methane that absorb infra-red radiation in the earth's atmosphere, thereby trapping heat and increasing the atmospheric temperature. Typically, sun's energy is transmitted to earth through visible light, ultra-violet radiation and infra-red radiation, along with other forms of radiation. Almost 30% of the energy thus received by the earth is reflected back to space from clouds, ice and other reflective surfaces. The remaining energy is absorbed by water and land and radiated back into the atmosphere. This radiated energy is absorbed by the earth's atmosphere which heats up the earth. The earth retains an average net temperature of 15 degrees centigrade, resulting from the inflow and outflow of energy. However, if there is an increase in GHGs, the atmosphere absorbs more energy and the overall temperature rises. This is known as global warming.

GHGs are produced by industrial activity. Since the beginning of the industrial revolution in Europe in the early 1800s and its subsequent spread around the globe, GHGs have consistently increased. Some of the prominent activities that produce GHGs are - production of electrical energy by burning fossil fuels such as coal, petrol and diesel; burning of fossil fuels for transportation; and manufacturing. Most industrial activity contributes to an increase in carbon dioxide. Since carbon dioxide remains in the atmosphere for a relatively long duration, it has the strongest contribution to global warming. Figure 8.1 shows the rise of carbon dioxide in the atmosphere, as measured on an island in the Pacific Ocean in the period 1958–2008.

Global warming is now attributed to changing climatic patterns around the world. There is substantial threat of ocean levels rising owing to the melting of ice in the polar regions. Many parts of the world are experiencing extreme weather conditions, something not known or seen earlier. Owing to changes in the climate, local habitats are also changing, causing extinctions in plant and animal species that are not adapted for these new conditions. Some scientists estimate that in the Asian region there will be substantial changes in rainfall patterns, and consequently the availability of potable and agricultural water; this will cause major geo-political upheavals, migrations and re-settlements.

KEY POINT

Industrial activity increases production of GHGs that cause global warming, which may lead to severe environmental problems.

Owing to the serious threat posed by global warming, many nations have adopted and are promoting "green" methods of manufacturing that contribute less to GHGs. An important

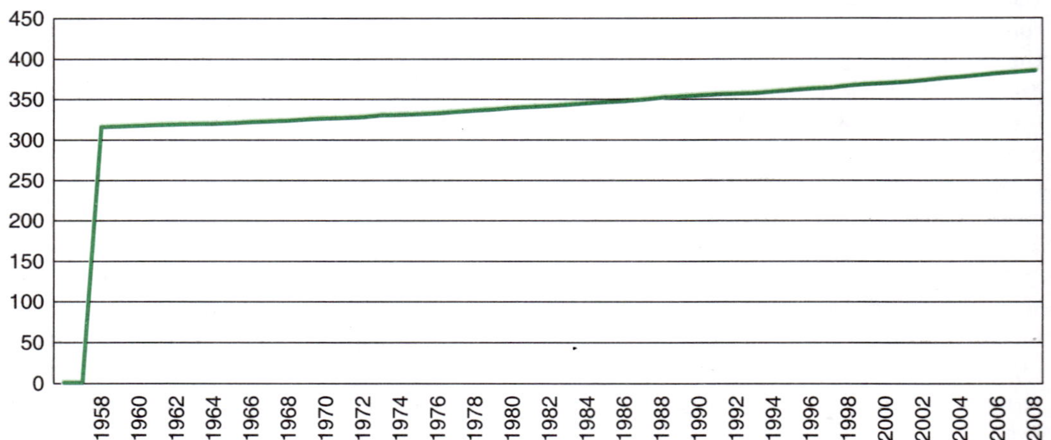

FIGURE 8.1 The increase in the quantity of carbon dioxide present in the atmosphere as measured in Hawaii, USA. The measure is parts of carbon dioxide per million by volume of atmosphere. The data shows the average across all months in the years 1958–2008.

Source: Carbon Dioxide Information Analysis Center http://cdiac.esd.ornl.gov/trends/co2/sio-keel.html

aspect of this is being able to measure the amount of carbon dioxide that is being released to the atmosphere. This is known as the carbon footprint.

8.3 CARBON FOOTPRINT

The carbon footprint of an organisation, or a city or a nation, is defined by the amount of GHGs produced to support human activities in a year. The definition is modified to include GHG emissions by people, events or products. Since carbon dioxide is usually the GHG of interest, as it has the most important impact on the environment, the measure of carbon emissions is most important and called the carbon footprint.

The measure of the carbon footprint is in kilograms of carbon emissions per year. For example, an organisation like Aircel may produce a few thousand tons of GHGs per year (where a reduction of 400 tons per year will be a significant decrease). Though this metric is easy to understand and state, it is not easy to measure. The carbon or GHG emission may be something that emanates from a process within the organisation and can be directly measured, or it may be related to an activity outside the organisation, such as generation of electricity, and not directly measurable. Many different methods and techniques have now evolved that help to measure the carbon footprint.

The carbon footprint for a product, say a computer, is calculated by assessing the energy requirements to make each part; the energy requirements to transport the parts from different places in the world; the energy required to assemble and process the assembled computer; the energy required to package, transport and install the computer; and finally, the energy consumed by the computer while working. Components of computers, say the mother board or the keyboard or monitor, are themselves composed of hundreds of components that are sourced through an extensive supply chain. Calculating the carbon footprint for the computer requires that the footprint for each component is also calculated and added to total for the computer as a whole. Processes such as painting or assembling also require energy, which may be obtained from fossil fuel sources, and thus these activities also contribute to the total carbon footprint. It will be clear that the calculation is difficult and detailed, requiring detailed knowledge of all components, their sub-components, etc., and how they are made. To help with this task, there are now many agencies and organisations including some online ones (such as those available at carbonfootprint.com and timeforchange.org).

KEY POINT

The carbon footprint of an organisation or product is measured by evaluating the impact of the complete set of activities and components deployed.

8.4 WHAT IS GREEN IT?

Green IT refers to the policies and practices that firms follow to manage IT to comply with green norms. Typically, for a firm that mainly uses IT for its business, for making products or for providing services, green IT practices would involve using IT in such a manner as to reduce carbon emissions or to use IT to monitor and manage carbon or other polluting emissions. So, for firms there are two aspects of green IT practices:

1. Use IT efficiently to comply with green norms.
2. Use IT to ensure other firm activities confirm to green norms.

Firms that are involved with making information technology products or those who provide information technology services, have to consider additional aspects of green IT. Design of IT products can follow green practices and this includes design of both hardware and software. The IT artefacts produced in this manner are thus compliant with green norms and the firms can assure their customers that environmentally sound processes have been used. Such an approach contributes to the bottom line of the firm and also to its reputation as a responsible firm.

KEY POINT

Green IT refers to efficient and green use of IT and relying on IT for ensuring green practices.

8.5 GREEN PRACTICES IN HARDWARE DESIGN AND MANUFACTURE

Information technology hardware goes through the same cycle of design, manufacture and disposal as many other products. The steps include design, manufacturing, packaging, transportation, usage, and disposal or reuse. Here IT hardware refers to products such as laptops, tablets, keyboards, mice, monitors, cables, processor boards, network routers, interface cards, etc. All these products are used with others to create the entire IT infrastructure. All these products are produced by a variety of manufacturers under different brands or as unbranded component goods.

At the design stage the artefact is envisaged with all the later stages - of manufacturing, packaging, transportation, use and reuse - in mind. Typically prototypes are produced that indicate what will be the environmental impact of all the later stages. The materials required, the energy required to transport them, whether the components are considered to be damaging to the environment during disposal (such as lead, cadmium, mercury, polyvinyl chlorides, polybrominated diphenyl ethers, and arsenic), and the energy required to assemble or make them constitute the environmental impact that can be assessed from the prototype. Designers can build in components that reduce or minimise such impacts, thus ensuring that the design is green.

IT product components are manufactured across the globe. Individual parts may be designed in one country, made and packaged in another, then branded and sold from a third. The entire supply chain contributes to the environmental impact of the product. To estimate the carbon footprint of an IT product it is important to add up the footprint of the component products, and then the carbon emissions from assembling the final product. The United Nations Environment Programme (UNEP) estimated in 2004 that to make a desktop computer 240 kg of fossil fuels, 22 kg of chemicals, including hazardous chemicals, and 1.5 tonnes of water are consumed. Burning of fossil fuels to make one desktop computer amounts to about 600 kg, at a very rough estimate, of carbon emissions.

KEY POINT

Green practices in hardware manufacturing require control over all aspects, including the design, transport and assembly of all components.

Manufacturing IT components also entails packaging them for shipping, then removing the packaging for assembly into other parts. This too adds to the carbon footprint. Packaging material is often designed for reuse and also components are sized to reduce the amount of packaging required. Some practices, such as not providing any printed manuals, but enabling them to be downloaded from a web site, also reduce weight and energy use.

8.6 GREEN PRACTICES IN SOFTWARE DESIGN

For any given hardware, such as a hard-disk or central processing unit (CPU), the operating system has a significant role in determining how efficiently the hardware is used. Software design has to include aspects of power and energy management for green IT practices.

Designers often consider software systems to be in two states - *active* and *idle*. In the active state, the software performs an activity, such as computing a spreadsheet, downloading a file, or playing a music file. In this state, the software relies on hardware units such as the CPU, the hard-disk or the compact disk player to run. In the idle state, software systems are ready for use but are not actually being used. A browser that is currently now rendering a new page or downloading data is idle, and may be ready for becoming active. The key issue for design of the software is to ensure that the energy used by the hardware is most in the active state and least in the idle state.

Computer scientists have developed many ways in which software can be designed to do its tasks more efficiently. It is known, for instance, that for many kinds of search tasks, where the software has to search through a bunch of numbers or text, some algorithms are more efficient than others. Such algorithms rely on certain techniques that take the least number of steps to come up with the answer. Such algorithms turn out to be energy efficient also, as they impose a lesser burden on the processors in the active state.

Another method for achieving efficiency in computation is by using multiple processors. Modern computers are built with dual-core, quad-core or octa-core processors, which means they have 2, 4, or 8 CPUs built into one CPU core unit. Such processors have the capability to take an active task and process it in parallel over all the CPU units. In such cases, the software has to provide multi-threading capabilities, where each thread is a processing activity that can run independently of the others, and in parallel on a different CPU. Multi-threading reduces the total energy requirement of the task, as the activity is shared by more than one CPU. Had the task run on one CPU alone, it would have taken much longer to complete. Besides, the energy used by one processor to run the entire task would be invariably more than the energy taken by multiple processors working on a part of the task.

Table 8.1 | Power Consumption by a Hard Disk Drive in Different States

Hard Drive State	Power Consumption (Watts)	% of Total Consumption
Idle	0.575 W	7%
Standby	0.173 W	2%
Read	2.78 W	35%
Write	2.19 W	27%
Copy	2.29 W	29%

8.6.1 Data Efficiency

Reading and writing data from and to secondary storage consumes a lot of energy. Software can be designed to minimise this energy consumption. Hard disks are widely used to store and retrieve data. These disks consist of a metal platter that rotates on a spindle and a read-write head that reads data written in concentric circles on the disk. The disk consumes power while rotating - the least power is consumed when it is in the idle state, and the most power is consumed when it spins up from the idle state for the read-write head to find the position on the disk from which to start reading. Software drivers that control the disk are designed to ensure that the disk goes into a high spin as few times as possible, and remains idle when not needed.

When large files, such as video or audio files, are being read from the disk, some software are designed to read as much data as possible, and buffer it, so that the disk does not have to start and stop frequently. The buffer is a temporary storage area in the RAM or Cache that stores the data read from the secondary disk storage. For example, if an application has to read 100 units of data from the hard disk and needs only 10 units at a time, it will have to start and stop the hard disk 10 times. However, if it can read 20 units at a time, where 10 are used by the application and 10 are buffered, the disk will have to be read only 10 times. Thus buffering reduces the energy required to read data for the application.

A similar logic applies to reading data from DVD and CD disks. These disks also have to spin to enable reading data from them, hence they consume a lot of energy. With data buffering, almost 70% of energy savings occur while using a DVD drive.

8.6.2 Context-Aware Design

Many hardware systems are designed to be context-aware and adjust their power use accordingly. For instance, a laptop will be aware when it has been disconnected from the power source and reduce screen brightness or hard-disk usage accordingly. Many devices now have screens that reduce brightness, as higher screen brightness consumes higher energy, when the ambient light is high. Context-aware devices use embedded software and operating system drivers to enable sensing and responding to the local surroundings.

8.7 GREEN PRACTICES IN IT USE

Use of IT products requires energy and consumables. Green practices require a careful understanding of how energy is consumed and how its use can be minimised. Further, green practices also require managing the use of consumables such as paper, batteries and toner. At an individual level users can reduce energy by adopting some green practices that are outlined in the Table 8.2.

Table 8.2 | Steps to Reduce Power Consumption in Laptop and Desktop Computers

1. Charging of batteries on laptops, tablets and notebook computers wastes energy as electricity is converted from AC to DC and the voltage is stepped down. This waste can be minimised by unplugging devices once the charging is done.
2. Battery life can be extended by frequent charges and also by ensuring that laptop and tablets power down or go into sleep mode when not in use.
3. Monitors consume about 20–30% of the power in a laptop or desktop system. Reducing brightness and turning off when not in use reduce power consumption by the monitor or display unit.
4. Most modern operating systems run background processes while the system is in use. Such processes consume energy by running the CPU or storage devices. Though such energy consumption is low, the un-needed background processes can be shut down.
5. When processors run at high speeds, they consume more energy. Modern processors can be "under-clocked" or speeded down when their high performance is not needed. Also, when needed, the processors can be "over-clocked" or speeded up (without having to acquire additional, faster, processors).
6. A lot of energy is consumed by hard disks during read-write operations where the disk has to spin. When the disk has not been de-fragmented, the read-write operations take longer and the disk has to spin more. De-fragmenting or joining together pieces of files on the disk helps to reduce energy consumption.

At the end of the useful life of hardware devices, some of which are often disposed after 3–5 years of use, their disposal adds to e-waste and pollution. One solution many firms have found is to increase the usable life of computers and components, either by re-using them in other configurations or by continuing to use them after installing compatible software that can run the applications needed. Many firms use open-source software on old computers to continue using them. Open-source software is re-configured so that it can run on the old machines to effectively run the applications.

Replacing and disposing a device requires care. Governments around the world have evolved careful norms to be followed while disposing off computers. In India, there are government approved organisations that collect and correctly dispose off e-waste. The process involves monitoring how the components are dismantled, where they are re-processed and how the resulting wastes generated are treated. However, much of the e-waste is disposed off inappropriately leading to pollution.

8.8 IT FOR GREEN PRACTICES

One key role of IT is that of monitoring, measuring and managing environmentally sustainable, or green, activities within the organisation. In the earlier sections we have seen how IT itself can be managed to reduce energy consumption, to reduce GHG emissions and also to reduce environmental pollution. In this section, the focus is on how IT can be used to manage and implement green practices in all functions and activities of the organisation.

Organisations are interested in the use of IT for managing greening for several reasons:

1. Green practices tend to increase cost of operations and monitoring would help to control these costs as well as reduce them.
2. Laws and regulations around the world now insist that organisations report on their activities that impact the environment - such as energy, water and material consumption, extent of re-cycling of materials and GHG emissions. This mandates all organisations to both monitor and report on these parameters.
3. The reputation and image of commercial firms and organisations are also affected by their efforts at sustaining green practices, and it is in their interest to monitor and show their efforts.

8.9 MONITORING VALUE CHAIN ACTIVITIES

In Chapter 4 we had seen how the value chain is a compact representation of activities in firms and organisations. Monitoring and managing greening activities can be understood from the value chain perspective. Each activity of the value chain may include green practices, in addition to the regular business and service tasks that are already included.

1. **Inbound Logistics:** Key tasks in this activity include procuring material from vendors, and storing and organising the material. Green practices in this function will involve - selection of vendors who are using re-cycled or environmentally friendly material; procurement from suppliers where least energy is spent and shipping distances are minimal; monitoring of energy consumption during storage, transportation and movement within buildings. IT systems assist by providing reports on energy consumed, material wasted or spilled, material balances, re-use of waste, material re-cycling, vendor activities and material flows.
2. **Production:** Sustainable practices in this activity include monitoring of energy, water and other resources consumption, re-cycling of components and parts, monitoring of waste and spillage. Some organisations practice "closed-loop manufacturing" where re-cycled products made by the same firm (discarded or exchanged by customers) are dis-assembled and reusable parts are included in the manufacturing process. All these activities can be monitored by IT systems and reported accordingly.

3. **Outbound Logistics:** Green practices in this function focus on optimising transportation for least energy and fuel usage, reducing waste and spillage during transportation, using green material for packaging, and re-cycling packaging material. IT systems provide key information and "dashboards" for these activities to be sensed, logged and monitored.
4. **Sales and Marketing:** Green activities involve informing customers and channel partners about the green practices being followed, the practice of re-cycling and the manner in which they can participate in these activities. IT systems can assist with informing and educating partners.
5. **Maintenance:** Green activities include informing customers of how product life can be extended, assisting them with greening activities and recovering old and used parts for re-cycling.

For all the above activities the information systems are used to collect data, store data in appropriate formats, run analysis on data and provide real-time and time-bound reports to management. The systems are usually integrated with the enterprise software or application software being used by the organisation.

KEY POINT

Systems monitor key activities within the value chain to provide information and analysis on green practices.

8.10 SMART CITIES

The phrase "smart cities" refers to geographical regions that have invested heavily in ICT infrastructure to facilitate the management of the region both for business and for the quality of life of its citizens. The word "smart" alludes to the idea that the growth and facilities of the region evolve with coordination, planning and greater efficiencies, as opposed to an unplanned and carefree or laissez-faire growth (which is growth without government or regulatory intervention).

There are many definitions of smart cities. Two examples are as follows:

1. The Government of India defines smart cities as – cities that provide core infrastructure and give a decent quality of life to its citizens, a clean and sustainable environment and application of "smart" solutions. The smart solutions are based on an IT infrastructure and include facilities such as electronic governance, waste management, water management, energy management, urban mobility management and other services such as education and healthcare.
   (*Source:* smartcities.gov.in viewed in Jan 2017.)
2. In Europe, one definition of smart cities that has gained attention is - a city is considered to be smart when "investments in human and social capital and traditional infrastructure (transportation) and modern communication infrastructure (ICT) to fuel sustainable economic growth and a high quality of life, with a wise management of natural resources, through participatory governance."

Both definitions thus emphasise use of IT and communications infrastructure, sustainability, quality of life and the efficient provision of services in cities.

8.10.1 Historical Origins

In developed countries, like the USA, the population in cities has grown significantly. For example, in the year 1900, the percentage of the US population living in cities was about 35%. This went up to about 75% in the year 2000. This growth has come from location of industrial production in urban centres, and the later proliferation of facilities such as education, healthcare, entertainment and transportation. Developed nations have also experienced massive migration of populations from rural to urban centres in search of work and better opportunities.

In India too, rapid industrial growth has led to increase in urbanisation or growth of cities. Table 8.3 shows the growth of five major cities in India.

Table 8.3 | Growth of Population in Six Major Cities in India, in the Decade 2001–11

City	Population in 2001 (millions)	Population in 2011 (millions)	Annual Population Growth Rate (%)
Mumbai	16.4	18.4	1.1
Delhi	12.9	16.3	2.4
Kolkata	13.2	14.1	0.7
Chennai	6.5	8.7	2.9
Bangalore	5.7	8.5	4.1
Hyderabad	5.7	7.7	3.0

Source: censusindia.gov.in

The table depicts the rapid growth of cities in India following India's policies of industrialisation and trade liberalisation since the 1980s. Cities such as Bangalore, Hyderabad, Delhi and Chennai experienced industrial growth through development of IT, manufacturing and services industries, which led to a massive demand for labour along with other resources such as land, water and energy. This attracted many people to migrate to these cities in search of jobs and employment opportunities. Though this growth has led to increase in wealth and improvement in the overall standard of living of people who were included in this, it has also led to massive problems of air and water pollution, inflation in real estate prices, traffic congestion, waste removal and management, shortage of services for schools, hospitals and emergency rescue, and reduction in public parks and amenities.

KEY POINT

Industrial growth in cities has led to population growth and demand for resources.

Bangalore is a case in point where the population has nearly doubled over the last decade and half, and this has created nearly insurmountable problems of congestion, pollution, resource depletion and shortage of amenities. The motivation for smart cities comes from a need to address these problems of cities where the power of IT can be leveraged to manage resources and improve conditions.

The next section highlights some of the facilities that IT can enable for the better management of cities and regions.

8.10.2 Facilities of Smart Cities

8.10.2.1 Sensing and Measuring

One of the foundations of smart cities is that of perceiving and recording various parameters of the city environment. This sensing is done by electronic sensors that are distributed across the city and provide data to connected networks that store and process this information. Data sensing is done for a vast number of phenomena, and the most popular ones are as follows:

1. Sensing of transport systems, including movement of individual vehicles, public transport, density of traffic at physical locations, speeds and range of travel.
2. Sensing of consumption of power and water usage, where smart meters relay data to central networks.
3. Sensing of particle density in air and water to gauge pollution levels.
4. Sensing of garbage production, accumulation and removal.
5. Sensing of land use, agricultural activity, soil erosion and construction activity.
6. Sensing of building temperature and illumination, arrival and departure of people, consumption of energy and water, and use of parking facilities.
7. Sensing of access to healthcare facilities, location of diseases, spread of diseases and availability of medical facilities.

With the above-mentioned sensing and measuring facilities, certain management capabilities are enhanced. The sections below delve deeper into the ICT architecture and management aspects of smart cities.

8.10.2.2 Smart Transportation

Many cities around the world have implemented ICT infrastructure for management of traffic. Traffic congestion has become a serious problem for rapidly growing cities where a large number of people need to commute on a daily basis and usually rely on their personal vehicles for doing so. Traffic congestion often has predictable patterns, such as rush-hour traffic, that sees huge surges in vehicles plying on the roads, over connecting flyovers and bridges, at intersections and in parking spaces. These patterns become the basis for understanding how traffic can be managed.

Sensing for smart transportation involves collecting data on traffic parameters in different ways. One of the widely used methods is that of using cameras mounted on traffic signals. Images from these cameras are viewed by people, usually traffic police, in large central command centres from where they inform individual policemen of the extent of traffic at particular junctions and whether any action needs to be taken. Policemen on the ground can then re-route traffic to avoid congestion build-up. An example of this is the Bangalore Traffic Management Centre in Bangalore City. This centre receives direct feeds from 180 surveillance cameras mounted on roads across the city. The feed from the cameras is displayed on a massive display screen and individual camera feeds are viewed on smaller monitors. Traffic personnel then instruct traffic policemen on the roads to direct and control traffic in different ways.

Another approach is to analyse the images streaming in from cameras to calculate the amount of traffic automatically. The processing systems are then able to compute the number of cars on different roads at an intersection and also the length of the queue that has built up. This information is then used to directly control traffic signals to slow down or speed up traffic on other roads that are connected. This information may also be used to re-direct traffic by flashing messages on road signs and on traffic intersections.

The information from surveillance cameras may also be used to identify different types of vehicles. For instance, in some cities, public transport buses are identified, and if there are a number of them at an intersection, then the road they are on is given priority for movement. This logic is also applied to vehicles such as ambulances, police patrol cars and other priority vehicles that are enabled to move faster than others. Sensors can also detect bicycles and pedestrians and enable them to cross intersections.

Some cities have historically used sensors embedded in the road asphalt to detect the presence of a vehicle. These sensors were connected to the traffic signal and the signal would turn green only if a vehicle was present. Modern versions of such sensors sense not only if a vehicle is present, but also how many are waiting in the queue and have been doing so for how long. Based on this information the signal is controlled.

A third method of sensing traffic is by monitoring mobile phones carried by drivers in cars. The basic idea is that cell towers for mobile phones near roads will register the mobile phone carried by the driver of the car. If one totals the number of connections to a particular tower, this could be an estimate of the traffic on the road. However, this is a rough estimate, as the tower will connect all people nearby, in homes or offices, walking on the street or in the vicinity, and they do not contribute to the vehicular traffic. Researchers have shown that sensing "handovers", that is, movement of phones from one mobile tower to another, as the phone is moving in the car, gives a better estimate of how many cars are on the road. This data on the number of cars is aligned with maps of city streets and this shows the flow of traffic on roads, which includes the volume of traffic, the direction and the speed at which it is moving. This information is then clubbed with data from cameras to estimate, with more accuracy, the amount of traffic and how it is likely to create congestion at various points in the city.

The latest trends are to use the traffic density and flow information to control traffic signals and traffic direction indicators, where available, to manage the flow of traffic in the city and avoid congestion. Experiments in some cities in different parts of the world show promising

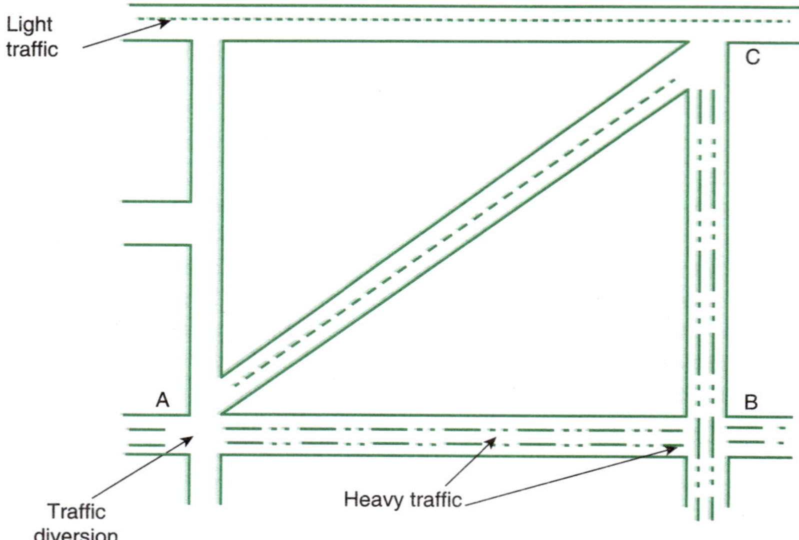

FIGURE 8.2 Diversion of traffic before a busy intersection. Traffic is diverted from intersection A, to prevent a buildup at B.

results, with upto 25% improvements in travel time. Measuring individual movement of cars and then assessing aggregate traffic patterns requires IT infrastructure to collect the data from millions of moving vehicles, aggregate it and then perform analysis on it. This is a significant cost for obtaining the benefit of reduced congestion.

Figure 8.2 shows traffic at three intersections – A, B and C. Traffic sensors show heavy traffic at intersection B. Diversion is then effected at A, towards C, that has lighter traffic.

Collecting movement information through GPS-enabled phones also helps individual commuters gauge their own position with respect to roads, bus stations and railway stations. Some smartphone-based apps enable the commuter to know how long it will take them to reach a particular place, say a train station, whether parking spots are available at their destination, and when the next train will arrive. This information enables commuters to make individual choices with regard to their travel. The IT infrastructure used for such systems relies on openly available information, such as traffic data, parking availability data, and train arrival and departure data.

Caselet Seoul's Owl Bus Service

Large cities around the world have to manage the problem of growth, where large sections of the city's population locate themselves at the geographical periphery, owing to limitations of availability of land and as prices of real estate are usually higher at the centre or older parts of the city. One of the problems that such geographical spread creates is that of transportation, where people have to find ways to commute to different parts of the city, some of which have limited facilities for public transport. In industrial cities, like Seoul, South Korea, the problem is compounded as people have to commute at different times of the day and night. Private transport providers, such as taxis or autorickshaws, are reluctant to travel to remote parts of the city at night and public transportation is not available.

The city of Seoul prided itself on its public transportation infrastructure; however, in 2012 it found itself with a problem of providing transportation to thousands of factory workers who had to travel to different parts of the city at night and were unable to do so. Public transport was available till midnight, and in the period from 1 am to 5 am there was very little for people to do but hope for expensive and unreliable private transporters. The city government decided to tackle this problem, but immediately ran into the issue of deciding of routes for buses. The city knew very little about the traffic demand and patterns at night - who and how many wanted to travel from where and to where.

One option the city planners had was to survey the residents of the outlying areas and find out their travel preferences. This approach had its challenges - the cost of such extensive surveying is expensive, the sample may not be representative of the actual demand and also the time taken to do such a survey would be many months, if not years. Given this, the city decided to look at the data that was already available - this was the data on call records of commuters in these outlying regions in the night, the text messages sent to taxis about pick-up points and the addresses of those who had made payments to taxis and private transporters at their destinations. This data was only collected for the night, in the window of 1 am to 5 am to understand the pick-up and drop-off points for night commuters. Three billion data points were mined and mapped to see how commuters travelled at night. In addition, the city planners also obtained the trip details of taxis that were fitted with digital tachography devices, which recorded the entire trip of taxis, including the speed at which they travelled. These devices had been fitted on all corporate and private taxis, for regulating their speeds, and the data obtained from these also showed the demand for routes by commuters at night.

After analysing the data, the city planners were able to come up with routes for "Owl Buses" that would play at night, in the window 1 am - 5 am, providing relief to night-time commuters. The buses became very popular and with a few months over a half million commuters had ridden on them. The Owl Bus service plied on the routes identified by data collected by the city on the prior trips of commuters, thus relying on smart technologies to design public transportation.

Sources:
http://blogs.worldbank.org/transport/what-does-big-data-have-do-owl
http://policytransfer.metropolis.org/case-studies/owl-bus-based-on-big-data-technology
http://dataimpacts.org/wp-content/uploads/2015/06/using-data-for-seoul-bus-routes.compressed.pdf

8.10.3 Smart Environment

The environment challenge of modern cities is that of conserving resources that are in short supply, such as water, and protecting some resources from pollution - such as water, air and land, and also protecting the audible environment from sound pollution. The environment challenge also draws on sustainable practices to limit GHG emissions, control global warming, and protect bio-diversity of flora and fauna.

8.10.3.1 Water Conservation

Many urban regions have a need to sense and monitor water resources as the growing population of these cities is creating shortages of this commodity. Varying rainfall patterns that replenish water bodies, draining out water from upstream dams or canals, and poor use of available water have forced many cities to manage water through smart methods. Water bodies such as lakes and reservoirs are monitored by sensors for their levels, the amount of inflows they have from streams and rainfall, and the amount that is consumed by urban water needs. These levels are sensed by water meters and the data is provided on a continual basis to a central system that computes the water levels.

Water-related measurements also include those of rainfall, humidity, soil composition, sunlight, topography and temperature. In rural areas, such data is provided to farmers to make decisions about cropping times, cropping patterns and irrigation.

Monitoring is also done with satellite image data that gives an indication of the spread of lakes and streams, flows in rivers and canals and the depth of water bodies. When waste water is released from urban areas in to the local lakes and reservoirs, this too is measured and accounted for. Researchers have developed many complex mathematical models that are used to predict availability of water from these water sources at different times of the year.

In many cities, one of the main challenges of water conservation is that of preventing leakages. Most older cities have water pipes that are many decades old and are underground, thus making them difficult to access and check. To address this problem, some cities are installing pressure gauges in the pipes that indicate the level and pressure of the flowing water. A lower pressure is usually desired as that leads to lesser leakage, where leaks are present. The system of sensors provides an accurate estimate of the extent, or stock, and flows of water in the network of pipes. When more water is demanded in some regions, the flows are increased by automated pump controllers that allow more water to be pumped into the system. Where water is in less demand, the flows are reduced and with that the water pressure is also reduced. This has the twin advantages of reducing leakages and also of reducing the energy required to pump water (as the water is pumped only when needed).

KEY POINT

IT sensors and motors are used to monitor and control stocks and flows of water in urban areas, based on demand and availability.

Cities are also encouraging water conservation at housing complexes and individual homes. In Bangalore, for instance, housing complexes and gated communities have to implement rain-water harvesting, as part of their compliance with municipal laws. IT is being used by these communities to monitor water levels in tanks and sumps. This information is used to control pumps to fill water and also to drain water when needed.

8.10.3.2 *Pollution Control*

Pollution control is enabled by monitoring air quality at different points in the city and aggregating this data to arrive at a comprehensive picture. Typical measurement sensors record data pertaining to levels of carbon dioxide, carbon monoxide, nitrogen dioxide, humidity, temperature and pressure. Some sensors will also monitor light quality and vibration levels, whereas others measure particulate matter and ozone. Such sensors are typically mounted on kiosks at points on city streets, on top of traffic signals, or on top of buildings. The data from sensors is aggregated and overlaid on a map of a city to obtain a visual image of the different components of air quality and their presence in the city. "Hotspots" of pollution are thus identified, where air quality is particularly poor and this is used to direct executive action. For instance, cities may divert traffic away from hotspots of pollution to control the air quality.

Sensors are also used to visually observe sensitive areas in the city - such as factories or warehouses, where there is a possibility of increase in polluting activity. These are surveillance cameras that may be observed by citizens on a volunteer basis and help to identify potential problem areas. The city of Pittsburgh in the USA has experimented with such an approach. Another approach for measuring air quality is to provide citizens with sensors that are connected to GPS-enabled smartphones that feed data from different points in the city to a central server. The advantage of this approach is that the sensors are mobile and check air quality where people congregate.

Water pollution is also a matter of concern for urban areas. Some cities have implemented sensors to monitor the extent of sewage flowing through the underground sewage system, both to treat the sewage before it is permitted to mix with other water bodies and also to control the extent of sewage that is produced and unleashed into rivers and oceans. Weather and rainfall measurement sensors are used to predict if excessive rainfall is likely, which often leads to overfilling of storm-water drains that lets untreated sewage into water bodies. With these measurements, infrastructure managers in cities can divert excessive water to alternate drains, without letting them enter the sewage system.

8.10.3.3 *Energy Management*

Conservation of energy remains a strong rationale for urban centres to use smart technologies. It is estimated that cities consume about 75% of the total energy requirements in the world. This consumption is for industrial production, in factories and offices, and also for running of services such as transportation, and for domestic consumption. A key goal of smart cities is to monitor and control energy consumption.

Energy management requires locating and measuring the generation, storage, distribution and consumption of energy. Each of these stages of the energy life-cycle requires sensing and monitoring for efficient management.

Energy generation is usually carried out by the traditional means of central power generation plants that use hydro power or are based on fossil fuels. In many cities, owing to uncertainty in power supply from these centralized sources, many industrial and other organisations install their own captive power generation plants that essentially rely on fossil fuels. Solar power has gained prominence in recent years, and many cities have begun to invest in massive solar panel installations, sometimes over rooftops and on buildings. Photovoltaic panels convert solar power directly into electricity, whereas thermal collectors convert solar energy into heat energy (such as solar water heaters). These sources of electricity generation may be located on individual buildings and homes in cities, thus creating a large mass of micro-generators that may be connected on a grid. Cities in some regions that have windy environments rely on wind energy obtained from massive wind turbines located on hilltops. In all these cases, the challenge is to sense and monitor the extent of energy production at all these sources and to decide on how these can be stored or distributed.

Electrical energy is typically stored in batteries of various forms. These batteries may be monitored to see when and how they lose charge and when they have to be recharged. Energy is also stored in superconducting magnetic energy coils and as potential energy in water pumped to higher positions, from which it can be released and converted to energy. These different storage mechanisms can be monitored by different sensors and their potential to release energy can be tapped for different requirements. Typical variations in energy needs include sudden peaks in demand, owing to weather changes, or gradual demand growth owing to industrialisation. Cities try to balance the different needs with different storage and monitoring facilities. The key objective of these efforts is to retain sustainability.

Energy distribution in smart cities follows the "smart-grid" concept where each energy generation and storage location is connected to a grid, along with the consumption locations. The function of the smart grid is to distribute energy from supply sources to demand points based on price expectations, contractual obligations and sustainability criteria. The key idea of smart grids is meet customer demand with existing energy sources without resorting to building new facilities, with an architecture that is resilient and can withstand natural forces and calamities. The smart grid is usually an interconnection of many micro-grids that operate independently of each other and are called to pull together only in times of need. Such an arrangement requires a strong communication backbone that is robust and constantly online.

8.10.4 Smart Buildings

One of the key aspects of energy management in cities is "smart buildings". Since buildings are the main consumers of energy, for air-conditioning, heating, lighting, ventilation, running machines, and for facilities such as parking, security and for running elevators and doors, it is important that each aspect of energy consumption within buildings is sensed, monitored and controlled.

Figure 8.3 shows a smart building that is designed as a commercial building with parking in the basement and several floors of office space on top. Such a building will typically have its own power generation facilities, such as through solar panels or a wind turbine on the roof, and also thermal generation and storage facilities in the basement. The building would be connected to a micro-grid from which it can draw energy when needed and provide energy when it has surplus of its own.

All the office floors of the building have sensors for measuring the quantity of light, the ambient temperature, and the extent of ventilation. These sensors would connect with nearby mesh routers that signal the conditions to a central control unit. In case the temperature or light condition has to be changed, the central control unit will send a signal using the mesh network to the actuators (or motors) to change the temperature by giving commands to an air-conditioner or to light switches to turn on or turn off lights. Many buildings also have motion and occupancy sensors that can detect presence of humans, and maintain certain light and temperature conditions. If humans are not present then the lights and temperature maintenance are automatically turned off.

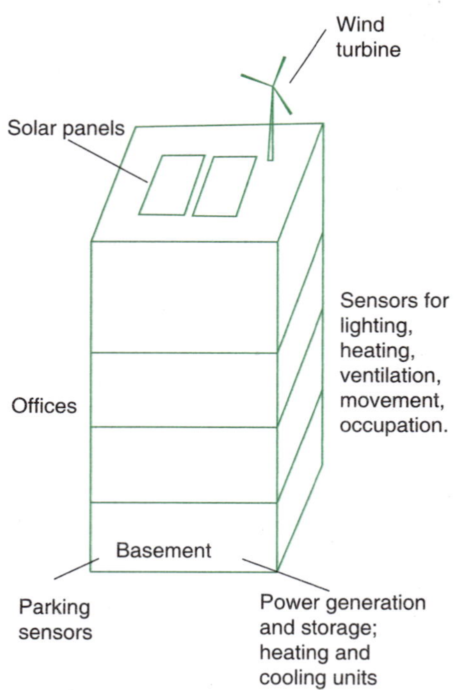

FIGURE 8.3 A smart building contains sensors to collect data on and control lighting, heating, ventilation, personnel movement and occupation within the building. It has facilities for energy generation – solar, wind and electrical energy – in the basement and on the rooftop. The building has sensors for parking, indicating occupancy levels of parking.

The building also has parking sensors that sense the number of vehicles in the building and also the number of parking spots available. This information would be available online and commuters intending to arrive at the building would know if they will find parking or not. If parking is already full, they may choose to rely on public transportation to commute.

The key challenge of smart buildings is to use IT to manage their energy requirements in a sustainable manner, where they draw on the grid only when required and try to remain dependent only on their own generation capacities. Meeting this challenge requires collecting data through many sensors and devising algorithms or programs that can achieve these sustainability goals.

8.10.5 Smart Living

There are many ways in which information technology is being used by people to enrich their lives. The idea of smart living in urban areas is that of people collaborating on online or peer-to-peer communities to sustainably impact and improve some aspect of their lives. Some examples that highlight aspects of smart living are as below

Open street maps are maps created by masses of people living in cities or rural areas. The idea behind OpenStreetMap (www.openstreetmap.org) was to have publicly available maps that are not owned by any corporation and are created and updated by people living in the areas that are mapped. The technology basis of OpenStreetMap allows registered users to walk, bicycle or drive around territories and mark them on digital maps that are uploaded on a central databases. The mapping work is done by volunteers who are registered on the OpenStreetMap.org site. In February 2017, there were over 3.7 million registered users of OpenStreetMap.

Citizens of cities around the world now collaborate through smart phones to rate facilities and services in their region. For example, there are many apps that rate restaurants, laundaries, healthcare providers, such as dentists, schools and colleges, and also government offices that provide citizen services. These ratings are provided by citizens who have availed of these services or consumed the products and provide feedback to other citizens and to the providers, largely to help improve the services. The breadth and quality of such feedback from citizens has improved vastly across countries, where citizens comment on all aspects of living in urban areas.

8.10.6 Smart Governance

The role of information technology in governance, referred to as e-governace in Chapter 5, is further enhanced through the concept of smart governance. The main idea is that the data and information required for governance and decision making is obtained from distributed and decentralised sources. Functions of governance such as monitoring, planning, execution of various policies are supported and enhanced by smart governance technologies and infrastructure. A few examples highlight these aspects.

Citizen participation in budget monitoring and setting was the goal of a smart governance project in some neighbourhoods in the city of Amsterdam. The idea was to have an IT infrastructure that could inform citizens about various allocations of budgets for neighbourhood development, the manner in which the budgets were spent and the outcome of the spending. The system allowed citizens to see and understand the budget allocation process, the details of where the money was being allocated, and see how the money was being spent. Further, citizens could also participate in the allocation process, helping set priorities for the spending - such as on roads, schools, playgrounds, etc. The system was a web-based application that enabled various neighbourhood councils to upload their data on a common platform, after which the data was presented in different views to citizens to understand and comment upon.

The coastal town of Rikuzentaka, in the Iwate Prefecture of Japan, was struck by a massive earthquake in March 2011. This was followed by a colossal tsunami, with waves more than 10 metres high, that effectively wiped out the entire downtown area of the city. Hundreds of buildings were destroyed, with a human toll of close to 2000 dead. The town was devastated, but its citizens resolved to re-build it and do it in such a manner that it would be environment-friendly and also be able to withstand future shocks like earthquakes and tsunamis. The challenge was to come up with a design that would be acceptable to those wanting to live there and also meet the cost and geographical constraints of the region.

The central government of Japan provided funds for the reconstruction, and by 2013, the authorities had drawn up a detailed plan for the new downtown and residential areas. The idea was to create a raised hill near the seaside that would host the new downtown area, including the business and shopping areas, and have the residences move uphill nearby. Residents were shown the plan; however, not all were convinced of its feasibility and how it would affect their lives. The authorities then drew up a virtual reality reconstruction of the entire plan, including details such as landscaping, roads, parks, forested areas, buildings, residences, schools, and other facilities. Citizens could now see the plan in three dimensions, with aerial views, cross-section views and also ground-level views. This helped them understand how their residences, neighbourhoods, offices and shopping areas would be located and would appear when rebuilt. Many then made suggestions for improvement and changes, which were visualized on the software. Citizens then gave their approval for the new plans and the construction of the new town could proceed. IT was used to build consensus for a new plan of a city, with active participation of citizens in both the design and approval processes.

8.11 MANAGEMENT ISSUES: CHALLENGES FOR MANAGERS

Implementing green IT and building facilities for smart cities present many challenges for managers. Four issues are highlighted below.

1. **Cost:** The cost of implementing software and hardware for green IT is a significant issue for most organisations. These efforts entail designing and building or buying new IT infrastructure that leads to increased costs. The challenge for managers is to ensure that the

subsequent benefits exceed the costs, where the impact of greening will have to be measured carefully and accounted for as a benefit. Managers also have to ensure that the long-term plans for IT include within them green practices to help reduce costs.

2. **Privacy:** One of the most important issues that arises with sensing and collecting massive amounts of data for green IT efforts and also with smart city projects is that of privacy of individuals whose data is being collected. This issue has been flagged in cities and countries around the world, where citizens feel that their everyday activities - such as driving to work, going to office, using water, using electrical devices - are being sensed, and the data from these is being stored and later analysed. The challenge for managers who are implementing IT within green practices in organisations or implementing smart city IT solutions, is to ensure that privacy concerns are addressed both for ethical concerns of citizens and for legal compliance.
3. **Surveillance:** Related to privacy is the issue of surveillance. Sensor data collected within organisations leads to the panopticon effect (covered in the previous chapter), where employees and others affiliated with the organisation are not fully aware of what is being monitored and when. Managers who implement green practices, say in smart buildings, will have to create policies that ensure data on employees movements, energy consumption, water consumption, etc. are used only in the manner specified (that is, for green compliance).
4. **Data Infrastructure:** Data from sensors is collected in very large quantities for the green IT and smart cities projects. The challenges that managers face in dealing with such large quantities of data are those of storage, management, disposal and compliance. Some of the questions they will need to answer are: How much data needs to be stored for the short term and for perpetuity? How should the data be made accessible to those within or outside the organisation (such as data analysts in a city or with a commercial third-party organisation)? What licenses should be used to make the data accessible? For how long should the data be stored? How should modified data be licensed and shared? Answers to these questions will enable them to formulate broad policies to manage the data infrastructure.

Chapter Glossary

Greenhouse gases (GHGs) These are gases such as carbon dioxide and methane that absorb radiation in the earth's atmosphere and cause the atmospheric temperature to rise.

Global warming The increase in the effective temperature of the atmosphere owing to the increase in GHGs.

Carbon footprint This the amount of GHGs that an organisation, or a region or nation, produces in a year, following from their activities.

Buffering Temporary storage of data in memory, used to reduce read or write operations, that also reduce energy consumption.

Context aware design Systems that are aware of the state they are in and reduce their power use accordingly.

Smart cities A broad concept that refers to cities, or urban regions, that use IT extensively to improve conditions of living and working.

Smart-grid A connected set of electricity generation and consumption nodes that are monitored by IT to balance demand and supply.

Review Questions

1. What is the concern that governments have about greenhouse gases and global warming?
2. How and why is information technology related to GHGs and global warming?
3. How can hardware be designed to reduce and control GHG emissions?
4. How can software be designed for green IT?

5. What is a context aware design?
6. How is IT used for green practices in the value chain?
7. When is a city considered to be "smart"?
8. What are some things that are sensed and measured in smart cities? Why are they measured?
9. What are the different ways in which transportation in cities can be managed with IT?
10. How can water conservation be effected with IT in smart cities?
11. What is the concept of a smart building? What facilities are provided in such buildings?
12. In what ways do citizens participate, through the use of IT, within smart cities?
13. How is smart governance affected?

Research Questions

1. Seek out and visit some organisation that has implemented green IT practices? List these practices and try to estimate how much energy they are able to save or how much pollution they are able to control.
2. For any particular brand of computing device, seek out their hardware and software design specifications and see if they follow any green practices? Do they follow the principle of context aware design?
3. Explore on the internet and find examples of smart cities. What kind of smart concepts have such cities implemented and how successful are they?
4. Search for examples of citizen participation in governance in the region in which you live. What are the ways in which citizens are participating and how effective are these practices?

Further Reading

1. http://www.livescience.com/37821-greenhouse-gases.html
2. http://cdiac.esd.ornl.gov/trends/co2/sio-mlo.html (Carbon Dioxide Information Analysis Center)
3. http://timeforchange.org/what-is-a-carbon-footprint-definition
4. http://www.greenit.net/whygreenit.html
5. Batty, M., Axhausen, K. W., Giannotti, F., Pozdnoukhov, A., Bazzani, A., Wachowicz, M., & Portugali, Y. (2012), Smart cities of the future. *The European Physical Journal Special Topics*, **214**(1), 481–518.
6. Mahesri, A., and Vardhan, V. (2004) Power consumption breakdown on a modern laptop, in *International Workshop on Power-Aware Computer Systems*, pp. 165–180, Springer, Berlin, Heidelberg.
7. Caragliu, A., Del Bo, C., & Nijkamp, P. (2011), Smart cities in Europe, *Journal of Urban Technology*, **18**(2), 65–82.
8. Calvillo, C. F., Sánchez-Miralles, A., & Villar, J. (2016), Energy management and planning in smart cities, *Renewable and Sustainable Energy Reviews*, **55**, 273–287.
9. Mattern, F., Staake, T., & Weiss, M. (2010, April), ICT for green: How computers can help us to conserve energy, in *Proceedings of the 1st International Conference on Energy-Efficient Computing and Networking*, pp. 1–10, ACM.
10. http://fortune.com/2015/08/20/smart-traffic-signals/
11. http://smartcitiescouncil.com/article/battling-traffic-jams-smarter-traffic-signals
12. https://www.wired.com/2011/03/cell-phone-networks-and-the-future-of-traffic/
13. https://www.researchgate.net/publication/248381445_Intelligent_road_traffic_status_detection_system_through_cellular_networks_handover_information_An_exploratory_study
14. http://www.libelium.com/smart_city_environmental_parameters_public_transportation_waspmote/
15. http://datasmart.ash.harvard.edu/news/article/monitoring-air-quality-and-the-impacts-of-pollution-679
16. http://www.libelium.com/smart_city_air_quality_urban_traffic_waspmote/
17. http://unhabitat.org/urban-themes/energy/
18. http://www.rcrwireless.com/20160725/business/smart-building-tag31-tag99
19. Malschaert, F. O. (2016), *Exploring the Road to Smart Governance: A Multiple Case Study of Institutional Change within Dutch Smart Governance Projects*, MS Thesis, Utrecht University.
20. http://smartcitiescouncil.com/resources/challenges-tohoku-reconstruction
21. http://www.cisco.com/c/en/us/solutions/industries/government/us-government-solutions-services/resources/case-studies.html
22. http://www.japantimes.co.jp/news/2017/03/07/national/tsunami-hit-rikuzentakata-rebuilding-high-ground-hoping-thrive-anew/#.WXHhHFdLfCI

Part II

FUNDAMENTALS OF IT

Chapter 9 Information Technology Infrastructure and Choices

Chapter 10 Cloud Computing and Internet-of-Things

Chapter 11 Networking and Telecommunication

Chapter 12 Information Systems Security and Control

Chapter 13 Information Systems Development and Project Management

Chapter 14 Managing Data Resources

Chapter 15 Business Process Integration and Enterprise Systems

Chapter 16 Decision Support Systems

Chapter 17 Artificial Intelligence

CHAPTER 9

Information Technology Infrastructure and Choices

LEARNING OBJECTIVES

After completing this chapter, you will be able to:

- Understand information technology infrastructures
- Get an overview of infrastructure decisions
- Learn about infrastructure components
- Understand infrastructure solutions

The information technology (IT) infrastructure consists of hardware, software, networks and services that are needed for an organisation to function. An IT infrastructure is built up according to the business needs of an organisation, and the type and kind of technology available. Many technologies today are driven by hype about their capabilities that managers have to be aware of.

The hardware consists of computers of different kinds and the devices that are attached to them that are known as the peripherals. The software consists of systems software that is used to run the hardware, and application software that is used to run the applications needed by the organisation. The networks consist of devices that connect the different computers of the organisation, and also connect the organisation to the internet.

Many organisations with a long history of using IT have complex systems in place. These present management challenges, as there is a complex mix of old and new systems working together, owing to which a number of comprehensive solutions have emerged such as enterprise systems and virtualisation. These are the newer forms of architecture in the domain of IT infrastructure.

MIND MAP OF CHAPTER TOPICS

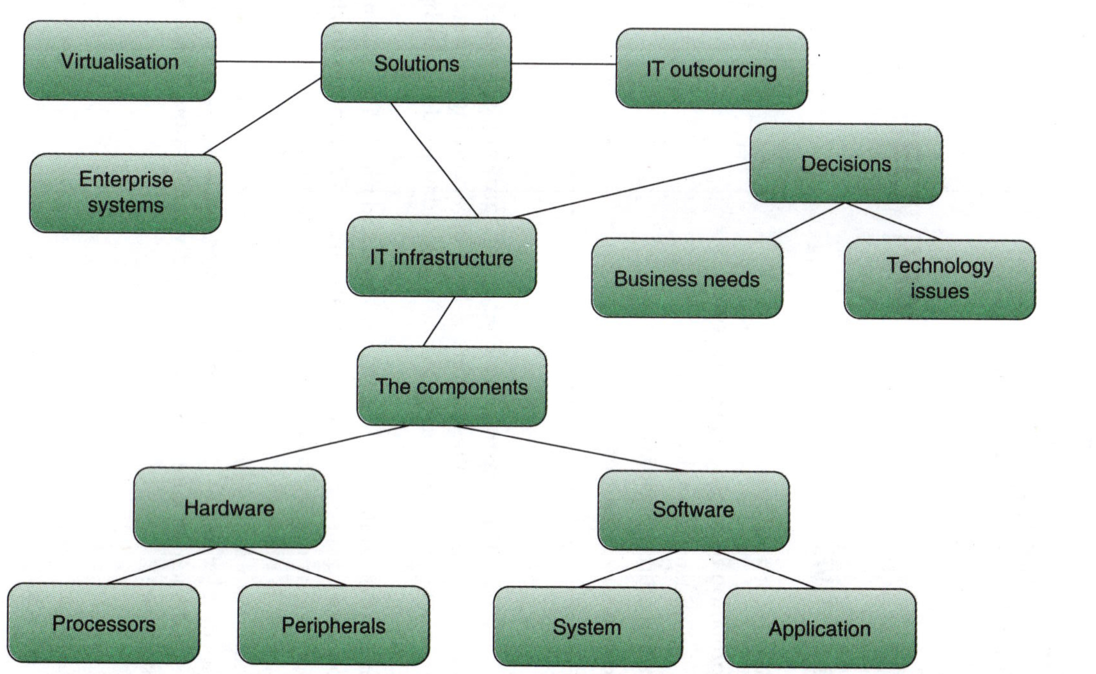

Tribhovandas Bhimji Zaveri (TBZ) is one of the oldest and biggest jewellery store chains in India. They were the first to offer certified solitaire diamonds and promote the concept of light-weight jewellery in the country. Apart from their stores across the nation, they have a training school for budding artisans and a force of 135 highly skilled master jewellers ensuring a unique touch to their jewellery. In 2010, the company operated in 15 locations across the country and employed 950 staff.

TBZ's IT infrastructure consisted of 35 servers, about 20 of which resided in a primary data centre and the rest were scattered throughout its Indian locations. This distributed architecture presented a management challenge to TBZ's IT team, which had to ensure that critical databases and applications met strict business requirements of availability and performance. The centrally located servers were also straining the data centre's air-conditioning facilities. Running 35 physical servers posed a strong management challenge of controlling the IT cost and overheads for TBZ. At this point TBZ decided to bring in data centre virtualisation to consolidate and centralise their servers as well as control costs.

TBZ chose the virtualisation product called VMware vSphere 4, which allowed them to manage their consolidated infrastructure from a single console. This reduced their hardware cost by Rs 4 million (about USD 89,000) over 3 years while achieving a server consolidation ratio of 7:1. TBZ was able to enhance the utilisation of its existing servers by boosting the average central processing unit (CPU) utilisation from the pre-virtualisation level of 3–4% to 70% and reduce the server requirements to four hosts. This minimised power and cooling costs. The solution also helped improve their uptime, from a mere 70% to 98%.
Kalpesh Dave, IT manager, TBZ said

> By deploying VMware virtualisation, we have consolidated our previously scattered servers into our primary data centre, which reduced our management load. The lower hardware requirement has also eased the strain on data centre facilities such as air conditioning. It has also enabled us to run on a single console and has reduced server requirement to four hosts.

He added that TBZ was planning to employ VMware to virtualise about 100 desktops to further reduce the IT management task.

VMware vSphere 4 is a virtualisation platform that helped customers control their applications, manage their security and ensure their security levels. At TBZ, the VMware platform ran high-end databases such as Oracle 11g, and a suite of applications on 60 virtual servers. The servers could run a choice of operating systems (OS) as needed by the applications. TBZ chose VMware as it was an award winning product (it won the Wall Street Journal 2009 Technology Innovation Award), backed by a strong company which had revenues of USD 2 billion in 2009. Furthermore, VMware was the top product among its competitors, with many CIOs choosing it over its rivals.

Investment was not a constraint for TBZ as it believed in having a full-fledged IT infrastructure. The applications were deployed in silos spread across three-tier applications, including client–server applications, which needed integration and consolidation. During 2009, when Dave decided to consolidate and virtualise their servers, TBZ zeroed in on the VMware virtualisation solution after careful evaluation of other vendors. Having finalised on VMware vSphere 4.0, Dave went ahead to rope in VMware's implementation partner, Network Techlab. TBZ invests about Rs 15 million (about USD 333, 000) on IT tools and technologies per year. As a result of server virtualisation and vSphere 4.0, the company witnessed great benefits. According to Dave, the process of implementation took only 2 weeks. The solution enabled management of a consolidated virtual infrastructure from a single console, reduced the server footprint to four hosts, and minimised power and cooling costs. The total investment that went into the deployment was around Rs 4.5 million (about USD 100,000). TBZ did not observe any hindrances during the implementation process though there were certain apprehensions earlier with regard to security.

According to Dave, the new infrastructure has enabled TBZ to reduce the number of people required to manage it. 'By deploying VMware virtualisation solution, we have consolidated our previously scattered servers into our primary data centre, which reduced our server management load', explained Dave and added, 'The fewer number of servers [just four blade servers] means a cut on future hardware spending and will reduce our data centre air-conditioning and power costs, resulting in a saving of Rs 4.0 million over the next three years'. The number of administrators required to run the environment went down to just 1 from 10 people, and the server performance improved by 30–34%. The time required to provision a new server (excluding hardware procurement processes) reduced from 1 day to just 20 min, the processor utilisation improved from a dismal 4% to 70%, while there was a drop in required rack space. TBZ estimated a 25–30% jump in its IT budget in subsequent years as the company planed to do some major upgrades according to its expansion plans for its retail outlets. Their main agenda was to virtualise about 100 out of 300 desktops to derive cost benefits.

9.1 WHAT IS THE IT INFRASTRUCTURE?

When the word infrastructure is used in the context of cities it refers to the facilities such as roads, electricity, water, transportation and other things that are necessary for the city to function. These are the underlying components on which a city is built and on which it functions. If any of the infrastructure elements were to be weak, like a city having poor electricity supply, then this affects the ability of the city residents to do their jobs, as electricity is required for doing most things. Any planning for the city, for example, its growth and modernisation, has to account for the parallel increase in the infrastructure facilities, without whose growth the city's growth is not possible.

Similarly, an information technology (IT) infrastructure consists of the facilities that are needed by an organisation to function. These facilities are in the form of hardware, software, networks and services that combine to form applications that are used by the organisation, such as e-commerce, materials management, accounting, customer relationship management (CRM), etc. The infrastructure components are the basis on which the organisation performs its various functions, and a lack of any component affects the functionality of the organisation. Also, planning for growth of the organisation requires that the infrastructure growth plan is accordingly determined.

KEY POINT

IT infrastructure consists of IT components and applications that enable the organisation to function.

Some examples of what constitutes an IT infrastructure are highlighted below. These examples are drawn from the TBZ case study.

1. Client computers such as desktops and laptops that employees of the organisation use, about 300 at TBZ. These have to be maintained through hardware and software upgrades. Most organisations will also include tablet computers, smart phones and hand-held computers.
2. Servers that host the applications needed by the organisation. At TBZ, after virtualisation, the firm used about 60 servers to run a number of applications.
3. Routers, switches, cables and wireless devices that constitute the networks used by the organisation. This will include the services obtained from external internet service providers.
4. Organisation-wide and function-specific applications such as email, databases, enterprise software, etc. At TBZ, these applications supported business applications at all the stores.
5. Support facilities for users, such as a Help Desk, for maintaining and upgrading hardware and software.
6. Physical facilities such as air-conditioned rooms and offices that house the hardware, software and personnel.
7. Training and development facilities for users and staff to enhance skills and also for problem solving.
8. Creating and maintaining standards for IT, including procurement.

The IT infrastructure of an organisation is different from its IT architecture. The difference is subtle but important. The IT architecture consists of the hardware, software and networks that enable and constitute the infrastructure of the organisation. The architecture may be designed in a suitable manner to meet the infrastructure needs, and as such many possible architectures are possible to meet the needs of the infrastructure. The architecture is a technical design of the computing *ecosystem* whereas the infrastructure is determined by the business and work needs of the organisation. An IT ecosystem, in this context, is the complete IT-enabled environment that exists for employees of an organisation to work in. This phrase is borrowed from biological systems to imply that all the elements in the system are interconnected and support each other.

KEY POINT

IT infrastructure is different from the IT architecture.

There are many decisions that have to be taken with regard to the IT infrastructure. These decisions are loosely categorised as those belonging to the business needs and those belonging to technology concerns. Business needs may be for any organisation, not necessarily a commercial firm alone, and point to the work the organisation does and the functions its employees have to perform. The choice for managers is to construct an infrastructure that will support the organisation's work. The technical decisions concern the technology itself – what is the most suitable technology for the task and what choices are available. These decisions impact the organisation because each technology choice entails long-term commitments, lock-in and switching costs. Some details regarding the two decisions are discussed below.

9.2 IT INFRASTRUCTURE DECISIONS

9.2.1 IT Infrastructure Questions: Business Needs

Following are IT infrastructure questions with regard to business needs:

1. **What business needs have to be met with the infrastructure components?** This question is self-explanatory and has to be answered by identifying the complete set of needs for which support is needed. Technology choices have to be based on what specific business needs are being met and will be met in future.
2. **How does the technology help the organisation compete?** For commercial firms, the infrastructure choices have to reflect their competitive needs. Therefore, they have to answer this question at the initiation of the technology acquisition process and, later, at the use stage of the acquired technology. Answers to this question often lead to insights on whether an application or service is needed or not. For non-commercial firms too, this question has relevance as it points to how the other organisations working in the same domain are coping with and addressing their infrastructure needs.
3. **Is the technology appropriate for the task?** This question highlights the issue of considering alternative technologies for addressing the needs of the organisation. A technology is considered appropriate for a task when it exactly meets the needs of the task. Inappropriate technologies are either excessive in scope or they have inherent shortcomings that do not meet the needs of the task in question.
4. **Is the technology the best in its class?** This question addresses the quality of the technology choice in comparison to the price paid for it. For many organisations this question is not relevant as they are more interested in the appropriateness of the technology rather than it being of the best quality in its class of products.

9.2.2 IT Infrastructure Questions: Technology Issues

Following are IT infrastructure questions with regard to technology issues:

1. **Is the technology scalable?** This question addresses the issue of future growth of the organisation. It asks whether the capacity of the technology can be expanded in the future to account for larger processing needs.
2. **Is the technology interoperable?** In an IT infrastructure, the components have to be able to work with each other. They should have built-in capabilities to allow them to work with different data standards, different file formats, different communication standards and so on. Interoperable technologies are the most suitable for complex infrastructures, however, such capabilities also introduce inefficiencies, so the choice has to balance these countervailing tendencies.
3. **What is the technology road map?** Many technologies are marketed by firms that have rights over their development. Before acquiring any technology it is worthwhile enquiring how the firm intends to develop and grow it, which is known as the road map. If a technology is to be evolved in the future, then this enables the adopting organisation to plan for upgrades and modifications. If the technology is to be terminated or its development is uncertain, as it has lived out its useful life, then the adopting organisation may choose not to invest in it.
4. **What is the renewal cycle?** This question is related to the issue of the technology road map, and refers to the innovation cycle of the technology. As the technology is developed, it will

have to be upgraded by the users, and this typically follows a cycle. This cycle informs the users of the need for investments required for updating the technology as well as the need to plan for the related changes that will be required in the organisation.

5. **Is there vendor support?** For many organisations that have to rely on vendors for supporting their IT infrastructure, this is an important question. Sometimes a technology can be purchased from dealers, but they are not able to provide support, for which a separate vendor is required. Availability of support is often an important variable for purchasing the technology.
6. **What will be the nature of the technology lock-in?** Any technology acquisition is bound to create a lock-in to the technology in terms of the data created, the formats used, the familiarity with and the training invested into it. Organisations have to be consciously aware of the lock-in being created and how much it will cost to switch to another competing or superior technology.
7. **Make or buy?** Organisations also have to decide whether they want to build infrastructure components in-house or buy them from a vendor. This is a complex question that requires a detailed assessment of the organisation's internal IT skills, the nature of the technology and the availability of suitable vendors from whom to outsource.

9.2.3 The Technology Hype Cycle

It is well known that there is a very high level of innovation in the IT industry. IT products appear on the market at a very high rate, and some also disappear equally rapidly. It is worthwhile for managers who have to adopt and manage these technologies to be aware of the trends in the industry and be in a position to take clear decisions regarding the technologies. Occasionally, technologies are brought out into the market by some firms, and then these are marketed as being potentially very successful technologies that are likely to solve hitherto unsolved problems. The language used is often hyperbole, involving exaggerations and extravagant statements about the technology, often referred to as 'hype'.

The Gartner Group, a leading technology consulting firm, has examined the hyperbole surrounding a new technology and come up with a *hype cycle* (see Fig. 9.1) that describes the manner in which the hype about a technology increases and then decreases in the news media.

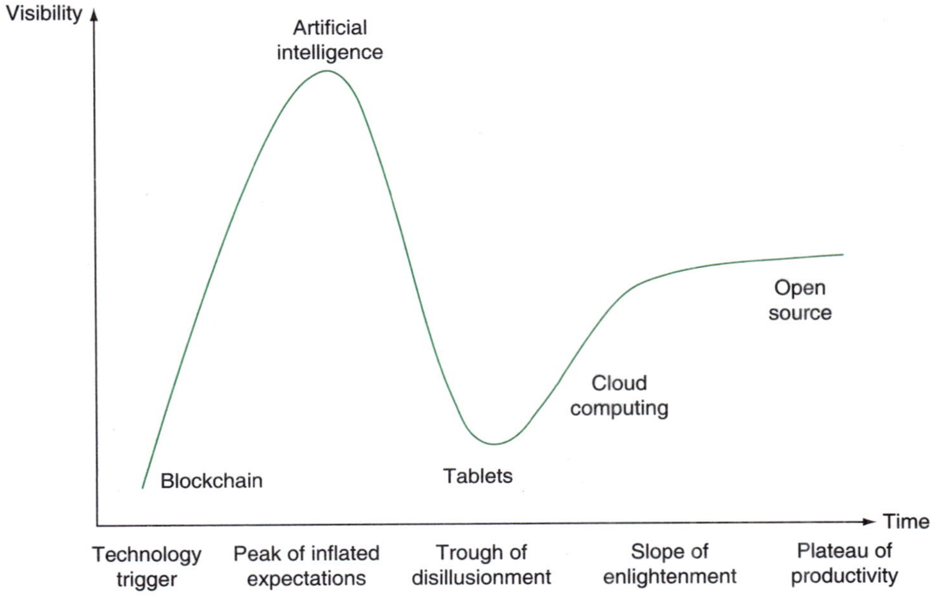

FIGURE 9.1 | Gartner's hype cycle — an illustration with examples drawn from the year 2017.

At the initial stages, when a new technology is announced, there is hope and anticipation. This triggers an increase or inflation in expectations, mostly in the technology media, which hypes up the technology. Media reports, television reports, interviews of the technology innovators, news about new firms being started up, etc. all add to the inflation in expectations. Soon, the media and users realise that the technology is either not mature enough to enter the market or not as good as the hype had entailed. This leads to a drop in the hype, or a certain disillusionment, and then as the technology improves, the true picture emerges. The hype around the technology disappears and the media and technology analysts are able to provide a better and more thorough analysis and assessment of the technology. At this point users are able to better understand what the technology can do and how it can be used within their domains.

KEY POINT

The Gartner hype cycle reflects the media coverage and hype about new technologies.

It is important to understand the hype cycle, more to be cautious about new technologies than to be scared away from innovations. Not all technology innovations are enveloped in such a hype cycle, and managers have to draw clear insights from the available knowledge about the value and use of a technology.

9.3 INFRASTRUCTURE COMPONENTS

The IT infrastructure consists of three broad categories of components:

1. Hardware.
2. Software.
3. Networks.

Hardware constitutes the computing equipment that is based on semi-conductor technology. Software constitutes the set of instructions that are written to drive the hardware. Networks consist of a combination of hardware and software whose main purpose is to move data. In a modern IT environment, none of these components can exist without each other. For instance, it is meaningless to think of having hardware without software to run it, or having software without hardware to run it on. It is possible to have and use hardware and software without networks but this is becoming increasingly rare.

In the following sections, the various components of hardware and software, and the various products are enumerated and described briefly. The objective is to have a broad understanding of the various kinds and categories of these products without going into an exhaustive enumeration of all of them. The discussion also touches on the issues of decision choices raised above.

9.3.1 Hardware

9.3.1.1 Processors

At the heart of every modern computer is a device that is principally responsible for doing all the computing and controlling other computer parts. This is called the processor or the CPU or the chip. A processor is made out of silicon and essentially contains a very large number of connected electronic elements called transistors. These transistors are arranged as computational elements, known as gates, which perform the basic computing operations such as adding, multiplying, subtracting and dividing. A typical modern processor consists of millions of gates that perform the essential computations of the computer.

The processors also have essential components that act as storage devices known as registers. The registers are fast storage devices that temporarily hold the data needed for computation. The gates read the data in the registers, do the computations and return the answers back to the registers.

The work in a processor is done in machine cycles. Each cycle consists of essentially two parts:

1. Instruction cycle.
2. Execution cycle.

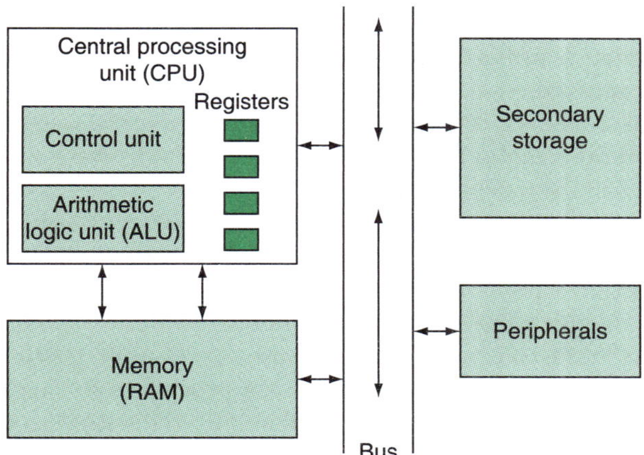

FIGURE 9.2 | Computer architecture.

A fixed number of things happen in both parts of the cycles, and the cycles are strictly timed by a clock. In the instruction cycle, the data and instructions are fetched from external memory and decoded for running them through the gates. This step reads data and instructions in the form of ones and zeros from the external memory [also called the random access memory (RAM) of the computer] that is associated with all processors. The instructions are decoded into a form that is understandable by the processing gates known as the instruction set. Each instruction states precisely how the data has to be moved through the gates for the processing. In this step, the data and decoded instructions are stored in the registers. The CPU consists of the control unit, the arithmetic logic unit (where the gates are located) and the registers. The bus is the pathway for transferring data around the computer (see Fig. 9.2).

In the second cycle, or the execution cycle, the instructions and data are fed through the gates and the results are stored back in the registers (see Fig. 9.3). The instructions that are acted upon could be related to transferring data (from one part of the computer to another), arithmetic operations such as addition and multiplication, logical operations such as the AND and OR, and control operations that determine a sequence of actions to take. Processors have specialised circuitry to handle various types of instructions, many of which are very complex.

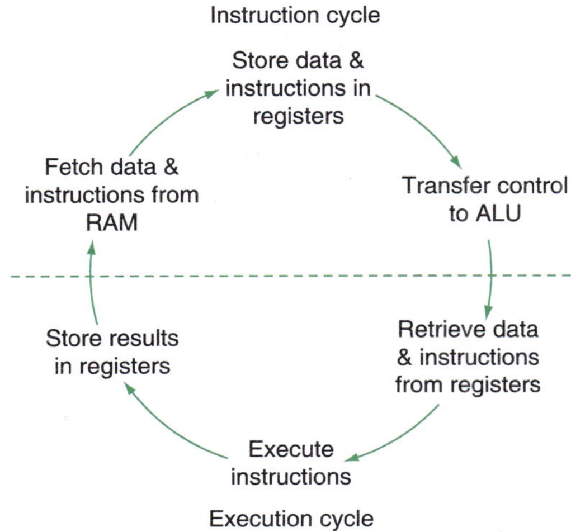

FIGURE 9.3 | The machine cycle.

KEY POINT

Processors run in cycles, which are measured in hertz-cycles per second.

Once a cycle is complete, the processor immediately starts another. The cycles are controlled by an internal clock that determines the speed at which the processor operates. A processor from a mainstream manufacturer could be rated to run at 3.33 GHz. One hertz is one cycle per second. A Gigahertz is a billion (10^9) cycles per second. A typical processor, in the year 2011, available in office computers runs a few billion cycles per second, where each cycle performs the entire set of operations in the machine cycle.

CPUs are designed with different kinds of architecture, where designers change the size of the registers, the type of instructions the unit can process, the speed of the clock and so on. The different designs of CPUs are possible and needed as there are careful trade-offs that have to be made. For example, sometimes the RAM of the computer is not fast enough to provide data to the CPU, which results in the CPU running *empty* cycles. Technically, this is called latency in the CPU. Designers often address the problem of latency by providing very fast memory, in addition to the RAM, which is called the *cache*. Data is transferred from the RAM to the cache at periodic intervals, and this is then provided to the CPU, which processes it and returns the results to the cache. Sometimes, the data in the cache is also outdated as the cache has not swapped it with the RAM, and this leads to a *cache miss*. Providing additional cache costs more, whereas lesser cache space leads to many misses and hence latency in processing.

Designers also build different kinds of instruction into CPUs. For instance, some processors are known as Complex Instruction Set Computing (CISC) chips, which have a large number of circuits (running into billions) that are dedicated to certain kinds of tasks, such as computations, movement of data and so on. The circuits are used when the required processing instructions appear in the data. When the instructions are not present the circuits are not used. An alternative design is to have a smaller set of instructions, called Reduced Instruction Set Computing (RISC), that allows the same circuits to be used repeatedly, and their combinations achieve all the different types of instructions. CISC processors are more expensive compared to RISC processors, which could be slower, but their performance depends entirely on the kind of tasks they have to do. A summary of several processor components is provided in Table 9.1.

Along with the processor, a computer consists of the main memory, called the RAM, a board on which these are located (also called the *motherboard*), a central pathway on which all the data travels, called the bus, a secondary storage device, called a hard disk, and a set of connection

Table 9.1 | Computer CPU Components and Their Meanings

Technical Term	Meaning
Registers	Very fast memory units built into the CPU. Data is written to and read from the registers during instruction and execution cycles.
Processing Gates	Lowest level of electrical circuitry that performs operations on data, such as addition, subtraction, etc.
Cache	Fast memory that is a supplement to RAM. Cache is faster than RAM, so it is used as a temporary store for data to be loaded into the RAM.
Complex Instruction Set Computing (CISC)	Computer CPUs that have billions of circuits to do different kinds of tasks.
Reduced Instruction Set Computing (RISC)	Computer CPUs that have a lesser number of circuits than CISC, and where the circuits repeat tasks.
Latency	When data is not moved fast enough in RAM then machine cycles run without data and are wasted. Designers try to avoid latency by using faster memory.

points to other devices, called ports. A typical desktop computer will have a configuration of a CPU, RAM, board, bus and ports, and hard disk along with peripheral devices such as a mouse, a keyboard and a monitor. The decisions about the configuration of each of these elements will vary along several characteristics that are discussed below.

9.3.1.2 The Computer

When the word 'computer' is used in everyday language, it evokes many types of devices as follows:

1. Desktops.
2. Laptop.
3. Servers.
4. Tablets and mobile phones.

A desktop is a personal computer that comes with a suitcase size casing and consists of all the elements that a computer needs. It is usually placed on or under a work desk, hence the name. Office desktops are connected to office networks. Desktop components are made by several manufacturers and are assembled by a few that brand and sell them. Hewlett-Packard, Dell and Lenovo figure among prominent desktop manufacturers. Desktops were at the maturity phase of their life cycle, by 2011 and their sales began to decline, as organisations preferred laptops. They key advantage of desktops was that they could be upgraded quite easily, as there is plenty of space in the CPU units to add or change the components.

Laptops are compact personal computers that range in size from that of a hardbound book to that of a small briefcase. All the components of a laptop are blended into one unit, including the monitor and the keyboard. An additional component they have is a battery that allows them to function without being plugged into the electric supply and hence they can be carried around and used anywhere (the batteries have to be charged by plugging into the electric supply). Many organisations have replaced desktops with laptops for many employees, especially for the employees who have to move frequently and work outside the office.

The current trends in laptops show that they are likely to remain strong in sales and evolution (see Figs. 9.4 and 9.5), both in India and worldwide, though there is a decline since the peak in

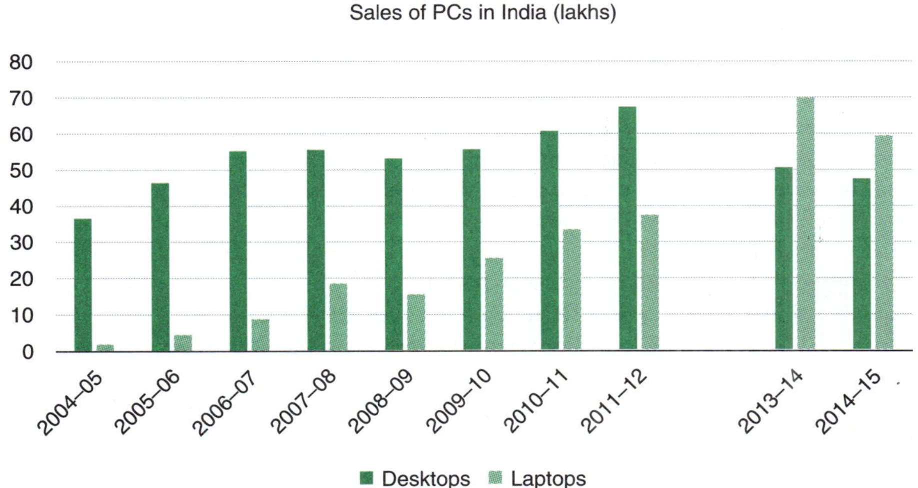

FIGURE 9.4 Trends in desktop and laptop sales in India 2004–2015, in lakhs of units (one lakh = one hundred thousand).

Source: Data obtained from the Manufacturers Association of Information Technology in India (MAIT).

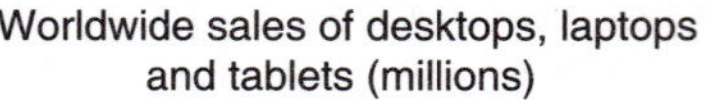

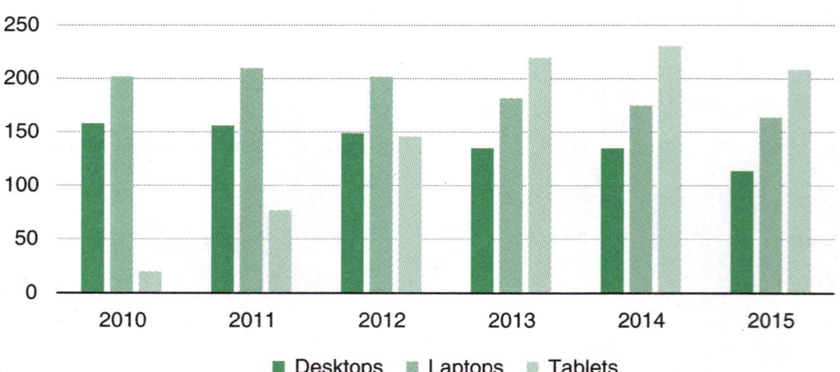

FIGURE 9.5 | Trends in desktop, laptop and tablet sales worldwide 2010–2015, in millions of units.

Source: www.statistica.com

2011, as usage of tablets has grown. They will be produced with faster processors, with possibly solid state storage making them lighter, and in a variety of sizes – from very small-screen notebooks and tablets to large laptops. Laptops typically have a smaller renewal cycle as they are more prone to physical shocks and mechanical wear. Laptops cannot be easily upgraded as the components within them are packed quite tightly and cannot be easily interchanged or replaced.

While acquiring laptops, organisations have to consider issues such as security features (where data has to be protected if the laptop is stolen or lost), the amount of processing the laptops will have to do, their ability to use various types of wireless and wired connectivity, the likely duration of one charge of the battery, and the size and weight of the laptop. Laptop purchases are usually more expensive than desktops, when compared feature by feature, but their usability is better as they can be carried around.

Servers and workstations are the third category of computers. Servers are used to provide applications to the entire organisation across its networks. Servers usually consist of high-speed processors and also have a high-capacity RAM. Some servers also have high capacity and fast hard disks although in modern servers storage is separated to another class of peripherals. Workstations are high-end desktop computers that have high-capacity CPUs and fast RAM and are used for specialised applications such as graphics manipulation and numerical processing. Servers are distinguished from *clients*, which are computers that demand and receive services from servers (see Fig. 9.5). Though servers mostly provide services, they also act as clients.

Servers are not designed for use as ordinary office desktops. They typically require a separate space that is air-conditioned and has extra backup for power supply. Servers are often available on racks, which are cupboard-like metal storage boxes in which a number of servers can be stacked up. Each individual server is a metal encased, rectangular box that is a half inch to a few inches in height, and is inserted into slots in the rack.

The server technology has improved significantly over the years. It is a deeply competitive field where manufacturers have introduced many innovations. One of the current trends is multi-core servers, where a single physical chip actually is more than one CPU, and these are used to distribute load when the need arises. Multi-core chips allow organisations to buy extra capacity and use it when required. As multi-core chips are bundled in the same box, they cost lesser than buying two individual servers. Multi-core servers also improve utilisation of servers and save on energy costs. Servers have a longer renewal cycle. Some servers have lasted even for decades because their processing capacity has not been exhausted and there is no need for replacement. Servers need renewal if the organisation's processing needs increase excessively, as sometimes happens with e-commerce servers.

9.3.1.3 Random Access Memory

RAM is volatile memory. It is able to retain its contents as long as there is power supply; if the power supply is stopped, RAM loses its content. This is in contrast to the secondary storage, like hard disks, which have non-volatile memory that retains its content even when there is no power available. Volatile memory is faster and can change its contents quite rapidly, which is why it is useful as RAM. The RAM speed is an indication of how fast the memory device is able to read or change its contents. RAM speeds are measured in nanoseconds; 1 ns is a billionth of a second. RAM speeds have evolved from hundreds of nanoseconds, over a decade ago, to about 6 ns in modern memory devices.

Choosing a RAM is quite simple: buy the fastest and largest RAM chips that can be afforded. Desktops and servers allow RAM to be upgraded if the applications so demand. However, this is not possible for laptops.

9.3.1.4 The Board and Bus

The board on which the CPU, RAM and other components are placed is also called motherboard. The original design of the motherboard was to enable modularity of all components. The idea was for designers to experiment with combinations of components of different types and from different manufacturers to obtain the best performance within cost limits. The motherboard used the bus as a central pathway for data to travel and through which the various components could interact. The evolution in bus technology has been significant, starting with a variety of bus architectures on the motherboard to the modern universal architectures that have blurred the distinction between connections inside the computer and outside.

The choices to be made with regard to the motherboard and bus technologies are based on the technology road map for the IT architecture and the manner in which it will allow components to interconnect.

9.3.1.5 Secondary Storage

The secondary storage used for desktops and laptops consists of two types:

1. **Fixed storage:** It refers to hard disks or solid-state storage devices with capacity sufficient to hold the operating system required to run the computer as well as the application software.
2. **Removable storage:** It consists of devices such as flash drives and compact discs; earlier floppy disks used to serve as the removable storage. The removable storage has rapidly evolved and settled on flash drives (see Fig. 9.6), which have no moveable parts, have large capacities and allow high-speed access. Fixed disks are also now being replaced with flash drives that have sufficient capacity.

The secondary storage used by servers has to be of much higher capacity than that used in personal computers. Historically, *tape drives* were used to store large amounts of data reliably and cheaply. These drives still provide the most cost effective and reliable storage available. Currently, a single tape can store about 1 TB of data. The drawbacks of tape drives are that they are slower than other drives, have to be manually loaded into the recording and playback units, and require a sequential reading process, as the tapes wind and unwind, which makes searching for data difficult and slow.

Data is also burnt onto compact discs that are then loaded onto multi-disc storage units, or disc jukeboxes, that allow the user to access any disc from the collection. Disc recording is usually slow, and multiple read-write operations on them are not easy. Typically, compact discs are used in applications where there is a need to write data once, and read many times.

Hard disks drives and solid-state storage devices (similar to flash drives) remain the most widely used form of the secondary storage for servers. Collections of many hard disks are used to create high-capacity storage systems that can be written to and read from rapidly. Such drives have very high capacities, running into hundreds of terabytes, and often have built-in backup

(a) (b)

(c) (d)

FIGURE 9.6 Images of a (a) floppy disk, (b) compact disk, (c) flash memory drive and (d) tablet PC.

Sources: Wiangya, Michelle Meiklejohn, Renjith Krishnan, David Castillo Dominici (Reproduced with permission from FreeDigitalPhotos.net).

devices that provide high security against disk crashes and data loss. Lately, the use of storage area networks (SAN) with hard disk arrays has become popular, where the storage unit is maintained separately on the network; however, to all the computers it appears to be an attached disk drive. SANs enable many users and computers to share the same storage, which can be effectively backed up and protected centrally. They also provide flexibility in scaling up as only the storage unit needs to be upgraded, not the computer boxes using the storage.

Some of the important issues with the secondary storage are those of

1. Security,
2. scalability and
3. recovery from disaster.

Data security is of utmost importance when shared resources are involved, and data management practices have to be strictly enforced. The business needs of many organisations now demand that the storage units be scalable, and the increased capacities be made available quickly. Recovery from natural and man-made disasters is also essential, for which many organisations rely on outsourced services that back up the entire data on SAN servers in remote, safe locations.

9.3.1.6 *Peripherals*

Of the peripheral equipment attached to CPUs, monitors have seen the most evolution - from monochrome cathode ray tube (CRT) monitors to high-density flat panel light emitting diode (LED) displays. The technology used to make monitors is the same as that for televisions, so the scale effects have reduced prices for all sizes and categories of monitors. The latest trend is of touch-sensitive monitors that will allow users to touch and point to objects on the screen along with a traditional pointing device such as a mouse.

Mouse pointing devices and keyboards use stable technologies. Printers have evolved to provide very high quality and resolution printouts at low cost. It is common to find scanners, faxes and printers all combined.

Almost all peripheral devices are now connected via the Universal Serial Bus (USB), which is now an industry standard. This means that organisations can invest in peripherals that work with USB and they will continue to operate with several generations of computers.

9.3.1.7 Tablet Computers

Tablet computers are made of a processor and memory that are mounted on a small board with provision for connectors and a device for user interaction. This device is a touch screen that allows users to type in and tap information as well as see the output. There are a large number of tablets available in the market, such as iPad or the Android tablets, though these devices are not as popular (in 2017) as they used to be. One of the early examples of a tablet built in India was the Simputer (see Fig. 9.7). Tablets computers use general-purpose processors to power their computing and make available a certain limited set of features to users.

Initially, tablets were used by organisations that had personnel who had to move about and also access or enter data on a frequent basis. For example, tablets were used in hospitals by doctors who wanted to quickly look up a patient's status or records. They allowed the doctor or nurse to quickly connect to a central server and recover the data. Tablets were also used by field personnel in organisations such as the armed forces, where the data related to field conditions was fed into the device and was later downloaded into central servers. Tablets are better for such applications than laptops or notebooks as they are easier to carry and their battery can last many hours.

Currently, all the features provided by tablets are available in many mobile phones, which combine the utility of a tablet computer with that of a phone. Mobile phones by firms such as Samsung and Apple have extensive computing facilities built in, and users can perform many tasks with them for which they would have otherwise required a computer, such as check email, write brief notes and prepare presentations.

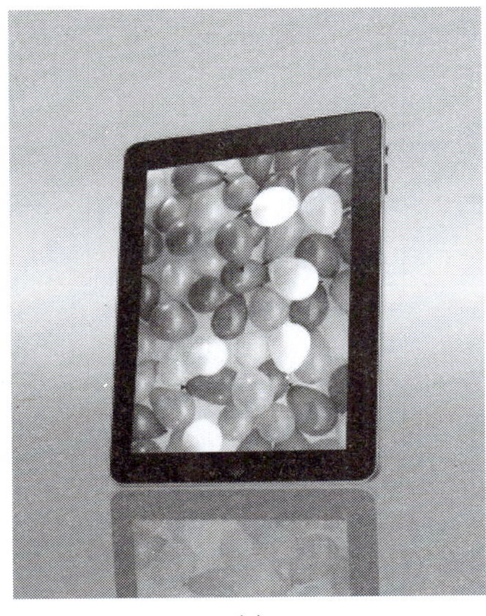

(a)

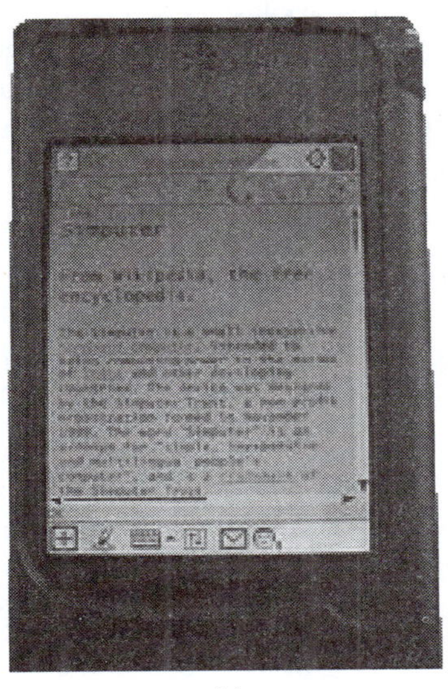

(b)

FIGURE 9.7 | (a) iPad and (b) Simputer.

Source: http://e123n.wikipedia.org/wiki/File:Simputer.png

9.3.2 Software

Software is the set of instructions that run hardware. When computers were invented, software was an integral part of the hardware, as the instructions were 'burnt into' the hardware. With the invention of the primary and secondary storage, it was possible to separate the software from the hardware. When a processor is started, it *boots* by reading the software instructions provided on the secondary storage. The software that controls the functioning of the processor and all peripheral devices is called the operating system (OS). The OS boots up the computer and takes control of all the components. It enables the computer to join a network, if available, and also allows users to interact with programs called applications.

Software is written in computer languages such as C, C++ and Java. These languages have an English-like structure that programmers can work with easily. After a program, known as the *source code*, is written in such a language, it is 'compiled' into a form that is loaded into the primary memory, that is, it is converted into binary form. Compiled programs are all in ones and zeros and are unreadable by humans. Software that is distributed only in the compiled binary version is called proprietary software, whereas software that is distributed with the source code is called open source software. A later chapter discusses open source software.

Software is categorised into two groups, by functionality:

1. Systems software that is used to manage the hardware, one example of which is an operating system.
2. Application software that is used by users to do their work. A word processor is an example of such software.

9.3.2.1 Operating System

The operating system controls all the hardware in computers. A typical operating system manages the work given to the processor, including scheduling various tasks and giving them priorities. For example, if a message is sent to the computer while it is processing a database file, then it is the operating system's job to determine whether the current task has to be interrupted or not, and how other tasks have to be queued up.

Another task of the operating system is to manage the primary memory or the RAM. It is itself loaded into the memory when the computer boots up and from then onwards it manages the rest of the memory space by loading and unloading programs. This activity requires keeping track of the available memory, the tasks that have to be loaded, how much space they will consume and what tasks have to be moved out of the RAM. For example, if a user is working on three applications simultaneously, say a spreadsheet, a word processor and a browser, the operating system has to load all of them in the RAM for them to be available (see Fig. 9.8).

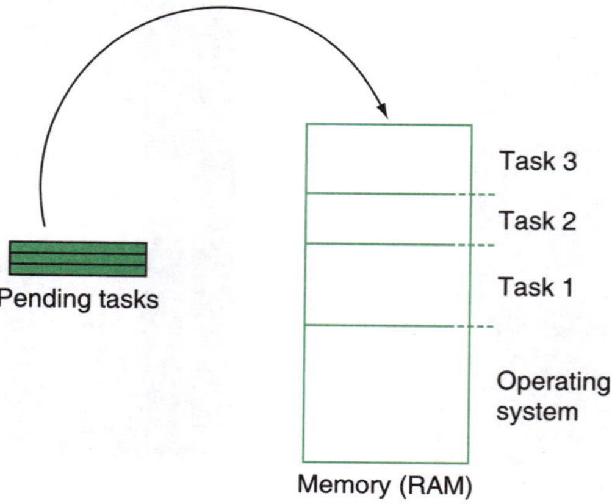

FIGURE 9.8 The operating system loads and unloads tasks in the main memory (RAM) and manages them.

It allocates space in the RAM for them to account for the programs themselves as well as the data the user might create. If the data is very large, say the user has a very large dataset in the spreadsheet, and this does not fit in the allocated space, the operating system has the ability to use the space on the hard disk, the secondary storage, to temporarily store the data and move it into the main memory (RAM) when required.

The operating system also manages and runs the *drivers* for all the peripheral hardware. A driver is a piece of software that is used exclusively to manage a device such as a keyboard, a mouse or a monitor.

The operating system also manages a user interface, which is graphical in most modern operating system, and allows the user to fire up applications, work with them and then close them. Most graphical user interfaces (GUIs) use the image of a window as the dominant theme to allow the user to interact with the system. The theme also uses the metaphor of the desktop, which is the opening screen that a user sees, and files, which are the data storage locations. Most GUIs also have a 'start' button, which is a sensitive area of the screen that can be accessed by a pointing device like mouse, and when pressed the button 'opens' a menu of choices for the user. This menu is a collection of files and applications from which the user can choose one.

KEY POINT

An operating system controls the hardware and allows the user to interact with the system.

Most GUIs also allow the user to configure the computer in a manner suitable to him/her. For instance, the user may want to change the appearance of the desktop, configure a new printer attached to the computer, delete files and folders (folders are files that contain other files) and so on. Most operating systems also allows the user to interact and control the computer with written commands, which act as a substitute to the GUI, from a special console window. These commands can be quite complex, sometimes allowing entire programs to be written, and allow the user to do a wide variety of tasks.

The operating system also runs the software that allows the computer to connect to others on the network, either through a cable or through a wireless connection. The operating system runs the drivers for the hardware responsible for doing the connectivity, called *network interface cards*, and then manages the connections by allocating resources to various applications that need them.

A key function of the operating system is to manage and maintain *user accounts*. An account is a collection of files and privileges that a user is given. Typically, most operating systems will allow one computer to have many accounts. With an account, a user is given an account name and a password. The user can access the resources of the computer, such as application programs, access to the internet, printing, playing music and so on only through his/her own account. Accounts enable the operating system to keep each user's files at separate locations and also allow different privileges to them. For instance, some user accounts will allow users to access a printer and some may not.

A *password* is a phrase or combination of numbers and letters that is a secret maintained by the user, and that allows the user to access the system. Passwords allow selective access to the system and help maintain security.

The operating system is responsible for the security of the computer system. It controls the manner in which files and programs are added to the computer, and monitors all incoming traffic from the network. An operating system uses a system of user privileges to allow only certain kinds of users to add or delete programs and files. For example, in most systems only the *root* account user has the privileges to add and remove programs. The root user is accessed by a password, which may be with an administrator in the organisation, and this root then controls all other users. A root user typically has access to all the parts of the system and also the passwords of all users in the system.

Harmful softwares, which are widely available on the internet, access systems by guessing the password of root users on servers. This is done by trying various combinations of words and letters that could be the password. Once the password of a root user is *cracked* then the entire system becomes vulnerable.

Some well-known and popularly used operating systems are described below.

Linux

Linux is a widely used open source operating system that runs a majority of the mobiles phones and tablets in the world, with the Android system, and is also widely popular on servers and also on desktops and laptops. Being an open source operating system, Linux is freely available to everybody and its source code is also made available along with the binaries. Linux is one of the most widely known open source softwares and as such there are hundreds of variations of Linux. Some popular brands of Linux are Android Ubuntu, Linux Mint, openSuse and Debian. Also, there are a very large number of open source application packages that work with Linux.

Linux has all the features of a modern operating system and can run on a wide class of hardware. One of its main advantages is its security - there are very few known viruses that infect Linux, and its protection levels have ensured that it is secure as a server.

Windows

Windows is a proprietary operating system sold by the Microsoft Corporation. Windows is particularly popular on desktops, but its variants are also used on servers. There are a vast number of application programs that work on Windows, and this gives it a competitive advantage. Many desktops and laptops come bundled with the Windows software.

The Windows system is threatened by over 1 million viruses that it can be infected with (according to a BBC report of 2008). The users of Windows also need to protect their computers with additional anti-virus and security software that comes at an additional cost.

MacOS

The MacOS is an operating system that works exclusively on the Apple Macintosh range of computers. This is a very stable, user-friendly and secure operating system. It has a vast range of applications that run on it. This operating system is widely regarded as one of the best designed for usability, as it allows users to work easily and productively, and manages the interface very well. It is not as popular as Windows but has a strong following in educational institutions and among the users who require graphics-intensive applications.

Solaris

One of the first operating systems to be developed was known as the Unix system, and was developed at the research laboratories of the AT&T Corporation in the USA. Later operating system has built on the concepts developed in Unix, and Solaris is one of those. Solaris is currently an open source operating system. It was originally developed by the Sun Corporation for running its high-powered servers. Solaris is a highly stable and secure operating system that is designed for high-performance computing, where the server can handle millions of transactions per second.

9.3.2.2 Application Software

Application software allows users to use the computer to do their work. Application software runs on the operating system, has to interact with it to access the hardware resources, and is managed by it. Application software is designed for a particular operating system and uses the facilities provided by it. For example, the word processing application called *Word* will run only on the Windows operating system as it is designed for it.

Application software can be selectively installed on the computer. For each kind of operating system, there are thousands of application packages available. Many organisations build their own application software as opposed to buying it off the shelf. The choice of building or buying is a difficult one that organisations have to undertake.

For open source application software, the source code is available along with the software binaries. With this users can modify the application to suit their needs. However, most commercial application software is not open source, and can only be tailored in a limited manner, depending on the facilities for configuring provided by the software.

There are a vast number of application programs that have been developed for a variety of applications. The following sub-topics identify major areas of applications and broad software development trends in those areas. Some of the applications are covered in greater detail in later chapters.

Databases

Databases are possibly the most important application software used by organisations. Their main function is to be a repository of data. They enable users to store data reliably and then retrieve it when needed in an efficient manner. Data has many forms, ranging from plain text data to multimedia data such as video clips.

One of the most popular databases is made by the Oracle Corporation of the USA. This database has capabilities to store vast quantities of data in its tables whose sizes can scale up to petabytes. It has built-in mechanisms for efficient retrieval, backup and security. The Oracle database is being used by organisations around the world, including commercial and public ones.

A close rival to Oracle is the MySQL open source database that also has very wide popularity. It has proved to be a highly stable and scalable database, with the advantage of being free of cost and having source code available. Many organisations have adopted MySQL and have tailored it for their needs.

For choosing a database, the important considerations are of the price, performance, stability, scalability and security. There are many small proprietary and open source database products that can meet the needs of small and medium organisations adequately. For mission-critical, high-end applications, it is important to choose a database that can meet the requirements for which products such as Oracle are strong contenders.

Database applications are not easily interchangeable and do create a lock-in when users opt for one. The formats on which data is maintained are often proprietary and not transferable to other products. Different database products also provide different data management facilities that are not available in all such products.

Enterprise Software

Enterprise software, also called enterprise resource planning (ERP) software, consists of application modules that can be used for the entire operations of an organisation. Historically, organisations used to buy or build software for individual departments and functions such as for finance and accounting, production, etc. These applications were tailored to the needs of particular departments or functions but could not, usually, interoperate with other applications. Organisations used to overcome this limitation, when there was a need to, by using software that would bridge the gap. This method was cumbersome and prone to errors. Then enterprise software came as a good solution to these problems.

Enterprise software enables all the functions and departments to work with the same standard of software, and interoperation is easy and convenient. The software allows data interchange between various functions on a real-time basis, and also produces periodic reports that aggregate data from across the organisation. The software allows management to have both a forest view of the organisation and a view at the level of trees and branches.

One of the most popular and widely used enterprise software products is SAP made by the German firm SAP AG. SAP has been adopted by organisations ranging from educational institutions and government departments to commercial organisations in different industries. SAP has modules for each function of the organisation that can be installed in sequence and then can interconnect easily. Furthermore, SAP has built-in configuration functions where applications can be tailored to the needs of the organisation.

Competitors to SAP include about 50 large and small proprietary ERP products and a host of open source products such as iDempiere, Openbravo and Compiere. The famous ERP products from SAP and Oracle tend to be expensive, so price is a major decision variable for organisations looking for such a product. The open source and smaller proprietary ERP products often have very stable and scalable modules for the needs of most organisations.

Office Productivity

A set of software applications has been developed primarily for the use of individuals working in organisations or at home. These are referred to as office productivity applications and consist of word processors, spreadsheets, presentation software, graphics manipulation software and databases among others. The goal of this package of tools is to enable the individual user to be more productive. Users can create or work on files that are relevant for their work, and then share these with others in the organisation.

The office productivity applications are very popular and are one of the main reasons people in organisations use computers. As files can be shared, these tools create network effects. The ability to share files enhances the value of using these tools more than that of individual use. An important issue for selection of the office productivity software is that of the data formats they use. Microsoft Office, which is one of the most widely used packages, uses proprietary formats for storing data. These formats are not shared by other packages. Open Office, the open source office productivity tool, uses open data standards, which can be used by any office application. Proprietary formats create a lock-in that is hard to overcome. For example, if an organisation has created a large number of spreadsheet files in the .xls format, which is a proprietary format used by Microsoft Excel, then this organisation is locked in to Excel as other spreadsheet packages may not be able to use .xls files. There are exceptions, though. For instance, Open Office can open .xls files in its own spreadsheet, but some functionality may be lost.

Utilities

Some software packages are designed to perform specific tasks related to managing files and data on the computer. These are referred to as utilities. Some examples of utilities are:

1. Compression software, which reduces the size of files so that the storage capacity can be used more efficiently.
2. Editor, a tool that allows users to write notes in plain text.
3. Calendar, a tool that allows users to maintain a schedule of activities.
4. File browser, a tool that allows users to see the files in their accounts and manage them, etc.

These software packages are usually provided freely with operating systems; however, some are sold independently. There are also a large number of utility packages available as open source.

Networking

A number of software packages provide access to the internet and to networking as such. The most popular application to access the internet is the browser, examples of which are Mozilla Firefox, Internet Explorer and Chrome. The browser allows users to 'surf' or move from page to page on the internet and also see videos or listen music on web pages that list them. Some web pages, especially commercial ones, are configured to work with only certain kinds of browsers. Organisations that need to access such pages frequently have to ensure that they have the right browsers installed.

Cross-platform browsers, such as Mozilla Firefox, are the most suitable for organisations as they function with any operating system, whereas browsers such as Internet Explorer work only with Microsoft Windows. Almost all browsers are available as free downloads, so there is usually no cost implications in deciding on them.

The most widely used application on the internet is email as it allows users to exchange messages asynchronously. Messages are sent across from organisation to organisation through email servers; however, individuals access the servers using email clients, Evolution on Linux or Outlook on Microsoft Windows, along with many clients available on Android and iOS mobile phones. The clients provide many features to users, allowing them to sort emails into folders, see emails in a certain order, such as chronological listing, filter out certain kinds of emails, view attached image or data files, store and locate addresses and so on. Email servers are also provided by external agencies like Yahoo and Gmail that allow users to create accounts that they can access on the internet through a browser or through an email client package.

Other popular networking applications allow various forms of communication over the internet. The Skype package, for instance, allows users to either communicate by exchanging text messages, referred to as 'chatting' or directly talk to each other by voice or over a video connection. The Skype package runs on many operating systems and is widely used as a low-cost and efficient means of communication. Peer-to-peer software allows users to exchange files directly over the internet without having to save the files on any server. Chat software allows users to exchange text messages in a peer-to-peer manner as also files and other data.

Multimedia Software

Multimedia software packages allow the user to either view or modify files containing images, music or video data. Among these packages is the popular package called Photoshop which is a proprietary software available only on the Windows operating system that allows users to modify image files. It is used extensively to modify photographs taken with digital cameras. The open source program, GNU Image Manipulation Program (GIMP), also does the same job and is available for many operating systems. Other software packages enable the modification of video and music files.

The choice of multimedia software is based largely on the capabilities and features of the program and the data formats they use. Proprietary programs, such as Photoshop, use proprietary formats but also provide an advanced set of features. Some packages are more suitable for professionals working as graphics designers, video editors or music editors, and for them the choice of software is based on features. However, for the casual users the feature selection is not important as their use is quite basic.

Software Development

There are a large number of application packages that have been written for the purpose of writing software programs. These range from complex programming environments, such as Eclipse, an open source package, which supports the software developer in many ways, to simple editors that assist with writing programs in languages such as Java or C. Currently, open source software development tools are widely popular and extensively used by developers all over the world, including those making proprietary software.

Software development tools assist programmers and developers in all aspects of the software development life cycle. They provide pre-packaged solutions for complex algorithms, graphical interfaces, networking tools, testing, de-bugging and maintenance. There is such a wide range of these tools that it is a complex job to select from them. Managers have to choose tools that their employees are familiar with or for which there is adequate training support available. Furthermore, the tools should have demonstrable competency, something that will have to be investigated before a tool is chosen. However, the most important requirement is that the tool should support the kind of application being developed.

Games/Entertainment

Games and entertainment software are very popular with home computers, and there is a wide range of such software. Many of these packages rely on high-performance graphics hardware and software that is able to render the complex images of games adequately on screen. Games are also an active area of development in open source.

Embedded Software

Most processors are designed as general-purpose processors, which means that they are capable of handling any type of computation that the software demands. However, there are processors available that have different capabilities, and have a different instruction set as compared to general-purpose processors. These special-purpose processors are used to control equipment such as machinery, hardware and fluid devices in cars. The software that is used for such processors is called embedded software, as the software too is written only for the processor chip and its limited instruction set. The software is resident on the processor chip in special memory modules. The chips have limited functionality and are designed to have a small 'footprint', which means that they use very little energy to run and use a tiny space in memory.

Embedded software has gained popularity of late owing to the widespread use of special-purpose chips in devices such as mobile phones, electronic health monitoring equipment, sensors in cars, consumer electronic devices (televisions and cable set-top boxes), cameras and sensors in industrial machinery (the latter are also referred to as Internet-of-Things or IoT devices, covered in Chapter 10). The embedded software is written in high-level languages such as Java and C, and then compiled specially for these chips. Open source software is used widely to both develop and compile the embedded software. Some of the latest chips have enough memory to hold an entire operating system, and many of these systems are based on open source operating systems.

9.4 NETWORKS

Networks consist of hardware and software components that enable organisations to create communication links both internally and externally or with the internet. Owing to the complex nature of this technology, a detailed discussion of networks is left to a later chapter.

9.5 SOLUTIONS

Organisations have built their IT infrastructure by assembling hardware, software and network components, and with few exceptions this has been the norm. This method represents a historical process where organisations outline their IT needs, budget and plan for them, and then execute the plan of acquiring IT. This results in a plethora of components that are interconnected and form a working infrastructure that is managed carefully and on which the organisation relies for its key operations. Such an infrastructure is fraught with many problems, as organisations realise over time. Some of these problems are outlined below.

1. When a technology is acquired, say technology A, it is ensured that it is compatible with other technologies, say B and C, which it has to interoperate with. This works until all the technologies are not upgraded. Later, when either B or C is upgraded, it may not be easy to ensure they interoperate with A.
2. Often technologies simply do not evolve further as has happened with some operating systems. For such 'orphan' products the manufacturer does not provide a migration path or road map, and users have to either support such products on their own or look for an alternative. This choice leaves them with the problems of interoperability.
3. Maintenance contracts and service contracts for different components of the infrastructure may have to be awarded to different vendors, as there may not be any single vendor who can manage all the different components. This leads to problems of managing many vendors and ensuring that they work together.
4. IT assets depreciate rapidly in accounting books. This happens due to the rapid obsolescence cycle of IT products. However, a fully depreciated asset, with zero book value, may continue to be a productive asset as it is still being used. It presents a challenge to accountants to identify its residual value or current value.

Owing to the problems of having a complex infrastructure, many solutions have emerged that address these issues. These solutions are a mix of hardware, software and networks that provide an alternative to the traditional IT infrastructure. Two such solutions that many organisations have adopted are cloud computing and virtualisation. Cloud computing is covered in Chapter 10.

9.5.1 Virtualisation

The virtual server is a technology that loosens the tight coupling between the hardware and the operating system. A virtual server is a software layer that is placed between the operating system and the hardware. This layer allows the same hardware to hold multiple operating system, while at the same time allowing multiple chips or processors to be used simultaneously, as if they were a single hardware unit. For example, if there are three processors A, B and C that an organisation has and uses, then in the traditional approach each of A, B and C processors would have an operating system running on it, which would allow multiple services to be run and enable users to use the system. However, the identity of A, B and C would remain distinct, and each server would have to be managed separately. With virtualisation, all the three servers can now be merged and would appear as one. The virtual software layer hides the difference between the processors and allows the operating system to pretend that they are running on one processor. Furthermore, the virtualisation software allows many operating system to be installed on the processors, where each would have its own dedicated resources of hard disk space, RAM and network connectivity. So, with virtualisation, the three processors A, B and C can now run several operating system, and within these several servers can be run (see Fig. 9.9). Users can now access each of the systems independently.

Virtualisation allows a better and more efficient utilisation of servers. If a load is high for a particular application then the server running this application can be given more resources than the other applications. Virtualisation also allows servers to be set up very quickly, because it involves simply adding an operating system and server software to the existing hardware. This feature is very useful for organisations that require servers to be set up quickly for a specific time-bound application, and when the application requirements are met, the server can be removed and the resources freed up for the other servers.

Virtualisation has allowed organisations, like TBZ, to consolidate many different servers into one single virtual server, making it a lot easier to manage. Virtual servers can share all resources such as printers and other peripheral hardware. Large and sophisticated storage devices can be used with virtual servers to provide extensive and reliable storage capabilities. Also, servers can be backed up effectively, thus allowing quick recovery in case of emergencies.

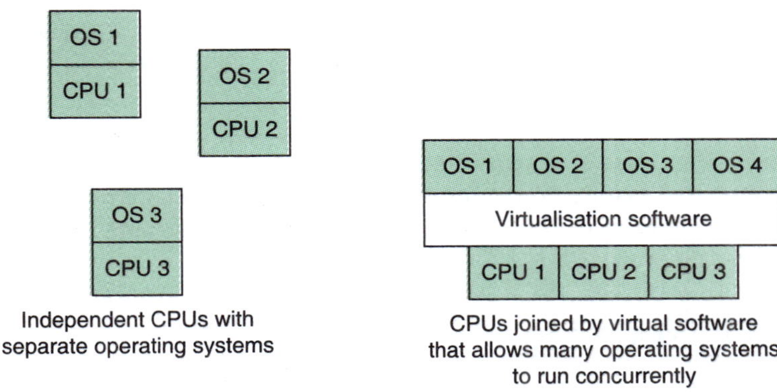

FIGURE 9.9 | Use of virtualisation software allows many CPUs to be used together to increase capacity and improve services.

Caselet Bring-Your-Own-Device (BYOD)

Employees of many organisations purchase and use their own mobile phones and tablets, which they also bring to the workplace. They use the devices for work activities – such as checking email, editing documents, reading reports, etc., along with their personal use. The trend of employees bringing their own devices was dubbed bring-your-own-device (BYOD) by the industry. Once this trend became prominent in organisations, it also raised management issues. The main issues were regarding data access from the organisation's systems and security of the devices. Since users brought a wide variety of hardware devices and platforms, there was no uniformity of screen sizes or formats that could be used to design reports from systems. Thus, for example, if the corporate ERP had to provide a report to be displayed on a mobile device, the size and display resolution of the device had to be estimated in order to ensure the report appeared visually similar to what the employees were used to on computers or laptops. The security problem was that of having a variety of unsecured devices entering the organisation's boundary with, possibly, viruses and other malware. Further, the managers also had to ensure that data made available on the devices was secure and could not be replicated and taken out of the organisation.

Managers and CIOs of organisations were, despite the challenges, upbeat about BYOD and wanted to enable it, as younger employees were keen on using their own devices. The problems were addressed in different ways. In Essar Group, a large and highly diverse company in India with interests in steelmaking and construction, the issue was of encouraging younger employees to bring their own devices and use the information systems present in the organisation to help them with their work and become more productive; one aspect was being able to work on their own devices from anywhere and at any time. Essar's challenge was to provide data in a useful manner from their enterprise systems to the mobile phones and tablets that employees brought with them. Further, they also wanted to secure the data and ensure that it was not taken out of the organisation. The answer that Essar found was to create a virtualisation layer of their software and applications, where this virtual layer was loaded on to the devices of users, with the result that each user device had two virtual environments, one for using for work and another personal. Virtualisation solved the two problems of data presentation and security: the enterprise systems were upgraded to provide data to the work environment in a manner suitable for the device, and it also prevented entering or removing data, thus securing the system. Essar's method was successful and led to wide adoption of the BYOD programme.

Other firms followed different strategies to implement BYOD, even though there was resistance from top management, in many cases, to allowing non-standard devices to proliferate within the premises of the organisation. The policies that supported BYOD were mainly based on having employees sign on to an enterprise app or programme from their devices while on the premises, and then using the data and processes available there. This ensured a measure of security and ease of use for the facilities that enabled the BYOD to work.

9.5.2 Enterprise Systems

Enterprise systems are a class of systems that allow multiple possible applications to be run in a centralised, coordinated manner. An example, discussed above, is enterprise resource planning systems. Another example is customer relationship management systems. This class of systems is covered in a later chapter.

9.5.3 IT Outsourcing

Managing the information systems of an organisation often requires using vendors to provide both infrastructure components and also to provide services (these issues were covered in Chapter 6). *IT outsourcing* refers to the process of contracting out the management of computing resources of an organisation. Outsourcing gained prominence in the early 1990s as many firms in the US and Western Europe started contracting IT companies from India to both create information systems and to manage their IT infrastructure. This led to a boom in IT firms in India, with the establishment of now famous companies such as Infosys, Wipro Technologies and Tata Consultancy Services.

The reasons why organisations outsource IT are many:

1. Organisations do not have sufficient capabilities, in terms of staff and skills, to do the functions they outsource (such as building a system or managing IT infrastructure).

2. The cost of managing a function internally is higher than outsourcing it leads to a natural choice of the latter. Many firms in the US decided to outsource system building tasks to Indian firms as the costs of software engineers in India was lower than that of the US.
3. IT management is often regarded as a staff function, which is not the major activity of the organisation, and it is difficult to hire and retain IT employees, as they do not see a career path for themselves in the organisation.
4. Organisations often choose to focus on their core activities, which may be manufacturing or service, and outsource all non-core activities to vendors. By this approach they can reduce their own management burden and have access to vendors who are highly skilled in their tasks.

For an example, consider the case of the Indian Institute of Management Bangalore (IIMB), a leading business school in India, deciding to renew its outsourcing contract for managing its IT infrastructure with ABC Technologies in 2009. IIMB is a relatively small academic institution, with less than a 1000 students on campus, about 300 faculty and staff, located on a 100-acre campus in south Bangalore. IIMB's core infrastructure consists of a campus-wide LAN, of both wired and wireless components, a central virtual server, which hosts close to 40 independent servers, and switches and routers to connect to the internet. IIMB had to manage over 700 desktop computers and laptops used by faculty, students and staff in offices, classrooms and computer laboratories. To manage this infrastructure, IIMB had a staff of three engineers and a manager. In addition, IIMB was in the process of implementing an enterprise software package that would require additional staff and IT resources.

IIMB's decision to outsource to ABC was based on the criteria mentioned above. The existing staff strength and skills were simply not enough to manage the complexity of the IT infrastructure. IIMB had already outsourced much of its systems management tasks since 2001, with the result that no new staff had been hired internally. The costs of hiring, training and retaining staff who could manage the systems was clearly going to be more than the cost of outsourcing. Besides, with the acquisition of new technology, it was imperative that the necessary skills required to manage these technologies be readily available, which outsourced vendors could provide. IIMB's core activities are academic in nature, consisting of teaching, research and interactions with the industry. Managing the IT infrastructure drew on time of faculty, staff and students, which could be well avoided by bringing a competent outsourced vendor. ABC Technologies is a major IT vendor in the country, with vast experience in managing such accounts. Their skills and experience convinced IIMB management to enter into an outsourcing contract.

Managing an outsourced vendor poses significant challenges and risks. Many outsourced deals in the early 1990s in the US did work very well, owing to many reasons. The main one was that there was a mismatch between the client's and vendor's expectations regarding the services to be delivered. In other cases, clients found that their own employees resisted the change, particulary when many employees were fired as their roles were absorbed by the vendor. Another reason was that many firms underestimated the costs associated with the contract, and with the ballooning charges decided to terminate the contract.

IT outsourcing contracts are based on several different models. These vary by the type of payment scheme, the location of the vendors, the ownership basis of hardware and software, and the management basis of resources. Some typical models are as follows:

1. **Time and materials:** In this model, the vendor brings skilled staff and resources, such as software and computers, to the site of the client to build systems. Such a model is best suited for clients who are not very sure of their requirements, and need the skills of the vendor to get going on their project. The vendor bills the client for the hours spent on the job (per employee) and the costs of the hardware and software used. Hence, the term 'time and materials' is used.
2. **Exchange based:** In this model, the client and the vendor draw up a specific contract on the nature of the work: (a) How long it will take, (b) what has to be completed and (c) how

much it will cost. Such a model can be used by clients who are sure of their requirements and can specify in advance what they want from the vendor. In such arrangements, the clients transfer control of all IT assets such as software licences, hardware and even personnel over to the vendor. The vendor may maintain personnel at the client site, and also have personnel dedicated to such a client at their own offices.

Though this model of outsourcing has many advantages for the client, it also involves many challenges. Many such outsourcing contracts have suffered as clients had not estimated their needs accurately, had not defined service levels expected from the vendor carefully, had not created sufficient flexibility in the contract to escape from a situation of lock-in and were unable to manage the client-vendor relationship carefully.

3. **Cloud based:** In this model, as was discussed earlier, clients enter into an agreement to use the cloud-based services of a vendor, with the arrangement that the vendor will provide the customisation of the software application and maintenance of it. The software and hardware assets are owned by the vendor and the staff also remain on the vendor's site. The contract is based on a fixed annual or monthly fee, plus a variable fee determined by usage. This model is suitable for client organisations that want a lower cost of operations and are also fine with standardised solutions.
4. **Joint ventures:** In this model, the client and vendor partner to form a third company, as a joint venture. Both invest capital, but the vendor provides the skill and personnel and the client becomes the first customer of this new firm. The objective is to scale up operations of the new firm by allowing it to seek new customers based on the special expertise it has gained by managing IT for its parent. If successful, such a model allows the parent client firm to realise profits, as well as have a reliable vendor for its own operations. However, such joint ventures may not succeed if they are not able to attract other clients and in such cases the parent firms may return to an exchange-based contractual arrangement.

Outsourcing has played a major role in developing the IT industry in India. Many US and European organisations outsourced their IT management to Indian firms, mainly for systems construction and maintenance. Indian firms used to maintain some of their employees at the client's premises, and these employees were referred to as onshore staff. For each onshore team there was an offshore team that resided in India and supported the onshore team's work. Owing to the time difference of about 12 h between the US and India, it would often happen that onshore teams, and their clients, would submit problems and requests during their working day, and the offshore team would work on it during its working day, when the onshore team was off work, and return the completed work at the end of day, which was early morning the next day for the client. This 'round-the-clock' outsourcing service proved very beneficial to the Indian IT outsourcing vendors.

Chapter Glossary

IT Infrastructure The information technology infrastructure consisting of hardware, software and networks are the facilities that are needed by an organisation to function effectively.

IT Architecture The hardware, software and network components that enable capabilities needed for the IT infrastructure of the organisation.

IT Ecosystem The complete IT-enabled environment that exists within organisations for employees to work with.

Technology road map The plans for the development and future growth of any technology.

Renewal cycle The period in which technology components have to be upgraded, as determined by their road map.

Central processing unit (CPU) The central core of the computer where all the computing and control activities take place.

Servers Computers that provide applications, data and services to other computers across the organisation.

Clients Computers that draw services and data from servers.

Random access memory (RAM) A very fast data storage device that is used by the CPU to do computing tasks. This storage is volatile, that is, the data is maintained in memory as long as it has electrical power.

Motherboard The basic hardware platform on which all the components of the computer are placed.

Secondary storage The storage that is slower than RAM but has much higher capacity to store both data and software applications. The secondary storage is not volatile and can store data in the absence of electrical power.

Peripherals Hardware devices such as monitors, keyboards, printers and cameras that connect to the CPU and provide needed services.

Operating system A software that is loaded into the CPU and that runs all the operations of the computer and peripherals.

Graphical user interface (GUI) The visual interface by which a user interacts with a computer. This is a part of the operating system.

Password A secret code, consisting of letters or numbers, which allows a user to access services of a computer or network. It is used for protection and security.

Application software A software that allows users to do the work for which they are using the computer. This software uses the operating system to access the services of the computer and other devices.

Enterprise software An application software that is used across the organisation and provides many services.

Office productivity An application software used by individuals in offices or at homes that allows creating documents, managing data and accessing networks among other things.

Embedded software A software that is used to run special-purpose processors, which are used in cars, home appliances, medical devices, etc.

Virtualisation Use of a virtual server is called virtualisation. A virtual server allows many CPUs to function as a single unit on which many operating systems and many applications can be run simultaneously.

Review Questions

1. Read the case at the beginning of the chapter and answer why TBZ considered using virtual servers for their organisation.
2. Define what is the IT infrastructure for an organisation?
3. What are some business needs on the basis of which the IT infrastructure decisions should be made?
4. Should the Hype Cycle of Gartner be taken seriously? Why?
5. Why should managers consider a technology road map before buying a technology?
6. What are the essential components of a computer processor?
7. What are the differences between registers, RAM, cache memory and secondary storage? You could do some research on the internet to know more about these different types of storage devices.
8. How are laptops different from servers?
9. What are tablet computers?
10. What is the difference between systems software and application software?

Research Questions

1. What are the challenges managers face while adopting virtualisation?
2. What are the new evolutions in processor architecture? Search on the internet to find out what new types of processors are being researched and designed?
3. Chapter lists only certain classes of application software. Can you mention any other, which are not covered? What are these applications used for?
4. Tablet computing has been declining, since 2015, after a very promising start. Why is it so?

Further Reading

1. www.tbztheoriginal.com/(accessed on October 2010).
2. www.expresscomputeronline.com/.../express intelligententerprise09.shtml (accessed on October 2010).
3. www.vmware.com/files/pdf/.../apac_in_09Q4_ss_vmw_TBZ_english.pdf.pdf (accessed on October 2010).
4. http://www.cio.in/case-study-byod-essar-way.

CHAPTER 10

Cloud Computing and Internet-of-Things

Learning Objectives

After completing this chapter, you will be able to:

- Understand cloud computing
- Know the rationale for cloud computing
- Know about the different types of cloud infrastructure and services
- Understand the challenges of migrating to the cloud
- Get an understanding of the economics of cloud computing
- Understand Internet-of-Things (IoT)
- Know about sensors and actuators
- Understand the architecture of IoT

Cloud computing enables computing infrastructure and services to be available over the internet. This provides many benefits to organisations, such as scalability, measured use, reduced setup time and many others. Cloud infrastructure may be private, public, hybrid or community. Cloud services are provided as an infrastructure (IaaS), a platform (PaaS) or as software (SaaS). Migration to cloud services entails challenges and opportunities. Cloud services are built on technologies such as Software Defined Networking (SDN) and Containers. The economic rationale of moving to cloud services includes avoiding capital expenses and purchasing capacity on an incremental basis.

Internet-of-Things (IoT) consists of a large number of sensors and actuators connected via the internet to sense and respond to their environment. IoT systems are used extensively in industrial operations, in healthcare, in homes and personal devices, amongst many others. Managing IoT requires dealing with massive volumes and variety of data. Designers rely on a four-layer framework to configure and manage IoT.

MIND MAP OF CHAPTER TOPICS

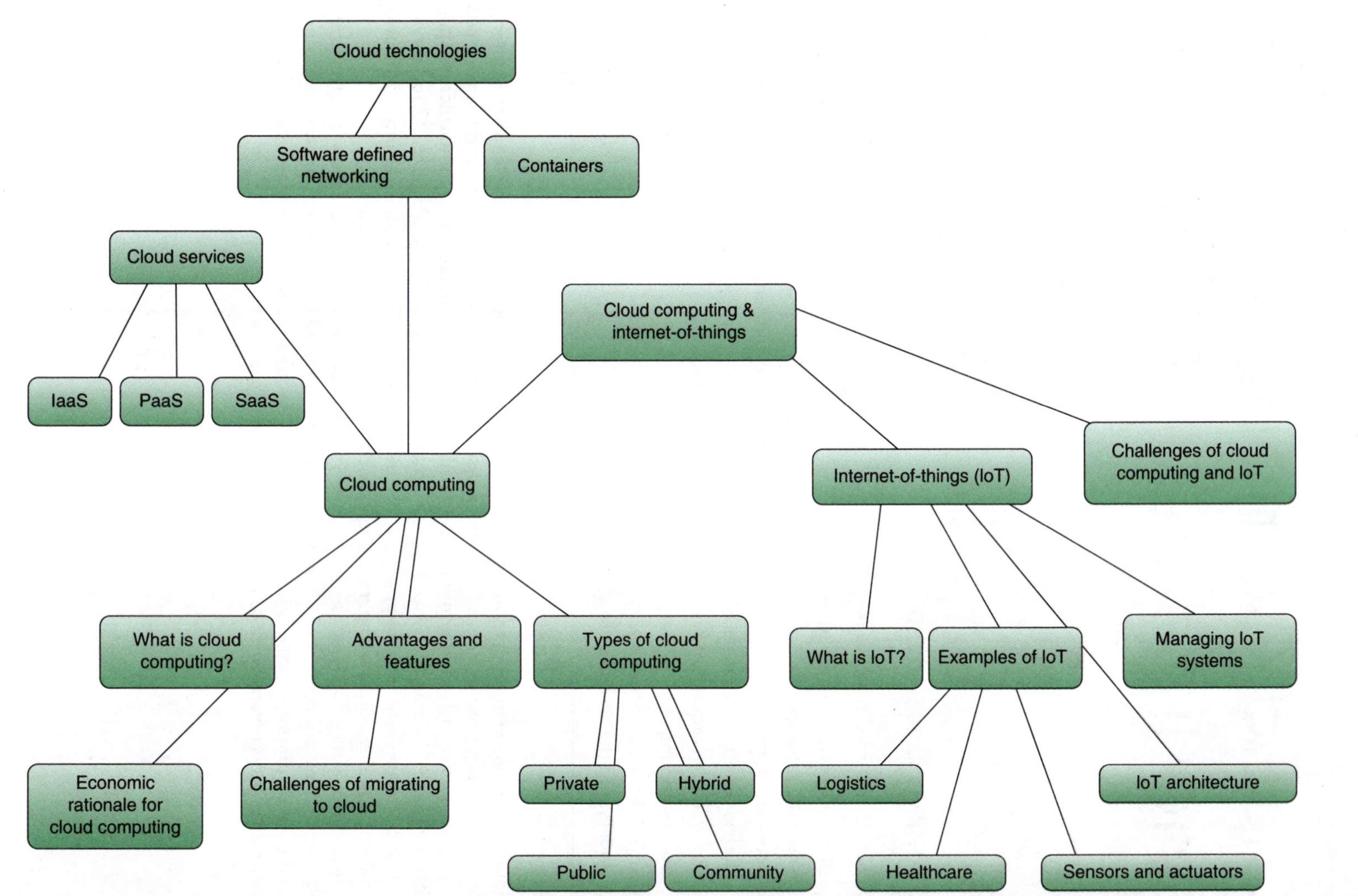

IDOS provides a Software-as-a-Service (SaaS) product that enables firms to manage their accounting data entry and set up controls. The product is suitable for a wide range of firms and organisations - in fact, any organisation that has to keep accounts can use IDOS. The idea behind the product is to allow employees in any organisation to enter data into their accounting system in a manner that is consistent with the organisation's internal policies and procedures. IDOS is like a "digital voucher" that can be used by any employee to file accounting data.

The idea for this product came from the problems that Cheruku Srikanth, one of the founders of IDOS, faced while working as a consultant for two large multi-national firms in the USA. These firms had 99% of their projects outside the USA, where they had field offices. Although they had wel-trained people working with their Enterprise Resource Planning (ERP) system at the head office, the problem was getting consistent and accurate data into the ERP system from the field offices.

Srikanth and his co-founder realised that this task was repetitive in nature and hence could be automated; and if automated, the cost of cleaning data could be reduced. Digging further into this matter they found that not all employees were qualified accountants and many were afraid of technology. The solution, they realised, was to provide a simple application that did not require domain knowledge and was easy to use. This way the people at remote sites would be encouraged to use it on their own. Also, correctly formatted data could be sent to experts with domain knowledge. These problems were not limited to US organisations alone. Detailed research showed that this problem existed worldwide in organisations of all sizes and types. So, if a solution could be found it would solve problems of many organisations worldwide.

IDOS provides a methodical step-by-step approach to maintain the internal controls on authentication and verification for different roles. The system checks for controls like approval, budget limitations, bills, etc. This is a system check at the transaction inception itself. When posting a transaction into a ledger there are many steps involved for verification, which accounting software like Tally or QuickBooks do not do. So, IDOS creates a structure where internal controls can be complied with at the creation of the transaction, so that audit can be in real time. The workflow is the same for any size of company. In addition, the system makes it possible to add or change rules for further customisation in a simple manner. The advantage of IDOS, as compared to an ERP system, is that it takes very little time to train users to understand and use the system.

Relying on the cloud as the infrastructure on which to host and launch the SaaS was key to the initial success of IDOS. The product was designed for clients who had geographically distributed offices or services, where accounting data had to be collected from diverse locations. For example, in the case of a client in India, Mother Dairy, a milk collection and distribution firm, accounting data on amounts paid to milk vendors or amounts collected from sellers had to be recorded from hundreds of buyers and sellers across a wide region. The data was collected on tablets or laptop computers that ran client's software that was connected to the IDOS application on the cloud. The data was entered and saved directly onto the cloud and made available to the management almost instantly. This widespread connectivity and availability allowed data to be collected at the point at which it originated, hence enabling immediacy and accuracy, and also allowed decision making with accurate and up-to-date data.

Another advantage of being on the cloud was that IDOS could roll out the product worldwide and also customise it for local conditions. For example, though the product was available to clients in both India and Venezuela, the language in which users saw the interface, on their client devices at their locations, was different. Those in India could see the user interface in English or a local language, whereas those in Venezuela could see in Spanish or English. Though the core product was the same, the presentation at different locations was customised according to the need.

To attract first-time customers and to draw attention to their product, IDOS relied on the well-known "freemium" model. They gave the client software to the potential user and created accounts for them. Users could now begin to make posts and add data to their accounts. This helped them see how the software functioned and also understand how they could use the software for their own work. The free account was available for a limited period, usually a month, after which a paid account had to be used. The benefit of having a cloud-based account for users was that when they switched to the paid version, they could pay for only the number and type of accounts and services they needed, initially, and then scale up as they wanted. IDOS too could customise the product to the users' needs based on their requirements and scale, letting them bill according to the usage of the product and not on a fixed charge.

IDOS did face initial resistance from generations of users who were used to the "hosted" model of software, where the software is on their premises and on their servers, without having to rely on an external cloud. The hosted model seemed to be more secure as it was on the premises of the client and could not be tampered with easily and also promised to enable better scalability and performance. Depending on the need, the hardware could be upgraded and scaled, and it was an asset created within the firm. The cloud seemed suspicious to them, particularly from the perspective of security: It was outside the premises of the organisation and the users had no idea of where the servers were located and how they were secured.

Another challenge to having an essential service on the cloud is that of connectivity. IDOS's basic proposition was that their product could be accessed from anywhere and at any time; however, this required internet connectivity at all times. This was a challenge in remote areas, such as in remote parts of India, where last mile data connectivity is not reliable or even available. Organisations that needed the service IDOS provided were aware of this challenge and questioned this. The point remains that last mile connectivity affects all types of products and services that are offered via the internet, including cloud-based products, and hence a hosted set of servers and clients would also be equally affected, thus the cloud-based model was not necessarily worse off.

IDOS succeeded in convincing their clients that the cloud-based model was indeed the best option, also by arguing that they were relying on Microsoft Corporation's Azure cloud, a cloud service that was considered reliable. This gave confidence to their customers who were mainly from the small and medium business segment. Larger customers too began to try out and then buy their product.

10.1 CLOUD COMPUTING

10.1.1 What is Cloud Computing?

The idea of cloud computing is that computing facilities and infrastructure can be obtained over the internet and do not always have to be hosted on the premises of the organisation. Cloud computing can be best understood by contrasting it with traditional organisational computing or hosted computing. Consider Fig. 10.1, which depicts a typical, traditional computing infrastructure in an organisation. The organisation has some servers (perhaps a web server, a database server, an application server, a storage server) and some client devices (such as laptops, desktops, tablets or smartphones) that run applications hosted on the servers. An organisation such as this would also be connected to the internet, from which it can access web services such as search, email, news articles and so on. The organisation would have to maintain this infrastructure by acquiring and maintaining the servers and the software that they use.

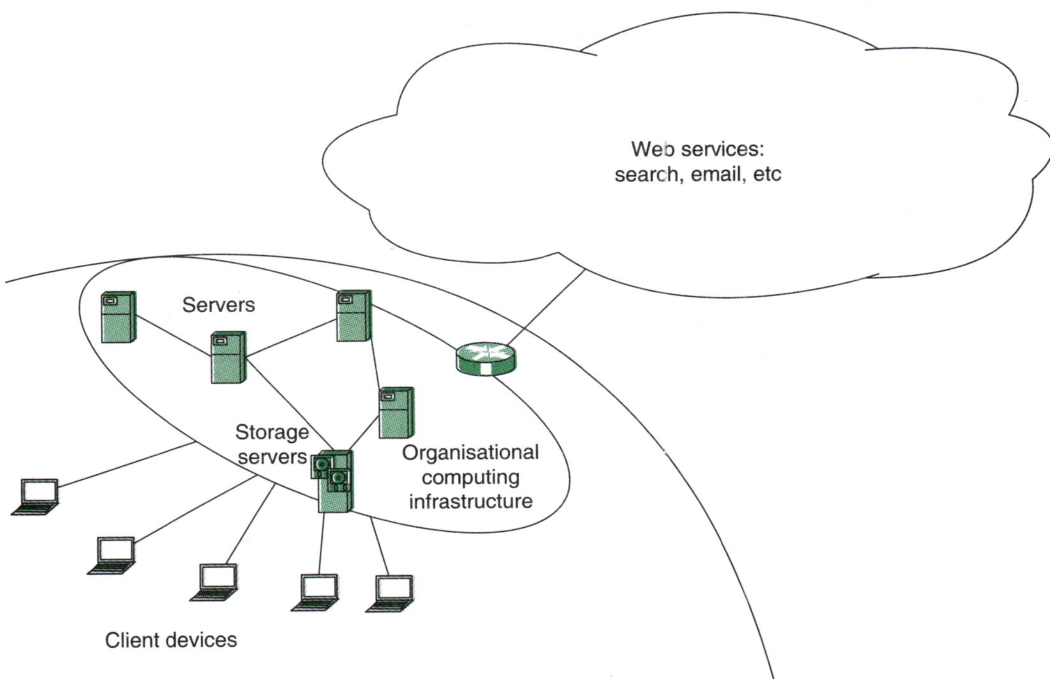

FIGURE 10.1 Hosted infrastructure. Here the organisation owns and maintains its own infrastructure of servers and draws on some web-based services from the internet.

Now consider Fig. 10.2, which depicts an organisation that is accessing servers from a provider on the internet. The different servers (application, database, storage, etc.) are now available via the internet and the organisation uses client devices and an internet connection to access these facilities. The servers are said to be on the Cloud. The organisation does not have to acquire or maintain these servers, as they are maintained by the cloud provider, and instead can focus on using them on a leased or rental basis.

The lead case on IDOS showed how the firm relied on cloud computing to offer its services to its clients. The clients accessed IDOS's products via the internet by simply logging on to the system. IDOS maintained all the hardware and software, doing the upgrades and customisations for their customers, transparently and without the direct involvement of their clients.

KEY POINT

Cloud computing enables computing facilities and infrastructure to be made available over the internet.

There are several differences in the ways in which computing infrastructure is both managed and accessed in the two scenarios presented in Figs. 10.1 and 10.2. These differences are what distinguish traditional hosted computing from cloud computing, and point to the advantages that cloud computing has. These differences are elaborated below.

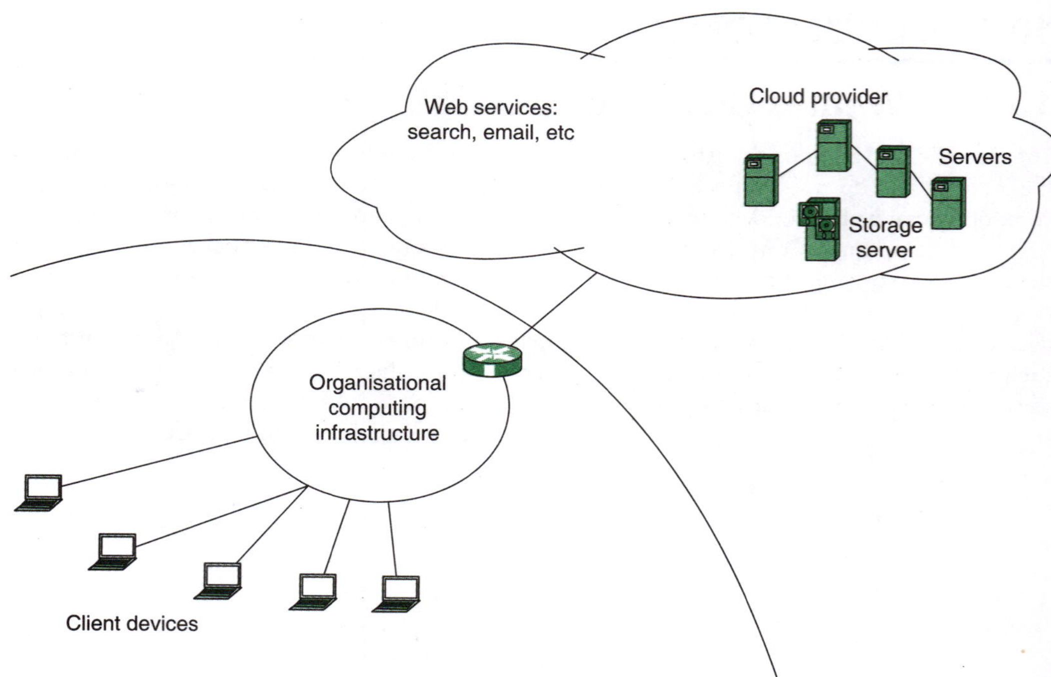

FIGURE 10.2 | Cloud infrastructure: Here an organisation draws on server and storage resources from the cloud and maintains a minimal infrastructure internally.

10.1.2 Advantages and Features of Cloud Computing

10.1.2.1 Scalability

Hosted facilities have a certain scale or capacity. For instance, typical computing facilities will be designed for a certain number of users (employees of the organisation or customers) or for a certain volume of processing (number of transactions to be completed per day or per hour). When these numbers change significantly - say when a firm experiences strong demand for its product and has to deal with a large number of customers - the organisation can scale up its facilities by buying new servers, adding more network capacity and buying more licenses for the software packages it uses. This takes time and careful management, and is prone to delays and cost escalation. The word *scalability* in this context refers to the ability of the IT infrastructure to address the needs of the increased demand.

When facilities are accessed from the cloud, scalability improves considerably. The client firm can acquire increases in infrastructure resources from the cloud provider and these can be provisioned rapidly. In many cases, the provider can make available increased resources in a real-time manner, based on the rate at which the demand is growing. The main advantage for the client firm is that they do not have to acquire, install and configure additional IT resources, and avoid the risk of delays. In this sense, cloud-based infrastructure is more scalable than hosted infrastructure. This is evident in the IDOS case, where IDOS provides a scalable infrastructure to its clients, where they can start with only a few accounts but can increase according to their need and as their business grows.

10.1.2.2 Elasticity

A concept related to scalability is *elasticity*. Elasticity refers to the ability of the infrastructure services to both expand and contract depending upon the demand. In a hosted facility, components that are acquired become assets and are permanently available for use. If not used, the capacity utilisation of these assets declines. However, in situations where demand declines, or the firm entirely drops a line of business, to explore another, utilisation of such assets may decline.

A cloud-based infrastructure permits reduction in resources, where specific resource parameters, such as the amount of CPU processing available, the amount of storage, the number of licenses for a software can be reduced as demand declines. This usually involves informing the cloud provider about the reduced requirements and switching them off.

10.1.2.3 Measured Use

Measurement of use of IT infrastructure services remains a challenge. Hosted services are typically assembled with components acquired from many vendors and may belong to different manufacturers and brands. When in use it is difficult to monitor their usage in a comprehensive manner and ascertain exactly how much each asset is being used.

Cloud services, on the other hand, are measured accurately and their design includes meticulous and thorough measurement of all services. A cloud provider can provide detailed reports to clients about the extent of use of resources along parameters such as the CPU utilisation in cycles per unit time, the memory usage in unit time, the data usage for read or write in bits per unit time, and so on. These measures provide a very accurate picture to the management about the extent of use or under-utilisation of resources. These parameters help with determining whether scaling up or down is required.

10.1.2.4 Usage-Based Pricing

Related to the facilities of scalability and measured use is the facility of usage-based pricing. Cloud services are priced in different ways, including number of users, number of resources used and amount of storage used, amongst others. The main issue is that the price can be set according to the usage and needs of the client.

When hosted infrastructure is used, the cost is based on the capital expenses required to build the infrastructure. The expenses are usually incurred over a period of time, possibly years, and they are usually depreciated over usage. The final cost of using the infrastructure is therefore difficult to estimate and is an approximate amount that is allocated as an overhead to different departments that use them.

Cloud-based infrastructure permits direct measurement of costs owing to the usage-based pricing models. Individual users or entire departments can know quite accurately how much computing resources they have consumed and how much they have been billed for the same. They can, thus, have an accurate estimate of the costs of computing they have incurred.

KEY POINT

Cloud services pricing can be based on usage and needs of the client.

10.1.2.5 Managed Services

A key issue with a hosted infrastructure is that it has to be managed by the organisation that has invested in the assets. The organisation has to hire systems personnel who design, install and manage the infrastructure. Even if the services are outsourced to a vendor, the organisation has to maintain a set of personnel who oversee and manage the vendor.

The situation changes significantly with cloud-based infrastructure, as the entire responsibility of building, maintaining and upgrading the systems is with the provider and is transparent to the client. Cloud providers upgrade hardware and software on their own facilities, without involving their clients. Clients then have access to the latest and upgraded facilities without having to build it themselves. IDOS, for example, maintains its own hardware, software and networking services that it provides to its customers; the customers do not worry about fixing bugs, upgrading or maintaining this infrastructure, which saves them the overhead costs and effort associated with the maintenance tasks.

10.1.2.6 Service Levels

Service levels specify the quality of the facilities available to users. Service levels may specify, for instance, the duration of time an infrastructure service has to be available without interruption or the speed or response level of a service over a period of time. Hosted infrastructure is set up with certain service levels, as determined by the current and forecasted demand on the system. Once installed, these levels are difficult to change or modify, as this would require changing infrastructure components or tweaking their performance levels.

On a cloud infrastructure, service levels can be specified and changed as required. This property is related to the scalability and elasticity of cloud facilities. When higher service levels are required, providers can provision this, usually at a higher price. When service levels do not have to be very high, these can be reduced, with consequent lower prices for services.

10.1.2.7 Ubiquitous Access

One of the significant advantages of cloud computing is 'anytime–anywhere' access. Since the facilities are located on servers accessible through the web, they can be accessed by clients from anywhere, either within or outside the campus of the client's organisation. Typically, large cloud providers set up servers across many geographic locations to address the issues of latency, or delay, that may appear in web access. If employees of an organisation are travelling in different countries, they can access their IT services through their web browser wherever they have an internet connection.

When infrastructure is hosted within the premises of an organisation, it is difficult to access these services from outside for several reasons - the organisation may not have created facilities for outside access, for security reasons; the servers may not be capable of being accessed from anywhere on the globe owing to their specific location; and the organisation may not have the bandwidth required to enable outside access to its servers from anywhere. These challenges are overcome by using cloud computing. For example, IDOS's business model was based on the property of ubiquitous access, where their product could be accessed from anywhere in the world, wherever their clients needed it. Also, this property let them offer their product in many different countries, with the provision that their users could access it from anywhere also.

10.1.2.8 Heterogeneity

For many large organisations, their hosted infrastructure was usually built up over time, with additions being made as the need arose and also as capital was available. This invariably resulted in many different components of the infrastructure that were based on different software and hardware - with varying operating systems, databases, memory components, CPUs and CPU racks. Such infrastructures are referred to as heterogeneous systems, owing to their having a wide variety of components. Heterogeneous systems are difficult to manage as they need a variety of different components and different standards by which they can be upgraded or maintained. Often, the required upgrades or replacement parts are not available as the firm that made them may have stopped doing so. Cloud infrastructure overcomes the problem of heterogeneity and upgradation problems for client organisations as they do not have to manage their own infrastructure - they rely on the cloud provider to do the needful.

Cloud-based infrastructure can also be heterogeneous, though, with different operating systems and different types of hardware used to do the computing. However, the main advantage of cloud services is that the heterogeneous systems can be managed easily. Through the method of virtualisation, the disparate components can be viewed and managed through a single interface. Different components can be grown or enhanced according to need by the cloud provider.

10.1.2.9 Reduced Setup Time

For hosted infrastructure, the time to set up a server or a network is significant, as it requires purchasing and installing physical components. Purchasing expensive hardware in many organisations often takes a long time as it requires floating request-for-proposals, evaluating bids, selecting vendors and then going through with the payment and purchase. Installation too may take a lot of time if civil works, that is, construction of rooms or facilities, is involved. Cloud services overcome all this, as there is no need to purchase hardware or do civil works. Cloud services are obtained over the internet and a good internet connection is all that is required. For example, obtaining an account from the cloud product provider, such as IDOS, takes very little time as only a client software has to be downloaded on a local computer and an account has to be created. This reduced setup time is a very valuable feature for firms that are starting up their business and need to act quickly to get their computing services functioning and ready. Cloud providers such as Microsoft Azure, or Amazon Web Services, have made it very easy to set up a cloud service, within minutes in some cases, and start using it.

10.1.2.10 Resource Pooling

One of the key features of cloud infrastructures is resource pooling or sharing of computing resources. The idea is that a cloud infrastructure is created with hundred, possibly thousands, of CPUs and memory devices that are linked together. Using virtualisation, and other methods, it is possible to provide only a tiny slice of computing resources to any one client, and similarly to other clients. The idea of pooling is that the slice of computing resources is not permanently dedicated to the client and can be made available, on demand, to other users when the client is not using the resource to its maximum capacity. For example, if IDOS provides 4 GB of memory to a particular client, and the client is using only 10% of it at any time, the IDOS's servers can provision the spare memory to another client that has a need for it, on a temporary basis. Resources of the services are thus seen to be in a pool that can be provided to clients as needed.

10.1.3 Types of Cloud Infrastructure

Cloud services are offered over different types of infrastructure - private, public, hybrid and community. Each is described in the following subsections.

10.1.3.1 Private Cloud

A private cloud is a cloud infrastructure that is created for a single client. This client is usually one organisation that wants the cloud infrastructure for its own private use, while at the same time being able to draw on the facilities of a cloud. Such a cloud infrastructure may be built on the physical premises of the client; in fact, the client may own the entire infrastructure. In such a situation, the cloud is no different from a classic hosted setup of servers.

Typically, a private cloud will consist of servers that are rendered as a cloud through virtualisation software. When connected to the organisation through a network infrastructure the cloud is available to all users. Such a cloud can be built with commodity hardware at a low cost. The drawback in such a private cloud is that the organisation has to both build and maintain the cloud, thus losing the facility of having someone else manage and upgrade the infrastructure. The advantage is that of security: since only one organisation is using the cloud and the physical server racks are also present on the premises of the organisation, it can ensure that access and data are secured.

KEY POINT

A private cloud is meant for a single client whereas a public cloud is shared by many clients.

A private cloud can also be hosted at a remote site. Here the client organisation can employ a cloud provider that creates the cloud infrastructure for the client and also maintains it. Security can be assured by the provider by physically separating the servers and dedicating them for use only by the client. Sometimes the provider may keep the client's servers in a separate cage or cell in a server farm, with its own internet cables and its own power backup facilities. This arrangement has the advantage for the client of having a private cloud that can be adequately secured, and also not have to manage it.

Though advantageous in terms of security, a private cloud also lacks some of the core advantages of cloud facilities in general. A private cloud does not permit sharing or pooling of resources, which limits the scale and on-demand advantages of a cloud infrastructure.

10.1.3.2 Public Cloud

A public cloud is a truly shared facility that allows multiple clients to use the resources provided. A typical public cloud infrastructure is created by a provider who sets up a large infrastructure of connected servers that runs virtualisation software. Different clients are then given space, computing power and bandwidth according to their needs, although there is no specific hardware specifically assigned to any particular client. In this sense, a public cloud is the closest to the definition of a cloud infrastructure. Amazon Web Services (AWS), Microsoft Azure and Google Cloud Platform are all examples of public cloud services. Each provider enables a number of services and cloud products that are made available to users, with different pricing and features.

10.1.3.3 Hybrid Cloud

A hybrid cloud is a combination of private and public cloud options. It was created to manage the problem of cloud 'bursts' with private clouds. When a private cloud runs out of computing capacity, for instance it runs out of memory or of computing power, this is known as a 'burst' and memory is provided in real time from a public cloud. The software that manages the cloud responds to bursts by provisioning extra resources from the public cloud as required.

10.1.3.4 Community Cloud

A community cloud is a shared computing infrastructure that may be set up as a private, public or hybrid cloud, with the caveat that it is used by a specified community of users, such as hospitals or banks, that have common needs in terms of specifications. For instance, a community cloud for banks may have special security and authentication software that is required by them.

10.1.4 Cloud Service Models

10.1.4.1 Infrastructure-as-a-Service (IaaS)

The IaaS model is based on providing data centre facilities to clients over the internet. This model is offered by firms such as Amazon Web Services, Google Compute Engine, Microsoft Azure and others. The data centres are virtual facilities that allow clients to rent hardware, such as one or many CPUs, memory and storage space, networking facilities, software to manage the facility, some basic security software, such as a firewall, and utilities. The facilities are identical to what would be created by actual purchase of hardware on premises, except that these are made available over the internet.

Vendors who provide IaaS products ensure the maintenance of hardware and software, provide service level guarantees (based on what clients need) and update the hardware and features as and when they are available.

The client or user can then install their own application software on the infrastructure they have rented. This includes system software, such as operating systems and networking software, and also applications that they need, such as databases, servers, enterprise software and so on. The idea is similar to renting an empty apartment, with basic facilities such as plumbing and utilities, like water and electricity. The furnishing and fixtures are provisioned by the renter, based on the latter's needs.

In this model, the responsibility of the provider is restricted to ensuring that the system is up and running as is promised in the contract, and does not extend to the applications and their functioning. IaaS pricing is based on usage - rentals may be by time units, such as minutes, hours, or months; and rentals may be priced on facilities provided, such as number of CPUs, extent of memory and storage.

IaaS facilities are often acquired by start-up firms who want to build or deploy a cloud-based product. They may not have the capital required to acquire all the needed hardware and facilities for their product and find it is easier to rent facilities at a fraction of the cost. Using the cloud also reduces the time required to have access to an infrastructure, considerably reducing the time to deploy their product in the market. This model is also used by firms that have established systems and want to try out something new, without having to buy and deploy new hardware. They can test out and experiment on the cloud, without touching their existing setup.

10.1.4.2 Platform-as-a-Service (PaaS)

The PaaS facility provides users with a number of tools and packages with which an IT solution can be built and deployed on the cloud. The PaaS model builds on and extends the IaaS model, where special software is included over and above the infrastructure. For example, a typical PaaS provided by vendors, such as Microsoft or Amazon, will have an infrastructure, with computing devices and memory and storage, and will also give additional facilities such as an operating system, programme development libraries, possibly an included database and other packages. The customer can use these tools to rapidly develop applications. The analogy for PaaS is that of renting a furnished apartment where most of the facilities for living are already available and the renter can start living there with only her personal effects.

PaaS is also widely used by start-ups and innovators who want to build an application quickly and deploy it in full scale. Most PaaS providers have facilities for 'plugins' or commercial products that clients can have access to, at a nominal cost. For example, clients who are building an enterprise application, on a PaaS cloud, can access an email or messaging 'plugin' application that helps them build mail or messaging features into their own product, without building these applications on their own.

10.1.4.3 Software-as-a-Service (SaaS)

SaaS is one of the oldest and best known ways of offering services over the cloud. Almost all internet users are familiar with applications such as email that are often provided for free by firms like Google and Yahoo! These applications are available to anybody with an internet connection and a browser. Further, these applications provide their full functionality regardless of the type of hardware or operating system from where they are accessed. The IDOS company offers its product as a SaaS product.

Zoho Office is another example of a SaaS product that has rich functionality and competes almost directly with desktop applications. Zoho's offering is a suite of office productivity applications, such as a word processor, a spreadsheet, a presentation tool, and others that are available on the cloud. A firm can rent the entire Zoho Office for its employees, and each employee user can then use the office tools on the internet, without having to download and install anything on their own computing devices. They can save their work on the cloud and also share their work with their colleagues easily. Zoho backs up all user files, upgrades their software and enables access to users from anywhere. Zoho prices their office suite on the basis of usage and clients need pay for only what they need. Zoho's direct competitor is Microsoft Office that earlier had to be installed, was priced on a per user licence basis and was available only on the device on which it was installed.

The SaaS model can be best compared to renting a fully serviced apartment where renters have to do little to run or maintain their surroundings, and focus instead on living and enjoying their apartment. The SaaS model builds on the IaaS and PaaS models, with the difference that the focus is on the application or functionality that is provided. SaaS application users have access to the application alone, and cannot change or manage the underlying hardware or systems software. Unless explicitly provided, users cannot also change any aspect of the application other than their own settings.

Many enterprise application sellers provide their product through the SaaS model. Salesforce.com is a prominent customer relationship management product that is available through their SaaS platform. Client firms rent accounts, for a given number of users, and their own customers, and run the application as if they had purchased and hosted it on their own premises. Salesforce.com assists its clients with customisation and management of the product, if required, and provides upgrades when they are available, otherwise clients run the software application on their own.

KEY POINT

IaaS provides data centre facilities, PaaS provides a software development facility, and SaaS provides applications over the internet.

Innovators and start-ups too rely on the SaaS model, as is evident in the case of IDOS. This model allows products to be made available to customers in a convenient manner, over any device and in any location where the internet is available. The model also enables potential customers to sample the product, possibly collaborate with others, and experience the features without the bother of downloading and installing anything.

A comparison of the three models IaaS, PaaS and SaaS is depicted in Table 10.1.

Table 10.1 | Comparison of Three Kinds of Cloud Services – IaaS, PaaS and SaaS

Feature	IaaS	PaaS	SaaS
What is provided	Hardware + System software + Networking software + System management tools	IaaS + Application development tools and libraries	Cloud-based Application
Management	Vendor manages infrastructure; everything else managed by client	Vendor manages infrastructure and development tools; client manages everything else	Vendor manages infrastructure and application; client manages user accounts only
Typical usage	Infrastructure for multiple servers and applications	Build and deploy new applications; maybe for new markets	Single application for focussed use

10.1.5 Challenges of Migrating to the Cloud

For organisations that have established and functioning hosted IS, the question that senior management face is that of deciding which applications or processes to move to the cloud. The answer has to follow from both sound technical and business logic, requiring careful thought and planning. The following are some reasons why moving applications to the cloud may *not* be suitable.

1. **Tight coupling between hardware and software:** Some legacy applications were written to tightly integrate with the hardware on which they ran. Applications on mainframe computers of past decades were written to take advantage of any special features of the hardware, such as specially designed storage or a special buffer, to improve performance. These software applications cannot be, in most cases, moved easily to other hardware environments and cannot be targets for moving to the cloud.
2. **Applications that do not scale:** A key feature of the cloud is its ability to enable scaling – it allows software to run faster and process more. However, if the application was not designed to scale up, there would be no point in moving it to the cloud.
3. **The cost is not justified:** The promise of the cloud is that it provides low-cost computing. However, this has to be seen in context. Legacy applications are often assets that are fully depreciated and have already provided a return on their investment. Purchasing cloud services, which may appear to be cheaper, may cost more when compared to very low costs of running legacy systems.
4. **IT staff may not have the relevant skills:** For organisations that have an IT department, it is quite likely that the skills required for working with the cloud are not available or are sparsely available. Since cloud technologies are relatively new, few of the older workforce would have familiarity with them. In such cases, unless reliable outsourcing vendors are available, adopting cloud solutions would be risky.
5. **Security is a key concern:** In situations where an organisation is strongly concerned about the security of its data and applications, it may hesitate to adopt the cloud. Though cloud vendors assure strong security of their data centres, buyers are sometimes worried about having their core data vulnerable to theft by hackers. Besides theft, a key concern is also of internet-based attacks that slow down server performance and affect the functionality of cloud-based applications. In such cases, firms are prone to host applications on their premises, rather than on the cloud.

The above are reasons why moving applications to the cloud are not advisable. However, there are some compelling arguments as to why moving to the cloud is an advantage and, sometimes, a competitive necessity. Some of these arguments have been discussed in earlier sections. Five major reasons for adopting the cloud are summarised here:

1. **Applications that have volatile demand:** Applications that are likely to grow suddenly and significantly are prime targets for moving to the cloud (even those whose demand is likely to shrink), as expanding scale rapidly and smoothly is possible on the cloud.
2. **Low business risk and commodity applications:** Applications that are not crucial for the business, and yet take up some management resources, are good candidates for moving to the cloud. Infrastructure for managing them is handed to third parties and host institutions can focus their resources on core activities.
3. **Applications that require collaboration:** Some functions require collaboration across departments or regions, and these can be moved to the cloud, as collaboration is easier over the internet. Sharing of data and files is facilitated by cloud-based applications.
4. **Big Data storage and analysis:** Applications that have large data streams with variety and high rates of accumulation are best stored on cloud servers that can accommodate the scale. Further, if analysis of these data streams is required, cloud facilities are the most appropriate for performing this.
5. **Capital available for infrastructure is low:** In situations where start-ups or innovators have low capital to build infrastructure for their applications, renting cloud facilities is the best option, as large scale and high performance can be obtained rapidly and with low cost. This is also applicable for fast time-to-market considerations, where start-ups want to set up quickly and reach their markets in short time. Here, renting cloud facilities is the quickest option.

10.1.6 Cloud Technologies

There are several key technologies whose invention and proliferation has enabled cloud technologies to grow. The most prominent technology is virtualisation, discussed in Chapter 9, that disassociates physical hardware from the computing facilities that are provided, effectively improving the efficiency of the hardware. Virtualisation is key for providing cloud services as the physical location and extent of the hardware is removed from what clients are provided in a virtual manner. Two other technologies, amongst many, are important for cloud services - software defined networking (SDN) and containers - which are discussed below.

10.1.6.1 Software Defined Networking (SDN)

The idea behind SDN is to virtualise the networking tasks. Typically, network hardware devices, such as routers and switches, are arranged in a fixed hierarchy and a rigid configuration. Any change in the networking topology or configuration requires changes in the hardware arrangements. This presents a problem for highly variable configurations of virtual cloud environments where networking devices may be needed temporarily and then reassigned to other CPUs and resources. SDN solves this problem by virtualising the networking tasks.

The principal idea behind SDN is separating the network routing tasks into two parts - one done by the control plane and one by the data plane. The control plane decides on the best routing of packets based on the current configuration of the network. This plane is aware of the latest status of the network and is able to decide how packets can be routed. The data plane is responsible for the actual routing and forwarding on the packets in the network. The advantage of this arrangement is that the control plane is free to solve the problems of routing through the complex arrangements of the network topology, without having to worry about the physical movement of packets. The control plane has a global view of the network, something that was not possible in traditional networking devices. The SDN as a whole has the facility to dynamically enable or disable devices, thus virtualising the entire network. This helps

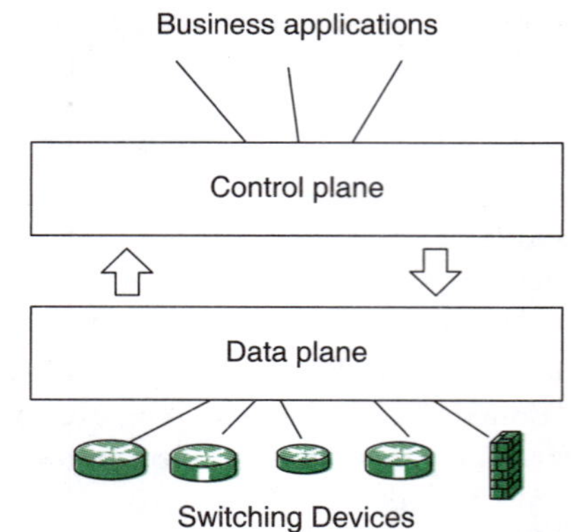

FIGURE 10.3 | Software defined networking.

with massive cloud data centre environments where virtual machines are created and collapsed according to the needs of the customers. The SDN consists of the control plane that interfaces with business applications and the data plane that directs traffic via the switching devices (see Fig. 10.3).

10.1.6.2 Containers

Containers are also a technology for creating virtual machines, similar to virtualisation, with the difference that they are 'lighter' and take less resources to run. Virtualisation works by creating a software layer on top of the hardware, where this layer consists of the operating system and the virtualising software, and then building independent 'machines' on top of this layer. These machines are created from different operating system environments. Containers simplify this idea by separating out the independent machines in the software layer that is controlling the hardware. This removes one layer of software, thus making containers 'lighter' or with lesser software code and also more pliable (Fig. 10.4).

Docker is a firm that makes containers that are widely used. Dockers are open-source code containers that can be deployed anywhere. The docker containers run applications in their own air-tight compartments with their own code libraries and dependencies and fully isolated from other containers that may be running on the same hardware. This property lets containers be highly suitable for cloud facilities.

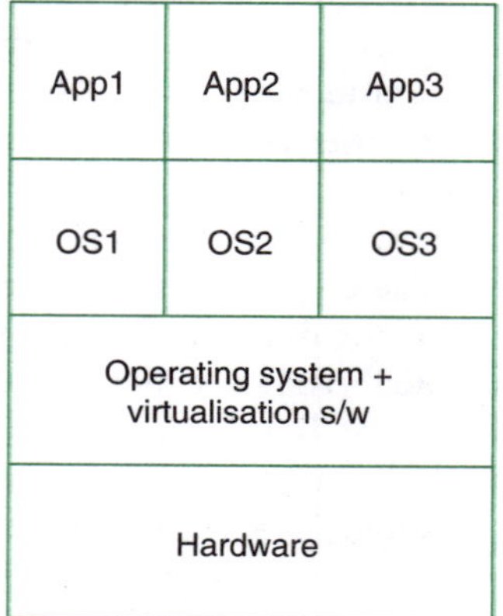

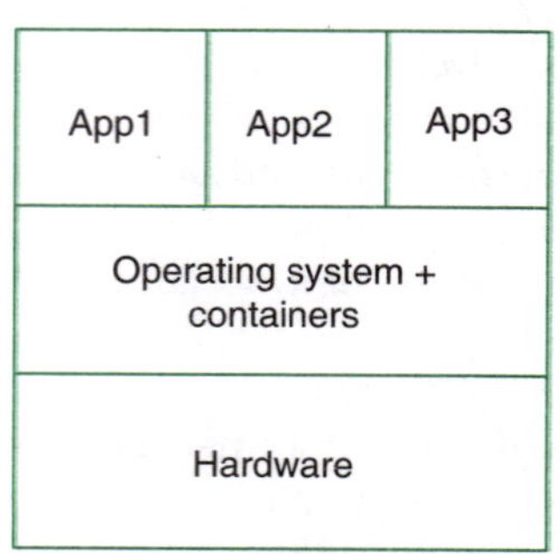

FIGURE 10.4 | Containers reduce the complexity of virtualisation systems.

10.1.7 Economic Rationale for Cloud Computing

Cloud adoption reduces investments in IT assets for organisations. This is the main economic motivation for them to adopt the cloud model of computing – where capital expenses of purchasing IT assets are converted to operating expenses of renting cloud services. The rationale for doing this is depicted in Fig. 10.5.

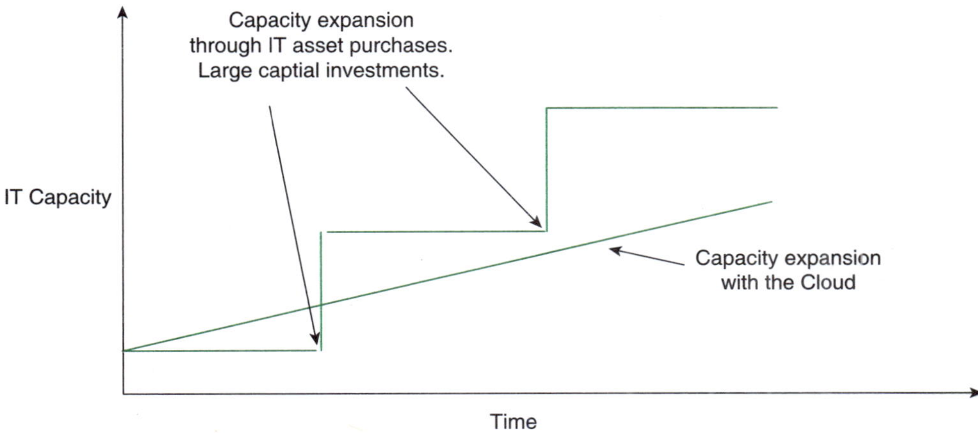

FIGURE 10.5 | IT capacity creation over time versus capacity expansion with the cloud.

Figure 10.5 shows that, over time, as the needs of the organisation grow, IT infrastructure capacity also grows. In the traditional hosted model, the capacity grows in steps. At some time point the organisation invests heavily in new hardware, software and networks and the additional increased capacity is created. This capacity remains relatively fixed until another, future, time point where the organisation may experience a demand for more capacity. When contrasted with the cloud model, the differences are quite stark. Capacity on the cloud can be purchased on an incremental basis as and when the need arises. Though the capacity increase need not be linear, as depicted in the figure, it does not also have to grow in steps, as in the hosted model. This is referred to as the Capex (capital expansion) versus the Opex (operational expenses) model of capacity expansion (Fig. 10.5).

When the hosted model is followed, large capital investments are required to create a certain installed capacity, which is incremented at a later point of time with additional investments. As is shown in Fig. 10.5, hosted capacity is increased in steps as opposed to a smooth manner with the cloud.

Managers will have to be careful about the cost of cloud services. The cloud option may appear to be cheaper at lower capacity levels but may become significantly more expensive as the capacity grows, then making the hosted option more cost effective.

10.2 INTERNET-OF-THINGS

10.2.1 What is Internet-of-Things?

The Internet-of-Things (IoT) consists of a large number of devices that are connected via the internet to sense and respond to conditions in their environments. The devices are typically sensors and actuators that exchange information with a controlling software for a defined purpose. For example, in the context of a smart city, there may be a large number of sensors in the water infrastructure that sense and collect information on water pressure and water flows. This information would be relayed over the internet to a software that would identify the location of the information and process it to determine if any action is required. In case action is required,

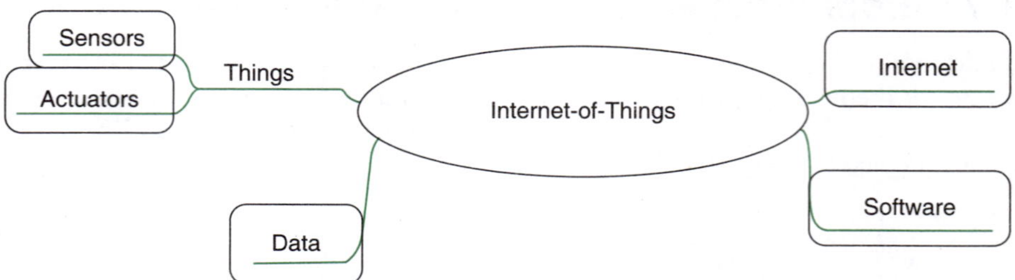

FIGURE 10.6 The Internet-of-Things consists of things, which are sensors and actuators, data from the things, software to analyse the data and the internet.

this information would be sent out over the internet to the actuators that can effect changes in the pressure and flow of water. (An actuator is a device that moves or changes the physical state of a machine. For example, an actuator may be a motor that responds to an electronic signal to open, close or change the position of a valve.)

IoT thus consists of sensors and actuators, data that flows to or from these things, the internet that enables the signals to flow, and software that can analyse the data from the sensors and determine control signals that will flow to the actuators (Fig. 10.6).

IoT is defined in various ways and is also named differently. The different definitions highlight different aspects of IoT, though the common elements include those given in the above figure. The things are the devices that sense the environment and convey the data, or make changes in it. Data is collected from the things and forms the basis of the entire ensemble. Software analyses and responds to the data in a manner suitable for the objectives of the network. The internet provides the connectivity that brings everything together. Cloud technologies form the basis of collecting, storing and analysing data that is obtained from the devices.

IoT is seen as a powerful method of control and coordination of different environments. Homes, offices, buildings, cars, personal devices, machines, amongst others, all have sensory devices, and some have actuators, and constitute the world of IoT. It is estimated that in 2017 there were 13 billion devices or things connected to the internet. Industry commentators and experts estimated that by 2020 there would be 20 billion devices connected to the internet and used in almost all domains of human activity.

Some industry experts also refer to the configurations of things connected to the internet as the Internet-of-Everything (IoE), while others refer to it as Internet 4.0. The latter is also called the Industrial Internet-of-Things (IIoT). IIoT is possibly one of the biggest application and focus areas of IoT. The sensors in IIoT are connected to a vast number of industrial devices and machines and that provide data on detailed and minute aspects of operations. This is a significant achievement as, so far, the use of the internet and its facilities was not significant in the operations domain. The data that is harvested from manufacturing and service operations is analysed to see where improvements can be effected. Research shows that even tiny savings, say a 1% gain in efficiency of energy use, result in massive cost savings (as the scale of operations is large).

KEY POINT

IoT are sensors and actuators that are connected via the internet, for responding to and control of events.

The use of sensors has also enabled a new business model, where specific devices can be marketed based on outcomes. For example, the Rolls Royce Company is a market leader in jet engines. It sold jet engines in the past to airplane manufacturers and then set up maintenance contracts to service those engines. However, with the advent of IoT, this model of doing business changed. Rolls Royce now embeds thousands of sensors in its engines and gives them to airplane manufacturers. The sensors record every aspect of the engine and send the data to the company over the internet. This data is used with complex software that simulate the performance of the engine, in real-time, as its 'digital twin'. The company knows how much the engine has run, how much wear its parts have experienced, and when certain parts have to be serviced or changed. Rolls Royce's customers pay for the service of the engine, based on how much it is used, and not for the total engine itself. This change in the business model is significant as, like in the cloud, it shifts the costs from buying up-front assets to paying for the engine service on a usage and measured basis. This model gives the manufacturer, Rolls Royce, a better handle on its product for servicing across its entire life cycle.

IoT deployments in different applications constitute a vast range of problems and solutions. The following subsections discuss examples from logistics management and healthcare.

10.2.2 Examples of IoT

10.2.2.1 Logistics Management with IoT

Radio-frequency-identification (RFID) tags are used widely to mark inventory and to identify them quickly. These tags are of low cost and through a radio signal can reveal information embedded in them. In a factory environment, they are very useful in tracking material. When goods are brought into a factory, say on a truck, RFID tags are read for each and every item in the consignment and also for the pallet or casing on which they are brought. The systems at the gate can record the time, date and exact quantity of input materials.

Once inside the factory, machine readers identify where each item or item group has to be stored and conveys this to devices on forklift trucks. Human operators, along with machine controllers, may then move the items to their storage areas or bins. The RFID information is used along with current inventory status information to determine both the exact location of the new inventory and also the path by which the forklift truck has to move and place the material.

The factory systems are updated with the new input material information. As material is consumed, their RFID tags are removed and the material balances updated. RFID tags are also deployed on finished goods, which when being moved out of the factory premises are scanned, their exact time and quantity of movement recorded with the systems. When paperwork has to be carried with the packaged goods, these may be scanned by human operators wearing virtual reality (VR) glasses. The scanned documents are digitally stored along with information about the goods consignment.

10.2.2.2 Healthcare with IoT

Modern healthcare devices include wrist bands and health bands that measure body parameters such as heartbeat rate, blood pressure and blood oxygen level. These parameters are relayed, using the Bluetooth wireless protocol, to smart phones that forward them to controlling applications. Hospitals use such devices to constantly monitor chronic care patients.

The Giraff project in Sweden is another example of the use of the IoT for healthcare. Giraff is a telepresence robot that is placed in homes where people need monitoring and round-the-clock care. The robot has a screen display and cameras on it, and the whole assembly is mounted on wheels. The robot can be remotely controlled by an operator to move it about in the house of the patient. Its cameras provide a feed about the activity of the patient and, if there is a need, enable the patient to can speak to an operator or nurse using a teleconferencing facility like Skype. The operator or nurse can move the cameras about and check the vicinity of the patient, zoom in on details, provide voice feedback and have the robot move back to a position from where it can monitor the location and be charged from an electrical connection. The sensors on this device are the cameras and microphone that convey information via the internet about the patient.

10.2.3 Managing IoT Systems

The examples discussed above show that there are numerous possible ways in which IoT systems can be used for providing innovative services and products. There are also significant challenges in providing IoT solutions. Some are discussed below:

1. **Massive data flows:** Industrial IoT systems require thousands of sensors fitted to machines and other devices that sense their environment, possibly, many times per second and

convert this into data packets, which consist of sensor readings, a time stamp and location information, and send this out over the internet to the controlling software. This amounts to thousands of readings per second that have to be moved onto the system to be collected, stored and analysed. This requires architecting the system in a manner that can handle the massive load without causing delays or breaking down.

2. **Massive volume of data:** Once the data is generated by the sensors and shipped to the central system, the problem of storing such massive quantities of data arises. In earlier systems, in the 1990s and 2000s, data emanating from such sensors was sampled, some data was stored and the rest was discarded. With modern IoT systems, however, managers are prone to keep all the data on cloud servers as they have access to advanced algorithms that can process all the data and make sense of it.
3. **Variety in data:** Sensors in industrial systems are made by different manufacturers belonging to vastly different industrial groups, who use a variety of standards and formats in which the data is generated. When data is acquired in different formats and standards, the challenge is to process them coherently, to make the analysis useful and relevant. The challenge for managers is to translate the many protocols of data and standards to a format that is useful.

10.2.4 Sensors and Actuators

10.2.4.1 Sensors

Sensors and actuators are key elements of the IoT. A sensor is a device that detects events or changes is its physical environment and provides an electronic output. Simple sensors collect the changes and report them as data. Smart sensors do some additional processing – they filter out duplicate data and send out data when specific conditions are met. Table 10.2 lists different kinds of sensors and some of their uses.

Table 10.2 | Different Kinds of Sensors and Their Uses

Type of Sensor	Usage
Temperature sensor	Detects changes in temperature or absolute temperature values. Wide applications in industrial machines for chemical and mechanical processes and in biological applications.
Pressure sensor	Measures the pressure of gases or liquids. Is used to measure the levels, flows and altitudes. Also used in touchscreen devices.
Flow sensor	Is used to record the rate of fluid and gas flow in pipes.
Level sensor	Is used to measure the level of liquids in containers.
Image sensor	Records images, including details of colour, intensity and brightness, for devices such as cameras.
Noise sensor	Monitors level and intensity of ambient noise. Is used to gauge noise pollution.
Air particle sensor	Monitors the level of air particles and gases such as carbon dioxide and other pollutants.
Proximity sensor	Detects the presence or absence of objects in the vicinity.
Moisture sensor	Measures the relative humidity of air. Is used inside buildings and factories.
Speed sensors	Measures the speed of objects, such as vehicles.

Sensor technology has advanced rapidly and there are many types and varieties of sensors available in the market. The choice of which sensor to use is driven by their characteristics, some of which are as follows:

1. **Data filter** – whether the sensor is able to filter out redundant data, to remove noise from the analysis. Sensors with such facilities are known as *smart sensors*.
2. **Power consumption** – sensors require a power source to function. Typically, the lower the power they consume, the more preferable they are.
3. **Size** – sensor sizes determine how and where they can be inserted in devices. Many sensors are small enough to be used in a wide range of devices.
4. **Sensitivity and accuracy** – sensors should be able to accurately and reliably record changes in their environment. The sensitivity range of sensors often limits and determines the applications for which they can be used.

10.2.4.2 Actuators

Actuators are tools or mechanisms that can change their own state or the state of other devices and machines. They are often motors that respond to electrical or data signals and change the state of something they are connected to. Actuators can be mechanical or hydraulic devices also, and change their state depending on the physical signal they receive. Table 10.3 mentions some actuators used in IoT systems.

Table 10.3 | Types of Actuators and Their Uses

Actuator Type	Usage
Electrical	Motors that convert electrical signals to mechanical motion, e.g., change the position of a valve.
Mechanical	Devices that convert motion or energy into a different movement, e.g., movement of gears or levers.
Hydraulic and Pneumatic	Devices that respond to pressure in liquids and gases, e.g., convert pressure in liquids into pressure on container walls.

Actuators may act locally, where they respond autonomously to changes detected by nearby sensors, or they may respond to changes as directed by the IoT system.

10.2.5 IoT Architecture

Given the complexity of IoT systems, analysts and designers have proposed several architectures that enable a comprehensive view of the entire stack of devices and software that constitutes an IoT system. At a very basic level, IoT is viewed as having three layers – the perception layer at the bottom, the network layer connecting to it and the application layer on top of that. The perception layer consists of sensors and actuators, the things of IoT, that are placed in the physical world and sense events and changes. The data from these sensors is passed on to the network layer through internet-connected devices, such as gateways, which collect, store and distribute the data to allocated sites. The application layer analyses the data and provides control directions that are sent back to the perception layer devices via the network layer.

A somewhat more detailed framework is composed of four layers as depicted in Fig. 10.7. The four layers are as follows:

1. **Device layer:** This layer consists of the sensors and actuators, just as in the perception layer, that generate the data from the environment and surroundings. Some frameworks depict a fifth, physical, layer below this layer from which information is collected.

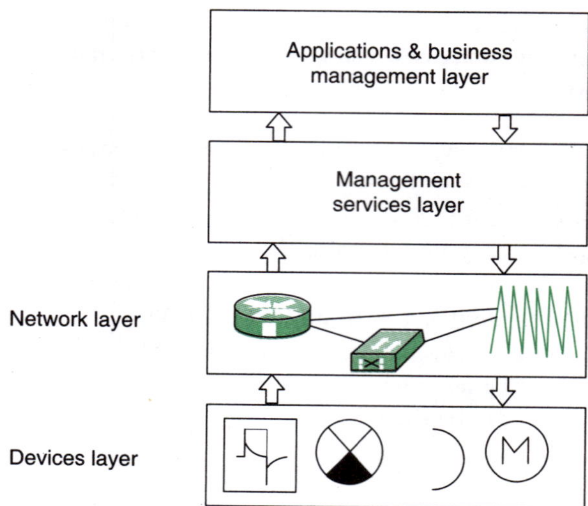

FIGURE 10.7 | Four layers of the IoT architecture.

2. **Network layer:** The layer consists of gateways, routers and switches that connect the devices to the internet. This layer also has the devices for wired and wireless connectivity that are based on protocols such as Bluetooth and Zigbee. These enable the perception devices to connect to and exchange data with other devices and software on the network. Many times specialised hardware is deployed at this layer to manage the speed, volume and intensity of data that is generated by the sensors.
3. **Management services layer:** This layer hosts the software that manages the entire IoT system. The function of this layer is to monitor and control the IoT devices, ensure that they are functioning, provision or remove their services if needed and ensure that they are responding properly within the network. This layer relies on the network layer to receive data from and to provide data to the devices.
4. **Applications and business management layer:** This layer analyses data for the high level business applications and ensures that the system is functioning according to the management priorities. For example, if the IoT is being used for an industrial application, such as inventory logistics, it is at this layer that the business rules for control of the devices are determined. This information will measure whether there is excess or shortage of inventory, for instance, and how this situation can be addressed. The data being generated by the numerous devices is abstracted at this layer to understand the manner in which the underlying operations are functioning and to convey any changes that may be required.

The layered approach to managing IoT systems, such as the framework in Fig. 10.7, enable the layers to be managed in an independent manner. Changes and upgrades in a given layer, say the devices layer, need be conveyed only to the layer above, the network layer, whereas the upper layers may continue to function as before. On the other hand, changes at the topmost layer, for business management, need not reflect in changes in any lower layers. This independence of layers enables designers to make changes and innovations at a given layer without disturbing the entire system.

Caselet Gnarus Solutions

Residential water supply is a problem in many parts of the city of Bangalore. The major source of water to the city is from the Kaveri river, where the river itself is close to a hundred kilometers away and water is piped in. With the growing size of the city, this water supply is inadequate and as a result many home owners rely either on groundwater that is pumped up to their overhead tanks or purchase water commercially, which is brought in truck tankers. In such a situation, one problem that residents face is that of knowing exactly how much water they have in their storage tanks, on the basis of which they can start or stop motors or place order for water tankers.

Gnarus Solutions has developed an IoT system that addresses this problem. They place sensor devices in water storage tanks in buildings that sense the water level and send out the data over a wifi gateway to a controlling software. The software processes the data and sends out updates about the water level to an app that may be accessed from the user's smart phone. Users who purchase Gnarus' solution have a reliable and handy way to know what the water level is in their home, at any time, and, if the level is below a threshold, have the software start a motor to draw up more water, or place an order with the water tanker supplier. The software also analyses the data to produce reports on weekly and monthly water consumption patterns. The user interface has visuals to depict water levels and also has the capability to display the results in several regional languages.

The app has additional features that can be used to alert plumbers, tank cleaners or electricians if potential problems arise and users want something fixed or their tanks cleaned. The system is designed for single homes or for large apartment complexes, where overhead tanks are sometimes difficult to access. The firm is also exploring the use of the solution in factories, hospitals, hotels and restaurants. They are also exploring the use of the solution in the supply chain of manufacturing units that have to move liquids in closed tankers and containers where the sensors can be deployed to monitor the levels.

10.3 CHALLENGES OF CLOUD COMPUTING AND IoT

Cloud computing and IoT present immense opportunities for innovation in products and services, however, they also present challenges for the manager. Some of these management challenges are highlighted below.

1. **Security:** Since its inception, cloud computing has always been questioned about security. Those adopting cloud services were doubtful about the security of their organisational and personal data being hosted on servers not within their control. Cloud service providers assured their clients of security, and also drew up contracts and warranties for assuring protection of their data. As cloud services grew and the market matured, security practices also matured and the risk for clients also reduced.

   For IoT, too, security is a concern. IoT devices and gateways remain points of entry, if unprotected, for malicious software to be inserted into the organisation. There are instances where IoT devices have been compromised to disrupt industrial processes for competitive reasons and also as acts of warfare. In some cases, monitoring of IoT devices is undertaken as a form of industrial espionage. Managers of IoT systems have to ensure that devices at the device and network layers remain secure.

2. **Privacy:** Privacy and surveillance are the other issues that have grown with the use of cloud computing and IoT. Devices that monitor individual parameters, for healthcare or fitness, invariably store data on cloud servers. This data is mined for insights on how the product and services can be enhanced and for design of new products. Privacy becomes an issue in such cases where explicit consent has not been sought for such analysis, and also where the data is used for purposes beyond what was specified in contracts with users.

   Privacy and surveillance issues also crop up in industrial IoT where worker performance is monitored along with machine performance. Managers will have access to a host of data on minute aspects of work that may violate applicable privacy laws. The challenge for managers is to ensure transparency and inform both employees and clients about potential privacy breaches and about the possibility of surveillance. Contractual obligations about data protection have to be maintained also.

3. **Internet access:** A major concern for many areas and regions is access to the internet. This is especially true for developing countries, like India, where, outside of urban areas, internet access through wired or wireless means is unreliable. This presents a severe challenge for cloud-based services and for the continued functioning of IoT systems that are installed in these regions. Managers have to ensure reliable connectivity through redundant access and backup systems.

Chapter Glossary

Cloud computing Method by which computing facilities and infrastructure are accessed over the internet, without being hosted on the premises of the organisation.

Elasticity Facility of cloud computing infrastructure that enables increasing or reducing computing capacity as needed.

Heterogeneity A mix of different kinds of hardware, software and network components within a particular computing infrastructure.

Private cloud A cloud facility that is dedicated to a single client, without any shared facilities.

Public cloud A shared computing infrastructure that allows many clients to access the resources.

Hybrid cloud A private cloud that also allows access to shared facilities when needed.

Community cloud A shared computing infrastructure that is used by a specific community of users who have common needs.

Infrastructure-as-a-Service (IaaS) Model of cloud service where computing infrastructure is provided to clients over the internet, where they install their own applications.

Platform-as-a-Service (PaaS) Model of cloud services where computing infrastructure is provided along with tools and software libraries to build applications.

Software-as-a-Service (SaaS) Model of cloud services where specific applications are provided to clients over the internet.

Software Defined Networking (SDN) The virtualisation of networking devices that enables better use of network resources.

Containers Software for creating virtual machines that are lighter and suitable for cloud environments.

Internet-of-Things (IoT) Devices connected via the internet to sense and respond to conditions in their environment.

Sensors Devices that collect data on specific aspects of their environment.

Actuators Devices that move or change their own state or of another device upon receiving a signal.

Review Questions

1. What is the definition of cloud computing, and how is it different from virtualisation covered in Chapter 9.
2. Consider the IDOS case. How could the firm have offered their product without the cloud? What are the special features of the cloud that helped them?
3. What are key differences between private, public and community cloud models?
4. What are the differences between IaaS, PaaS and SaaS?
5. How are the different cloud service models beneficial for start-ups and innovators?
6. What are some of the challenges of migrating applications to the cloud?
7. Why is the cloud an attractive option for hosting applications?
8. What is the significance of SDN for cloud services?
9. How are containers different from virtualisation technologies?
10. What is the difference between the hosted and cloud models of computing capacity creation in terms of costs and investments?
11. What is IoT? What are its key components?
12. What are the advantages of using IoT in manufacturing environments?
13. What are the challenges of managing IoT systems?
14. What are the functions of the different levels of the IoT architecture?
15. What are some of the major challenges of deploying cloud and IoT solutions?

Research Questions

1. Research on the internet to find out how cloud service providers like Amazon and Microsoft price their services and products? What type of measures do they use to vary the prices of their products?
2. Find a start-up in your region that has offered its product or services over the cloud. Examine why they chose the cloud and what cloud model is most suitable for them.
3. Cloud offerings can be seen as both services and products. What is the difference between the two and how do cloud businesses resolve the difference (if any)?
4. IoT is used extensively in smart cities solutions. Search on the internet for an example and see how IoT is deployed.

Further Reading

1. https://www.swan-forum.com/resources/a-layered-view/
2. Rayes, A., and Samer, S. (2017), *Internet of Things—From Hype to Reality,* Springer International Publishing, Cham, Switzerland.
3. Gilchrist, A. (2016), *Industry 4.0: The Industrial Internet of Things*, Apress.
4. Khan, R., Khan, S. U., Zaheer, R., and Khan, S. (2012, December), Future internet: The internet of things architecture, possible applications and key challenges, in *Frontiers of Information Technology (FIT), 2012 10th International Conference on* (pp. 257–260), IEEE.
5. Wu, M., Lu, T. J., Ling, F. Y., Sun, J., and Du, H. Y. (2010, August), Research on the architecture of internet of things, in *Advanced Computer Theory and Engineering (ICACTE), 2010 3rd International Conference on* (Vol. 5, pp. V5-484), IEEE.
6. Tan, L., & Wang, N. (2010, August), Future internet: The internet of things, in *Advanced Computer Theory and Engineering (ICACTE), 2010 3rd International Conference on* (Vol. 5, pp. V5-376), IEEE.
7. Kavis, M. J. (2014), *Architecting the Cloud: Design Decisions for Cloud Computing Service Models (SaaS, PaaS, and IaaS),* John Wiley & Sons.
8. Williams, B. (2012), *The Economics of Cloud Computing,* Cisco Press.
9. Hugos, M. H., and Hulitzky, D. (2010), *Business in the Cloud: What Every Business Needs to Know About Cloud Computing,* John Wiley & Sons.

CHAPTER 11

Networking and Telecommunication

Learning Objectives

After completing this chapter, you will be able to:

- Understand life of a packet
- Get an overview of structure of the network
- Learn about network services and layers

The internet functions by moving packets of information across networks. A packet is a basic unit of information and is created by the software being used by a user, who wants information from the internet. This packet passes through various software layers and devices to reach its destination, which may be within or outside the user's organisation. The servers at the destination respond to the request, created by the packet, by creating packets of their own which then travel the internet on the return journey.

At a higher level, the networks can be seen as a collection of servers that provide basic services demanded by users on the networks. These servers include web servers, email servers, database servers, print servers and so on, which provide specific shared services to users. The host or client computers are said to use these services.

Telecommunication networks are made of devices such as cables, hubs, switches, routers, wireless access points and servers. These hardware devices enable service providers to provide internet services for organisations through wired or wireless means. The internet consists largely of a set of services run on the hardware devices, based on shared standards of communication, known as protocols.

For managers, the decisions regarding the network infrastructure revolve around identifying the networking needs and levels, the kind and type of services required, the scalability of the network, the security that has to be enabled and the type of standards that are adopted.

MIND MAP OF CHAPTER TOPICS

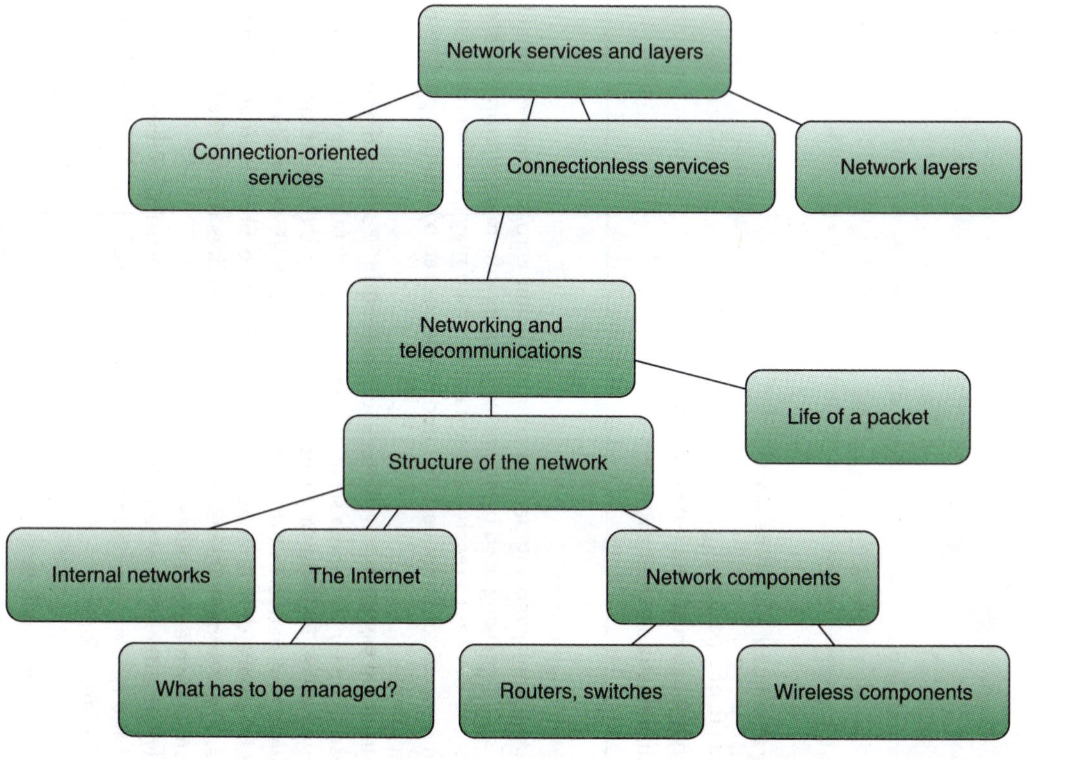

AirJaldi Networks is a firm that provides wireless connectivity for internet access in remote and mountainous regions. It specialises in providing internet access to communities that are geographically isolated and do not have easy access to electricity or telephonic connectivity. It has evolved a technology based on hardware components that are readily available and on open source software that is both affordable and suited to the needs of the environment.

Building infrastructure for internet access for rural communities in developing countries like India is not economically attractive due to the high cost of reaching users with low purchasing power. Following the deregulation of Wi-Fi for outdoor use in India, AirJaldi was established in 2005 as a social enterprise in Dharamsala in the mountainous state of Himachal Pradesh, India. In alignment with their organisational vision to help in the deployment of licence-free wireless networks, build the capacities of network operators and users, and undertake research to develop technologies that enable simple deployment of affordable, feature-rich wireless networks, AirJaldi launched the Dharamsala Community Wireless-Mesh Network in cooperation with the Tibetan Technology Center. The AirJaldi network provides internet access and Voice over Internet Protocol (VoIP) telephony services to about 10,000 users within a radius of 70 km in the rural mountainous terrain characterised by extreme weather. The network has eight long distance directional links ranging from 10 km to 41 km with 10 endpoints. In addition, the network also has over a hundred low-cost modified consumer access points that use a wide variety of outdoor antennas.

AirJaldi provided connectivity only to fixed installations and did not offer wireless access to roaming users or mobile devices. A cost-sharing model was used to share the operational costs with the network subscribers. The network was financially sustainable and was growing rapidly.

The rural supply–demand gap in broadband and internet services in remote and inaccessible areas with a relatively small number of users was the main development problem AirJaldi decided to address. The challenges in particular were:

1. High infrastructure costs.
2. High bandwidth costs.
3. Low reliability and quality of service.
4. Network security.
5. Bandwidth-hogging applications and users.
6. Absence of local expertise and reliable connectivity for remote experts.

AirJaldi designed networks that extended existing broadband services by interconnecting wireless routers to provide access to a larger area. AirJaldi's technology is based on the identification, modification and deployment of affordable equipment suitable to the needs and conditions of rural areas. The mountainous terrain creates line-of-sight limitations. The router and other components are mounted mostly on low masts placed on rooftops or high places. The easily installed nodes are small and unobtrusive, and their low emitted radiation and power requirements make for a very low ecological footprint, which means that the minimal amount of electrical power is used to run the network. Conventional point-to-multipoint networks cannot overcome the line-of-sight problems. AirJaldi's network designers chose mesh networking, as this topology offered much larger area of coverage. A variety of antennas are used to enable significant extension of the range of each node and area of coverage. The mesh nodes act both as points of connectivity for users and as relays to other nodes.

Electricity supply in rural India, if available, is extremely unreliable. Due to its fault tolerant design, mesh routing proved to be essential in retaining established connections in such places. Through research and intensive testing, AirJaldi also designed selected hardware platforms fitted with power supplies and charge controllers capable of handling wide power fluctuations. Each node was supported by a battery backup. In places where electricity supply was erratic or non-existent, a solar power supply was used.

The main obstacle facing network operators in rural areas of developing countries is the low economic viability of broadband internet networks run on expensive commercial technologies due to relatively few and dispersed users. The typically high cost of internet upstream bandwidth in such areas adds significant challenges. Furthermore, frequent upstream congestion and long hours of total service downtime – often resulting in slow, limiting and erratic service – are common.

The central network management system allows operators to maximise the network abilities. Its design is based on the analysis of network traffic trends on the Dharamsala network and clarification of users' needs. AirJaldi's objective was to find ways to ensure uninterrupted internet connectivity and maximise the utilisation of available bandwidth with minimal impact on the end-user's experience. The Information Society Innovation Fund (ISIF), a grant programme aimed at stimulating creative solutions to Information and Communication Technology (ICT) development needs in the Asia Pacific region supported AirJaldi in this endeavour. ISIF places particular emphasis on the role of the internet in social and economic development in the region.

Network bandwidth that was an expensive resource in many developing countries escalates operational costs for a rural internet Service Provider (ISP). AirJaldi developed a unique set of solutions to meet this challenge, collectively referred to as the 'Bandwidth Maximiser' (BwM). AirJaldi's BwM combines local content caching and filtering with tools that enabled the use and load balancing of multiple upstream connections. An irritant that the AirJaldi network support team faced was the large user base of the Microsoft Windows OS. Windows updates consume significant bandwidth as it was the second highest rated website in terms of usage, within the AirJaldi network, with almost 5% of the bandwidth used.

The software packages used by AirJaldi for its networks and support systems were predominantly free and open source (FOSS). They tightly integrated their code with the open source software tools to develop special features for traffic optimisation, high-level network encryption, status and performance reporting of nodes and to recover from various problems. In addition, they enabled remote diagnostics and provided hot-spot services. They contributed to open source by making all technical information about their work available. Although AirJaldi's BwM product is fully replicable, familiarity with networking, particularly FOSS-based networking, is required.

Future Directions

The designers of the network have documented their learnings clearly:

> In overcoming these challenges we have learned three important lessons that we argue apply to IT development projects more broadly. First, designers must build systems that reduce the need for highly trained staff. Second, a simple redesign of standard components can go a long way in enabling maintenance at lower costs. And third, the real cost of power is not the grid cost, but is the cost of overcoming poor power quality problems.

In order to simplify the deployment and upgrade of the infrastructure and individual components of its network and its backup and recovery process, AirJaldi focussed its research on development of four virtual machines, each with a specific role:

1. For routing and the firewalling of the network.
2. For caching.
3. For hosting a network monitoring solution.
4. For integrated billing and customer management.

AirJaldi is building additional networks in other rural locations in India. The ExtremeCom 2010 workshop was hosted by AirJaldi and planned around its Dharamsala network's locations and facilities, thereby giving participants a great opportunity to be involved in a real-life network deployment. The mountainous town of Dharamsala presented a unique mix of cultures and traditions and was also a starting point to a number of spectacular trekking trails.

11.1 LIFE OF A PACKET

We begin this chapter by discussing the life of a packet, which is a basic element of network traffic. A packet is a collection of information that basically consists of the message that the packet is carrying and a header, which contains information about where the packet is going and what it contains. A packet is what is mainly used to communicate over the internet. Other elements of communication are also used, but understanding the role and relevance of a packet will help reveal the various components and services of the internet.

Consider a situation where a user clicks on a web page to obtain some information. This may be a link on a site such as Yahoo! or Google, which the user clicks to access the information on the site to which the link points. Websites are viewed through software programs called browsers such as Mozilla Firefox or Internet Explorer. When the user clicks on a link, the browser responds with some actions. It takes the address listed on the link and creates a packet of information. The packet has the link address on its header, and its body contains a request for the page indicated by the link. The packet is created by the application software, such as the browser, as well as the operating system on which the application runs.

KEY POINT

A packet is the basic element of the internet, consisting of a message and an address.

Once the packet is made ready by the application, it is pushed out of the user's local computer, either a desktop or a laptop, onto the local area network (LAN) where the user is working. This LAN is the network that connects the various computers and network devices of the organisation in which the user works. The LAN typically connects devices in a single physical location, like a building, and not multiple locations or offices. Before pushing the packet out onto the LAN, the user's operating system may provide the address for the *proxy* server on the LAN that may be used to inspect and then direct the packet onto the internet.

A *switch* on the LAN then picks up the packet, reads the header information and then directs the packet in the right direction. Traffic on the LAN will consist of various types of packets, with different types of content payload, and headed in various directions. For example, a packet may be headed for a printer, containing information about the material that has to be printed. Another packet could be from an email server, headed towards a client machine where a user wants to read email.

Packets do not have an entirely smooth ride on the LAN. They may enter into collisions, or get caught in loops, going round and round the network without being able to reach their destination. Furthermore, they may also encounter malicious traffic that destroys or corrupts their contents. When packets do not reach their destination in a specified period of time, the software on the user's computer will realise that something is wrong and will send out another packet with the same content.

Once packets reach the switch on their part of the LAN, they are directed to that part of the LAN that will lead them to the proxy. The switch acts as a director of packets – it reads the destination information on headers and then directs packets in the correct direction.

At the proxy, the contents of the packet are examined. A proxy enables the organisation to control the kind of addresses that can be accessed. For example, if the packet is addressed to a site that the organisation wants to avoid, such as a site with pirated software or music, then the proxy prevents the packet from moving further. The packet is destroyed. Furthermore, the proxy also prevents outside traffic from entering the organisation's network.

After being cleared by the proxy, the packet travels through the *firewall*, which is another filter for packets. Firewalls are set up to filter out any traffic that is not of the right type, such as email or web traffic, and also check for the addresses that are permitted. Firewalls are usually set up at the gateway of the network, and they effectively monitor all traffic movement. Nowadays, many organisations only use a firewall to monitor traffic, avoiding the use of a proxy.

From the firewall, the packet moves to the *Router* that routes or directs the packet on the correct internet path. Packets headed to the same address do not necessarily follow the same path through the internet. Routers send packets in a direction that will eventually take them to their destination. Routers essentially determine the next 'hop' for the packet, or the next node in the network that has a router and that can direct the packet further. Usually, there are many directions in which any router can direct a packet, and the choice is determined by factors like current load on a route, availability of connections, etc.

KEY POINT

The internet is a network of networks over which packets travel.

Once on the internet, which is a network of networks, the packet travels along various cables, wireless paths, satellite links and also undersea optical fibres. Its path is determined by various routers on local networks that are used to direct traffic. Each network on the internet is a set of computers linked to each other via switches and LANs, and then to the internet with their routers. Packets arrive at the intervening routers from various directions and are moved along according to their destination. While traversing the internet, packets need not take the shortest or most efficient path to their destination. What is more, packets belonging to the same page or file of information may take different paths to arrive at the destination.

The packet thus bounces from one router to another until it finds itself at the router of the organisation it is seeking. Here it is directed to the firewall, where it is permitted into the host organisation only through the relevant port. For example, web traffic uses port number 80, and the packet has to show this destination information. Once it does so, the firewall lets it through port 80 into the organisation's network. The firewall also checks if any other packet is masquerading as a legitimate packet, and if so, this packet is eliminated.

Inside the firewall, the packet is sent to the web server (see Fig. 11.1). The web server is a software that directs all traffic from outside to its relevant destination internally, and all requests from inside to the internet outside. The web server looks up the information, such as a page, which the packet is seeking and responds by setting up the mechanism to convert the page into packets and send them off to the requesting organisation. These packets are then sent off on a similar journey as the requesting packet – through the proxy, through the firewall and from the router onto the internet.

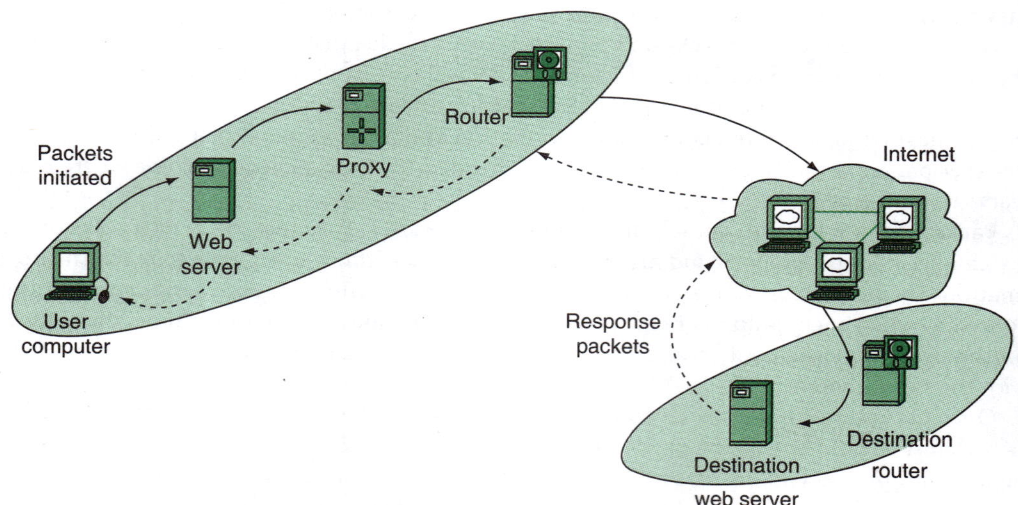

FIGURE 11.1 Path of packets from source to destination. A packet travels through many devices in the organisation in which it originates before moving to the internet.

11.2 STRUCTURE OF THE NETWORK

11.2.1 Networks in the Organisation

As is evident from the 'life of a packet' discussed above, any organisation's network consists of a number of elements. These elements or components function together to enable users to access various services within the organisation and also outside, on the internet. The components are often invisible to users, who simply see the application, such as a browser, that they are working with. The components operate in the background and perform a complex set of operations that enable the services of the network to be realised. Different components of the network are described below.

11.2.1.1 Packet Switching and Circuit Switching

Packets allow many messages to be sent over a medium at the same time. The method of creating and sending packets is called packet switching technology. Packet switching is a modern method of transmitting messages and is often compared to circuit switching. To understand the difference between the two one has to understand the elements of a network. A network is understood to consist of nodes and links. Nodes are end points from which messages originate, terminate or are re-directed from. Links are the channels by which the messages travel. All nodes and channels have limited capacity, where the capacity of a channel is known as the bandwidth in networking terminology.

In circuit switching, when a message is sent from one node to another, a part of the channel is blocked or dedicated for this exchange (see Fig. 11.2). For as long as the message takes to travel through the channel, that part of the channel is blocked. This is the method by which most landline telephones used to work earlier. In packet switching, the message is broken up into parts and the parts are sent across one at a time.

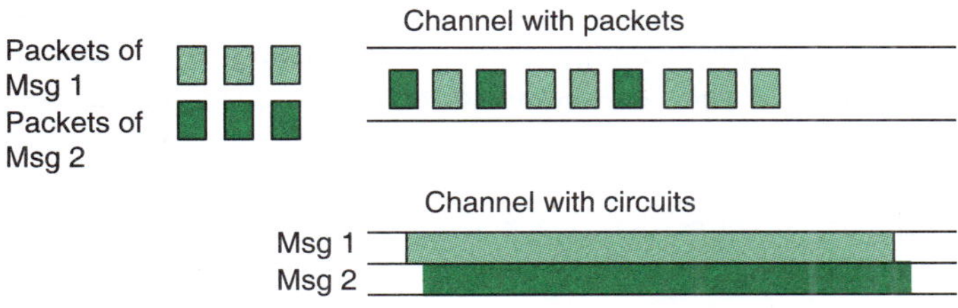

FIGURE 11.2 | Packet switching versus circuit switching.

Consider a conversation between two persons over a telephone landline. Even if the persons talk animatedly, it is certain that there are many silences in their conversation (say between words and phrases). At these points, the circuit is still blocked for this conversation only. Other messages cannot be sent overy this channel, even though it is carrying nothing (during the silent moments) at most times. With packet switching this problem is solved, as when one sender pauses, packets from other messages can be sent over the line. Packet switching is thus more efficient at using the entire bandwidth of the channel. Circuit switching, on the other hand, is better at assuring the speed of transmission of messages over the dedicated line.

11.2.1.2 Servers

Servers are computers on the network that host data or applications that can be shared by users. Servers such as web servers allow many users on the network to use their services to access information on the internet. Mail servers, another example of servers, help send and receive messages on behalf of users in the organisation. A server is called upon by a *client*, which is the software that accesses the server. In other words, a client demands services, while a server provides them, and hence their names.

Servers are at the heart of any network. Networks are created to exploit the resources on servers. Had this not been the case, each client machine would have had to maintain its own software that is now provided by the server, thus introducing high redundancy and inefficiency. Servers are usually very fast and powerful computers that can provide services to many clients. There are many types of servers used in organisations, some of which are described below.

File Server

It provides a space for and access to files created by the user. Many organisations create *accounts* for users on file servers, which are a private space dedicated to the user and where the user can store files of different sorts. On file servers, users can create folders and store files in them. They can access these files from different parts of the network. For example, a user can create a file while at a meeting, using a computer in the meeting room, store the file on his/her file server account and then access the file again from his/her personal computer in his/her own office.

Application Server

It provides access to different application programs. For example, an application server in a university may provide access to students to software applications required for academic purposes, such as *Matlab*, a software for mathematical calculations or R, a software for statistical analysis. These software packages are often expensive and bulky to store on individual computers, so users can access them off the servers. This arrangement is especially useful for proprietary software, as the user organisation may buy an application software with only a few licences to keep costs down, and then allow users to share the software directly from the server.

Email Server

It provides email services to users in an organisation. Email is a widely popular network application and is used almost universally. An email server provides a mailbox facility to users, an email address, a space in which to receive messages and an application from which to create and send messages. Additionally, email servers store email addresses and personal data of users, and also of those that the user frequently interacts with. Currently, email servers are quite sophisticated and can help users manage their mailboxes by the following services: providing filters by which to sort and store mails under different subject headings; pushing email to hand-held devices such as mobile phones; checking for and removing harmful software, such as viruses appearing as attachments, and wasteful files such as spam; and allowing users to store details of appointments, a calendar and data of personal contacts.

Print Server

It enables users to access shared printers through the network. Many organisations place printers at a convenient location in the office where many users can print files, especially when they need access to high-quality and special-purpose printers (for colour printouts or for large format printouts). Many organisations use shared printers instead of personal desktop printers to save costs.

Web Server

It allows users to access the World Wide Web and also to store information that others can access. Most organisations now use a web server to store their web pages that can be accessed by their clients or partners outside the organisation. Web servers can often be hosted, or maintained, off the premises, at the location of an internet service provider. In this case, the organisation does not physically maintain the server but accesses it over the internet. To users this action is transparent, and they see the web page as if it were on their own premises.

Database Server

It is used by organisations that have large data storage and data management needs. The database server hosts a database application program that works with other applications to store, share and manage data. For example, an organisation could have an accounting software that uses the database server to store and manage all its data. This software could be resident on the application server and use the database server across the network. In addition, the database server may also be used by an inventory application or a client management application. The server thus becomes a common service available to many applications.

Proxy Server

It is used as an intermediary between clients in the organisation and other servers. One role it plays is to act as a temporary server, or cache, which stores information frequently demanded by many clients. The cache services the clients, instead of them going directly to the main server repeatedly, for the same information. This saves time and congestion on the main server. A proxy server is also used to act as a filter, particularly when it is used with a web server. It restricts packets that cannot be sent out and also removes packets that should not enter. In this sense, it acts as a firewall or gateway filter. A proxy is sometimes used to enable shared access to certain servers. For example, if a server with protected information is being used by the organisation then it may use a proxy to both limit and share access to this server.

11.2.1.3 Hosts/Clients

Hosts are the end systems, such as desktop computers and laptops, with users. They are also called clients as they demand services from the servers. Hosts are attached to the network through *network interface cards* (NICs). Hosts provide users access to facilities on the network.

Host computers such as desktops and laptops have operating systems equipped with the needed software to connect with the organisation's LAN and with the internet. Hosts run client software such as browsers and email programs that enable users to access specific services.

Host computers are largely client in nature in that they demand and receive services from the servers on the network. However, it is possible that sometimes hosts too act as servers when they share files or programs with other hosts on the network. For instance, some users share files through peer-to-peer networks, where their hosts act as servers.

11.2.1.4 LAN and WAN

A local area network (LAN) connects the computers within a physical location like a campus or a building. It uses internet technology to maintain the connections between the devices, such as the routers, switches, servers and clients. Thus, a LAN creates a network within the organisation.

A wide area network (WAN) refers to the connection of the organisation to the internet. A WAN connection is typically provided by an internet service provider (ISP), who provides a cable or a wireless connection to the organisation (see Fig. 11.3). ISPs may consist of different types of providers, and this is discussed later.

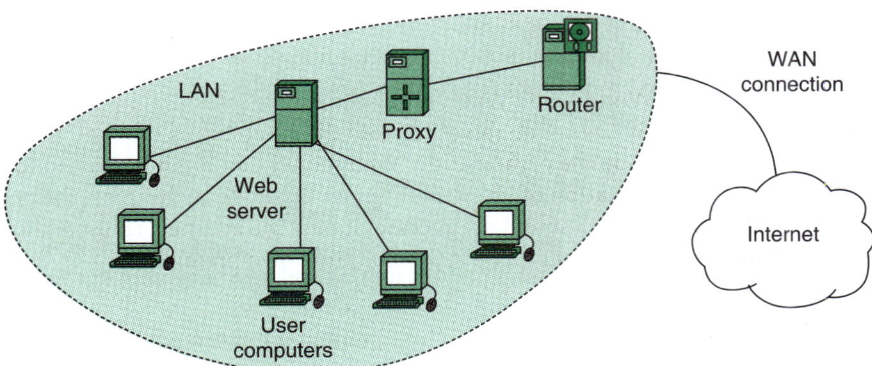

FIGURE 11.3 | LAN versus WAN connections.

11.2.2 Network Components

11.2.2.1 Cables

Cables are the physical devices by which the network is connected. The usual cables in organisations are unshielded twisted pair (UTP) copper cables that are inserted into a wall socket to connect a desktop computer (see Fig. 11.4). The wall socket is wired to connect to a switch or a hub. The twisted pair cables are rated according to their capacity. Category 5 (CAT 5) cables

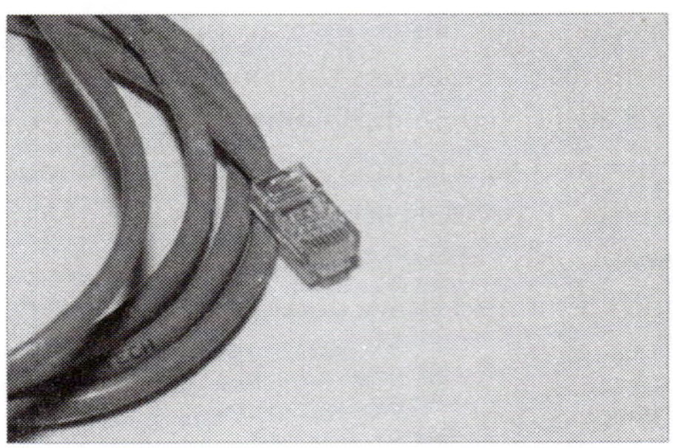

FIGURE 11.4 | LAN twisted pair cable.
Source: PublicPhoto.org.

can handle data transfer rates of 100 million bits per second (mbps) and Category 6 cables can handle 1000 mbps or gigabits per second.

Cables can also be made of glass fibre, also known as optical fibre cables, in which case they are able to handle much larger speeds and volumes of data. Optical fibre cables used for network connections have speeds ranging to terabytes per second (data obtained in September 2017). These cables can be brought up to the desktop, but they are mainly used to create the backbone or the underlying cable infrastructure of the organisation. Fibre cables are harder to handle, to bend and twist, and so they are not used extensively to connect desktops. Furthermore, fibre cables are far more expensive than copper cables.

11.2.2.2 Wireless Devices

Modern organisations also use wireless connectivity within their offices. This connectivity is obtained by radio waves. Organisations buy special routers that operate with the wireless protocol called Wi-Fi (Wireless Fidelity). Wi-Fi enables the router to connect to the computer. Packets from the computer are converted by the Wi-Fi card of the computer into radio wave pulses that carry the digital information. Wireless transfer is determined by different protocols or standards. The 802.11 is a set of standards approved by an international body for wireless communication. One standard in this set is 802.11b [that allows up to 11 megabits-per-second (mbps) data transfer rates] and another is 802.11g (that allows up to 54 mbps). 802.11g is a later standard that operates on a different frequency than 802.11b and also has a better range and performance through obstacles such as doors and walls. Many other standards on the 802.11 series have been developed over the years. By 2017, standards that can deliver data at 7 gigabits per second (802.11 ad) are being deployed.

A wireless device allows offices to create wireless LANs quite easily. As cables do not have to be laid and maintained, a wireless network can be set up quite quickly and cheaply. Desktop and laptop locations are not fixed, as users can locate themselves in any part of the office that receives the Wi-Fi signal.

Wireless devices are also called access points. These points are connected to the wired network via cables. Once set up, the access points also act as routers in that they are able to address and locate a large number of computers in their range. These computers or laptops connect to the LAN only through the nearest access point. Access points can also use security codes, wherein users have to use a password to access the network. This is a useful feature for many businesses and home users who have a risk of unauthorised users gaining access to their wireless networks.

11.2.2.3 Hubs and Switches

Hosts and client computers are connected via cables to hubs or switches. Hubs are local network devices that connect a number of computers to a router that further connects them to the internet. Hubs are the most basic of all network devices. They establish a simple connection between hosts and servers.

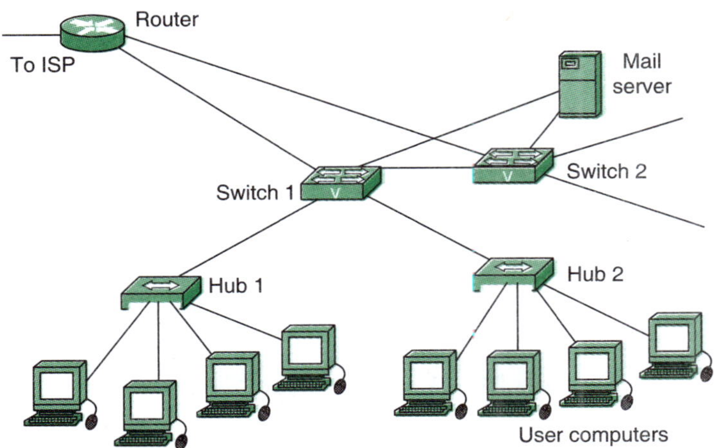

FIGURE 11.5 | Hubs and switches connected to the router.

A typical hub could have 6 or 12 or 24 ports. A port is a connection gateway that allows a cable to be inserted, and this cable can then be connected to a computer at the other end. Each port connects to all other ports via a simple connection. So when one computer in the hub wants to send information to another, it sends packets to the hub that redirects them to all the other ports, and the port for which the information is meant receives the packets. This method of communication is not very efficient as the packets are sent across to all the ports, even the ones for which they are not intended.

In a typical office, a hub would be placed in a corridor or a floor and could connect all the computers and printers located there, with one connection going over to the router in the organisation that enables internet access. Hubs are relatively inexpensive and have found wide usage over the years.

Most modern organisations, though, have replaced hubs with switches. Switches too have a number of ports – 12, 24 or 48 – that can be connected to hosts or to other switches and routers. The difference between hubs and switches is that when packets are sent to switches they are not re-directed to all the ports, but are only sent across to the port for which they are designated. This frees up a lot of traffic congestion in a device and makes it more efficient.

Modern switches are used to connect or bridge parts of the network within an organisation (see Fig. 11.5). For example, one department may have forty computers and printers connected to one switch. This department switch could be connected to the switch of another department, say on another floor of the building, which itself may have another 40 computers on the network. The switches would allow traffic to flow between the departments and also allow them to connect to the internet through a central router.

Many switches are 'intelligent' in that they read information in the packets, can use filters and can implement security policies. Switches can be managed, as new policies can be written into the devices, allowing them to deal with new kinds of traffic.

11.2.2.4 Routers

Routers are possibly the most important devices on the internet (see Fig. 11.6). They provide the link from the external world of the internet to the internal network of the organisation. Routers act on the internet as direction providers, bouncing off packets in the direction that they need to be or pushing them into the organisation's networks if that is the destination.

When an organisation arranges to buy an internet service or *bandwidth* from an external provider, the router is the device to which the external provider will fix their internet cables. The router has its address registered on the internet. All the traffic that is meant for the organisation is now sent to this address.

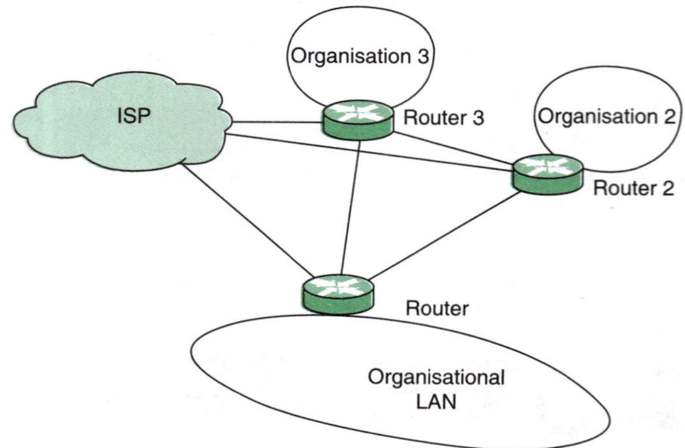

FIGURE 11.6 | A router connects the organisation to the internet.

The core function of the router is one of directing traffic. Whenever it receives a packet, it reads the destination address of the packet, and then looks up a table to determine which of the many other routers it is connected to should receive this packet. This information is carefully calculated by the router and is based on one of several protocols or agreed upon rules that it follows.

A protocol for the router determines how it decides on the direction for each packet. An example is the Router Information Protocol (RIP) that is based on updates sent by various routers on the internet as to the best way to proceed towards a destination. This information is shared, once every few minutes, between the routers and is used to update tables. If a link goes down or is choked with traffic, the routers near the problem site will warn others of the problem and they will change the manner in which packets will be forwarded (by selecting an alternative path and forwarding this information to all other routers to update their tables).

Inside the organisation, the router is used to connect to the internet and also direct traffic internally. Routers are often used to create virtual LANs (VLANs), which are subnetworks of users within the organisation who may be in the same physical location but may belong to different user groups. For instance, students and professors in the same university may be on different VLANs, allowing them different access rights to the internet, as also to resources on the LAN.

11.2.3 The Internet

The internet is a vast array of networks and end hosts connected to each other. It is best understood as a network that moves packets from one end to another through a vast array of wired and wireless connections and routers. At its core, the internet consists of very high speed routers that move traffic at massive volumes between one part and another. At its periphery are end devices that send or receive data.

Along with the host devices described above are a number of other devices that operate over the internet and that are now gaining popularity. A digital photo frame is one such device. These photo frames are kept at homes with internet connections, and look like ordinary photo frames. The difference is that they access the internet and display photos they receive from there. So families can leave these frames with relatives and upload photos onto them from remote locations, and relatives can see them directly. Another fun application has a web access device built into a pop-up toaster. It can access local weather information from the internet and then imprint or burn this information as an image on the toast.

There are many internet devices that act as sensors. Some are installed in buildings and relay a stream of information about activities in the building or about the light, temperature and humidity conditions, which can then be monitored for changes and adjustments. Some sensors are embedded in remote and human-inaccessible locations and provide information on geological conditions. All these devices use the facility of the internet to relay information.

The internet is maintained by a number of telecommunication service providers around the world. Those closest to user organisations are called *Tier-3 providers*. They own and maintain cables or satellite-based links and lease these to organisations that want internet access. They maintain large capacity routers and servers that route traffic and also host the addresses of the client organisations (addresses are discussed later). Examples of Tier-3 providers in India include Tata Teleservices and Reliance Telecommunications. These service providers control traffic via their servers and allocate bandwidth according to the contracts they have with their clients. Some clients may buy shared bandwidth, for example, 8 mbps shared 1:4 with other users. This means that the client will receive an 8 mbps service that is shared with other users, and at any point of time they are guaranteed to receive only one-fourth the bandwidth (or 2 mbps). At other times they may receive more bandwidth, depending on the usage of the other clients sharing the service. The service provider has to ensure that this service level is always maintained for the client.

Some Tier-3 service providers also enable other facilities such as providing a firewall for protection against viruses, worms and other malicious software. The protection is provided at the node at which the client organisation connects with the internet, so it is of quite high reliability. Other services include providing *bandwidth shaping*, where clients take higher bandwidth during peak hours and lower during non-peak hours, thus getting a price discount, and also obtaining better service.

Other Tier-3 service providers also enable internet traffic to be routed through mobile networks such as GSM (the Global System for Mobile Communication). The GSM service picks up packets and routes them through to mobile devices using special protocols such as the GPRS (the General Packet Radio Service). Mobile phones, which have the capability, can thus receive and send internet packets through such a mix of protocols. All facilities and applications of the internet are now available over mobile phones.

Tier-3 service providers buy or lease internet connectivity from Tier-2 providers. Tier-2 providers operate in large regions such as a continent or a large country such as India. They invest in and maintain large networks of fibre optic cables that can move massive volumes of data and also have huge routers that can route the traffic. Tier-2 providers usually operate through Tier-3 firms, although they sometimes sell bandwidth directly to large customers too. Tier-2 providers deal with capacities in hundreds of mbps per second (see Fig. 11.7).

Tier-1 consists of the core providers of internet services. Tier-2 providers buy services from Tier-1 providers, who operate at the global level. Tier-1 providers are large multinational telecommunication firms that maintain massive intercontinental networks of cables, undersea

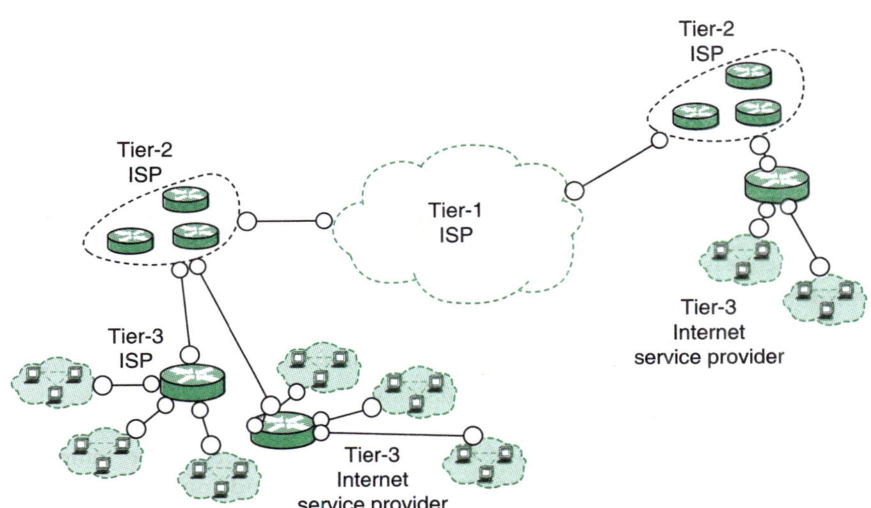

FIGURE 11.7 | Internet service providers (ISPs) at different tiers.

cables, and satellite links. They manage capacities of gigabits per second and have massive routers placed at several locations across the world. They lease bandwidth to regional providers and create points-of-presence (PoP) in specific locations, which are nodes from where other providers can tap into the networks. Examples of Tier-1 providers include Sprint, NTT and Tata Communications.

11.2.3.1 The Last Mile Problem

Most countries around the globe have built up considerable capacities for internet access and penetration. These include developing countries, which have made considerable efforts to build up the backbone networks using Tier-3 and Tier-2 service providers. However, many developing countries and regions are troubled by what is known as 'the last mile problem'. This problem is that of providing internet services to individual homes and establishments. The lead case on AirJaldi is an example of a service that solves the last mile problem.

The basis of the last mile problem is economics. It is economically viable for commercial telecommunication firms to set up backbone services by laying cables across towns and cities. However, it is not commercially viable for them to lay cables to each individual home and building; the costs for doing this are prohibitive.

The first solution to the last mile problem was of providing internet connectivity through phone lines. Phone lines in most countries had been provided by government investment or subsidies and many city and town homes already have these. Devices called modems could be used to dial into servers provided by telecommunication firms and these could connect to the internet. *Dial-up connections* were limited to very low bandwidths known as *baseband* connections [usually about 56 kilobits per second (kbps)]. Soon the *digital subscriber line* (DSL) technology was developed which could deliver much higher bandwidth (of 2 mbps or more), also known as *broadband* connections, and these could be used with phone lines too. In many developing countries, this has become the norm and many individual users and business establishments connect to the internet through DSL connections.

An alternative to DSL is the *cable modem* that provides internet connectivity through television cable connections. As many subscribers have had cable connections installed, it is commercially viable for the cable provider firms to provide internet services on the same media.

> **KEY POINT**
>
> The last mile problem is that of providing internet connectivity to individual homes and establishments.

In regions where cable or telephone lines did not already exist, like many rural areas in developing countries, governments and commercial providers are exploring WiMax (Worldwide Interoperability for Microwave Access) technology. This technology can provide up to 10 mbps speeds through radio waves. The advantage of this technology over Wi-Fi is that it can serve clients across very long distances. WiMax has strong advantages over DSL and cable in coping with the last mile problem and is gaining popularity in many parts of the world.

With the wide availability of mobile phones, which are able to access the internet over 34 and 44 connections, and with most people accessing the internet over their mobile phones, the problem of the last mile has been largely reduced.

11.2.4 What Has to be Managed?

For organisations that use networks and have integrated their operations around the available network services, there are several management challenges. Questions about the design, performance and maintenance of the network have to be answered, as also the manner in which it will support the operations of the organisation. Following are some issues that are pertinent in this context:

1. **Network architecture:** Organisations have to design the basic architecture of the network that would be most relevant for them. This would entail answering questions such as:
   (a) What services have to be offered over the network?
   (b) How many users will access this service now and in the future?
   (c) What are the categories of users in the organisation and what are their networking needs?
   (d) How will the network be accessed and used by those outside the organisation?

(e) How will the network connect diverse offices and regions?
The architecture will determine the number of servers, the type of servers, the kind and type of VLANs required, the number of switches and routers needed, etc. This is a technical design based on the business needs of the organisation.

2. **Service level:** For many organisations that have networks in place, the important question is what the service levels should be. This entails deciding on the internet bandwidth that the organisation has to subscribe to and also the internal bandwidth requirements. The number of concurrent users, the number likely to demand services from outside, and the kind of services demanded will determine the service levels. For example, an educational institution may decide that at any time it should be able to host 50% of its students, simultaneously, on its internal networks without any deterioration in quality.
3. **Security needs:** In organisations that have adopted networking technologies, it is imperative that they also plan for their security needs. Many networks are directly targeted by adversaries on the internet, sometimes for trivial reasons, and sometimes for reasons of competition and espionage. Organisations have to clearly frame a security policy and implement an architecture that supports the policy. This is covered in detail in another chapter (see Chapter 9).
4. **Open or proprietary standards:** Organisations do have the option of choosing basic application and data standards that are open or proprietary. Adopting open standards implies they can rely on widely available network components that can be assembled in a plug-and-play manner. Proprietary standards entail constructing the network with special components that the organisation has to build or acquire from vendors. Proprietary standards could provide a competitive edge for some firms, though this would be rare.

Caselet Videoconferencing in Courts

One of the most dramatic measures that have affected the legal process in some Indian courts has been that of the use of videoconferencing. Judges, lawyers, defendants and litigants have found that this technology is able to save much time and money for all concerned.

It is well known in law enforcement circles that high-profile undertrials, particularly those who have political links, are prone to escape during the process of transfer from the prison to the court. There are instances where police have had to use public transport, or minimal security measures to transport undertrials, and the latter have used this opportunity to escape. This creates a huge burden on the police, as they have to answer for the incident and also take measures, which are expensive, to find the escapee again.

Videoconferencing helps in such cases as with this telecommunication technology judges and lawyers can interrogate and question prisoners remotely. Typically, videoconferencing involves placing video camera equipment at the prison where the undertrials are located and at the court where the judge can interview them. The cameras are linked through telecommunication technology, where audio and video are transmitted over Transmission Control Protocol/Internet Protocol (TCP/IP).

For a particular trial in the state of Karnataka, in 2006, five undertrials had to be brought to Bangalore from different cities. As there was a strong security concern with regard to these five persons, the judge in Bangalore permitted the case to be conducted via videoconferencing, providing a huge relief to the police and jail wardens concerned. It is estimated that the state saved about Rs 1.26 crores (about USD 286, 000), mainly from reduced transportation costs.

All the courts of New Delhi have installed videoconferencing equipment and routinely hold trials over this medium. Courts in other states such as Gujarat, Bihar and Maharashtra have also followed suit.

The benefits from videoconferencing are not only from reduced costs of transportation, but also from reduced corruption, speedier trials (as there are no delays of transportation or of prisoners escaping), lesser number of adjournments and more accountability of public officials. Furthermore, sensitive cases, such as those involving minors, can be handled more discreetly. Observers claim that videoconferencing in courts has reduced the number of pending cases in many courts by a significant amount.

11.3 NETWORK SERVICES AND LAYERS

11.3.1 Connection-Oriented Services

A connection-oriented service on the internet is one in which a feedback loop of acknowledgements is used to support exchange of data. For example, in a connection-oriented service like email, each packet of data, sent from the client to the server or from the server to the client, is acknowledged with another packet sent to the sender as confirmation. In such a service, it is guaranteed that packets would reach their destination, as there is explicit confirmation of delivery.

A typical connection-oriented service sends out a packet of information from a sender to a receiver, and the moment the receiver receives the packet, it responds with an acknowledgement packet. If the packet does not reach the receiver, then after a certain period of time the sender resends the packet and continues to do so as long as it does not receive a confirmation. It continues on this loop until the maximum time limit is reached, at which point it terminates the exchange with a message saying that the exchange has ended as it has run out of time. Every packet received by the receiver is confirmed in this manner.

Connection-oriented services are heavy users of bandwidth as they have to send out a confirmatory message with every packet received. This uses up bandwidth and slows down the process, while ensuring a guaranteed delivery of the message.

11.3.2 Connectionless Services

Connectionless services do not send out confirmatory messages upon receiving packages. The receivers in such services do not respond at all. Senders send out packets to receivers – all the packets may be in a bunch or spread out. Each packet is received and collected into the message, without any acknowledgement.

Connectionless services are faster than connection-oriented ones, but they are less reliable. There is no way of knowing if some packets have arrived or have been dropped during passage as there is no explicit accounting for them.

11.3.3 Protocols

The internet today is a collection of *protocols* that enable services. A protocol is an agreed upon standard by which devices exchange information. The protocol specifies the manner in which the exchange has to be initiated, how it has to be executed, how data has to be formatted and exchanged and how the exchange has to be terminated. The protocols are, in that sense, procedures by which the devices proceed on an exchange of information (see Fig. 11.8).

Humans too use protocols to exchange information. For example, if you meet a stranger on the street and want to ask about the time, you may proceed with a sentence that is similar to: 'Excuse me'. If the stranger responds to you with a nod or a verbal: 'Yes' then you can ask the question: 'What is the time?'. If the stranger does not respond to your request then you know that the exchange cannot proceed further. This protocol of exchange is a cultural norm and will vary from culture to culture. For example, in some cultures it may be fine to ask right away: 'Excuse me, what is the time?' This protocol precludes an initial intimation of a request.

Human protocols allow transactions to proceed in a reasonable and orderly manner. They are necessary for strangers to interact and proceed with a known and reliable set of informal rules for the interaction. Furthermore, humans know how to react when a certain protocol is violated or a rule is broken. Machine protocols serve the same purpose.

11.3.3.1 Internet Protocol

The Internet Protocol or IP is one of the fundamental and most basic protocols for the internet. It essentially provides a means of addressing and locating devices. The IP is a connectionless

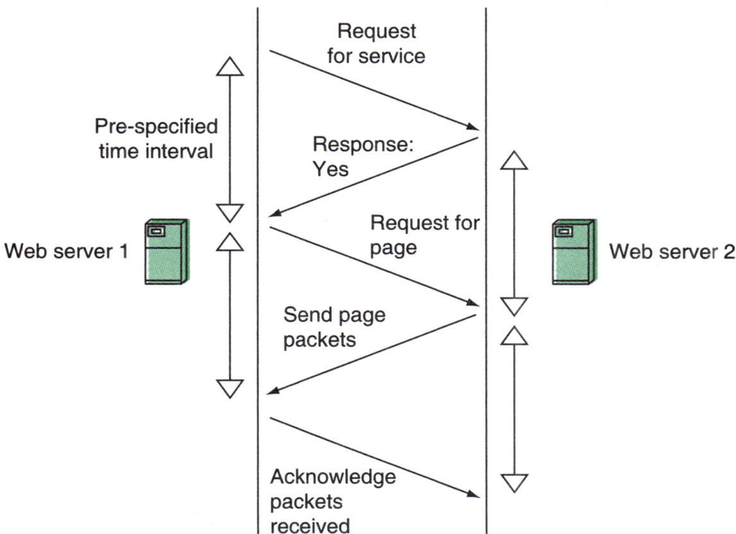

FIGURE 11.8 Example of a protocol for communication between two web servers.

Note: For each initiation from web server 1, there is an appropriate response from web server 2, within a specified time period.

protocol, which means that it only supports finding and locating addresses but does not guarantee the transfer of messages.

The basic IP address consists of a set of four numbers separated by dots or periods, for example, 163.123.12.100. Each number is called an octet and is represented by exactly 8 bits (or 1 byte) in binary notation. The entire address is thus represented by 32 bits.

For most users of the internet, addresses are identified by names (also called host names), such as www.yahoo.com or www.google.com or www.uc3m.es, which correspond to known institutions or businesses such as Yahoo, Google or the University Carlos III of Madrid. For each of these host names, there is at least one unique 32-bit number address that represents the host name on the internet. For instance, www.yahoo.com is represented by the address 69.147.76.15 (this is one of the numbered addresses that represent yahoo.com). Each name is thus translated into a number that is understood by the Internet Protocol. This translation is done by the domain name server (DNS) protocol. Many famous addresses on the internet, such as www.google.com or www.mit.edu, often have many IP addresses pointing to their host name. This is to facilitate ease of use for users around the world - for users in India the address www.google.com will translate to an IP address that can be accessed faster from their region.

The 32-bit addressing scheme is known as the IP version 4 scheme or IPv4. When only 32 bits are available for creating addresses, it is clear that there is a limit to the number of addresses that can be provided on the internet. This number, corresponding to 2^{32}, is quite large, at about 4 billion addresses. This, however, is not enough for the current demand and growth of the internet. So there is a move to use a 128-bit addressing scheme that will provide 2^{128} addresses (or 3.4×10^{34} addresses). This larger scheme for addressing is known as the IP version 6 standard or IPv6.

For an institution to obtain an IP address, it has to apply to an agency within its country. Worldwide the addressing scheme is maintained by the nodal agency ICANN (Internet Corporation for Assigned Names and Numbers), which runs the Internet Assigned Numbers Authority (IANA). The ICANN is located in the USA and is charged with the responsibility of maintaining and assigning globally unique addresses for all institutions using the Internet Protocol. The IANA assigns responsibility of address assignment to regional internet registries (RIRs) that assign unique numbers in their regions or nations. The IANA assigns blocks of numbers to the RIRs which further distribute them in their regions. The RIRs are responsible for resolving any address related conflicts that may arise in their region.

IP addresses are assigned to organisations, and within organisations to particular servers, such as web servers or email servers, and to host systems. Some of these addresses are *public addresses* in the sense that they can be understood by the public IP system that is maintained by routers and *domain name servers* (DNS). Public IP addresses are located by router address tables and by DNS tables that identify the addresses underlying the names (such as www.yahoo.com).

Institutions can also maintain a large pool of private IP addresses. These addresses are known only inside the institution and are not revealed outside. For example, it is quite common for institutions to use the series of addresses beginning with 192.168.0.0 or 17.16.0.0 to assign to computers and devices on their internal LAN. The reasons for having public and private IP addresses are:

1. Public IP addresses have to be purchased by institutions, and owning a large number is expensive. This is also a recurring cost.
2. Private IP addresses have no cost associated with them and any number of them can be generated and assigned, as needed.
3. Translation protocols, such as *Network Address Translation* (NAT), allow private addresses to be translated to public addresses that can be used over the internet.

It must be noted that for a device to use a service over the internet, such as requesting a web page, it must have a recognisable public IP address. But if devices within organisations have private addresses, then how will their addresses be recognised? This problem is solved by the NAT protocol, which operates from the router of the organisation and gives each packet with a private address a public and recognisable one. This is done only temporarily. Once the transaction is complete, the NAT protocol recovers the public address and gives it to the next internal packet that is seeking a service. In this manner a pool of, say, 256 public addresses that an organisation may own can be shared by thousands of devices with private addresses.

Private IP addresses can be assigned within the organisation to devices in a fixed or static manner, or in a dynamic manner. A static IP address means that a particular device always has the same, fixed IP address that is not shared by anyone else. A dynamic address means that a pool of addresses is shared by devices within the organisation, so one particular computer may have different IP addresses at different times. Static addresses are used when the number of users is fixed, and they use their computers at about the same time. IP addresses are written into files in their computers and remain the same throughout their lifetime of usage. Static addresses are resolved easily by the routers and switches and work faster. Dynamic addresses are assigned by a protocol known as *Dynamic Host Control Protocol* (DHCP). The DHCP assigns an IP address to a device whenever it is booted up within the network of the organisation. The DHCP looks up a table of available IP addresses, from the internal pool, and assigns an address to the device. This address may change the next time the device boots up. This protocol has the advantage that the address pool can be shared and it is also secure, as no particular IP address is tied to a computer and the computer hence cannot be targeted by those seeking to do mischief.

KEY POINT

IP addresses are unique locations assigned to servers and other computers connected over the internet.

11.3.3.2 *Transmission Control Protocol*

The Transmission Control Protocol (TCP) along with IP is synonymous with the internet. In fact, the internet is said to be constituted by TCP/IP. The TCP is a connection-oriented protocol that is used by a large number of services including email, the Web and file transfer. Every packet that is sent using TCP has to be accounted for by acknowledging its receipt, and also the packets have to be numbered and assembled at the receiver's end. The TCP ensures that the complete information in the file is transferred and is in the order in which the user desired it to be.

The TCP uses an elaborate procedure to establish contact between senders and receivers. This entails a series of messages in the form of data packets, which constitute a *handshake* or commitment to exchange information. A handshake is initiated by sending a request for a connection, then waiting for an acknowledgement from the recipient. The wait is strictly timed, and if no signal is forthcoming, the sender sends the request again. The protocol proceeds in such a manner until the connection is established and then information flows follow. The termination of the connection is also regulated and follows a strict procedure.

The TCP also implements *flow control* or traffic control over the movement of packets. When a network is congested, packet traffic is often dropped from routers or switches, and this forces the sending and receiving servers to re-send packets and acknowledgements. In such situations, the TCP adjusts either the size of packets or the window waiting for acknowledgements. It makes adjustments to suit the needs of the network, and as the performance improves or deteriorates further, the parameters for flow control are further adjusted.

The TCP enables services such as email, web browsing and file transfer through specific ports on host devices. For example, the protocol for web browsing, which is known as the Hypertext Transfer Protocol (HTTP), uses the TCP as its underlying mechanism for transferring information and uses port 80. This port is dedicated to HTTP packets and routers. Firewalls allow traffic to go through port 80 only when they are marked as HTTP by the TCP. Email is based on the Simple Mail Transfer Protocol (SMTP) and also uses TCP as its underlying mechanism for transport. Email uses port 23 and all packets marked for this port have to be SMTP packets for the internet devices to allow them to pass.

The TCP's elaborate routines for handshaking and establishing connections are also a source of vulnerability. Some mischief makers on the internet use the request for connection of the TCP to make servers hang and wait endlessly for information, thus, slowing them down. One such type of mischief is known as denial-of-service (DoS) attack, wherein mischief makers send requests to servers using the TCP and then hang up the connection. The recipient responds with an acknowledgement and then waits for further information, but nothing comes through and the connection times out after waiting needlessly. The mischief makers send multiple requests, repeatedly, and make the server wait endlessly for information, while not attending to other, regular requests. These issues are covered in detail in Chapter 12.

KEY POINT

The Transmission Control Protocol (TCP) establishes a connection between senders and receivers of messages on the internet.

11.3.3.3 User Datagram Protocol

The User Datagram Protocol (UDP) is a connectionless protocol that is used to transmit packets from sender to receiver in a fast but unreliable manner. Many multimedia applications use UDP, such as the YouTube.com service that hosts videos, as a large number of packets have to be sent to the user reasonably quickly. Here, the disadvantage of lost packets is not important as a few lost packets will not hurt the overall video, but a slow transmission rate will not be acceptable. UDP is also used by services that request quick, but small pieces of information, for which reliability is not important.

11.3.4 Layers

The protocols of the internet are arranged in layers. These layers are conceptual in nature and have to be understood as groups of protocols that perform distinct tasks. The topmost layer is known as the *Application Layer*. The protocols at this layer, such as HTTP and SMTP, provide specific services such as access to the Web and email. These protocols allow the user to directly interact with the programs and demand services. They are specifically designed for that purpose. However, the Application Layer Protocols are not able to send the information that they capture in packets directly to switches or routers or to other destinations on the internet. They are also not able to move the individual bits along copper cables or radio waves. These detailed jobs are left to the other layers.

The layers of the networks are thus functional divisions of tasks (these tasks are outlined in Table 11.1). The lowest layer is known as the *Physical Layer*, and it has a set of protocols that are usually implemented in the hardware of the network devices, which move bits along copper cables or through wireless media. When manufacturers of network devices build new media, such as new types of fibre or copper cables, they have to work with the protocols at this layer and the layer adjacent to it. The manufacturers do not have to worry about the details of how the user will use the cables to surf the Web or send emails, as those tasks are left to the upper layers.

Table 11.1 | Network Layers and Their Functions

Layer	Purpose
Application	Supports network applications such as email, the Web and file transfer. Protocols such as HTTP, SMTP and FTP are used at this layer.
Transport	Transports Application Layer messages between clients and servers. Use of connection-oriented and connectionless protocols such as TCP and UDP.
Network	Determines the address of devices and the routing of messages between them. Uses the Internet Protocol and others.
Link	Transfers messages from the Network Layer along links in the network, such as routers and switches. Uses protocols such as Ethernet and Wi-Fi.
Physical	The protocols in this layer are used to move bits along different media and from various devices.

Layers permit designers and engineers to invent and innovate on the services of the internet without having to bother about all the details of movement of bits or packets at all layers. They can innovate on services at a particular layer and only worry about its interaction with the layer below it. For example, the layer just below the Application Layer is the Transport Layer that is responsible for the actual movement of packets and their control, and this layer has the TCP and UDP protocols. When users create innovative services, such as transmitting video images to mobile devices, they have to work only on designing a protocol at this layer, which will handle the packets efficiently. They need not think about other layers.

Owing to the layered nature of protocols, and their relative independence in functioning, the internet has seen immense innovation in the services and protocols that it uses. Many commercial enterprises have evolved and gained prominence by creating protocols and services that provide a new and unique feature for users of the internet.

11.3.5 Ethernet Topologies

The Ethernet protocol is widely used within LANs. As it is one of the oldest protocols, it has many different physical configurations through which it can be implemented. These configurations are known as topologies. Two of the most widely used topologies are known as the *star* and *bus* topologies.

In the star topology all devices on the network are connected to a central hub (see Fig. 11.9). The hub routes all messages to the nodes on the network. Each node is connected to the hub on a point-to-point basis (there are no intermediate devices) and communicates directly with it. The hub directs all traffic between the computers and also connects the computers to other devices, such as switches. Hubs have a number of ports on them, either 16 or 32 or 48, thus limiting the number of computers that can be linked to them. The star network has the advantage that nodes can be added or removed from them at will, the network can be monitored from a central point, and capacity can be added to the device. Its drawback is that it constitutes a single point of failure, if the hub faults then the entire network is affected.

In a bus topology all the nodes are connected to a single central channel called the bus (see Fig. 11.10). It acts as a communication medium onto which all the nodes can send messages. Each message travels to and fro on the bus and whichever node is the destination, picks it up. All the nodes thus *listen* to messages on the bus to receive the one intended for them. To send a message on the bus, the nodes have to first check and see that it is not busy with

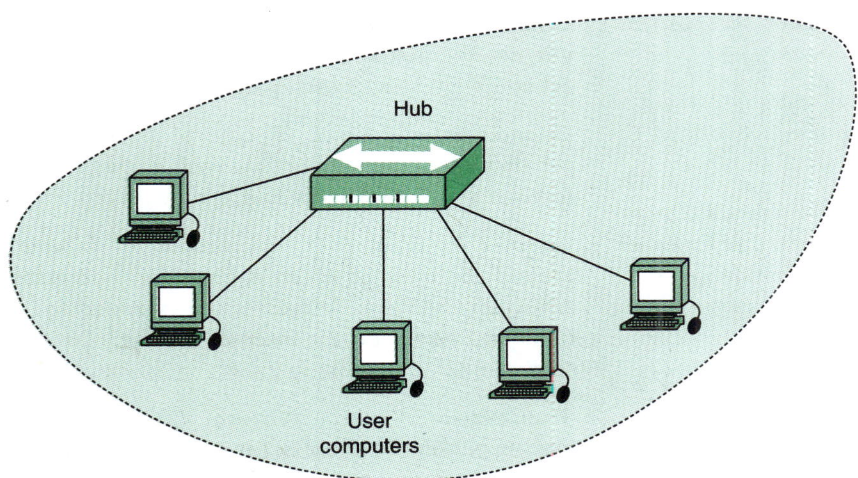

FIGURE 11.9 | Star topology. All devices on the network are connected to a central hub.

another message. If the bus is busy, then the sending node has to wait for a random amount of time before trying again. This is done to prevent collisions on the bus and is formally referred to as carrier sense multiple access/collision detection.

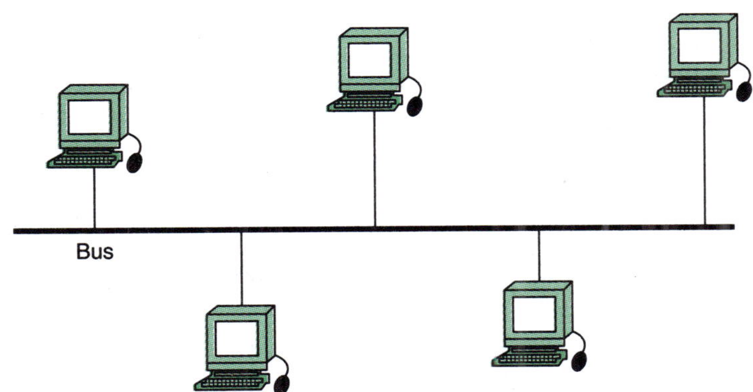

FIGURE 11.10 | The bus topology.

Chapter Glossary

Packet A basic element of the internet that carries information. Each packet has a header that specifies the source and destination addresses for the packet and the nature and type of the content it is carrying, among other things.

Local Area Network (LAN) A network connecting various computers inside an organisation.

Proxy A server that manages the connection between the computers in an organisation and the internet.

Switch A device that manages traffic on the LAN. It directs packets in the correct direction on the network.

Firewall A device that permits or blocks traffic to and from the internet into the internal network of an organisation. It protects the organisation's network from malicious intrusion.

Router A router connects different networks on the internet and primarily re-directs packets. Routers also connect the internal network of organisations to the external internet.

Server A server is a computer that provides shared services to other computers on the network.

Client A client or host computer demands services from servers on the network.

Network Interface Card (NIC) This card is present in computers and lets them connect to the network of the organisation.

802.11 (Wi-Fi) This is an international standard maintained by the Institute of Electrical and Electronic Engineers (IEEE). It refers to the manner in which wireless fidelity (Wi-Fi) routers connect to computers. This standard determines the speed at which data packets can travel.

Hub A device that connects computers on a network and enables basic packet movement.

Tier-3 service provider Internet service providers who operate at the local and regional level and provide cable or wireless connections to organisations.

Bandwidth The capacity of internet connections, measured in millions of bits per second (mpbs).

Dial-up connections Internet connections enabled by service providers through landline telephones. These connections are enabled by special devices called modems that were built into computers.

Digital Subscriber Line (DSL) A high-bandwidth connection enabled through landline telephone connections.

Broadband connection A high-bandwidth connection specified at more than 256 kpbs in India.

Connection-oriented service A type of service on the internet for exchange of packets, which requires explicit acknowledgement of each packet transmitted and received.

Connectionless service A type of service on the internet that does not require that each packet transmitted or received be accounted for and acknowledged.

Internet Protocol (IP) A protocol for moving packets around the internet which is based on addresses and an addressing scheme. Addresses are provided for organisations and nodes on the internet to which packets can be sent.

Transmission Control Protocol (TCP) A protocol for moving packets on the internet that is connection oriented.

Public address An IP address that is visible on the internet. This is a specific address of an organisation that others can see and send packets to.

Domain name servers Servers that translate human-readable internet addresses, like www.yahoo.com, into the numerical addresses that are used by the IP.

Dynamic Host Control Protocol (DHCP) This protocol allows computers within an organisation to share a pool of IP addresses. A computer takes an address temporarily from a pool when it is booted up, and the address is returned to the pool when the computer is shut down.

Review Questions

1. How and where does a packet originate? What are the important devices that move a packet across the internet?
2. What is the role of a file server?
3. What is the role of an email server? Can an email server reside outside the organisation where the email is being used? Why?
4. How are client computers connected to the internet?
5. What is the 802.11 series of numbers used for?
6. What is the difference between a hub and a switch?
7. What is the function and role of routers on the internet?
8. Differentiate Tier-1 service providers from Tier-3 service providers.
9. What is "the last mile problem?"
10. What are the important issues for managers to consider regarding networking within an organisation?
11. Differentiate between connection-oriented and connectionless protocols?
12. What is the main job of the Internet Protocol or IP?
13. What is the main function of the TCP?
14. Read the AirJaldi case and answer: What were the main challenges AirJaldi faced in providing internet connectivity in the region where they operate? How did they overcome the challenges?

Research Questions

1. What are the main advantages that IPv6 will provide over IPv4? How will this benefit the common user?
2. How does a router route packages? Use the traceroute service available on the internet to trace the routing of

packages from different parts of the world to your own institutional router.

3. There is talk in the news media about "Internet 2." What is this and how will it be different from the current internet? Research this on the internet and answer in terms of how the protocols will differ.
4. Read the Airjaldi case and determine the following: What were the chief elements of the technology used to create the wireless network? What were the innovations Airjaldi introduced to implement the network?

Further Reading

1. Kurose, J.F. and Ross, K.W. (2005) *Computer Networking: A Top-Down Approach Featuring the internet*, Pearson Education, Singapore.
2. http://drupal.airjaldi.com/system/files/Beyond+Pilots+Keeping+Rural+Wireless+Networks+Alive.pdf (accessed on June 2011).
3. http://drupal.airjaldi.com/ (accessed on June 2011).
4. http://isif.asia/groups/isif/ (accessed on June 2011).
5. http://extremecom.org/(accessed on June 2011).
6. Narasimhan, B. (2006) Haazir Ho [Present Yourself], *Real CIO World*, **1**(5), 53–56.

CHAPTER 12

Information Systems Security and Control

Learning Objectives

After completing this chapter, you will be able to:

- Get an overview of threats to the organisation
- Learn about technologies for handling security
- Get an overview of wireless technology
- Understand managing security

The modern organisation, being highly networked, is constantly under threat from harmful software and from the malicious intent of certain people. Viruses and worms are rampant and infect millions of computers, wreaking heavy damage on data and productivity. Malicious coders, called crackers, also attack organisations to infect them or to steal data or money. Some crackers simply attack the services of organisations to bring them down or make them ineffective. Many technologies have evolved to address the threats from the internal and external environment of the organisation. These technologies protect data by encrypting it, or protect organisations by monitoring the incoming and outgoing network traffic. Wireless technology is used by many organisations, and it poses unique security challenges. Managing security means ensuring the organisational users' confidentiality, authentication, integrity and access of digital resources. Security management involves managing people, technology and processes – all of which impact and determine security – from the perimeter of the network till the client computer.

MIND MAP OF CHAPTER TOPICS

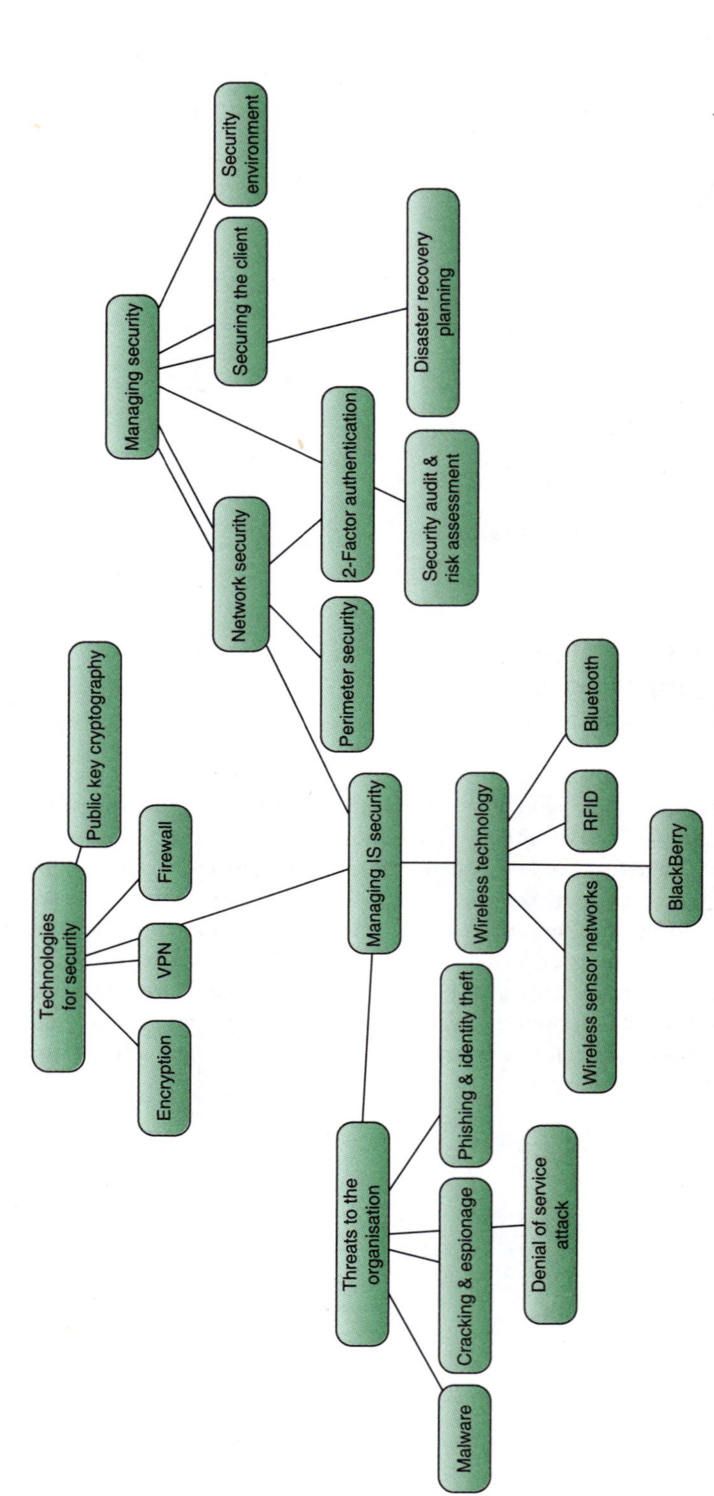

CASE STUDY: THE STUXNET WORM

Stuxnet is the first known worm specifically designed to target industrial organisations in a specific country. The worm targeted a power station and a uranium enrichment plant at Natanz, in Iran, between June 2009 and April 2010. These were the seeds of over 12,000 infections that were to follow. Waves of at least three new variants of the worm were launched at Iranian industrial facilities subsequently.

The origin of the worm remains a mystery. According to published reports, it is believed to be a joint USA–Israel project. The goal of the initiative was to destroy or delay Iran's ability to build nuclear weapons, which it did by up to 5 years. A director of security research at McAfee Avert Labs, said, 'Those behind the attacks had a level of financing that enabled intelligence gathering prior to the attacks'. According to a manager at Symantec's security response team, 'They weren't just after information, so a competitor is out. They wanted to reprogram [the chips] and operate the machinery in a way unintended by the real operators. That points to something more than industrial espionage'. Stuxnet was first detected by VirusBlokAda, a little known security firm based in Belarus.

Stuxnet could be the blueprint for future offensive endeavours in cyber space. In most cases, cyber espionage and cyber war are being juxtaposed as they both use the same mechanisms to tap on vulnerabilities. However, the motivation of the cracker is very different from that of a cyber attacker. In both the cases, the attacker's identity and motivation are unknown and hence there is no policy on who should be responsible for mitigation of such risks. The combination of sophistication, funding and processes behind the development of Stuxnet could be a wake-up call for policy makers. Stuxnet has introduced a new spate of public questions about covert operations carried out with malware and USB sticks rather than warships and missiles. As more commerce and political activity moves online, it is reasonable to expect that military experts would look at cyber space as a potential new theatre for war.

The late 1990s and early 2000s saw widespread cyber threats like the 'Melissa' and 'I Love You' viruses. This gave birth to a multibillion dollar anti-virus and worm-protection software industry. Cyber attacks have grown with a vengeance in the late 2000s. The denial-of-service (DoS) phenomenon has apparently become a tool of war. A 15-year-old Canadian with the handle 'mafiaboy' launched the first documented DoS attack in 2000 against numerous e-commerce sites, including eBay and Amazon.com, shutting some down and wreaking havoc that cost an estimated USD 1.7 billion. In 2007, a DoS attack against Estonia crippled the country's digital infrastructure, paralysing government, media sites and a bank. A massive cyber attack against Georgia crippled the banking system and disrupted cell-phone services. The Pentagon reported some 360 million attempts to break into its networks in 2010, up from just 6 million in 2006. Attacks have mushroomed so quickly that the Defense Department of USA reportedly plans to establish a new military command focused solely on computer warfare, as the country is 'under cyber attack virtually all the time, every day'. Security experts such as Bruce Schneier say a cyber war is escalating, much in the way nuclear arms build-ups characterised the USA–Soviet Cold War of the 1980s. All sides have more capabilities than needed and little dialogue happens on the subject between affected parties.

Stuxnet surfaced in July 2009 when it infected MS Windows machines via USB keys, commonly used to transfer files rather than the internet, as the targeted industrial systems are usually not connected to the internet for security reasons. The mechanism targeted a zero-day vulnerability in MS Windows file sharing, and spread using the AutoPlay feature for USB sticks and other removable drives. Microsoft issued an emergency fix, but researchers found that other methods were used as well by Stuxnet, including a printer-sharing bug, patched much later by Microsoft. Once on the corporate network, the worm was designed to find the programmable logic control (PLC) software, manufactured by Siemens and running inside an Iranian uranium enrichment centre, and redesign it to give new instructions to the machinery it controls. Stuxnet went after vulnerabilities in the process control systems which automate the most critical parts of an industrial facility's processes – temperature, pressure and the flow of water, chemicals and gases. Stolen digital certificates from JMicron and Realtek avoided detection by Microsoft's driver installer.

Before Stuxnet, the most popular vectors of infiltration, for malware, into the users' machines were popular client-side applications like browsers and plugins. The Stuxnet attack is different and is termed 'semi-targeted'. In such an attack, while the payload is focused on the Supervisory Control and Data Acquisition (SCADA) systems, the computer systems that monitor and control industrial machinery and infrastructure, the malware propagates promiscuously. Self-replicating code, as that in worms, not only spreads very fast but also becomes highly visible. Researchers therefore feel that malware developers have moved away from such methods of penetration to Trojans that spread through infected URLs, Microsoft Office documents and PDFs compromised with zero-day exploits (zero-day exploits refer to infections occurring on the day the system is started). Stuxnet was written in multiple languages, including C, C++ and other object-oriented languages and had a 500 MB footprint indicating that there was a large enough team that spent significant amount of time and money on developing this worm. An expert commented,

> This is not developed by a hacker sitting in his basement. It required a development team, a QA team and a level of expertise of not only procuring zero-day vulnerabilities and obtaining signed certificates, but procuring the knowledge to also infect PLCs. They had to have a testing environment to find out if it worked. It opens a whole new avenue in the research community and new level of vigilance for highly sophisticated threats to come in the future.

A security vendor said,

> In reality, there will always be vulnerabilities. It's easy to see how control systems can be open to attacks, and it's easy to see why they might be targeted. Hopefully, Stuxnet will be a wake-up call because the next volley in the cyber war could hit even harder, and we need to be ready for it.

According to Alexander Gostev, Chief Security Expert at Kaspersky Lab, who played an active role in identifying the threat and cooperated closely with Microsoft to resolve the issue, the statistics relating to the initial Stuxnet variant shows epidemics in India (18,307 infections), Iran (11,952 infections) and Indonesia (14,010 infections). 'The number of infected computers increases by about a thousand every day, and this is only what our monitoring systems show us. In other words, it is merely the tip of an iceberg'. According to Jeffrey Carr, author of *Inside Cyber Warfare*,

> On July 7, 2010, a power glitch in the solar panels of INSAT 4B satellite resulted in 12 of its 24 transponders shutting down. As a result 70% of its direct-to-home (DTH) customers were without service. The Indian Space Research Organization (ISRO) is a Siemens customer. According to the resumes of two former engineers who worked at the ISRO's Liquid Propulsion Systems Centre, the Siemens software in use is Siemens S7-400 PLC and SIMATIC WinCC, both of which will activate the Stuxnet worm.

The fact that JMicron and Realtek, the two companies from where Stuxnet stole digital certificates, have offices in the same industrial park in Taiwan raises more suspicion that it may have been an insider's job. The assessment on a possible Chinese government hand is well backed up, yet considered to be 'low to moderate'.

12.1 THREATS TO THE ORGANISATION

All modern organisations use information systems that are networked and connected to the external world via the internet. Though this brings access to a vast ocean of useful information and services, it also poses a tremendous security challenge. The threats to the modern information systems environment are many and varied. Security threats arise from the malicious software that enters the organisation from outside, from internal users who have malicious intent or from accidental loss or exposure of internal information. The sections below explain some of the threats faced by organisations.

12.1.1 Malware

Malicious external software that pose a threat to the security of organisations come in many forms. One of the most widely prevalent threats is that of *viruses* which are software packages that harm the organisation's information technology assets. Viruses typically enter the organisation through various applications of the internet or through devices such as USB memory sticks, and then spread within the network to many hosts. There are millions of viruses that harmfully impact computer systems. A cousin of the virus is the *worm*, another malicious software application that spreads relentlessly across networks and chokes them up. A third type of malicious software is called *Trojans*, or Trojan horses. Trojans typically reside in the computer and allow malicious software or users from outside to invade the computer and use its resources. Spyware is a type of software that also resides in the computer and secretly relays information about the usage of the computer to agents outside.

A common term used to describe the various kinds of malicious software mentioned above is *malware*. Malware are a massive security problem for Chief Information Officers (CIOs) of organisations and require careful planning and large investments to manage. Analysts estimate that huge losses worldwide are caused by malware. The loss is computed on the basis of productivity lost owing to downtime of computers, the costs for cleaning up and replacing data, the costs for additional security measures and the costs from direct loss of business. Commercial firms lose data if malware enters their premises, and it costs them much to clean up, but they also lose reputation as a firm among their clients and partners. Managing security is thus a very high priority for organisations.

The impact of malware on business and organisations is massive. It runs to billions of dollars on a worldwide scale, and in 2016 the estimated economic losses were about $450 billion. Table 12.1 depicts the sources of economic losses from cybercrime across the world.

Table 12.1 | Economic Losses Incurred from Cybercrime across the World

1.	Losses from piracy and theft of confidential business information.
2.	Losses from theft of money and customer profile information.
3.	Social cost of implementing laws and monitoring mechanisms for sites hosting illegal content.
4.	Damage to reputation of organisations and loss in stock valuations.
5.	Increased cost of acquiring security technology.
6.	Opportunity costs of lost business.

Source: McAfee's Center for Strategic and International Studies report 'The Economic Impact of Cybercrime and Cyberespionage', 2013.

12.1.1.1 Examples of Malware

A worm is an autonomous software that acts by penetrating computers and networks by mainly replicating itself. Each unit of the worm finds security loopholes to enter networks or individual computers, replicates itself so that its copies can seek out other computers and network components to infect, and each instance of the worm then continues its work. Worms as such do not do any harm to the infected computer system or network components; they simply consume storage space and network bandwidth while they propagate and spread.

Worms spread very rapidly when they infect a system. A famous worm, known as the *SQLSlammer*, started to propagate rapidly in a few minutes. It multiplied and spread across the network, and also opened pathways for its progeny to follow. This led to an explosive growth of malware in the systems of the infected organisation and paralysed and crashed many systems.

ILOVEYOU Worm

The ILOVEYOU worm, also called the 'love bug' by the media, gathered much attention from around the world for the havoc that it wrought in major organisational systems. ILOVEYOU appeared in May 2000 and spread rapidly across Microsoft email servers. It was a worm that came as an attachment in an email message, with the subject line of the message reading 'I Love You'. If the recipients opened the attachment by double-clicking on it, the worm would fire a program that allowed it to replicate itself, and further look up all the addresses in the recipient's Windows mailbox and send itself to them. Thus, the worm replicated itself through email.

The worm used a particular weakness of the Microsoft email server and clients, that of allowing, by default, users to run programs that had been sent as an attachment to them. Users, however, were not aware of this weakness, as the attachment showed up as a text message, with a '.txt' extension (thus indicating that it could not be executed), where the user tried to see the text by double-clicking on it. Microsoft corporation was heavily criticised for this error in design, and soon remedied it by disallowing email attachments to be executed as a default.

The ILOVEYOU worm did harm to the systems too as it made changes to the Windows registry so that it would always be invoked when the system was booted up. (The Windows registry is a set of files that holds configuration and running instructions for the personal computer; it is part of the operating system.) Furthermore, the worm replaced many types of image and document files (files with extensions such as '.jpg' or '.doc') with copies of itself.

It was later detected that the worm was originated in the Philippines, written by two college dropout computer programmers. They wrote the entire worm in the Visual Basic scripting language and released it through their local internet service provider (ISP). From the Philippines the worm spread to Hong Kong and then on to the rest of the world through email attachments. At its peak it choked up systems across large organisations, including government departments, defence establishments and commercial institutions. It also affected many systems in India. It is argued that the worm used *social engineering* to spread, as human users were enticed to click on the email messages sent to them and thus propagate it. At the time of its release, this worm was declared the most virulent malware ever.

The Philippines government apprehended the programmers who had released the worm, but was unable to prosecute them as there was no law in the Philippines, at that time, which explicitly banned the creation and release of worms. The two programmers were set free after a mild punishment, however, the government was prompted to enact a law to address such crimes. In India too, in the year 2000, the IT Act was passed by the Parliament to provide legal support to authorities to monitor and prosecute cyber crime.

Conficker Worm

The Conficker worm was detected in late 2008, and soon became one of the deadliest worms in computing history. The worm propagates only via the Windows operating system by relying on its vulnerabilities such as shared folders and insecure passwords. Users who had insecure passwords, such as dictionary words, or had shared folders with others without carefully protecting them, or had left their computers unsecured while on the network, were the prime targets that inadvertently enabled the worm to spread.

The Conficker worm works by first entering a system through the internet as an email attachment, through USB memory sticks or through shared files. After entering a system, it maps out the other computers on the network, particularly those that have insecure passwords or non-updated security software. It then sends replicas of itself to these computers, and continues bringing the new computers to its own network. The Conficker worm is supposed to use all known infection techniques to spread itself; it also downloads patches for itself from the servers of its authors to continue propagating against efforts to control it!

The Conficker worm affected almost 9–15 million computers in dozens of countries around the world. Of these, India was reported to be in the top 10 affected countries, as computed by an anti-virus software firm. The worm affected major government and defence departments such as the French Navy, the armed forces of Germany and the City Council of Manchester. The worm was often updated by its authors, and specialists around the world confirm that there are at least five different versions of it that attack different vulnerabilities in Microsoft-based personal computers. The Microsoft Corporation has responded by releasing several patches and security updates for its operating system and also announced a large prize to anyone who is able to give information on the perpetrators of the worm.

12.1.2 Cracking and Espionage

The words *cracking* and *hacking* are often used interchangeably. Cracking is the act of breaking into computers or computer networks illegally. This is usually done by expert programmers who find ways to break into networks by identifying weaknesses in their security or by uncovering passwords or some such method that is not strictly legal. The programmers' intention of doing so is often mischief to show how clever they are at breaking secure systems. Sometimes their objective is to steal information, digital resources or money.

Hacking also refers to the same act, but sometimes hacking is also done for useful reasons, known as *ethical hacking*, where expert programmers break into systems to expose weaknesses rather than to do any harm. Although the two terms are now confused, technically, many people believe hackers are always ethical and are the most competent at programming.

In the current business environment and with the widespread use of e-commerce, cracking has assumed very large dimensions. Many countries have passed laws to address cyber crime, which most directly refers to the acts of cracking to steal money or digital assets. The estimates of different agencies vary, but the underlying story is the same – millions of dollars are being stolen from banks, credit card firms, e-commerce firms, governments and private businesses by crackers. For example, in 2010 some crackers from Ukraine cracked the security of a bank in the USA and did systematic wire transfers to move money from the bank to a bank in the Ukraine. This was done with the connivance of some bank employees. In another example, some crackers broke into a credit card firm's databases and removed information pertaining to thousands of users. This information was then sold to marketing agencies who wanted to target the users with customised sales.

KEY POINT

Cracking is the act of breaking into computer networks illegally.

Cracking is done in many ways, most of which exploit some weakness, human or technological, in the security of systems. One method of cracking is *reverse engineering*, where crackers identify the kind and type of system that is being used and then uncover its security mechanism. For example, some crackers who wanted to steal from gambling machines in casinos in Las Vegas, in the USA, first identified the type and manufacturer of the machines being used. They purchased similar machines, removed the central processing unit (CPU) from them and, through reading the assembly language code written in the CPU, discovered how the CPU determined when to release a straight flush of cards that would earn a lot of money for the player. They did this by finding a flaw in the random number generator (a software for finding a sequence of numbers that are random in nature), and then replicated the manner in which the chip computed numbers and the sequence in which they would appear. This allowed them to predict accurately when the required number would appear and the machine would display a straight flush. Using this method the crackers were able to win millions of dollars from the casinos over several years (until one of the crackers was caught).

Another method used by crackers is that of *social engineering*, which is the manipulation of unsuspecting users to extract private information from them. Here, the trick is to exploit the insecurity and lack of knowledge of human users. For example, one common trick crackers use is of calling an unsuspecting user over the phone, pretending to be operators from a local bank, in which the user has an account, or from an ISP, which the user accesses, and asking him/her about any technical problems. Users often give away details about their account names, and possibly, passwords without verifying who the callers are. In other cases, crackers join as employees of computer firms to visit users' homes on support calls. They note down details of accounts used, account names and other details such as the names of the user's family members. People often use the names of their family members as passwords, which helps crackers to break into their accounts from remote locations. Unsuspecting home users, in particular, are vulnerable to such social engineering as they are not aware of the value of maintaining security.

KEY POINT

Social engineering is the act of manipulation of employees to break into organisational networks.

Social engineering is also used in organisations where crackers befriend employees and ask about their everyday work in casual conversation. They are able to identify security procedures, operating hours, the nature and type of security software used, the names of key employees and often the Internet Protocol (IP) addresses of important servers. Using this knowledge they are able to hack into the servers of such organisations. There are several examples of banks, schools and government departments where crackers have used these techniques to break into systems and steal information, or use these systems to break into other systems.

Another reason why crackers break into organisations is for industrial and political *espionage*. After breaking into a system, crackers leave behind software that forwards email messages from key individuals to certain destinations that they can access later, or simply log in and read and download files. Cracking for espionage and warfare is now common practice by countries such as the USA and Israel, as shown in the Stuxnet case study at the beginning of this chapter. This is also known as cyberwarfare. The intelligence agencies of the USA routinely monitor online traffic of the defence departments of rival nations. The extent of this espionage is not revealed, however, reports suggest that this is quite widespread.

12.1.3 Phishing and Identity Theft

Phishing is another cyber crime that is perpetrated through social engineering. Phishing is done with fake websites that masquerade as real ones. A typical scenario for phishing is as follows: Person A receives an email message from his/her bank, saying that he/she has to upgrade his/her login and password details for security reasons. The email also provides a link on which A can click and be directly transferred to the bank's website. A does click on the link and is taken to a web page that looks entirely like his/her bank's page. He/she types in his/her login and password and finds that he/she is not able to enter the page and only gets an error message. What has happened is that A has been directed to a fake website that has a similar appearance to that of the bank. When A types in his login name and password into the space provided on the web page, he/she has inadvertently given away vital personal information to somebody.

In the above case, the phishing attack only went to the extent of extracting the victim's login name and password. In many cases, fake sites are designed to extract more details from the victim. The idea of phishing is identity theft, where crackers are manipulating unsuspecting users into revealing personal details that they can exploit later. In a case in India, crackers had sent an email asking users to log into the Indian Income Tax Department's website and enter their personal details. The crackers had gone into great detail to ensure that the fake website looked as authentic as possible, thus, not raising any suspicion among users who had been directed there. Figures 12.1 and 12.2 show the real and fake websites of the Indian Income Tax Department.

Another form of identity theft takes place by snooping and *keylogging*. As many people in India still use public internet cafes in urban and semi-urban areas, many crackers use keylogging software to steal their personal data. A keylogger is a software that when installed stays in the random access memory (RAM), and keeps a record of all keystrokes on the keyboard. When customers in an internet cafe sit at a computer with a keylogger installed, all the keys they press to do their work are recorded, creating a clear record of all the text they have typed in. The crackers can later extract all private details, such as account login names, passwords, bank account numbers, etc. from the logs available in the software. In a case in Bangalore in 2007, a team of thieves used keylogging software to obtain identities and passwords of over 100 people from internet cafes, and used this information to transfer out over Rs 1.2 million (about USD 27,000) from 28 bank accounts.

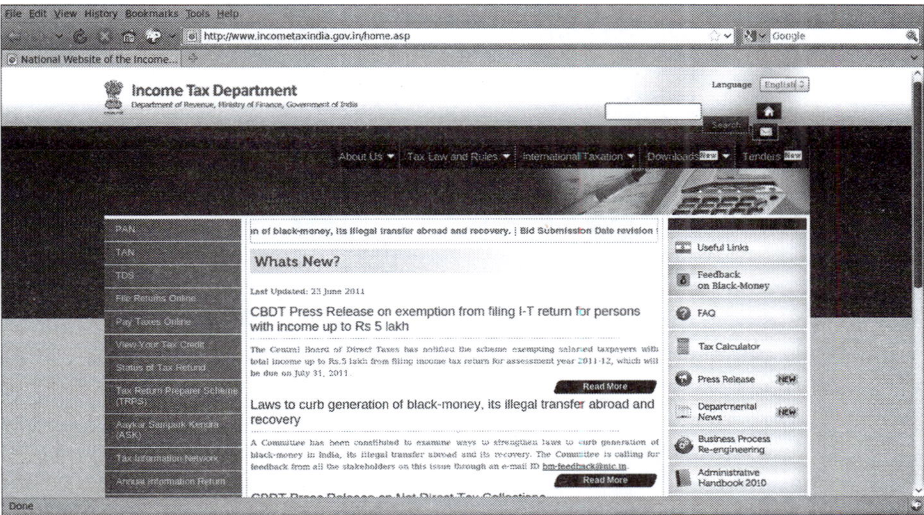

FIGURE 12.1 | Image of the real website of the Indian Income Tax Department.
Source: http:// www.incometaxindia.gov.in/home.asp

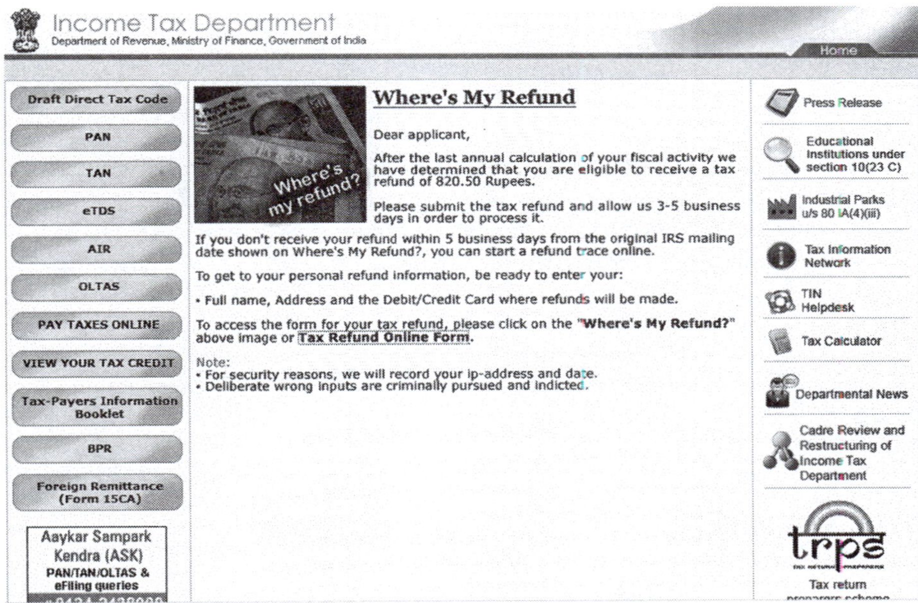

FIGURE 12.2 | Image of the fake website of the Indian Income Tax Department (as of June 2011).

12.1.4 Denial-of-Service Attack

A denial-of-service (DoS) attack is a method by which crackers pull down or slow down the services of a website. Attacks of this sort make the website appear to be slow and unresponsive to normal users. DoS attacks are typically targeted at famous websites such as Amazon.com or Yahoo.com, as also against government and institutional websites.

One type of DoS attack relies on the three-step handshake of connection-oriented protocols. A connection-oriented protocol, such as Hypertext Transfer Protocol (HTTP, the protocol used for reading web pages), requires that the sender first send a connection request, the server responds to this with an acknowledgement and then the sender sends a specific request for a page. After the second step, the server waits a specified amount of time for the third-step request from the sender, and then times out (which means it stops waiting). Web servers that deal with a very large number of clients, such as those of Amazon.com or Google.com,

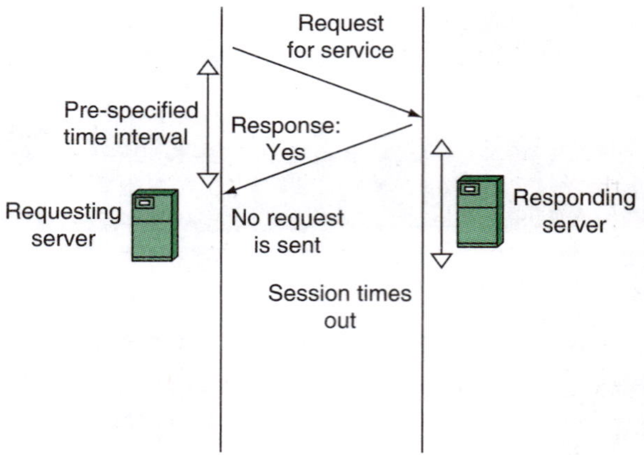

FIGURE 12.3 | Denial-of-service attack.

Note: The requesting server sends a request for service; the responding server sends a response; but the requesting server does not respond, thus, allowing the connection to time out.

KEY POINT

A Denial-of-Service attack is aimed at disabling or drastically slowing down the functioning of prominent websites.

are capable of handling a few thousand requests per second. For each request they follow the three-step handshake and then continue with providing the information. Crackers exploit this handshake by sending out a request – the first step – to which the server responds, and then the cracker client does nothing, letting the server time out the connection request. During a DoS attack, such requests are sent by the thousand and for each of them the server waits a few seconds and times out, effectively doing nothing (see Fig. 12.3). However, legitimate users seeking information from these sites have to wait in a queue to be served.

Crackers create DoS attacks by manipulating web servers (which attack other servers) to send many connection requests. They also change the IP address of the requesting server by spoofing the address. IP spoofing is a trick by which packets sent to the victim server are given a fake IP address, so that it appears that the server is receiving requests from many different IP addresses and not from a single machine of the cracker. However, IP spoofing is easy to detect, so crackers use multiple machines to launch attacks, and also spoof the IP addresses. This makes it very difficult to identify the IP address of all the attacking computers and block them. This is known as a distributed DoS (DDoS; see Fig. 12.4).

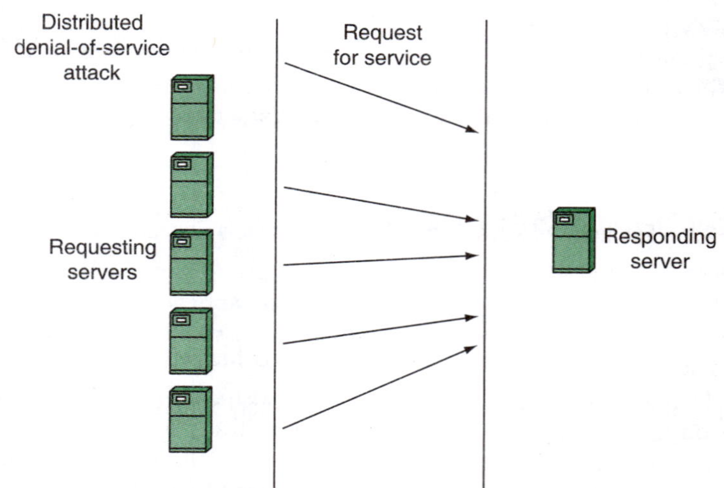

FIGURE 12.4 | Distributed DoS attack.

Note: Many requesting servers send service requests to the responding server, which responds, but the requesting servers allow the connection request to time out.

To launch a DDoS attack, crackers first have to capture and control computers from around the world. Typically, crackers enter networks, such as those of universities or government departments, which have many computers connected to the internet. If the security of these networks is not strong then crackers infiltrate and control many of these computers. These computers may be servers that are left running continuously on the campus or host computers that are never detached from the network and never shut down. Under the control of crackers, these machines act as *zombies* or *botnets* that send service requests to the victim servers. As these zombies are located around the world and not owned by crackers, their identity is not spoofed. In many DDoS attacks, thousands of such zombies have been used to send requests to servers.

12.2 TECHNOLOGIES FOR HANDLING SECURITY

In response to the threats being faced by organisations, different types of technologies have been developed. These technologies counter or deter threats from malicious software and people, and protect users. Some of these technologies are explained below.

12.2.1 Encryption

Encryption is a technology by which a message or data is transformed or translated into a form that is not easily readable by anyone. Encryption is an ancient technology, once used by kings and emperors to send coded messages to their commanders and confidants, particularly during times of war. An encrypted message could be apprehended or stolen by the enemies, but it would not be easy to decipher its contents. Encryption allows a message to be coded or scrambled, and also returned to its original by using *keys*. In computing terminology, the original message to be encrypted is usually called a *plaintext*, whereas the coded message is called a *ciphertext* (where cipher refers to a key). Consider a plaintext message – 'send more tanks' – that has to be encrypted. This message can be transformed by reversing the order of words and their letters as 'sknat erom dnes'. In this example, the plaintext is the first phrase and the ciphertext is the second phrase (which does not make sense in the English language). In this case, the key is 'reverse'. This is a rather trivial key for this particular example, but when used in conjunction with other keys it can create a very effective encryption. Table 12.2 shows examples of several other types of keys that can be used to encrypt the given message.

In the first example in the table, the key is to shift each character by five letters. This is done by considering all the characters in a row (see Fig. 12.5) and looking at the character which is five places away from the one to be replaced. For example, letter 's' is replaced by 'x' which is five positions away from it in the first row of characters.

In the second example, the key first reverses the text and then shifts each character by 5. In the third example, the characters are shifted by 19 spaces. Note that after 'z' the row cycles, beginning with 'a'. The fourth key is an arbitrary assignment of numbers to letters. Here, the

Table 12.2 | Examples of Keys, and How the Plaintext Is Converted to Ciphertext

Key (plaintext = 'send more tanks')	Ciphertext
Shift 5 (shift each letter by five characters)	'xjsi htwj yfspx'
Reverse and Shift 5 (reverse the order of the letters and then shift by five characters)	'xpsfy jwth isjx'
Shift 19	'lxgw fhkx mtgdl'
S=16;e=3;n=67;d=234;space=21;m=59; o=34;r=39;t=94;a=10;n=57;k=34	'16367234215934393219410573416'

	a	b	c	d	e	f	g	h	i	j	k	l	m	n	o	p	q	r	s	t	u	v	w	x	y	z
5	f	g	h	i	j	k	l	m	n	o	p	q	r	s	t	u	v	w	x	y	z	a	b	c	d	e
19	t	u	v	w	x	y	z	a	b	c	d	e	f	g	h	i	j	k	l	m	n	o	p	q	r	s

FIGURE 12.5 | Examples of encryption of English alphabetic characters.

Note: The first row depicts English alphabets in their normal sequence. The second and third rows show the alphabets resulting from the application of Shift 5 and Shift 19 keys.

space between words in the plaintext is also replaced by a number and the ciphertext is a long string of numbers. Figure 12.5 shows the application of Shift 5 and Shift 19 keys to encrypt the message 'send more tanks'.

When an encrpyted message is sent to a party, the key has also to be sent to them. This process of encryption is known as *symmetric key* cryptography. The receiver can use the key to decrypt the message by reversing the method by which the ciphertext was created. If the key is not available then decryption becomes very hard.

The keys shown in the examples above are relatively easy, and given some time many people would be able to solve the problem of discovering the keys. In modern electronic systems, highly complex keys are used to encrypt messages. The encryption may involve a series of transformations in the plaintext, for example – reversing, dividing into blocks of few characters and exchanging the blocks, shifting by 5, then shifting again by 23, then replacing all characters by digits and so on. The larger the number of steps involved, the larger the key, and hence larger the amount of time required to both encrypt and decrypt the message.

Symmetric key encryption is used extensively to protect data on wired and wireless networks. Various innovative methods of protecting the key have been found, where the key has to be shared between sender and receiver and is the most vulnerable to crackers.

12.2.2 Public-Key Cryptography

The weakness of the symmetric key cryptography is the need to send across the key. Throughout the history of encryption, the problem that many have tried to solve is to have an encryption mechanism that does not require a key to be sent. Keys are the weak point in the encryption process because if a key is leaked, the message can easily be compromised. Senders have to go to extra lengths to ensure the key remains safe and secure.

Public-key cryptography solves the problem of having to send a key secretly to the receiver of the message. The method followed here is of having a *pair* of keys called the *public key* and the *private key*. For any pair of sender and receiver, let us call them Alok and Bani, the message can be encrypted using a public key and decrypted using a private key (see Fig. 12.6). The process followed is as follows: When Alok wants to send a message to Bani, he uses Bani's public key to encrypt the message and sends it across to her. Bani receives the message and decrypts it with her private key. Alok is able to access Bani's public key, as she has made it public, by leaving it on her website or has emailed it to Alok.

When Bani wants to send a message to Alok, she has to acquire Alok's public key, possibly from his website, and then encrypt the message and send it to him. Like Bani, Alok can decrypt the message by using his private key.

FIGURE 12.6 | Sending a message with a public-key encryption.

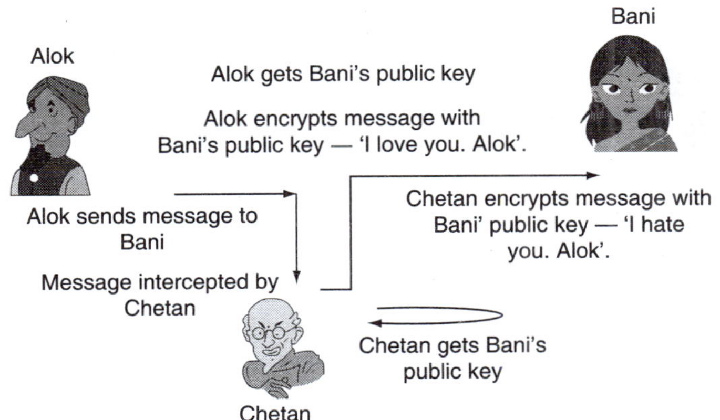

FIGURE 12.7 | The problem of impersonation with public-key encryption.

Why is system secure? Let us assume that a third person, Chetan, is interested in spying on Alok and Bani. Let us further assume that Chetan is in a position to intercept Alok's encrypted message to Bani (see Fig. 12.7). Can Chetan now read the message? After all, he can simply get hold of Alok's public key from Alok's website and decode the message. But this is not possible. Even though Chetan can get hold of Alok's public key, he needs Alok's private key to decode the message. The two keys that Alok uses, the public and private keys, are created as a pair and only the private key can be used to decrypt the message encrypted by the public key. As long as Alok can protect his private key (which he does not have to send to anybody), his message will remain encrypted.

Public and private keys are created from very large prime numbers. The first technique to create pairs of keys is attributed to Ron Rivest, Adi Shamir and Leonard Adleman. This technique is known as the RSA encryption technique. Prime numbers are difficult to find, especially large prime numbers. A pair of large prime numbers is used to derive a key. The process involves taking the product of these numbers from which an amount is subtracted and then a division is performed. The key so derived is unique. When a message is encrypted with a public key, it is practically impossible for someone to guess what the private key will be for decrypting the message. If the keys are based on small prime numbers, crackers can search for and find them within a reasonable period of time. But if the numbers are very large, it can take hundreds of years even on very fast computers to find them. The power of public-key encryption lies in this difficulty.

KEY POINT

Public-key cryptography relies on two keys, public and private, that are used to encode and decode messages.

In practice, RSA encryption is enabled by private firms that create and sell pairs of keys to users. Firms, such as Verisign, provide such keys and also authenticate them at the time when a connection is electronically established between the sender and the receiver. The *authentication* ensures that the keys have been obtained from a reliable source and are secure. After authentication, the sender receives the receiver's public key and encrypts and sends the message.

Digital certificates are also used to authenticate the owner of a public key. Such certificates are issued by security agencies, such as Verisign, and assure that the user's public key is being obtained from the designated source, and not from an imposter. Thus, the digital certificate associates public key with an agency or person or organisation with a name, an address and other reliable identity data.

Authentication is also required to ensure that no one is impersonating the sender. For instance, if Chetan wants to send Bani a message pretending he is Alok, all he has to do is take Bani's public key (easily available) and encrypt the message (the method for encryption is also easily available) and send it to Bani. Since Chetan can sign the message as Alok, Bani cannot really tell that it is not from Alok. Thus, Chetan can easily impersonate Alok (see Fig. 12.7). This problem of authentication can be solved by using a digital signature, which follows the public-key principle. To ensure that Bani receives an authenticated message, Alok first encrypts the message with his private key, and then with Bani's public key. When Bani receives the message,

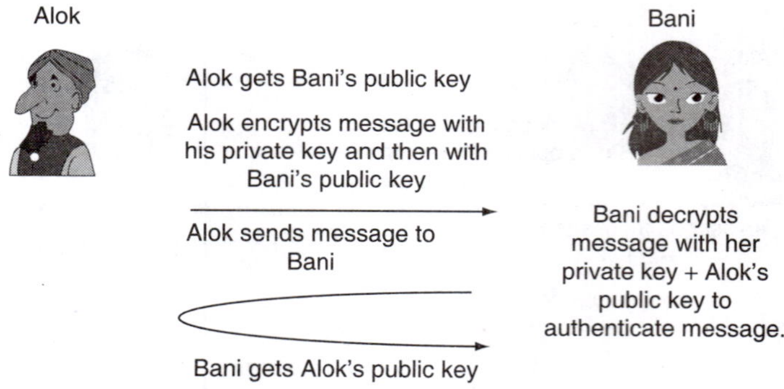

FIGURE 12.8 | Authentication with public-key encryption.

she can first decrypt it with her private key. She will now have a message that is encrypted with Alok's private key. This Bani can decrypt with Alok's public key. If the message does indeed decrypt with Alok's public key, Bani is assured that the message is from Alok as no one else could have encrypted it with Alok's private key. This authenticates the message for Bani. Meanwhile, Chetan can intercept Alok's message, but he will be unable to unlock it as that would require Bani's private key. Furthermore, Chetan cannot impersonate Alok as he does not have Alok's private key (see Fig. 12.8).

This method of authentication using the public-key technology is known as a digital signature. Many countries, including India, have enacted laws [the IT Act 2000 in India is amended as Information Technology (Amendment) Act, 2008 or ITAA 2008] to give legal backing to digital signatures, as this technology is used extensively by business establishments to exchange documents. Documents exchanged by such a mechanism can be upheld in a court of law in India, with the assurance that they are secure and have not been faked.

12.2.3 Firewall

KEY POINT

A firewall acts as a filter for both incoming and outgoing traffic in a computer network.

A firewall is a filtering and protection device that is usually a combination of software and hardware. As was explained in Chapter 8, a firewall protects the organisation against malicious crackers and intruders. At a basic level, a firewall is a packet filter device that monitors both outgoing and incoming packets (see Fig. 12.9). It is usually placed at the perimeter of the organisation's network, inside the router that connects the organisation to the ISP and the internet. It is possible to write a set of rules in the firewall that check the content of packets and allow or disallow them. For instance, one can write a rule that specifies: 'disallow all packets from youtube.com'. This rule will specifically check for packets whose source address is youtube.com and bar them from entering.

Packet-level filtering can be applied to packets of different protocols and services, to packets with specific source and destination addresses, and to packets using specific port numbers. It is quite common for organisations to ban traffic on port number 23, which is used for an internet application called *Telnet*. Telnet allows remote users to login to machines within the organisation, a practice that is considered to be insecure and that has been consequently banned.

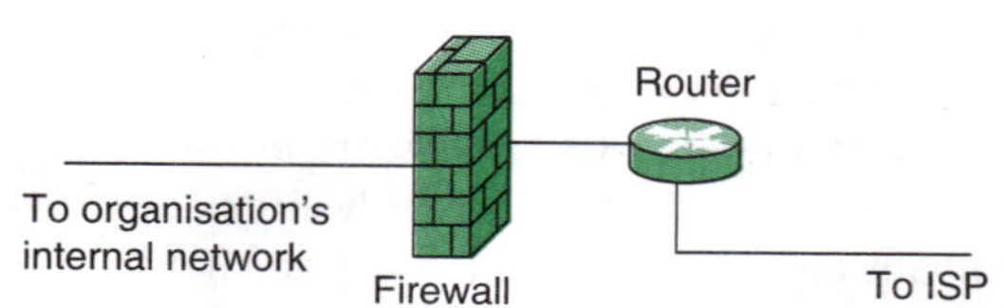

FIGURE 12.9 | Firewall in a typical organisation.

A more advanced version of filtering is achieved through application-level filtering. Here, the system administrator has more flexibility in designing security policies. For example, in application-level filtering, a specific, trusted user can be allowed to access the Telnet facility, whereas other users can be barred from doing so. This particular user may have established a need for this with the organisation and is being permitted to do so. The user would have to be authenticated by the firewall through a login, and then can be allowed to use the application. This facility can be applied to all higher level applications, such as email, file transfer, etc. by the firewall.

Although, firewalls serve as very effective security devices, their one drawback is of slowing down traffic at the perimeter (every packet has to be examined, and this takes time). To overcome this drawback, firewalls are often built into hardware and hence realise huge speed advantages. Some router manufacturers offer firewalls built into their products.

A technique known as deep packet inspection (DPI) is often used by many packet filtering devices. By this method, packets are inspected for their header information as well as content. As the actual payload of a packet is inspected, DPI can uncover malware such as worms within packets, protect against DoS attackes and harvest data for managing the security infrastructure. As DPI involves inspection of data, it has led to issues of privacy and censorship.

12.2.4 Virtual Private Network

A virtual private network (VPN) is a technology that enables clients or employees of an organisation, who are outside the network, to connect to the organisation's network securely. A VPN is a kind of 'tunnel' through which clients can connect to the organisation's network while using the public internet. The need to use a VPN often arises when employees are travelling or working from home as tele-commuters, and they use the internet to log into their computers at work. A VPN allows them to securely enter the organisation from outside.

A VPN connection relies on authentication and encryption. Most organisations provide a VPN server to their clients or employees, who log into the server with a password that acts as the authentication. Once logged in, all the packet traffic flowing in the connection is encrypted, enabling the tunnel to be formed. Since traffic on the internet is usually not encrypted and employees often log in from public internet kiosks, this mode of transmission allows a secure connection. VPN connections often are able to go through firewalls via a special channel, allowing users to connect to all the facilities and features available on the organisation's computing network.

For example, consider a protected network on an educational campus. Students on the campus can access online facilities such as email, educational software, library software and publications, etc. while using campus computers. When they are off campus, such facilities are restricted as firewalls disallow outside users from accessing campus resources. This is where VPN servers are used. Students are given VPN accounts on this server, which lets them login from outside, and once logged in, they can access all the digital facilities on campus.

Caselet Bangladesh Bank Heist

$81 million was stolen from the Bangladesh Bank, the central bank of Bangladesh, in February 2016 by means of fake money transfer requests. The perpetrators had infiltrated Bangladesh Bank's network and used spyware to identify the manner in which employees of this bank made money transfer requests through the SWIFT system. SWIFT (Society for Worldwide Interbank Telecommunication) is an international interbank money transfer network that operates a closed computer network whose 11,000 members can make requests to transfer money from any bank in any country to another bank. The system resolves exchange rates in real time and enables over 25 million communications a day.

In this particular instance, the perpetrators knew that each request made by the bank employees was printed by a particular printer in the bank. They installed malware that blocked the printer, on a Friday afternoon, and then made over thirty large-value money transfer requests out from the Bangladesh Bank's account to accounts in the Philippines, Sri Lanka and other Asian countries. The total amount requested for transferring out was about $851 million.

The requests were forwarded to the Federal Reserve Bank of New York, where Bangladesh Bank had an account, and this account was used further to transfer the funds to other bank accounts. The employees of Bangladesh Bank noticed the problem with the printer and requested for it to be fixed. It was fixed sometime later and a whole slew of printed messages showed them that many transfer requests had been made, amount to almost a billion dollars. Since this was a weekend in New York, they could not immediately request to block the transfers; however, by Monday most of the transfers had been blocked.

Of the few transfer requests that were cleared in New York, $81 million was sent to the Rizal Commercial Banking Corporation of Philippines, to accounts that had been opened just a year before. The money was then cleared from these accounts to some casino in Philippines (where these institutions are legal) and were never recovered. These money transfers were legal according to Philippines law. A particular transfer was sent to an account in Sri Lanka and was routed through a bank in Belgium. The request in this case had a spelling error, where the destination account was meant to be 'Shalika Foundation' whereas the transfer message spelt it as 'Shalika Fundation.' The spelling error was spotted in Belgium, the transfer was stalled to seek an explanation and was later stopped by Bangladesh Bank.

An international investigation was launched to identify the criminals but no clear picture emerged. Of the $81 million, some amounts were recovered; however most of it was lost. The SWIFT system was not faulted in this case as it had not been breached; the transfers were made in a legal manner and according to the procedures of the system. The fault lay with the breach at Bangladesh Bank. It was later found that banks in other countries had also been broken into in such a manner.

12.2.5 Wireless Technology

In modern organisations wireless devices and technologies proliferate. Examples of wireless devices include remote controllers for televisions or monitors (or key fobs for cars); wireless keyboards; wireless mouse; laptops with Wireless Fidelity (Wi-Fi) connectivity; mobile phones; laptops and mobiles using Bluetooth technology; and a Global Positioning System (GPS) client. All these devices rely on radio waves of different frequencies to connect with each other to share information. All the technologies available for wireless rely on specific ranges of radio frequencies, called the bandwidth or spectrum, and deploy different methods for sending and receiving messages. These technologies also have different capacities for carrying data, and varying distances to which the data can be carried. For example, the Bluetooth technology can transfer data over a few metres, whereas a WiMax router can send and receive data over many kilometres. Strong security issues are associated with wireless technologies. Given below are brief descriptions of some wireless technologies currently used by organisations.

12.2.5.1 Wi-Fi Routers

Wi-Fi, which is a contraction for 'Wireless Fidelity', is a communication standard approved by the IEEE for wireless communication. Many devices use Wi-Fi, such as phones, laptops and tablet computers. So this standard of communication has become very popular. Wi-Fi is popularly used with 'hotspots' or access points that are routers, which use the Wi-Fi standard to provide wireless internet connectivity. A typical hotspot in a home or office is connected by LAN cable to the internet. It allows devices such as laptops, mobile phones and tablets to connect to the internet through it. The hotspot acts as a router as it allows the devices to share a pool of IP addresses, provided by the router, which allow the devices to communicate with the internet.

Wi-Fi routers are sometimes used in a mesh network (see Fig. 12.10). Here, the hotspots act as relay devices that carry forward the network connectivity from one device to another, therefore, only one device needs to have a connection to the internet through an ISP, and the others can relay and share this connectivity.

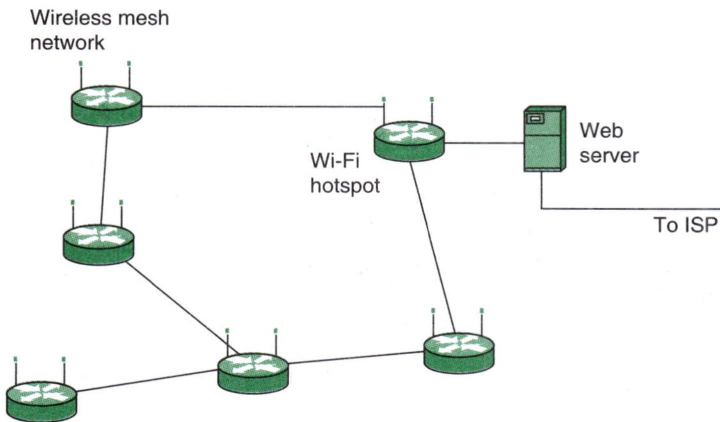

FIGURE 12.10 | Wireless mesh networking.

The Wi-Fi standard is specified by the IEEE 802.11 series of specifications. Each specification refers to a particular bandwidth and type of connection. For instance, one standard allows up to 54 mbps of data traffic with a range of 100 feet within buildings. With clear line-of-sight outside buildings, such Wi-Fi routers can be detected several hundred metres away.

Connecting to Wi-Fi routers could be in an unsecured manner, where anybody could simply lock into the signal available and use the connection. Or the connection can by secured, where gaining access to the router requires entering a password as authentication. Unsecured Wi-Fi routers have been a source of many security problems.

12.2.5.2 *Bluetooth*

This is another standard that is used to wirelessly connect devices. The Bluetooth standard connects devices such as mobile phones with headsets, laptops with printers, laptops with mice and keyboards and so on. Bluetooth was created for connecting personal devices rather than connecting devices at home or in the office. As such the Bluetooth standard offers lower data transfer rates and operates over a short distance, however, it is a more secure method of communication.

12.2.5.3 *RFID*

Radio Frequency Identification (RFID) is a technology by which tiny radio receivers and transmitters are embedded in devices or objects from where they can be identified. These radio receivers and transmitters are typically embedded in 'chips' (tiny encasements), which can then be mounted practically anywhere. The RFID chips work with 'readers' that send out radio signals to find if any are available in the vicinity. Upon receiving the query radio signal, the chips respond by sending out a unique signature, which identifies them. The RFID devices may be active or passive. Active devices require an energy source, like a battery, to broadcast signals. Whereas, passive devices can use the energy of the reader's signal to respond. When objects are embedded with RFID chips they are said to be tagged.

Following are some examples of how RFID tags are used:

1. The YES Bank, a large retail bank in India, uses RFID tags to identify their customers. In a YES Bank branch in New Delhi, in a neighbourhood that typically has wealthy customers, YES Bank has given wallet cards with RFID tags on them to its high net worth customers. When these customers enter the bank branch, a reader located near the entrance reads the RFID tag the customer has in his/her wallet or purse (or perhaps in a briefcase) and sends

a signal to the branch operatives. The customer's name, photo, profile and brief banking history is immediately made available to the operative who will greet the customer and take him/her to a separate office to attend to their needs. High net worth customers appreciate this gesture as they like to be recognised and treated especially while visiting their bank, and it also saves their time.

The challenge in implementing this technology was in ensuring that the reading signal is able to reach the RFID tag that the customer is carrying. The signal has a limited range (a few metres) and has to penetrate through clothing or any accessories the customer may have kept the card in. Furthermore, the identification has to be quick, the signal has to be decoded, matched with existing records and the customer's profile retrieved even as the customer walks the steps into the branch office.

2. JustBooks is a private book-lending library that started out in Bangalore in 2009 and has spread to many cities in India. The library works on a membership basis, where enrolled members walk into a JustBooks store in the neighbourhood, and borrow books from the shelves. Members can have a fixed number of books borrowed at a time, but have no restrictions on when they will have to return the books or how many they can borrow overall.

   Membership cards have RFID tags, as also all the books in JustBooks stores. After selecting the books they want, members can walk up to kiosks where they identify themselves with their cards, and then log the books they have selected, which are detected by their RFID tags. Members can thus check-in and check-out books without human intervention. The RFID tags are also helpful in locating books that have been misplaced from shelves in the store. The tags reveal the location of the books and these can be corrected by store employees.

Other applications of RFID tags include managing inventory in large warehouses by tagging all items, charging cars at toll plazas through RFID-tagged display cards (which can be read by readers placed at the toll gate), and for use on public transportation where RFID-tagged passes allow users to travel without having to purchase tickets. There are now dozens of different types of applications to which RFID tags have been applied across the world. The prices of tags are quite low, owing to their mass production and they are likely to gain more uses in future.

12.2.5.4 *Wireless Sensor Networks*

A sensor is an electronic device that is used to measure some aspect of the environment it is located in. For instance, sensors can measure temperature, humidity, movement, colours of light, size of particles and so on. Typically, sensors make a measurement and report this to whoever or whatever has initiated the sensing. Wireless sensors are used to sense some parameter and send out signals about the measured value over a wireless network. A wireless sensor network (WSN) consists of such wireless sensors and wireless networking devices (like Wi-Fi routers) that can then relay the messages from the sensors to any pre-specified destination.

WSNs were originally developed for warfare, where the sensors could sense information about a war zone and relay it back to a control centre. Later they have found widespread use in monitoring forests for fires, monitoring traffic junctions for pollution, and for sensing temperature and humidity conditions in buildings to control air-conditioning, among many others. In India, WSNs are being used for sensing agricultural regions for what is termed 'precision agriculture'. In this form of agriculture, hundreds of wireless sensors are distributed over the agricultural region, extending over many acres, and the condition of the soil, its humidity and its chemical composition, is transmitted wirelessly back to a centre from where specific soil treatments are determined. The sensors ensure that the treatment is targeted at the specific spot where the condition has been detected, and not spread over the entire acreage. Such precision in agriculture has resulted in increased yield for crops, such as grapes, in Maharashtra in India (in Nashik), with reduced input costs.

12.3 MANAGING SECURITY

One of the most important tasks of the CIO is to manage the security of an organisation's information systems (IS). The security policies, the practices and the choice of technology all have to be designed and implemented in a manner that ensures security. This section examines the different decision-making issues a modern manager faces with regard to IS security.

On the question of what facilities and features have to be managed to enable a secure IS infrastructure in an organisation, the following four features are important:

1. **Confidentiality:** One role of security is to ensure confidentiality - each message is accessed and read by only the intended recipient(s), not by anyone else. Message confidentiality entails many things: (a) Only the sender should know that the message has been sent; (b) only the sender/receiver should know if a message has been sent and when and how; and (c) only the sender/receiver should have access to the content as well as the meta-details about the content of the message.
2. **Authentication:** Authentication entails confirming the identity of both the sender and the receiver of the message. Security within systems has to ensure that authentication is provided and guaranteed.
3. **Message integrity:** Both the sender and the receiver should know if the contents of the message are intact. The contents should not have been tampered with, corrupted or altered in any manner. If there is any alteration, the sender/receiver should be informed about this.
4. **Access and availability:** Secure systems should also ensure they are accessible and available to designated users at all times. Disabled access or inefficient access is a security failure.

12.3.1 Securing the Network

12.3.1.1 Perimeter Security

Of the servers in an organisation, those most prone to be attacked by crackers are the email, web and DNS servers. These are widely used servers that provide internal users access to many services on the internet, and are typically the first to be attacked. To secure these servers, they are often isolated from the rest of the organisation's network into a separate virtual network called the demilitarised zone (DMZ) shown in Fig. 12.11. This DMZ is then protected by a firewall, and extra care is taken to manage its security. The advantage of a DMZ is that even if one of the servers in the DMZ is compromised, the rest of the network is isolated and not threatened.

When users of the organisation have to access services from outside, say through a VPN, then the VPN server is maintained within the DMZ. The DMZ thus acts as a buffer to allow users to enter and after their authentication permit them to access other services.

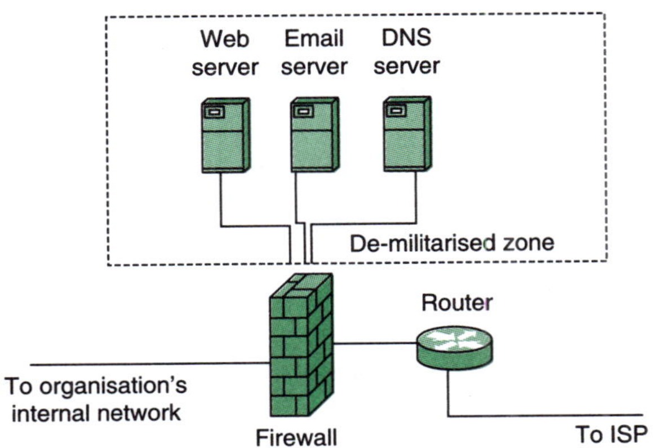

FIGURE 12.11 | Typical layout for a demilitarised zone (DMZ).

12.3.1.2 Two-Factor Authentication

Many services that have to be accessed from outside the organisation require special security management. When employees access corporate databases from the field or access corporate services from home, it is essential that they have more than a single form of authentication. This is to ensure that impersonators or crackers are not able to copy their keystrokes and gain illegal access.

A special type of authentication process is referred to as *two-factor authentication* (TFA). Usually, authentication, such as logging into an email account, is based on single-factor authentication. The user types in a login name and a password. The password is the single secret known only to the user that allows this authentication to proceed. In TFA, two factors are used - such as a password and a physical token. For example, for most bank debit cards (the cards used to withdraw cash from ATMs), TFA is used. The first factor is the card itself, which belongs to the user, and the second factor is the password the user types in to access his/her account. The double security is ensured by a unique card that belongs to the user and also a unique password known only to the user. Either one by itself will not help authenticate the account.

TFA is being used by organisations quite widely now. The second factor is usually a card, a mobile phone, or a unique number device (an electronic device that displays a unique number every few seconds), or a biometric scan (such as that of a fingerprint) where the first factor is usually a password. TFA allows CIOs to maintain strong security and facilitates easier detection when a breach has occurred.

12.3.2 Securing the Client

12.3.2.1 Desktop Firewalls

With strong protection at the network, it is also important to maintain security at the level of the end-systems. Desktops and laptops have also to be covered with security technology. Most modern operating systems now provide a personal firewall or a desktop firewall. (Personal firewalls can even be purchased as independent software packages.) Such firewalls monitor traffic at the network interface of the personal computer. They are especially useful for those desktops that are left connected to the internet continuously, especially at home, and use a fixed IP address. Such desktops are susceptible to attack and capture by crackers for using them as zombies in DoS attacks. Desktop firewalls monitor packet traffic into and out of the computer and filter out suspicious ones.

12.3.2.2 Password Policy

Many client computers or desktops are not configured to have password protection. This means that they can be booted up and all their services accessed immediately without any authentication. Although most modern operating systems now disallow this practice, it is still quite common for personal computers within offices and homes. This constitutes a serious threat to security of the individual computer and through that to the entire organisation of which it is a part.

Every organisation has to insist upon and maintain a strict password policy that mandates that every personal computer is password-protected (many current systems can also allow TFA through biometric technology). Furthermore, passwords must be updated frequently and should follow a pattern that is not easily detected. Some rules that many organisations use with regard to password management are as follows:

1. Passwords must consist of letters and numbers (such as 'xptillgp6' or '*ppefgrv8') and should not resemble dictionary words. Furthermore, passwords should not be based on names of family members ('bbosy56' is better than 'latha23', where Latha is a family member).

2. Passwords should be changed frequently, every week or every month.
3. Passwords should not be written down, or shared or spoken out loudly in office settings.

Another security policy that is advisable for personal computers is not to allow users to work with them in the Administrator mode. The PC operating system allows an Administrator mode, which has all privileges for changing settings and configuring the core functionality of the computer. Most users operate the PC in a User mode, which is their 'account' that has their login name, and that has lower privileges for making changes to the system. Running the system in the Administrator mode is insecure, as worms and viruses can wreak a lot of damage from within this mode, as the malware have all the privileges to do so.

12.3.3 Creating a Secure Environment

Security within an organisation is maintained and sustained through an active culture of security (people), of having the right tools (technology), and of having the right procedures and practices (process) in place. A secure environment can be initiated and achieved as a start, however, it takes active involvement of people, technology and processes to sustain it.

Users have to be informed of security priorities and principles, and also trained in using security software. People are often the weakest link in the security chain as they do not follow basic security rules such as:

1. They do not change their passwords regularly or use dictionary words as passwords.
2. They use computers at public kiosks and use insecure channels to communicate.
3. Many of them use storage media (such as USB sticks) at public kiosks and then use the same in their offices, thus, increasing the exposure to viruses and worms.
4. Many office users in India share their passwords with secretaries or co-workers. Overcoming these problems requires creating a culture of security where users are both aware of and competent with security policies and practices.

Security practices too have to be developed carefully to meet the needs of the organisation. High security does imply higher costs of doing business, as every process will have to be secured before it is initiated and completed. However, reducing security policies entails costs of damage from virus and worm attacks. At the very least, an organisation's security practices should include:

1. Regular updates of anti-virus software for all personal computers and servers.
2. Reminders to users for updating passwords, and also forcing updates.
3. Disabling, as far as possible, the use of storage devices that have been used outside.
4. Strict policies for control of guest access to organisational networks.
5. Having a fair use policy for all employees and members that outlines what is considered appropriate use of information technology resources (see Table 12.3 for an example of a Fair Use Policy).

Security technology within the organisation has to be acquired and upgraded according to the needs of the organisation. The technology has to suit the nature of business or activity the organisation is engaged in and the relative exposure to risk this entails. Educational institutions, for instance, maintain open networks and an open environment for students to experiment with and use their IT. Their needs for security will be very different from those of a bank, which has to maintain very high levels of security. The choice of technology will largely be determined by the perceived and historical incidences of security violations within organisations. The CIO will have to decide the high-priority areas for security, and focus on those with an understanding that the low-priority areas will be prone to violations. The technology should be such as to contain the damage security violations can incur.

Table 12.3 | Example of a Fair Use Policy Statement at a University (a Hypothetical University)

Fair Use Policy at a University

Philosophy

The A University provides access to computing resources such as computers, networks, printers, email and internet access to all students, faculty, staff and guests. The access is provided to support the educational, research and administrative needs of the users. The purpose of this Fair Use Policy is to establish the grounds on which the computing resources can be used by all, with a view to enable equitable sharing, and disable misuse.

The A University assumes that all users are acting independently and responsibly while using A's computing resources. It further assumes that the highest priority for use of these resources is for teaching/learning, research and administration. Uses of computing for recreation and personal benefit are of low priority.

Code of Conduct

- Etiquette for using networks and email
- List of unacceptable uses of computing resources

Penalties for Violation

- Warnings
- Suspension of use rights

12.3.4 Security Audit and Risk Assessment

A security audit is a process by which the security features, technologies and practices of an organisation are scrutinised. The object is to find vulnerabilities, identify any risks, and conform to regulatory and contractual requirements. A typical audit will include examining log files on servers, testing known security weaknesses in software, examing data and server access rights, and interviewing users and system administrators about secuirty practices, among other tasks. Auditing is done by security experts who base the checks on the established security policies and objectives of the organisation. Successful audits will verify that the organisation conforms to its own security objectives and policies. However, an unsuccessful audit will imply that the organisation has to re-engineer its security policies and practices, and fix the problems that have been identified.

Security audits help a firm achieve its security goals, particularly with regard to compliance. In the Indian situation, the Indian IT Act 2000 has clearly specified compliance norms for organisations. If an organisation is found violative of these norms, they could face stiff penalties, including jail terms for its executives. For example, if a malicious email, with terrorist connections, originates on the premises of an organisation, the organisation is obliged to isolate and inform authorities about the author of the email. If the organisation is unable to find the source of the message, it could face dire legal consequences. To prevent such a fate, organisations have to run audits to ensure their security procedures are adequate.

An important aspect of the security audit is risk assessment. Risk assessment implies computing a rupee or dollar value for the possibility of a particular security failure. For example, the risk of a virus breaching a firewall and spreading across an organisation has to be assessed in terms of the money lost owing to loss of work, loss of data and expenses incurred for finding, isolating and eliminating the virus. With such a value, management can decide how much to spend on security infrastructure. Clearly, if the risk assessment is Rs X for a particular threat, management would be hard pressed to spend much more than Rs X for preventing the risk.

Risk assessment is difficult as it requires estimating potential losses, all of which may not have direct monetary implications. For instance, the loss of data at a bank may have intangible costs such as loss of client confidence that will be hard to quantify. However, risk assessment is required to complete a security audit and cannot be ignored.

12.3.5 Disaster Recovery Planning

Physical strucutres of all organisations are susceptible to natural disasters such as fires, earthquakes, flooding and (for those in coastal areas) tsunamis. Furthermore, man-made disasters such as terrorist attacks or arson are also possibilities that organisations have to account for. In the internet age, another threat arises from attacks from malware or targetted DoS attacks. A challenge that many CIOs face is that of recovering from a disaster. Some questions they have to face are: (1) How soon can the IT infrastructure be resurrected to full functionality? (2) How much will it cost to recover from a disaster? (3) How can it be minimised by planning? (4) Can a partial recovery work, and if so, what parts have to be recoverd first?

The terms disaster recovery (DR) planning and business continuity planning (BCP) are often used interchangeably or together. They refer to the idea of having a plan in place that will lead to resumption of normal business with the IT infrastructure after a disruption caused by a natural or man-made disaster. Organisations have evolved many different strategies for DR/BCP based on their needs and available resources.

One strategy many organisations follow is that of mirroring their data centres. Mirroring entails creating an exact copy of the entire database of the organisation. Mirrors can take backup copies of data even as they are created through business transactions at the organisation. Mirrors thus have an exact copy of the data and if the original database fails or is harmed, the mirror can be used to recover whatever data is missing. Mirrors can also be created by scheduled backups, those that are not done in real time but at specific intervals such as after every few hours, or daily or weekly.

Mirrors are often referred to as redundant facilities, and are used to create copies of the original data. For example, Kuoni Travel India provides outsourcing services for travel to various clients across the world. One of its requirements was that of ensuring business continuity and high uptime for its servers, which were maintained in Mumbai and London. Kuoni decided to create redundancy by duplicating its servers and VPN connectivity. This ensured not only highly reliable and scalable infrastructure for Kuoni, but it also enabled a sound disaster recovery plan.

As real-time mirroring is very expensive, some organisations rely on periodic backups. However, the backups are stored at highly secure facilities that are not on the campus or building of the organisation. Such backup facilities are known as co-location facilities. Co-location facilites have temperature and humidity controlled rooms where data servers are located, highly reliable power supply, their buildings are designed specially to resist fire and withstand earthquakes, and are secured against water flooding. Such facilities often have extra fuel for their backup power supply ready on the premises, to ensure that power supply can last for as long as needed. In India, many such co-location facilities are in Chennai, as Chennai has the lowest risk of several possible natural disasters. In the USA, many co-location facilities are located in the Arizona desert where the risk of sudden natural disasters is also low.

Chapter Glossary

Virus A malicious software program that infiltrates and spreads in organisational networks, infects personal computers and usually destroys files and data.

Worm A malicious software program, much like a virus, whose main goal is to infiltrate and choke networks.

Trojan A malicious software program that infiltrates computers and secretly allows external software and people to invade the computer and use its resources.

Spyware A malicious software code that infiltrates personal computers and secretly relays information to outside persons.

Malware A common term used to describe various kinds of malicious software.

Cracking The act of breaking into networks and computers illegally.

Hacking Hacking has the same meaning as cracking, but it is sometimes also used to signify expert or high-quality programming.

Ethical hacking The act of breaking into networks, not for malicious reasons but for the purpose of exposing their weaknesses.

Reverse engineering Where crackers identify the type and kind of system being used, and then uncover its security mechanism.

Social engineering Use of social methods, such as be-friending, to target victims and extract vital information to break into their networks and computers.

Phishing Use of fake websites to lure customers into revealing their private information.

Denial-of-Service (DoS) attack Slowing down the services of a website or computer system by sending it many fake service requests, thus, denying service to genuine users.

Distributed Denial-of-Service (DDoS) attack Use of many captured computers on the internet for a DoS attack.

Zombie/botnet A captured computer on the internet, which is used by crackers to launch DDoS attacks.

Encryption Transformation of a message into a coded form that is not easily readable.

Symmetric key A key to decrypt an encrypted message that is sent to the receiver.

Public key A key that is part of a pair, which is used to encrypt a message. It is openly available.

Private key A secret key that works with the public key to decrypt the message encrypted with the public key.

Authentication A process by which the identity of a sender or receiver is verified.

Virtual Private Network (VPN) A technology that enables clients or employees of an organisation, who are outside the network, to connect securely to the organisation over the public internet.

Two-factor authentication Authentication done by two independent methods.

Review Questions

1. Read the Stuxnet case and answer the following questions:
   (a) How does the Stuxnet worm propagate and spread?
   (b) Why was it created?
   (c) How is it different from other worms created before?
2. What is the main difference between viruses and worms?
3. What is cracking?
4. How is social engineering done?
5. How is phishing effected?
6. How is a denial-of-service attack created? What is the difference between DoS and DDos?
7. If the plaintext message is ‘the key is seven’, then what will be the ciphertext with a shift key of 19?
8. What is the difference between a public key and a private key in public key cryptography?
9. How does a firewall function?
10. Why are VPNs needed?
11. What are the four essential features of a secure network?
12. Why is TFA more secure than the single-factor authentication?

Research Questions

1. Visit a commercial organisation that has been affected by a virus or worm. Examine how much damage was done by the worm and costs involved in both recovery and work time lost.
2. In your own organisation (college or workplace), explore how users maintain their passwords. How secure are the passwords? Are they updated regularly? Can social engineering be used to crack them?
3. Explore the security measures used by your own organisation's computing infrastructure. Identify the measures used for securing the network and those for securing individual client computers.
4. What are the different kinds of encryption techniques that have been used historically? Search your library for books on encryption, or on the internet, and explain at least three different encryption techniques.

Further Reading

1. An article 'Stuxnet under the microscope' in IEEE Computer Society, 2011 is availabe at: http://www.computer.org/portal/web/computing-now/stuxnet-under-the-microscope (accessed on 26 September 2011).
2. Mimoso, M.S. (2011) *Schneier on Stuxnet malware analysis*. The article is available at: http://searchsecurity.techtarget.com/news/1528091/Schneier-on-Stuxnet-malware-analysis (accessed on 26 September 2011).
3. Keizer, G. (2010) Is Stuxnet the 'best' malware ever? *Computer World*.
4. James, R. (2009) A Brief History of Cybercrime, *Time U.S.* The article is available at: http://www.time.com/time/nation/article/0,8599,1902073,00.html#ixzz1GI-1Yhy1n (accessed on September 2011).
5. http://en.wikipedia.org/wiki/Bruce_Schneier (accessed on September 2011).
6. An article on cyber war threat in BBC News Technology is available at http://www.bbc.co.uk/news/technology-12473809 (accessed on 26 September 2011).
7. An article 'Stuxnet is the Tip of the SCADA Exploit Iceberg' is available at: http://www.nitrosecurity.com/company/press-releases/stuxnet-is-the-tip-of-the-scada-exploit-iceberg/?keywords=Stuxnet (accessed on September 2011).
8. http://www.kaspersky.com/news?id=207576178 (accessed on September 2011).
9. http://www.securelist.com/en/blog/280/Myrtus_and_Guava_Episode_4 (accessed on September 2011).
10. http://www.oreillynet.com/pub/au/3720 (accessed on September 2011).
11. An article 'Did the Stuxnet Worm Kill India's INSAT-4B Satellite?' is availabe at: http://blogs.forbes.com/firewall/2010/09/29/did-the-stuxnet-worm-kill-indias-insat-4b-satellite/ (accessed on September 2011).
12. An article 'Why Steal Digital Certificates?' is available at: http://blog.eset.com/2010/07/22/why-steal-digital-certificates (accessed on September 2011).
13. An article 'Conficer Virus Excessively Infecting Indian Computers' is available at: http://www.spamfighter.com/News-12392-Conficker-Virus-Excessively-Infecting-Indian-Computers.htm (accessed on June 2011).
14. An article '6 in Net for Cyber Bank Robbery' is available at: http://www.indianexpress.com/news/6-in-net-for-cyber-bank-robbery/250621/ (accessed on June 2011).
15. An article 'JustBooks RFID Implementation Upgrades Library Inventory Management and Customer Experience' (2010) is available at: http://www.printedelectronicsnow.com/news/2010/09/03 justbooks_rfid_implementation_upgrades_library_inventory_management_and_customer_experience (accessed on November 2011).
16. Swedberg, C. (2008) Yes Bank Uses RFID to Personalize Service, *RFID Journal*. The article is available at: http://www.rfidjournal.com/article/view/4381/1 (accessed on November 2011).
17. An article 'Kuoni Standardizes to Cut Risk (2010)' in *Computerworld* is available at: http://www.computerworld.in/articles/kuoni-standardizes-cut-risk (accessed on November 2011).
18. https://www.wired.com/2016/05/insane-81m-bangladesh-bank-heist-heres-know/ (accessed on August 2017).
19. http://www.reuters.com/article/us-cyber-heist-philippines/bangladesh-bank-heist-was-state-sponsored-u-s-official-idUSKBN1700TI (accessed on August 2017).
20. https://www.economist.com/news/finance-and-economics/21719492-much-remains-unknown-sophistication-crime-clear (accessed on August 2017).
21. https://www.cnbc.com/2017/02/07/cybercrime-costs-the-global-economy-450-billion-ceo.html (accessed on August 2017).

CHAPTER 13

Information Systems Development and Project Management

Learning Objectives

After completing this chapter, you will be able to:

- Learn analysis of business processes
- Get an overview of Life Cycle Models
- Understand project management

The construction of systems is a difficult task that requires careful analysis, design and planning. One of the first tasks for building systems is to understand the requirements or functions of the organisation for which the application is being built. This is known as analysis and entails understanding the business processes that need to be supported with computerisation, followed by a detailed exploration and documentation of the specific functionality required from the system. The analysis tasks can be performed by using techniques such as data flow diagrams and use cases.

Gathering requirements is one of the early steps in the Waterfall Model, which is the classic method by which systems are analysed, designed and built. It has well-defined steps, each of which has clear goals and deliverables. Alternatives to the Waterfall method, such as Rapid Prototyping and the Spiral Model, overcome the shortcomings of the classic method. Modern methods of agile programming bring an entirely new perspective to software development and are gaining wide popularity. Tied to the methods of systems development are the project management issues which ensure that the methods are indeed functional. Project management involves careful vendor selection, team composition and project estimation.

MIND MAP OF CHAPTER TOPICS

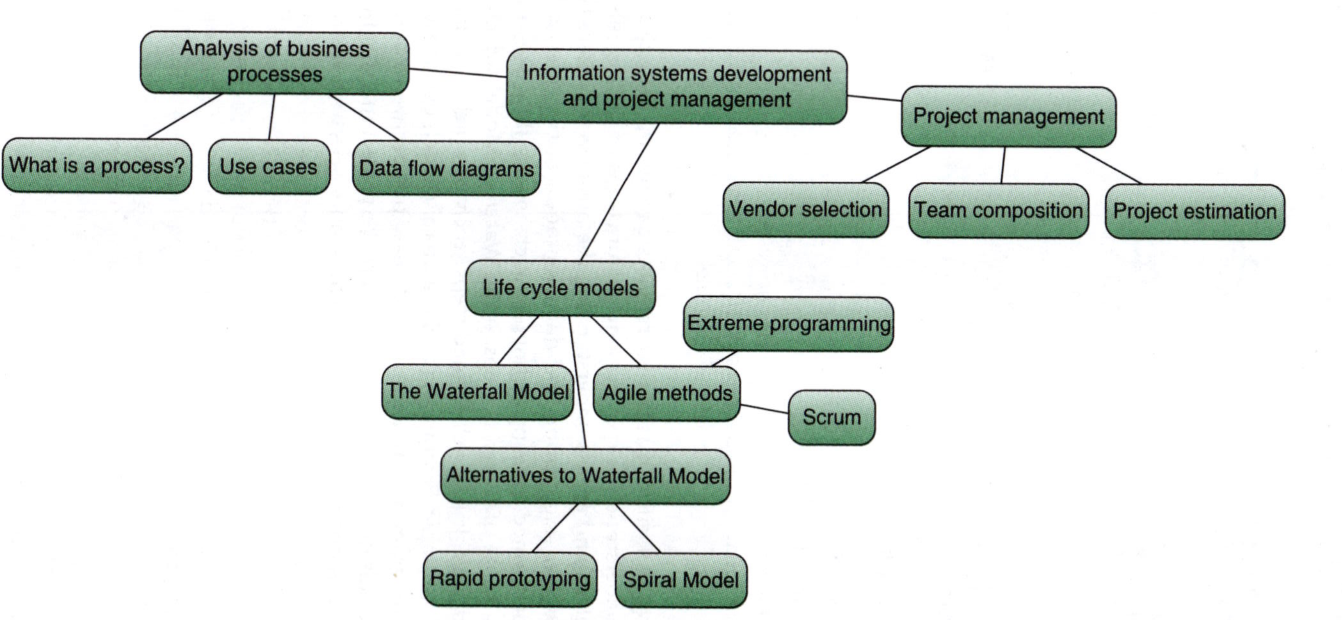

CASE STUDY: AMIS FOR FARMERS IN BANGLADESH

One of the challenges farmers in Bangladesh face is that of getting the best possible price for their produce. Agricultural produce consists of food crops such as paddy and wheat, along with vegetables and fruit, and cash crops such as jute. When the produce is harvested, farmers have to find a wholesale market where they can sell it, as well as ensure that they get a good price for it to cover their investment and turn a profit.

The challenges that farmers face are formidable: Most live in remote areas without much access to transportation to markets, most are marginal farmers who eke out a living on small plots of land and cannot invest in resources to find the best markets for the produce, and many are illiterate and unable to access printed information. Furthermore, the traditional hold of moneylenders and local wholesalers is very strong preventing farmers from straying from local markets to seek better opportunities.

The problem of small and marginal farmers is common to the nations of the subcontinent, including India, Bangladesh, Nepal and Pakistan. Many small Indian farmers are suffering from a severe economic crisis: They are not able to recover the input costs for their crops from the revenues they obtain. This has led to large-scale farmer suicides in some regions, and in other regions farmers have simply given up farming and have moved to cities to work as labour.

When a young Bangladeshi researcher, Sirajul Islam, decided try and use information and communication technology (ICT) to alleviate the problems of farmers in Bangladesh, he faced twin challenges of identifying what technology to use and how to design it so that farmers could use the technology effectively. One of the first things Sirajul learned was that the effort of the government to provide agricultural commodity prices to farmers was a failure. The government was collecting information from different markets and posting them on a website. Farmers in most parts of Bangladesh had scant access to the internet, let alone the ability to navigate through the website to find the information they were interested in.

Bangladesh has a population of 186 million (in 2010) with a population density of 1000 per square kilometre, making it one of the most densely populated countries in the world. Moreover, 72% of the population lives in rural areas, where the agricultural sector constitutes 20% of the total domestic product. About 50% of farmers are said to be below the national poverty line, pegged at an income of USD 1.25 per day. In 2010 the adult literacy rate was 55%.

Sirajul found that there was no clear answer to the question of how information could be disseminated to the farmers. He then decided to conduct an extensive study by which he could ascertain what information farmers wanted, what kind of ICT they were comfortable with and how the information could be communicated to them. He went to 13 (out of a total of 64) districts in Bangladesh, and surveyed over 400 farmers from 50 villages. He also conducted focus group discussions, by getting together a bunch of farmers in a village and having a discussion around their needs. He spoke to government officials, district officials, prominent citizens in the region, local politicians and policy makers, and wholesalers and retailers of agricultural products.

Sirajul found that of all the ICT services, mobile phones have the highest penetration in Bangladesh. Mobile penetration was at 45% (in 2010), as compared to a penetration rate of 0.6% for the internet. One of the most important findings of the survey was that income levels were not significant in predicting who would own a mobile phone. This meant that even the poorest farmers owned or had access to a mobile phone. This demand for a mobile phone was determined by lifestyle issues, as many rural people are young and wanted to own a mobile, as well as the need to communicate to family members residing elsewhere.

Bangladesh villages also have the 'village phone' (VP) ladies, women who rent out phone use. These women are entrepreneurs who acquire a mobile phone and allow residents of their neighbourhood to use the phones for a nominal charge. This has increased access of rural residents immensely. VP ladies have subsequently increased the scope of their services, providing rental access to fax, computers and also the internet.

Phone users were more comfortable with using the voice features than the text-based SMS service. This discomfort had to do, partly, with the low literacy levels of the population. However, Sirajul's study showed that the levels of usage of text services were increasing, along with a better understanding of how to use the system.

His study also showed that the farmers still relied extensively on relatively primitive modes of farming and transportation. For instance, the bullock or ox-cart and hand-cart were frequently used for transporting goods. Farming relied heavily on manual labour, as opposed to electric-based machinery (electric power supply is very poor in rural Bangladesh). They also relied on price-boards at local agricultural markets to access price information.

Given the state of agriculture and the nature of ICT penetration, Sirajul formulated a design of an Agricultural Market Information System (AMIS). The system relied on the mobile phone as the essential mode of delivery of market information. The detailed design of the system is briefly mentioned below.

The input data to the system would consist of price information related to various commodities and the markets in which they are being sold. Price information collectors would spread to all the different markets and yards and collect price information at different time points during the day. This information they would send back to a central server using text messages. The text messages would be aggregated under different categories and market heads with the help of a software package on the central server. The information would then be disseminated to farmers on a 'push' and a 'pull' basis. Farmers subscribed to the push service by specifying the produce and markets for which they wanted the information and this could be sent to them through SMS. Each broadcast of information would consist of the name of the produce, the highest and lowest prices for the day and the market at which that price was recorded. On the pull system, farmers could text their query to the central server, and then the server would respond with the relevant price information.

The design of the entire system – how data would be collected, how it would be aggregated, how it would be verified and how it would be disseminated – was based on the requirements that Sirajul had gathered from his surveys of all stakeholders. He had to make many design choices, about the manner and details of data collection and dissemination, which were made based on the needs and priorities of the farmers and the possibilities that could be exploited. Although many farmers were aware of and used mobile technologies however they could not articulate, and this was also not expected, how the system had to be configured. They did clearly articulate their needs and the resources available to them to access any information that is available.

Sirajul eventually implemented the AMIS, which was called PalliNET, for farmers and experimented with it for about 6 months. The results showed that farmers were comfortable with the system and used the market price data that was SMSed to them.

13.1 ANALYSIS OF BUSINESS PROCESSES

13.1.1 What is a Business Process?

A process in a business is any activity that requires movement of information between individuals, departments or functions. Furthermore, a process is an activity that is of value to the organisation and necessary for it to achieve its goals. A process can be quite complex consisting of many tasks ranging across many individuals and many departments. On the other hand, it can be a simple one involving only one individual sending out a single message. Processes have to be understood in their context and also their rationale.

Processes revolve around the movement of information. For analysis we begin with understanding a process mainly by understanding how information moves, and why this is required. It is important to contrast business processes with other types of processes that do not involve information. For instance, the manufacturing process of mixing chemicals is not a business process. However, the information that the chemicals have been mixed, and its communication to a management information system is a business process.

Many business processes are standard and cut across organisations, whereas other processes are specific to a particular organisation. For example, the process of making a wage payment to an employee is standard across all organisations, whereas receiving a cheque from a customer may not be prevalent in some. It is useful to identify standard business processes, as they can then be supported with information systems that have these processes built in. Many software packages have in-built standard business processes that organisations can use as they are. For other processes, software has to be specifically created.

13.1.2 The Business Analyst

The task of understanding and documenting business processes is often done by an Analyst. The business process analyst is often a specialist position in many software and consulting organisations, which is staffed by persons who are trained in using the methods and tools of systems analysis. Their job is to understand processes in the context in which they arise by talking to those who manage and are involved with the processes. They document the processes in a manner that is easily understandable by all and can be used to create designs for systems.

By nature, business processes are often obscure and mired in details. For example, in a government office, to give a clearance for a particular task, the officer in charge may have to consider many binding laws and regulatory conditions. The process of giving the clearance then becomes a matter of what the officer knows of the many cases he/she has seen. After many years, officers and managers often internalise these processes and are not able to specify all of them quickly or in great detail. The job of the analyst then is to work with such officers to understand the full complexity of the situation and the processes involved.

13.1.3 Analysis Tools

A number of diagramming techniques are used to understand, analyse and document business processes. These tools are available as software packages. The tools are used to create graphic representations of business processes whose main aim is to communicate. Since business processes are mainly known to those engaged within them, the purpose of tools is to create a precise document that others can read and understand.

Such tools are part of what are referred to as *structured methodologies*. Structured methodologies are step-by-step ways by which processes are understood, analysed, designed and constructed. As they are structured in nature, it is assured that each step will build on an earlier step, and the design and implementation progresses from concepts and principles to modules and systems. Structured methodologies rely on many tools and proceed in a top-down manner.

Different tools serve to analyse and describe different aspects of business processes. They also focus on different levels of detail. Given below are brief descriptions of some tools and the purpose for which they are used. In Section 13.1.4, one tool, the data flow diagram, is explained in more detail.

13.1.3.1 Flow Diagrams

This is a high-level tool that describes processes as a collection of tasks and information flows between them. Flow diagrams are used in Chemical Engineering to draw diagrams of chemical flows in a factory. Another version of flow diagrams is also used in Electrical Engineering to depict flow of electricity. For business processes, flow diagrams may consist of elements to depict tasks, flow of information, information stores, start points and endpoints. Figure 13.1 shows a basic activity flow diagram. The rectangles indicate activities or tasks that are performed, the arrows indicate information flows, the circles indicate data stores, and the small circles show the start and endpoints. The objective of creating such a diagram is to depict the flow of information between activities. It gives a higher level view of what information is used by tasks and what information is produced by them. It also shows what tasks are relevant and have to be included in the analysis, and which ones are not (they will not be shown).

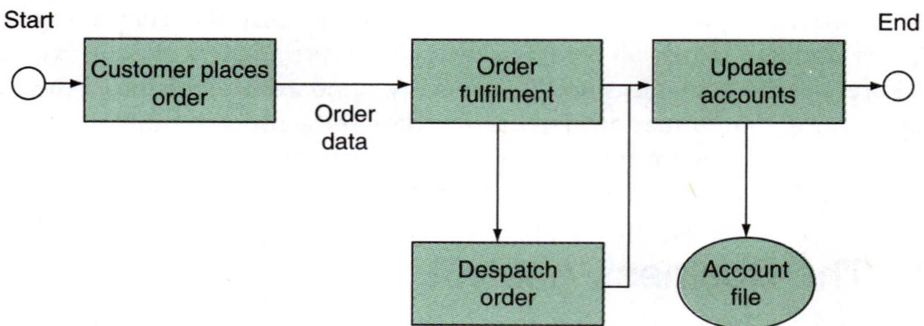

FIGURE 13.1 | Example of activity flow diagram.

13.1.3.2 Flow Charts

One of the earliest methods for depicting logic was the flowchart. This tool was developed to illustrate the logic and flow control of a computer program, also called an algorithm. This tool is widely used to show how a program will use data, decisions and processes to complete a computation.

The elements of the flowchart are shown in Fig. 13.2. They consist of a start/stop symbol, a rectangle to denote a process step or a computation, a diamond shape to represent a decision, a parallelogram to represent data input/storage and arrows to indicate flows. These symbols represent programming steps and control, but flowcharts have been adapted and used to depict business processes also.

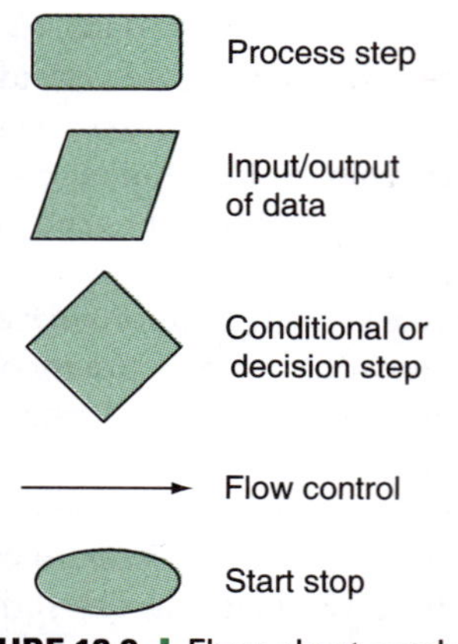

FIGURE 13.2 | Flow chart symbols.

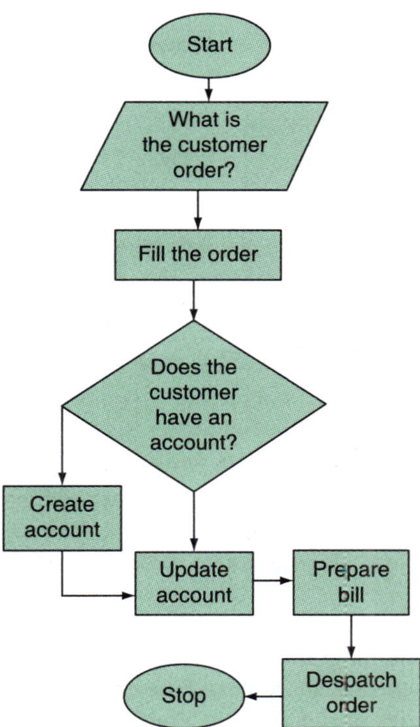

FIGURE 13.3 | Example of flowchart.

Figure 13.3 shows a business process by using a flowchart. The details of the steps are as in the previous example depicted in Fig. 13.1. A customer places an order, the order is filled and the accounts are updated. And, if the customer is a new one, a new account is created, the bill is prepared, and the goods and bill are despatched. This diagram has a decision point where it is checked whether the customer has an account or not. There are two possibilities at the node, and for each a different route is specified.

Flowcharts do not show all details of information flows. They are appropriate for the low-level depiction of activities and how they are sequenced. They are typically used in conjunction with other tools to specify details of activities and the logic for them.

13.1.4 Data Flow Diagrams

Data flow diagrams (DFDs) are widely used by analysts to gain an understanding of the sources of data in an organisation, the processes that modify data, the storage of data and the manner in which data flows between these elements. DFDs are typically drawn in a sequence of hierarchical flows where each diagram, lower in the hierarchy, shows more detail than the earlier one. The details show each process consisting of more detailed processes.

Data flow diagrams consist of only four elements that are used repeatedly to document the processes in any organisation. Each element has a particular meaning and that meaning is strictly adhered to in the diagram (no new interpretations are allowed). The elements of the diagram are thus easy to understand, and all those who are involved with creating them, whether technically trained or not, are able to have a shared understanding of the analysis.

The elements of the data flow diagram are depicted in Fig. 13.4. The first element is the process, depicted by an oval shape. The process is any task or activity that takes data as input and produces some data output. The second element is the entity, depicted by a rectangle. The entity in a data flow diagram (DFD) represents a person or department or organisation that is a source or termination of data. Entities either produce data or receive it. The third element

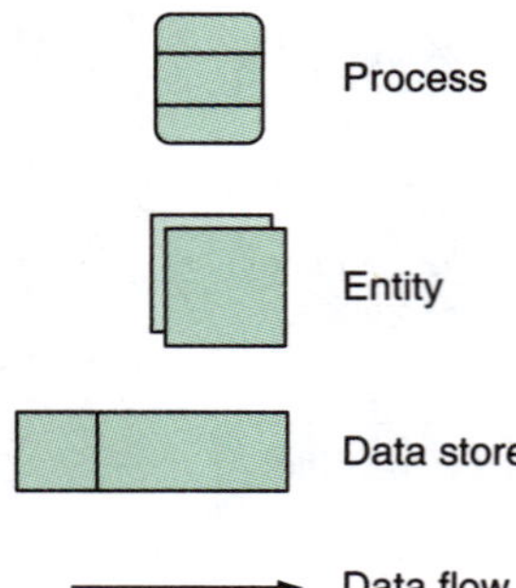

FIGURE 13.4 | Elements of the data flow diagram.

of the DFD is the data store. This represents a file or storage unit where data is maintained and from where data may be read. The fourth and the last element is the flow, represented by an arrow. Arrows show the flow of data from the other elements. They are always labelled to show the type and nature of data. Flows are also directed to show the origin and destination of data.

An example of a DFD is shown in Fig. 13.5. The top part of the figure shows the context diagram. The role of the context diagram is to identify who the entities are and what the main process is through which the entities share data. The context diagram helps circumscribe the analysis, or show the boundaries of the analysis. For the system being considered, other entities in the organisation are not relevant and hence not included. The single process, the order processing, is what is of most relevance. Other processes in the organisation that are not related to order processing are not included in the diagram. The diagram thus clearly shows the scope of the system that is being analysed. The data flows in the context diagram show the

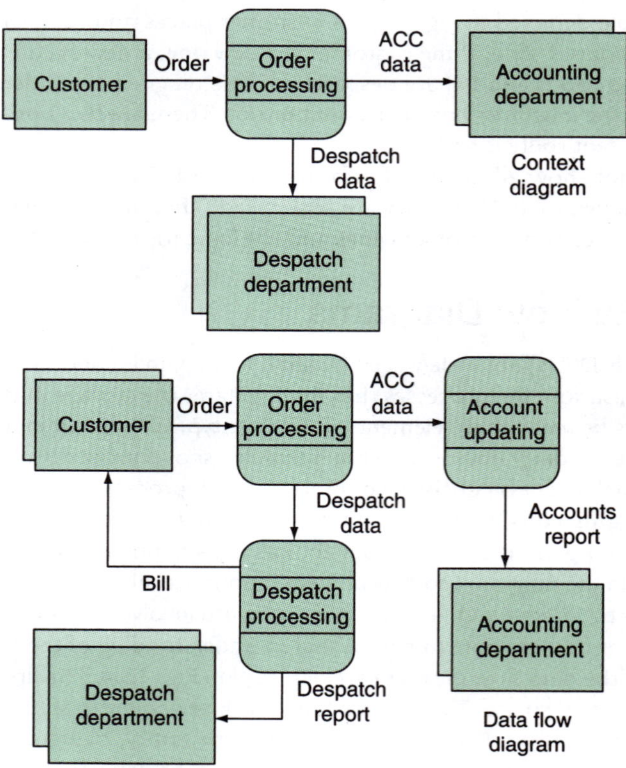

FIGURE 13.5 | Example of data flow diagram.

most important information that is used within the system. Detailed data flows are shown in later diagrams.

The lower part of the diagram depicts a detailed DFD. The order processing process is now broken into three processes

1. Order processing.
2. Account updating.
3. Despatch processing.

When a customer entity places an order, a data flow labelled order is shown to carry data to the order processing bubble. This process then produces two further data flows - one to the account updating process and another to the despatch processing process. Data carried by the data flows to these other processes is used to trigger further processes. Despatch processing creates a despatch report and a bill that are sent to the despatch department and the customer, respectively. Account updating produces a single report that is sent to the accounting department entity.

There are several points to note about a data flow diagram. First, a data flow diagram does not necessarily show the order of flows or the sequence in which things happen. It simply marks the direction and content of data flows. Whether one process precedes another cannot be read or interpreted from the diagram. Second, a data flow diagram does not depict the internal logic or decision points of any process. How the data is processed inside any process is not evident in the diagram.

Data flow diagrams capture the *what* of any system (i.e. What has to be done? What are the inputs?), as opposed to the *why* and *how*. They are a powerful tool to rapidly scope a system and outline its basic functionality.

As an example of how to construct a data flow diagram, consider the following business scenario.

13.1.4.1 DFD Example

A university wants to create an online registration system for its students. When a student wants to register, he/she may log into the system and check for available courses. The system presents some alternatives to the student who then makes some choices. The system interacts with a course scheduling module to ensure that the courses and ample seats for them are available, and the student can register for them without clashes of timing. The information about the student's choices is communicated to the concerned professors and also to the accounting department.

The context diagram for the above scenario is depicted in Fig. 13.6. It consists of a single process called the Course Registration System. Interacting with this process are two entities, the student and the Professor. Basic information flows between the entities and the system are marked.

At the next level is the detailed data flow diagram. The student entity provides information to the Course Registration System regarding courses needed. The Course Registration System passes information to the Scheduling System that provides information to the student about available courses and their timings. A separate data flow from the Scheduling System indicates to the student the courses that have been registered. This system also sends a report to the Professor entity regarding the registrations. The Course Registration System also sends data to the Accounting System that then stores the data in a data store called Student Accounts. The Scheduling System stores data regarding registration for courses in the Courses and schedules data store.

The above example is a simple description of the manner in which data flow diagrams are created from business processes. Here a notable point is that there is no sequencing of data flows and processes. It is important to note what data flows between, say, the student and the Course Registration System, not the sequence and logic by which this flow occurs. Furthermore, details of the three processes depicted in the figure can be expanded in lower level diagrams.

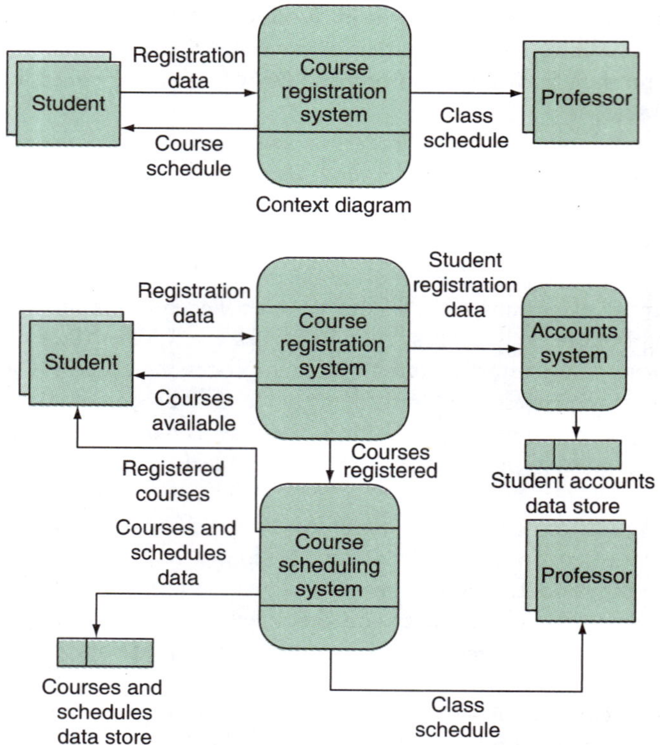

FIGURE 13.6 | Course Registration System – data flow diagram.

13.1.4.2 Some Cautions While Creating DFDs

Data flow diagrams are easy to understand and can be created reasonably quickly. However, to be useful some cautions have to be taken to ensure that the diagrams are accurate.

1. All processes must receive at least one data input and produce at least one data output. Without an input they cannot possibly be functional, and if they do not create an output, either to a store or to an entity or to another process, then their role is questionable.
2. All data stores and entities must either receive or give out at least one data flow. If any data store or entity does not either receive or emit one data flow, their presence in the diagram is questionable.
3. All data flows must originate or terminate at a process. This implies that data flows cannot directly connect entities with other entities, or data stores with other data stores. Furthermore, data flows cannot directly connect entities with data stores. Connecting two entities with a data flow is a very common error while creating data flow diagrams.
4. Entities depict groups, departments or individuals. In the above example, it is correct to denote all students at the university as a single entity. The system is designed for all of them, even when it is known that many of them will have different behaviour patterns with respect to the system. When the entity is a single individual, such as a manager, then the analysts have to be certain that this particular individual is the source or destination of data.

13.1.5 Use Cases

Use case is another powerful technique that is used for business process analysis. At a very basic level, a use case is a text description of a process or activity in which some user is involved. Use cases describe the activity in some detail with the objective of clarifying what is needed from the system and in what way should it respond. Use cases are often used as a discovery tool, where users in an organisation, or customers who interact with a system, or citizens who use an online system, are asked to describe in their own words what they expect from the system. These descriptions can then form the basis for more detailed analysis with, say, a tool like data flow diagrams.

Use cases may be brief, describing the process in a few lines and some other details, or may be about a page in length or may be very detailed. Use cases are used extensively in many system development methods and are developed to a level of detail based on the progress of the development project. In many situations, using a simple template is enough to create a brief use case.

Use cases are used as part of the formalisd software development methods known as the Rational Unified Process (RUP) and the Unified Modeling Language (UML). These techniques also use a formal visual method for creating use cases, which is supported by software.

It is possible to create use cases using a template. The elements of the template that have to be filled out are:

1. **Name:** Each use case has to be given a name appropriate to the process. It should capture the essence of the process and also be unique. For example, customer call; citizen request; order fulfilment.
2. **Description:** A brief text description of the use case.
3. **Actor:** Each use case has to involve an actor that is an external agent or entity. The actor initiates the case and also receives some output from the system. Actors are humans, such as citizens or customers, or they are other systems that are external to the system under study.
4. **Precondition:** Each case has to have some preconditions that have to be met. If the precondition is not present or met then the case fails. For example, a precondition for a citizen to reach an online system is access to the internet.
5. **Trigger:** An event or a time at which a use case is initiated. Triggers are different from preconditions; their occurrence is necessary for the process described in the use case to be initiated, with or without the presence of preconditions.
6. **Scenario:** This is the description of the steps or the sequence of events that happen or are likely to happen when the actor interacts with the system. This is the most likely set of events that are planned for and will be formally built into the system.
7. **Alternate paths:** These are the likely alternatives to the scenarios described above. Alternate paths show the possible ways the process behaviour could proceed in, and the manner in which the system could respond. This is a detailed step often left out of initial use cases.
8. **Business rules:** These are rules or principles by which the organisation is run. These could be accounting rules to make tax calculations, or the sequence in which a form will be processed. These limit and scope the manner in which the system will respond to actors and triggers.

An example of a use case is provided in Table 13.1.

Table 13.1 | Example of a Use Case

Use Case Name	Process Order Request
Description	A customer places an order for a catalogue item on a website. The order is recorded and the customer's credit card is checked for sufficient funds.
Actor	Customer
Precondition	The customer has selected one or more catalogue items.

(Continued)

Table 13.1 | (Continued)

Use Case Name	Process Order Request
Scenario	• The customer places an order based on a catalogue item and provides information about his/her account. • The account information is recovered and the customer's credit card details are accessed. • The credit card is verified to see if sufficient funds are available. • If the card has sufficient funds, the order is placed firmly and a despatch request is posted. • The customer is informed of the order details and the expected date of delivery.
Alternate scenario	• If the customer does not have an account then a new account is created. • If the credit card is not verified then the customer is asked if he/she would opt for a cash-on-delivery option.

13.2 LIFE CYCLE MODELS

When the commercial computer industry was born in the 1950s in North America and Western Europe, customers paid for the hardware and the software was provided along with it. Software was developed using principles of engineering, with an emphasis on design before implementation. As the industry grew, there emerged for-profit companies that would create only software, as partners to the hardware companies. The software companies followed creative practices for building software, as software, unlike hardware, could easily be modified and changed because costs of repeat manufacture were very low and no materials were consumed. The software industry grew immensely, and with it grew the problems of 'spaghetti code' and the need for extensive and scientific testing.

In the 1950s the bulk of the costs of the system purchased by any organisation was the hardware (over 90%), as shown in Fig. 13.7. As software grew and became more complex, along with the ability to deliver more complex solutions to address complicated needs, it also grew as a total cost of the system. By the mid-1970s, software constituted about half of the total cost, and by the mid-1980s it was about 80% of the cost of the system. These increasing costs demanded that the production of software had to be streamlined, and aligned more with hardware production methods.

Large contracts for software, with millions of lines of code, required a formal and structured manner in which the code could be written. This need led to the creation of what are known as Life Cycle Models. These models specify a technique by which the coding for the software is preceded by design which is preceded by analysis. Coding is followed by the formal steps of testing and implementation. The first such model was known as the Waterfall Model, depicted in Fig. 13.8.

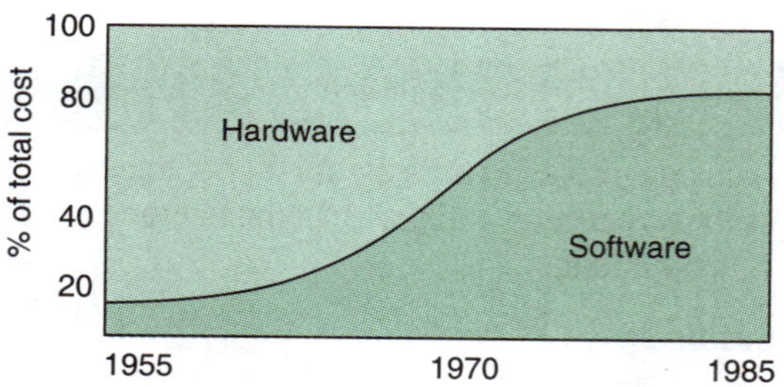

FIGURE 13.7 | Large organisation hardware/software cost trends.
Source of data: A view of the 20th and 21st Century Software Engineering by B. Boehm, 25 May 2006.

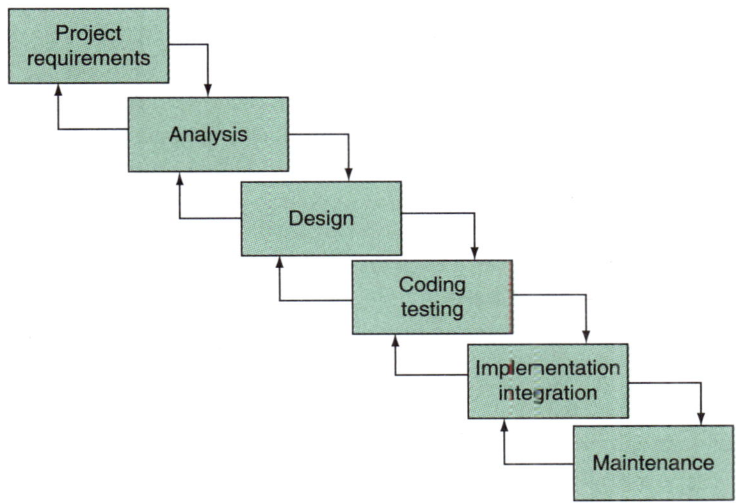

FIGURE 13.8 | The Waterfall Model.

This model depicts six stages arranged in steps, or a waterfall; the project proceeds along each stage, with the ability to loop back to a previous stage if necessary. Each stage consists of a number of activities that have to be performed and milestones that have to be met. Often the first three are considered the most critical and important parts of the life cycle, called the upper stages of the cycle. The lower stages are more involved with coding and implementation, and though no less important, they are often left to technical management.

The model is called a life cycle as it refers to the entire life of the software, from creation to retirement and replacement by another. Seen in this light many software projects have very long life cycles, spanning decades, whereas many have short cycles, lasting only a few years.

13.2.1 Waterfall Model

13.2.1.1 Project Requirements

In the first stage of the Waterfall Model, the overall scope of the project is established. The main problem that has to be solved with the system is determined and carefully scoped. Questions that are asked at this stage include: What is the purpose of the proposed system? Who will use the system, which departments, which employees? Will the system interact with other systems in the organisation, and if so, for what purpose? Will external entities such as customers or citizens interact with the system and in what capacity? How long will the system last, what is its expected life cycle? How long will it take to design and implement? How much money has to be allocated for its completion? Who will be responsible for managing its implementation and use?

An important task of this stage is a *feasibility analysis*. This task establishes whether the project is feasible - whether the project is possible at all, given the financial, technical and managerial capabilities of the organisation to go ahead with the project. Once the feasibility is firmly established, it marks a go signal for requirements to proceed further.

The project requirements provide a road map for the project, with important details such as budgets allocated and time frames. Top management has to be involved with this phase of the project, however small or large the project may be in terms of budget or time required. The project team leaders who will have to manage the project through its life have to be directly involved in making and committing to the decisions.

The output from this stage of the life cycle is a document that clearly outlines the scope of the project, the budget, the personnel involved, the likely milestones and the key success indicators. The last head is a set of measures by which the management can estimate how the project is progressing; it includes measures such as person hours on the project, documentation completion, lines of code, team size and budgets spent among others.

13.2.1.2 Analysis

This stage is also called the Requirements stage where the basic objective of the system is explained in as much detail as possible. At this stage the most important question that is asked is – What should the system do? To answer this question, it is important to ask potential users of the system what they expect from it. Typical questions at this stage include:

1. What are the main inputs to the system?
2. What will be the various outputs from the system?
3. What kind of subsystems is required?
4. What processes will the system automate?
5. Which processes will be changed to account for the new system's improved performance?
6. What is the expected increase in efficiency?
7. What kind of data will be stored by the system?
8. What kind of reports will be created for external entities?
9. Which other systems of the organisation will the system interact with?

There are many tools by which the analysis is conducted. Some of them such as flow diagrams, data flowcharts, data flow diagrams and use cases have already been explained. Analysts may select one or more of these tools and meet with various stakeholders of the system to record the requirements for the system. Stakeholders are those who are connected to the system in a direct manner, and sometimes indirectly, and whose use or non-use of the system will determine its success. Stakeholders are interviewed by analysts to understand their needs from the system, both currently and in future when they integrate their work with the system.

Analysis also requires working with the documentation and work flows currently existing in the organisation. These documents indicate the data requirements of the organisation, and the work flows are the manner in which data flows. Detailed analysis also involves understanding the subtle and often unspoken methods by which work is accomplished, thus explicating tacit codes in the organisation's work.

The analysis is best conducted by trained personnel, particularly, those who understand the business domain and have a deep knowledge of the tools of analysis. For example, in the banking and finance domain, the best systems analysts are those with knowledge of this sector and who also have deep skills in using analysis tools. Analysts have to use rigorous documentation techniques to ensure that the requirements they unearth are adequately recorded in the requirements document.

The output from this stage is a detailed requirements document that specifies the objectives of the system and what is needed to be done to realise these objectives. After this stage, analysts may feel the need to revise some of their estimates for project budgets and time estimations in the project requirements documents prepared in the first stage.

13.2.1.3 Design

Once the analysis is complete and a document containing what has to be done is available, the next step of designing is how the goals have to be achieved. The objective of the Design stage is to provide clear and precise guidelines as to how the system will be built. Details about the logic to be used, the screens to be used, the manner in which decisions will be made and the rules that will be followed are specified. If the analysis outlines what the system should do then the design tells how the system should do this.

The questions asked at the design stage are as follows:

1. How are the data inputs to the system to be collected?
2. What is the nature of the user interface?
3. What are the menu options that will be provided?
4. Where will the data be stored?

5. What kind of data files is required?
6. How will the data be normalised (will it be normalised)?
7. What are business rules used for computations?
8. What is the exact logic for computing certain values?
9. What are the systems, sub-systems and sub-sub-systems that have to be constructed?
10. What will be the architecture for the entire system?
11. How are the different components to be integrated?
12. How much of the system will be off-the-shelf software?
13. How much will be built?
14. How much of the system construction will be outsourced?

A number of tools are used at this stage to specify the design for the system. These tools include flowcharts, structure charts, hierarchy charts, and Computer-Aided Software Engineering (CASE) tools. CASE tools are software environments that provide graphical tools for designing software, and some can also create code on the basis of these designs (see Fig. 13.9). Many programming languages permit quick creation of software prototypes that are used as design tools. A prototype can be created with a CASE tool or with a software programming tool, and it is a working model of the system. The prototype does not have the full functionality of the finished system, but resembles some of the functionality and the look-and-feel that allows users to understand how the software will function eventually and suggest what they would want additionally from it.

The design phase is highly technical in nature, and mainly the technically skilled members of the system-building team are responsible for the final outcomes. They work closely with the analysts and often change the analysis document as more details of the system are fleshed out.

The output of the design stage is a design document that specifies the system in great detail, but does not necessarily contain coded programs. Prototypes may be used for the design but are not a required output from this stage. The idea of the design phase is to de-couple it fully from coding and testing so that the design can be built independently of coding considerations.

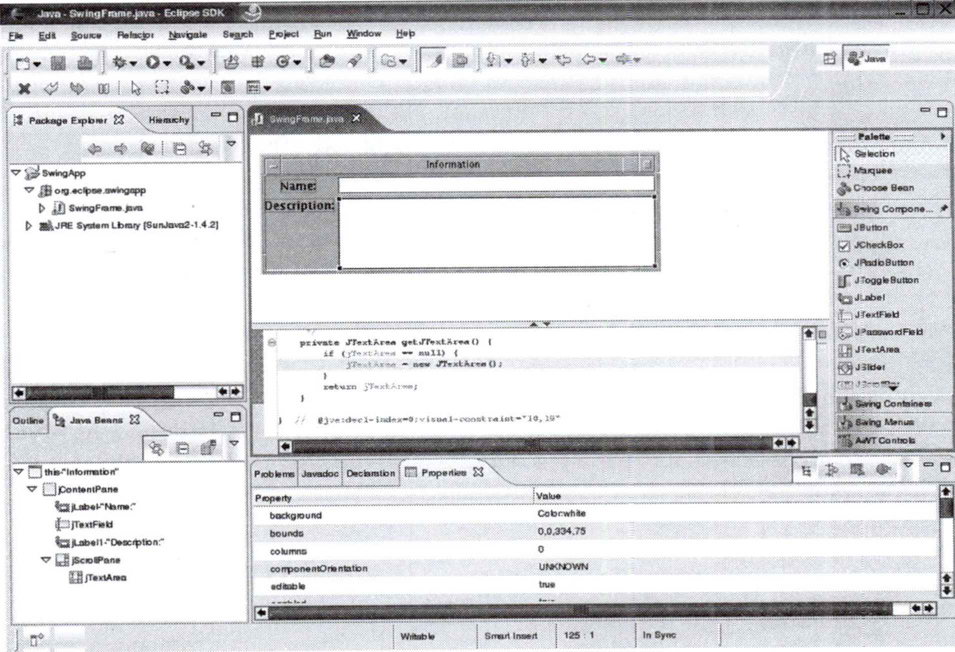

FIGURE 13.9 | The eclipse case tool.

When the design is complete, it can be handed over to the coding department or to an outside agency to build the system. The design document is thus a blueprint for the entire system.

13.2.1.4 Coding and Testing

This phase involves building the system by writing the software. Coding involves creating software with high-level programming languages. Modern programming languages offer many facilities for reusing pre-built modules through objects. The code is built according to the design specified in the design document.

Some issues that arise at this stage are:

1. What platform (which is a combination of an operating system and programming language tools) will be best suited for the system to be built?
2. What coding and documentation practices will be followed?
3. How will the team structure be constituted?
4. What will be the reporting requirements for the team?
5. If some modules are being outsourced, how will the outsourced part be managed?

An integral part of coding is testing the modules produced. Test suites are created, which are a set of problems the program is run on to see how it performs. Tests are conducted for individual modules called *stub testing*, and for some modules clubbed together called *integration testing*. Testing reveals the flaws in the logic and the implementation of the system. At this stage, coders may return to the design documents and modify them to ensure that the changes made at the coding stage reflect in the design.

Coding requires the involvement of the most skilled programmers and project managers of the system team. Their work does not involve users or analysts. It is usually recommended that they be provided isolated facilities within which they can work, meet and discuss the progress of the project. Specific milestones are reviewed by the management and resources such as team members and hardware, networks and software licences are provided.

13.2.1.5 Implementation and Integration

Once the system is at a stage where it can be released for use, the implementation phase begins. This stage also involves testing, which implies testing the system with the targeted users. Potential users are identified and trained with the software interface. Trial data is created along with dummy processes with which users can interact. The system runs through as many types of possible scenarios as can be anticipated. Problems are detected and recorded.

Software released to users for testing is often said to be on the *Alpha* test phase. This phase returns results regarding the use of the software in conditions that are close to what would be the case in actual use. Reports regarding problems are attended to and the software is revised. After this phase, the software is released to a larger audience, and this is known as *Beta* testing. Here, the software is in near *production mode*. (A software package is said to be in production mode when it is being used to the full capacity for the purpose it is created for.) Beta testing is more rigorous as it forces the software to encounter situations it has not seen before. This often requires updating the software with patches and fixes.

The testing phase includes integration of the software with the everyday processes of the organisation. After users are trained, the processes of the organisation have to be, usually, modified to accommodate the new software and match the speed and efficiency it introduces. Integration also implies creating new jobs with updated job descriptions and writing new process manuals describing the new methods of working.

Many organisations choose a one-time cutover to the system. The older methods, perhaps using an older software or by manual means, of completing processes is abandoned and the new software is adopted. This has problems as users have to cope with the changes and learn new tools quickly. However, the advantage of a one-time cutover is that it eliminates the old system in one go and there is better adoption of the new system. Another option is the parallel cutover where the old and new systems exist in parallel for a certain period of time, which allows users to both get used to the new system while continuing their work as before, and also gradually migrate their data and files over to the new system. Though this method has its advantages of giving users more time to get used to the new system, it allows some to linger with the old system that may create problems of migration to the new system later.

Usually, large systems take a long time to be tested and made fully operational. At the level of production mode use, more problems will invariably show up that had not been seen or anticipated before. Some of the bugs may be serious in nature requiring an overhaul of both the design and implementation. This is particularly true when the systems have to integrate with other systems in the organisation.

13.2.1.6 Maintenance

The maintenance phase is for the continued use of the system. This phase is initiated once the system has been tested and installed into production. This phase entails recording problems and feature enhancements. Problems are attended to and feature enhancements are attempted when they are possible within the existing structure of the system. Enhancements that require substantial changes and an overhaul of the system are not attempted, however, this is a difficult call to make. Some problems with the system may be large enough to require an entirely new system, kicking off another life cycle, while others may be managed within the maintenance phase of the current cycle.

Maintenance is often outsourced to firms and agencies that have specialist skills in this task. Some systems are often in continuous production for decades after they are developed. They are maintained by agencies that have skilled employees who know the old technology and can create updates and patches for the system to remain relevant. For example, some systems that were created for large insurance agencies with the COBOL programming language, a language that is not used any more to create new programs, about 30 years ago are still in production use. Some outsourcing firms have a pool of programmers who are skilled in COBOL and have taken up the task of maintaining these programs.

13.2.2 The Waterfall Model in Perspective

The Waterfall Model and its variations have been used extensively for software development for almost four decades. Standards for the software development process and certifications for the same are based on the Waterfall stages of development.

The Waterfall Model has also become the basis for awarding software development contracts and managing them. The phases of the model are treated as milestones that are monitored and linked to progress reports and payment releases. Government agencies around the world have developed standards for software development projects based on the Waterfall Model. Some inter-country collaboration agreements for development of joint software packages, say for trade purposes, assume the Waterfall Model as the basis for formalising the steps of the agreement.

Despite its wide acceptance, the Waterfall Model also has its share of problems and criticisms. The strongest critique is based on the linear and bureaucratic manner in which the method progresses. In many cases, the feedback aspects of the model are ignored, and the model is treated as consisting of a linear progression of stages, without much feedback to alter the previous stages. Contracts for software development often ignore feedback altogether, treating, say, the analysis phase as completed once the analysis documents are ready, with the implied assumption that the requirements cannot change or be modified in later stages. This has often led to a crisis in the project, where it is realised at the design or implementation stage that certain requirements are not feasible, given the resource constraints of the project. If the requirements are changed then this is called *scope creep* by vendors, and accommodating the new requirements attracts extra charges. In many contracts, scope creep is explicitly accounted for and any requirements changes after the analysis phase are charged a steep penalty price.

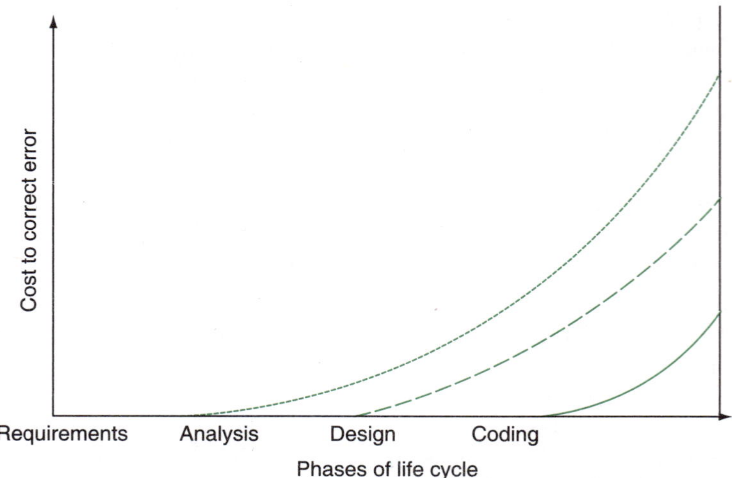

FIGURE 13.10 | Cost to correct errors detected at different phases of life cycle.

The second strong critique of the Waterfall Model is that it slows down the development process, particularly for software that is not very large in scope. With its strong emphasis on analysis followed by design, some developers argue that small software projects suffer from delays. Smaller projects do not need extensive analysis or design; only brief outlines of these are sufficient to go directly to the coding phase. Furthermore, the documentation requirements are also considered to be tedious, particularly for small projects. Many analysis documents run into hundreds of pages for large projects. However, many argue that for small projects these are not required.

When the Waterfall Model is used, the costs of finding and fixing mistakes vary according to the stage at which the mistake was detected and fixed. Figure 13.10 shows the nature of costs incurred for fixing bugs. If an error is introduced at the requirements phase and this is not detected till the maintenance phase then the cost of fixing the bug is the highest. If the error is found at an earlier stage, the cost for rectifying the error is lower. Similarly, if an error is introduced at the design or coding phases, the cost of rectifying it is lower if it is detected in the earlier phases than in the later phases. The figure also shows that the increase in costs for fixing errors increases non-linearly.

The cost of identifying and rectifying errors, as depicted in Fig. 13.10, has two implications. First, the project managers have to ensure that at the analysis and design phases no serious errors are introduced, or extreme care is taken at these phases to ensure that the design is near-perfect and can go for coding. This approach is followed by many organisations and for large projects - with close to 500,000 software lines of code. In these cases, almost 50% of the effort within the project is dedicated to analysis and design. Second, the project managers may follow a variation of the traditional Waterfall Model with having short durations of analysis and design followed by coding and testing. The entire system is thus not analysed and designed completely, but is done in manageable parts. This approach has led to a number of alternative approaches to software development, which are described below.

13.2.3 Alternatives to the Waterfall Model

13.2.3.1 Rapid Prototyping

Prototyping in software development implies creating a working model of the system, not the entire system. Rapid Prototyping is a formal method by which the system is built in a sequence of cycles of the Waterfall Model. The phases of analysis, design, coding and testing are compressed into a shorter time frame. A partial system is built, and then this is used for analysing more

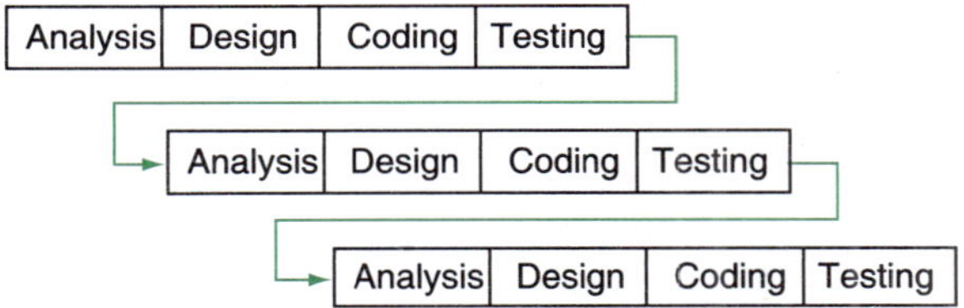

FIGURE 13.11 | Rapid prototyping.

detailed requirements for the next prototype. Detailed documentation is not done. A larger prototype is then built, again going through the phases of analysis, design, coding and testing. The working prototype that is now obtained is larger and more complex than the previous one, and is closer to the eventual system that is desired. The first prototype is now discarded, and the second one becomes the basis for the next round of prototyping (see Fig. 13.11).

The advantage of rapid prototyping is that it allows incremental development of the system, thus, reducing the amount of initial time spent on analysis and design, and giving the systems team a chance to see whether some requirements are feasible or not, and what more can be designed into the system. The prototypes allow for a better understanding of the eventual system and also reduce the analysis and design flaws that may be introduced. A disadvantage of this method is that effort is wasted in building the initial prototypes that are discarded. Furthermore, the reduced documentation becomes a problem once the final system is in place. Without the detailed documentation, systems maintenance becomes difficult as the maintainers do not know the reasons why certain parts of the system were created.

13.2.3.2 The Spiral Model

The Spiral Model was developed in 1987 to address some of the concerns raised by system developers about the Waterfall Model. The Spiral Model uses an iterative approach, where prototypes are built successively in a spiral of expanding capabilities. It was originally designed for large projects, those that require considerable time and effort to build and would run into millions of lines of code. The model is not an alternative to the Waterfall Model as much as it is an enhancement.

The stages of the Spiral Model are depicted in Fig. 13.12. The model is depicted as a spiral that increases its diameter along the orthogonal axes. The spiral starts in the top left quadrant,

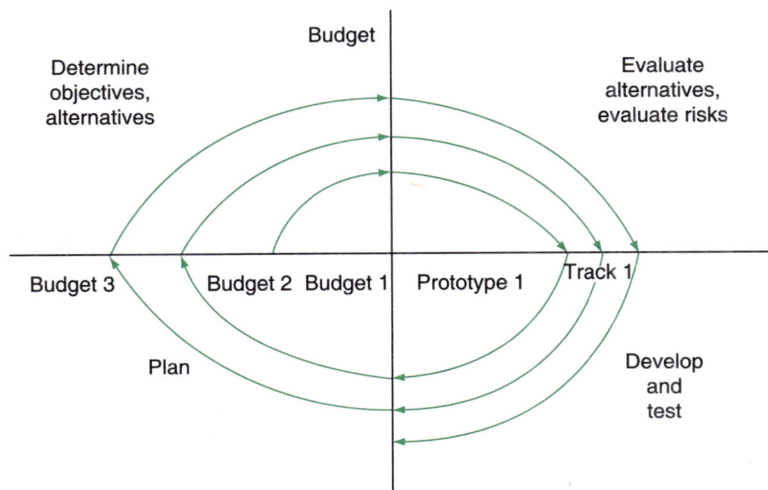

FIGURE 13.12 | The spiral model of software development.

and this is the first stage. The spiral is kicked off by a felt need for a system and an assessment of the alternative ways in which the need could be addressed. Objectives of the system are estimated along with estimates of the budget.

In the next stage, as depicted in the top right quadrant, the alternatives are evaluated. For each alternative, the evaluation involves estimating the risk associated with the development. For example, if the two alternatives for a system for setting up a database are – using a proprietary software or using an open source alternative, then these two choices would be assessed for their risks. Risk assessment involves assigning estimates to the construction, use, value and eventual success of the two alternatives. It involves identifying uncertainties in the project and manner in which this could be dealt with. This stage may include benchmarking the project against other similar projects, interviewing developers and users regarding the effort, and simulating or visualising the conditions under which the software would be used. Once a risk profile has been created, the prototype is developed.

At the next stage, represented by the lower right quadrant in the figure, the prototype is tested and evaluated. This provides a detailed idea of the requirements of the system, now that the prototype can be tested, as also the features that are missing. Using the detailed requirements as well as the risk profile determined in the previous stage, the next stage is started. This stage is marked by the lower left quadrant in the figure. Here plans for the next iteration in the spiral are made. These plans are based on the lessons learned from the first prototype and its evaluation. The plan includes the life cycle of the product, including all stages of analysis, design, testing and coding.

As the next cycle of the spiral is initiated, the activities of setting objectives, determining alternatives and setting a budget are initiated again, followed by the next stage of determining the risks for the alternatives. A new prototype is built, followed by its evaluation and a new set of plans for the next iteration.

The Spiral Model of iterations ends when the risk analysis shows that the system is well enough understood to go into the final round of analysis, design, coding and testing. The requirements are known well enough now, and so the focus is on the design of the eventual system and the testing.

The Spiral Model is a risk-driven model that explicitly models risk and uncertainty in the development process. The entire focus is on understanding and controlling risks to reduce the chances of eventual failure of the system.

13.2.4 Agile Methods

The late 1990s saw the evolution of software development methods known collectively as the *Agile Methods*. Drawing inspiration from manufacturing quality processes, these methods relied on short analysis–design–coding–testing cycles, with close user interaction and flexible team compositions to build software. The underlying emphasis in the Agile methods is on reducing and controlling risk. Shorter life cycles ensured that bugs and design flaws were detected early, and the user involvement throughout the project ensured the requirements were addressed adequately.

The Agile manifesto, a document outlining the beliefs of the developers who invented the Agile techniques, defines the fundamental propositions of these methods. The Agile methods rely on creating programs quickly and with close interaction with the customer. Requirements are never frozen and change is welcomed to ensure that the customers' needs are attended to right through the end of the project. Developers are given autonomy and responsibility to work on their own and seek out quality measures for the project. The Agile methods also require suitable working conditions like an open working environment and a limit on the number of hours that can be worked on in a week so that developers remain motivated and productive.

Different agile methods have different means by which they address the objectives of the manifesto. Two of the methods that have gained popularity are Extreme Programming and Scrum. These methods are described below.

13.2.4.1 Extreme Programming

Extreme Programming has gained wide popularity among the Agile methods. It embodies most of the objectives of the Agile manifesto and has been demonstrated to be effective for small- to medium-scale projects. As a method, Extreme Programming has a few core ideas.

1. **Stories:** All activities are initiated by stories that users tell about what they want from the system, how they go about doing their work and what processes they follow among others. These stories are then written on index cards and the writing is done rapidly. The stories constitute the initial analysis for the system.
2. **Short releases:** Modules for the software are released quickly and often. A module is determined by the users and the developers jointly, based on the highest priority of features wanted. Here, users have a priority as to what they want to see first, and the developers guide this choice based on cost and resources available. The releases are made as frequently as every day.
3. **Testing:** Releases of code are tested as soon as they are created. In fact, while planning for the module, the test sets are created and a module is considered completed after the tests are satisfied. This manner of testing is known as *unit* testing.
4. **Iteration:** The iterations in Extreme Programming are based on the features needed in the releases. The system is put into production the moment the release is made, or it is placed in the central repository (a repository is a central collection of code). The units are integrated and the whole package is tested. If it fails then the latest changes are reversed. If the changes are accepted then this starts a new iteration with another story and another set of features.
5. **Refactoring:** The design of the system evolves and changes as the system is built up from the modules. Refactoring, or changes, is done as the integrated system needs them.
6. **Pair programming:** All the coding is done by a pair of developers. One writes the code and the other 'looks over his/her shoulder' to see how the code fits in with the rest of the system and how it can be thoroughly tested. Programmers have to be highly skilled in doing their task and they have to work rapidly.
7. **Work environment:** The entire team is located in one room, with the programmer pairs at a centre table/computer. At least one customer is always available for evolving the features and to write the stories. In total, 40-h work weeks are desired. However, occasional overtime is permitted, but not for successive weeks.
8. **Metaphors:** Both the developers and the users work with metaphors to visualise their system. Metaphors are words or phrases that resemble some desired feature or attribute, but are not exact. Metaphors help seek out different meanings that the users may have about what they want, and explore different possible ways of achieving the same.

Extreme Programming is successful because it allows the developers autonomy in understanding the problem clearly and designing the system accordingly. The close interaction with the customers also enables continuous dialogue and an understanding of implicit and tacit codes that are often missed in formal meetings. Furthermore, its emphasis on continuous testing and integration ensures that the evolving system is always working and meets the customers' needs.

13.2.4.2 Scrum

The Scrum method relies on the idea of evolving the requirements for the project and the needed activities on the basis of work completed rather than on plans. The word 'Scrum' is borrowed from a particular team formation used in the Rugby sport. In such a formation, the team gains possession of the ball and jointly moves forward with it. This approach of a cross-functional team going the distance as a unit, passing the ball back and forth – this is what agile scrum is about.

The project proceeds in a series of *sprints*, which have fixed durations of 2 or 4 weeks. In each sprint particular and defined objectives are met; a tested system is built for that portion alone, and what further needs to be done is determined on the basis of the completed work. A sprint commences with a sprint planning meeting that is time-boxed to a few hours—usually 4 hours for a two-week sprint.

Scrum involves defining a number of roles for the project members and the creation of a number of artefacts.

1. **Product owner:** He/she is a customer or client who determines what the system should be and how it should behave. He/she is a part of the team and is always involved.
2. **ScrumMaster:** The scrum is facilitated by the scrum master who is responsible for removing any impendiments the team faces. The scrum master is not a project manager; the team is expected to self-manage and the scrum master acts as a facilitator. He/she also acts as a project coordinator.
3. **Team member:** He/she is a member of the team, who participates in building the software.
4. **Product backlog and sprint backlog:** These are requirement documents that state what has to be achieved for the project and for each sprint. Each backlog is essentially a high-level requirement specification that is fleshed out and detailed during the sprints.
5. **Burn down chart:** This is a record of backlogs that have been completed. For a sprint, the burn down chart shows what has been completed on a daily basis, giving the team a focus for what needs to be achieved.

Note the lack of documentation in the above list, such as design specifications or test plans. This is consistent with the agile manifesto of 'completed functionality over comprehensive documentation'.

During a sprint, meetings to review the progress and create the burn down logs are highly structured and controlled (see Fig. 13.13). A daily meeting is held for exactly 15 min in the same place and at the same time (first thing in the morning). All may attend the meeting but only the 'pigs' are permitted to speak. Pigs are the product owner, the ScrumMaster, and the team members, or all those who are committed to the project; commitment implies they are accountable to the progress of the project. Others are not permitted to speak, and are termed 'chicken' as they are only involved with the project but do not have a commitment. Meetings determine what has been achieved during the previous day's sprint and what will be achieved today. The ScrumMaster determines if there are any obstructions to the progress, and if so, these are resolved. After this meeting, the team members meet to discuss various areas in which collaboration is required.

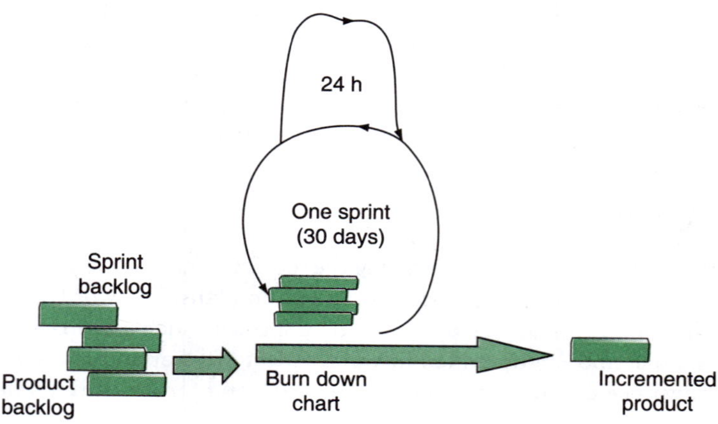

FIGURE 13.13 | The scrum process.

To summarise, during a sprint, the scrum team selects tasks from the sprint backlog, conducts software development activities including analysis, design, coding, testing and implementation for the selected tasks. This is done in an incremental manner by completing one backlog item at a time. The team meets during the daily scrum to review progress, plan activities and collaborate with each other. The burn-down chart is used to track progress and take corrective actions. The output of a sprint is an increment to the software that is potentially shippable.

As compared to requirements elicitation in the Waterfall model, requirements are captured as epics and user stories that are maintained in a product backlog in Scrum. A *user story* describes a functionality that is of value to a user and is usually described in the format: 'As a user...., I wish to...., so that I can.' In other words, it captures who conducts the action, what action is performed, and the reason why the action is performed. The start point for a user story is an *epic*. Epics are the initial set of functionalities defined as part of the product vision. An epic is split into multiple user stories by the product owners in discussion with the business users.

The difference between Scrum and Extreme Programming lies mainly in the diffuse manner in which Scrum proceeds. Requirements are specified at the high level and get focused and tightened only as the development progresses. Furthermore, requirement changes are considered to be inherent in the product evolution process, and after each sprint changes can be quite significant.

13.3 SOFTWARE PROJECT MANAGEMENT

The frameworks or methodologies for software development present a structured manner in which software can be constructed. However, the frameworks do not include a large number of issues that arise as a project unfolds. Some of these issues are common to projects of all kinds, whether for software development or for some other activity, and some are widely different. For software project management, the most substantial issues have to do with finding requirements, managing a team, ensuring the final product works, and trying to stay within budgets of time and money.

The project management issues arise in all contexts of software development, regardless of the particular methodology followed.

13.3.1 Top Management Support

Possibly one of the most important issues for software project management in the current organisational environment is that of obtaining and retaining top management support. Top management buy-in to the project is required from the start, even while the project is being conceptualised. The requisite resources have to be allocated and then supported for the duration of the project.

The distinct advantages of having the top management involved are many. Large and medium-sized projects, in particular, require integration with other systems within the organisation, which the top management can facilitate. The vision and high-level requirements for the software are provided with assistance from the top management, ensuring that the software integrates well with the larger goals of the organisation. Vendor involvement and selection are facilitated with negotiations at the highest levels of the organisation. Also, for the organisation to accept the new system, the top management is indispensable for providing the motive and rationale for the new system, ensuring personnel training and re-assignments.

13.3.2 Team Composition

The team that is involved with the overall design, implementation and maintenance of the system has to be constituted carefully. Teams have to have a balance of skills and experience in project management. Ideally, teams should last the duration of the entire project cycle, however long the cycle may be. Rules for team composition are hard to define, as they are so dependent on context. However, some avoidable issues can be highlighted as they are known to be serious problems.

1. The project leader should be an individual who commits to the entire duration of the project. A replacement should be clearly identified and groomed, in case the leader has to be away for unavoidable circumstances.
2. Skills of team members should be carefully documented and made known. This will ensure that others know who can do what, and so they can call upon them when needed.
3. Team members should be comfortable working with each other. More importantly, if there are known problems with individuals, they should be addressed early in the project by the management.
4. The leader should have overall accountability and responsibility for the project. He/she should be the person one is to turn to if things are not going well. The leader should also be the person to be held responsible if the project fails.

In modern, large organisations, it is often the case that teams are distributed across the globe and work jointly using electronic networks for communication. System building assumes a more difficult form in such situations, although the above critical concerns have to be addressed.

13.3.3 Vendor Selection

Organisations nowadays use vendors extensively to build and help maintain their systems. Vendors are often hard to identify, particularly those with special skills. Industry associations provide directories that list software vendors and their skills. In India, the National Association of Software and Services Companies (NASSCOM) is a well-known association that maintains a database of vendors. This is a good starting point. Most client firms will make it a point to evaluate a vendor thoroughly before they are selected. Some points for evaluation are:

1. The number of projects the vendor has completed of a similar nature in the past. This should also include the size of the projects, the time taken for completion, the kind of technology used and whether the clients were satisfied with the project.
2. The skills base of the vendor depends on: (a) How many employees they have with particular skills, (b) how many have been with the firm for long, (c) what has been the training imparted to them and (d) how have they gained experience.
3. A site visit to the vendor's premises to see the working conditions as well as the assets the vendor has to use for the work. This would indicate how deeply the vendor can commit to the project.
4. For long-duration and large projects, the financial position of the vendor should also be evaluated. Some firms demand bank guarantees from vendors against successful completion of the project. Only financially sound vendors are able to produce such guarantees. As small vendors cannot produce such guarantees, the client organisation has to rely on financial records to assess the vendor.

It is also important that tenders and call-for-proposals floated to ask for bids from vendors should not be biased to favour one or the other vendor. The wording of the tenders has to be vendor-neutral, particularly avoiding words or phrases that identify with a particular vendor.

13.3.4 Project Estimation

At the initiation phase of projects, one of the most difficult problems managers face is that of estimating the size of a project. This entails estimating the resources that will be required by the project and the effort involved. The entire planning for the project is based on these estimates and if they are wrong, the project success is jeopardised.

Project estimates can be over or under. If they are overestimated, it means that the project will eventually take less resources than planned for. If underestimated the projects will take more resources than planned for. Some argue that it is better to overestimate than to underestimate, as excess resources are not a problem but less resources are. For vendors who are bidding for a project, overestimation leads to a high cost estimate for the project thus making their bid potentially uncompetitive. If their bid is an underestimate, which they also win then they will incur higher costs for the project than they had bid for, thus cutting into their profits. For client organisations, overestimation leads to committing resources more than required, thus leading to higher costs and management problems; underestimation leads to scarce resources that have to be procured, possibly at a high expense.

13.3.5 Function Point Analysis

This is a technique to estimate the size and effort required to build an information system. The estimate is given by one measure, called the *function point*, which shows how complex the project is. For example, a project with a function point of 200 can be estimated to be built in a certain number of person hours. This estimate is independent of the platform and software tools used. The function point estimates are based on two broad categories of computing requirements:

1. **Data functions:** It indicate the variety of data input and output needs and how they have to be built.
2. **Transaction functions:** It indicate the processing required within the system. Transactions are categorised into various sorts such as communication, manipulation, writing, etc., and the efforts required for these are then estimated based on some industry benchmarks.

Function point analysis has been shown to be quite effective in providing an estimate of the size and complexity of the system. However, it cannot account for project-based specificities such as changes in the project scope and requirements, skill levels of developers, availability of platforms and so on.

Caselet The Vasa Story

In 1625, the King of Sweden, Gustavus Adolfus, contracted the construction of four massive warships that would give his navy, then at war, an edge over their rivals. The contract was given to a firm of shipbuilders known as Henrik and Arend Hybertsson. Over the next three years the design of the ships underwent many modifications and changes, and eventually a single ship, known as the Vasa, was completed. The ship was launched on 10th August 1628, and after sailing for barely a kilometer, the ship keeled over, from a light gust of wind, and sank in the Stockholm harbour. For its time, the Vasa was considered to be a state-of-the-art ship, with two dung decks, as all other ships had only one, and would have been the pride of the King's fleet. The ship was recovered from under water over 300 years later and scholars have since examined why it sank so abruptly and on its maiden voyage. The answers are varied and have much to do with project management.

Initially, the King ordered four ships to be built, with different keel lengths. Once the shipbuilders assessed the amount of timber they had, they planned to build only three ships. Subsequently, the King lost many ships in a deadly sea battle, and insisted that the two smaller ships be built on a priority basis to replace the lost ships. As the construction proceeded, the King changed his mind several times, to have more armaments, more guns, more gun decks and different keel lengths. The changes in the requirements are depicted in the figure.

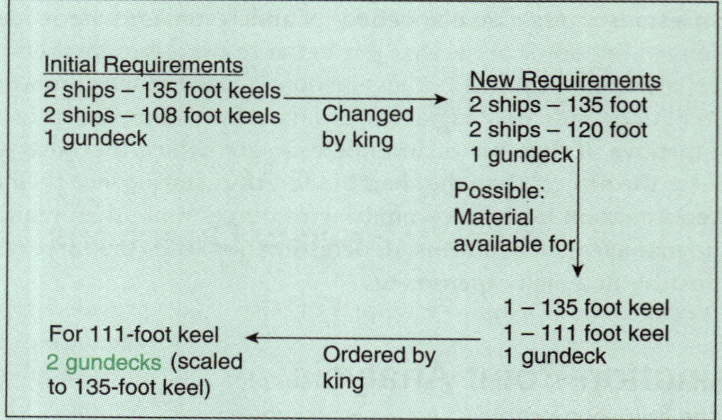

The changes in design and specifications were not documented, and no sketches, drawings or measurements were made on paper. The shipbuilders relied on rough measures and approximations to construct the ships. Once a single ship was settled on, owing to the many changes in the design, the centre of gravity of the ship was raised and it became unstable. The instability was one of its major flaws. Other challenges in the construction of the ship were also many. The master shipwright, Henrik Hybertsson, passed away after a prolonged illness almost two years after the ship had been commissioned and construction had begun. The task of constructing the ship was now passed on to his successors, whom he had briefed during his illness, but who were unaware of the details of the project and had to make many adjustments. Further, owing to the pressure of completing the task, many workers were pressed onto the project, and it became difficult to coordinate activities.

Once the ship was ready, it was tested for stability and sea-worthiness. Thirty men were asked to run from side to side in the middle of the ship. The Vasa began to rock violently and the test was halted. The Admiral of the Swedish navy was presented and saw the test, but he deemed it important to halt the eventual, formal launch of the Vasa. The King had demanded heavy ornamentation on the main deck of the ship, with the use of gold and other heavy metals, which further raised the centre of gravity of the ship.

Once the Vasa sank, a judicial inquiry was held and nobody was found guilty and held responsible. The Vasa story has many lessons on project management, including managing changing requirements, excessive schedule pressure, lack of formal documentation, neglect of test results and dealing with the loss of the project manager.

Chapter Glossary

Business process Any business activity that involves movement of information between people, groups or departments.

Business analyst A person who has the responsibility of understanding and documenting business processes.

Flow diagrams A high-level illustration of tasks and the movement of data.

Flowcharts A diagram that depicts the logic and flow control of a computer program.

Data flow diagrams A high-level diagram that illustrates data flows between people, processes and data storage.

Use cases A technique for conducting business process analysis that involves descriptions of tasks, people and information that flows between them.

Prototype A scaled down version of a software program that is used for analysis of business processes.

Stub testing A way of testing software that involves examining how responses from independent modules will impact the complete package.

Beta test Testing of software that is nearly complete, has all the features and can be conducted under conditions similar to the real environment for which it has been created.

Parallel cutover Releasing a new software in an environment where the old methods of doing tasks are also kept alive.

Scope creep Increase in the requirements of a software module, much after the requirements phase is over.

Unit testing A method of software testing that involves testing independent modules extensively.

Review Questions

1. What is a business process? Give two examples of business processes.
2. Review the elements of a flowchart. Then draw a simple flowchart for the following problem: A customer sends an email requesting some information. If the request is about a product, send a product brochure to the customer by email. If the request is for something else, refer to the request to a representative by forwarding the email.
3. Review the elements of a data flow diagram. How are they different from a Flowchart?
4. Draw a data flow diagram for the following problem:

   A system at a library, called the Library Information System, allows a user to check out a book. When the user requests to borrow a book, the book details are provided to the system, along with the user's details. The date of the checkout and the due date are printed out and given to the user. The system then stores all the details in a file.
5. When are use cases applied? What are some basic elements of a Use Case?
6. Why has software engineering assumed importance in the modern context?
7. Identify the stages of the Waterfall Model and describe their main goals?
8. Describe some limitations of the Waterfall Model?
9. What is Rapid Prototyping and how is it an improvement over the Waterfall Model?
10. How are agile methods useful? Why are they preferred over the Waterfall Model?

Research Questions

1. What are the different kinds of tools used for software development using the Waterfall Model? Some are mentioned in the text, can you find more?
2. Identify some weaknesses with the agile methods? Are they suitable for all types of projects? Are they suitable for all types of firms?
3. Visit a library in your institution (or in your neighbourhood). If they use an information system for lending out books - try to draw DFDs to analyse their lending processes. Try to capture as much detail as possible. If the library does not have an information system, then sit with the librarian to find out what kind of system would they need and draw DFDs for the same.
4. Search the internet or in your library for information on systems development projects. How many of these were successful and how many failed? How is project failure measured?

Further Reading

1. Gomaa, H. (2011) *Software Modeling and Design: UML, Use Cases, Patterns, and Software Architectures*, Cambridge University Press, Cambridge.
2. Beck, M. (1999) Embracing Change with Extreme Programming, *IEEE Computer*, **32**(10).
3. Boehm, B. (2006) A View of 20th and 21st Century Software Engineering. Proceedings of the 28th International Conference on Software Engineering, ACM, New York, USA.
4. Nerur, S., Mahapatra, R. and Mangalaraj, G. (2005) Challenges of Migrating to Agile Methods. *Communications of the ACM*, **48**(5), 72–78.
5. Islam, M.S. and Grönlund, Å. (2011). Factors influencing the adoption of mobile phones among the farmers

in Bangladesh: Theories and practices, *International Journal on Advances in ICT for Emerging Regions*, **04**(01), 3–13.

6. Islam, M.S. and Grönlund, Å. (2011). Bangladesh calling: Farmers' technology use practices as a driver for development. *Journal of Information Technology for Development*, **17**(2), 95–111.

CHAPTER 14

Managing Data Resources

Learning Objectives

After completing this chapter, you will be able to:

- Understand the need for data management
- Get an overview of database concepts
- Learn about database design
- Get an overview of data warehouses

Data as a resource of any organisation has gained critical importance in recent years. It has to be managed carefully with the objective of ensuring access, reliability and security. Databases consist of simple structures such as fields, records and tables. When assembled within an architecture, these simple structures provide an immensely useful yet manageable resource for organisations. There are many types of database designs, the most popular being that of tables related to each other, called relational database. Commercial implementations of such databases are called database management systems (DBMS) that have many features to easily create, update, query and manage data. All such systems rely on SQL, a computer language that allows easy definition and manipulation of tables and relations.

Modern database requirements are modelled by entity-relationship (ER) diagrams that provide a high-level user view of a database structure. This view is then translated into the actual design, called schema, of the database. When organisations accumulate large masses of data, the focus shifts from simply using the data for transactions to that of using the data for help in decision making. Data is separated out into special tables called warehouses that are then used for analysis. Big Data is the form of data that has massive volume, velocity and variety, and is often used for organisations for key insights.

MIND MAP OF CHAPTER TOPICS

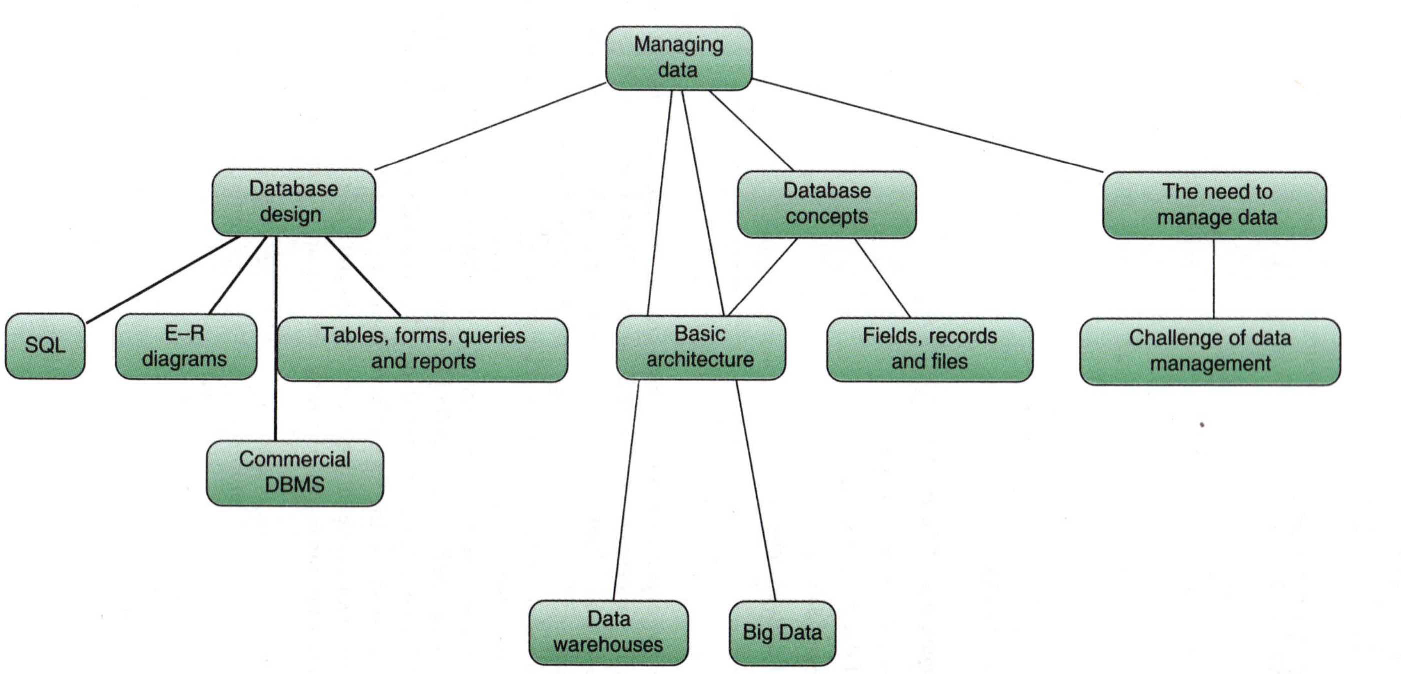

CASE STUDY: UNIQUE IDENTIFICATION NUMBER IN INDIA

For citizens of India, mobility from one state to another is a problem. If one moves, say, from Uttar Pradesh to Karnataka, then in the new state of residence, one will have to obtain a new driver's licence, open a new bank account, obtain a new permit for cooking gas cylinders, get a new electricity connection, re-register an old vehicle in the new state, and, if needed, get a new ration card. This is because these documents cannot be transferred easily from Uttar Pradesh to Karnataka, as there are no legal provisions to do so. As these documents require considerable time and effort while getting them for the first time, applying and waiting to get them a second time is a huge waste of effort.

It is partially to address this problem of transfer of documents that the Government of India initiated the Unique Identification Number (UID) scheme. Under this scheme, every citizen of India will be provided a unique number that will be backed by an infrastructure to verify and authenticate the number. A special organisation, called Unique Identification Authority of India (UIDAI), was created in 2009 for this purpose, and was charged with issuing the UIDs to citizens. The UIDAI will eventually provide a unique 12-digit number to all citizens of India with the assurance that the number is unique (each number is associated with a unique citizen), is verifiable and is valid across India.

Many citizens of India already have several documents that provide them with unique numbers:

1. Most have a Voter Registration Card that has a unique ID.
2. Many citizens have an official driver's licence issued by their state, which has a unique number.
3. Many citizens also have a passport, issued by the Government of India, which has a unique number.
4. Many citizens have a card for income tax payment (called the PAN card) that uses a unique number.
5. Many citizens also have a ration card that also uses a unique number.

However, not all citizens have a need for or use all these cards. For instance, the number of income tax payers in India is a small fraction of the population (as agricultural income is not taxed and a bulk of India's population relies on agriculture). Furthermore, most citizens do not have a passport, as they don't need to travel across borders, and many do not have a driver's licence either, as they do not own a motorised vehicle. The ration card is meant for people below the poverty line, but can be issued to any citizen of India. Thus, most or all of these cards that provide a unique number are not available or are of little real use to all citizens of India. It is in this context that the UID becomes important.

An UID number can provide a basis for uniting these disparate identification projects under a common umbrella. Thus, a citizen who has a PAN card and also a driver's licence can be seen, through the unique number, to be the same person. This will reduce redundancy in the issuing of unique numbers as well as control fraud and misuse of the numbers.

As envisaged, the UIDAI will issue a unique number to citizens based on biometric authentication. This number is called *Aadhaar*. With a scan of ten fingerprints and the iris, each citizen will receive a unique 12-digit number. Aadhaar can be used by banks, or the tax authorities, or schools, or the ration card agencies to issue cards or validation documents to citizens. The idea is that if a citizen presents a bank card to a merchant for some commercial transaction, the merchant can verify that the card belongs to the particular individual by checking against the UIDAI database. This verification service will be made available at a reasonable cost by the UIDAI.

Aadhaar, in this sense, becomes what in database terminology is called a *primary key*, a unique identifier for a record that can be used across the database and across applications without worry of duplication. Various agencies like banks, the tax authority, the passport agency, the motor vehicles department and the public distribution system can then use Aadhaar to issue their own verification and authentication documents. A citizen can move from one part of the country to another, and with Aadhaar he/she can retrieve or use his/her card anywhere and be assured that his/her identity is authenticated.

The role envisaged for Aadhaar is best captured by the Chairman of the UIDAI, Mr. Nandan Nilekani, 'The name Aadhaar communicates the fundamental role of the number issued by the UIDAI the number as a universal identity infrastructure, a foundation over which public and private agencies can build services and applications that benefit residents across India'.

1. Aadhaar's guarantee of uniqueness and centralised, online identity verification would be the basis for building these multiple services and applications, and facilitating greater connectivity to markets.
2. Aadhaar would also give any resident the ability to access these services and resources, anytime, anywhere in the country.
3. Aadhaar can, for example, provide the identity infrastructure for ensuring financial inclusion across the country - banks can link the unique number to a bank account for every resident, and use the online identity authentication to allow residents to access the account from anywhere in the country.
4. Aadhaar would also be a foundation for the effective enforcement of individual rights. A clear registration and recognition of the individual's identity with the state is necessary to implement their rights - to employment, education, food, etc. The number, by ensuring such registration and recognition of individuals, would help the state deliver these rights.

Source: uidai.gov.in (accessed on June 2011).

Aadhaar in India is similar to a unique number given to citizens in other countries. In the USA, all citizens are required to have a Social Security Number (SSN) that was originally designed to provide them with social security - such as pension, medical care, job-loss compensation and so on - but it is now used for many different purposes such as for opening a bank account, obtaining a driver's licence, getting a credit card, being registered for medical insurance, enrolling in school or college and so on. Such schemes for providing social security, along with a unique number, are prevalent in European countries too, such as Spain and France. In all these countries, the unique number is used for many transactions other than social security, including those of credit card purchases, property purchases and college enrolment.

The Aadhaar scheme has come in for a fair measure of criticism. For a country as diverse and complex as India, critics argues, such a scheme is not suitable. Some argue that the Aadhaar scheme will link many vital sources of information about individuals under a common source and thus compromise individual privacy. Those with dubious intentions can snoop into online and computerised records of individuals and have access to a vast store of information, something that is not possible without a primary key. Others contend that, in the case of poor and marginal citizens, obtaining and maintaining such a number will become an additional burden, and instead of helping them, it will further impede their ability to make a living and function effectively. Still others argue that Aadhaar will become another tool in the hands of a corrupt and power-hungry bureaucracy, which will extract further rents from those unable to understand the value of this scheme and how it can be used effectively.

14.1 THE NEED FOR DATA MANAGEMENT

14.1.1 History of Data Use

In the early years of computing when programs were written on large mainframe computers, the practice was to include the data required for a computation within the program. For example, if a program computed the income tax deductions for personnel in an organisation, the data regarding the personnel and their income was maintained within the program itself. If changes were required, say, when a new employee joined the organisation, the entire program for income tax calculations would have to be modified, not just the data alone. Changes to data were difficult as the entire program had to be changed, and further, the data was not available to other programs.

With advances in programming languages, this situation changed and data was maintained in separate files that different programs could use. This improved the ability to share data, but it introduced problems of data updating and integrity. If one program changed the data, other programs had to be informed of this development and their logic had to be altered accordingly.

A start in organising data came with the idea of the relational data storage model, put forward by British scientist E.F. Codd in 1970. Codd, then working with IBM in the USA, showed how data could be stored in structured form in files that were linked to each other, and could be used by many programs with simple rules of modification. This idea was taken up by commercial database software, like Oracle, and became the standard for data storage and use.

14.2 CHALLENGE OF DATA MANAGEMENT

Consider the following facts:

1. Researchers estimate that the total amount of data stored in the world is of the order of 295 exabytes or 295 billion gigabytes. This estimate is based on an assessment of analog and digital storage technologies from 1986 to 2007. The report (by M. Hilbert and P. Lopez appeared in *Science Express* in February 2011) states that paper-based storage of data, which was about 33% in 1986, had shrunk to only about 0.07% in 2007, as now most of the data is stored in digital form. Data is mostly stored on computer hard disks or on optical storage devices.
2. The consulting firm IDC estimated (in 2008) that the annual growth in data takes place in two forms:
   (a) *Structured:* Here data is created and maintained in databases and follows a certain data model (explained in Section 14.4.4). The growth in structured data is about 22% annually (compounded)
   (b) *Unstructured:* Here data remains in an informal manner. The growth in unstructured data is about 62% annually.
3. The large online auction firm eBay has a data warehouse of more than 6 petabytes (6 million gigabytes), and adds about 150 billion rows per day to its database tables (in 2010).

The above examples highlight the incredible amounts of data that are being created and stored around the world. Managing this data so that it could be used effectively presents a strong challenge to database systems: the systems not only have to store the data but also have to make it available almost instantly whenever needed, allow users to search through the data efficiently, and also ensure that the data is safe and uncorrupted. Different aspects of the need for database systems are discussed in the sections given below.

14.2.1 Data Independence

Databases allow data pertaining to an activity or a domain to be maintained independently. This independence means that the data is stored in separate files in a structured manner, and the creation and updating of the data is done independent of its uses. For instance, in a college, a database of students is updated when a student joins or leaves the college, changes address, changes phone number and so on. This is independent of how the data is used by programs for course registration or for the library. Furthermore, the programs and applications that use the data are not aware of where and how the data is maintained; they only need to know how to make simple calls to access the data.

14.2.2 Reduced Data Redundancy

One goal of databases is to reduce data redundancy. Data redundancy refers to the duplication of data in different tables. If data on students is maintained in two or three different databases in the college then for one change, say in a student's mobile phone number, all the databases have to be changed. Reduced data redundancy ensures that minimal storage is used for the data. With the rapid increase in data over time, conserving space is an important management challenge.

14.2.3 Data Consistency

It is important that data users have access to consistent data, that is, the data is the same regardless of the application through which the user accesses it. Consistency implies that the integrity of the data is maintained (the data has not been changed or corrupted in a manner unknown to the system); the data is valid, which means that the data is the correct one to use for the moment; and the data is accurate, which means that the data being used is the one that was designed to be used. Consistency requires careful management of data updating, deletion, copying and security.

14.2.4 Data Access

Data stored in databases must be accessible efficiently. Very large databases, such as those maintained by eBay, have to be managed in a way that when users search within them, their results should be available within a matter of seconds. A search in eBay results in a response within a few seconds, even though the system has to search through billions of records. Furthermore, the response from the database has to be presented to the user in a manner that is easy to read and understand, which requires further processing.

14.2.5 Data Administration

Data administration entails deciding who can *create*, *read*, *update* or *delete* data. Many organisations have strict controls over who can create or delete data fields or tables. This is determined by the needs of the organisation and the roles defined for database administrators and users. Read access is usually provided to those who need to only see and use the data, but not modify or change it in any way. Update access is also carefully restricted to those who have the rights and privileges to do so. Modern database systems enable sophisticated ways in which these four functions can be enabled or disabled for users and administrators.

14.2.6 Managing Concurrency

A serious challenge for modern databases, especially those used for e-commerce applications, is that of managing concurrency. Data is often maintained on many servers, distributed across a wide geography. Concurrency entails ensuring that changes or updates to a particular element in a table are reflected across all the distributed servers where users access the data. This is an element of managing consistency, particularly for distributed databases.

14.2.7 Managing Security

A substantial threat to modern databases is from crackers and unauthorised users. Database systems have to provide a layer of security, over and above the security systems in place at the organisation, which ensures protection across transactions and all administration tasks.

This also means that internal tampering and mischief with data is carefully monitored and controlled.

14.2.8 Recovery from Crashes

Databases are crucial to the internal working of an organisation - they are both a resource and an asset. With the high levels of transactions happening within the IS of organisations, it is imperative that the data is secured against failure. Modern database systems provide a sophisticated system of backup, mirroring and recovery that allows rapid recovery from crashed servers.

14.2.9 Application Development

Databases enable applications to be developed using the facilities of data management provided by them. E-commerce sites, for example, create a web presence that includes search, display, selection, sale and payment for products, which rely on databases that provide all the relevant data, and store data, for the transactions. Applications may be local to a function or department or shared across many departments, and they may share data from the databases. Database systems provide special languages by which their data can be manipulated, and hence can be used by application developers.

14.3 DATABASE CONCEPTS

A database is a collection of files that have stored data. The files and the data within them are related in some manner - either they are from the same domain, the same function, the same firm or some other category. The files in the database are created according to the needs of the function or department and are maintained with data that is relevant for the applications the department runs.

An example of a database in an organisation is an 'Employee' database. This will correspond to the human resources function of the organisation. The 'Employee' database may contain files related to employee details, their employment history, their benefits details, their leave history, their family details, their medical compensation details and so on. The files are related to the employee concept, although they contain different data, depending on the applications that will need the data. Computations regarding medical reimbursements, for instance, will read data from the files related to the employee's status, benefits and medical history.

Consider another example of a 'Product' database. This may contain files related to the types of products, the details about product features, the prices and history of prices of products, the regional and seasonal sales figures of products and the details of product designs. Such files could be used by the manufacturing department to determine production schedules, by the marketing department to determine sales campaigns or by the finance department to determine overhead allocations.

14.3.1 Fields, Records and Files

A file in a database consists of particular spaces, called structures, in which data is maintained. The basic structure of a file is called a *field*. A field is a defined space, of specific dimensions, in which data is placed. Data is read from and can be deleted from fields. When defining or designing a field, the contents of the field have to be specified exactly. For instance, if the field has to hold the date of birth of an employee, it has to be specified how the data will be stored (in dd-mm-yyyy format or mm-dd-yy format), and what kind of characters (numbers, in this case) will be permitted. There are several other dimensions that specify a field and are held in a *metadata* file. (A metadata file contains details about how data is stored in files, and provides information on how the data can be used and managed.)

A collection of fields is called a record. Each record is like a row in a spreadsheet; it consists of a pre-defined number of fields. In most cases, the sizes of the fields are fixed; this ensures that the total size of a record is also fixed. Records are a collection of fields that have meaning in the context of the application. For example, consider the two records of a student file given in Table 14.1.

Table 14.1 | Two Records of a Student File

Aadhaar Number	First Name	Last Name	Year of Birth	Major
234577643239	Aamir	Khan	1968	Physics
–	–	–	–	–

Table 14.1 shows five fields that define a record. Each field contains data pertaining to some aspect of a student - roll number (Aadhaar number in this case), first name, last name, year of birth and the subject in which the student is majoring. The data in each field is written in characters or numbers. For each record, there should be at least one field that uniquely identifies the record. This ensures that even if there are two students with exactly the same name (say Aamir Khan), with the same year of birth and the same major, then there is at least one field that will distinguish the records of the two students. In Table 14.1, Aadhaar number is the unique identifier. In other cases this could be an employee number, a tax number or even a random number generated by the system. This unique field is called a *primary key*.

A table is contained in a file (see Fig. 14.1). Each table may contain a few records or a very large number of records. A database consists of many files. Modern database systems allow table sizes to include billions of records. Furthermore, very large tables may be split and stored on different servers.

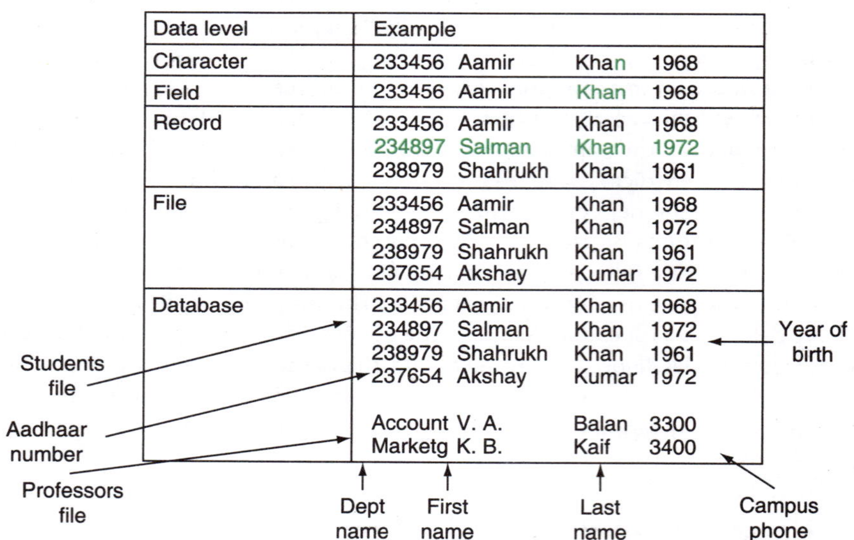

FIGURE 14.1 | The basic elements of a database – fields; records and files.

In relational databases, the tables are related to each other. These relations allow data to be linked according to some logic and then extracted from the tables. A detailed example of this is provided in a later section.

14.3.2 Basic Architecture

Databases may be organised and used in many different ways. The most basic use is as a *personal database*. Individual users create databases for their personal use in organisations or at home. A personal database may be on a personal computer at office, on a mobile phone or on a tablet

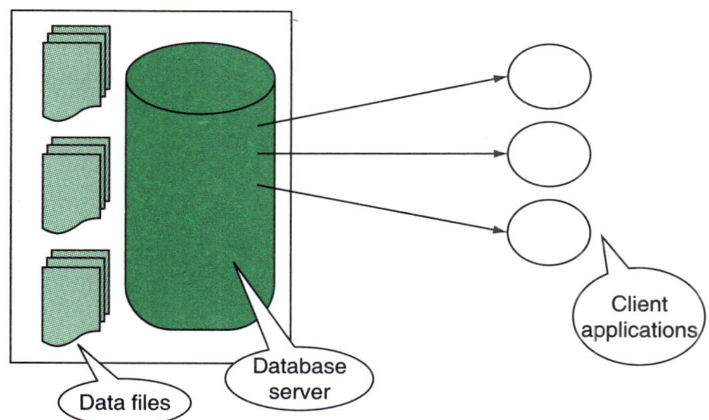

FIGURE 14.2 | Client–server architecture of a database.

computer. The data in these databases is fed and updated by the user, and is principally used by him/her. For instance, a contacts database on a mobile phone is a personal database. All the data is entered and used by the mobile phone user. The design of the database is not created by the user (such databases are often provided as off-the-shelf applications), but the use and maintenance is only by the user.

Personal databases are highly tuned to the needs of the user. They are not meant to be shared. These databases also cannot be shared, as they reside on personal devices; and this is a limitation of these systems.

Workgroup databases or function databases are designed to be shared across employees in an organisation, either belonging to a group or to a functional department. Such a database is maintained on a central computer, along with applications relevant for the group or department. Users access and update the data on the central database from their local computers.

Enterprise or organisational databases are accessed by all members of the organisation. These are typically organised in the client–server mode (see Fig. 14.2). A central database server provides database capabilities to different applications that reside on other computers. These client applications interact with the database server to draw on data services, whereas the database server is managed independently. An advantage of these database servers is that they can be made highly secure, with strong access restrictions, and can also be backed up carefully to recover from crashes.

While designing client–server databases, a prime issue to be addressed is – where the processing should take place. If data processing has to be done on the client from, say, three tables then these tables have to be moved across the network to the client, which should have enough computing capacity to do the processing. If, on the other hand, the computing is done on the server then the clients have to send processing requests to the server and await the results, and this puts a lot of load on the server. Clients such as mobile phones or personal computers often do not have the processing capacity to deal with large amounts of data, so the processing is invariably left to the server.

The architecture often used in enterprises is referred to as three-tier architecture (see Fig. 14.3). Here the clients interact with application servers, which then call upon database servers for their data needs. Here the load of processing for applications and for data is spread across two sets of servers, thus enabling greater efficiency.

Databases may be centralised or decentralised within organisations. Centralised databases are designed on the client–server model, with a two-tier or three-tier architecture. Decentralised or distributed databases have tables distributed across many servers on a network. The servers may be geographically distributed, but for the applications they appear as a single entity. One type of distributed server has the entire database replicated across many servers. This is called a *homogeneous* database (see Fig. 14.4). Those users who are close to a particular server are able to

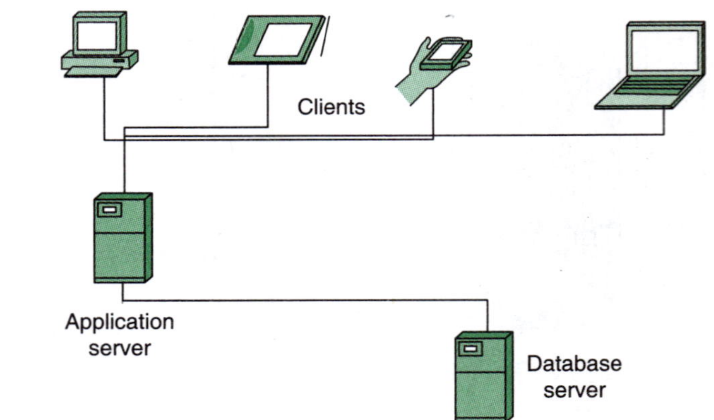

FIGURE 14.3 | Three-tier database architecture.

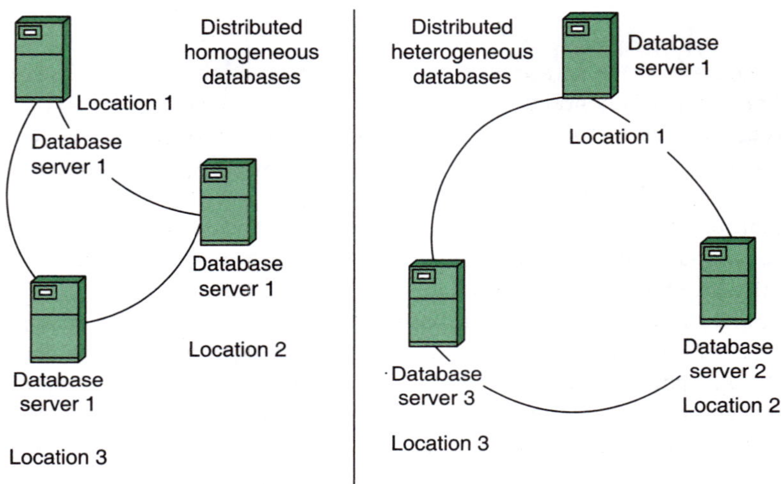

FIGURE 14.4 | Distributed databases with homogeneous and heterogeneous architectures.

access data from that particular one, whereas others access data from other, physically closer servers. When data is changed on any one server, it is also changed on the others.

Distributed databases can also be federated in nature. It means the databases across the network are not the same; they are *heterogeneous*. In such an architecture, when application servers draw on the databases, special algorithms pull together the required data from diverse servers and present a consolidated picture. This architecture is useful where the data entry and management of servers is particular to a region. For example, multinational banks use federated databases as their databases in different countries operate on different currencies and exchange criteria, and rely on local data. For applications requiring global data, the applications use special logic for analysing the disparate data.

A special class of software is used to connect disparate databases and these are known as *middleware*. As databases can have different data structures for the same kind of data, the middleware software allows the databases to read and write data to and from each other. For example, the data field for 'student name' may have a space for 30 characters in one database and 40 characters in another. The fact that they are referring to the same concept is captured by the middleware that enables the translation from one to the other. The middleware is also used by the Application Layer to read and use data from many databases. In modern web-centric applications, the middleware plays a major role in allowing the use of distributed databases by application servers.

14.4 DATABASE DESIGN

Among different types of databases, relational databases are the most widely used. Relational databases consist of tables, or files, linked together by 'relations' that are specified according to the needs of the application that will use the data. Such a relational design has a mathematical basis, as was shown by E.F. Codd in 1970, and can be manipulated to extract and input data into the database efficiently, while ensuring integrity and consistency.

Other types of databases include the hierarchical, object-orient, network and object-relational types. The *hierarchical model* of organising data involves creating a structure in which data is maintained in a tree-like manner (the 'tree' is actually an inverted tree with the root at the top and branches below), where the topmost structure is the root from which the lower structures inherit values and properties. This model is not widely used now, but there do exist certain applications where it is highly suitable. The *object-oriented model* relies on structures that are objects, which include data and procedures that act on data. Object-oriented databases are designed to work well with object-orient programming languages, which are popular high-level languages, and can efficiently integrate the database with the application. The *network model* places data objects and relations in a graph-like structure. This model too is used in special applications. The *object-relational model* enables the use of objects in relational tables. Data is maintained in objects, and these are related to allow reading and updating of the data with specified procedures. Many modern database systems support this model, and it is gaining popularity.

Although there are several competing models, the relational database model remains the most popular. The rest of this section focuses on the design of relational databases.

The first design issue for a relational database is that of designing the tables that will hold the data. Tables consist of records, which are constituted by fields. The manner in which tables are constructed depends on the DBMS being used. Most modern DBMS allow tables to be created using a visual interface, with tool bars and drop-down menus. However, tables can be created by using the SQL language also. Figure 14.5 shows the opening window of an open source DBMS called Base (which is part of the Open Office suite).

Figure 14.5 shows a sample database called 'Classic Models'. The database is for a firm that makes and sells toy models of classic cars, planes and ships. The data is about customers, products, employees, payments, offices and orders. (This database is freely distributed under the Eclipse Public License, as part of the Eclipse Birt project. Details can be found at www.eclipse.org/birt)

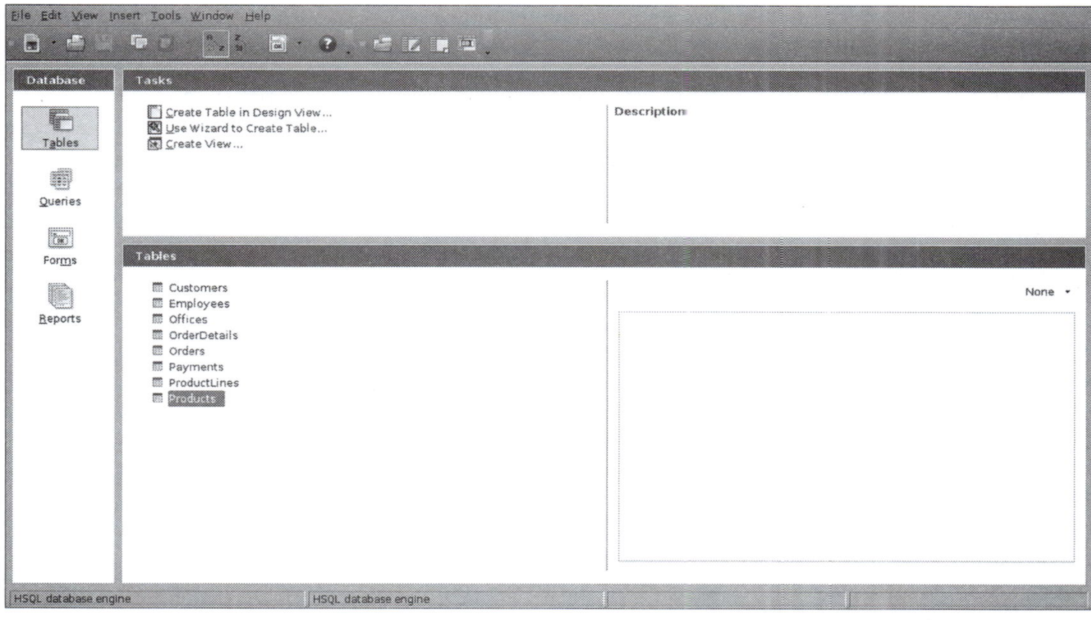

FIGURE 14.5 | The opening screen of the base DBMS showing the 'Classic Models' database.

14.4.1 Elements of Databases

Using the Classig Models database, we can now understand how the elements of a database can be created in a DBMS. The following sections show how tables, forms, queries and reports are created in the DBMS.

As is seen in Fig. 14.5, the DBMS has four categories of objects in the left panel:

1. Tables.
2. Queries.
3. Forms.
4. Reports.

14.4.1.1 *Tables*

A table is the basic data structure that consists of fields and records. When the 'Tables' feature is selected in the left of the screen, the system shows all the tables already in the DBMS. Each table has been designed to include certain fields. The design of the table can be seen by selecting any table and then opening it in Edit mode (this can be reached by a menu that appears on right-clicking the mouse, or through the 'Edit' menu item on the top of the screen). Figure 14.6 shows the Customers table in the design view.

The screen (Fig. 14.6) lists all the fields, also called attributes, of the table. Some fields are specified as numbers (such as integers) whereas others are specified as text characters. The first field is called the `customerNumber` and it is declared to be a field type of 'integer'. This implies that the `customerNumber` field will contain only integer-valued numbers. If any other type of data is placed in the field (say some text values), this will constitute an error, and the DBMS will not allow it to be stored. In the lower half of the screen is a window in which the properties of the field can be provided. For instance, the length of the field, its default value and how the data has to be formatted are specified. The properties also specify whether a value for this field has to be supplied or it can be left blank.

The properties of all the fields are similarly specified. The system treats each field differently. For example, for mathematical calculations, only number-based field types will be used. A field containing data about, say, prices will be a numeric field, whose values can be added, subtracted, etc.

14.4.1.2 *Forms*

Once a table is designed, it can be populated with data. One way to write data into tables is by using a *form*. A form is a user interface of a table (or set of tables) that allows specific users to enter or change data in tables (Fig. 14.7). Forms can be designed using the graphical interface of a DBMS. Forms are always built on top of a table or several tables. Once the Forms item is selected in the Base screen, it shows that a form can be created by using a wizard or it can be designed directly. A form allows a particular user, or set of users, to update data regarding some aspects of a table, and nothing else. For example, in the Customers table, one form (Fig. 14.8) can allow some users to only change the address and phone numbers of the customer and nothing else.

14.4.1.3 *Queries*

As a form enables entry of data into tables, a query allows reading of data from tables. At its most basic level, a query allows selection of data from a table according to some criteria. For example, the Customers data table can be queried to extract the names, phone numbers and credit limit of customers from Finland. The design for this query can be done with a wizard in Base, as shown in Fig. 14.9. Figure 14.10 shows the table that results from running the query on the Customers table.

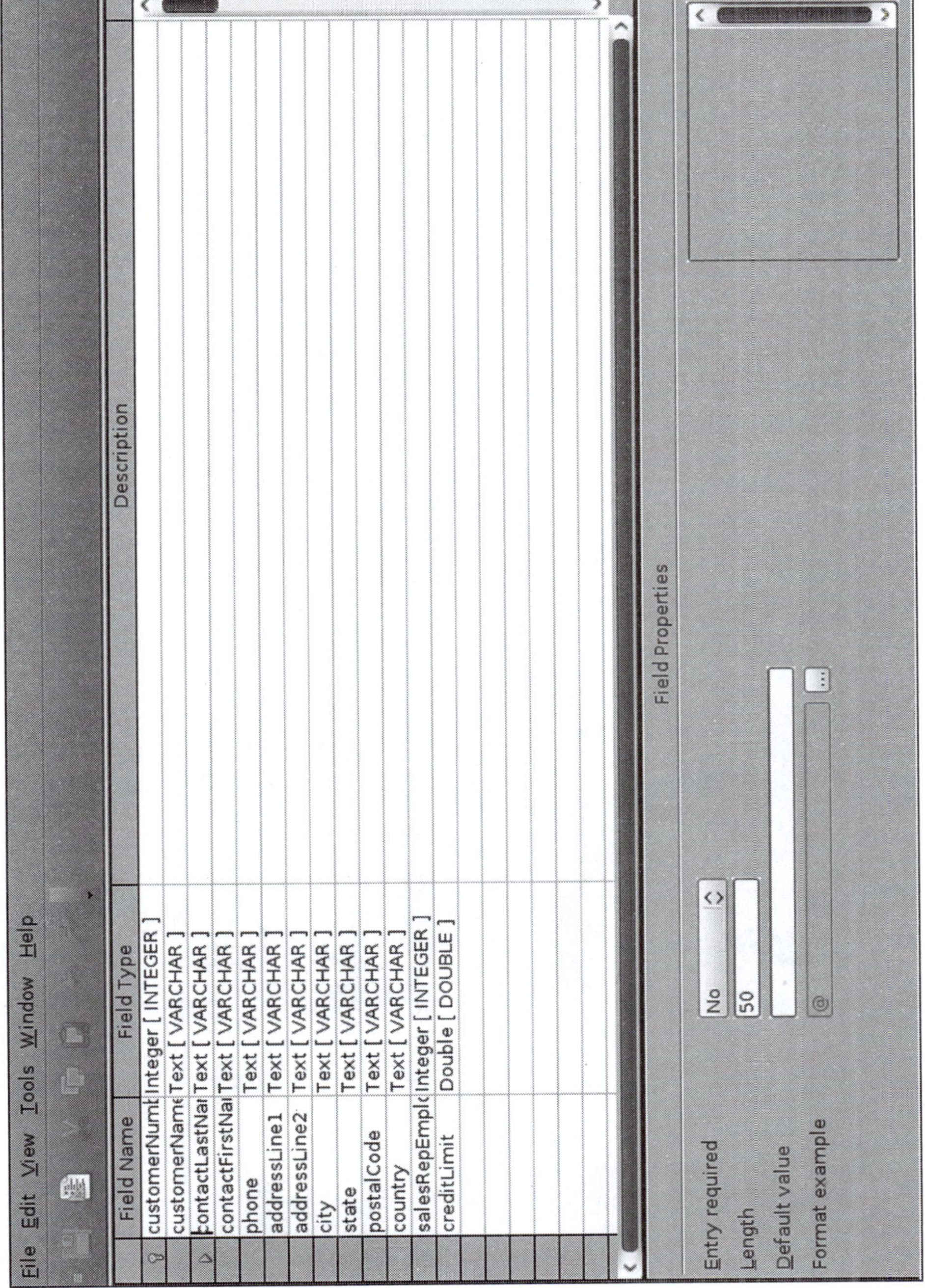

FIGURE 14.6 | The design view of the customers table.

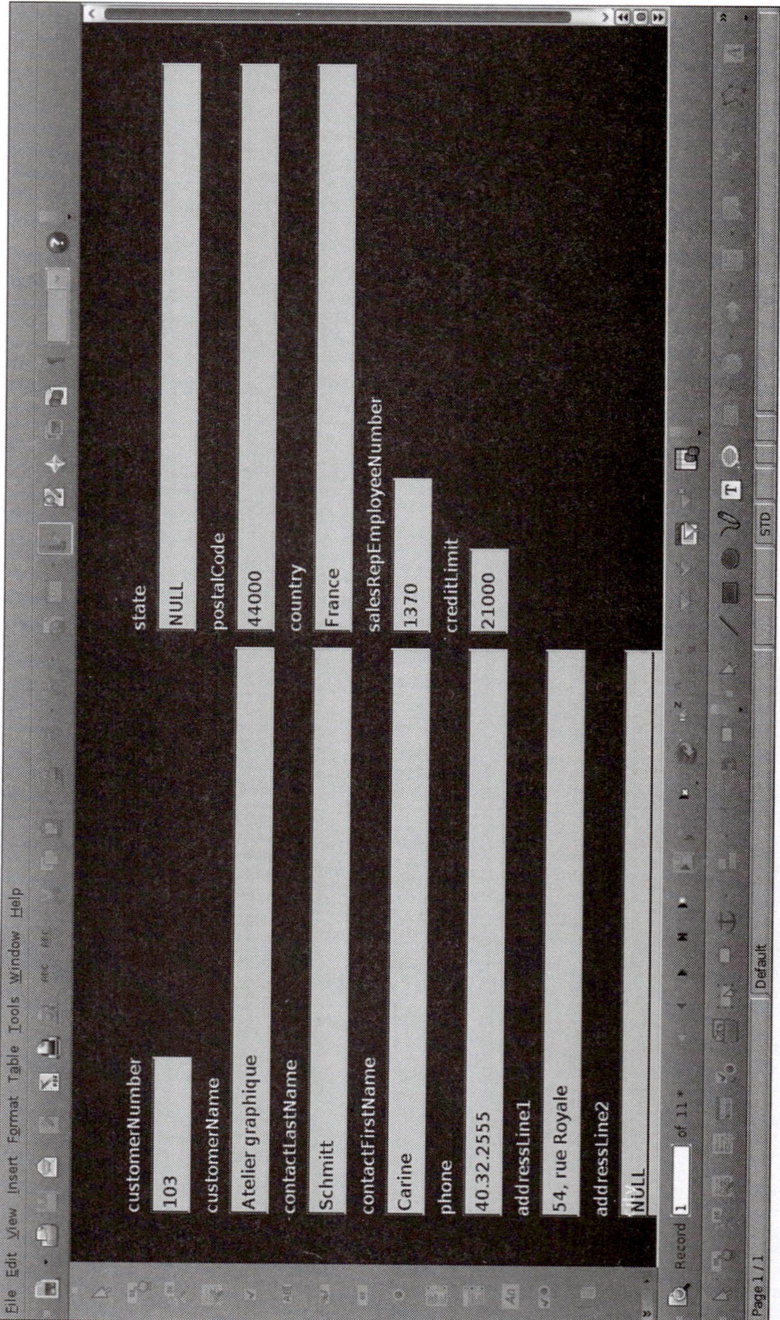

FIGURE 14.7 | Form for entering data in the customers table.

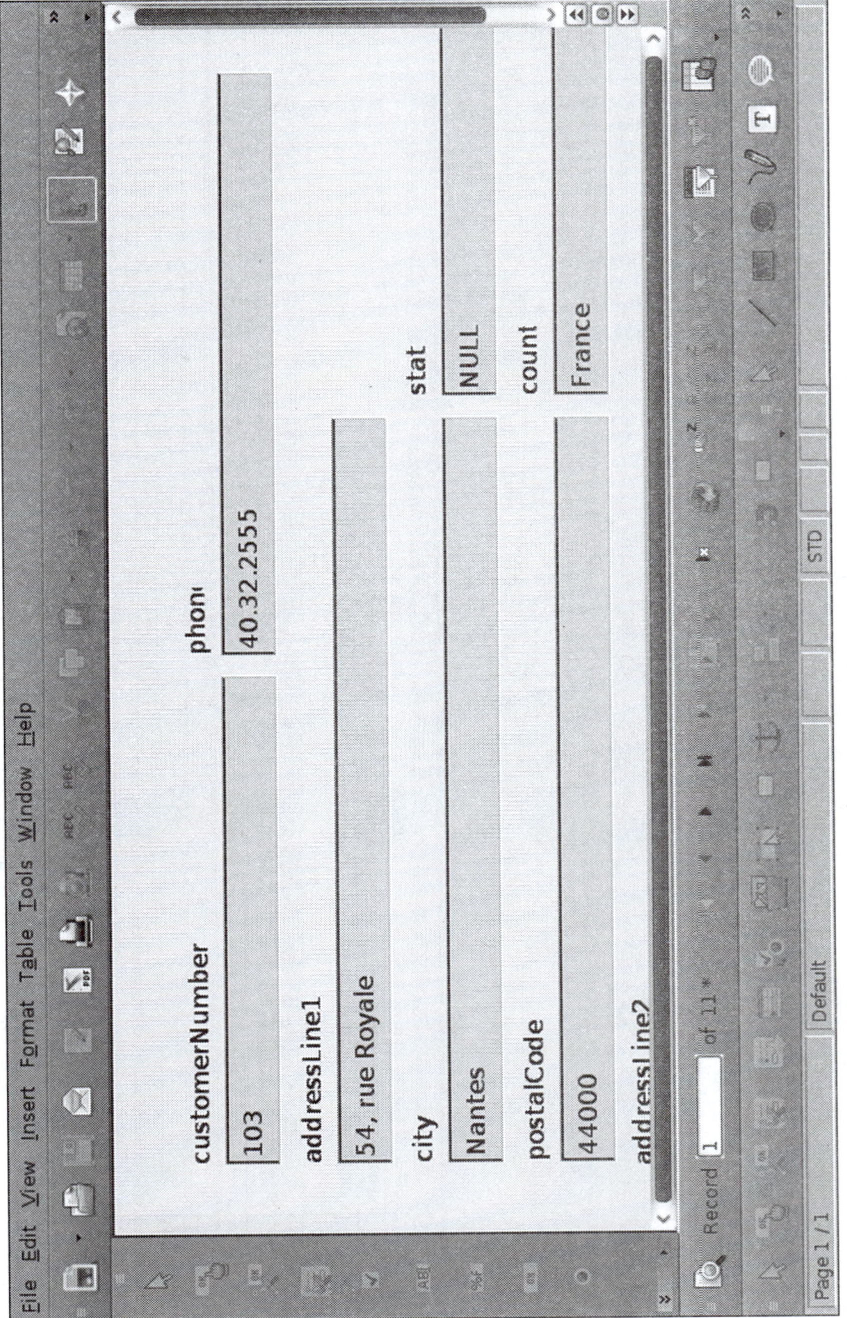

FIGURE 14.8 | Form for changing data in some fields of the customers table.

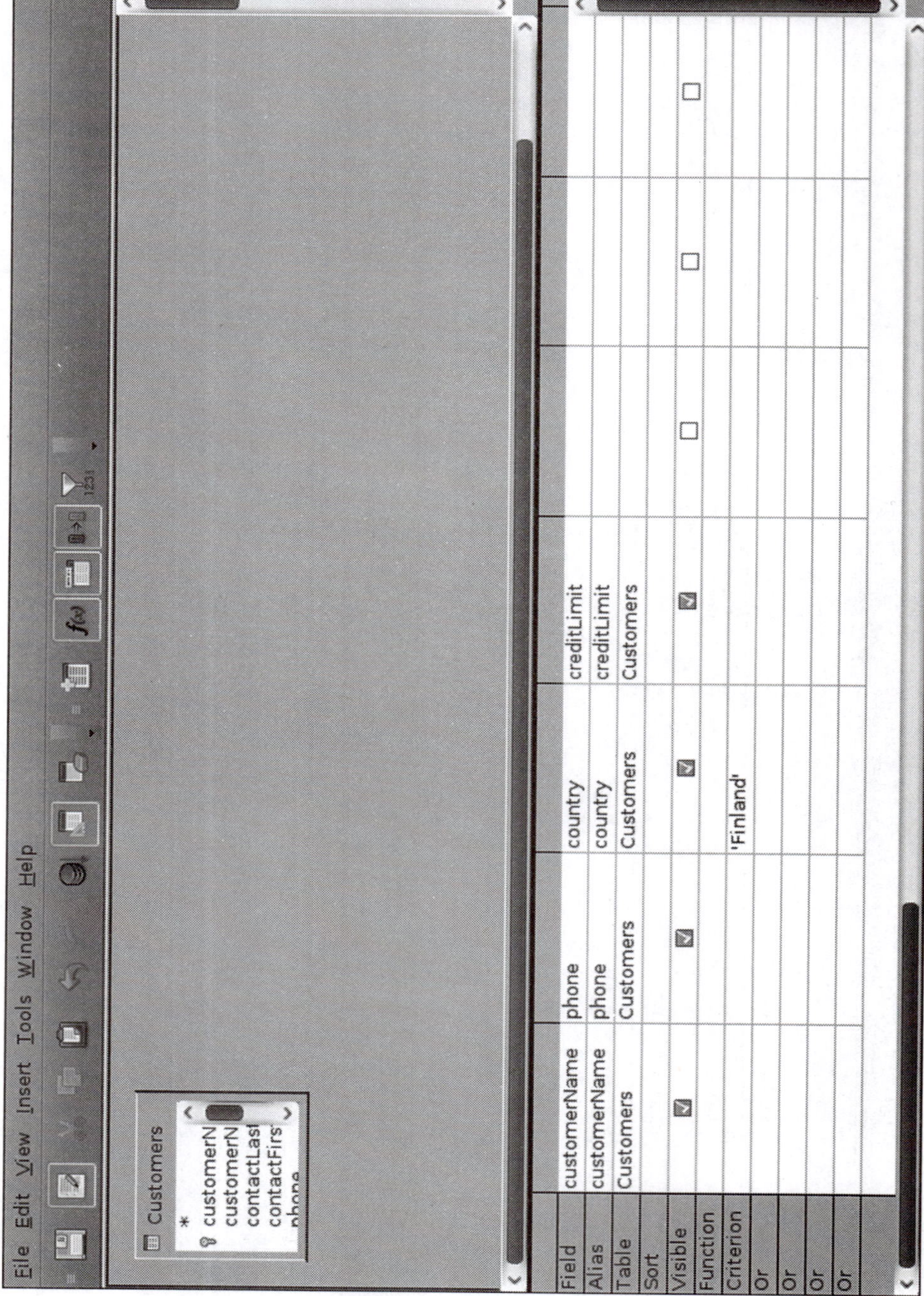

FIGURE 14.9 | Design of query for identifying customers from finland in the customers table.

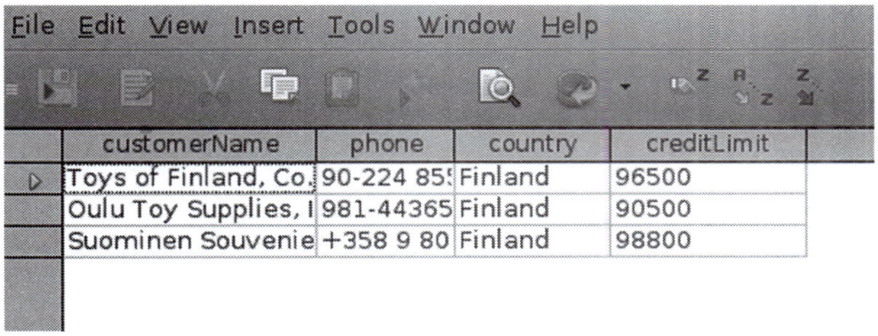

File Edit View Insert Tools Window Help

customerName	phone	country	creditLimit
Toys of Finland, Co.	90-224 85!	Finland	96500
Oulu Toy Supplies, I	981-44365	Finland	90500
Suominen Souvenie	+358 9 80	Finland	98800

FIGURE 14.10 | Results of running the query about customers from finland on the customers table.

The query acts as a data filter on the table to which it is applied. It keeps in data that is specified, and removes the rest. As such, a query can be designed to show any particular *view* of data from the database. The desired view can include all records pertaining to some criteria or portions of records relevant to some criteria (Fig.14.11).

Queries can also be run on tables *joined* by relations. A query can extract some fields from one table, some other fields from another table and present them as a single table to the user. The selection of records from these tables can be done according to some specified criteria. Joining of tables implies drawing a relationship between two data tables, based on some common parameter, such as a primary key. The key acts as a link between the tables and allows them to be queried together. The criteria for selection can be inclusive, that is, the selection will include all records that meet the criteria, or exclusive, that is, the selection will leave out records that meet a certain criteria and include the rest. The design of queries is based on the relational language of databases and can be quite sophisticated. Figure 14.12 shows a query design that joins two tables, the 'Customers' and the 'Orders' tables, to obtain a list of those customers whose orders have not been shipped. The query uses '<>' symbol to select those values not equal to 'Shipped'. The data obtained from the query is also shown in Fig. 14.12.

The above examples show that two tables can be related to extract data. However, in relational databases more than two tables can be related. It is usually the case that all the tables in a database are related in some manner. The relationships depend on the business problem to be solved. The manner in which tables are related in a database is called *schema*. An example schema for the Classic Models database is shown in Fig. 14.13. It consists of all the tables and the relations between them.

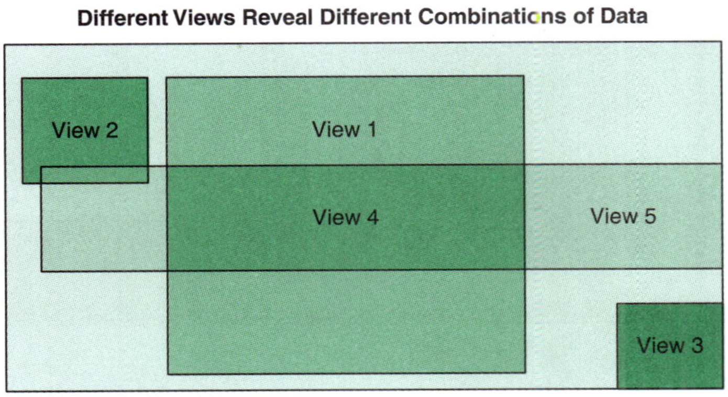

Different Views Reveal Different Combinations of Data

View 2
View 1
View 4
View 5
View 3

FIGURE 14.11 | Views of data using queries.

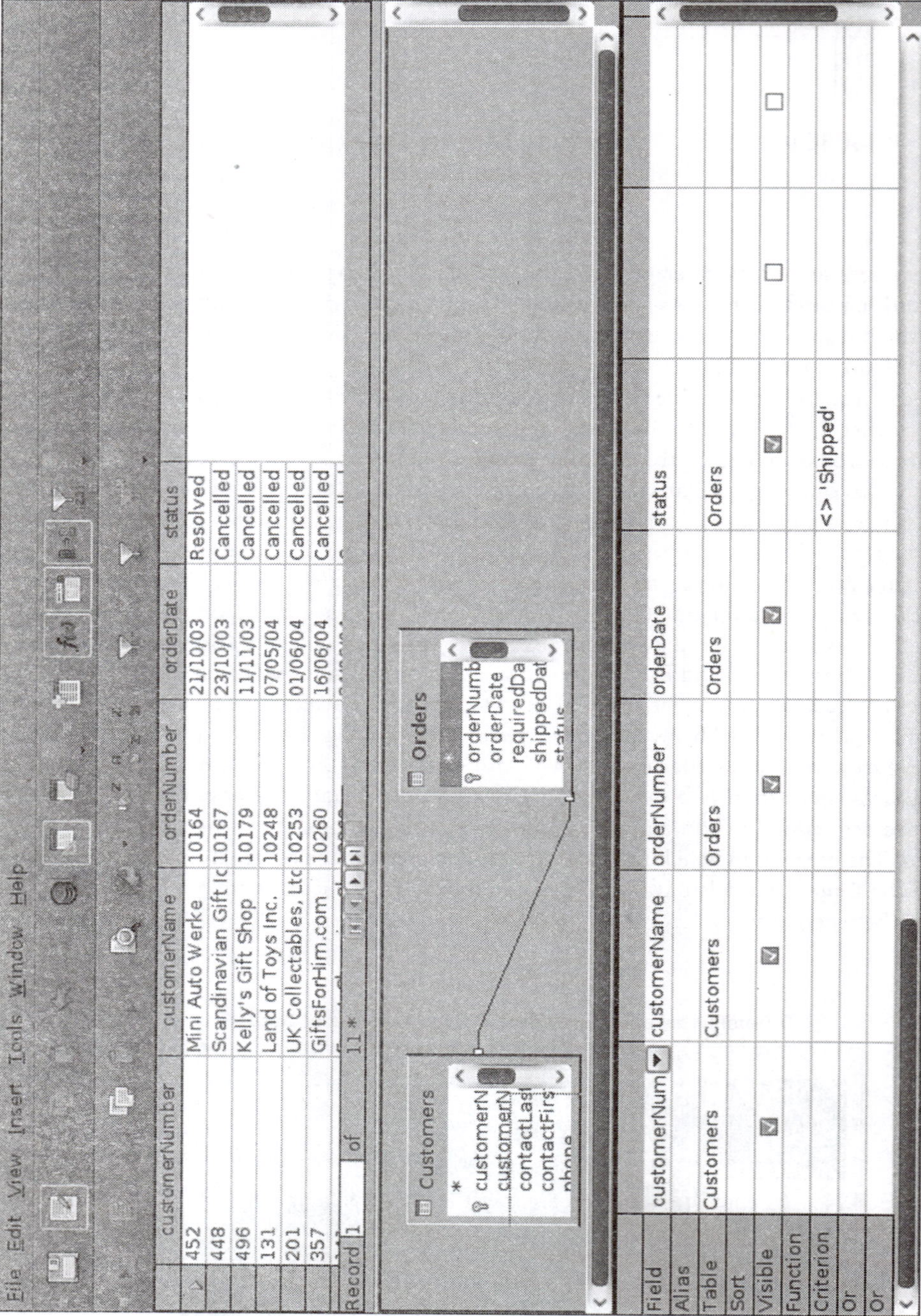

FIGURE 14.12 Query that joins two tables 'Customers' and 'Orders' to select those customers whose orders have not been shipped. The results of the query are also shown.

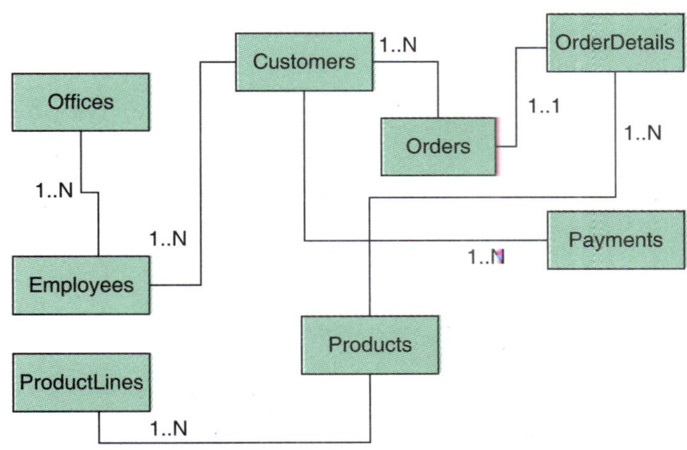

FIGURE 14.13 | Schema for classic Models database. The numbers of the relations indicate cardinality (covered later).

14.4.1.4 Reports

Another facility provided by a DBMS is that of creating reports. These reports are similar to queries in that they present selected data from tables. In reports, the data is presented in a useful and readable format (see Fig. 14.14). Reports are also used to do calculations and computations on the data in tables. For example, a report can draw on data from incomes and tax schedules, and present the total tax liability in a neat format. Reports also have facilities to include charts to display data graphically. This enables creating highly presentable documents.

Customer Number	Customer Name	Order Number	Order Date	Status
452	Mini Auto Werke	10164	10/21/03	Resolved
448	Scandinavian Gift Ideas	10167	10/23/03	Cancelled
496	Kelly's gift Shop	10179	11/11/03	Cancelled
131	Land of Toys Inc.	10248	05/07/04	Cancelled
201	UK Collectables, Ltd.	10253	06/01/04	Cancelled
357	GiftsForHim.com	10260	06/16/04	Cancelled
141	Euro + Shopping Channel	10262	06/24/04	Cancelled
145	Danish Wholesale Imports	10327	11/10/04	Resolved

FIGURE 14.14 | A report fragment showing 'Orders not Shipped'.

14.4.1.5 Metadata

Information regarding the data in tables – for what purpose it is created, by whom, who maintains them and so on – is referred to as *metadata*. This information shows how the tables are structured and what kind of data is stored in them. The latter apsect, which focuses on the data rather than the table structures, is also known as a *data dictionary*. For a typical table, say, the Customers table, a data dictionary is shown in Fig. 14.15.

File:	Customers
Prepared by:	R. Hirani
Date:	10-2-2010
Approved by:	V. Chopra
Date:	11-2-2010
Owned by:	Marketing
Master:	Clients
Access:	Sales data entry Op, marketing Op, accounts receivable manager
Data Element:	ID
Description:	Customer identification number
Other names:	None
Value range:	1000–9999
Data type:	Alphanumeric

FIGURE 14.15 | Data dictionary for the customers table.

Metadata is very important for managing and sharing data. Image files, for instance, carry metadata about the image content, the type of image, when it was captured, when it was modified and so on. This data allows the user to adequately store the image so that it can be retrieved for appropriate applications. Metadata also points to how the data is structured and how it can be processed. Metadata is very useful when data has to be migrated from one database to another. For example, if a customerName field data has to be migrated from one database that allows 50 characters to store the data to another database that allows only 40 characters, then the migration program can determine an appropriate way to truncate 50 characters to 40. Metadata helps identify where and how to modify the data to remove 10 extra characters.

14.4.2 SQL

SQL is an acronym for Structured Query Language, a language that is used to define and manipulate data in database tables. SQL was developed along with the relational database concept. Currently, there are various versions of SQL, all of which conform to an international standard.

The most common use of SQL is to query databases. The basic structure of an SQL language query expression consists of three clauses:

1. `SELECT`: The clause lists the desired fields that have to be included in the query.
2. `FROM`: The clause lists the tables from where the data has to be drawn.
3. `WHERE`: The clause specifies the values of the fields that have to be included, or the conditions that have to be met to include the field. Consider the simple query below:

```
SELECT customerName, phone, country
FROM Customers
WHERE country = Finland
```

This query will include the fields '`customerName`' and '`phone`' from the Customers table and select those records whose value for the '`country`' field is Finland. In this example, the `WHERE` clause uses the '=' operator. Other operators that can be used are '>' (greater than) or '<' (less than) or '<>' (not equal to). These operators can be used with numerical values, as shown in the following example:

```
SELECT customerName, phone, creditLimit
FROM Customers
WHERE creditLimit > 50000
```

Queries with SQL can also be used to join two tables to extract data from both the tables, based on some conditions. The join is defined by some common element in both the tables. As an example, consider the following SQL commands:

```
SELECT Customers.customerNumber, Customers.customerName,
Orders.orderNumber, Orders.orderDate, Orders.status
FROM Orders, Customers
WHERE Orders.customerNumber = Customers.customerNumber
```

The commands above use the '`.`' notation to indicate which fields are to be selected from which table. So, the '`Customers.customerNumber`' indicates that the `customerNumber` field is to be selected from the Customers table. The '`status`' field is, as shown, taken from the Orders table. The `WHERE` clause states that all the records collected by the `SELECT` clause must be such that the `customerNumber` from both the tables match. This ensures that only those records are selected that conform to the same customer in each table. Such an operation in relational languages is known as a *join*.

SQL clauses can also relate more than two tables. To extend the example above, it is possible to write a command that relates three or even more tables together, given that all the tables have one field common with one other table (to create the join).

SQL also allows for data definition – creating tables with commands, and data manipulation – adding and updating data in tables. Data definition uses commands such as *Create*, *Alter*, *Truncate* and *Drop*; each command does approximately what its English language meaning suggests. Data manipulation commands include *Insert*, *Update* and *Delete* used to add and modify data in tables.

Although the graphical user interface used by databases, such as Base and Access, precludes the need for SQL-type commands, the SQL commands are a simple and compact way of doing the same things. Often, SQL commands are used to do some very complicated tasks that would be hard to execute using a graphical interface. The SQL language provides a powerful means to access highly complex databases with perhaps thousands of tables that are related through thousands of relations. Many expert database programmers often use only the SQL commands to manage commercial databases and leave the graphical interface for casual users.

The SQL commands are also the means by which application programs call the database and read, update and modify data. Extensions of SQL, called Procedural Stored Modules, allow programmers creating applications in other languages, such as C or Java, to write SQL commands that will seamlessly integrate the application with the data from the tables. These languages allow sophisticated logic to be used to manipulate tables and data, consistent with the needs of the application.

14.4.3 Commercial DBMS

There are many commercial DBMS available in the market, both as proprietary and as open source products. Each product has captured a market share owing to some unique feature. Each of them also uses a version, or dialect, of SQL. Table 14.2 lists some commercial DBMS along with their features.

Table 14.2 | Features of Commercial DBMS

Product	Features
Oracle	Released in 1979, this is one of the earliest commercial relational DBMS in the market. It has been the most widely used database, with a 44% market share reported in 2007. Oracle has the distinction of being the first commercial DBMS that popularised the relational database concept of using distributed tables for the first time and also used the SQL standard. Oracle also supports the largest table size (the number of records in a table) among all databases. This product remains the best option for enterprise-wide databases, providing a complete range of DBMS features.

(*Continued*)

Table 14.2 | (Continued)

Product	Features
DB2	DB2 is a DBMS popularised by IBM, one of the pioneers of computing in the world. DB2, along with Oracle, is one of the first to implement SQL. DB2 has a strong presence in the enterprise database market although it has versions that can be run as personal and workgroup databases. In 2007, DB2 had a market share of 21%.
SQL Server	This product is offered by Microsoft Corporation and has the third highest market share of 18.5%. This product is largely a workgroup database, meant for smaller departmental or functional applications rather than the enterprise.
MySQL	MySQL is an open source database, as it was first developed using open source principles, and one version of it still remains in the public domain. MySQL has a commercial version that is now owned by the Oracle corporation, and this had a market share of less than 1%. However, the open source version has a massive market share in terms of installations, as MySQL powers many websites across the world, including famous ones such as Wikipedia, Google and Facebook. Furthermore, MySQL is used extensively by many open source projects that require a database, and it has a presence in thousands of products. MySQL is also used extensively by enterprise customers.
PostgreSQL	This is an object-relational DBMS that is also open source in nature. Its commercial market share is negligible (as it is not sold directly), but it has a very strong presence in many online sites such as gaming sites, Skype, Yahoo! and MySpace. PostgreSQL is considered to be one of the most advanced implementations of a DBMS.
Teradata	Teradata DBMS was started in 1979 and was one of the first to create what is now known as data warehouse. Teradata's speciality is that of very large databases that are run on high-end hardware. Teradata had a market share of about 4% in 2007.

14.4.4 E–R Diagrams

The task of a database design is often accomplished by creating Entity–Relationship (E–R) Models. These models provide a high-level view of the data requirements of an organisation. A set of diagrammatic tools are used to create such models, and these are known as entity-relationship diagrams or E–R diagrams.

E–R Models are descriptions of the business requirements of data. They are not the actual, physical data model (of tables and relationships) that is maintained in databases, but they are the first step in designing and creating a physical data model. E–R Models are used to extract the business requirements of data and the rules by which data are related. In this sense they are similar to Data Flow Diagrams, with the difference that they focus on the need for and use of data. E–R Models essentially focus on the user side of systems and model how the user sees and will use the system. The users may belong to different groups and departments, such as customers, employees and students. They may have different needs to transact and use data. When their needs are documented within E–R diagrams, it is important to note that this is one of the views of the database that will be visible to them. In this sense, E–R Models help arrive at a possible design, which can then be elaborated upon to create an entire schema.

An E–R diagram essentially consists of data *entities*, *relationships* between entities and *attributes* that describe the entities and relationships. A data entity is any object, person, place, concept or transaction (or event) on which data has to be maintained by the organisation, for which the analysis is being conducted. It is usually easy to identify basic entities for any organisation as

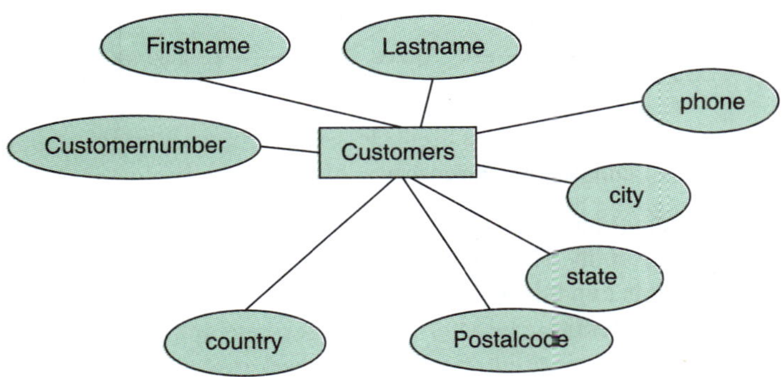

FIGURE 14.16 | Customers entity with attributes.

they pertain to the very core of the activities organisations are engaged in. For a business organisation, entities such as customers, orders, products, employees, departments, warehouses and stores would be included quite naturally. Similarly, for a university, the most natural entities would be students, professors, courses and classrooms among others.

Entities are described by attributes (see Fig 14.16). Each entity has to be described by at least one attribute. The attributes are properties or facts about the entity. For example, a customer will have attributes such as name, address, phone, identity number and so on. There is no limit on the number of attributes that can be used to describe an entity. The number of attributes used is dependent on the business requirements of the organisation. For instance, if an organisation contacts its customers only via digital networks then there is no need for it to maintain attributes related to the physical address of the customer.

Of the attributes used to describe an entity, at least one should be unique valued. This attribute will constitute the primary key of the table described in the previous sections. This unique-valued attribute may be generated by the system, or may be selected according to the requirements of the organisation. For example, universities may choose to use the roll number of students as the primary key of the student entity so as to display this value on reports.

Attributes may require a value (i.e. be forced to have one, such as the name of a customer) or may not (such as the phone number of a customer). The latter are called *optional* attributes. Attributes may also be single-valued or multi-valued. For example, the first name of a customer may be multi-valued (allowing the customer to enter one or more middle names), whereas the system may ensure a single-valued last name for the customer. Furthermore, attributes may be directly stored in the table, or may be derived from other values. For example, the tax liability of an employee may be stored directly in the attribute, or may be computed from the salary value.

Relationships identify natural links or associations between entities. For E–R Modelling, they are used to show how entities have to be treated and how data from different entities can be associated. For example, an entity called 'Student' can be related to an entity called 'Course'. The natural association between the two is that students take courses. When associated in this manner, a question arises: Do students in the entity take all or many or one or none of the courses in the course entity? This question raises the issue of *cardinality*, or the number of entities in a relationship.

A 'Student' entity will consist of many *instances* of students (e.g. Aamir Khan, Shahrukh Khan, etc.). Similarly, the 'Course' entity will consist of many instances of courses (Physics, Chemistry, etc.). The cardinality of a relationship shows how many students, minimum and maximum, can take how many courses. The maximum and minimum number of the cardinality is determined by the business context. For example, a university may specify that a student may take no courses, or may take a maximum of six courses. Similarly, the university may specify that each course can be taken by no student (i.e. it has no enrolment) or may be taken by a maximum of 75 students (see Fig. 14.17). Should a student be listed as a student instance of the 'Student' entity even if he/she has not taken any course? This question has to be answered in the context

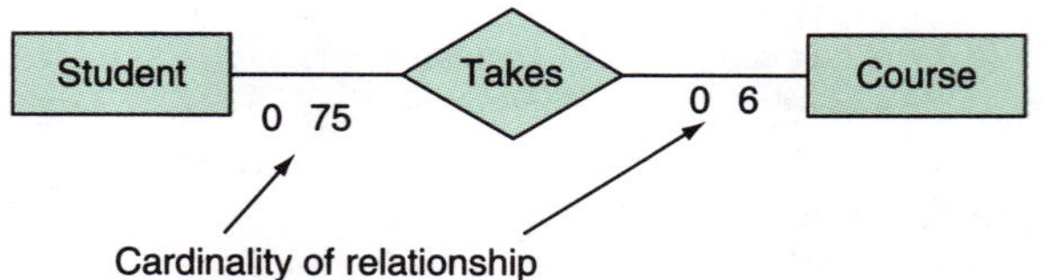

FIGURE 14.17 | E–R diagram showing relationship of the Student entity with the Course entity. The relationship is 'takes'. The cardinality shows that students can take 0–6 courses, while each course can be taken by 0–75 students.

of the university concerned. Many universities may allow a student to remain as a student even though the person is not enrolled in any courses. Similarly, the database may maintain an entity instance of 'Course' even though the course has no students enrolled.

Cardinality for relationships between entities can be of many types, as illustrated in Table 14.3. Some examples of the various types of relationships between entities are depicted in Fig. 14.18.

Table 14.3 | Types of Cardinality for Relationships between Entities

Cardinality	Relationship
0 N to 0 N	Zero to many instances of one table can be related to none or many instances of another table.
1 to 1	One, and only one, instance of one table can be related to one of another table.
0 N to 1	Zero to many instances of one table can be related to exactly one instance of another table.
N to N	Many instances of one table can be related to many instances of another table.

Some relationships become quite complex as they are explained within the modelling process. For instance, the relationship called 'Enrols' designates the entity 'Student' taking a 'Course'. Enrolment itself is a complex transaction – it is done at a particular date, it may require payment of fees, it may have requirements of pre-requisites and so on. In such situations, where the relationship requires maintaining data, it is often converted to an entity. This requires careful analysis at the database design stage.

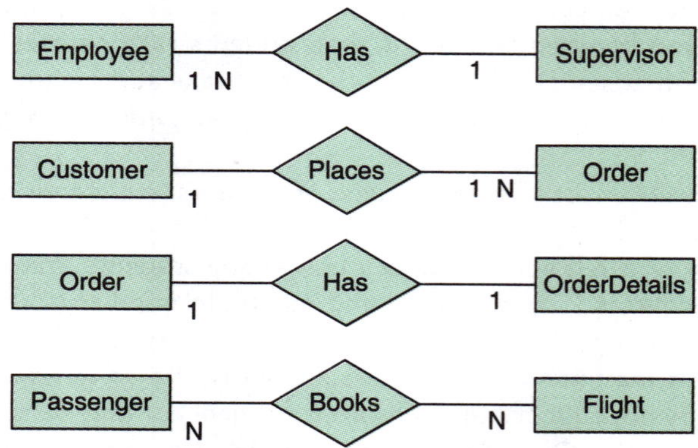

FIGURE 14.18 | Different types of relationships between entities.

14.4.5 Normalisation

While designing databases, it is important to keep in mind the issue of redundant or repeating data. Redundant data creeps into the system if the design of the database is such that it does not explicitly prevent it. Normalisation is the process of table design where groups of fields (or attributes) are kept together. Redundancy is removed by this process as only the most pertinent fields are kept in a table and the others that are needed are used from other tables.

For example, consider Table 14.4. It contains data that is used to create an invoice for the Classic Models dataset. The two customers in the table – Atelier graphique and Dragon Souveniers Ltd – have placed one order with multiple products. For each order an order number and date is recorded and then the product codes and names are listed. For each customer and order number there are three products in the invoice. It is not possible to maintain a table in such a form in a database, as each field has to have a single value.

Table 14.4 | Data for an Invoice

customerName	customerNumber	orderNumber	orderDate	productCode	productName
Atelier graphique	103	10100	06/01/03	S10_1678	1969 Harley Davidson Ultimate Chopper
				S10_1949	1952 Alpine Renault 1300
				S10_2016	1996 Moto Guzzi 1100i
Dragon Souveniers, Ltd.	148	10107	24/02/03	S12_4473	1957 Chevy Pickup
				S12_4675	1969 Dodge Charger
				S18_1097	1940 Ford Pickup Truck

To avoid multiple entries in the product code and product name fields, the table is now converted to the form as shown in Table 14.5. The values for the customer's name and number and also for the order number and date have been inserted in the rows for the two other products in the same order. Now, each row in the table is identified by two keys, the customer number and the order number. However, it will be clear that the rows are not uniquely identified by these keys alone.

Table 14.5 | Data Converted to 1NF

customerName	customerNumber	orderNumber	orderDate	productCode	productName
Atelier graphique	103	10100	06/01/03	S10_1678	1969 Harley Davidson Ultimate Chopper
Atelier graphique	103	10100	06/01/03	S10_1949	1952 Alpine Renault 1300
Atelier graphique	103	10100	06/01/03	S10_2016	1996 Moto Guzzi 1100i

(Continued)

Table 14.5 | (Continued)

customerName	customerNumber	orderNumber	orderDate	productCode	productName
Dragon Souveniers, Ltd.	148	10107	24/02/03	S12_4473	1957 Chevy Pickup
Dragon Souveniers, Ltd.	148	10107	24/02/03	S12_4675	1969 Dodge Charger
Dragon Souveniers, Ltd.	148	10107	24/02/03	S18_1097	1940 Ford Pickup Truck

The first table is converted to the second one, to bring it to a form known as the First Normal Form or 1NF. A table is said to be in 1NF when it contains no repeating entries in any field. The process of converting the table to 1NF is the first step in normalisation.

The table above, though, presents several challenges. If a customer calls and asks for a change in the order, or cancels an order, it is possible that the data is entered incorrectly (say the name of the customer is misspelt or an incorrect product code is entered for the product). To avoid such possible problems, it is best to further break up the table so that only the most relevant changes need be made. One way to do this would be to have three separate tables: one for customers, one for orders and one for products. These are further steps in normalisation of tables to reduce redundancy.

Data normalisation is done to convert tables to second and third normal (2NF and 3NF) and beyond. Currently, the tables can be converted up to the sixth normal form too, however, this depends on the context of the application in which the database is being used.

Though normalisation is useful and reduces redundancy and consequently anomalies and discrepancies in data, it is also leads to inefficient processing. Normalisation is very useful for maintaining and updating data, however, for using data in an organisation it is best to have the most relevant data in a single place. Thus, many database managers also denormalise data (i.e. aggregate separate tables) so that constant use is easier and requires less processing.

14.5 DATA WAREHOUSES

Since the inception of desktop computing, in the mid-1980s, around the world, there has been a proliferation of data use and needs for data storage. Almost all employees of organisations, above a certain size, now use computers and produce, modify or read data. For very large organisations, the amount of data that is used on a day-to-day basis could be as high as in petabytes. With this huge explosion in data, organisations felt the need for:

1. Consolidating much of the data from various databases into a whole that could be understood clearly.
2. Focusing on the use of data for decision making, as opposed to simply for running transactions.

The need for creating data *warehouses* arose from the above two needs. The technology of data warehouses draws on enterprise databases to create a separate set of tables and relations that can be used to run particular kinds of queries and analytical tools. Warehouses are different from transaction databases, as users can run complex queries on them, which are related to the functions of the enterprise that need not affect the transaction processing.

To create a data warehouse, data is extracted from transactional tables and pre-processed to remove unwanted data types and then loaded into tables in the warehouse. The extraction process requires making queries into transactional databases that are currently being used.

This is a challenge as the data tables may be distributed across various servers, and the data may be changing rapidly. The data obtained from these tables is maintained in a *staging* area, a temporary storage area, where the data is *scrubbed*. The idea of data scrubbing is to remove clearly recognisable erroneous data. This task is often difficult, as errors are not obvious - say a misspelt name or a wrong address - and require careful examination to remove them. At the scrubbing stage, data is not corrected in any manner; it is invariably removed from the collection of raw data.

Once the data is scrubbed or cleaned, it is loaded onto the tables that constitute the warehouse. When an organisation is creating a warehouse for the first time, the entire data is loaded into a database, using a particular design. Subsequent data that is obtained from the transaction databases is then extracted, cleaned and loaded incrementally to the earlier tables.

Data pertaining to a particular domain or a problem to be analysed is maintained in data *marts*. For example, a mart may be created to examine sales data alone. This mart will collect data related to the sales activities across the organisation and store them in the warehouse. However, it will exclude the data related to production, finance, employees and so on. The mart can then be analysed for particular problems related to the sales trends, sales predictions and so on. Furthermore, the mart may be updated on a periodic basis to include the fresh data available.

Data in warehouses can be stored in tables with timestamps. This is the *dimensional* method of creating warehouses. The idea here is to store data in a single or a few, unrelated tables that are given one additional attribute of a timestamp (that indicates when the data was collected or created). For example, one table in a dimensional warehouse may include data on customers, sales, products, orders, shipping and a timestamp of each transaction. Each timestamp will pertain to one particular event in the life of the organisation when a transaction occurred and the data was created. Such a table can be analysed to examine trends in sales, fluctuations in orders across seasons and so on.

Another method of storing data is in the regular tables-and-relations format of relational databases. Here too an additional attribute of a timestamp is included within the tables.

Various kinds of analysis can be conducted on data available in warehouses including data mining, online analytical processing and data visualisation. These different methods are designed to extract patterns and useful information from very large data sets. Online analytical process (OLAP) is used to analyse and report data on sales trends, forecasts and other time-series-based analyses. Such analyses allow managers to see and visualise the data in a form that shows interesting and unusual patterns that would not be easily visible from the analysis of transaction data alone.

In modern organisations, ones that have a strong online presence and collect data from customer visits to websites and transaction data from different types of e-commerce sites, the extent and size of the data is such that analysing it for patterns is almost impossible, unless a warehouse is used. For example, one firm analyses data, using OLAP, from millions of visitors to different pages of its website to dynamically place advertisements that would conform to the visitors' interests, as determined by the regions on the page the visitor hovers over or clicks on.

Data warehouses are an active area of development and have strong commercial potential for database vendors. Almost all major commercial vendors of DBMS have products that can be used to create and manage warehouses.

14.5.1 Data Mining Uses

Data mining means extracting patterns and knowledge from historical data that is typically housed in data warehouses. Data mining is a loose term that means many things at the same time - data storing, data analysis, use of artificial intelligence techniques, statistical pattern recognition and others. The original idea of data mining came from the field known as 'knowledge discovery in databases' (KDD). KDD is a sub-field of artificial intelligence and is concerned with finding useful, human-understandable knowledge from data. Several other terms are now used to describe the same ideas - business intelligence, data analytics and web analytics. These concepts are covered in Chapter 16.

Data mining is used with data accumulated in data warehouses. Following are some examples of data stored in warehouses that are used for mining:

1. **Click-stream data:** This data is collected from website pages as users click on links or other items on the web page. Data on where a user clicks, after what interval, what page the users goes to, does the user return and visit other links, etc., are collected. The data are mined to identify which links are most frequently visited, for how long and by what kind of users. The online search firm, Google, has initiated an entire field of mining click-stream data that is known as web analytics.
2. **Point-of-sale purchase data:** Data obtained from retail sales counters is the classic data set to which mining software was applied. The data pertains to the item quantities, price values, date and time of purchase, and details about customers that are obtained from point-of-sale terminals. The data is used to perform 'market basket' analysis, which essentially shows what kinds of items are typically purchased with each other. In a famous case, a large retailer found from a market basket analysis that men in a certain part of the USA were likely to buy beer and diapers on Thursday evenings. This was an unusual finding and the retailer sought to explain why. It was later learned that many families with young children planned their weekend trips on Thursday evening, at which point the women would ask men to go and buy diapers from the store. The men would take this opportunity to buy beer, also for the weekend. The retailer used this information to announce promotions and increase sales of both these products.
3. **Online search data:** This data is about search that users type in search boxes on web pages. Many organisations collect the text typed in by users while they are searching for some information. This text data reveals what users are interested in and is mined for patterns. The data collected pertains to the search texts typed in, the time at which they are typed and the number of times different searches are done. Many online retailers, such as Flipkart, mine this data to identify what users are interested in and then make product suggestions based on association rules. For example, users searching for books on Java programming may be offered what others have seen and purchased, including associated books on programming they have not considered.
4. **Text data:** This is text data that is posted by users on web pages, blogs, emails, wikis, twitter feeds and others. Many organisations have found that by mining this data they can glean interesting insights and trends. Many tools and software programs have been created recently to mine text data. One example is provided by the online site called Wordle.

The www.wordle.net site hosts an application that mines text submitted to it. The application counts the frequency of words appearing in the submitted text and then creates a word 'cloud' with the most frequent words appearing as the largest. For example, Fig. 14.19 has a word cloud of the text of a portion of the Constitution of India. Text from Part III of the Constitution, comprising of the Fundamental Rights, was submitted to wordle.net. This part consists of about 13 pages of printed text.

14.6 BIG DATA

The huge volume of data that are now produced by both humans and machines, at a very high rate and with massive variety, is now referred to as Big Data. The popularity of Big Data grew with the analysis of opportunities which presented to those who could manage and make sense of the data. The initial set of successful applications drew data from internet services such as Google search and social media sites and was able to draw interesting insights from the analysis of these. The data that such services provided was highly unstructured in nature - that is they did not follow a well-defined schema to which they could be fitted and stored on standard relational databases.

Big Data was differentiated from regular data owing to the high volumes in which it was produced, the high rates at which it originated and its unstructured and variable nature. These three properties of Big Data are known as the three 'Vs'. These three Vs were later extended to four Vs to characterise Big Data, and these are - volume, velocity, variety and veracity.

FIGURE 14.19 | Wordle cloud for text from part III of the constitution of India pertaining to fundamental rights.

14.6.1 Volume

It was estimated that as of 2016, about 2.5 exabytes of data was produced per day, by people and organisations and devices around the world. To have an estimate of how much this is – consider that a typical laptop in 2016 would have a capacity of about 1 gigabytes of secondary storage. An exabyte is a billion gigabytes of storage. Some industry analysts predict that by 2020, 40,000 exabytes of data will be produced annually. This massive volume of data is produced from various sources – from people participating on social media sites and making posts, sharing images and videos; from sensors attached to IoT devices; from online transactions for banking and e-commerce; and from scientific research and experiments such as weather analysis, astronomical observations, etc.

14.6.2 Velocity

Velocity of data refers to the rates at which data is produced or accumulated. For Big Data environments, this rate is very high. For example, a set of sensors attached to a jet engine may produce over 300 gigabytes of data every one minute. Other examples of the high velocity of data are shown in Table 14.6.

Table 14.6 | Velocity of Data from Different Sources. Data pertain to 2016 unless otherwise noted

Source	Volume of Data
YouTube videos	300 hours of video uploaded every minute. This is about 1.6 terabytes of data per minute.
IoT devices	A jet engine produces about 300 gigabytes of data per minute.
Emails	There were 187 million emails generated per minute, worldwide.
Social media	There were more than 455,000 tweets generated per minute. 15 million text messages were sent every minute. Facebook logged 4 million posts per minute (in 2014).

Sources: Varied.

14.6.3 Variety

Variety refers to the fact that Big Data is produced in many different forms, from structured, to semi-structured to unstructured data. Metadata too is a distinct variety of data. Unstructured data constitutes almost 80% of Big Data and consists of text or binary files that are independent and not relationally linked to other files. Unstructured data may be produced by devices or computing equipment, by humans interacting with various applications, or application programmes that generate data as a by-product of their processing. Unstructured data may be in many different forms, examples of which are: log files from servers, collection of tweets, collections of text, video or audio posts on social media sites, logs of chat sites, etc.

Semi-structured data is that which has some inherent structure, either corresponding to a hierarchy or a graph. This type of data too does not have any relations between the files. Semi-structured data is often maintained in XML (Extensible Markup Language) or JSON (Java Script Object Notation) languages that are used for exchange of data that is readable by humans, as well as by computer programs. Data stored in such formats is text-based and one of the major sources for such data is sensors. Sensors used for IoT often encode data into JSON or XML-based formats that are easily transmitted and processed.

Two other sources of variety in Big Data are structured data and metadata, both of which have been explained earlier. Metadata is particularly crucial for Big Data analysis as it provides information on the source of the data and some indication of its authenticity.

14.6.4 Veracity

The characteristic of veracity refers to the validity of data. Big Data often has noise that is generated at the source. People type in incorrect names or hashtags, enter wrong or misleading addresses, use pseudonyms during online conversations, pass off blogs as authentic news sources and so on. Noise is also collected from sensors in the form of incorrect data readings, missing data values, incorrect setting of data filters and so on. Data that can be used to process for valuable information is considered to be signal, whereas the rest is considered to be noise. High values for signal-to-noise ratios are always preferred, and is the same for Big Data environments.

There are several Big Data database products that are used in the industry, the most prominent of which are Hadoop and MongoDB. These databases are able to process massive volumes of data across distributed databases. Their architecture is very different from traditional, relational databases. A detailed discussion is beyond the scope of this chapter.

Caselet Big Data in Flipkart

Flipkart is one of the largest e-commerce firms operating in India. Flipkart has close rivals in Amazon.in and Snapdeal.com that also run e-commerce marketplaces and have a massive presence across all categories of products. These three big rivals corner over 90% of the market share in e-commerce in India, with Flipkart owning about 70% of the total in early 2017.

Flipkart relies extensively on generating, storing and analysing Big Data to help with its operations. The firm generates close to 5 terabytes of data per day that it stores and analyses for various purposes.

One of the tools that Flipkart uses is called Qlikview and this collects data on the customer's browsing history. The tool records how many times a customer visits a page, logs in, which products the customer browses, the navigation path of the customer, the number of times the customer clicks, the page till which the customer reached, the page at which the customer navigated away, the time at which the customer exited, and what the customer eventually purchased, amongst other details. This data is collected by different systems in Flipkart's infrastructure and then fed to the Qlikview system. Qlikview aggregates all this Big Data and provides a dashboard to manage for further analysis.

Managers typically use the last 90 days data, using a rolling horizon, for analysis on Qlikview, though most recent data is given preference. Data that is beyond the horizon, older than 90 days, is maintained in a data warehouse.

A key analysis that managers conduct is that of knowing the page from which customers bounce away, after navigating to it. This suggests to them that the price listed on the page is not suitable and then can take action (by lowering the price or matching it with rivals). Sometimes customers may search for a product, based on some search words, arrive at a page and then bounce away. This suggests to managers that the search objects associated with the search terms may not be appropriate and hence some action could be taken in that regard.

Another application for monitoring user-clicks is that for placement and pricing of banner ads. Flipkart charges clients for placement of banner advertisements, for example, when a user is searching for mobile phones, a particular brand may be displayed, and if the user clicks on the banner displayed, the rate for the advertisement is increased, and if the user lands up buying that particular brand then the price is increased further. The placement of the advertisement on the page is also decided by the user behaviour.

Flipkart has created a set of sales events, calls 'Big Billion Day' sales. These events are heavily advertised and carry special discounts on many items, and attract a very large number of visitors. The preparation for these sales events is based on the analysis of prior such events and managers use this analysis to decide on prices, the inventories of goods to be maintained and the placement of advertisements.

Another area in which Flipkart analyses its Big Data is that of logistics. Managers see the customer pin codes of delivery locations and based on an analysis of frequency, access and the number of package delivery services available, decide on how future deliveries can be made. The idea is to reduce the time of delivery for the customer, and also reduce the costs for the company.

Chapter Glossary

Database A software program that enables storage, access and use of data by other software applications.

Field A defined space of given size, which stores the basic elements of data.

Record A collection of fields.

File A collection of records, also called a table.

Metadata Contains details about how data is stored in files; provides information on how the data can be used and managed.

Primary key A field that contains data that uniquely identifies a record.

Personal database Databases created and used primarily by single users.

Database server A database software that runs on an independent computer and provides services to client applications.

Distributed database A database whose tables are maintained on various different servers.

Middleware Software that is used to connect distributed databases to different client devices.

Relational database A database whose tables are associated through special links called relations.

Database Management Systems (DBMS) Software package that has tools for creating, updating, accessing and managing data within a database.

Forms Special objects used within DBMS to update data in tables.

Queries Special objects used within DBMS to access data from tables.

Reports Special objects used within DBMS to present data and analysis in an appealing manner.

Joins Relations created between tables.

Data dictionary A special data structure to store metadata.

SQL A high-level computer language to create, update, access and manage databases.

Entity Any object, place, person, concept or transaction on which data is maintained in a database.

Attributes Properties of entities.

Cardinality The order of a relationship between two entities.

Data warehouse A massive database that is created from organisational data to enable analysis and to assist with decision making.

Data scrubbing Removing erroneous data from data warehouses.

Data mart A data warehouse containing data pertaining to a particular domain.

Review Questions

1. What is the need for data management? Why is it difficult to manage data?
2. Describe some of the challenges of modern database management.
3. What is the difference between fields, records and files?
4. Why is a primary key needed?
5. What is the difference between a personal database and an organisational database?
6. What is the advantage of three-tier architecture?
7. Why is middleware important?
8. Is it possible to query two or more tables at the same time? How?
9. Why is it important to maintain metadata?
10. What are three basic SQL commands and what do they achieve?

Research Questions

1. Study the library database in your university or institute. Try to draw a schema of the basic entities of the database and the relations between them.
2. Seek out examples of how organisations use data stored in warehouses. What decision making issues are the organisations trying to address?
3. Search the internet for the concept of 'Big Data'. Find out what it means and how organisations deal with this kind of data.
4. Download and install Open Office or Libre Office on a personal computer you have access to. Then dowload the Birt database that is discussed in the text (the source is also mentioned). Recreate all the forms and queries in the text. Then create a few queries on your own.

Further Reading

1. An article 'How much Information is there in the World?' in USC News, February 2011 Is available at: http://uscnews.usc.edu (accessed on June 2011).
2. An article 'eBay's Two Enormous Data Warehouses', in DBMS2, 2009 is available at: http://www.dbms2.com/2009/04/30/ebays-two-enormous-data-warehouses/ (accessed on June 2011).
3. Hoffer, J.A., Prescott, M.B. and McFadden, F.R. (2007) *Modern Database Management,* 8th edn, Prentice Hall, NJ.
4. https://zephoria.com/top-15-valuable-facebook-statistics/
5. https://www.lifewire.com/how-many-emails-are-sent-every-day-1171210
6. https://blog.microfocus.com/how-much-data-is-created-on-the-internet-each-day/
7. http://wersm.com/how-much-data-is-generated-every-minute-on-social-media/
8. http://www.business-standard.com/article/companies/flipkart-claws-back-market-share-from-amazon-until-march-2017-naspers-117062600660_1.html
9. Erl, T., Khattak, W., & Buhler, P. (2016), *Big Data Fundamentals: Concepts, Drivers & Techniques*, Prentice Hall Press.

CHAPTER 15

Business Process Integration and Enterprise Systems

Learning Objectives

After completing this chapter, you will be able to:

- Understand business process integration
- Get an overview of enterprise resource planning systems
- Learn about supply chain management systems
- Get an overview of customer relationship management system
- Learn about challenges of enterprise systems implementations
- Understand international information systems

Organisations execute complex business processes as part of their work. Business processes consist of activities that transform inputs into desired outputs. Computerisation leads to automation of processes across departments and organisations. Enterprise systems integrate complex business processes, providing a means to re-engineer old processes and also to replace existing, legacy systems. ERP systems integrate functions across the enterprise through a common platform that includes modules for finance and accounting, marketing and sales, human resource management and operations management. Supply chain management (SCM) systems integrate vendors and suppliers of the organisation through a common system to help in coordination, planning, order management and transportation efficiency. Customer relationship management (CRM) systems integrate the functions of sales force management, call centres, direct selling and customer support. Enterprise systems face numerous challenges of implementation, including loss of competitive advantage, high costs, managing change and selecting appropriate vendors.

International Information Systems help integrate the functions of organisations that have a presence in other countries, or of multinational or transnational organisations. An important benefit of international systems is that they allow firms to outsource functions to different countries.

MIND MAP OF CHAPTER TOPICS

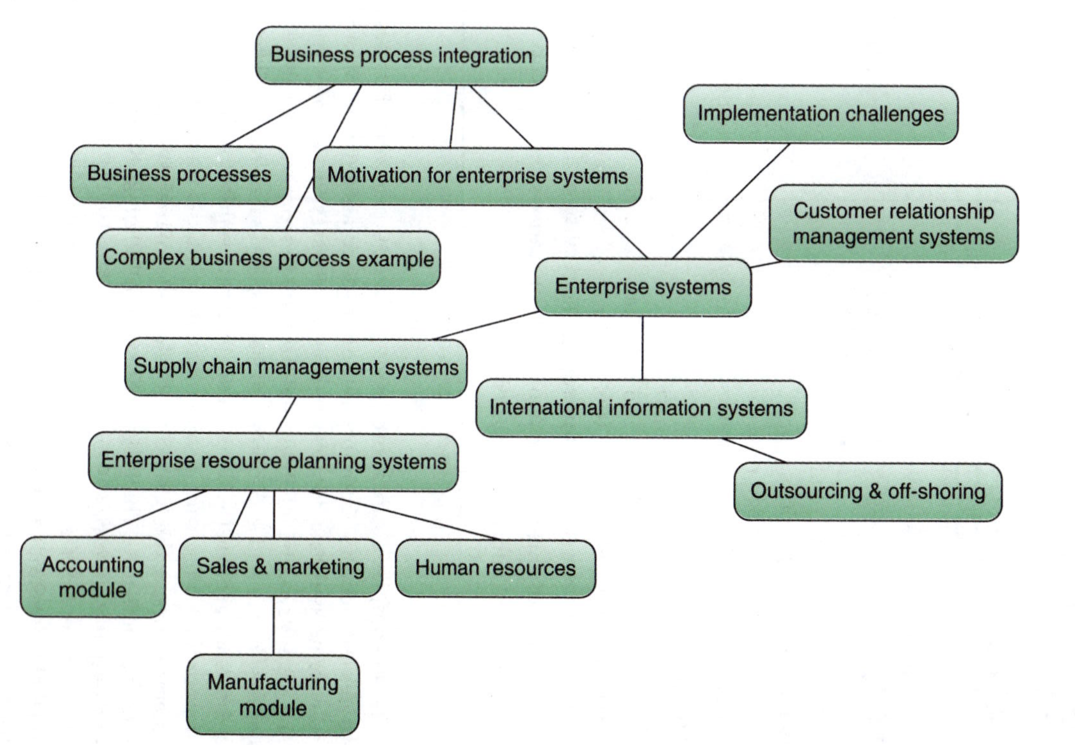

CASE STUDY: ERP VIA THE CLOUD AT OXFORD BOOK STORE

When Oxford book store opened on the swanky Park Street of Calcutta in 1920, it catered to a select clientele who read English books. Ninety years later this book store still thrives and has expanded its operations to over 20 stores across India, and also boasts of an online book store. In its modern form, the book store offers a wide selection of books, a pleasant ambience for customers to sit and browse books, weekend events such as book readings and musical performances, and also a cafe that serves tea with snacks. The stores include stationary, toys and gift items, along with books from different languages, magazines, music discs and film DVDs.

Oxford book store's drive to modernise and upgrade its offerings is a response to the tremendous rise in competition both from other book stores and from online book sales. Over the last decade, brands such as Landmark, Crossword and Strand have created a chain of book stores to address the demand of a growing urban population interested in English language books. These chains specialised, initially, in imported books, which were usually hard to find anywhere in India. With the tremendous growth in the book publishing business in India, the stores have started selling many books written and published in India, along with the international bestsellers.

The book publishing numbers in India were impressive – the county had about 19,000 publishers, publishing about 90,000 titles a year and the number of titles was growing at about 30% per annum (in 2011). Organised retail outlets, such as Oxford book store, accounted for only 7% of the total market, and the rest were sold through informal channels such as university book stores, textbook stores, railway station stalls, footpath book sellers and so on. The online retailers too had a significant share of the market, accounting for almost 2 million books a year.

Despite the large number of publishers and titles being published, as well as the presence of organised retailers, the demand for books was an unmet need. There were very few book retail outlets outside of the major metros and some towns. The online retailers had an issue with gaining the trust of customers and could not reach out to those in unserved locations.

Oxford book store was able to spot the potential of growth in the book market, reflected in the unmet demand, as well as the growing competition in its current urban markets. It wanted to scale up its operations by opening newer stores and establishing its presence. However, it had a severe problem.

Like all book retail outlets in India, Oxford book store had very poor inventory management. They had a large number of books in inventory that did not move.Besides, each store in the chain managed its own inventory, with the result that a single book could have multiple codes in different stores; therefore the management found it hard to say how many copies of a book they had. Oxford added 50,000 titles to its stocks every year, to the 200,000 titles it already had. It added 150 stock-keeping-units (SKUs) every day, and required computerisation to manage this large inventory.

Oxford book store was a medium enterprise, with a gross turnover of Rs 250 million. It wanted to create information systems that would help it manage its inventory of books across all its stores in India. It also needed the information systems to help it scale to both more retail stores (with a target of 100 stores in India and abroad) and an online store. But Oxford's management did not want to do this with a heavy investment, in millions of rupees, in information systems; they wanted a solution that suited their medium size.

The Chief Technology Officer (CTO) of Oxford book store, Subhasish Saha, said 'Management was looking for a model that would allow Oxford book store to leverage its full IT potential without [a] large one-time IT capital investments or [compromising on] issues of scalability'. The solution they sought had to have low upfront investment, and also allow them to cover their entire operations and enable them to scale. The solution Saha settled on was that of using an ERP system from SAP, not purchased outright, but acquired through the Cloud. This meant that a high down payment was not required, but the expenses could be paid on a monthly basis and charged to operational expenses.

The ERP package enabled them to have their entire inventory, across all stores, on a single system. It integrated their point-of-sale terminals with the inventory, thus allowing them to see their stock position on books on a current basis. Furthermore, the system also provided for payroll and accounting functions. With a total cost of Rs 10.8 million, to be paid out in installments, this also met Oxford's investment constraints.

The biggest challenge for the implementation, as is the case for all ERP implementations, was that of finding a vendor who could not only roll out the system but also remain as a long-term partner for the duration of the project. Oxford book store eventually settled for the Tata Consutancy Services (TCS) as the vendor, banking on the latter's strong reputation and due to the fact that the system would be available on the TCS cloud service called iON. TCS provided technical, project and business consulting for the implementation.

The results of the implementation were very impressive. With the improved stock management, Oxford book store was able to increase retail sales, reduce costs on slow inventory and also improve online sales. Online sales increased by as much as 100%, and the total revenues increased by Rs 34 million. Furthermore, Oxford could create special offerings like the Gems program, where private firms could offer Gems points to their employees as rewards, which could be redeemed at Oxford stores.

The system also streamlined operations across all the stores, giving Oxford a platform to open more retail outlets. Some critics argue that the pay-as-you-go model is more expensive in the long run, as the total payouts, after some time, exceed the initial down payment costs. However, Saha counters that 'The technology adoption strategy for Oxford has been relying on a no-CAPEX model. It is true that when the cost is calculated for five years then there won't be much difference. But with a proprietary solution we would have to face the one-time payment, maintenance and upgradation challenge'.

15.1 BUSINESS PROCESS INTEGRATION

15.1.1 Business Processes

In an earlier chapter, we had defined a business process as any business activity that involves the movement of information between individuals, groups or departments. This definition was used in the context of systems analysis and of defining requirements for information systems within organisations. In the current context, the definition of a business process remains largely the same, with a small difference: business processes are understood as activities within or across organisations that involve some inputs, which are transformed to produce desired outputs. A business process, in this larger sense, then may involve inputs that are not just information but actually are transformations that act on all types of inputs to produce outputs that are desired by the organisation. Here is a notable difference that processes are now to be understood as happening within or across organisations.

Business processes have a telescopic character: the nature of a business process may extend from being one that is elementary to one that is very complex. Furthermore, a process may consist of sub-processes, which are also processes in their own right. While analysing processes, an analyst will strive to understand the most elemental business processes that constitute more complex processes, which further constitute more complex processes and so on.

Complexity of a process may extend to the number of activities, persons and departments it includes as well as the amount of time and effort it takes to complete. Some processes, for instance, of securing a payment, may involve several parties across several organisations and take a short time to complete. In contrast, a process of making a batch of mechanical parts by machining in a factory may take only a few inputs and steps, but may extend across a large span of time.

One of the aims of building information systems has been to identify and map basic processes that can be automated to build highly complex systems. Such automation can improve the speed and accuracy of the processes as well as help reduce costs of conducting them. Though this goal has been achieved with large-scale computerisation within organisations across the world, it has led to a consequent increase in the complexity of processes in terms of the nature of involvement of people, departments and organisations and also in the nature of processes. The old manual processes tended towards simplicity at the individual, atomic activity level, with complexity arising from multiple processes combining to form higher level processes. But the modern computerised atomic processes are highly complex even to start with.

KEY POINT

Business processes are activities that transform some input into desired outputs.

As an example, compare the task of buying a film ticket in India by the manual method, which is still prevalent in many theatres in India, with buying the ticket online. The manual method means going to the film theatre personally, or through an agent, and appearing at a counter where the ticket vendor can sell the buyer a ticket for a film that will run the same day or at some future date. The buyer has to provide information about the type of ticket, economy or premium ticket, the show for which it is required and the date for which it is required. The buyer usually has to buy the ticket using a cash transaction. The ticket purchased is printed on paper indicating the correct date and time for the show. The theatre management has to ensure that sufficient tickets are available at the ticket counter for all the shows for which tickets can be purchased in advance. The manual process for buying the ticket thus involves sub-processes of the buyer arriving at the window (after, perhaps, waiting in a queue), informing the vendor about the time and date of the show, providing the money, and the vendor then giving the buyer the relevant ticket after ascertaining that tickets for the desired show are available. Pre-requisite processes involve printing sufficient number and type of tickets by the theatre management.

The process of buying a ticket online is simpler for the buyer but far more complicated, considering the number of sub-processes it invokes. A buyer can use a website, such as www.bookmyshow.com, find the film and theatre that he/she is interested in, select the theatre, the show time, the seats, the price of the ticket and then order the purchase. The buyer can then purchase the ticket using a credit card, a transaction that involves sending information to a bank or a credit card agency, verifying the credit available, enabling the transaction and then verifying the card owner's details. Once the card enables the purchase, the buyer prints out the ticket receipt.

Table 15.1 | Manual and Online Processes of Buying a Cinema Ticket

Manual Process		Online Process	
Pre-conditions	**Steps**	**Pre-conditions**	**Steps**
	Going to the theatre	Website is updated with the latest information	Logging on to the website that sells tickets
Counter is opened at a specified time	Queuing at the ticket counter	–	Selecting a particular theatre
Tickets for certain dates are to be sold	Specifying the date and the type of ticket	–	Specifying the date, time, seat preference
Physical printed tickets are available	Providing cash and receiving the ticket	Payment gateway has to be enabled and is available	Payment with credit card or other method and printing ticket, receiving SMS
–	–	Ticket printer is updated with information	Receiving ticket at the theatre before the show

Note: Pre-conditions are the arrangements that have to be made to enable the steps of the processes.

The online sites also send an SMS text message to the buyer, if a mobile number is provided, to indicate the details of the purchase. This involves another organisation that enables the sending of the SMS. Once the buyer arrives at the film theatre, he/she has to provide the details of the purchase to an automated kiosk or at the counter to receive her tickets that will allow him/her to enter the hall to see the film. The prior arrangement the management of the film theatre has to make is to arrange with the website to list their films and provide details about show times, hall seating arrangements and prices. The website management has to enable the buyer to select the tickets and also enable an easy payment through multiple possible gateways. The purchase has then to be listed by the management at the theatre in their kiosks and counters to issue the final tickets to the buyer.

The two examples clearly show that the manual method of ticket buying requires a fewer number of sub-processes but is more expensive for the buyer in terms of transaction time (see Table 15.1). In contrast, the online method is very convenient for the buyer, but takes a much larger number of sub-processes, involves a larger number of agencies and has much greater information flows.

The online method of ticket purchase is an example of the manner in which business processes have been integrated to serve a common purpose. Ticket purchasing is simplified for the buyer who, however, is unaware of the complex processes involved in the simple ticket purchase.

In other business processes, the complexity can be much higher than in the above example. An example is provided in Section 15.1.2.

15.1.2 Example of a Complex Process

Certain business processes require a large number of steps to be initiated and completed before the processes are themselves complete. These steps could involve persons and groups from different departments within the organisation, as also groups and people from other organisations. The complexity of such processes arises from the number of steps and the boundaries across which those steps have to be executed, as also from the choices that may be required to be made to complete the entire process. Within the execution scenario, there may be certain steps that can be reversed and certain steps that cannot be reversed.

Now, we examine a complex process in some detail. The objective is to gain an understanding of the people, departments and organisations that are involved as also of the information and material flows that are required. The process is based on a hypothetical book store, much like Oxford book store discussed in the opening case. The process steps are as follows:

1. A customer arrives at the store website and makes a book selection. The customer then logs in to a store account that he/she already has, and selects a book for payment.
2. The system checks for the customer's credit or debit card account, which it finds.
3. The system then checks with the partner bank if the customer's card can be charged. Upon receiving a confirmation, the credit/debit card details are transmitted to the bank, and the bank then asks the customer for security information (after redirecting the customer to its site). If the security is cleared, the credit transaction is completed.
4. The store receives a confirmation of the transaction from the bank and confirms the order for the customer.
5. The order details, including the customer's address, the title of the book and the quantity order are then transmitted to the shipping and inventory management modules.
6. The inventory management module will check if the book is available from stock, and if so, where it is located. If it is not in stock, then the purchasing module is informed that will then pass the request for this item to a vendor. If the book is in stock then it is located and the shipping module is informed.
7. The shipping module then passes the order and address information to the stock and shipping clerks, who can physically obtain the book from the shelves and package it for shipping. The clerks also include a receipt and a shipping invoice with the package. The receipt is obtained from the accounts department.
8. The shipping module also checks whether the customer has cancelled the order or the order has been cancelled for some other reason (such as the bank reporting a default on credit) or the order has been postponed or delayed. If the order has been cancelled then the shipping module cancels the shipping instructions.
9. Once the physical shipping of the book is started through a logistics or shipping agency, the details of the shipping number are recorded and may be sent via email or SMS to the customer.
10. When the amount from the customer is received from the bank, the accounts module is updated with the cash credit.
11. The details of the book are recorded by the marketing and sales department in order to keep track of fast-moving or popular titles that could be offered on discount or for special promotions. The marketing department may inform the procurement and inventory section of the demand for the book and whether to order more copies.
12. The inventory department may also perform checks on the number of books available in stock for the title and place further orders or not. Consolidated reports based on the inventory and marketing inputs may be prepared for relevant product managers to evaluate and recommend further action.
13. When the book is received by the customer, the information is recorded and the customer's account is updated.

As shown in Fig. 15.1, there are at least four departments - information systems, marketing, accounts, inventory and shipping - involved in the process of selling and shipping a book to a customer online. As all the possible outcomes of the process were not explored, this is a minimum number that is involved in the process. The example also shows engagement with two external agencies (the bank and the shipping agent) for the process to complete. Since the process is highly automated, the people involved are few - the shipping clerks, the delivery agents and the managers who decide on inventories. Reports generated from this process, and many other such processes, will however reach managers in all departments including those at the very top.

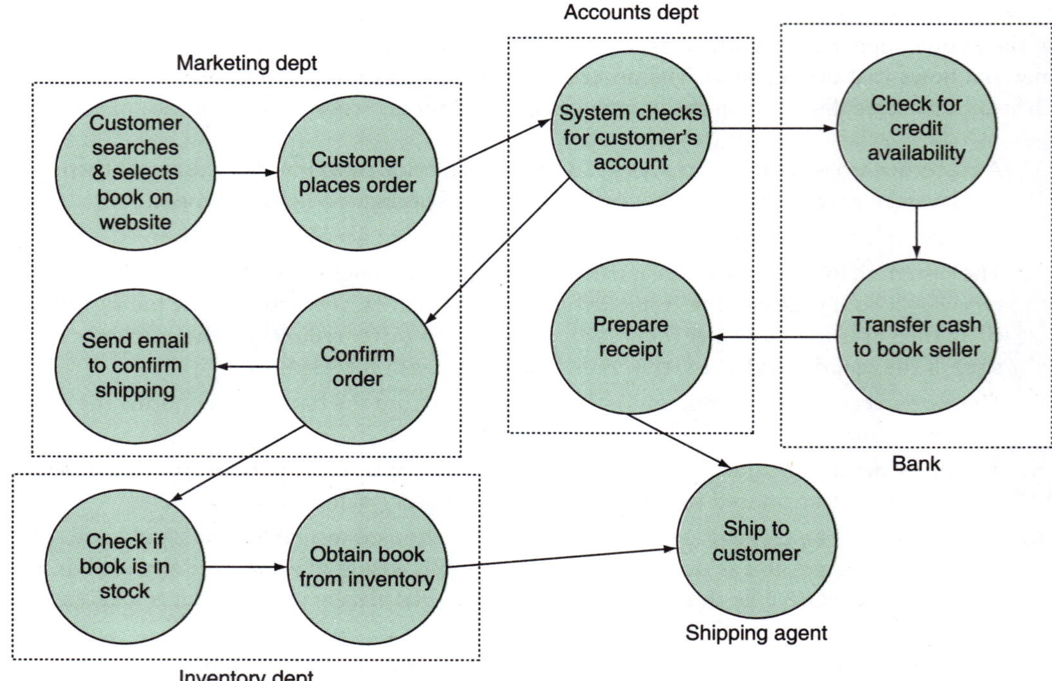

FIGURE 15.1 | Example of complex process of an online book order and execution involving many departments and two external organisations.

This example shows the complex nature of processes and the massive integration required between people, departments and systems. With the use of information systems, many of these processes can be integrated with automatic flows of information from one department or system to another.

15.2 MOTIVATION FOR ENTERPRISE SYSTEMS

In a landmark paper that appeared in the *Harvard Business Review* in 1990, Michael Hammer argued strongly for what came to be known as *Business Process Re-engineering*. Hammer's fundamental insight was that large-scale computerisation of processes in organisations was automating manual processes but not changing or re-engineering them to use the power of computers. As an example, Hammer showed that Ford Motors, a large automobile manufacturer in the USA, created three documents for ordering and receiving goods. Each of these documents, one from the ordering department, one from the receiving dock and one from the vendor, were sent to the accounts payable department, where a clerk had to match these documents to verify that the correct order had been received. Ford found that it had 400 employees in the accounts receivable department to do this work, while a rival, similar sized firm had five employees for the same task. Ford then thought of re-engineering the accounts receivable process, where the ordering department entered all the details of the order online, and the receiving clerk checked the goods against the purchase order available in a database. This way the work of the accounts receivable department was reduced. Hammer showed that this method of re-engineering allowed managers to integrate and streamline work processes, using the power of computer technology, rather than create automated versions of tedious manual processes.

The 1990s also saw the rise of what are now termed as enterprise systems. The most visible of these systems were called enterprise resource planning (ERP) systems, whereas the others were (later) termed supply chain management (SCM) systems and customer relationship management (CRM) systems. Such systems also encouraged organisations to think of process integration and put into place processes that utilised the computing power enabled by them. Furthermore, such systems also forced organisations to align their processes along the best practices within their industries. For example, an ERP implementation entails that the accounts receivable process in manufacturing organisations be conducted in a manner very similar to the way it had been designed within the ERP, which had undertaken research to ensure the 'best practices' of the industry were included.

Enterprise systems also gained popularity as they enabled firms to bring together a number of legacy systems within one platform. The idea was to bring 'islands of information' under one umbrella. Many large commercial firms, by early 1990s, across the world had invested in distributed, departmental information systems that automated the processes and work for their departments. Exchange of information between departments and having high-level views of joint data was difficult and presented many challenges. Data was not maintained in the same formats, and there was little coordination regarding updating the same data. Besides, the systems were built on a heterogeneous set of hardware and software (mainframes running Unix, desktops running Windows, etc.) and thus data migration was much harder. Enterprise systems pulled together these departmental information systems under a common, standard platform to overcome many of these problems.

Enterprise systems also helped organisations move from obsolete technology, acquired at high cost many years ago. One of the problems that spurred deployment of enterprise systems was the *Y2K problem*. This problem, in the 1990s, refers to the impending arrival of the year 2000. Many software programmers, who had started writing code in the 1970s and 1980s, when they were required to use the year value for some calculations, used the last two digits of the year rather than the entire set of four digits. For example, they used 69 instead of 1969. Computations that required dividing by the value of the year used two digits. Systems managers realised that in the year 2000, the last two digits would be zeros, and this raised a fear - it was well known that dividing by zeros within computer programs throws errors. Organisations had two options - either to check all their software for any place where a possible division by the year could occur, or change their software to newer packages where this problem had been resolved. Many opted for the second option and decided to buy enterprise software anyway, as these could address the integrated computing needs of the entire organisation. This drove up the demand for enterprise systems and many firms started their roll-outs before the year 2000. Millions of dollars were spent on these systems. It is a remarkable irony of history that the Y2K problem turned out to be a non-problem. The dawn of the year 2000 triggered no catastrophic failures of systems as had been predicted.

The multiple reasons for organisations to adopt enterprise systems are depicted in Fig. 15.2.

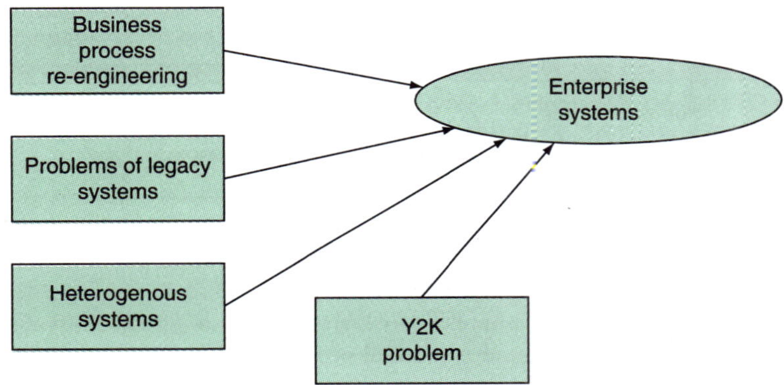

FIGURE 15.2 | Motivation for enterprise systems.

15.3 ENTERPRISE RESOURCE PLANNING SYSTEMS

ERP systems constitute the most important enterprise systems currently being used. The term ERP evolved from Material Resources Planning (MRP) that were systems developed to integrate functions of manufacturing, such as managing inventories, parts purchases and production planning. An MRP system allowed managers to provide inputs about product demand, including the different items demanded and the time at which they are required, and the system then determined the type, number and time duration in which various intermediate parts had to be assembled. It also tracked inventory levels for parts, and using scientific models determined when these parts had to be replenished to ensure a smooth manufacturing process.

Inspired by the manner in which MRP managed different systems used for manufacturing on the shop floor, software engineers tried to integrate the data and operations for all the other functions of the organisation. This led to the evolution of ERP.

One of the pioneers in the world of ERP systems is the German company SAP. Starting in the late 1970s, SAP had a vision of creating a common platform for all the major functions of any commercial organisation. The company was started by engineers who had worked in IBM and who knew the challenges of integrating data across functions. SAP remained a relatively unknown player in enterprise systems until the 1990s by when some very large firms around the world had deployed SAP very successfully across their enterprise.

SAP currently is synonymous with ERP software. It is one of the largest software product firms in the world and has deployments in 100,000 companies across 120 countries. The firm itself employs about 50,000 people, and it partners with over 2000 companies who act as SAP specialists and implementers. SAP is available in 40 languages and in 50 different currencies.

Owing to the popularity of the ERP software concept, several competitors to SAP have emerged over the years, many of which have been bought out or have not survived. Currently, the strongest competitors to SAP are Oracle, Microsoft (with a product called Microsoft Dynamics), Ramco, Epicor and Infor. Almost 70% of the market share is with SAP, Oracle and Microsoft, with the balance distributed between over a dozen smaller vendors. The smaller players include open source ERP products such as Adempiere, OpenBravo and Compiere.

An ERP package consists of four fundamental modules – manufacturing, finance and accounting, sales and marketing, and human resources – that are supported by a central database (see Fig. 15.3). Each module fully implements the functions that it is designed for, and additionally brings the best practices in terms of processes. The modules may be implemented independently but the core database remains the same.

The SAP ERP package further distinguishes between modules and business processes. The modules represent functions such as marketing or accounting, whereas the business processes are integrated, and they implement a number of transactions or steps that may cut across modules.

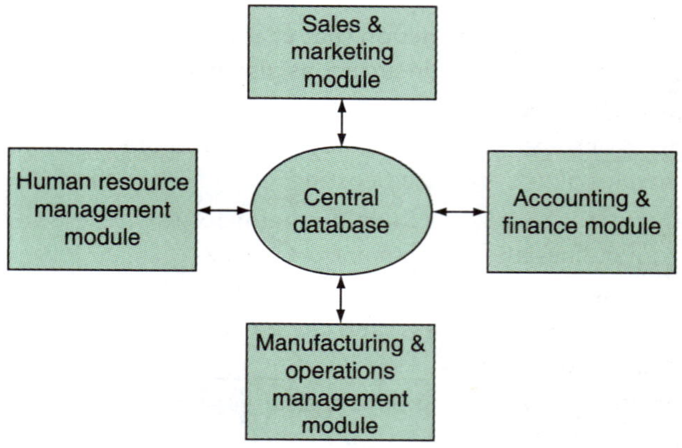

FIGURE 15.3 | Important modules of an ERP package supported by the central database.

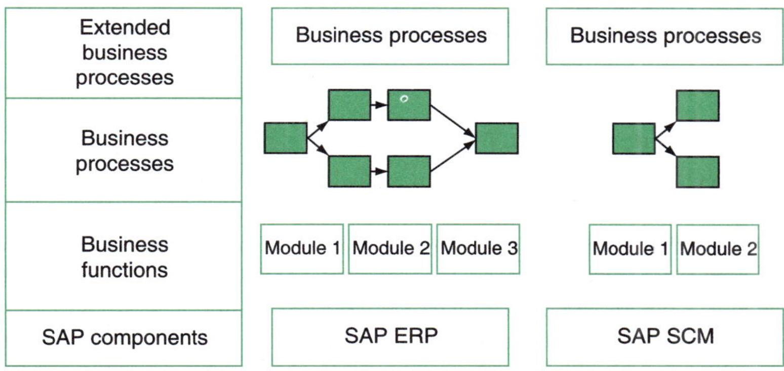

FIGURE 15.4 Depiction of SAP components that support business functions and processes that cut across departments and organisations. SAP ERP and SCM packages are shown.

Source: Adapted from *SAMS Teach Yourself SAP in 24 Hours* by G.W. Anderson.

SAP business modules include within them a large number of operations or functions that are routinely used by organisations (see Fig. 15.4). A brief description of these operations is described below.

15.3.1 Finance and Accounting Module

Finance and Accounting Module includes:

1. **General ledger accounting:** It is a place to record all the business transactions occurring across the organisation.
2. **Accounts payable and receivables:** It is a place where the data pertaining to vendor payments is recorded, along with cash and monies received from customers.
3. **Asset accounting:** It is a place where data about transactions involving fixed assets is maintained.
4. **Funds monitoring:** It is a set of operations where revenues and expenditures are monitored, along with a facility to plan and monitor budgets.
5. **Governance and risk:** It is a facility to monitor and govern the organisation's regulatory requirements. These functions help the organisation monitor its compliance with various laws and regulations.
6. **Overhead cost controlling:** It is a function that enables the organisation allocate, monitor and assess the overhead costs being incurred, as also helps in controlling these costs.
7. **Activity-based costing:** It is a function that allows the firm to charge overheads to activities such as sales, operations and customer management, and obtain an analysis of overheads based on the principles of activity-based costing.
8. **Profitability analysis:** It is an analysis function that helps the organisation views the profits from different product lines and departments.
9. **Business planning and budgeting:** It is a function that enables management to see the dependencies between profits and loss, and the balance sheet and cash flows, and create plans for budgets.
10. **Cash management:** It allows firms to have a clear view of their liquidity, both in terms of current status and future flows.
11. **Credit management:** It enables firms to have a clear view of credits allocated, pending, management and control.

15.3.2 Human Resource Management Module

Human Resource Management Module includes:

1. **Workforce process management:** It is a place where data on employee performance, benefits and work record is maintained according to legal requirements. These functions enable management to view the record of and make decisions about employees.
2. **Manager self-service:** It is a module that allows managers to view the profile of employees to seek out top performers and those with specific skills, calculate costs associated with employees, and estimate salary enhancements and budgets.
3. **Enterprise compensation management:** It is a place where data and analyses regarding salaries, benefits, bonus awards, salary trends, salary adjustments, budgets and planning, and compensation management are conducted. This module helps keep track of salary trends within the industry to help management attract and retain the best skilled and talented employees.
4. **E-Recruitment:** This module helps organisations track candidates for employment through online databases, notifications and hiring facilities.
5. **Organisational management:** This module helps with analysing the structure of the organisation in terms of its reporting and functional hierarchy, and helps analyse how different structures could be evolved and how they could be staffed.
6. **Organisational learning:** This module allows managers to assess the qualifications and skills within their workforce and plan for training and education for skills development. The module enables planning for company-wide training programs, budgeting for them and managing their execution.

15.3.3 Manufacturing and Operations Module

Manufacturing and Operations Module includes:

1. **Production planning and control:** This module maintains data on all production-related activities such as raw materials, sales forecasts and plans, production schedules, bill-of-material for different products, orders for repetitive manufacturing, costs of production data, just-in-time production plans and so on. It is a high-level module for managing the production function.
2. **Material management:** This module is responsible for managing inventories of consumable and non-consumable items in the firm. The module manages the inventory that includes purchasing, billing, storage in warehouses and bins, confirming invoices, as also material planning.
3. **Plant maintenance:** This module helps manage different manufacturing plants by keeping data on plant equipment, maintenance schedules, service routines, equipment details, equipment warranties and contracts, and orders.

15.3.4 Sales and Marketing Module

Sales and Marketing Module includes:

1. **Sales management:** This module helps in managing a sales force by keeping data on sales force distribution, sales calls, sales contacts, customer contacts and call information, regional sales data, contracts and so on.
2. **Marketing management:** This part helps in planning for campaigns, costs of campaigns and analysing competitor data.
3. **Distribution management:** This module complements the production module in keeping track of product distribution centres, the needs of various zones and warehouses, and the unmet demand.

Many of the tasks of the sales and marketing function of the ERP have now shifted to CRM systems, which is discussed later.

15.4 SUPPLY CHAIN MANAGEMENT SYSTEMS

Supply chain management (SCM) systems evolved alongside MRP and ERP. The basic purpose of such systems is to integrate suppliers and vendors of the host organisation that will allow processes to be integrated across organisational boundaries. A supply chain of an organisation consists of the vendors and suppliers who provide materials, parts and services to the organisation. In a larger sense, a supply chain consists of organisations and entities, which demand as well as supply goods and services that ultimately provide services or products to an end customer. The supply chain is thus a system of organisations, people, technology and information that enable material to be moved and processed to a form that the end customer consumes.

As a supply chain example, consider the manufacture of a book that is sold at Oxford book store. A book is made by a publisher who supplies it to the warehouse or retail store of Oxford. The publisher makes the book by obtaining the contents from the author, typesetting it on a software and then printing out many copies of the book on a printing press. Inputs to the printing press are paper and printer's ink along with other chemicals that are used to clean and operate the press. The printing press itself is manufactured by a hardware manufacturer. The publisher buys paper from a paper manufacturer and printer's ink from an ink-making factory. The paper manufacturer makes paper by taking wood pulp as input along with chemicals such as starch, dyes, calcium carbonate, sodium carbonate, zinc and many others. The paper manufacturer also requires specialised equipment to pulp, bleach, stain or colour and dry the paper. This equipment is supplied by different manufacturers. Ink is made from pigments, dyes, resins, lubricants, solvents, particulate matter and many other chemicals. Ink manufacturers source the ingredients from chemical manufacturers, who further source them from agricultural produce and materials obtained from mining, and from by-products of chemical processing. The supply chain ends at either mined materials or at agricultural produce, as these are the only things not of human manufacture.

The supply chain is also referred to as the logistics chain. In this chain, there is a flow of materials from suppliers to assemblers or manufacturers or sellers (see Fig. 15.5). At the end of the chain are the final customers who use the product. It may also happen that some users send the material back into the chain.

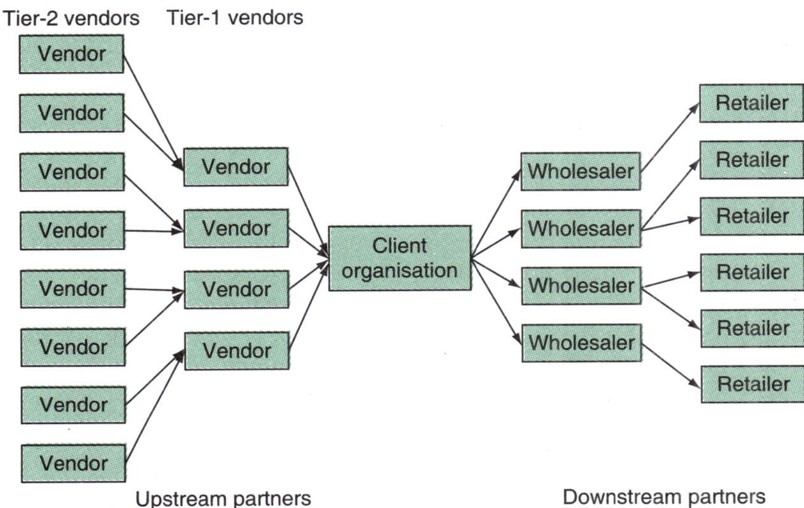

FIGURE 15.5 A supply chain showing Tier-1 and Tier-2 upstream and downstream partners. Upstream and downstream partners are with reference to the client organisation.

Oxford book store is one of the links in the chain that channels books to the end-user, the customer. The management of Oxford book store has to manage that part of its supply chain, which is of direct interest to it. The suppliers the management deals with directly are referred to as first tier or Tier-1 suppliers. It is notable that the suppliers of books are not the only Tier-1 suppliers for the book store. There are other vendors who also provide essential services and goods to them, such as:

1. Logistics firms will bring books to their stores and warehouses.
2. Banks provide them with financial services.
3. Advertising agencies can help them with marketing.
4. Human resource training companies may help them with training their staff and workers.
5. Telecommunication firms may provide them with internet and mobile phone services.
6. A software firm may assist them with maintaining their website.
7. A security firm may provide them with retail security and protection.

All such vendors are also part of the book store's supply chain and assist it with doing its business.

Tier-2 suppliers, in the context of the book store, are those who supply goods and services to Tier-1 suppliers. These may consist of a large number of manufacturers, service agencies and financial agencies. These, in turn, will be supported by Tier-3 suppliers. The purpose of SCM systems is to provide a coordination and planning platform to link Tier-1 suppliers (and sometimes Tier-2 suppliers too) with the activities of the parent organisation.

The ideas of managing supply chains originated in Just-in-Time (JIT) manufacturing that gained popularity in the 1980s. The idea of JIT manufacturing is to principally reduce inventories to as low levels as possible. Manufacturing units manage suppliers and delivery schedules in such a manner that the inventories are delivered just when they were in need, or just in time. Pioneered by the Japanese automobile manufacturer Toyota, JIT has many advantages:

1. It reduces costs associated with buying and holding inventories for many days in advance.
2. It reduces wastage.
3. It reduces the need for storage space.
4. It forces management to maintain stronger links with their suppliers and thus reduce uncertainties in supplies, and it leads to supply stability.

The computer manufacturer, Dell, also used JIT systems strategically to reduce its inventories from 60 days of stock to almost nothing, thus gaining considerable market share as a reliable supplier of computers.

An integral part of the philosophy of JIT is continuous improvement to reduce waste in the manufacturing process. JIT adherents use the principle of having the right amount of material, at the right time and at the right place. This requires close coordination between suppliers and clients, and thus SCM systems are a natural fit for the modern implementations of JIT.

One of the central problems of managing supply chains is that of having accurate demand information. If the demand information is accurate and is available sufficiently in advance then the planning that the vendors in the chain can do will be highly accurate. Accuracy implies that the manufacturers will be able to stock the right amounts of inventories for the manufacturing schedules and also accurately allocate their employees to tasks.

If the demand information is not accurate and suppliers are not able to plan their production accurately then this leads to losses for them. If the inventories of raw materials are maintained at levels that are too high and the materials are not being consumed on schedule, this means high costs of storage, working capital costs, and possibly costs from loss of goods. To prevent this from happening, suppliers may land up stocking lower quantities of raw materials, taking the risk of running out of materials if the demand increases suddenly.

Small fluctuations in demand at various points of the supply chain result in fairly high fluctuations in inventories at the end of the chain. This phenomenon is known as the *Bullwhip effect*.

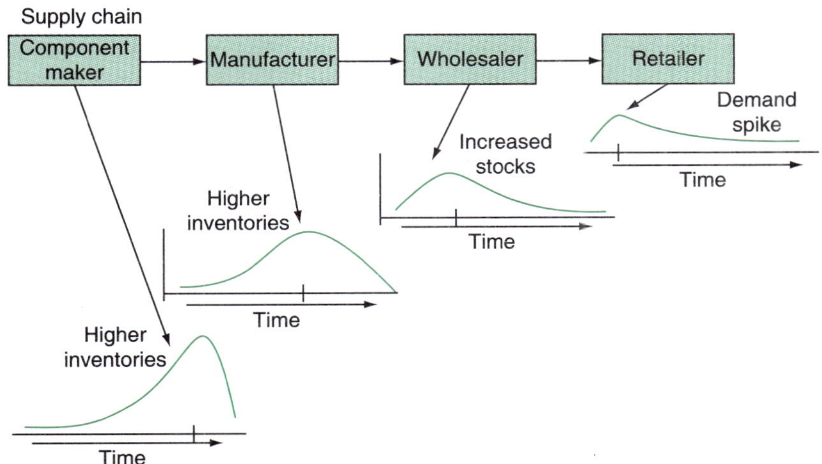

FIGURE 15.6 Depiction of the Bullwhip effect. Small spike in demand at the retailer results in very high increase in inventories at the end of the supply chain.

This happens because each supplier in the chain is trying to accommodate variability in demand from a downstream client, with excess buffers of stock. As the demand is unpredictable, the buffers tend to be conservative and excessive. This forces suppliers further upstream to carry even higher inventories and so on (see Fig. 15.6). The Bullwhip effect has been shown to occur in many international supply chains where the demand variability in some markets, say the USA markets, leads to manufacturing firms having to maintain high levels of inventories in China or Malaysia.

SCM systems are usually integrated with ERP systems for production, planning and control of manufacturing. SCM systems are often identified as planning systems or as execution system. SCM planning systems focus on demand forecasting and planning, whereas the execution systems help the actual transactions by enabling flow of information. Some important tasks, for planning and execution, which SCM systems execute are:

1. **Order management:** The system helps select orders and execute them. Vendors and clients can see the pending tasks and their priorities based on due dates and price values, and set up a plan by which to execute orders. This allows vendors to align their delivery dates with those of the client.
2. **Manufacturing scheduling:** On the basis of the orders received, the demand, the available inventories, and availability of equipment and personnel, the schedule of production activities is drawn up. These tasks also create job schedules for personnel, helping with setting targets and deadlines.
3. **Demand assessment:** The system tracks downstream manufacturing activities and creates a demand profile for upstream vendors. The vendors can then plan their own activities based on the demand forecast.
4. **Distribution management:** The system can help organise the movement of finished goods and parts from vendors to clients. This allows for careful just-in-time planning of stocks to reduce inventory costs.
5. **Transportation management:** Related to goods movement is the issue of arranging goods carriers, like trucks or railway rakes, which can enable smooth transport. The system enables coordination of these vehicles.

SCM systems may be designed to enable a build-to-order (demand-pull) regime of production, or a build-to-stock (supply-push) regime. The former relies on accurate demand forecasts, JIT inventory management and close management of all aspects of the chain, to ensure demand is met. Whereas, the latter entails building to a pre-determined production schedule and then moving finished goods as demanded. In the context of global markets and e-commerce-based marketing, the demand-pull system is beginning to dominate production.

15.5 CUSTOMER RELATIONSHIP MANAGEMENT SYSTEMS

The idea of CRM systems is to integrate all functions related to sales and marketing on a common platform. These functions include those that require support to sales and marketing staff and also those that directly enable customers to interact with the client organisation. Although CRM systems evolved independently, they are now integrated with other enterprise systems.

The origins of CRM lie in the sales force automation systems that grew with the rise of personal computing around the world in the 1980s. The systems would automate the processes of recording sales calls by salespersons; recording customer data and reading historical customer data; processing and relaying orders to the department; and enabling managers to plan for sales campaigns and field personnel. The use of call centres too emerged in this period. A call centre implies a facility in which customers could make phone calls to a particular number and have a representative of the company speak to them about orders, shipments, payments, order tracking, delivery schedules, return of goods and refund of payments. Call centres evolved as customer support mechanisms. In parallel, firms also realised that it is possible to reach out to customers via phones and started campaigns known as telemarketing, where sales representatives would call customers and market their goods and services. Calls would be made to customers who are already in the database of the firm, or to others, known as *cold calls*, who are likely customers. Telemarketing too relies on a database of customers, which record details about who was called, when the call was made, and what response was obtained.

The 1990s saw the growth of e-commerce around the world, with a variety of goods and services marketed and sold through the internet. This phenomenon gave rise to a demand for sales and marketing services geared to the needs of online customers. If customers purchased, say, a rail ticket online, and needed to verify or change some value in it then a facility was provided by which they could call a sales or marketing support agent and make their queries. This required that the sales support agent had to have details about the transaction available at hand and be able to respond to the queries.

CRM systems evolved to consolidate these different activities - call centres, telemarketing and online e-commerce and support - and enable them through a common platform. A firm called Siebel was the first to market such a system. Started in 1993, Siebel grew from a firm making sales force automation software to one that had a suite of applications to help sales and marketing. Siebel's key idea was to integrate data related to customers under a single window such that sales personnel could have all the necessary information to make their sales and also improve their relations with the customer.

CRM applications are a way to enhance and embellish customer *touch points*. Touch pionts are interfaces at which the marketing establishment of a commercial firm interfaces, directly or indirectly, with a current or potential customer. This term also has a larger connotation – referring to any interface of the firm with stakeholders such as customers, employees, shareholders, the government, etc. Firms that market a product or service (or a brand associated with these) have to manage the touch points carefully, to ensure that the correct information is transmitted. CRM systems assist with this task.

CRM systems provide functions for broadly two kinds of activies - analysis and execution. The systems that support analysis (also referred to as analytical CRM) are based on data obtained from organisational data repositories, such as data warehouses, and use data mining and analytics to make demand forecasts, provide customer profiles, predict consumer behaviour, assess competitor strategies and so on. The systems that support execution (referred to as operational CRM) provide background data and analysis to personnel on the sales and marketing teams. Functions such as telemarketing or email-based publicity are assisted by the operational CRM.

Examples of various facilities created by CRM are as follows:

1. **Manage customer data:** The CRM system maintains data on customers that not only pertains to the details about the customer – such as name, address and demographic profile – and the products the customer has purchased, but also maintains a history of the contacts with the customer. A CRM system for a bank, for instance, will maintain data on when a potential customer called or visited the website of the bank, when the customer enrolled and who he/she talked to at the bank, when he/she began transactions, whom he/she has talked to or contacted over the years regarding different services, and how many calls he/she has responded to. With such data available to them, sales personnel can recall any prior transactions with the customer, showing that they are aware of the customer's needs.
2. **Manage sales force:** The CRM system allows sales managers to track activities of sales force personnel and plan their tasks. The CRM system supports sales personnel by providing access to data about customers, order, delivery status, invoice status, payments and payment histories. Furthermore, the system helps sales personnel follow up on leads and record details about their visits and conversation. The system also enables creating quotes, based on the current prices of products, in the field.
3. **Marketing management:** The system can be used to plan for and execute marketing campaigns and then systematically analyse the results. The system can help plan events, campaigns, promotions and retain data and results related to these. Marketing managers can then use customised analysis to assess the impact of their campaigns. The system can show maps, charts, graphs and dynamically adjusted visuals of marketing activities across regions and products. Some special add-on analysis products can also enable managers to simulate scenarios to decide on their campaigns.

Some special marketing tasks that the CRM system enables are that of cross-selling, up-selling and bundling.

1. **Cross-selling:** It enables sales personnel to offer complementary products to customers; the system helps them by providing information on the customer's past purchases, for example, a laptop, and then showing what complementary products can be offered to them, for example, a printer.
2. **Up-selling:** It offers higher value or higher priced goods to customers. For example, a customer, who has purchased a basic mobile phone, may be offered a smart mobile phone when it is known, from the customer's profile, that he/she can afford the product.
3. **Bundling:** It is the act of clubbing together products to help the customer get a better price on all than on any one alone. The system can help the sales personnel offer this, based on the customer's profile and estimated preferences.
4. **Service support:** The CRM system can provide data and analysis regarding all activities related to servicing customers – feedback reports, payment information, delivery information and so on. This support is used mainly by the call centre and help desk personnel.

As with other enterprise systems, CRM systems too are designed with industry best practices built in. For instance, the process of customer call handling is standardised within CRM packages to represent the best practices followed in the industry. CRM systems enable processes to be built on existing and future databases of firms.

The ideas of relationship management are extended to employees and partners too. Systems known as *employee relationship management* (ERM) and *partner relationship management* (PRM) follow the same principles as CRM but are targetted for use by employees and partner organisations. PRM are used by vendors to manage their clients through electronic means. The difference between PRM and CRM is based on the fact that vendors typically have to deal with fewer clients, their clients are usually organisations, and vendors have a more interactive relationship with clients. Vendors use a PRM to reduce the costs associated with a sales force that establishes and maintains contact with clients; the electronic interface serves to do the same.

15.6 CHALLENGES OF ENTERPRISE SYSTEMS IMPLEMENTATIONS

Enterprise systems have faced severe challenges of implementation and even failures. The Foxmeyer Drug Co in the USA went bankrupt after a failed ERP implementation. Researchers estimate that about 75% of ERP implementation projects fail; the failure implies excessive overrun of budgets or outright inability to perform after implementation.

One of the most famous cases of failure of a CRM project was that of a Siebel implementation at AT&T. AT&T was one of the largest telecommunication firms in the USA and had a huge mobile phone business. It had implemented Siebel software to allow customers to interact with its staff, maintaining a history of all the interactions. In 2003, AT&T upgraded the Siebel software to a new version and this resulted in large-scale problems. Servers crashed routinely and millions of customers were left unserved. The problems with the CRM were that it did not allow creation of new customer accounts, would not allow customers to change their numbers under the new number portability laws in the USA and also blocked call access for many customers. Many of their customers moved to their competitors. This had a profound impact on AT&T's business and it later was bought out by a rival firm.

Much criticism too has been levelled at enterprise software. The most prominent one is that by adopting industry practices, as embodied in the software, firms are losing their competitive advantage. After all, say critics, many firms derive a competitive advantage by how they do the same things as their rivals albeit in a better manner, so customers come to them. If every firm in the industry follows the same practices, they will be indistinguishable from each other. Another criticism is that the enterprise-level focus forced by enterprise systems is, in many cases, so severe that it shuts out the innovative ways in which employees can change their work practices to meet the demands of the market. Such systems deaden the innovation potential of employees. Other critics argue that the changes forced by the system ruptures the organisational culture, quite adversely, in many cases.

However, despite the criticism enterprise systems have been adopted widely across industry segments, as also by small and medium enterprises and by government agencies. The current trend of providing enterprise services through the cloud model, by firms such as Salesforce.com, has lowered many of the implementation risks as also the costs.

15.6.1 Managing the Implementation

Possibly the most important issue in ensuring the success of enterprise systems is that of managing change effectively (see Fig. 15.7). Such systems introduce massive changes in terms of procedures and practices that the firm's employees are used to. Large systemic changes pose

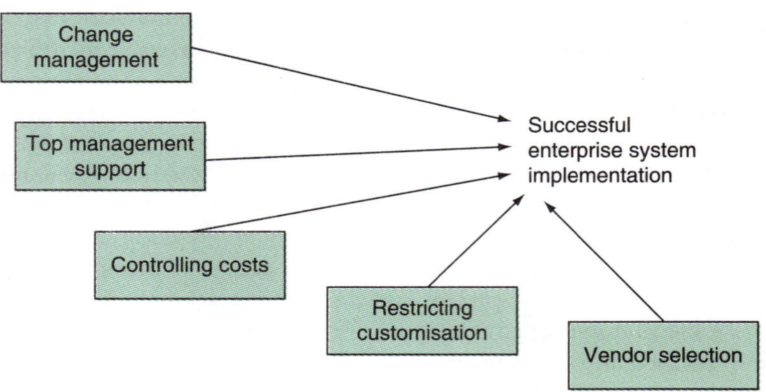

FIGURE 15.7 Issues having a bearing on the successful implementation of an enterprise system.

a threat and raise the levels of anxiety in the firm. Job roles are changed and redefined, the employees are trained for using the system in a manner that suits the new processes rather than what the employees were comfortable with, and the flexibility that they enjoyed, in many cases, is replaced by a rigid process.

Change management entails training staff in the new procedures, creating new teams and defining new tasks, creating new reporting relationships, and creating a new culture in which employees will work. This requires careful and sensitive handling of involved employees, right from the start of the project. Key employees from departments and groups have to be recruited for guiding the system's implementation, and they have to be encouraged to participate freely rather than resist the system.

Although change is not easily accepted, it is achieved after employees begin to see the visible benefits of the system through reduced workloads or through the effective use of the system. The management has to tread carefully and nurture this change when it becomes visible.

The second most important criterion for the successful implementation of an enterprise system is that of the *top management support*. Almost all the successful cases of ERP deployments show that the top management was deeply committed to the project and supported it all through the implementation steps. The top management has to be involved from the start and stay with the project management team right through the duration of the project. They should openly take responsibility for the success of the system and announce rewards and incentives for its successful operation.

The top management is also the key ingredient for change management. Their acceptance, support and encouragement of change make possible the creation of new cultural norms and business practices. In several large and successful ERP roll-outs, the top management spent much time talking about the project to employees, participated in meetings and training workshops, wrote on personal web pages and emails to staff and spoke to news media about the project. They created a positive environment for the new system and celebrated its success.

Controlling costs is the other critical issue in ensuring the success of the enterprise system implementations. The costs of implementing and running an ERP system range from USD 400,000 to about USD 3 million, depending on the size of the company. These figures are from a study conducted in 2007, and are much lower than an average of USD 15 million per firm, which was found in 2003. These figures are largely for USA and European commercial firms. In India, the average figures are reported to be in the range of Rs 6–9 million (USD 130,000–200,000) for an ERP system implementation per firm. These are the figures that are arrived at after the implementation is complete and firms know or can approximate the total amounts they have spent. The initial estimates that they had for the projects were, invariably, lower.

Of the many items that managers usually underestimate, training of staff and personnel is the most frequent. Since almost all employees of the firm are affected and have to learn the new system, this cost grows as people realise the challenges of entering and using data that affects many others in the firm, and demand more help and training. Another area of increased costs is *customisation* of the package. As the implementation proceeds, many firms realise that the changes in processes being demanded are not possible or difficult and then they resort to customisation, which requires extra work from the vendor and hence extra costs. Customisation also leads to further demands on testing and integration, which also add to the cost. Other areas that add to increased costs are data conversion and migration (from old formats to the formats required by the system); costs of consultants who are hired to solve specific and hard problems; costs of time lost by the best employees in helping with the new system rather than working on their own tasks; and the loss in productivity immediately after an implementation as employees have to work with an entirely new system.

Project management and *vendor selection* are also key issues for the success of the project. Project management entails that the management and the implementation team have to keep a sharp tab on the deadlines and milestones. If these are missed, it is certain that later milestones will also be missed. Delayed implementations cause loss of morale and a poor image with all stakeholders. Key to the success of the project is the implementation partners. Few firms have internal skills to manage an enterprise system implementation on their own. They invariably rely on the vendor to do the implementation or a third party, who act as consultants. The selection of this partner is very important as the partner needs to have the necessary skills, experience and a cost structure that matches the expectations of the client firm. There are many examples of lawsuits against implementation consultants by clients as the project went sour or failed totally and wasted millions of dollars.

15.7 INTERNATIONAL INFORMATION SYSTEMS

In a world now connected by the internet, the basis of trade and global transactions is International Information Systems. Just in terms of trade, the value of transactions crosses over a trillion US dollars per day. There are over 2 billion users on the internet, according to the internet Stats Today website (in May 2011), and they account for close to 7 exabytes (or 7 billion gigabytes) of global traffic per month (according to a forecast by Cisco Corporation in 2011).

Many organisations, especially commercial firms, now have a global footprint, which means they have a presence in many countries around the world. For example, ArcelorMittal, the largest steel producer in the world, has a presence in 60 countries. Firms in the initial stages of having international business either act as exporters or importers of goods and services. Many firms in India export textiles, chemicals, ore, software and auto parts to customers in different parts of the world. Others import goods from them. Firms that have a stronger presence in the international market have offices in many other countries where they do business. Their main line of business could be exporting goods or parts or services to customers in those countries. They create offices as legal entities in foreign countries and comply with their laws and regulations. Such firms are known as *multinationals*. Infosys of India is a multinational as it maintains an office in many other countries where its employees work to develop software. Infosys is headquartered in India, and its offshore offices serve to continue Infosys's work there. The Taj Hotels chain is another multinational corporation that has hotels in many parts of the world and its headquarters is in India.

Some firms maintain entirely different entities in different countries of the world, including separate headquarters in some countries. So a firm may have originated in the USA, but now has headquarters in India, China, Australia and so on. The offices in different countries work independently although they may be in the same line of business as the original firm. Such firms are called *transnational* companies. HSBC bank, a bank originating from Hong Kong in China, is also a transnational as it has independent banks in many countries of the world. Figure 15.8 depicts differences between multinational and transnational organisations.

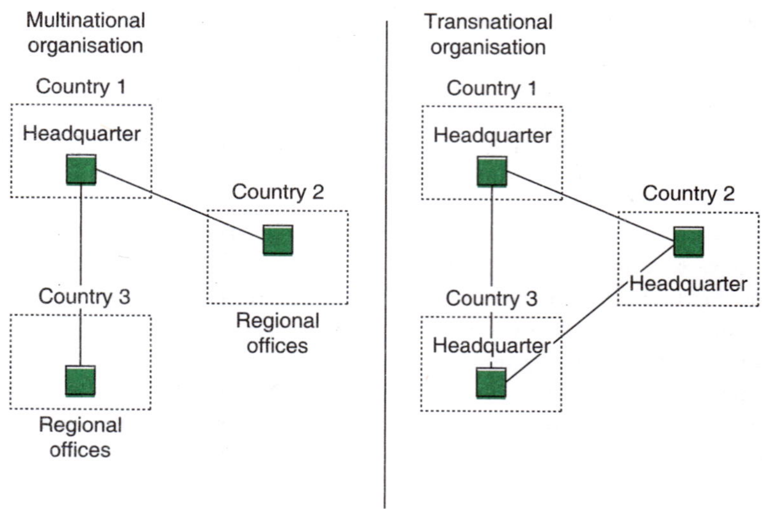

FIGURE 15.8 Differences between multinational and transnational organisations.

The needs of these different types of firms with regard to information systems are different, as they have different ways of doing business. Export- and import-oriented firms mainly need to interact with their clients to understand delivery schedules for exchange of documents and for transfer of monies. Some firms in this category will be part of the foreign firm's supply chain and thus may have systems that are part of the client firm's SCM. In such situations, they have to maintain their systems to comply with the demand and supply schedules determined by the client's enterprise system. In most such cases, the vendor firms also have to invest in and maintain enterprise systems that match those of their clients.

The most complex requirements for international information systems originate from multinational firms. The challenge of such firms is to coordinate information systems for sharing of data and processes. Data sharing across countries and time zones requires careful handling of currencies, languages, time stamps and legal requirements. Varying currencies are usually handled by US dollar denomination, which means that when currency data (related to prices or value) is shared across nations, the local currency values are converted to US dollars that are converted back to other currencies where needed.

Time stamps on data, which is needed in some cases (such as the time when a credit card transaction occurs), are usually handled by recording the time and the location. When needed, this time is converted to the time at the firm's headquarters, according to a world clock such as the Greenwich Mean Time (GMT). Similarly, the transactions are recorded in the local language along with the location information. When needed, these are translated to English, which remains the predominant language of business.

Possibly the most serious challenge for international information systems arises from shared processes, where the processes have to cross borders and legal requirements. Consider, for example, the case of collecting sales or value added tax (VAT) from customers in different countries for the sale of the same product. For example, if centralised information systems, located in the USA, are being used in a different country, say India, then the Indian tax laws are applicable for the transaction instead of US tax laws. This situation can be addressed by using business rules for the local country that account for the tax requirements. However, complications arise if tax computations have to be based on components of the goods being sold – whether they are made in India or abroad, whether they are made with certain kinds of imported or indigenous materials or not and so on – and then blended with the conditions operating in the USA. Such situations call for case-by-case handling which results in increased costs.

Processes that extend across national borders require that there is a shared understanding of the nature of the tasks and what they demand. For instance, if a process requires entry of data, manually, immediately after receipt of goods, this has to be followed exactly in all the countries where the process is shared. If this practice is not followed exactly in some places then the aggregated data pertaining to receipt of goods will not be reliable. This issue is also governed by local cultural practices and local customs. If it is not customary for employees to record anything on certain days, say on a religious holiday, then this task will not be completed on that day.

15.7.1 Outsourcing and Off-Shoring

One of the strengths of Indian IT firms has been in the area of outsourcing and off-shoring of services related to IT and back-office processing. *Outsourcing* refers to moving some processes of the firm to a partner or a vendor. Outsourcing is prevalent in all organisations to a larger or lesser extent. Many organisations outsource tasks such as photocopying or managing a cafeteria, tasks that are best managed by specialised vendors. With the advent of information technology, more sophisticated tasks, such as building and maintaining software or running a website, are also outsourced. Outsourcing contracts specify the nature of the task, the manner in which it has to be executed (for instance, whether the vendor's employees will be on the facilities of the client), and the manner of payment. Outsourcing is useful for reducing costs and acquiring expertise. Vendors who specialise in a task (say making websites) will be the best resource to hire for a firm that does not have internal employees who can do this. Furthermore, vendors can be hired at a cost lower than what it would cost to do this internally.

Off-shoring has to do with moving business processes overseas to some other country. This idea originated in high-cost countries like the USA and some European countries, where some firms thought that moving processes such as production of goods, like software, to countries that have lower costs of raw materials and also lower wages would help them be more competitive. So, many manufacturing firms in countries like the USA started moving the facilities first to countries such as Mexico and others in Latin America, and then to China, where lower labour and material costs let them make the same goods at a lower cost. India became a major destination for software goods and services for the same reason.

The use of international information systems for outsourcing and off-shoring is significant in both enabling the phenomena and also allowing them to grow to a massive scale. These systems enable many ways in which clients and vendors from different countries and organisations can collaborate. Some examples are given below.

Outsourcing vendors from Bangalore can see and share the data, application and systems of clients in the USA in real time. They can monitor activities on, say, a database server, and respond to emergencies or technical needs of clients rapidly.

Many organisations in the USA and Western Europe have outsourced and off-shored their help desk and customer support processes to vendors in India and other countries. When customers call help numbers in the USA, they are directed to an operator in Delhi or Bangalore who is able to look up their transaction data on a server located in the USA and respond to their calls.

Many systems development teams in the client organisation work closely with outsourced vendors, who are off-shore, by communicating through chat sessions, email, video sessions, teleconferencing and using social media. Documents about the development are maintained on shared servers. The messages of the teams are also saved for further referencing.

For some clients in the USA, calls for fixing software bugs or for offline support on applications are logged on to shared servers. When the employees in the USA go off work in the evenings, it is usually the time engineers in India, who are the outsourced support vendors, and are going in to work in the morning. The logged complaints are attended to during the day in India and reports about remedies and measures taken are submitted. When the American clients return to work the next morning, they are able to see these reports.

Caselet: Using Blockchain Technology for Managing Supply Chains

Blockchains are software artifacts that enable the creation of what are called *public ledgers* that are a record of transactions maintained on widely distributed clients and servers. These blockchains or public ledgers have some strong properties :

1. Once a ledger entry is made, it cannot be tampered with, and it becomes a permanent entry.
2. The entries in the ledger are visible to all collaborating parties.
3. The blockchain data is maintained on distributed entities that are secure and cannot be hacked.
4. Blockchains provide a proof of authenticity, in the sense that only the verified and legitimate party can make the ledger entries.

Blockchain technology thus provides many advantages for use within supply chains. Firms such as IBM have started using these extensively.

One of the challenges of managing supply chains is that of trusting all the partners and players in the many transactions. A global supplier has to ensure that the goods being imported from many different countries have been shipped, that the relevant papers have been included, the documents related to local customs and local shipping regulations are included, payments have been received, and of course, ensuring that no information is leaked and no fraudulent entries are made. Traditionally, ensuring authenticity and correct information on all these tasks has required a massive infrastructure of documents, information sharing, trusted intermediaries and reliable contract handling. Blockchain technology provides a modern alternative that eases many of these tasks.

With a blockchain-enabled supply chain, a global supplier can rely on knowing exactly when a particular shipment has been made, as this will be recorded on the blockchain (as a block entry that is *chained* with prior entries). The entry into the ledger can be accompanied by a *smart contract* that enables the release of funds, depending on who has to receive and who has to provide the funds, the moment the entry is made. Such smart contracts assure the blockchain owners that monies are released the moment a task is completed, without the need for oversight and availability of intermediaries (such as banks).

When a shipment is made, and recorded on a blockchain, the relevant documents that are to accompany the shipment are included in the ledger entry. This arrangement ensures that all pertinent documents are included within the transaction. This also ensures that all the correct parties receive the documents are the time when the shipment is completed.

These blockchain entries provide complete transparency of the supply chain transactions. As transactions are completed and recorded they are made visible to all the trusted parties who have access to the public ledger. Recipients of goods can now be assured as to when the goods will arrive and also how they will be transported. In supply chains where certain conditions have to be maintained, say of temperature or pressure, this information is also recorded on the blockchain and made available to partners. Upon receipt too, suppliers can verify how the goods were transported and the conditions under which they were stored and moved.

Another advantage of blockchain data for the supply chain is that the information is available across the chain and demand forecasts can be accurate. For example, the moment of a customer, at a retail outlet, purchases a good, this can be recorded and reflected using blockchain technology and the entire ripple of demand arising out of this sale can be known in advance. This information can be used to overcome the problems of the bullwhip effect as demand forecasts are generated from actual sales data on a real time basis.

Blockchain technology enables vendors and suppliers to see clearly the demand arising out of various locations on the supply chain and to anticipate future demand. Blockchains assure that the data is updated, reliable and assured.

Chapter Glossary

Business process Activities within an organisation that require some inputs that are transformed into desired outputs.

Process re-engineering Changing manual processes by using computerisation to make them more streamlined and integrated.

Y2K problem The problem perceived by the computing industry in the 1990s to occur owing to the arrival of the year 2000.

Supply chain The set of vendors that provide raw material, parts and services to a client organisation.

Cross-selling The act of offering complementary products to buyers.

Up-selling The act of offering higher priced products to buyers and current clients.

Bundling Offering several products to a customer with a price discount.

Multinational An organisation that has a headquarter in one country and offices in other countries where it does business.

Transnational An organisation that has headquarters in many countries, and it functions independently in each country.

Outsourcing The act of moving some processes of an organisation to a partner or vendor.

Off-shoring The act of moving business processes to another country, usually to an outsourcing partner.

Review Questions

1. Identify and document three business processes in your college or organisation. Do any of these processes cut across departments?
2. What is business process re-engineering?
3. What is the Y2K problem? How did it arise?

4. What is an ERP system? What are its major components?
5. Briefly identify the main functions of the finance and accounting module of an ERP.
6. What is a supply chain? Give two examples.
7. What is the function of SCM systems?
8. What are the main functions of a CRM system?
9. What criticisms are levelled against enterprise systems?
10. What are the main issues to manage for a successful ERP implementation?
11. How are international information systems different from the ones that only operate in domestic locations?
12. What is the meaning of outsourcing and how is it different from off-shoring?
13. How do multinationals differ from transnationals?

Research Questions

1. Visit a firm that has implemented an ERP and study all the processes that it automates.
2. Critics argue that enterprise systems reduce a business firm's ability to compete. How is this possible? Look for some examples of this.
3. Suppose you wanted to manufacture a tablet computer in India. Do some research to find out what components you would need? Then search further to find out the supply chain for each component.
4. For the firm you visit in Question 1, identify the complex process that you saw and describe it in detail. How many internal departments and external agencies did it involve?

Further Reading

1. Pathak, A. (2011) Publishing in India Today: 19,000 Publishers, 90,000 Titles, Many Opportunities. The article is available at: http://publishingperspectives.com/2011/07/publishing-in-india-today-19000-publishers-90000-titles/ (accessed on July 2011).
2. Gupta, V. (August 2011) Oxford Bookstore boosts efficiency using cloud based solution. *Information Week*.
3. Chidambaram, V. With SaaS ERP, Oxford Bookstore increased its revenue by Rs 3.4 crore. The article is available at:

   http://202.138.100.134/case-study/erp-solution-delivered-saas-style-bumped-oxford-bookstores-revenue-rs-34-crores (accessed on July 2011).
4. Koch, C. (2004) Project Management: AT&T Wireless Self-Destructs. *CIO.com*
5. Koch, C. and Wailgum, T. (2007) ERP Definitions and Solutions. *CIO.com*.
6. Anderson, G.W. (2011) *SAMS Teach Yourself SAP in 24 Hours*, Pearson Education.
7. Hammer, M. (1990) Re-engineering work: Don't automate, obliterate, *Harvard Business Review*.
8. Rettig, C. (2007) The Trouble with Enterprise Software, *Sloan Management Review*.
9. Byrnes, J. (2003) Dell Manages Profitability, Not Inventory, *Working Knowledge*, HBS Press. The article is available at:

   http://hbswk.hbs.edu/archive/3497.html (accessed on November 2011).

CHAPTER 16

Decision Support Systems

Learning Objectives

After completing this chapter, you will be able to:

- Understand decision support systems
- Learn about components of DSS
- Understand analytics and business intelligence
- Learn about knowledge management

Decision support systems (DSS) are used extensively across organisations to assist managers with making decisions. DSS are different from management information systems as they are used on an as-needed basis and created for solving special types of decision problems. Decision making by managers involves the phases of intelligence, design and choice, and DSS help mainly with the choice part. DSS support structured and unstructured types of decisions. A typical DSS consists of a database, a model base, where mathematical models of decision making are maintained, and a user interface. Modern approaches to decision support include analytics and artificial intelligence techniques for predictive and real-time analysis of data. Use of tools such as Neural Networks, Decision Trees, Clustering and Visualisation are quite extensive.

Knowledge management (KM) is the practice of codifying the knowledge of individuals and organisations in a manner that it is available for all to use. Knowledge may be of many different kinds - declarative, procedural, explicit and tacit. Knowledge also has a life cycle in which it is created or captured, developed, used and reused, and then it degrades. Knowledge management can be effected by a top-down hierarchical approach or by using a market approach. Some technologies for KM include Expert Systems, Content Management Systems and Mind Maps.

MIND MAP OF CHAPTER TOPICS

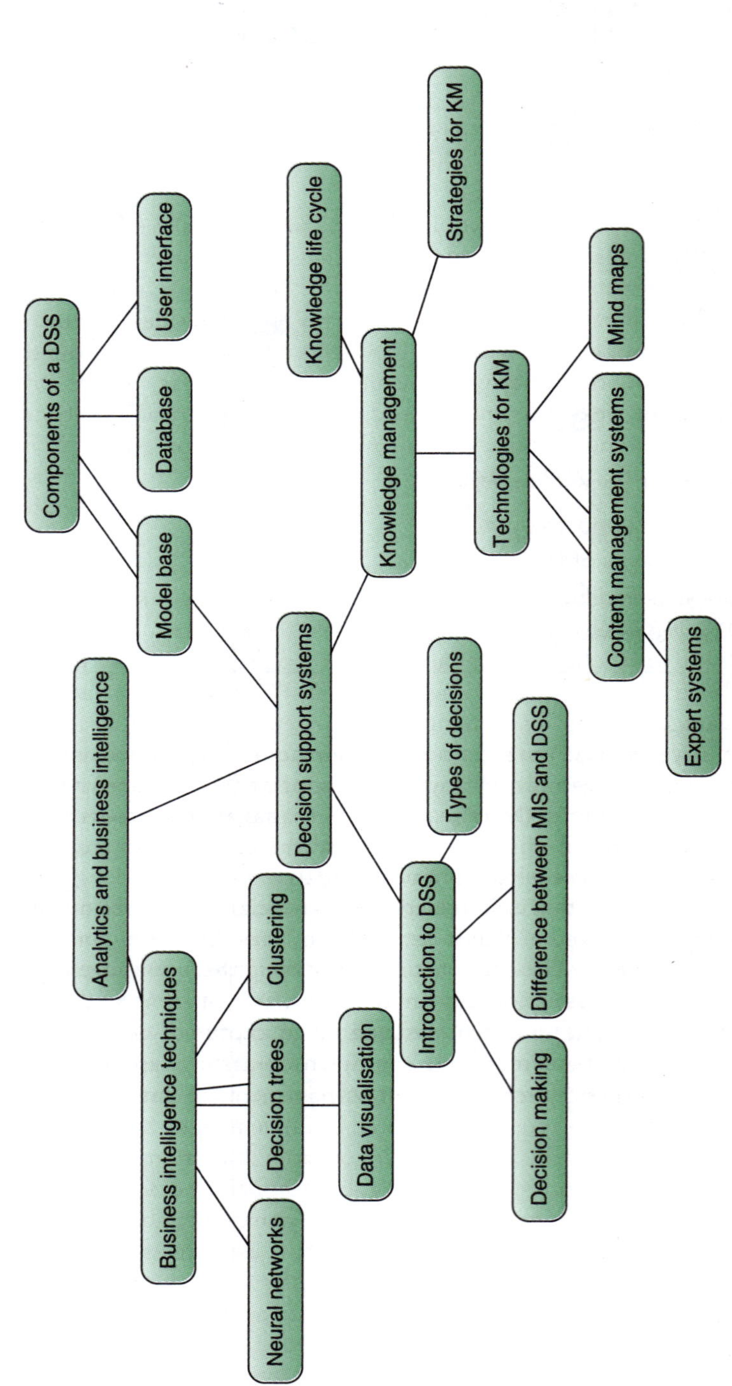

CASE STUDY: REVENUE OPTIMISATION AT TAJ HOTELS

The Taj Hotels Resorts and Palaces group is one of the largest hotel chains in India, and also in the world. It has 93 hotels in 55 locations in India (in 2011), with 16 more internationally in places such as the UK, the USA, Africa, Australia, Maldives and Malaysia. The Taj hotels are known for their excellent service and high quality of properties. One of the most luxurious and expensive hotels in the world is a Taj group hotel, which was a former palace.

The Taj group is distinguished in India, as the Taj Palace Hotel in Mumbai was one of the first luxury hotels in India, having started in 1903. It stands as an icon of Mumbai, next to the Gateway of India. The Taj Palace Hotel was also the first to be electrified in Mumbai. The group was also one of the first to convert an erstwhile palace into a hotel, the Rambagh Palace in Jaipur, and a fort, the Aguada Fort in Goa, into a hotel. The Aguada resort is unique as it is built within the walls of a former Portuguese fort.

The Taj group has seen a massive growth in their business throughout the 2000s, spurred by a massive growth in the tourism industry along with the overall growth in the Indian industrial sector. The period saw a steep increase in the demand for hotel rooms by both tourist and business travellers. The Government of India provided the trigger for this demand by reducing taxes on air travel and thus allowing the low-cost airlines sector to bloom, increasing the number of airports and also increasing the capacity of existing airports in cities such as Delhi, Mumbai, Bangalore and Hyderabad. The Government also initiated tourism related publicity campaigns abroad that have increased the awareness of and attraction for Indian destinations. Campaigns such as 'Incredible India' and 'Atithi Devo Bhavah' drove India's rankings up as a tourist destination. In 2008, the global tourism magazines *Conde Nast Traveler* and *Lonely Planet* rated India among the top five destinations in the world.

The demand-supply gap in hotel rooms is immense in India. According to industry experts, in 2008, the demand exceeded the supply by 100%. The total number of rooms available at that time was about 110,000 in over 1000 registered hotels. The industry demand has driven the prices to rise at the rate of about 25% annually, with occupancy rates rising at 80%.

To manage its large fleet of hotels, the Taj group uses IT extensively. It has implemented an ERP package to manage supplies and finances. The system has helped hotels manage a very large stock of inventory items such as shampoos, cooking oils, etc. The hotels also use a system to manage room reservation centrally. This system is supported by a call centre that can handle over 2000 calls daily. Furthermore, the group uses a CRM system that keeps track of all users, what rooms they usually book, in which hotel and what their preferences are. With such a system, managers can plan for prices of rooms and bookings.

A problem that hotels face is that of limited supply. A hotel only has a fixed number of rooms that it can offer in a day, and so the value it can realise by providing fixed prices is also limited. Following a strategy, that most hotels do, of maximising their room utilisation leads to a situation where the maximum value is also fixed.

However, many experts offer a way to overcome this maximum by a technique of revenue optimisation (RO). Here, the hotel managers can use a forecasting system to determine what their demand is and then take chances of offering higher prices to lesser customers to obtain higher value realisation. The Taj group experimented by implementing such a package.

The Taj managers found that they have a pattern of room utilisation across cities, with Delhi and Mumbai at a higher utilisation than Bangalore. But, they also noted that the revenues realised at Bangalore were higher. This was a result of a peak demand period in Bangalore (around the Dussehra period, usually in October, when many tourists arrive to see the festivities in neighbouring Mysore city), when higher prices could be charged.

RO works on the principle of offering rooms at higher prices to lesser number of visitors, rather than lowering prices to fill up occupancy. If a group of four demands four rooms at Rs 10,000 (USD 220) each then the management has the option of refusing them the bookings, hoping to offer the rooms at Rs 15,000 (USD 330) each. This would bring a higher realisation, an additional profit of Rs 5000 (USD 110), even by booking only three rooms. However, here is a catch - the management should be reasonably sure that three new customers will ask for rooms, even at the higher price of Rs 15,000. Or else, the hotel will lose the revenue that was sure to come from the lower price of Rs 10,000!

The RO software is a decision support software that forecasts demand based on past record of reservations. It allows the managers to price each room based on the highest value that can be realised. The software uses a mathematical model to show the managers the risks associated with denying reservations at a lower price and waiting for buyers who will pay the higher price. Thus, the managers can make the decision with confidence, based on the rigorous analysis carried out by the RO system.

The value of decision support with the RO system, experts note, is that it takes the focus away from cost minimisation that IT is usually used for, and focuses the attention on profit maximisation. The Taj group was able to use the RO system very effectively. After introducing the system, the group increased its revenues dramatically, with average room rates increasing by as much as 35%.

The techniques of RO work effectively in situations where demand exceeds supply and this can be accurately predicted. A hotel can afford to turn away customers, and go against the conventional wisdom only if they have the confidence that they can charge higher revenue from the other customers who will arrive later. This confidence is provided by the system that relies on historical data of demand and the patterns that it can determine about seasonal usage, variations in demand and changing preferences.

16.1 DECISION SUPPORT SYSTEMS

Decision support systems (DSS) are a kind of application software used by organisations to help make decisions regarding day-to-day operations or about long-term plans and strategies. These systems typically use data available within the organisation to analyse and present alternative scenarios to managers. The systems may use data from outside the organisation too, where the challenge is to ensure that the data is relevant and reliable. The following example on the use of a DSS will help clarify the manner in which the system is used.

A manager in a large manufacturing facility has to decide on the number of lots of raw material to start processing on a daily basis. The factory manufactures extruded metal pipes that are used in the energy industry. Each lot consists of short and thick pipes that are passed through several stages of cold extrusion, then cooling and processing to retain the structural properties of the metal. At each stage, the extrusion machines are limited and highly specialised for the dimensions of the input and output extrusion pipes. The manager has to decide carefully how many lots to select at the input stage, as too many lots will cause unwanted queues and bottlenecks. In contrast, too few lots will underutilise the expensive extrusion machines.

The manager uses a DSS to make his decisions (see Fig. 16.1). The DSS takes as input the current status of the shop floor: How many lots are currently being processed, what is the status of queues at various machines on the shop floor, the time available for the processing (or when the final products are due for the current lot to be processed), whether there are any machines undergoing maintenance and how long that will take and so on. With this information the DSS is able to compute alternative scenarios for the manager regarding the type of and number of lots to release into the system and the time they will take to get processed. The alternative scenarios are computed on the basis of a mathematical 'model' already built into the system. With the system, the manager can try 'what-if' scenarios for his decisions – what if one additional lot is included, or what if two additional lots are included, and how will this affect the final outcome, how will the queue sizes change and so on.

KEY POINT

Decision support systems help managers with day-to-day or long-term decisions.

It is important to note from the above example that the system only helps the manager make the decision – it does not make the final decision by itself. The system does not replace the manager; it simply assists the manager to arrive at a decision. Furthermore, the decision is structured in nature because the number of variables that have to be decided on are known clearly, which are the kind and number of lots to release. Also, there is a pre-existing model of the problem, one that is used to arrive at the possible scenarios of interest to the manager.

DSS are widely used in organisations. They may be used to select stocks to invest in the stock market, to determine which routes to follow to supply goods to various retail outlets, to determine which employees to enlist for a given project or to determine how to allocate budgets to different products based on their sales. The lead case of Taj Hotels shows an example of how decisions about room rates are made with support systems. Such decisions are helped by predetermined models that allow the decision maker to input the relevant data and then compute

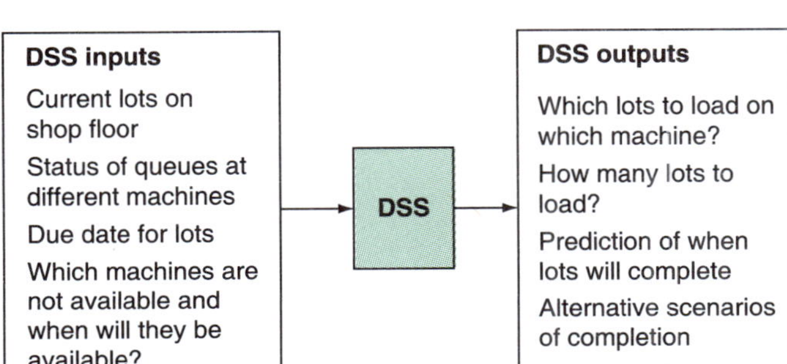

FIGURE 16.1 Example of DSS inputs and outputs for decision making at the shop floor of a manufacturing facility.

various alternative scenarios. DSS are used individually by managers and executives, and also by groups that are working on a particular problem domain.

16.1.1 MIS and DSS

Management information systems or MIS have been covered in an earlier chapter (Chapter 3). MIS essentially present data to managers in various forms and from various sources. The intent of MIS is to enable managers to see the data pertaining to the functioning of the organisation in a summary manner that enables both a bird's eye view as well as a penetrating view of the data. MIS too process the data but in a manner as to show different views and summaries. DSS, on the other hand, are designed to help managers with decisions, and the analysis is meant only for a particular decision.

DSS are used infrequently, mostly on an ad hoc basis, when a decision has to be made, whereas MIS are used regularly. DSS analysis allows the manager to assess various scenarios and alternatives, whereas MIS reports have a fixed output and format. Furthermore, DSS are designed for users and managers across the hierarchy of the organisation. Those who work in situations, which can be assisted by DSS tools, rely on them. In contrast, MIS reports are largely used by higher management in the organisation, who need to see summary and regular reports. Broad differences between MIS and DSS are listed in Table 16.1.

Table 16.1 | Differences between MIS and DSS

Management Information Systems	Decision Support Systems
Provide managers with data and reports on a regular basis	Support managers for decision making on an ad hoc basis
Reports are targeted for specific users, especially management	Find use across the organisation, by whoever needs help with problems.

16.1.2 Decision Making

What is it that managers do when they make decisions? This is a fundamental question that needs to be answered before one can think of using DSS to support decision making in any meaningful manner.

Herbert Simon, the Nobel Prize winning researcher, showed that humans went through three essential stages in the act of problem solving. He called these the *Intelligence*, *Design* and *Choice* stages. Decision making can also be considered as a type of problem solving. When making a decision, humans tend to follow Simon's Intelligence-Design-Choice Model, shown in Fig. 16.2. In the first stage, that of intelligence, they collect information about the issue from the

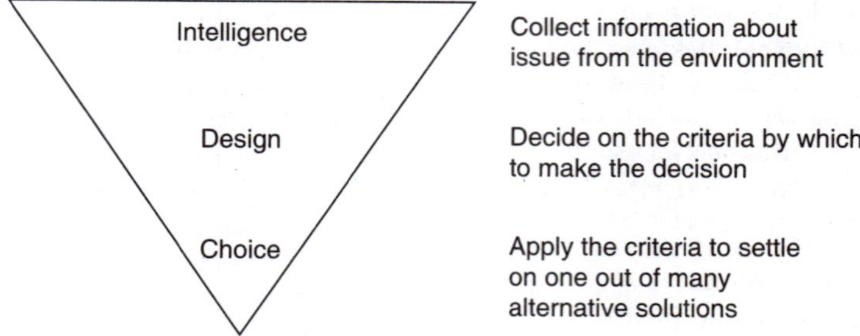

FIGURE 16.2 | Phases of problem solving in the Intelligence–Design–Choice Model.

environment and the surrounding context. For example, if a person is faced with the problem of travelling from Bangalore to New Delhi, a distance of about 2000 km, then in the intelligence stage the person will seek all possible information of how to travel - by air, by train, by bus or by a personal vehicle. This inquiry is open-ended and will involve searching for all possible avenues by which the problem can be solved.

Once the intelligence information is available, the decision maker moves on to the next stage which is the design stage. The question addressed at this stage is - What criteria should be used to decide between the alternative possible solutions to the problem? This question requires the decision maker to settle on the criteria that are important, and then select or rank-order them. For example, the choice of cost and time may be the most important criteria for the decision-making process. In our example of the Bangalore–New Delhi journey, it may also be specified that no more than a certain amount of money may be spent and no more than a certain amount of time can be used for the journey.

At the next stage, that of choice, the criteria are applied to select the best answer from the available choices. For example, based on the criteria of cost and time available, it may be best to travel to Delhi from Bangalore by train. The criteria may be weighted and these weights are applied in a formal manner, often with the help of a mathematical model. Once a solution is available, the decision maker may be satisfied with the answer or may return to earlier stages to redo the process.

KEY POINT

Human decision making involves the steps of intelligence, design and choice.

At the choice stage, the criteria and parameters for the decision help curtail the amount of search required to arrive at a decision. If the criteria are not specified sharply then the number of alternatives to be considered to arrive at a decision may be very large. This stage may also require returning to the intelligence gathering activity, and then to the design stage to change or modify the criteria and the weights used to apply them.

In his seminal work, Herbert Simon also showed that decision makers have *bounded rationality*, implying that they are restricted in the number of choices and criteria they can actually bring to bear in a decision-making situation. These limitations exist, in part, because of the limits on the cognitive abilities of humans or, in other words, the limits on the number of things that people can think about at a time. Most people are content with a satisfactory answer, not necessarily one that is the best or optimal.

DSS are designed to support mainly the choice stage of the decision-making process. Managers can enter the relevant data into the system, select or prioritise their criteria and let the system decide on the final solution. Mathematical models are usually built into the system to help analyse the data and arrive at solutions. Some modern software also assist decision makers in the intelligence stage, where they seek out pertinent information from organisational databases or from the internet.

16.1.3 Types of Decisions

DSS are typically used to support what are called *structured* decisions. In a structured decision-making scenario the relevant criteria, the data needed and the method of analysis are usually known and can be modelled by the system. For example, the *travelling salesman problem* is a very well-known structured problem (see Fig. 3.8 in Chapter 3). In this problem, the data on the number of cities the salesman has to visit, the distance between the cities and the criterion for selecting the tour for the salesman (which is the lowest cost route that he can take calculated on the basis of distance), are all known. The problem is to then find the best solution among the many possible tours the salesman could go on. DSS effectively tackle such structured problems. However, it should be mentioned that the travelling salesman problem is very hard to solve, especially if the number of cities exceeds 30.

Unstructured problems do not have clearly defined parameters or criteria for selecting solutions. For example, finding the best candidate for filling the position of a chief executive officer of a firm is an unstructured problem. The criteria may not be sharply defined, the parameters by which to describe and evaluate the candidates may also not be sharply identified, as they pertain to subjective concepts like personality, leadership skills, vision, motivation and so on. Unstructured decision problems are usually solved by imposing some form of structure in order to apply the analysis and select the best candidate. For example, to choose between several candidates for the chief executive officer position, the decision makers may create a scale on which to rank the candidates on the subjective parameters. These ranks can then be used objectively to select the best candidate.

A large class of problems are of the nature of semi-structured problems - where some parameters are specified, but other parameters have to be determined by studying the problem domain carefully. The problem of finding the best marketing campaign for a product, for example, is a semi-structured problem where some parameters such as the budgets, the target population, etc., are known, but others such as the effectiveness of the media may not be known. DSS are used in cases of semi-structured problems with some assumptions and some imposition of structure.

16.2 COMPONENTS OF A DSS

A DSS consists of three main components, the database, the model base and the user interface (see Fig. 16.3) that are described below.

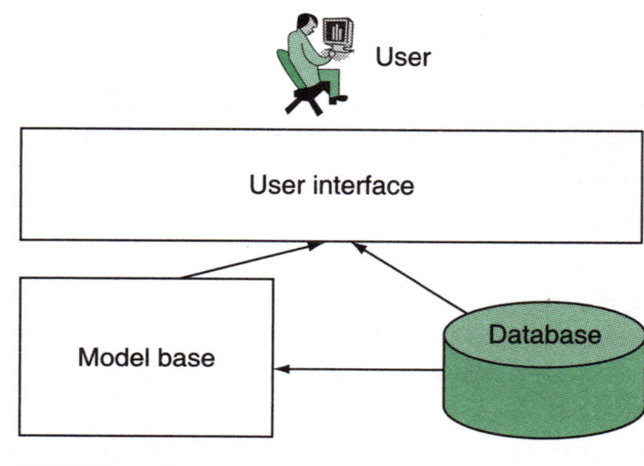

FIGURE 16.3 Components of a DSS: The database, the model base and the user interface.

16.2.1 The Database

A DSS relies on a database component that stores, manages, retrieves and presents data in a suitable manner. The DSS database relies on organisational databases, and as such has functionality similar to that of databases covered earlier. The difference is that the querying and reporting of data are done by and for the DSS itself.

16.2.2 The Model Base

The model base consists of the mathematical or other models that are used to compute the answers for the problems posed to the system. Model bases typically consist of various types and kinds of models that are designed for different problem domains. For example, the model base may consist of an algorithm for solving the travelling salesman problem and another one for inventory management. The models are derived from known solutions to problems and may be tailored to the organisation's needs.

Each model in DSS needs particular kind of data that it draws from the database. The data has to be provided in a form that the model can use, and this often requires pre-processing of the data. Provided below are some examples of models that are used in DSS and the input data they require.

16.2.2.1 Models of Brand Management

Marketing managers have to make decisions about the products and brands that they are responsible for. One aspect of their job requires assessing the current position of the brand in the market with regard to its competitors, while another part requires deciding on what steps to take with regard to price, promotion, retailing, distribution, etc.

A DSS to support brand management requires input data about the sales of the brand at all stores and retail locations, similar data about competitors, the prices at which all are sold, the number of units on display, the number of days on display, the number of product returns and so on. Once the data is available, the system presents analysis of the brand's current competitive position, its possible pricing to increase sales, the required inventory levels at different stores and so on.

The analysis is based on theoretical models of pricing and demand, and on inventory and sales models.

16.2.2.2 Models of Portfolio Management

Finance managers of firms have to make decisions regarding investment in various financial instruments. These instruments consist of different kinds of stocks, bonds, mutual funds and derivatives. The investment decision is based on the data about the prices of these products, their expected returns, the risk profile they have, and their market volatility among other parameters.

Models for making the portfolio decision are based on theoretical models that determine how much to invest over a given time horizon in the different investment vehicles. The models show alternative investment scenarios and enable the users to vary their risk profile or preferences to see their impact on the portfolio allocations.

16.2.2.3 Models of Human Resource Management

Many organisations have to solve the problem of employee allocation. They have to decide which employees to allocate to different projects they have. The inputs required for this decision are about the employees, their experience, skills, job preferences and their current allocation to different tasks. The models in the system use theoretical models of resource allocation, with constraints, to identify which employees should be allocated to what tasks. For the models to arrive at accurate decisions the details about the requirements of various tasks also have to be specified.

16.2.3 The User Interface

The third component of the DSS is the user interface. This is a software application that allows the user to access the database easily and also put the data into the model base for analysis. The user interface may consist of the typical tools and icons available on any interface, such as drop-down lists, buttons, menus, text-entry boxes, dialog boxes and so on.

User interfaces also guide the user to select models appropriate for the problem by providing tips and suggestions. The design of user interfaces is based on how humans solve problems and the guidance is according to how the user progresses with using the data for building models. User interfaces now also have a component that is able to interpret natural language. The user types his/her problem in English, for example, and the then the system interprets the user's commands to come up with an appropriate model. The user can select or reject the model and then further refine the requirements of the problem

16.2.4 History of DSS

The idea of using computers for assisting with decision support co-evolved with the use and development of computers. When computers were limited in their capacities, in the 1960s, they could be programmed for a few activities and also only a small amount of data could be

Table 16.2 | Customer Payment Data

customerNumber	checkNumber	paymentDate	amount
103	HQ336336	19/10/04	6066.78
103	JM555205	05/06/03	14,571.44
103	OM314933	18/12/04	1676.14
112	BO864823	17/12/04	14,191.12
112	HQ55022	06/06/03	32,641.98
112	ND748579	20/08/04	33,347.88

analysed (owing to limitations of memory size and speed). The DSS tools developed at those times were designed to help with specific tasks that could be modelled adequately. These systems were known as model-driven DSS (this name was given later), and were based on numerical or statistical or computational models of business, for applications in accounting, finance and production. The model parameters were specified in advance, and given data about a new situation, could compute various values for use by managers. Managers could also change the data values to see the effect on the eventual result. This was known as 'what-if' analysis.

When the first spreadsheets were developed in the 1980s and became popular applications on personal computers, they allowed users to build numerical and statistical models, which could be used with data sets for decision support. What-if analysis gained popularity as data could be easily changed in spreadsheets to see what effect they had on various parameters. For example, budget planning is often done on spreadsheets. The numbers in a spreadsheet for the budget can be easily changed to see the effect they have on the overall budget.

A tool that gained wide popularity in spreadsheets is the pivot table. A pivot table allows data to be summarised, sorted, cross-tabulated and aggregated quickly. The tool allows the data to be visualised in different ways, enabling decision makers to see the patterns and trends in their data. For example, Table 16.2 depicts the data from the Classic Models payments table (discussed in Chapter 14). The data is arranged in rows, corresponds to the payments made by different customers on different dates. A simple pivot table (Table 16.3) shows the data aggregated according to customers, to show what payments they made on what dates. The pivot table leaves out the check numbers data, which is not relevant for this analysis.

Pivot tables are available in all popular spreadsheets. Even today they are a very powerful decision support tool.

As computational power improved in the newer versions of computers, the decision support paradigm shifted to a more data-driven approach. Large volumes of data were available to organisations from databases, and these could be analysed with various tools, including models. This field evolved into what is now referred to as data mining, analytics and business intelligence.

Table 16.3 | Pivot Table Showing Individual Customer Payments

customerNumber	paymentDate	amount
103	05/06/03 19/10/04 18/12/04	14,571.44 6066.78 1676.14
112	06/06/03 20/08/04 17/12/04	32,641.98 33,347.88 14,191.12

KEY POINT

Group decision support assists a set of people working together to make decisions.

Group Decision Support systems (GDSS) emerged in the late 1980s with the goal of enabling a group of people to participate in a decision-making exercise jointly. The need for such types of decision-making systems arose from the fact that in most organisations, high level decisions are typically made by a group at a meeting. While they could work on individual DSS, the real value of the system would be if their group thinking was somehow captured. The design for such systems was proposed by academics who studied group decision-making behaviour in laboratories and arrived at a number of features that would assist the group.

The typical design of a GDSS involved group members sitting at computer terminals in a room, with a central, shared projection facility that shows the computing results of the group. All the computers are linked to the GDSS software that coordinates the activities of the group members, and also manages the data and models that the group uses. A facilitator starts the process and coordinates activities for the group. Group members can make contributions to the data or models or ideas being discussed, at any time, and anonymously, if needed. A session at a GDSS meeting is expected to involve phases of idea generation, consensus building, idea consolidation, evaluation, and policy writing.

1. At the idea generation phase, the GDSS provides facilities for electronic brainstorming – which is the process of free thinking on a problem and adding ideas for possible solutions. The system enables contributors to add suggestions and comments to existing ideas, while developing independent lines of thinking.
2. At the consensus building and idea consolidation phases, the participants may vote on the best ideas, or fill out an electronic questionnaire to rate the best ideas and suggestions. Ideas may be depicted graphically as maps or node-link graphs, illustrating the relations between concepts.
3. At the evaluation phase, the system may enable polling or rating to identify the best solutions to the problem.
4. At the policy writing phase, where the solution found by the group is elaborated into a policy text, the system helps with providing modelling tools, data and analysis tools to elaborate on the solution and write its implications.

GDSS also account for disagreements and conflicts in the decision-making process. Stakeholders of different ideas can be recorded, and the history of the process can be revealed to show the origin of conflicts, and point to how they can be resolved.

Many commercial GDSS tools were developed, along with physical facilities where such sessions could be conducted. The evaluation of these tools showed that they were quite successful in helping groups arrive at decisions collectively. Some drawbacks included slowing down the process of conversing and restricting the easy flow of ideas.

Currently, GDSS tools have been largely replaced with online collaboration tools such as wikis, Googledocs and rating systems, which many organisations have adopted internally.

Along with the growth of GDSS, decision support systems specifically targeted at senior executives were also designed. These are known as executive support systems (ESS). These systems have similar capabilities as DSS, with the difference that they rely on heavy use of graphical presentations. ESS typically have a dashboard display where they depict the status of different parameters of the organisation in graphical format. The emphasis in dashboards is on depicting the current state of the organisation, via the parameters, along with facilities to drill-down to uncover details.

16.3 ANALYTICS AND BUSINESS INTELLIGENCE

Modern organisations are rich with data. Owing to large-scale computerisation efforts, almost all processes, activities and interactions within the organisation are available in accessible databases. This rich data environment has spawned a variety of software applications that rely on the principles of decision support systems (DSS) and enable organisations to change their competitive strategy. These applications rely on fast computing architectures, a large collection of historical data, access to data being produced currently in the organisation, and computing software that enables complex models to be used for analysis. This approach to using data analysis is widely known as *analytics*.

Firms have changed their ability to compete in markets by using analytics in ways that are new and innovative. One problem that has received considerable attention is that of *predictive* analytics. In predictive analytics, the challenge is to use historical data effectively to predict aspects of the future that are important for the business. For example, a loan processing officer in a bank, which specialises in providing loans to small businesses, has a rich historical data bank on the loans given in the past, the characteristics of the firm the loans were given to, the repayment schedule and the performance of the borrower for returning the loan. For a new loan applicant, the officer can use the historical data and run it through the analytics software to predict how the current applicant will perform. The officer relies on the power of the models, based on statistics and other techniques, to have a very good estimate of the risks involved and can make a better decision as compared to his/her counterpart in a rival lending agency that does not use such kinds of analytics tools.

Predictive analytics has many applications in business. For example, mobile phone services firms have a problem of their customers 'churning' away, or switching services to rival firms. Such customers are dissatisfied with offerings of their current provider, or are attracted by better features or services of other firms. Some firms use analytics to determine which of their thousands of customers are likely to churn away, or switch their service to a rival firm, and then these customers are provided incentives, such as reduced prices, to stay on. The prediction of churn is based on the relative decline in usage, offers by rival firms, change in calling patterns and complaints from customers.

Large manufacturing firms have to manage a pool of suppliers who provide them with the essential raw materials to run their manufacturing activities. One management challenge these firms face is that of predicting suppliers who will default on supplies or on delivery. Predictive analytics is used to analyse past patterns of activity of all such supplier firms and understand the trends in the patterns. For example, if a supplier has had a recent history of delays in delivery, or quality problems, or batch-size problems, analytics can highlight this and enable the management to correct the problem before it assumes serious proportions.

Customer relationship software is used to monitor a commercial firm's interactions with its customers. Based on patterns such as buying activity, level of transactions, use of credit and so on, the firm can offer promotions and deals to its customers. The analytics results point out the customers to whom offers can be made profitably versus others.

Another area in which analytics is used increasingly is that of *real-time analysis*. Firms that have large-scale ongoing transactions, such as e-commerce firms, want to monitor and analyse trends. Software applications monitor the stream of transaction data in real time, that is, soon after the transaction data is created, and measure the data for trends. Such monitoring allows firms to make pricing, load balancing and resource allocation decisions quickly. Furthermore, these applications create a *dashboard* of monitors that provide a continuous stream of input data to be seen in a summary. The dashboard interface resembles the dashboard in a car, showing performance indicators with graphical displays.

For example, an e-commerce firm uses real-time analytics at a call centre to monitor the load on various operators who answer customer calls. The operators are assigned to calls based on the type of information required, and if the load increases on a set of operators, the software suggests moving the load to others. The entire operation is monitored by the software, and the data trends are compared with past trends and also with loading policies. An insurance firm uses alerts about competitor prices, which are provided to all its agents on a real-time basis, to enable them to price their products competitively.

16.3.1 Business Intelligence Techniques

Analytics relies on a number of computational and statistical techniques that were developed in the field of artificial intelligence. When applied to business problems, these are known as business intelligence techniques. Brief descriptions of some business intelligence techniques are provided below to highlight the kind of problems that can be solved and the kind of data that is required.

16.3.1.1 Neural Networks

A neural network is a mathematical model of neurons in animal brains. The network consists of nodes and links between them. One set of nodes are called input nodes, and input data is provided to these nodes. These nodes are connected to many others in a specified manner. Another set of nodes are called output nodes and here the computations of the network are terminated. When data is provided to an input node, the idea is to move the data through the network, and as this is done, certain calculations are performed. Data is 'moved' through the network by allowing it to be used in calculations from a source node to a destination node that is connected by a link. Data from a particular node cannot be used in a node to which that particular node is not linked.

Each link in a neural network has a weight. This weight is initially randomly assigned. In the most widely used form of neural network, data is propagated through the network in a single direction, from input to output nodes. The weights on the links are used to make the calculations as the data is moved.

Neural networks are used in two types of analytics problems:

1. Classification.
2. Prediction.

A classifier takes input data and puts it in one of several known categories. For example, neural networks are used to determine if a loan should be given to an applicant at a bank. The network has to be given past data of sanctioned loans given, and whether the borrower had paid them back according to the contract. The input data can include the amount of the loan, the profession of the borrower, the income of the borrower, his/her debts, age, gender and the reason for applying for the loan. The data may contain details about the borrower's repayment history, and the defaults on the repayment, if any. Most importantly, the data also contains specific categories of giving or denying a loan (see Fig. 16.4). The neural network is then 'trained' on the given data, where the details of each loan processing instance are provided along with the final decision of whether the loan was given or not. The training procedure is built into the software, and consists of elaborate mathematical procedures that adjust the weights on the links in the network. Once trained, the network will be able to tell from the given input data whether a loan was approved or denied. When the data on a new case is given to the network, it is able to classify the applicant as one to whom to give the loan or deny.

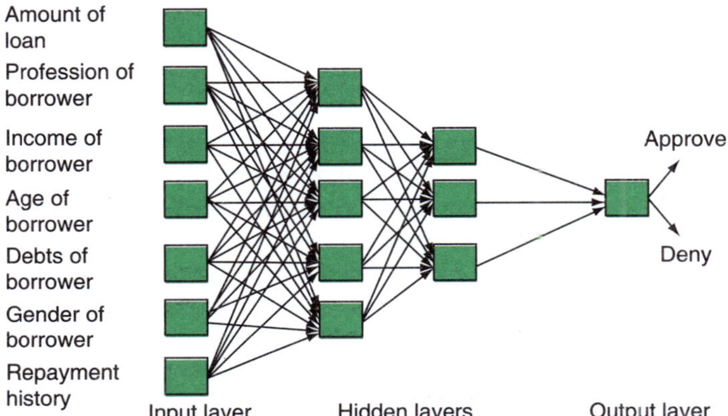

FIGURE 16.4 The neural network for loan processing problem. The input layer consists of seven nodes. The output layer consists of one node. The inner layers of nodes are called the hidden layers.

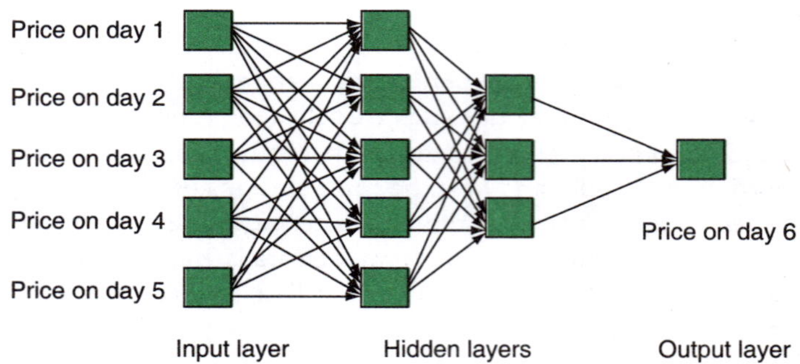

FIGURE 16.5 The neural network for stock price prediction. The network consists of five input nodes and one output node.

Classifiers are used to distinguish between categories of objects and groups. Classifiers are used to distinguish between promising customers and not-so promising ones, reliable and unreliable borrowers, products that are likely to be more successful than others, suppliers who are likely to be more reliable and so on. Classifiers require historical data on which to train the neural networks, and then can adequately classify objects based on the decision situation.

Prediction problems involve forecasting a number or a value for future, based on past data. Neural nets are used to predict the movement of stocks, the price fluctuation in exchange rates, the volume of sales for different products, the capacity utilisation for airlines and so on. Prediction requires a long stream of past data on which the neural networks can be trained. For example, for a given stream of data on prices of stocks, the training is done by giving as input, say, 5 days of data about certain stock prices, where the output is the price on the sixth day (see Fig. 16.5) Thousands of data points are used to provide values for the ten input and one output data required. Once properly trained the neural nets can predict the next day's price of a stock, based on the last 10 days closing prices of the same stock.

Construction of appropriate neural networks for the decision problem at hand is a challenge. There are a number of design problems that have to be solved, such as: How many nodes are required, how are they to be connected, what training algorithm should be used (of the many available), how should the data be broken up into sets for training the networks and so on. In most cases, these design issues are resolved by experimentation. Various networks are trained and tested, and the one that gives the lowest error on a data set, which is distinct from the set the network is trained on, is selected as the best network for decision support. The design, training and testing of neural networks for specified tasks is a time-consuming activity. However, once the networks are trained, they can be used very efficiently.

16.3.1.2 Decision Trees

A decision tree is used in a manner similar to neural networks, but only for classification problems. A decision tree is built with past data and is used to classify fresh data from the same type of problems. An example of a decision tree is shown in Fig. 16.6. The figure shows a decision tree for the problem of deciding to give a loan to an applicant. The tree begins with the most important parameter for making the decision, which is that of the 'income' of the applicant. This parameter is assumed to have three different values, those of 'high', 'medium' and 'low'. For each of these values there is a branch of the tree. If the applicant has a high income, then the tree considers the next important parameter on that branch of the tree, which is 'repayment history' of the applicant. This parameter then becomes the starting point of another branch of the tree, where two values are considered 'good' or 'poor'. If the repayment history is good then the decision to give the loan is a 'yes'. The yes node does not branch anymore and is considered a terminal or a decision node.

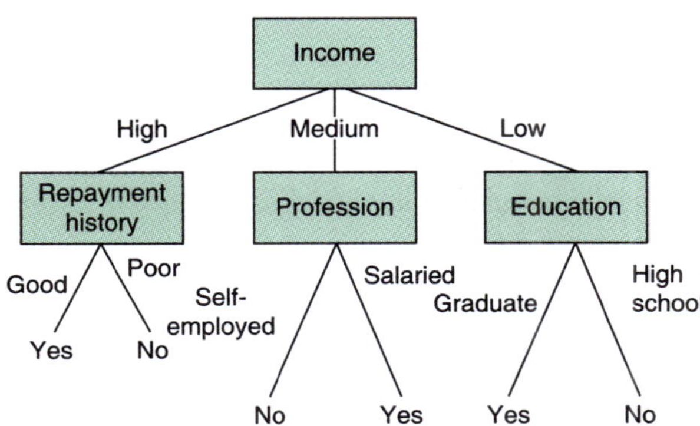

FIGURE 16.6 | The decision tree for loan approval.

Going back up to the 'income' node of the tree, we find that the value of 'medium' income leads to another branch, where the next parameter is 'profession'. This parameter has two values 'self-employed' and 'salaried'. These branches end in terminal nodes with the decisions of 'no' and 'yes'.

The third branch from the 'income' node has a value of 'low' and leads to a node called 'education' which has two values 'graduate' and 'high school'. All the branches of the decision tree terminate in decision nodes.

A decision tree allows a decision maker to determine the most important parameters for a decision from historical data and use these to arrive at the best decision. Each tree is constructed by seeing data from past transactions and the decisions that were taken in those cases. The method for constructing the tree relies on a statistical technique. In this sense, the decision tree is similar to a neural network in functioning. However, it has one advantage in that it specifies which parameter is the most important for the decision. In the given loan example, the most important parameter is 'income'.

Decision trees can be very simple, or very complex. The simpler they are, the better it is for the decision maker. Consider a decision tree that is another solution to the same problem of classifying a loan applicant (see Fig. 16.7). The tree here has only one node and three branches. The branches end in terminal nodes with decisions. This tree is very small and robust. It will have an answer for all applicants very quickly, and this can be determined with hardly any calculations. However, decision trees can become quite complex and have thousands of nodes and branches, depending on the size of the decision problem. A simple and small tree is the most general and has the most robust answers for most types of problem situations.

The construction of decision trees is far easier than that of neural networks. The algorithms that construct decision trees also determine the number of nodes and branches required. The designer has to ensure that the number of cases to train the tree are adequate, and also test the tree for errors of classification. Another advantage which decision trees have over neural networks is that the data can consist of text values also, whereas neural networks can only handle numerical data.

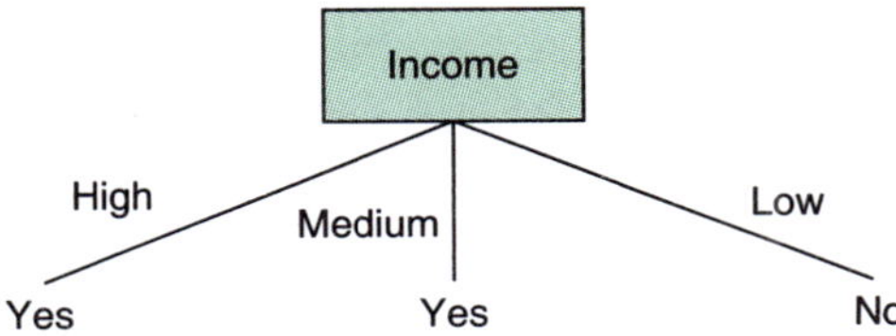

FIGURE 16.7 | A simpler decision tree for a loan approval process.

16.3.1.3 Clustering

The method of clustering helps a user identify patterns in data. It allows one to see how data is aggregated, and understand what type of groups exist in the data. The methods rely on statistical techniques to create the groups or clusters, so there is high reliability in the information obtained. Clustering techniques are usually used to discover patterns, which may be confirmed by other techniques.

For example, consider data about the sales of a product such as car. The data will have details about the buyers, such as the age, gender, income level, education level and family size; it will have details about the purchase context, such as the location of sale, the time and date, whether a deal had been provided, how long the customer took for the decision and how many alternatives did the customer consider. It will also contain details about the product, such as the type of car, the number of doors, its capacity, its mileage and so on. When such data is available on thousands of car purchase transactions, groupings within the data may be discovered by using cluster analysis. For instance, the cluster analysis may reveal that most buyers of sedans, or large family cars, buy them when a deal is available and typically in the last quarter of the year, such as in the period October to December. Such information is useful for marketing managers to plan their strategies and target specific consumers through advertisements and campaigns.

16.3.1.4 Data Visualisation

There is a famous Chinese proverb that translates loosely as 'a picture is worth ten thousand words'. This proverb highlights the power of visuals and images to convey meaning, something that would take a lot of effort to express in words. In DSS design, too many modern designers have adopted advanced visualisation techniques to assist decision makers. See Fig. 16.8 for example of data visualisation.

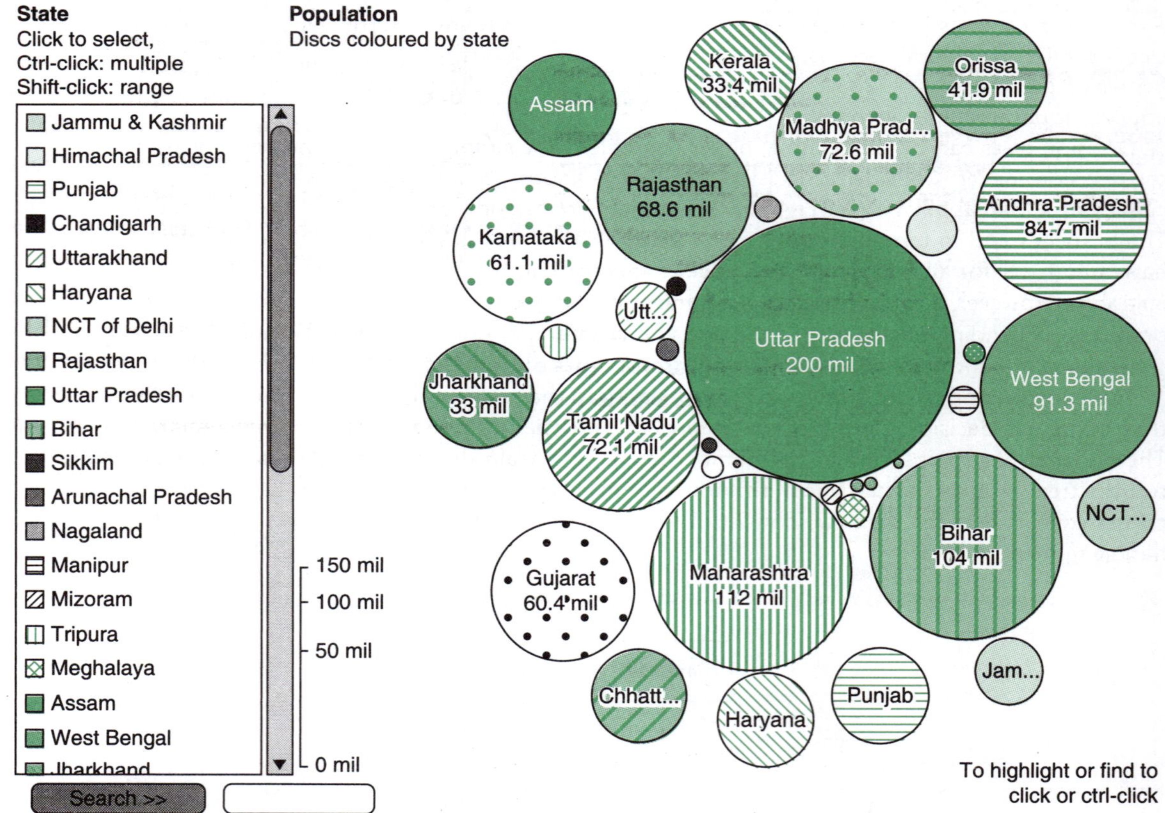

FIGURE 16.8 | Bubble chart of populations of different states of India.

Source: Visualization created at Many Eyes, an online application is available at http://www-958.ibm.com. (Reproduced with permission).

For data analysis, there are many graphical techniques that are well known and are available to most users of software packages. These techniques include scatter plots, charts of various sorts, histograms and box and whisker plots. These techniques are used extensively to render summary data or provide a graphical description of data. The data sizes may run to thousands of data points. However, a simple histogram can show how data is aggregated, and a scatter plot can show how data is distributed. When data is static and does not have many variables, these techniques are usually adequate for helping decision makers.

However, when data becomes complex, with many variables and with wide deviations in the variables, or when data is not static, that is, there is a continuous stream of data that has to be understood, then more complex data visualisation techniques are used. Some techniques reduce the dimensions of data, that is, they reduce the number of variables in the data and then allow the user to make judgements, visually, about the entire data set. Other visualisation techniques present the dynamic data stream as a set of plots on a screen that is constantly changing, or as a scale, as on the dashboard of a car, which is showing some parameters of the data.

Many techniques are used to show extreme data points and outliers in data. The objective of these techniques is to show if there are certain data points that are not part of the main data set, or they are outliers, and need special attention. Outliers are difficult to identify through statistical techniques, and sometimes humans can spot them visually.

Dynamic data visualisations are also used by presenters to dramatise and emphasise a point. For example, to show trends in, say, usage of computers, a presenter may show the increase in the use of computers over a 10-year period not as a simple increasing graph, but as a dynamic graphic of a rising and expanding bubble, where the size of the bubble depicts the number of computers, and the vertical position of the bubble shows the population of users, both of which are increasing. This type of presentation impresses upon users the fact that not only is the number of computers increasing, but the number of users is also increasing.

16.4 KNOWLEDGE MANAGEMENT

Knowledge management (KM) refers to the practices that organisations follow to identify, capture, store and reuse the insights and experiences of their employees and the codified experiences that are stored in their data and information repositories. Knowledge is itself a difficult term to define as it has many meanings and connotations. In the organisational context, knowledge is separated from, and is at a higher level from, both information and data. If data is raw facts about things stored in databases, and information is the processed data, then knowledge is insight obtained from information about things related to the organisation and to the context.

Knowledge is understood in the knowledge management context in many different ways. Traditional approaches of representation categorised knowledge in two different ways:

1. **Declarative knowledge:** It is about invariant facts or descriptions. For example, the room number in a building in which an office is located is declarative knowledge. It has a context in which it has a meaning, and this remains fixed as long as the context remains.
2. **Procedural knowledge:** It has to do with how things are done. For example, how to find an office in a building is procedural knowledge.

These two types of knowledge differ in the way they are represented in DSS and other systems.

In the organisational context, knowledge is categorised as either *explicit* or *tacit*. (1) Explicit knowledge is that which has been codified in some manner and is available within organisational systems. It could reside in documents, manuals, procedures implemented in application systems or a DSS. Explicit knowledge is available to all without the requirement of a person who has to enable the access to the knowledge. (2) Tacit knowledge, on the other hand, is the uncodified knowledge possessed by individuals in the form of insights and experiences that only they can access and provide to the others. Tacit knowledge cannot be made explicit and explained to others or codified in text or systems. It is the knowledge that people know through practice or what they have learned over the years that cannot be verbalised. For example, recipes of exotic dishes are explicit knowledge that are codified in recipe books or on websites. Such knowledge is often only an indication of the tacit knowledge required to actually cook the dish. Tacit knowledge, in this case, would refer to how the materials have to be prepared, how the ingredients have to be added, what signs to look for to see if the dish is ready and so on. Tacit knowledge is often some things individuals may not even be aware of consciously – such as how a tennis player responds to a serve, something he does instinctively but may not be able to explain verbally. Or how a mechanic in a factory may know that something is wrong with the sound of a machine but may not be able to say why.

KEY POINT

Explicit knowledge is documented and can be accessed through systems, whereas tacit knowledge is known only to people.

Knowledge is also categorised as either *expert* knowledge or *casual* knowledge. The difference between the two, for example, is the difference between the knowledge possessed by a surgeon performing open-heart surgery, and an individual tying a shoelace. The former requires years of training and practice to do competently, whereas the latter can be learned after a few tries. Both types of knowledge consist of tacit and explicit parts. The difference between expert and casual knowledge lies along a continuum, with states such as partial expert and novice in between. For example, computer programmers may be experts with many years of experience, specialists with a few years of experience, competent programmers or just beginners. Their levels of knowledge and understanding of the programming tasks will vary along an axis, with few experts at one end and possibly many beginners at the other.

Knowledge is also *contextual* and situational. Knowledge about how to operate a machine or use ERP software is grounded in the context of the organisation where the person has learned and acquired the knowledge. The person may transmit that knowledge to others, but the context has to be accounted for. To apply to another context, the knowledge has to be made abstract, or some principles have to be extracted from the context that can be applied elsewhere. For example, a person who has gained expertise in configuring an ERP package in one organisation has to apply the basic principles of such configuration in some other organisational context; the other organisation may have entirely different procedures and practices for which the principles will have to be applied.

16.4.1 Knowledge Life Cycle

Scientific knowledge about the world and nature are considered to be universal and unchanging. The theory of gravitation that explains how planets move and how stars change their positions in space has remained the same since its discovery (by Isaac Newton). Other scientific theories about the origins of the earth, the origins of life, the evolution of humans and so on, do have an unchanging character, but with the advancement of science some theories are replaced by others. For example, the nature of matter, based on particles, has constantly evolved, beginning with the theory of atoms and molecules to that of fundamental particles today. Knowledge, thus, has both invariant and varying parts.

Organisational knowledge, typically, has a life cycle in which it is created, developed, used and reused, and then it degrades and is replaced by other knowledge (see Fig. 16.9). The value of knowledge increases as it is created and developed. It is at a maximum when it is used and reused and begins to decline thereafter. Knowledge may degrade gracefully or sharply. *Knowledge creation* is the process of identifying and capturing knowledge. Within organisations, people

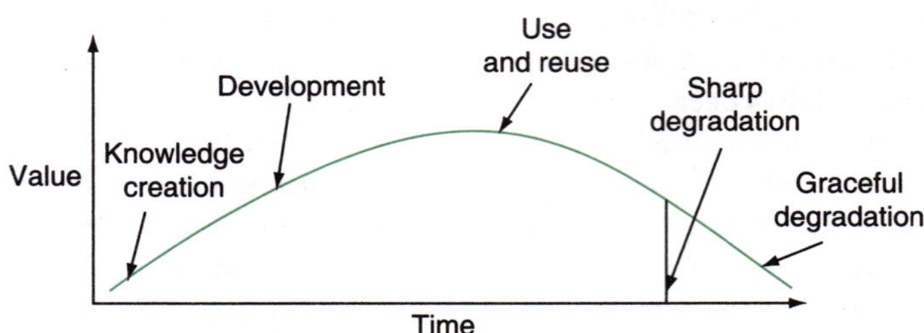

FIGURE 16.9 | Value of knowledge.

may find that some knowledge is of value, identify what is to be captured, and then codify this knowledge or identify the person who has the knowledge. The codification or the act of 'person-to-documentation' transfer entails the person(s) having their insights encoded as text or as rules within a software application. This task may also entail upgrading knowledge encoded earlier to reflect newer variations and also the new context that may have emerged.

Knowledge development is the task of validating the knowledge to ensure that it is from an authentic source and is accurate. For example, knowledge about making changes to a particular manufacturing process, like machining, may require that engineers validate that the change is indeed from a reliable source (an expert) and also that the change will not disrupt existing methods. Knowledge development also entails preparing the knowledge for reuse. This will mean transferring the documents to searchable databases or creating templates or *frequently asked questions* (FAQ) documents to help people use the knowledge. Such development has to ensure the users are able to apply the knowledge to their special context, which may be different from the context in which the knowledge was created or captured.

Knowledge use and reuse refers to the tasks of applying the stored knowledge in situations where it is required. For example, users in an organisation may search a knowledge repository to find out how to create a Kiviat diagram with some data that they have collected. Knowledge about this may be stored in a document in which a user has used Kiviat diagrams to show data in a different context. Users will now have to interpret the manner in which Kiviat diagrams were created in the document and apply it to their own situation. The three important steps for using stored knowledge are: first search for and find the relevant knowledge, identify the abstract principles outside of the context of the knowledge, and then apply the principles to the current situation. Knowledge use and reuse can be facilitated by a person who has insight about the context and specific knowledge. Finding such a person becomes part of the first step, that is, search.

Knowledge *degrades* when its usefulness declines within the context in which it was created and captured. Degradation may be 'graceful' where the knowledge slowly becomes less useful, or may degrade suddenly. For example, knowledge about using a particular kind of hardware, say a pager, degrades slowly as people stop using pagers. However, knowledge about how to file taxes may degrade sharply owing to a change in tax laws.

The value of some forms of knowledge too has a life cycle. At the point of creation or capture of knowledge, the value is low as the organisation is not using the knowledge. At the point of development, the value increases as the knowledge has gained in credibility. When knowledge is being reused repeatedly, it has the highest value. As changes in the context and in the organisation erode the usefulness of knowledge, its value declines, either gracefully or sharply.

16.4.2 Strategies for Knowledge Management

16.4.2.1 Identify Knowledge Needs

Organisations have to identify what their knowledge needs are. Firms that are engaged in manufacturing need knowledge about advances in manufacturing processes, where to find better and cheaper materials, regulations regarding their industry, where to find skills and labour and so on. A service firm such as a hospital, for instance, will have different knowledge needs - what are the latest treatments for different kinds of diseases, who makes certain kinds of equipment and drugs, and from where can surgeons and other skilled personnel be hired. The needs will vary for each organisation based on their domain, their geographic location and their particular orientation.

It is essential for management to identify their key knowledge needs in different domains. The knowledge needed by the organisation usually belongs to two categories:

1. **Knowledge about the external environment:** It includes knowledge about competitors, the industry, government regulations, the economy and about innovations happening in the world.

2. **Knowledge about the internal workings of the organisation:** It refers to knowledge about how different things in the organisation are done and the facts relating to the organisation. In large organisations, people develop specialised knowledge about many things internal to the organisation that are not known to others. This knowledge is often the key to the efficiency of the organisation as a whole.

Having identified the knowledge needs of an organisation, management can organise the KM function in different ways.

16.4.2.2 Hierarchic Approach

In the hierarchic approach to KM, it is the top management that creates and sustains the KM infrastructure. Knowledge needs are identified for the different functions of the organisation. Experts and experienced persons are also identified, as the ones who will provide the key knowledge inputs. A method of selection and validating the knowledge inputs is put in place, as also information systems technologies that will enable the use and reuse of the knowledge.

Knowledge capture in such situations is done by codification and personalisation. Codification involves identifying the needed knowledge and its sources and then transferring the explicit portions into documents or text or system processes. Experts are consulted for this process and their knowledge is also codified. Care is also taken to ensure that the abstract rules are extracted from the knowledge while codifying so that it can be applied in different contexts. In the personalisation part, persons are identified and recognised as being most knowledgeable in a domain. Arrangements are made to enable users access the experts on a one-on-one basis when needed.

To maintain such an arrangement, the management has to ensure that sufficient incentives are provided to experts and key personnel for their time and efforts spent on knowledge management. Experts often have to be taken away from their work during the codification process, and also during one-on-one consultations, which has to be compensated adequately.

16.4.2.3 Market Approach

In a market approach to KM, the management is not centrally responsible for the KM effort. The management simply creates a set of enabling technologies and environments in which the knowledge is created and used by demand and supply conditions. For example, many firms allow employees to use email list servers, personal web pages (or blogs) and wikis to communicate with others. Such media can become the platform for a KM market, as employees can post their 'demand' for some knowledge, and those who have the knowledge can post the 'supply'. There is no explicit effort on the part of managers to either induce people to ask or respond.

In a market model, there is no explicit coding process, nor a validating process. During reuse, there is no quality guarantee of the knowledge being recovered. There is also no assurance that the desired knowledge will be available. But market models work best to involve diverse people in different groups or functions. For example, a multinational firm used a market model to locate experts in different parts of the world. This could only happen when a demand for something specific, technical in nature, was posted, and someone from somewhere in the organisation saw the demand and responded to it.

A market model is sometimes supported by providing incentives to the most useful posts by any individual. This requires a mechanism by which users rate the knowledge provided, and the best rated ones get the rewards. This acts as a simple mechanism to encourage employees to devote their time and effort to helping others.

The market model does not work well in a fast-changing environment where context changes rapidly, and the degradation of knowledge is sharp. Markets also do not work well where search costs are high - where the effort required to find and answer is very high. Since the knowledge is not explicitly coded for a context and a situation, users find it hard to seek and understand the knowledge.

Despite the considerable effort put in by many organisations to manage knowledge effectively, there remain some challenges. One of the main challenge is that of incentives of employees to contribute. It is well known that employees have to compete with each other to rise in the corporate or organisational hierarchy. Much of the competitive advantage over co-employees comes from their superior knowledge about their work, which also leads to superior performance. When asked to share this knowledge with others, it leads to a contradiction at an individual level. If experts freely share their expert knowledge with whom they are competing for promotion, how will they have an advantage? This contradiction has led to many failed efforts at KM.

16.4.3 Technologies for Knowledge Management

16.4.3.1 Expert Systems

Expert systems are softwares that reflect reasoning by expert human beings. They are designed to capture the knowledge that expert humans have about certain domains. Once built, expert systems can be used by lay users as consultation systems, where they can respond to questions by users by querying their knowledge base. The systems can also explain their reasoning to the users, thus showing how a particular answer was arrived at.

Expert systems originated in the 1980s in the domain of medical systems. Researchers working in the discipline of artificial intelligence were keen to try and capture the expert knowledge that doctors gather over years of experience, and build it into computer software. In one of the pioneering efforts at Stanford University, a system known as Mycin was created. Mycin consisted of about 600 rules that captured the knowledge of doctors, particularly in the domain of identifying bacterial infections and prescribing antibiotics. Mycin was created by interviewing doctors over a period of many months to arrive at the rules. Rules are representation of the knowledge of the doctors. They are in the form of if-then statements that can be implemented in a computer program. An example of a Mycin rule is given below:

```
IF
1) The stain of the organism in grampos, and
2) The morphology of the organism is COCCUS, and
3) The growth confirmation of the organisms chains
THEN
There is suggestive evidence (0.7) that the identity of the organism
is streptococus.
```

With such a rule, the expert system can inquire about the parameters such as the 'stain' and morphology from the user, and establish the presence of 'organism chains' and then make a recommendation about the identity of the organism. In combination with other rules, the system could make very sophisticated diagnosis. When evaluated against human doctors, Mycin performed very well.

Expert systems were subsequently developed for many applications such as drilling for oil, loan processing, shop-floor scheduling, mortgage evaluation, process control of machines, combining of chemical compounds and many others. The crucial requirement for expert systems is having a human expert who can be queried and modelled.

16.4.3.2 Content Management Systems

Content management systems (CMS) are used to store all types of files within organisations. Such systems are typically designed to be used through a browser and allow many individuals and groups to both deposit and retrieve documents and files. A typical CMS consists of a database with a front end that allows access to users. Files stored on the CMS could be of any type – unstructured text documents, word-processed documents, audio or video files, links to websites and other software. Some CMS allow *workflows* to be implemented. Workflows are sets of permissions given to some files that allow the file or document to be seen and modified by people in a pre-specified order.

CMS are typically used as repositories of codified knowledge. They allow users to easily search through the files as also add comments to and rate particular items. Within some universities, for instance, CMS are used to store all the reading materials, grades, student homework, student files and other material related to education. Such CMS are also referred to as learning management systems.

16.4.3.3 Mind Maps

Mind maps are diagrams that have a central idea as a node in the middle, around which are links to related ideas, concepts, themes, objects, files, text and so on. A mind map can be made collaboratively to capture knowledge about processes or phenomena. Participating users can add to the mind map details about what they know and also sources from where knowledge can be obtained.

There are many software tools available that allow mind maps to be created in a collaborative mode. Most tools are available on a web server or in the cloud through a web browser. The beginning of this chapter (and all the chapters in this book) has a mind map of the theme and related concepts covered in this chapter.

Caselet Decision Support at Mitra Biotech

One of the challenges for cancer treatment is that no two patients respond to the same drugs in the same manner when patients are detected with one of about a hundred types of cancer. Doctors have to literally guess which of the many drugs available for treatment, or combinations of drugs, will help reduce the proliferation of cancer cells. This decision is helped by certain tests that can be performed and one of them examines certain bio-markers - such as cells, molecules, genes or enzymes - to see whether the drugs have affected them or not. These bio-markers work in the negative, which means that if the cells are not affected then the drug or drugs are not effective, but they don't say which drugs are working. Another test uses mice, where mice are grafted with human cancer cells and certain treatments are given to them to test the effects. Though this provides slightly better results, the testing takes several months.

To solve the problem of finding the right drugs for cancer treatment, a start-up called Mitra Biotech has developed a decision support tool for doctors. The technology basically creates a micro-environment where different drugs can be given to cancer cells in different incubators. The patient's tumour samples are placed in these incubators and different combinations of drug treatments are given to them. After this treatment, the cancer cells are tested for 17 different parameters to identify the effect of the drugs on cell death, tumour growth, enzymes and growth patterns of the cells. These parameters are then combined to create an 'M-Score', an overall metric that indicates the effectiveness of the drug. This M-Score can be obtained in a week's time, thus cutting down on the total time required to arrive at a treatment plan.

The M-Score measure was created by testing the algorithm on thousands of sets of treatment data to identify the weights for the parameters that would find the most accurate results. The system that was built to compute the score acts as a decision support tool for doctors - they can feed the tumour cells of the patient to the system, specify various drug treatments, see the results on the different parameters and then see the computed M-Score to evaluate the effectiveness of the drugs.

The main advantages of the system are that the patients are not treated with drugs to see if they are effective or not, as excess drug dosage sometimes leads to toxicity. The system also reduces the cost of this analysis, as drugs are expensive and experimental treatments too cost a lot of money. The system also reduces the time required to arrive at the correct treatment for the patient.

Chapter Glossary

Intelligence The phase of problem solving and decision making where the person seeks information about the problem.

Design The phase of decision making where the person determines the criteria by which to find the best solution.

Choice The third phase of decision making where the person uses the criteria to select the solution out of many available.

Bounded rationality The idea that humans can consider only a certain number of criteria and a restricted number of options to make decisions.

Structured decisions A situation in which the criteria, the data needed for the problem and the method by which to make a decision are known.

Unstructured decisions A situation in which there are no clear parameters or criteria by which to make a decision, and what data to use is also not precisely known.

Analytics Techniques by which complex models are applied to large collections of data available within organisations to solve problems and seek insights.

Predictive analytics Techniques that use past data to predict future trends and scenarios.

Real-time analytics Using modelling techniques to monitor activities within the organisation, using transaction data.

Dashboard A set of graphical displays that show certain parameters in a real-time manner.

Neural networks A mathematical model of the brain that is used to assist with solving problems of classification and prediction.

Classification Techniques by which data on objects and transactions are categorised into groups.

Prediction Techniques by which historical data are used to forecast future data.

Decision trees A technique by which a hierarchy of classifications is created.

Clustering Techniques by which natural groupings and aggregations are revealed in data.

Data visualisation Techniques by which data properties are displayed graphically.

Declarative knowledge Knowledge about factual matters.

Procedural knowledge Knowledge about how things are done.

Explicit knowledge Knowledge that is codified in text or some other tangible manner.

Tacit knowledge Knowledge that is known to humans in the form of insights and experiences, and that cannot be easily verbalised.

Expert knowledge Knowledge possessed by humans who have extensive experience in a domain.

Contextual knowledge Knowledge that is specific to a situation or a location.

Knowledge creation The task of explicitly encoding knowledge or recording who has the knowledge.

Knowledge development The task of validating and verifying the knowledge to ensure it is from an authentic source and is accurate.

Knowledge use The act by which organisational knowledge is applied in situations where it is required.

Knowledge degradation The process by which knowledge becomes less useful in a given context.

Expert systems Systems that encode human knowledge and reasoning in a set of rules, pertaining to a domain, which can be applied to solve problems in the same domain.

Content management systems A system used to store and retrieve documents. The documents may be stored and accessed by any group within or outside the organisation.

Mind maps Diagrams that depict a central node around which are arranged, through links, related ideas, concepts and themes. These diagrams can be created and shared by a group.

Review Questions

1. What is a DSS and how can it help managers?
2. What is the difference between an MIS and a DSS?
3. What are the phases of decision making? In which phase can DSS be most helpful?
4. What is a structured decision? Explain with an example.
5. What is an unstructured decision?
6. What are the main components of a DSS? What are their roles?

7. What is predictive analytics? Give one example.
8. How are neural networks used for predictive analytics?
9. What is a decision tree?
10. What is the technique of clustering used for?
11. What is knowledge management (KM)? Why do organisations use KM?
12. What is the difference between declarative and procedural knowledge? Give examples of each.
13. What is the difference between explicit and tacit knowledge? Give examples of each.
14. What is expert knowledge?
15. Describe the knowledge life cycle?
16. In what ways does knowledge degrade?
17. What is the advantage of the hierarchic approach to KM over the market approach?
18. Why do KM efforts fail?
19. How is knowledge captured in an Expert System?

Research Questions

1. Give an example of a decision that requires considering many parameters and many choices. How does bounded rationality play a role in this?
2. Draw a decision tree for the decisions you make to choose a restaurant to go to. You could use parameters such as 'reputation of restaurant,' 'type of food,' 'price' and 'distance from home.'
3. Visit a local firm and talk to an experienced person within the firm who is working on a problem or a project. Identify the rules that he/she follows to solve problems, such as the rules mentioned in the section on Expert Systems.

Case Question

Why did the management of the Taj Hotels resort to revenue optimisation? What problem did they need assistance with?

Further Reading

1. www.tajhotels.com (accessed on July 2011).
2. Narasimhan, B. (May 2006) Hit the Suite Spot, *Real CIO World*.
3. Hotel Industry is Poised for a New Growth Phase, *The Financial Express*, 20 March 2008.
4. Davenport, T.H. (2006) Competing on Analytics, *Harvard Business Review*.
5. Dennis, A.R. and Vessey, I. (2005) Three Knowledge Management Strategies: Knowledge Hierarchies, Knowledge Markets, and Knowledge Communities, *MIS Quarterly Executive*, **4**(4).
6. http://www.cio.in/case-study/mitra-biotech-prescribes-perfect-cancer-drug-using-data-analytics
7. https://qz.com/786426/mitra-biotech-in-just-seven-days-this-indian-biotech-firm-can-tell-cancer-patients-the-ideal-course-for-their-treatment/

CHAPTER 17

Artificial Intelligence

Learning Objectives

After completing this chapter, you will be able to:

- Learn about the origins of and current status of the field of Artificial Intelligence
- Understand different theories of achieving intelligence in machines
- Learn about different machine learning methods and techniques
- Understand the managerial challenges of AI and its applications

Artificial Intelligence (AI) began as a quest to build human-like thinking and problem-solving capabilities in computers. The field has made great progress from the 1950s onwards, and today programmes are able to demonstrate near-human-like capabilities in playing games, general knowledge and perception tasks, amongst many. AI researchers have been concerned with defining what constitutes human-like intelligence and also how it can be designed in algorithms. Early research showed that representing problems and searching for solutions was the most promising approach. This approach required searching through states that would lead to the solution. Other methods required searching through actions to come up with plans to solve problems. Since representation required stating rules and representations carefully, which was difficult, machine learning methods were found to learn solutions from masses of data.

One of the most important machine learning (ML) methods uses relies on a network of artificial neurons to learn to solve problems of classification and prediction. The learning is done by changing the weights on the links in the network. Later research has shown that networks with many nodes, deep learners, are able to solve difficult problems of image and audio perception. Classification of data is also achieved by ML methods such as induction learning, Bayesian learning and learning from analogies. Genetic algorithms are a class of learners that explore solutions and discover ways of solving problems through novel search methods inspired by evolutionary biology. Reinforcement learning is an ML method that relies on cues from the environment, such as rewards, to learn how to sequence actions to solve problems.

AI systems have deep implications for managers in organisations, as they have to deal with the challenges such systems bring to aspects of competition, skill acquisition, errors and how to manage data acquisition, job loss and division of work between humans and machines.

MIND MAP OF CHAPTER TOPICS

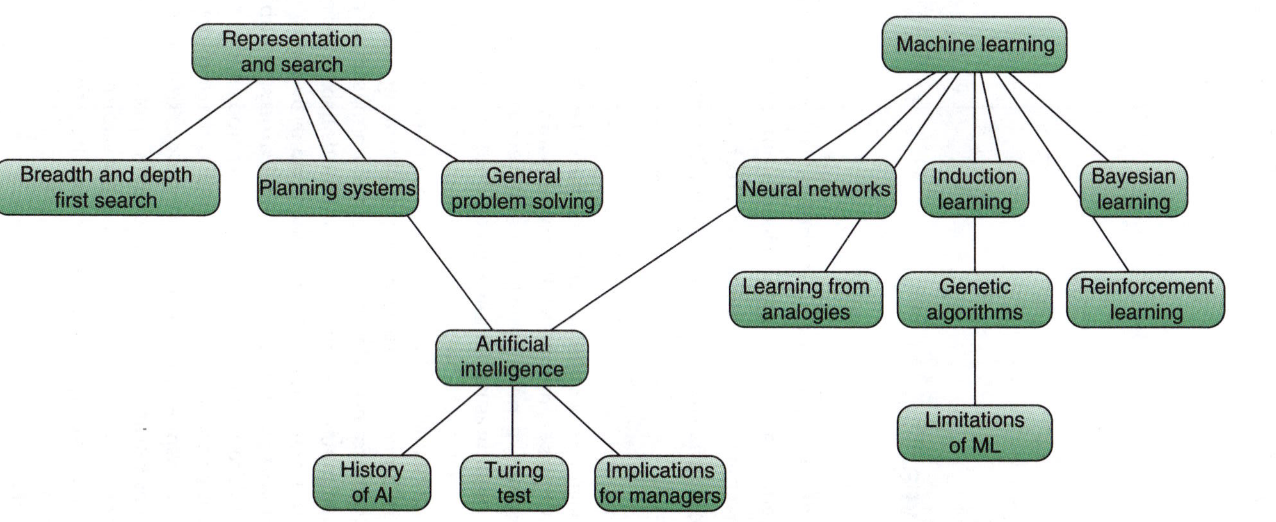

CASE STUDY: IBM'S WATSON

The game of Jeopardy! is a popular television show in the USA. The game is based on general knowledge and in its usual format has three contestants who are given turns to pick a category from which they are given clues, from where they have to find the answer, within a specified time. If they are unable to answer then the other two contestants can bid, by pressing a buzzer, to answer the question. There is a reward associated with each question and is given to whoever answers correctly in the specified time. The game is challenging as it requires the contestants to make sense of the clues very rapidly and state the answer. The other challenge is that sometimes contestants can bid for a reward with the rider that it may be doubled if the question is answered and forfeited if not. The winners of individual shows win money and also have an opportunity to compete again, in a later show. Some contestants win repeatedly and are declared as champions, who eventually receive very large monetary rewards.

In the year 2004, the IBM computer firm in USA planned to design a system that could compete effectively in a Jeopardy! contest. The system was called Watson and was designed with several AI methods and techniques to play the game. The methods included understanding proper English, separating the clues from the stated question, identifying the context of the clues and then searching through the possible combinations of answers to find the correct one.

An example clue in Jeopardy! would be phrased as follows: 'the town in India in which the leader of India's independence movement was born.' The context of the question is gleaned from the category, and the individual clues have to be extracted from the meaning of the question. To understand the clues the software has to extract 'the leader of India's independence movement' as a separate concept and find a name or an instance for it. Since there were many leaders of India's independence movement (such as Gandhi, Nehru, Maulana Azad) the system has to use some logical method by which to identify 'the leader,' and once the answer is isolated as Gandhi, then the problem becomes that of finding Gandhi's birthplace.

In 2011, Watson was ready for a live competition and was pitched against two champion Jeopardy! contestants – Ken Jennings and Mark Rutter. The system was trained through many trial rounds where it competed against other contestants in a live situation. Watson was permitted to respond to the question, that is, press the buzzer, electronically and it had five seconds to come up with the correct response. Watson also computed bid amounts for the challenge rounds. The system beat the two champions in the first as well as the second round of the game. This victory by Watson became big news as a computer programme was able to beat champions in a complex task that requires deep knowledge and human ingenuity in solving clues both quickly and without error.

Watson's success was based on having a massively parallel architecture of hardware that enabled many algorithms to run simultaneously to search for the answer. All the tasks – of speech recognition, of understanding the tests, of logical reasoning, of search through databases and of synthesis – were done by many algorithms in parallel, were evaluated, and the best answer was selected as the response. The system did make mistakes and got answers wrong or took too long to find an answer. It was prominently weak on answering questions with few words for clues.

At the time when Watson won against the human champions, it relied on about 200 million pages of data in both structured and unstructured form stored in its database. While competing, Watson was disconnected from the internet, though it did have access to the entire contents of Wikipedia stored offline.

Watson's principal ability was to read documents written in English and analyse their content for knowledge about basic facts. For instance, it was able to read the Wikipedia page on Mahatma Gandhi and register basic facts about his date of birth, the city in which he was born, where he was educated, what kind of education he received, and so on. This information was not available in structured form and so Watson parsed the text and deduced these facts. The system did not work entirely on its own, it was guided by human trainers who asked pertinent questions and assisted the system to focus on relevant facts.

After winning the Jeopardy! contest in 2011, IBM decided to extend the facilities built into the system to other domains. For example, Watson was trained on a large number of articles appearing in scientific journals of medicine. The articles were specifically focused on cancer treatment. The system was then trained to answer questions about cancer diagnosis and treatment.

This was a special facility of Watson that was marketed by IBM to hospitals to assist doctors. The system was given more data on patient characteristics, doctor's notes and the clinical profiles. Watson was then consulted by doctors in a question-answer mode. Hospitals such as the Sloan Kettering Memorial Hospital in New York and many others around the world adopted the system. By late 2017, the results were varied - some hospitals found that the suggestions by Watson, on diagnosis and treatment of cancer, were adequate, whereas others thought the system was not mature enough to give reliable answers. A few hospitals pulled out of their contracts with Watson. IBM engineers, though, continued to build Watson's capabilities by enabling additional features such as the ability to read and analyse medical images, to analyse the sequence of genes in a tumour and recommend treatments, and to examine the literature on neuron diseases and recommend the genes responsible for causing them.

IBM has located Watson's core processing capabilities on a cloud, allowing various products to be developed, along with those in medicine. One such product analyses data on cyber security incidents and is able to predict potential threats and cyberattacks within a firm's computer system. Another product reads and analyses data related to insurance and can assist with insurance claims and contracts.

Though Watson's recommendations in cases of cancer treatment or fighting cybercrime or for insurance are not better than what human specialists can arrive at, they provide justifications and explanations that support the human decision makers. To this extent Watson's achievements appear to be impressive.

17.1 INTRODUCTION AND HISTORY OF AI

Seeking human-like intelligence and behaviour in machines is an ancient goal in Western philosophical traditions. The drive to build machines that could display abilities of thinking, such as playing chess or answering questions, is reflected in scientific, mathematical and philosophical texts, as well as in fiction. The first attempts to build computing devices, such as adding machines and 'calculators', were not intended to be intelligent but were perceived as giant brains in popular culture. Fiction writers have added to the mystique and possibilities of intelligent machines that can talk and behave like humans, either as positive or negative characters.

In the 20th century, research and developments in many fields led to the fundamental ideas that drove and also birthed the phrase *artificial intelligence* (AI). Developments in general purpose computing devices, as envisaged by mathematicians such as Alan Turing, and the consequent constructions in the UK, USA and Germany, opened up possibilities of advanced computing. Later, the design of operating systems, methods for managing random access memory and high level programming languages provided the tools to advance computing in general and AI in particular. In the 1940s, neuro-scientists, McCullough and Pitts, developed a mathematical model of neurons (the cells that constitute brains) that was to be revolutionary in advancing AI methods of learning and pattern recognition. Other disciplines that contributed to the growth and interest in AI included economics, psychology and linguistics, where advances in theories prompted explorations in AI.

In a workshop in 1954, organised by four researchers – Herbert Simon, Allan Newell, Marvin Minsky and John McCarthy – the phrase Artificial Intelligence was coined and the workshop demonstrated several software programs that could solve problems, play games and perform tasks that required human intelligence and problem-solving skills. One program, the Logic Theorist, could prove theorems in first-order logic. Another program was able to play checkers at a very advanced level. Later, as the field grew, researchers demonstrated various capabilities of programmes that would require human intelligence to perform, such as proving mathematical theorems, playing chess, understanding written sentences and reasoning about actions.

As computing power improved and programming languages became more sophisticated, AI programmes also began to demonstrate capabilities that went beyond demonstrations and trials. A set of systems were developed, such as Caduceus at the University of Pittsburgh and Mycin at Stanford University, which could behave like expert doctors in diagnosing patients and identifying infections. These systems were designed by teams of researchers who worked on the logic of the programs as well as the knowledge required to solve difficult problems, such as in medicine. These systems were called *expert systems* as they behaved like human experts and had knowledge built into them that a human expert would require many years of experience to acquire. It was quickly realised that expert systems could be used in many domains, such as banking, manufacturing, stock markets, insurance and medicine, and many firms came forward to build and deliver such systems commercially. These were the first examples of commercial products based on AI.

KEY POINT

The term artificial intelligence was coined at a workshop in 1954, which was attended by the four founders of the field — H. Simon, A. Newell, M. Minsky and J. McCarthy.

The commercial development of AI faced many challenges and the main one was of scalability – the moment the problems were scaled up to 'real-world' instead of scaled-down sample domains, the programs could not deal with the complexity and the speeds required.

In 1997, an AI program, Deep Thought, beat the reigning world champion, Gary Kasporav, at chess. This was widely believed to be the first demonstration of a full-scale AI program in a live situation. This demonstration paved the way for more programs that operated in live domains.

Robotics developed in parallel with AI, with an emphasis on specialised and autonomous hardware that could be deployed for various activities that required human level abilities of perception, hearing, touch sensitivity, mobility and coordination. Researchers developed robots that could drive cars, control planes, burrow into the earth, clean rooms or move packages. Special hardware for sensing and responding was blended with software that provided reasoning and problem-solving capabilities.

Over the last two decades the developments in computing technology and sensors has given a boost to AI and robotics. Cloud computing has made available massive computing facilities at low cost and in huge scale that has enabled many commercial AI programs to be deployed.

The advances in sensor technologies, such as in IOT devices, has enabled the development of robots such as drones that can carry and drop packages, autonomous cars, factory assembly robots and even robots that cook and prepare meals at restaurants.

17.2 THE TURING TEST

In an influential paper in 1950, Alan Turing, a British mathematician who had proposed the fundamental basis of computing devices, wrote an answer to the fundamental question 'Can Machines Think?' This question had come up in many quarters amongst philosophers and academics, amongst journalists and in the popular media and also within the nascent community of computer scientists. Turing stated that the answer lay in giving precise definitions of what constituted machines and what constituted thinking. He defined machines in the same manner as he had proposed earlier, as devices that had a memory store, a set of instructions and a means to carry out the instructions on the input data. These abstract devices, called Turing Machines, were capable of general computation.

Defining thinking was much harder and for this Turing devised a test, where if any machine is able to pass the test it would be because it was thinking. This was called the Turing Test. As Turing visualised it, the test consisted of the arrangement depicted in Fig. 17.1.

The arrangement consists of the three players – A, B and C. C is separated by a physical partition so that he or she cannot see or hear A or B. C interacts with A and B over a teleprompter, by typing in text. A and B are also seated at independent teleprompters and interact with C. C is the interrogator and asks A and B a series of questions to determine their gender. A and B, who know each other's gender, can respond in any manner they like and generally try to make it very difficult to guess whether they are male or female. Since C cannot see or hear them C is forced to rely on the type-written answers to guess their genders. In the game, C has to interrogate various pairs of A and B, of varying genders, to guess whether they are male or female.

Turing argued that after a few trials if one of A or B is replaced with a computer program and C has the same probability of guessing the genders of A and B, then the computer program can be considered to display thinking. In other words, the computer program has to show the same level of cleverness and wit and command over language as a human player while responding to C's questions. Such a program would have to understand ordinary English language questions, understand the tacit rules of conversation over a teleprompter and also understand the nuances of gender practices, habits and knowledge to be able to deceive the interrogator. Turing called this the Imitation Game.

KEY POINT

The Turing test compares the performance of a computer program with that of human in a live interaction situation.

The Turing test compares the performance of a program with that of human in a live interaction situation. Similar to the Watson program, discussed in the lead case, the program undergoing the Turing test has to understand the questions typed in real time, understand the context of the question, understand various parts and how they are linked and search through a database of facts and knowledge on the basis of which it can arrive at an answer. The program also has to assume or create plausible persona, of a man or woman, and construct a profile of tastes, preferences, background and family history. The program has to assimilate all this information and formulate grammatically correct English language statements. Though Watson has part of these abilities built in, it does not have all the capabilities required to pass the Turing test.

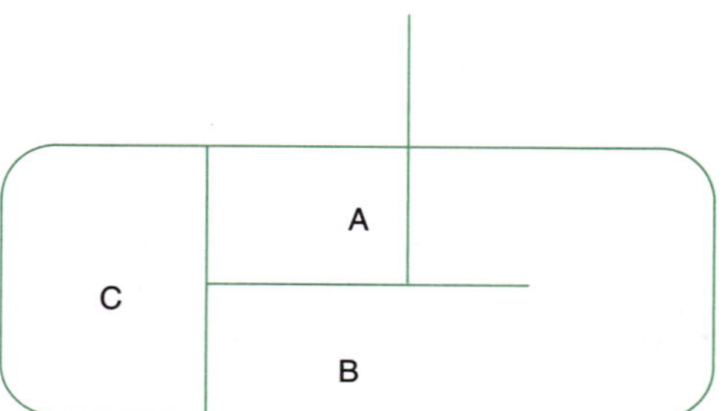

FIGURE 17.1 | Arrangement for Turing test.

In the paper, Turing also set out an agenda for how a computer program to play the Imitation game and win the Turing test could be built. This outline incudes building in reasoning capabilities that outline how thought is made possible, and also a set of learning abilities that enable the program to grow its own knowledge and reasoning abilities. Turing emphasised this aspect, stating that building child-programs that could learn knowledge of the world was a better way of proceeding than encoding massive amounts of knowledge in computers. Turing's thoughts and ideas became the basis of further development in the field of AI, and over the last almost 70 years AI has emphasised reasoning and learning programs that now dominate the field.

17.3 REPRESENTATION AND SEARCH

Two of the founders of the field of AI, Herbert Simon and Alan Newell, said that the very basis of intelligence and problem solving amongst humans was searching through a representation of the problem. A representation is a way of stating or framing the problem such that a solution can be searched. Through detailed studies of human thought processes they showed that humans represented problems as structures of symbols, and then searched this structure until the solution was found.

17.3.1 Example of Representation and Search

Consider the puzzle stated below:

A farmer is traveling with a goat, a bale of grass, and his pet lion. He comes to a river and finds that there is only one boat available and it has only two spaces in it. The farmer realizes he has to make several trips on the boat to move his items. But he is puzzled as to how to do this: if he leaves with the bale of grass, the lion may eat the goat; if he leaves with the lion, the goat may eat the grass. If he leaves with the goat, the lion will not eat the grass; however, once he is on the other bank and leaves the goat there to return and collect the other items, he will be in a quandary again; if he takes the grass and leaves it there, the goat may eat it and if he takes the lion across, the lion may eat the goat.

This simple puzzle can be solved by a consideration of the different ways in which the farmer can move the items in his 2-seater boat (see Fig. 17.2). The farmer has to 'search' through possible combinations and arrive at the solution. Most children are able to solve this puzzle after a few tries. These tries are the search they are engaging in.

A representation for the farmer's problem may be stated as follows:

```
Initial state: Farmer, goat, lion, grass, 2-seater boat on one bank
of river.

Goal state: Farmer, goat, lion, grass, 2-seater boat on other bank
of river.
```

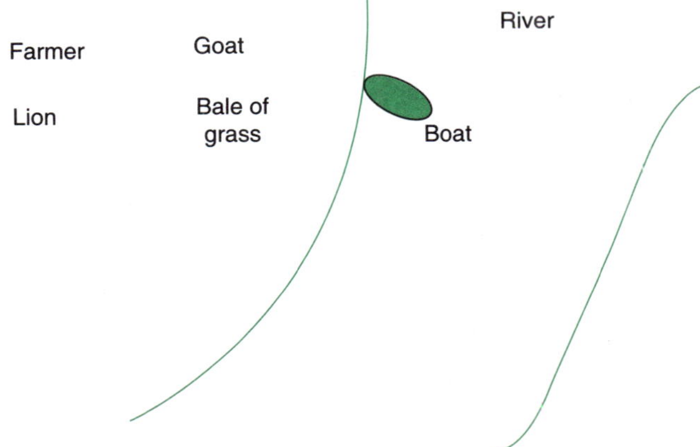

FIGURE 17.2 | The farmer's problem.

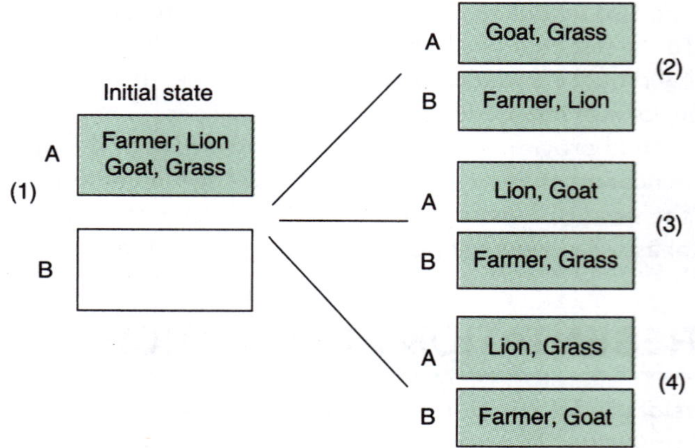

FIGURE 17.3 | First 4 states of farmer's problem.

The implicit constraints of this problem are that only the farmer can row the boat, he can carry only one other item on the boat, and the farmer cannot do any other thing, like tying the grass up on a tree branch the goat cannot reach. Once these constraints are understood, children realise that the problem is one of moving the items with the farmer in the boat.

One possible way to solve the problem using the representation above is as follows:

If A and B designate the banks of the river then the problem is of moving all the items from A to B, two at a time, with the farmer always included (as the one who rows the boat).

Initial State:

Figure 17.3 shows that from the initial state three other states are achievable by moving different items with the farmer. The new states (2) and (3) are not feasible states because they violate conditions of the puzzle – the goat can eat the grass in (2), and the lion can eat the goat in (3). Only state (4) is feasible, as the lion won't eat the grass.

Figure 17.4 shows that further movement of items reaches states (5) and (6), where in (5) the farmer returns with the goat, or he can return alone to side A, which is state (6). State (5) is a return to the initial state, and we may abandon this state. Further search may proceed from (6); see Fig. 17.5.

The states achievable from (6) are (7) and (8) where either the lion or the grass is carried to side B. The states achievable from (7) and (8) are shown in Fig. 17.6.

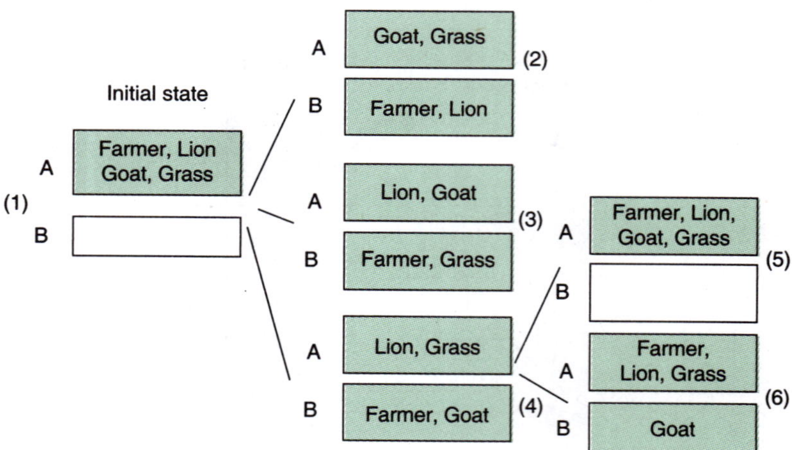

FIGURE 17.4 | States (5) and (6), reached from (4).

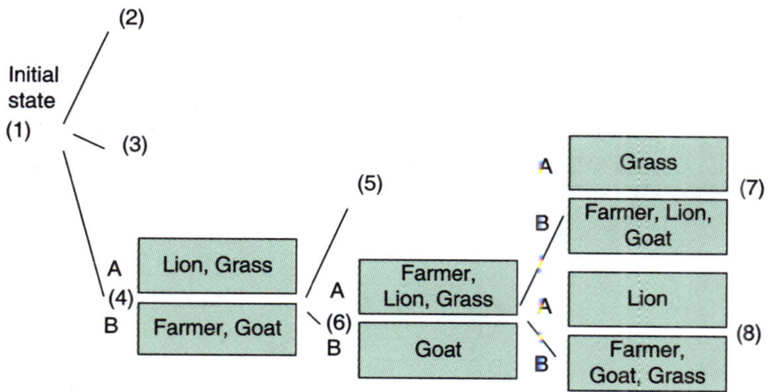

FIGURE 17.5 | States (7) and (8), reached from (6).

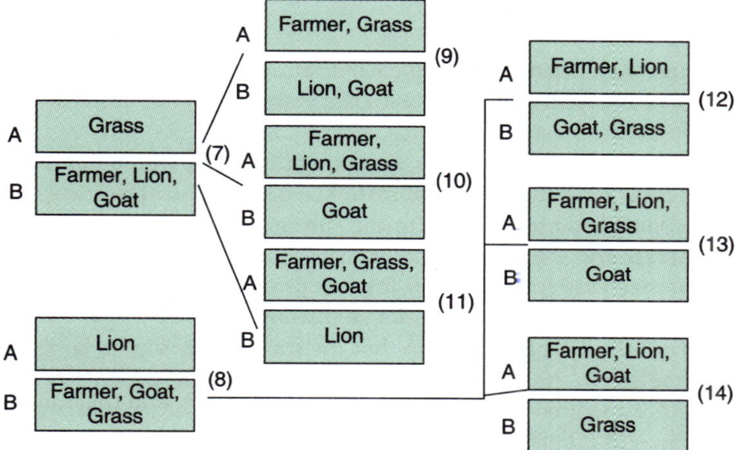

FIGURE 17.6 | States (9), (10) and (11) reached from (7); and states (12), (13) and (14) reached from (8).

States (9) and (12) are infeasible as the lion and goat are left together and in (12) the goat and grass are left together. All the four remaining states (10), (11), (13), (14) can be expanded now to see whether the goal state is achievable. Figure 17.7 depicts the expansion of states (10) and (11).

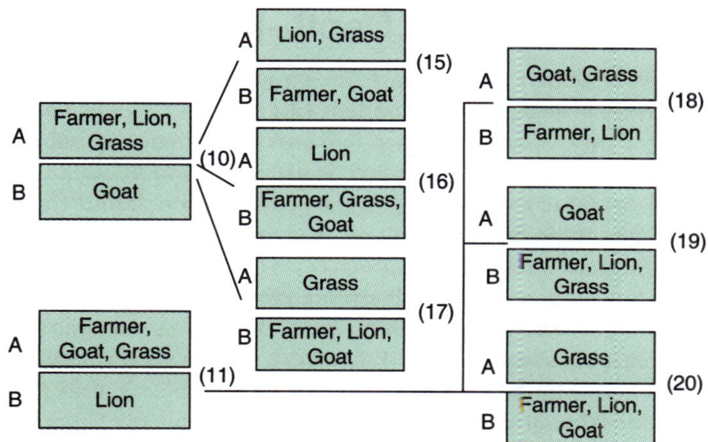

FIGURE 17.7 | States (15) through (20).

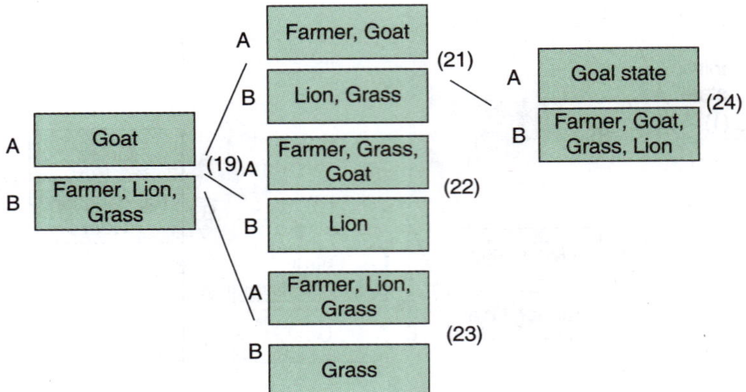

FIGURE 17.8 | States (21) through (24). State (24) is the goal state.

Of the new states generated, it will be clear that state (19) will lead to an answer - the farmer has to return to bank A and return with the goat to bank B. These steps are depicted in Fig. 17.8.

The solution to the problem is found by searching through a whole number of states, called the *state space*, and testing whether the goal state has been found. The states in the state space are generated by *operators* that are applied to the current states to arrive at new ones.

Newell and Simon found that the way to achieve general intelligence in computer programs was to build in the needed representation for any problem and then enable the program to search through the state space to arrive at the goal state.

It will be clear from the example problem that the state space is quite large. Even for a simple problem like the one given, the state space could run to several dozen states (many of which are repetitions) before the goal state is found. The challenge for general intelligence is to find a method of searching that cuts down on the number of states searched. The term Newell and Simon applied to this method of searching is *Heuristic Search*, where a heuristic is a rule-of-thumb or 'trick' by which the search could be pruned to find a solution rapidly. For most real-world problems the state space is very large, running to millions of states and heuristic search is the only viable method of finding an answer.

The states space depicted in the figures above are often referred to as trees. The tree is rooted at the initial state and the branches show the various ways in which the states are generated. The objective of heuristic search is to keep this tree as trim as possible and try to ensure that the goal state is found as quickly as possible.

17.3.2 Breadth-First and Depth-First Search

Two broad categories of search methods are known as *breadth-first* and *depth-first* search. In breadth-first search every branch from any node is first examined to see if a goal state is available before the branches are expanded further. In depth-first search, any one branch is selected, tested for the goal and if not found, this branch is expanded and one branch is selected from there to expand and continue the search. If a particular path is found to be exhausted, the search returns to the other branches and explores them in depth. The act of returning to explore sibling branches is known as 'back-tracking'.

Breadth-first search is exhaustive and will explore every branch at every level. If a goal state exists, it will certainly be found by the search method. Depth-first search is not exhaustive, but is likely to find the goal state sooner. In depth-first search there is no guarantee that a solution will be found. In the example shown above (the farmer's problem), breadth-first search was used to find the solution (though all the branches are not shown in the figures). Most real-world problems use a combination of these approaches. Where good information about the problem is available to guide the search, depth-first search is used.

17.3.3 Planning Systems

Representation of knowledge and conditions in the world and searching through such representations forms the basis of most systems in AI. Computer programs are created with representations that enable creating the state spaces for a wide range of problems, and search heuristics have been devised to quickly and efficiently comb through the state space.

In the initial developments in AI, the key focus was on building representation for difficult problems and then using novel search methods to find the solutions. Some of the first AI systems that were commercially successful were Expert Systems that represented knowledge as a set of rules, which are elaborate if–then statements that solved problems in special domains such as medical diagnosis, oil exploration, factory-floor scheduling and many others. (Expert Systems were discussed briefly in Chapter 16.) Such systems relied on a form of depth-first search to run through the database of rules to find answers.

Another class of systems that were commercially developed were known as planning systems. These systems represented problem situations where sets of activities had to be performed and required advanced planning, hence the name, and this involved a search through many combinations of those tasks. A simple example illustrates the challenges involved.

Consider the tasks required to make an omelette. The list will vary according to the recipe followed and one such is provided below.

1. Break the eggs	2. Add oil to the pan
3. Fry the onions and chillies	4. Cut the onions
5. Cut the chillies	6. Heat the pan
7. Beat the eggs	8. Fry the eggs

The eight tasks above clearly have more than one sequence in which they can be followed. For an AI system to do this correctly same pre-conditions have to be specified – frying can only be done after the oil is heated, frying of onions and chillies follows cutting them, eggs can be beaten only after they are broken, etc. However, there are some activities that can be done in any sequence – add oil to the pan, heat the pan. One solution to the omelette making plan is:

1 – 7 – 2 – 6 – 4 – 5 – 3 – 3

Another solution could be:

4 – 5 – 2 – 1 – 7 – 6 – 3 – 3

Similarly there could be many other solutions that satisfy the pre-conditions and achieve the goal. The representation for such problems can be of the form

```
Action { }; Precondition { }; Effect { }
```

where *Action* states the name of the action and the includes what the action is supposed to do; *Precondition* refers to the conditions that must exist for the action to work; and *Effect* refers to the resulting state after the action. A possible action for the omelette problem could be:

```
Action {Fry (something)};

Precondition {Raw (something) and Chopped (something); or Beaten (something)};

Effect {Fried (something)}
```

The above representation describes either a state (Cooked or Chopped) or an action (Fry). The (something) following the state or action is a variable that can have any of the values of the problem domain. For the action Fry, the variable could be bound as follow: Fry (Eggs), Fry (onions and chillies).

The planning system would need a number of such actions – for Chopping, Beating, Heating, and Adding; and a number of states that the actions can achieve. The Goal state for the problem of making an omelette would be: `{Fried (eggs) and Fried (onions and` `chillies)}`. With these actions and states the system could search combinations of actions that would complete making the omelette, or achieve the Goal state, where the constraints, say of chopping before frying, are taken into consideration by the action representations.

The challenge for such planning systems is that an adequate representation could have thousands of actions, with many preconditions and effects, and states, thus making the problem of searching through combinations of them run to billions or trillions. A problem representing scheduling activities on a factory floor, for example, would have thousands of actions and states, resulting in a dense search space.

17.3.4 General Problem Solving

The problem of knowledge representation is not simply that of finding the most compact set of actions that, when searched efficiently, will find the solution for the given problem. This approach works for a narrow domain and problems restricted to that domain. A representation of knowledge about cooking an omelette or a Biryani will work for cooking alone and may not have any answers for how a flat tyre can be replaced or how a cancer patient can be treated.

This restriction prompted AI researchers to explore general problem-solving systems that would be able to represent knowledge about the world, in general, and about domains, in particular. A part of this challenge is reflected by the Turing test that requires the system that replaces A or B to have a vast repository of knowledge about the world, using which it could set up and solve complex problems. This challenge is also reflected in the design of Watson, a system that can answer factual questions about a vast range of topics, though it is not able to solve planning problems.

General problem-solving systems require that the knowledge about the world, the representations of actions and preconditions and effects, also known as production rules, are encoded by humans. This is a near impossible task as humans themselves are incapable of speaking out and encoding all that they know. For example, humans can recognise faces and tell one from another, but they cannot articulate or encode directly how they do this. There are so many complexities within tasks – recognising a face, recognising songs, walking, hitting a cricket ball – that production rules for them cannot be identified and coded with all possible details.

This problem is far better solved by machine learning algorithms that can infer knowledge from vast amounts of data. The problem of recognising faces can be 'taught' to machines by providing a large number of examples of images of faces and other objects, with appropriate classifications of each and machine learners can then distinguish images of faces from others. In the sections that follow several machine learning algorithms are discussed.

17.4 MACHINE LEARNING

17.4.1 Neural Networks

Artificial Neural Networks (NNs) are, as was mentioned in Chapter 16, used for classification and prediction problems. The neural networks are mathematical representations of neurons in brains and they are widely used to solve machine learning problems. At a very basic level, a neuron is a node in a network that receives many (sometimes one) inputs and produces an output based on some computations. A typical artificial neuron is modelled as depicted in Fig. 17.9.

In this artificial neuron there are three inputs – d_1, d_2 and d_3 – that enter the neuron, which is also called a node. Each input link has a weight associated with it, referred to in the figure as w_1, w_2 and w_3. Within the neuron a sum is computed, which is simply the addition of each weighted data point. This weighted sum ($w_1d_1 + w_2d_2 + w_3d_3$) is then passed through a transfer function. The transfer function transforms the input number to an output number based on some mathematical formula. For example, the transfer function could be: *If weighted sum is > 0, then the output is 1; else the output is 0*. This transfer function is known as a step function.

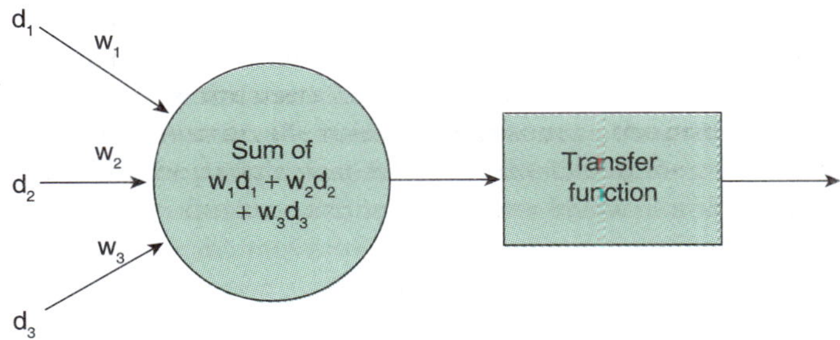

FIGURE 17.9 | A neuron or node calculates the weighted sum of the inputs and passes it to a transfer function.

Another example of a transfer function is: the output is Tanh(weighted sum), where Tanh is the trigonometric function Tan hyperbolic.

As an example, consider the neuron depicted in Fig. 17.9. Let the values for the weights and data be as shown in Table 17.1.

The weighted sum for these weight and data values will be: $0.5 * 1 + 0.2 * 0 + 0.1 * 0 = 0.5$. If the step transfer function is used, then the output from this node will be 1.

When such simple neurons are connected together in a network then they can reproduce the behaviour of very complex phenomena. A typical neural network used in business will have several layers of neurons or nodes, where the first layer is called the input layer, and is the layer where data is input; the last layer is called the output layer; and the in-between layers are called 'hidden' layers, as they are hidden from both the input and output layers. There could be many neurons in each layer and this will depend on the complexity of the phenomenon that is being modelled.

Figure 17.10 depicts a network with an input layer that has 4 nodes, two hidden layers with 9 and 7 nodes each and one output layer with 2 nodes.

Table 17.1 | Sample Values for Weights and Data Inputs

w_1	0.5	d_1	1
w_2	0.2	d_2	0
w_3	0.1	d_3	0

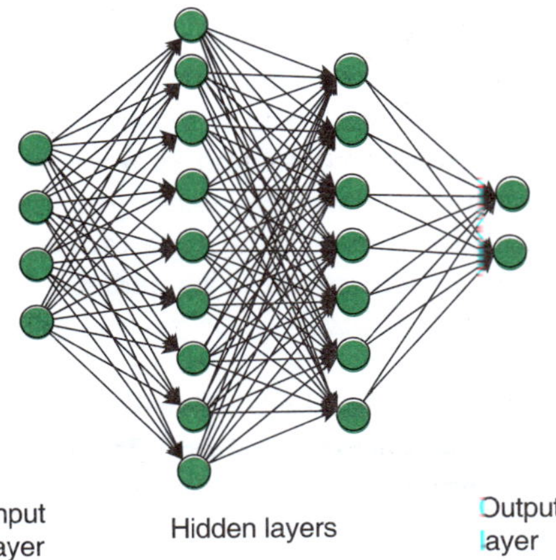

FIGURE 17.10 | The three layers of a neural network.

For most neural networks the flow of data is in the forward direction, from the input layer to the output nodes. As the data moves through the network, the earlier neurons become the source of input for the later ones. These networks are typically referred to as *feed forward* networks.

The outputs from the networks are always numbers. These numbers are interpreted in different ways. For example, if a network is designed to decide whether or not to grant a bank loan, the output could be a 1 or a 0, where a 1 corresponds to an approval and 0 to a reject. Another network could output a number that corresponds to a numeric value – say the amount of loan to be granted.

17.4.1.1 Learning in Neural Networks

Neural networks are *trained* with large amounts of data. The training essentially involves adjusting the weights on the links connecting the nodes of the network. This change in the weights is how the network learns to compute the right answer as output for the given input. The right answer is known as the desired output. This desired output could be, for example, the predicted class for the input data, which is part of the data on which the NN is trained.

To illustrate how weights are changed or updated, consider the example of the single neuron given in Fig. 17.9. Table 17.2 shows the values that are input as data to the network, the weights on the links and output from the network. The last column depicts the desired output, which depicts what the output from the network should be and this may not exactly match the actual output.

In Table 17.2, the desired output is different from the actual output. The neural network weights may be changed to match the desired output with the actual output for the same data set. For the given problem, if w_2 is changed to +0.2, the actual output will match the desired output.

For the simple problem in the table, the weight can be changed by visual inspection. If there are thousands of weights in a network (corresponding to links between nodes across many layers), then changing them is not easy. A further complication is that for different combinations of input data, the desired output may be the same (or for the same input data the desired output may be different). To handle this complex problem of changing and updating weights, neural network designers use an algorithm known as *Backpropagation*. Amongst many other weight update algorithms, Backpropagation has been shown to be very successful and is also able to handle the complex situations of input data and desired outputs mentioned above.

The basic principle that Backpropagation works on is that of comparing the desired output with the actual output, for some given input data, calculating the difference (if any) and then adjusting the weights by small amounts. The algorithm first changes the weights in the links connecting to the output neuron(s) and then the weights on the links connecting the hidden layers, and then the weights on the links connecting the hidden layers to the input layer. The weights are thus changed in a 'backward' manner, moving from the output layer to the input layer, and hence the name Backpropagation. New input data is then provided to the network, the output is again calculated, and if it is different from the desired output the weights are again updated. The weights are changed over many iterations and eventually close the gap between the actual output and the desired output for all data points.

KEY POINT

Backpropagation works on the basic principle of comparing the desired output with the actual output for some given input data, and then adjusting the weights of the network by small amounts.

The design of neural networks requires attention to many issues: the number of layers of neurons in the network, the number of neurons in each layer, the nature and type of the transfer function and the manner in which the input data is arranged and provided to the network. Many different networks are often constructed and trained, for the same data set, to see which

Table 17.2 | Sample Weights and Data for Training a Neural Network

w_1	w_2	w_3	d_1	d_2	d_3	Actual Output	Desired Output
0.5	–0.2	0.1	0	1	0	0	1
			1	1	0	1	1

performs best. Many different types of training methods are also used to arrive at the best performance. Performance of the network is measured by seeing how it classifies data that has not been used for training the network.

17.4.1.2 Deep Neural Networks

Although the idea of neural networks was invented in the 1940s and considerable progress was made in their design and applications, they remained difficult to scale up as large networks took many iterations to train, and hence a long time to train, to converge to an answer, and the results were not always satisfactory. Some innovations were made, since the 2000s, in the design and construction of neural networks that included very large networks, combined with very large data sets that showed significant improvements in time to train and also in performance. These networks are called *deep neural networks* and the field is often referred to as *deep learning*.

Deep neural networks (DNNs) show excellent performance in perceptual tasks - they can recognize images and can convert speech signals into text very well. In 2016, their performance showed dramatic improvements and some DNNs were able to surpass human capabilities in image recognition and categorisation.

DNNs rely on the principles of Backpropagation for training the weights and also on the idea of feed-forward networks for flow of data. The difference is in the number of layers. Whereas shallow or traditional networks relied on one or two hidden layers, DNNs typically have dozens or more hidden layers. In one type of DNNs, called convolutional networks, the initial layers are used to focus on parts of the input data (or pieces of an image for image recognition) which are then pooled, in later layers, based on their similarity. This pooling of parts of images allows the network to break up the input data into similar regions or features. For example, when images of faces are given to the DNN, the eyes, ears, nose and mouth become features that are extracted by the network and trained on. With this form of extraction there is no need to label the features as an eye or nose or mouth; the network is able to do this on its own from the given data. Labels, or categories, may be provided at the output layer to say whether the image is that of a particular person or someone else.

In 2017, convolutional DNNs were applied in dozens of firms and start-ups for recognition tasks. Some DNNs are designed with about 20 layers with thousands of neurons in them, which results in millions of weights. Some of the major applications include recognition of images in self-driving cars, which require processing thousands of images per second; detection of faces in public areas for security purposes; labelling of images containing particular objects, such as traffic signs, birds or animals and other objects, which are used for classification and recognition tasks. Convolutional DNNs are also used to convert spoken natural language to text, and these applications are available on almost all smart phones. Firms such as Samsung, Intel, Google and Qualcomm are building systems that recognise images and speech for use on various kinds of mobile devices; all such systems are based on DNNs.

17.4.2 Induction Learning

The discussion on Decision Trees in Chapter 16 showed that such trees can be used for classification problems with discrete data. The decision trees were based on a broader class of techniques known as induction learning, where the word induction means drawing conclusions from data without any prior hypotheses. Consider the data in Table 17.3. The table shows data regarding bank loans for 14 different cases. The first row of data shows a case in which the loan was not given (the decision of a grant is in the last column), whereas the third row has a case where a loan grant was given. In all of the 14 cases, the loan grant was approved for 9 cases and denied for 5.

Figure 17.11 shows a tree that is constructed from Table 17.3. The root of the inverted tree is the Income parameter. This parameter is the most significant or important for making decisions about loans. The tree shows that the other important parameters are Repayment and

Table 17.3 | Data on Bank Loan Granted in 14 Different Cases

	Income	Repayment	Profession	Education	Grant
1	High	Good	Self-Em	HighSch	No
2	High	Good	Salaried	HighSch	No
3	Med	Good	Self-Em	HighSch	Yes
4	Low	Good	Self-Em	Grad	Yes
5	Low	Poor	Self-Em	PostGrad	Yes
6	Low	Poor	Salaried	PostGrad	No
7	Med	Poor	Salaried	PostGrad	Yes
8	High	Good	Self-Em	Grad	No
9	High	Poor	Self-Em	PostGrad	Yes
10	Low	Poor	Self-Em	Grad	Yes
11	High	Poor	Salaried	Grad	Yes
12	Med	Good	Salaried	Grad	Yes
13	Med	Poor	Self-Em	HighSch	Yes
14	Low	Good	Salaried	Grad	No

Profession. The tree may be interpreted as a set of rules guiding how loans should be granted. These rules may be read off the tree as follows:

```
If the Income is High & the Repayment is Good; Then the Loan Grant
is a Yes.
```

For the rule above, there are two examples that support the rule. This rule is read from the tree by starting at the root node and going down to the *leaf* node where the decision (shown as a Yes or No) is depicted. Another rule that can be read from the tree is:

```
If the Income is Low & the Profession is Self-Employed; Then the
Loan Grant is a No.
```

In total, there are five decision rules corresponding to the five leaf nodes in the tree. The rules help managers make decisions about loan grants based on the prior data available to them.

Decision trees are constructed by considering past data on the parameters used for the decision and the final decisions taken. The root parameter for the tree is determined by a method

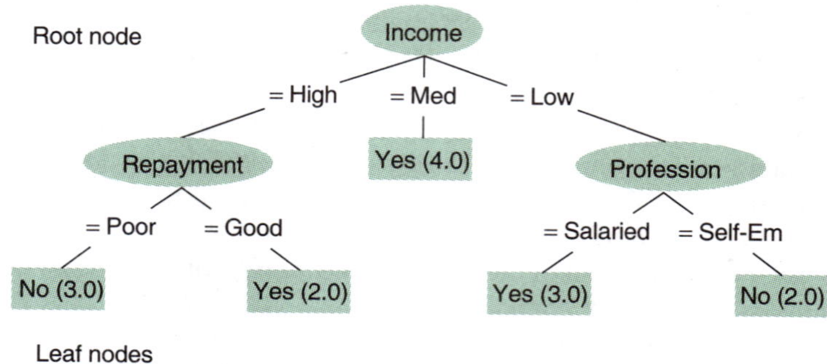

FIGURE 17.11 | Decision tree for loan granting problem.

that involves finding the parameter that has the lowest *entropy* for the given data set. Entropy is a statistical measure of the complexity of information in a data set. Subsequent branches of the tree are also determined by the entropy measure. As the tree is grown, some parameters may not enter the tree at all, and some may enter more than once. In the tree above (in Fig. 17.11) the parameter of Education does not enter the tree at all.

Decision trees are used extensively for classification problems in business and are similar to neural networks in their performance and accuracy. One limitation of decision trees is that they can be used only for problems that have discrete answers for the decision. For example, for the loan problem the decision is either a Yes or No, and so decision trees can be used for such decisions; however, if the decision was a continuous valued answer, such as the amount of the loan, this could not be derived from a decision tree.

17.4.3 Bayesian Learning

The learning problem that induction learning solves is that of classifying data in some categories in a compact manner, such that when a new example is seen, it too can be classified. Another form of learning that solves a similar problem is known as Bayesian learning. This method of learning is based on Bayes' Rule, which computes the probabilities of data belonging to certain classes.

Bayes' rule is fundamentally based on conditional probabilities, which are different from simple probabilities. The simple probability of having rain, stated as Probability (rain) or P(rain) may be 0.5. This states that there is a 50% probability of it raining. A conditional probability considers more information. The conditional probability of rain may be stated as P(rain | clouds). This is read as the probability of rain given that there are clouds. Bayes' rule then allows the evidence to be accumulated as probability values. One way to state Bayes' rule is

```
P(cause | effect) = P(cause) x P(effect | cause) / P(effect)
```

The term P(cause | effect), read as the probability of the cause given the effect, is known as the *posterior probability*, as this is computed based on the information in the right-hand side of the Bayes' equation.

The sample probability of the cause, P(cause), is known as the *prior probability*, something that we already know. The other probabilities on the equation's right-hand side, the conditional probability P(effect | cause) and P(effect), also have to be known in advance. With the prior probabilities known, the posterior probability can be computed. This is the updated Bayes' probability.

For example, consider the following prior probabilities:

```
P (get a loan) = 0.27

P (income is medium) = 0.35

P (income is medium | get a loan) = 0.08
```

The posterior probability is

```
P (get a loan | income is medium) = 0.27 x 0.08 / 0.35 =0.06
```

The above example relies on some prior probabilities to estimate the posterior probability of getting a loan with the condition that the candidate's income is medium. The value of P(get a loan) is 0.27. The figure indicates that the bank has given loans to 27% of those who have applied. The value of P(income is medium) is 0.35, which means that of the people who apply to the bank for loans, 35% have a medium income. The conditional probability P(income is medium | get a loan) is 0.08 gives the percentage of medium income people who were given a loan by the bank. The posterior probability then calculates the probability of getting a loan for a person with a medium income. This last probability is 0.06 or 6%, which is much lower than the prior probability of 27% of getting a loan.

Bayes' rule is a probabilistic method of updating prior beliefs in some phenomenon of interest. The learning in Bayesian learning is the method of updating beliefs on the basis of new data and evidence. As the evidence arrives, probabilities of the phenomenon increase or decrease.

In a very widely used application, Bayes' rule is used to estimate whether an email received in a mailbox is spam or not. The data for the application consists of email that users classify as spam or useful. The software then scans the words and phrases in the email and updates the probability of P(email is spam | indicative words). When a new email is received, the presence of the indicative words is evaluated and if the probability is above a certain threshold, then the email is classified as spam. Though this approach requires a lot of computation, it still works well in practice.

17.4.4 Learning from Analogies

Another form of learning, known as instance-based learning or learning from analogies, relies on finding a match from previous examples to find the classification for data. When people are asked to identify a fruit, for example, whether a citrus-looking fruit is a lemon or an orange, they will do so based on how close the particular fruit is to either a lemon or an orange. If its colour is closer to yellow or green, then it is more likely a lemon. The only reasoning required here is to find out whether, on some parameters such as colour, shape or size, the object belongs to one category or other. This method of classification, through analogies, is very efficient and can be successfully deployed in practical applications. The requirement for the learning algorithm is a large data set of prior examples that have clear classes for the categories.

One of the classification techniques that uses this idea is known as the *k*-Nearest Neighbour (kNN) algorithm. This algorithm compares the object to be classified with *k* neighbours, where *k* is any number from 1 to *n*, where *n* is the number of case examples available. The way this works may be illustrated by the example of loans discussed above. Consider the five examples in Table 17.4.

The classification of the new case, in the sixth row, is not known. Using kNN this classification can be estimated. With $k = 1$, we find that the case has the closest match with the data on row #4. (The values for all the parameters - Income, Repayment, Profession and Education - match exactly with the case.) Hence, the classification for the new case will be the same as that of row #4, as this is the nearest neighbour, and is a 'No' for a loan grant. This is the closest analogy for the case.

What would happen if $k = 3$? In this situation the new case would have to be compared with 3 of the closest neighbours and the majority classification would be its classification also. It will be seen that for the 3 nearest neighbours, 2 have a classification of 'Yes' (row #1 and #5) and one has a classification of 'No' (row #4). Rows #1 and #5 have 2 matches with the case. Thus, with $k = 3$, the new case would have a classification of 'Yes,' going by the majority.

The above example thus poses a challenge: which value of *k* is the most appropriate for classifying the new case, as with $k = 1$, the answer is a 'No' and for $k = 2$, the answer is a 'Yes'. The way to solve this problem is to have a test set of cases (where the classification is known in advance) and to run this test set against different values of *k*. Usually, the *k* value for which the lowest errors are obtained on the test set is then chosen as the most suitable. *k* values are also chosen as odd numbers to ensure a majority value is obtained.

Table 17.4 | Case Examples for Bank Loan Grants

	Income	Repayment	Profession	Education	Grant
1	Med	Poor	Salaried	HighSch	Yes
2	Low	Good	Self-Em	PostGrad	No
3	Med	Good	Self-Em	PostGrad	Yes
4	High	Poor	Salaried	Grad	No
5	High	Good	Self-Em	Grad	Yes
6	High	Poor	Salaried	Grad	??

17.4.5 Genetic Algorithms

A class of learning algorithms is inspired by evolution and is known as genetic algorithms. The main idea is that by following the steps of evolution – such as reproduction, variation and adaptation – the algorithm is able to find solutions to problems. The representation of the problem is done with the help of strings of information (numbers or letters) that are treated as genetic information that are used to generate 'offspring' strings that have within them solutions to the problem. The genetic information in the strings is subjected to variation through methods of crossover and mutation and then they are tested for their 'fitness' to solve the problem. The most successful offspring are then used for further evolution. The fitness tests involve the ability of the offspring strings to solve problems of classification, prediction or any other type of problem.

The main challenge for this kind of learning is to find an appropriate representation that will allow the problem and solutions to be stated as strings that can be both manipulated and then evaluated for fitness. The evaluation has to be done by a function that can provide a fitness score to show how good a particular string is in solving the problem.

As an example, consider the problem of granting a loan. One rule for giving loans could be:

```
If Income = Low and Profession = Self-Employed, Then Loan = No.
```

Such a rule could be encoded in a string as follows: Let three positions of 1s and 0s represent the Income (say, 101 is High, 010 is Medium, 001 is Low); let the next 2 positions represent Profession (say, 01 for Self-Employed and 11 for Salaried); and the last one position represent the Loan grant (say, 1 for Yes and 0 for No). The string that would represent the rule given above would be

```
001 01 0
```

(for a total of six digits). Many such strings, of six digits, could be generated to create a *population* of rules that reflect the data in the Loan grant problem. If they are randomly generated, many would not make any sense (for example, a string such as 000 00 1 would not make any sense within the representation we have).

An evaluation function could then be created to test which of the strings make sense and find some appropriate rule to classify the data. This function could be used to select the best of these strings/rules from the population to let them be used for producing offspring. Variations in the offspring strings could be introduced through crossover and mutation. In the offspring population thus created, the evaluation function could be used to again evaluate the new strings/rules to identify which ones perform best on the given data. This would then lead to another selection of strings to continue the breeding process. In each generation there would always be strings better at solving the problems than in the previous generation.

Genetic algorithms have been used very successfully to find rules for managing robots, for solving hard problems of logistics (such as the Traveling Salesman problem) and also for designing neural networks (which solve other problems). A type of genetic algorithms are used to directly create computer programming code that can perform functions such as play games or solve problems. These systems are known as Genetic Programming systems.

As learners, genetic algorithms can search through a vast range of possible solutions. These learners can also seek out and invent entirely novel ways of solving problems, and have been used effectively in many domains.

17.4.6 Reinforcement Learning

Reinforcement Learning (RL) is based on the idea that an agent has to perform a series of actions that will lead to a goal, and this series of actions has to be learned by the agent through rewards and punishments. The agent knows a set of actions it can take and it can see the state it is in currently, but the outcome of the actions is not known in advance and how they have to be applied is also not known. The agent observes the state of the world, takes an action, the state changes and a reward is given to the agent. The agent now has to learn which actions to take in any given state to maximize the reward it receives.

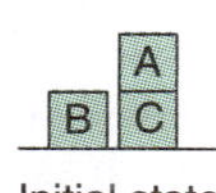

Initial state

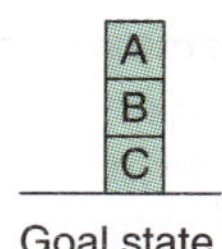

Goal state

FIGURE 17.12 | The problem of stacking blocks.

Rewards and punishments are provided to the agent from the environment, as is the information about the state. These rewards are used to update a function that uses a numerical value to identify the best actions for each state encountered by the agent. Unlike earlier learning methods, in RL, the agent is not provided with a set of classes or categories of right actions to take; it has to learn this through trial and error. For this reason, RL is known as an unsupervised learning method. Learners based on RL have been very successful in training robots to move and navigate through environments, and they have also been successful as online trading agents for auctions and financial transactions.

As an illustration of RL, consider the simple problem of stacking blocks that a robot has to complete. The initial state and the goal state for the problem are shown in Fig. 17.12.

In the initial state block B and block C are on the table. Block A is on block C. The goal state for this simple problem is to create a stack with block A on block B and block B on block C. Consider a robot that can perform three actions: Pick(x), where x is any block; Stack(x,y), where any block x is placed on y (where y is clear); and Ontable(x), where block x is placed on the table.

One possible sequence of actions that will solve the problem is

Pick(A) → Ontable(A) → Pick(B) → Stack(B,C) → Pick(A) → Stack(A,B)

This sequence of actions is something the robot has to learn. Now consider another sequence, which has many wasted moves:

Pick(B) → Ontable(B) → Stack(A,B) → Pick(C) → Stack(C,A) → Pick(C) → Ontable(C)
→ Pick(A) → Ontable(A) → Pick(B) → Stack(B,C) → Pick(A) → Stack(A,B)

For each move the robot makes the state of the problem changes. For example, from the initial state if the Pick(B) action is applied, the new state will have block A on top of block C, and block B in the grasp of the robot. This state is visible and accessible to the robot. Other aspects of the environment are not known or considered (the amount of light in the room, whether there is enough strength in the battery of the robot, etc. are not considered).

For every action that the robot performs, it receives a reward. This reward may be a 0 if the state achieved is not the goal state. Once it achieves the goal state, the robot will receive a reward of 1. A reward of 0 may be considered a punishment. The learner continues trying actions to go from the initial state to the goal state, and receives a reward for each action. After having achieved the goal state, the learner continues with the task of moving from the initial state to the goal state and accumulates the rewards it receives. The accumulated rewards are reflected in a mathematical function, sometimes a table, which learns the best sequence of actions to move from the initial state to the goal state. Over time and after many trials the robot will learn the most efficient way to achieve the goal state.

Successful reinforcement learners require a finite reward as a means to learn the best sequence of actions. These learners *converge* to an optimal sequence of actions based on the function values learned by the rewards received from the environment. Though there are no guarantees that a learner will converge to desired sequence, for many practical applications reinforcement learners have performed quite well.

17.4.7 Limitations of AI and Machine Learning

Though AI and machine learning have made impressive progress in many domains, there are significant challenges in their implementation and development. As organisations move to adopt AI, they will have to take cognizance of and manage these challenges.

1. Many AI systems cannot explain how and why they came up with their conclusions and answers. Particularly, for neural networks the response to inputs is based on a network of weights that cannot be understood easily.

2. Learning systems train on and eventually reflect biases in the data that may distort their performance. The biases may be on the racial codes or language use aspects of computer generated output, which may offend human respondents.
3. Many AI systems still operate in limited domains of operation, such as object classification, disease classification, market predictions, etc., where they provide deep analysis and results; however, they lack general intelligence abilities. General intelligence and the ability to reason with common sense is still a challenge for most AI systems. For example, a system that may have deep knowledge of cancer diagnosis and treatment may not know how to solve simple crossword problem.
4. Systems of perception, such as image recognition and speech understanding, work fine in certain domains, such as recorded camera images or speeches, but their performance degrades in live situations with varying and adverse environmental conditions.

17.5 IMPLICATIONS FOR MANAGERS

Managers in all industries, domains, regions and at almost all levels will feel the impact of a general-purpose technology like AI. They will have to address many challenges in managing AI and ML technologies to effectively compete and grow their own organisations. Some challenges are as follows.

Most AI and ML technologies need prior data to train the algorithms. In some cases the data requirements are massive, running to billions of records. Managers will have to create resources and opportunities for data collection within their existing IT infrastructure, with adequate labels and classes, to ensure data is available for intelligent algorithms.

A significant and emerging need for design and deployment of AI is that of skilled engineers and scientists. In 2017, many commentators said that appropriately skilled personnel for these tasks were in short supply. Managers were seeking training and skilling resources, such as online courses, to train their employees.

Managers will have to decide on the appropriate division of work between people and machines. Some tasks, requiring judgement and decision making, will invariably require people; however many other tasks can be transferred either completely or partly to intelligent machines. The right balance of this division of work will be determined by each context and circumstance.

Persuading organisational personnel and staff about the challenges and opportunities of AI/ML technologies will remain as one of the most difficult tasks of managers. Though awareness of such technologies is high, there is a pervasive apprehension that intelligent machines will displace more jobs than they will create.

Managers will also have to actively seek new areas of innovation in products and services with such technologies. These constitute both a threat to existing products and services and also an immense opportunity for innovation.

Chapter Glossary

Artificial intelligence The name of the field that attempts to build human-like capabilities of thinking and problem solving in computers.

Expert systems Computer programmes that have deep knowledge about domains and can solve problems in those domains with the same depth as human experts.

Turing test A test of thinking capabilities in computer programmes designed the by computer pioneer Alan Turing.

State-space A vast number of intervening steps that lead to the solution of a problem.

Operators Methods by which states in a state-space are generated.

Representation Manner by which the state-space of a problem is defined.

Breadth-first search A method of looking through the state-space that systematically explores every option at each step.

Depth-first search A method of looking through the state-space that examines a limited number of options at each step of the search.

Planning systems A representation of problems as a set of actions that needed to be performed to arrive at the solution.

Machine learning Methods by which knowledge and solutions are inferred from available data.

Neural networks Mathematical representations of neuron cells in brains, which can be trained on data to solve problems of classification and prediction.

Backpropagation A method by which neural networks are tuned, through changes in parameter values, to learn the training data.

Induction A method of drawing conclusions from data without prior hypotheses.

Posterior probability The probability of an event computed from prior information about the event and related conditions.

Genetic algorithms A class of machine learning methods that are inspired by biological evolution.

Reinforcement learning A method of machine learning that learns actions based on rewards.

Review Questions

1. What were the origins of AI? Why did it catch the imagination of researchers?
2. What are some of the significant milestones in the development of AI?
3. Is the Turing test designed to test for intelligence or for general conversational abilities? Explain.
4. Can Watson be considered to have successfully passed the Turing test? Why?
5. Can you find any other solutions for the Farmer's problem, perhaps with more number of steps? How?
6. Figures 17.3 through 17.8 show the steps to the solution to the Farmer's problem. Is the solution shown an example of depth-first or breadth-first search?
7. Two solutions for solving the planning problem are shown in Section 17.3.3. Can you identify another solution?
8. How are weights used in NNs?
9. How are weights trained in NNs?
10. What do the leaf nodes indicate in a Decision tree?
11. What is Bayes' rule and how is it used for updating probabilities?
12. What is the basic idea on which Genetic Algorithms are based?
13. How are rewards used in Reinforcement Learning?
14. What are three challenges the managers face with regard to deploying AI?

Research Questions

1. Read up further on the Watson system of IBM. What are the kinds of machine learning methods and problem-solving methods that are built into it?
2. Logistics management is a very profitable and important problem for modern businesses. What are some AI methods used to solve logistics problems?
3. Open source software packages such as R and Weka have built-in modules for many ML methods. Find a data table, from many available on the web, for a classification problem. Run the data through a neural net, a Naive Bayes classifier and a Decision Tree. Which gives the best results for this data set?
4. AI has a potential to replace many humans at their jobs. Is its potential being realised? Is there a possibility of massive unemployment due to AI? Research answers to these questions on the internet.

Further Reading

1. "The Business of Artificial Intelligence: What it Can—and Cannot—Do for Your Organization." Brynjolfsson, Erik and Andrew McAfee. *Harvard Business Review*, July 2017.
2. "What's Driving the Machine Learning Explosion?" Brynjolfsson, Erik and Andrew McAfee. *Harvard Business Review*, July 18, 2017.

3. "What Artificial Intelligence Can and Can't Do Right Now." Andrew Ng. *Harvard Business Review*, November 09, 2016.
4. "Computer Science as Empirical Inquiry: Symbols and Search", Newell, A. and Simon, Herbert. A., *Communications of the ACM*, Vol. 19, No. 3, 1976.
5. Buchanan, Bruce G. "A (very) brief history of artificial intelligence." *AI Magazine* Vol. 26, No. 4, 2005.
6. "Computing Machinery and Intelligence" A.M. Turing, *Mind*, 1950.
7. LeCun, Y., Bengio, Y. and Hinton, G. "Deep Learning," *Nature*, Vol 521, pp. 436–444, 2015.
8. *Machine Learning*, Tom Mitchell, McGraw-Hill, 1997.

Part III

SOCIAL ASPECTS OF IS

Chapter 18 ICT for Development and E-Governance

Chapter 19 The Society of the Internet

Chapter 20 Open Source Software

CHAPTER 18

ICT for Development and E-Governance

Learning Objectives

After completing this chapter, you will be able to:

- Understand the use of ICT for development
- Learn about types of ICT interventions
- Understand ICT4D projects
- Get an overview of e-governance concepts
- Learn about e-government and e-participation

Information and communication technologies (ICT) include the set of technologies that deliver digital content and processes. ICT can reach masses of people at a low cost and conveniently, and assist with providing services which can help with development. Development is understood as increasing per capita income of people, especially in countries where there are a large number of poor people, and also increasing their freedom to lead better lives. The premise of ICT for development is based on the fact that citizens of rich countries have a greater access to ICT than those in poor countries. Overcoming this difference, also known as the digital divide, is considered to be a priority for many governments. ICTs can be used effectively for development by disseminating needed and useful information; they can allow transactions to happen between citizens and government at a low cost; they can enable citizens to organise around political issues; they can assist with providing education for those without easy access to educational facilities; and they can help with providing warning about natural calamities. ICT for development projects such as Radio Sangham, Video Volunteers and e-tuktuk have achieved many of these development goals.

E-governance is the use of ICT for the governance of a state. In a country like India, e-governance has assumed a very important role with the governments both at the Centre and in the States giving it a high priority. E-governance moves through many stages of evolution as the technology and departments mature with the processes. Design and assessment of e-governance projects requires understanding the needs of demand-side and supply-side stakeholders, the economic costs and benefits of the project, and the priorities of development. Implementation challenges for e-governance projects include implementing data standards, legal issues, resistance and corruption. E-government is the use of IS within and across government departments. E-participation, which is at a nascent stage in India, is the use of ICT in the democratic process.

MIND MAP OF CHAPTER TOPICS

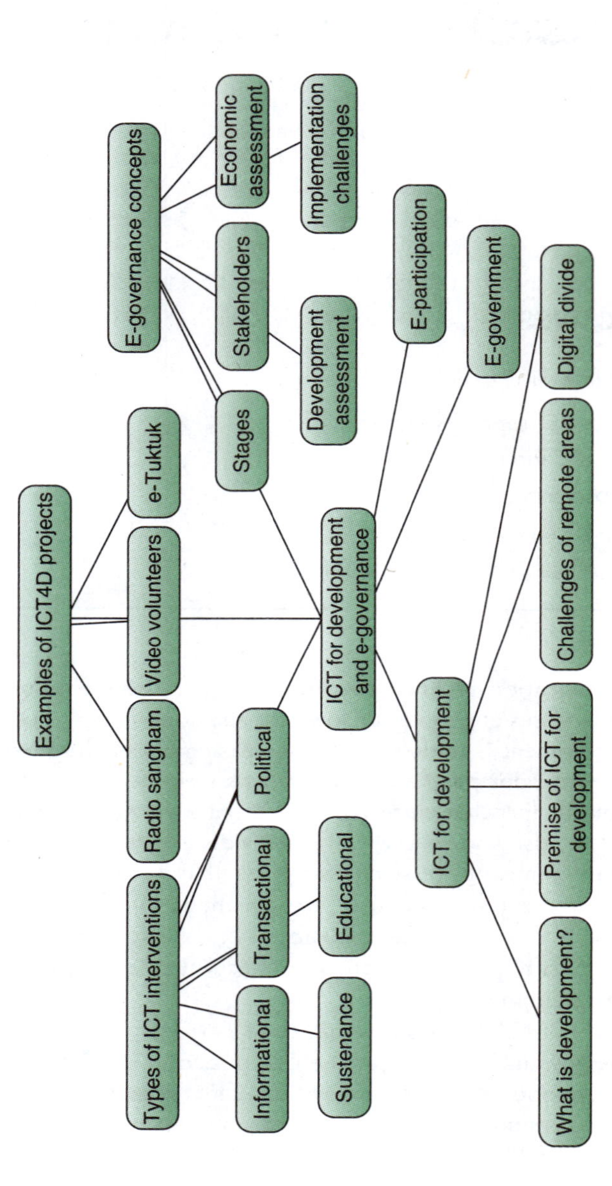

CASE STUDY: THE BHOOMI LAND RECORDS SYSTEM OF KARNATAKA

The Bhoomi land records system of Karnataka state in India is a classic example of an e-governance system. The system was introduced in 2001 to provide easy access to land records to the farmers of Karnataka.

Land-owning farmers in Karnataka maintain many records that establish their ownership to the land. The main document is a tax record, known as *khata* in Kannada language, which establishes the ownership details. Another document maps the piece of land and shows its boundaries and adjoining geographical regions. The land record, or *pahani* in Kannada, is an official document that establishes a farmer's ownership status. It contains details of the land, details about the crops farmed on the land, and details about any loans taken against the land parcel. The pahani is not an official ownership document, but is a document that establishes ownership status along with other details. The land record is mainly used by farmers to obtain bank loans.

Historically, land records were issued by the Village Accountant or VA. The VA would issue a land record upon a request from a farmer, and would manually fill out the required fields. All the information had to be updated, and this used to take a lot of time to complete and fill out accurately. For instance, the VA had to verify the amount and kind of crops produced, the extent of loans outstanding against the land, and the amount of water used for irrigation among other things. Since one VA would account for typically three to six villages in Karnataka, they had a lot of work to do when the demand for land records was high. Farmers would face considerable delays in obtaining the document, and sometimes even had to pay bribes to speed up the process. At the time of planting crops, when farmers would typically seek loans, the demand for land records is very high and the VAs are under a lot of pressure to write the land records quickly.

The government of Karnataka had decided to computerise land records and had made efforts to do so since the early 1990s. These attempts to computerise failed owing to the problem of updating the records soon enough. By the time they had the computer records in place the information regarding crops harvested was out of date. In the final round, the government planned to digitise the records while at the same time having the VAs update the information relevant to it.

Bhoomi kiosks are maintained at *taluk* headquarters. A taluk is part of a district. (It is a sub-district.) On average, it takes a farmer about half a day to reach the taluk. The taluk headquarter typically houses several government departments that operate at the sub-district level. Since the late 2000s, Karnataka state has also permitted access to Bhoomi services through several hundred kiosks available across the state.

Farmers access Bhoomi by waiting at a window from which a computer operator takes their requests. They identify their records by providing a unique identifier that is the record number, also known as the *khata* number. With this number, the operator pulls up the record on the screen which is verified by the farmer and is then printed out. The computer operator signs the record to authenticate it and also sticks a hologram sticker on it, as a proof of authenticity. Farmers pay Rs 15 (about USD 0.35 in 2009) for the record.

Farmers can also log requests for land mutation in the Bhoomi system. A mutation is a request to change the khata owing to change in ownership from sale or inheritance of land. The process of mutation is complex and involves verification of the land parcel, confirmation that it is available for mutation, and a background check on loans taken against the land. A mutation takes at least 6 weeks to complete, usually much more. When farmers file a mutation request at a Bhoomi kiosk, their requests are logged on a queue and are processed off the queue. Farmers are given a queue number and can use this to verify their status.

The computer records are updated by the VAs on a regular basis. Three times a year they visit the farming lands, verify the crops sown and harvested, and then go back to the taluk headquarters to update each record. This is a tedious process and some attempts have been made to use hand-held computers to ease this process.

Bhoomi kiosks consist of desktop computers that host the database and report creation software. Only the records for a particular taluk are maintained at a kiosk. Each computer is backed up by an un-interrupted power supply. The state has signed a contract with a private firm to maintain the computers, printers, power supply and other peripherals.

Since its inception Bhoomi has been used quite extensively, particularly for obtaining land records. Currently (as of 2009), it hosts about 20 million land records, and is used by almost 800,000 users annually. The revenues generated by the sale of land records are sufficient to sustain the operations of the kiosks and also create a surplus.

An early study focusing on Bhoomi users showed benefits of the system: users found it easy to use; they could obtain a record in a few minutes; most did not have to pay a bribe to get the record; and the data on the record was largely accurate. Subsequent studies confirmed these initial findings, but did point to some irregularities such as tampering with data, mild forms of corruption, and downtime of computers owing to power outages.

Other studies have shown that Bhoomi mainly benefits the land-owning classes of Karnataka and leaves out a large section of farmers who do not have title to land. Bhoomi's design does not address the concerns of landless farmers.

18.1 ICT FOR DEVELOPMENT

ICT stands for information and communication technologies. Information technologies include the entire gamut of technologies that deliver digital data-based content, including the computers of all kinds such as desktops, laptops, hand-helds and servers, and network technologies that link computers together and create the internet. Communication technologies include the existing analog technologies such as radio and television as also digital mobile phones.

Taken together, the ICT represent a powerful set of technologies that when accessed by masses of people can assist with providing health care, education, safety, access to relevant information, government services and other developmental services. ICT can handle and manipulate large quantities of information in various forms, and can move them over large distances efficiently and cost effectively. With regard to this, they are considered highly suitable for development of communities and even entire nations.

18.1.1 What is Development?

Although the word development, and what it means, is contested by many, to most economists and political scientists it connotes an improvement in the income, usually referred to as the per capita (or per person) income, of a community or nation. When the United Nations and the World Bank refer to development, they are essentially basing their policies on per capita incomes. The multilateral agencies divide the nations of the world into three categories:

1. Less developed countries (LDCs).
2. Developing countries.
3. Developed countries.

The classification is primarily based on the per capita income, where a daily per capita income of less than USD2 would mark a nation as an LDC. A low per capita income but a high potential to generate incomes, measured by low vulnerabilities to agricultural variations, export shocks and natural disasters among others, and a population relatively well off with regard to nutrition, health and education, would place nations in the developing country category. By this calculation, India is categorised as a developing country.

Amartya Sen, a leading development economist and a Nobel laureate, argues that development should be more concerned about human freedom than about income levels. He states that development is not an end by itself but a means to an end, where the ends are freedom from hunger, poverty, deprivation and illiteracy. This form of development is achieved by having certain freedoms that enable citizens to live their life in a fruitful and full manner, unencumbered by deprivations. These freedoms include:

1. Political freedom, or the ability to participate in agenda setting and selecting elected representatives.
2. Economic facilities where citizens are free to participate in markets, including being able to sell their labour and skills.
3. Social opportunities that allow citizens to live healthy and informed lives that enable them to participate in political and economic activities.
4. Transparency guarantees where citizens have the freedom to know about and see all that is being done for and in their communities.
5. Protective security where all citizens are secured from basic deprivations such as poverty, disease or natural calamities.

With such freedoms citizens can choose and shape a life of their own that fulfils their aspirations as human beings.

Though Sen's theory does not entirely oppose the development arguments of other economists, it centres on the ideas of freedoms as opposed to income. This helps focus activities and policies of development on areas not entirely directed at employment and income generation. In this vein, it is easy to see that the ICT use and deployment too should not be entirely directed at employment and income generation but also at providing or enabling the basic freedoms as outlined by Sen.

18.1.2 The Premise of ICT for Development

Information and communication technologies have the potential to start or speed up development in a developing or less developed country – that is the premise of the entire project called ICT for Development or ICT4D (the number '4' in the acronym replaces the 'for' in the original phrase). Many international multilateral funding agencies have concluded that ICT does support development and have provided funding and policy support for such efforts by nations.

The strongest evidence of the ICT–development relationship comes from the data on ICT penetration in developed countries, contrasted by the data from developing and less developed countries. As an example, Table 18.1 shows data from two developed countries, Sweden and USA, and two developing countries, India and Nigeria, to show the contrasts in ICT penetration and per capita incomes.

Table 18.1 | Comparison of Per Capita Income and ICT Penetration in Four Countries

Country	GDP (2016) in USD	GDP per Capita (2016) in International Dollars	ICT Development Index (2016)
USA	18.6 trillion	57,467	8.13
Sweden	514 billion	49,175	8.41
India	2.2 trillion	6,572	2.65
Nigeria	404 billion	5,867	2.44

Sources: ICT Development Index (http://www.itu.int/net4/ITU-D/idi/2017/index.html)
databank.worldbank.org/data/download/GDP.pdf
https://en.wikipedia.org/wiki/List_of_countries_by_GDP_(PPP)_per_capita

The data in Table 18.1 clearly shows the marked difference between developed and developing countries with regard to internet penetration, PC penetration, mobile phone penetration and broadband users.

Leaders around the world are convinced that ICT has a positive impact on development, and increasing ICT access and penetration is a priority for many developing nations. Even if one argues that the increased ICT usage has happened because of higher per capita incomes, it is difficult to tease out clearly the cause and effect. Have USA and Sweden developed because of higher levels of ICT penetration or have they achieved higher levels of ICT usage because they already had a higher per capita income? This is a difficult question to answer as there are many causes for any nation's economic growth and only one criterion cannot explain such complexity.

18.1.3 The Digital Divide

Table 18.1 shows the differences in access to digital technologies between people of developed and developing countries. Developed countries, it has been shown, have greater access to digital technologies and hence greater resulting productivity. This is because employees engaged in production or service in developed countries can use the digital technologies to enhance the volume and quality of work they do, and hence improve productivity. In this situation, productivity is defined as the output, be it in things made or people serviced, of a manufacturing industry or a service industry per employee. Employees can increase productivity by using the technologies for helping their own work.

Since about 1975, the gap between rich and poor countries, in terms of access to telephones and the internet, has increased dramatically. The rich countries have invested heavily in technology and increased the rate of ICT penetration in their populations. Poor countries, in relative terms, have lagged behind. The story is a bit different for middle-income countries that have increased penetration starting around the early 1990s and have recorded substantial growth in penetration rates. The digital divide is thus different for different income levels of countries.

The digital divide refers to this gap in ICT penetration between developed and developing countries, and points to the differences in productivity that arise because of it. Within developing countries, the term also refers to the gap in access to ICT and services between urban and rural citizens, those with higher education and those with less education, those with higher incomes and those with lower incomes, and those who are conversant with English and those who are not.

18.1.4 The Challenges of Remote Areas

In developing countries, remote and interior areas, which are away from large population centres like cities, are typically difficult regions for deployment of ICT. One of the main challenges in these regions is lack of access to electricity. For example, in India, electricity is available only for few hours of the day, or not at all, in large sections of rural areas. For instance, only 44% of all rural Indian households were electrified (compared to about 87% electrified homes in urban areas) in 2007. In India, the problem of electricity deficiency is related not only to low electricity generation but also to difficulty in distribution to remote and difficult terrains. Even in urban areas where electricity is available to most, the supply is often erratic, with wide fluctuations in voltage and uncertainty in continuous supply.

The non-availability of electricity leads to many deficiencies. Devices such as televisions, computers, radio transmitters and mobile phone towers cannot function, and hence investors are reluctant to put them up. Many solutions have been found in portable devices, such as radios, laptops, mobile phones and personal-digital assistants, which use batteries. However, charging batteries does remain an issue. Some have resorted to solar power for charging batteries and also for powering computers and servers.

The other problem of remote areas is connectivity. Signals for mobile phones and terrestrial radio transmitters are unable to reach over long distances and remote areas. Even if users have devices, they are unable to receive signals and see, hear or read the messages.

18.2 TYPES OF ICT INTERVENTIONS

18.2.1 Informational

Many ICT4D implementations are designed to provide relevant information to those residing in remote areas. The idea here is to provide information about markets, the economy, crops, weather, examination results, and other information, which is of value to those living in remote areas and who do not have access to traditional media such as newspaper, television and the radio. These implementations also provide information in a form that is different from other media; the information is based on specific queries; it could be highly individualised and personal, and is needed on an ad hoc basis.

Implementations of informational systems have taken various forms. The best known of these is the information kiosk. These are small physical centres containing essentially one or two computers, a printer, an internet connection and a reliable power supply. The kiosks are run by operators who enable users to seek information off the internet for a small fee. Kiosks are very popular around the world and have been implemented in many countries, though with mixed results. As their main basis for sustenance is a paid transaction, they have not always been commercially viable.

Information can also be provided through other means such as websites, SMS messages over mobile phones and through radio broadcasts. The degree of specificity of the information will vary according to the media, as broadcast media such as the radio and SMS broadcasts can only carry general information. Websites, on the other hand, can carry general information as well as very specific information, which is made available through query systems.

18.2.2 Transactional

Transactional systems allow the users to perform some required business through them. A transaction could be a download of a form, or filing of taxes or request for a service. Transactional systems are more complex and require additional knowledge of computing technology from users. Users have to be aware of the facilities available and be in a position to avail of them. Transactional systems can be simple in terms of providing access to a form or collecting basic information, or they can be very complex requiring detailed data entry and working through many interface screens, such as filing and paying taxes.

Transactional systems in developing countries are typically provided through kiosks that are usually manned. The personnel in charge of these systems maintain and update them, while helping out users. For example, the Bhoomi e-government system of Karnataka is a transactional system as it allows users access to documents and also register for services. These systems are manned by operators who help the users if they are not conversant with computer systems, and also with queries and follow-up actions.

The main difference between informational and transactional systems is that transactional systems provide something more than information, such as forms, or the ability to pay, or a document. Such transactions are legal, and in cases where the government is involved, are official documents.

18.2.3 Political

Systems that enable political interactions and participation fall in this category. An example of such a system is the one that allows citizens to engage in a discussion with candidates up for an election over a website using text or audio or video facilities. The system enables the citizens to express their views and try to set the agenda for the candidates. Citizens interact with all the candidates, read their views, send in questions and requests, and organise debates and speeches by the candidates. This is a direct way of accessing and influencing the political agenda of parties and candidates.

Political systems enable richer participation by citizens. Instead of passively consuming news about candidates and issues, they can actively engage in the political process. Citizens can use electronic media such as the internet or SMS or the radio to participate. Even after elections, systems can be used to monitor candidates and their political activities. For example, social networking sites maintain current reports on the activities of candidates, records of discussions by elected members, data on political funding and sponsoring, corruption and graft data, and reports on activities of the bureaucracy. News and data are pooled and aggregated to further empower citizens.

18.2.4 Educational

Educational systems enable students and teachers to interact electronically. These systems provide educational content to areas where such knowledge is not available, or to regions where infrastructure for schooling or college education is not available. For example, some systems are used to provide subject knowledge to students in remote areas by teachers who are located in distant cities or towns. Students are able to view content and interact with the teachers over the internet.

Educational systems are either used to supplement teaching resources, such as additional material in the form of online videos, or to provide entire courses over an ICT media. The latter include distance learning courses and degrees offered to students in remote areas.

18.2.5 Sustenance

ICT devices can also be designed to provide sustenance to rural populations. For instance, systems have been designed to warn fishermen off the coast in Kerala of impending storms or bad weather conditions. These early warning systems work on radio signals and inform the fishermen of adverse conditions. Such systems can be used to provide warning at appropriate times, information about government policies that protect against natural disasters, provide assistance with obtaining loans and provide assistance with medical diagnosis.

Such systems for sustenance have to be designed that address the needs of the local community and involve their active participation. Local conditions will specify what are the natural disasters that can occur and how the systems can help against them. For example, the conditions and requirements of a coastal region will differ vastly when compared to a semi-rural, hinterland. Systems for providing insurance, banking, and health care will have to be tailored to the specific needs and conditions of the local population. Furthermore, the systems have to be designed with a clear and conscious choice of services for different classes, castes and professions of people. A single approach with all such segments does not work as effectively.

18.3 EXAMPLES OF ICT FOR DEVELOPMENT PROJECTS

18.3.1 Radio Sangham

Radio Sangham is a project in the Medak district of the Andhra Pradesh state in India. This is a community radio project started by two women volunteers to meet the needs of the community for news, commentary and cultural programmes in the local dialect. The initial broadcasts were made on loudspeakers in the village centre where people would gather to hear the programmes that were played from tape recorders. The operators prepared news items, community discussions and interviews, and cultural offerings such as songs and recitations. The programmes were aired in the evenings for 2 h after the farmers had returned from their work.

Radio Sangam received funds from various multinational donor agencies, such as UNESCO, to set up an FM broadcasting station. After setting up the station, it had to wait for a licence from the government to be able to begin broadcasts. This licence was granted in 2008, and it became one of the first community radio stations in India to obtain one.

The two volunteers at Radio Sangam are local women, belonging to a Dalit caste, who learned how to use the equipment to record and edit their programmes. They spend the day preparing the programmes, and then air them in 2 h in the evening. They also have a call-in section where local residents, in the 25 km radius of the broadcast, call from mobile phones to ask questions or place requests. The broadcast reaches a population of about 50,000 residents of about 100 villages.

The radio station is backed by a non-governmental organisation called the Deccan Development Society (DDS) that started experimenting with the idea of providing electronic broadcast and narrowcast media to local woman who were non-literate or semi-literate. When the narrowcasting was initiated in 1998, it immediately became popular with the local population as it dealt with news and issues of interest to them and in the local dialect. The idea was initially dismissed as 'Radio of Beggars' but later it garnered respect from even its critics as it sustained over 10 years and was able to obtain a licence to broadcast on an FM frequency.

DDS trained the women volunteers, and it has trained a total of about 5000 women in that region. Currently, 10 trained volunteers move across villages, acting as reporters and recording interviews and news items digitally. They then edit these recordings with guidance from the station coordinators. The volunteers are able to manage the complex electronic editing and management software for audio files on their own.

Radio Sangham is an ICT project that is both informational and political in nature. It provides relevant information to its listeners in their preferred language. It is political in nature as it enables women to voice their concerns in a free and open manner without the control of large private interests or the state. This freedom enables them to seek out change in their society by overcoming gender and caste oppressions and engage with the larger society as equals.

18.3.2 Video Volunteers

Video Volunteers (VV) is a project that enables people living in under-privileged communities to voice their views and opinions through videos. VV engages with residents of such communities by providing the video recording, editing and playback equipment and then training them in the use of these devices. Volunteers from the community record and edit videos on the issues that are important to the community. These videos are then shown in the community and discussions are arranged around the issues raised.

VV engages with communities by working with them directly or in partnership with other NGOs. They select volunteers from the community who are excited about creating videos on issues of importance to them. These volunteers are then trained on the equipment. They learn to shoot video segments and edit them on computers. Professionals work with them for 12–18 months to teach them how to make high-quality films. Each film involves interviews, commentaries, songs and sequences featuring the local community members. Typically, each film is an hour long and is shown to the community in a public place with a digital projector. After the film is screened, the viewers discuss the issues raised by the film, and if there are problems that need to be addressed, concrete steps are suggested.

The volunteers, who are trained in film making, form part of the community video units. These units consist of local journalists and film production specialists, who are specially trained by VV and whose job is entirely devoted to making and screening films. VV started their project in 2003, and since then they have trained over 150 community producers and have screened video films for more than 200,000 people. As of 2009, there were about 15 community video units operating in different parts of India and Brazil, and they have produced more than 100 films that are screened in about 350 villages and slums. Many of the videos produced by these communities have been purchased by mainstream television stations.

The VV project addresses the informational needs of its target audience by providing news and editorials on the activities in their location. Residents are informed on issues such as the state of civil works, the activities of elected officials, specific law and order situations, criminal activities of residents and so on. Such reports are created in an investigative journalism format and shown as video magazines. Residents learn about such issues only through this media as it is very specific to their locale and is largely ignored by the national or regional news and television networks.

The VV videos are also political in nature as they help project the voices of people at the margin, whose concerns are typically not mainstream news. The videos produced by the volunteers have helped bring about change. For example, at a locality, the videos forced the authorities to complete civil works that had been long neglected and were shown up in films; in a poor neighbourhood, one video pointed out the cheating being practised by a local merchant who sold controlled price commodities at inflated prices, and this was immediately redressed by the youth in the community; videos have brought up issues such as domestic violence, sexual harassment and caste discrimination. These videos help highlight local voices and issues that are otherwise not visible. For example, in one video the topic of marriage of girl children was addressed, and the interviewed women pointed out that with girl children being married off early, the biggest loss to them is that they are not able to play anymore. This contrasts sharply with the community activists opposed to child marriage, who highlight the aspect of inhuman practices of child marriage and loss of education for the girl child.

18.3.3 The e-Tuktuk Project

The e-tuktuk project in the Kothmale district of Sri Lanka is a very interesting experiment for connecting rural populations with radio and the internet. A tuktuk in Sri Lanka is a three-wheel motor vehicle, also known as auto-rickshaw in India. The e-tuktuk is a three wheeler that is equipped with a radio transmitter, a laptop computer, an internet connection (enabled through a mobile phone and also through a wireless local-loop technology), a generator, some loudspeakers, a printer, a scanner, a camera and a phone. The e-tuktuk can travel to remote destinations and transmit radio programmes on a narrow bandwidth (called narrowcasting) and also connect to the internet. They are self-sufficient in terms of electric needs as the generator can charge up the batteries.

Kothmale is a remote and mountainous region in Sri Lanka. The idea of creating a mobile telecentre was to enable many villages have access to electronic services, and at the same time create a community by sharing news, making the content and using the common facility. The e-tuktuk project was launched in 2006 and since then has seen huge success.

A typical e-tuktuk session starts when a tuktuk arrives at a village centre. The programme operator plays songs or news on the narrowcast radio and also on the loudspeakers. Some residents may ask for information to be obtained from the internet, which the operator looks up using his laptop and then broadcasts the answer both on the radio and on the loudspeakers. Programmes of local interest are often produced by village residents, for which the e-tuktuk is equipped, and these may then be broadcast in the same village and in other villages. Thus, information related to local needs - pertaining to agriculture, school results, bus timings - is obtained and broadcast in the village.

The e-tuktuks are sponsored by multilateral funding agencies, which is the only means of their financial sustenance. The operators as yet do not have a means of earning revenues for their efforts and for maintaining the e-tuktuks.

18.4 E-GOVERNANCE CONCEPTS

E-governance is a contraction of the term 'electronic governance'. The idea behind e-governance is using electronic means, namely digital computers and networks, to assist in the governance of a state.

In modern parlance, the word 'governance' is the act of ruling over a state or a geographical region, where the ruler is an elected government or a body empowered to rule by some other means. The ruler has to enact laws, implement programmes, address the needs and concerns of citizens, and provide an overall framework of administration. Governance, in this sense, is all that government bodies do - administer, enact laws, pass legislations, implement programmes, set up organisations, conduct elections, interact with citizens and so on.

Electronic governance, or e-governance, refers to the use of electronic means to assist in ruling and administration by a body with the powers to do so. E-governance entails reaching out to a vast citizen population, interacting with business and other organisations, and effecting governance in partnership with these *stakeholders*.

In India, e-governance has a high priority for both elected leaders and bureaucratic officials. Over the years, the Central governments as well as State governments have spent large sums of money in setting up and implementing e-governance mechanisms to reach out to citizens and provide a plethora of services. For instance, the Central government currently has high priority projects for issuing a unique identification number to all citizens, a portal for paying taxes, conversion of all manual land records to electronic form, computerised property registration, computerisation of all village councils (panchayats) among others.

E-governance has been a priority for governments across the world. In developed nations such as Sweden and the USA, most citizens interact with the government mainly through electronic means. Almost all the information that governments provide is available through websites, and most forms and information requirements of people are also met through online sites. In Sweden, citizens receive a pre-filled and pre-calculated tax form from the government annually at the time of paying taxes. Citizens can then accept or modify the calculations by responding online or by sending a message from their mobile phones. If needed, they can also request a face-to-face meeting with tax officials. In the USA, citizens can file their taxes online as also file manually by sending in their tax papers. Requests for specific documents such as passports, birth certificates, social security cards and so on, can be filed electronically. Furthermore, in the USA, almost all data exchange between government departments is done electronically.

18.4.1 Stages of E-Governance

It has been observed that e-governance development in a nation proceeds in stages (see Fig. 18.1). These stages evolve over time and represent increasing complexity of the services provided by the government.

1. At the start, governments and departments mostly provide informational e-governance. This implies providing information about various services and activities of the government; websites are created and used to provide citizens this information. The only requirement for the departments is to ensure that the websites are available at convenient hours and relevant and updated information is provided. After obtaining information, citizens have to use other means, such as physical presence, to complete their interaction with the government.
2. At the second stage, government departments provide basic interactivity, such as allowing citizens to download forms or data according to their needs. This is a small improvement over providing information, but it is an important step as it allows citizens to obtain forms and print them out at their convenience. They do not have to physically visit offices and wait in queues to obtain forms. With such facilities, citizens in remote areas can visit nearby computer kiosks and, for a nominal fee, obtain forms without making a trip to the government office in a city.

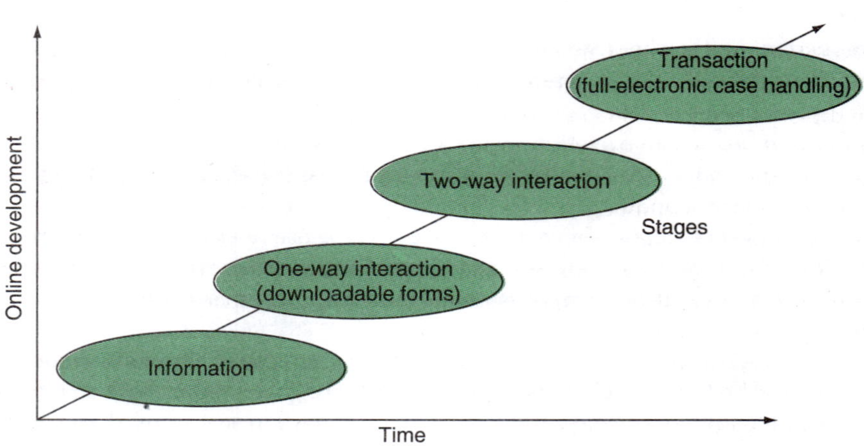

FIGURE 18.1 | Stages of e-governance evolution.

3. At the third stage, we have a two-way interaction, wherein citizens can seek specific information or forms or services, and these are provided by the government department. This is an improvement over the previous stage, as the information and services are specialised to the needs of the individual citizen. Tax payment is an example of the two-way interaction: a firm or an individual can create an account on a website and then file information regarding tax payment. This information is specific to the user and is entered into the website as such. A confirmation message is usually given to the user regarding the information he/she has uploaded. At this stage, if there are further inquiries that the user has or wants questions answered that are complicated in nature, the transaction shifts to the manual mode. The user meets or talks to an official of the department to complete the transaction.
4. The fourth stage is transactional e-governance where the full transaction is completed online. There is no manual interaction either by meeting or talking personally. From the previous example of paying taxes, a transactional stage would imply that all interactions that users have with the department would be through the website or the facilities provided on the site.

18.4.2 Stakeholders

Stakeholders of an e-governance system are those who are impacted by the system or have an impact on the system in some manner. Stakeholders of the system have an interest in its success or failure, and are beneficiaries of the consequences of the system's implementation. It is best to understand stakeholders from the perspective of being from the demand side or from the supply side.

Supply-side stakeholders are those who are interested in the design, deployment and continued maintenance of the e-governance system. They are the sponsors and managers who ensure that the e-governance project is initiated, funded and completed on schedule. They are not necessarily the primary users of the system. For the case of the Bhoomi system of Karnataka, the supply-side stakeholders include the project sponsors (including high-level state officials), the project coordinators and the officials who run the kiosks.

Demand-side stakeholders are those who consume and rely upon the services of the system. They may benefit directly by using the system, such as farmers or other citizens, or they may be agencies that benefit from the usage of the system. On the demand side, stakeholders' use or non-use of the system often determines its fate. For example, in the case of Bhoomi, the closest demand-side stakeholders are the farmers. Agencies such as banks, courts and the police, who benefit because farmers use the Bhoomi system to obtain land records easily, are also stakeholders.

18.4.3 Economic Assessment

The economic implication of an e-governance project is often measured by considering the costs incurred to implement the project as seen against the benefits derived. Costs are measured by taking the project costs, which are allocated as an overhead cost over the duration of the project; and the operating costs, which include the costs of these heads: personnel training, space rental, computer consumables such as paper and toner, and maintenance of the facilities.

Benefits are often computed on the basis of the revenues derived from the paid services of the e-governance project. For example, for the Bhoomi project, users have to pay a fee of Rs 15 to obtain a land record from the system. This revenue is a benefit of the system, and is sufficient to cover the operating costs of running Bhoomi.

18.4.4 Developmental Assessment

An economic assessment of costs and benefits can show how successful a project is, however, the analysis is limited to the concerns of the project, and the facilities the project provides. A different idea is to measure an e-governance project on a developmental basis, where the larger issues and concerns of development can be assessed. E-governance is to be seen largely as a developmental project similar to ICT4D projects discussed earlier. This implies that e-governance is assumed to assist in development – improvement in the incomes, security, education, health and other indicators of individual citizens' welfare.

Development assessment is a complicated topic. Some examples will help clarify the issues. In the case of Bhoomi, it is clear that the reason why farmers need and buy land records is to obtain bank loans. In addition, these records are used as surety in courts and in jail, and to establish identity in some situations. Bank loans directly affect the ability of farmers to improve their income (provided they use the loan for buying materials needed for farming). However, the other uses of land records are also important and contribute to their value. Furthermore, land records do not mean much to landless or tenant farmers of Karnataka. As they do not have title access to land, they cannot effectively avail of farming bank loans although their principle means of livelihood is farming.

18.4.5 Implementation Challenges

E-governance projects face many implementation challenges. Most of these arise from the complex nature of the interaction of technology with archaic manual government processes. Mentioned below are some challenges particular to the Indian context.

18.4.5.1 Design

Possibly, some of the most difficult problems in e-governance implementations arise from the perspective of design. It is clear that e-governance projects so far have been designed primarily from the perspective of supply-side stakeholders. High-level officers in the government, who are knowledgeable about information technology, take up projects to computerise services and tasks that mostly conform to their priorities. They do not conduct extensive and detailed requirements analysis to determine the nature of the required technology support and the manner in which it can be deployed. In situations where a large and diverse population's needs have to be addressed, the requirements exercise is difficult and time-consuming and is thus ignored. Some of the design practices and choices that are important are described below.

1. **Location:** The physical location of a kiosk or e-governance facility has to be carefully planned, particularly in rural areas. First, the facility has to enable access to all residents of various communities that reside in that area so that none is barred or voluntarily avoids the facility owing to religious, caste or gender reasons. The location has to appear to be neutral and secular, and encourage all, and those particularly from marginal communities, to use its services. Second, the location has to be physically close to the targeted users, particularly if the services being offered can be of regular use, such as obtaining information or news. Third, the facilities have to be located with access to basic amenities such as electricity, water and transportation. This enables continuous functioning of the services and also easy access to maintenance personnel.
2. **Local Language:** The e-governance services provided on computers have to be customised to the local language, and also in a visual orientation, to assist those not literate. In areas with low literacy rates, touch-screen computers with appropriate graphics are useful. Some attempts at voice-enabled services have also proved useful.
3. **Portfolio of Applications:** Kiosks providing e-governance services in remote areas have to provide a bouquet of services that can address the needs of a sparse population. The applications could include services such as sale of land records, online application for birth and death certificates, internet browsing, access to and filing of forms, credit applications, school examination results and so on. These paid services would provide revenues to sustain the kiosks as well as permit users to perform a number of activities in one trip to the kiosk. Rural kiosks have also started partnering with other organisations such as the post office and private firms to add to their service offerings and use their

facilities optimally. E-governance kiosks in urban areas, such as eSeva and Bangalore One, provide a number of services to increase their revenues and cover their overheads for maintaining the facilities. It is important to note that the facilities provided in kiosks are highly specific to the region. The needs of the local population change as the location and region change. A standard kiosk portfolio common across an entire state or many states is not a feasible idea.

4. **Scale:** One of the challenges that some services face is that of scale. For example, the *Jaankari* e-governance service in the state of Bihar allows citizens to call in and file applications under the Indian Right to Information (RTI) Act. Citizens call in and file a specific request for information that Jaankari forwards to the relevant agency and then follows up if the information sought is not sent. When the service was introduced in early 2007, it was a huge success as many citizens called in their requests (each request was charged a nominal sum, which was charged to the telephone bill). The success story spread quickly and attracted more people to the service. Soon the Jaankari service was overwhelmed with calls for information and they found that they could not keep up. In late 2009, the service was suffering from a lack of personnel and is attracting criticism from the public.

The *Lokvani* e-governance project in the Sitapur district of the state of Uttar Pradesh had a similar service, where for a nominal fee citizens could file at a kiosk an online complaint for a government claim or service (such as getting a cheque cleared or a road completed). Lokvani collected the claims on a central server and then despatched them to the relevant department for redress. Lokvani's initial success, as citizens' complaints were addressed, led to a positive feedback that encouraged more citizens to file complaints. In this case too, the departments were overwhelmed and could not sustain the activity of responding to complaints.

In both the cases, the design of the systems did not account for the scale increases that resulted from positive feedback. Other systems, such as the Drishtee system of Haryana, have also suffered from a similar weakness. Scale has to be addressed from the perspective of the capacity of the front-end system that users interact with as well as the back-end processes and services that have to meet users' needs.

18.4.5.2 *Data Standards*

E-governance projects have to store data for perpetuity. This means that the data is created for the public and has to be maintained that way forever. It cannot be kept in a manner that future generations will not be able to access it freely. Furthermore, data has to be maintained in a format that can be shared. For example, when the Bhoomi system of Karnataka was created, it replaced numerous manual data formats in which land records were maintained, as these were in different languages such as Tamil, Marathi, Urdu and Kannada among others. The new format used one language, Kannada, and a fixed set of fields for the data. This format is useful for the state of Karnataka, but it may not be suitable for other states that had different forms of writing land records.

Common data standards allow sharing and pooling of data. Once the data pertaining to a particular application, say land records, is available in a standard form, data from different states can then be pooled to obtain useful reports. Furthermore, the standard allows building of complex applications based on the available pooled data, such as creating cadastral maps of the land and linking them to the records.

18.4.5.3 *Legal Issues*

Governance processes are driven by underlying laws and legislations. All the paperwork requirements, the need for signatures and approvals, and the manner in which the work flows are determined by historic laws and the amendments made to them. For example, the documents related to land use, purchase and transfer in the state of Karnataka are controlled by close to

50 laws including the Karnataka Land Reforms Act of 1951 and the Karnataka Land Revenue Act of 1964.

When Bhoomi was introduced in Karnataka, it had to be designed in a manner that was in conformity with the existing laws. However, since printed records were not included in the existing laws, a new legislation was introduced to make Bhoomi land records legal and the process for doing so was specified.

All e-governance efforts in India are thus restricted by government regulations. Many officers who design e-governance systems try to re-engineer or modify the processes, bound by laws, by either re-interpreting existing laws or by modifying them. The success of e-governance efforts is often based on the successful re-engineering that can be introduced for modification of processes.

18.4.5.4 Resistance

E-governance systems are often resisted. The resistance may be from supply-side stakeholders who are opposed to computerisation or from demand-side stakeholders as e-governance changes the old ways of working that they were used to. Resistance often comes from the users who fear that new, unfamiliar technology introductions will challenge their existing work practices. For example, the introduction of the Bhoomi system in Karnataka was opposed by the village accountants as it changed a significant aspect of their work and also introduced new forms of work.

There are different reasons for resistance to e-governance systems. One has to do with employees and users fearing the unknown new technology, and fearing job-loss or loss of skills. This is often overcome by informing and training the users on the new technology. Resistance to change is the other cause of opposition to e-governance, which is independent of technology and has to do with the users being familiar and comfortable with existing work practices, routines and procedures. Employees who have worked for long with existing procedures, and have mapped out their careers along lines they are familiar with, oppose disruptions imposed by technology. It is often the case that employees see the new technologies as a threat to the power and prestige they enjoy, particularly if their power derives from access to or control of information. This resistance can only be overcome by showing the benefits of the technology and reducing fears about its role in the organisation.

18.4.5.5 Corruption

India ranks 87th in the Corruption Perceptions Index of the Transparency International, released in 2010. This index ranks countries according to the perceived corruption within them. The countries that are the least corrupt have the highest ranks and include Denmark, Sweden and the Netherlands among others.

E-governance is often promoted and championed in India to reduce corruption. Many elected leaders and government bureaucrats firmly believe that e-governance can reduce corruption by improving efficiency and transparency in government processes. Whether e-governance reduces corruption is still an open question. It can have certain impacts but a lot depends on the underlying causes of corruption.

Corruption is categorised into two types. The first is called *exogenous corruption*, mainly caused by government procedures and red tape. When people encounter delays in getting their work done, they pay bribes to officials or their agents to speed up the process. This type of corruption is also called 'grease money' corruption, where money is used to speed up work. E-governance can directly help in reducing this form of corruption as computerisation directly affects the speed and processing capacities of government departments. For example, in the case of Bhoomi, when the issuing of land records became faster due to the new system, there was a reported reduction in the bribes paid by farmers.

The second type of corruption is called *endogenous corruption*, which arises when bribe payers are trying to overcome some government restrictions or rules to get their work done.

For example, when some agents pay bribes to obtain a licence or permit to sell some goods, which they would otherwise have not got, they are overcoming government rules by paying the bribe. Another example is when bidders for a tender or proposed work pay a bribe to have their bid considered, for which they are otherwise not eligible. In such cases corruption arises owing to collusion between the two participating agents, possibly a government official and a private firm, and it is very difficult to use e-governance to reduce this type of corruption.

Corrupt officials often oppose and resist e-governance systems as it threatens their ability to extract bribes. This is typically the case in offices that have entrenched corruption with most officials participating in extracting bribes. In such cases, though e-governance may be enforced through authority, the employees will resist strongly and try to subvert the system. Furthermore, the possibility is high that corrupt practices will re-emerge in different forms. For example, cases have been reported where officials at computerised offices have demanded bribes to correct the errors introduced 'by accident' during data entry.

18.5 E-GOVERNMENT

E-government is an aspect of e-governance where the systems that are built are meant primarily for internal use within the government. These systems may provide interfaces for interaction with other government departments or with firms outside government. However, they do not have an open public interface. If e-governance is for providing electronic governance services to the public, then e-government is the use of electronic services by the government for its own use.

E-government systems can be categorised as Government-to-Government (G2G) systems and Government-to-Business (G2B) systems. G2G systems are no different from information systems used in commercial firms (as described in Chapter 2) – they allow a government department to streamline its work processes; they allow the employees to communicate through various means and they allow individuals to work on their own specific tasks.

18.6 E-PARTICIPATION

Information and communication technologies are being increasingly used to assist in the democratic process along with the governance processes described above. The term used to describe the phenomenon of people using digital means to participate in a democracy is called e-participation.

A typical democracy, like India, has citizens participating in the process of selecting and voting for candidates, the elected ones of which form the various levels of government. The process of democracy in democratic countries across the world involves several steps. These have to do with identifying candidates, selecting them through a voting process, having agendas of various people recognised and addressed, having information about the priorities of elected representatives and their activities related to the democratic agenda and so on.

E-participation systems help in the democratic process by informing voters about the candidates who are seeking election, providing a platform for citizens to voice their concerns and turn them into agendas for action, enable citizens to connect in a virtual forum from which they can collectively voice their issues, get a means to have informal 'straw' polls on the popularity of issues and candidates, and follow the election cycle in a convenient manner.

Candidates and elected representatives too are using voter information systems that provide them with information on the citizens in their ward or district. These systems help before the elections by providing candidates information about agenda items, distribution of citizen groups across geographies, spread of opposition parties and so on. After elections, representatives use such systems to monitor citizen demands and concerns and also the projects they have initiated. Some representatives use such systems to inform citizens of the work they are doing and of their thoughts on matters of concern to citizens.

Currently, many candidates and representatives in Europe use social networking tools like blogs, wikis and twitter to inform and interact with citizens in their constituencies. Citizens have also created sites with similar technologies to connect with each other, and also communicate their views to the representatives. Such systems support the democratic process by enabling greater information to reach both the citizens and their representatives.

E-participation is in its infancy in India. However, many notable politicians have created blogs and websites where they inform citizens of their views. Online citizens groups have also sprung up websites that organise people around specific issues and also during elections. *Jaago Re* is a campaign promoted by a commercial firm that encourages first-time voters to register and vote. Jaago Re mainly operates through its website. Another effort is the National Election Watch campaign that provides information about candidates on its website. Its goal is to inform citizens about candidates, their legal status (as several candidates who go up for elections have criminal backgrounds), their work in their constituencies and their popularity with citizens.

It is as yet unclear what effect these e-participation efforts have had on the democratic process. However, they are popular and are being used by representatives and citizens alike.

Caselet E-Office

E-Office is a suite of software that enables easy movement of files within government offices. E-Office is based on the Indian Government's Manual of Office Procedures (MOP), which is a document that provides a formal and legal method of conducting official work in India. The system helps to digitise files and documents and also to manage the process by which they are recorded, read, marked, moved and stored in the office. It was designed with a view to strictly follow the MOP, which is widely accepted across all central and state departments, including public sector units and autonomous government bodies.

E-Office was initiated in 2008–09 and the first prototype implementation was in 2010. The National Informatics Centre (NIC), a department of the Central Government of India, had a dedicated team of 60–70 engineers who worked on the product and continued to support it. The basic design followed the principles of an enterprise resource planning system, where all data were maintained in a central database from where they are shared by different applications and processes. At present the central repository is hosted locally within the organisation; however, it can be easily hosted on the cloud.

Since its launch, several government departments, across Indian states as well as in the centre, have successfully installed e-Office and are using it. The installation takes only a few weeks if the basic hardware is in place. If the hardware is not available, the procurement and installation process takes a little longer. Once installed, the learning curve to use the software is low and employees start using it reasonably quickly.

A typical use case is as follows. A document arrives by courier to a department or office that is using e-Office. This document would be a physical copy with many pages. The clerk who receives the document makes an entry in an online form, stating when the document arrived, from whom and for whom it is addressed. The document is then digitised by scanning, and the digital document is then stored on the system. The receiving clerk then assigns the document to the department or person to whom it is addressed. This initiates a workflow and the document is marked to the next recipient. The next recipient may then read the document and mark on it online and forward it to someone else, or place it in a repository for storage (assuming no further action is required). Depending on the rank and privileges of the officer, he or she may create suitable workflows for further processing of the document.

The system records the entire passage of the document, who has seen it, who has marked on it, who has forwarded it and where it resides currently. Further, the system can also show for how long the document has remained in the system before it was worked on, and if it has been delayed or processed in advance.

E-Office has been adopted in over 25 state and central departments and over 80,000 government employees were using the system (by early 2016). The cost of implementing the system was quite reasonable, as it was only a few hundred thousand rupees for each installation. Since it is built with open source components, the basic technology is quite robust and secure. It uses the highest levels of encryption and security to ensure that the files are always secure and are only accessible to those who have the explicit authority to see it.

Chapter Glossary

Development Usually means improvement in the individual incomes of people in a community or nation.

Digital divide The difference in access to ICT services, such as the internet, mobile phones, computers, radio and television, between peoples of nations and regions.

E-governance The use of ICT to rule over a state or region, including in enacting laws, implementing programmes and taking care of the needs of citizens.

Stakeholders Those who are impacted by a system or have an impact on the system in some manner. The impact may be through design and implementation or through use or non-use.

Exogenous corruption When government procedures and red tape give rise to bribery to 'speed up' procedures.

Endogenous corruption When bribes are taken to overcome some government procedures, rules or restrictions.

E-government An aspect of e-governance where information systems are used primarily within or between government departments.

E-participation The phenomenon of citizens using ICT to participate in the democratic process.

Review Questions

1. What is the most widely used meaning of development of a nation?
2. What is Amartya Sen's view of development? How is it different from the widely held view?
3. What is the basic premise of ICT for development? Why are developing countries interested in ICT?
4. What is the digital divide?
5. Name different kinds of ICT interventions and give examples of each.
6. How are Radio Sangham and the e-tuktuk project different from the perspective of the development goals they achieve?
7. What is the meaning of e-governance?
8. What are the main stages of e-governance evolution?
9. Who are stakeholders in an e-governance project?
10. How is economic assessment different from development assessment? Give examples.
11. What are the main challenges of designing e-governance systems?
12. Why should data standards be used for e-governance projects?
13. Why do people resist e-governance systems?
14. How does corruption impact e-governance?
15. How is e-governance different from e-government?
16. What is the difference between e-governance and e-participation?

Research Questions

1. Review the Bhoomi case and identify at which stage of e-governance evolution can the Bhoomi system be said to have achieved.
2. Are you aware of any ICT for development projects in your city or town? Visit the site and examine whether the project is informational, transactional or of any other type. Why?
3. What is the status of e-governance in other countries in the world. Search the internet to find out the extent and variety of use of e-governance in Singapore and Sweden.
4. Search for and find any e-participation sites in India. How effective are they and what design changes can be made to improve them?

Further Reading

1. Sen, A. (2000) *Development as Freedom*, Oxford University Press.
2. Layne, K. and Lee, J. (2001). Developing fully functional e-government: A four-sage model, *Government Information Quarterly*, **18** (2), 122–136.
3. De, R. (2007) Antecedents of Corruption and the Role of E-Government Systems in Developing Countries, *Proceedings of Ongoing Research, Electronic Government 6th International Conference, EGOV 2007*, Trauner Verlag Schriftenreihe Informatik 24, 167–174, Regensburg, Germany.
4. Prakash, A. and De, R. (2007) Importance of Development Context in ICT4D Projects: A Study of Computerisation of Land Records in India. *Information Technology and People*, **20** (3), 262–281.

CHAPTER **19**

The Society of the Internet

Learning Objectives

After completing this chapter, you will be able to:

- Learn about the services of the internet
- Get an overview of technology of the internet
- Understand social issues connected with the internet
- Learn about social networks in the enterprise

The internet is a vast network of people, groups and organisations around the world. It is a social force that is impacting society in many ways. The main service of the internet is search, the ability to seek and find relevant information reasonably quickly. Another important service is the ability to network easily with others – to create online communities – through the use of social networking sites. The other services include the ability to create personal web pages or blogs, the ability to share files and information on a peer-to-peer basis, and to create virtual worlds for gaming and business use. The services are enabled by a number of technologies, specifically designed for the internet, which include web page creation using Hyper Text Markup Language (HTML); wiki shared authoring; Twitter, instant group communication; community rating of sites; community-based categorisation of sites and the ability to mix technologies through mashups.

The internet has impacted the social issues of identity, where people can present themselves in various forms and roles. The internet also has deep consequences for privacy as people and organisations adopt social media and open up information about themselves, their friends and communities and their activities. Social media is also driving conventional broadcast media and impacting, practically, politics and social movements in many countries. Collaboration has taken an entirely new form through the internet, with massive participation in creating sites such as Wikipedia and open source software, efforts that are unprecedented in history. The internet also shows that despite the open and free nature of participation, order naturally emerges in communities.

MIND MAP OF CHAPTER TOPICS

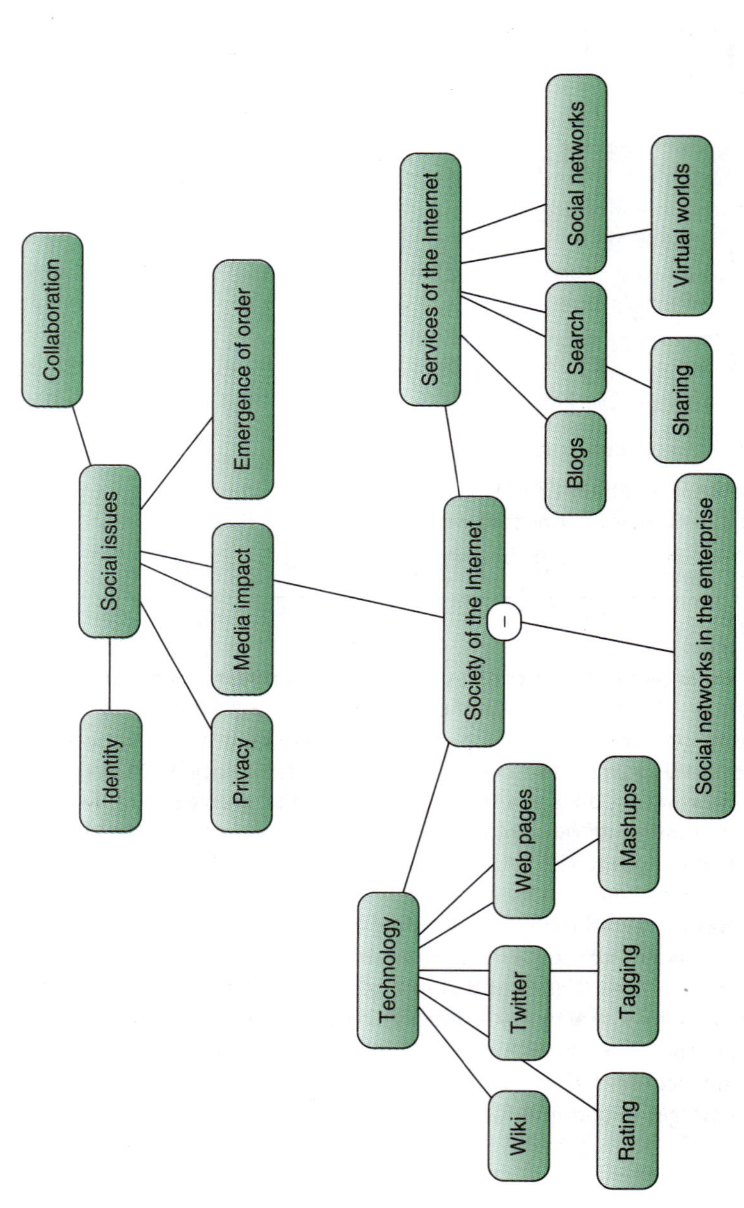

CASE STUDY: SOCIAL MEDIA IN POLITICAL UPRISING

Organising political activity requires gathering masses of people at a place for a cause, and getting across a message to them for further action. Throughout history political action has relied on leaders reaching out to people by meeting with them personally or by using media. When the political action is by those not in power, their ability to use traditional physical and electronic media is restricted. However, in the modern internet and digital era, the conditions have changed to allow even those without power to be able to access media.

An example of this is the uprising and revolution in the small North African country of Tunisia, which erupted in December 2010. Tunisia had been ruled by a dictator, called Zine el-Abidine Ben Ali, for 23 years. Although Tunisia was rated as a politically stable country having friendly relations with its neighbours in Europe and also with the USA, and a relatively better-off economy, however, its citizens were repressed. Ben Ali did not permit democratic means of expression by Tunisian citizens: He had jailed and tortured thousands of dissidents, he had controlled and restrained the media and had shut down civil society. Tunisian citizens had for years been losing their means of livelihood owing to the policies of Ben Ali, but they had no recourse to political change for betterment.

The situation came to a sharp focus when a street vendor, whose wheelbarrow full of produce had been confiscated and who had been beaten by the police, set fire to himself in a public square. This sparked a round of protests from ordinary citizens and the protests began to spread. The speed at which the protests spread across Tunisia surprised the dictator who immediately offered jobs for the unemployed, but the protests and riots did not stop. Ben Ali had to flee the country within a month.

Social network sites such as Facebook and Twitter had a role to play in the revolution in Tunisia. Young people with mobile phones and access to the internet spread the stories about the protests (despite a clampdown in the official media of the country), took pictures and videos and uploaded them online, and sent messages about organising rallies. At some point, the government tried to shut down internet traffic but to no avail.

Soon after the incidents in Tunisia, a Facebook page by a software engineer appeared about the repressive regime of Hosni Mubarak, the President of the neighbouring country of Egypt. The author, Wael Ghonim, was an employee of the internet firm Google, and soon after he created the page, he was arrested and disappeared from public view. The happenings in Tunisia had already stirred revolutionary feelings in Egypt, and Ghonim's Facebook page added fuel to the people's latent anger. Egypt for long had suffered police brutality, lack of democracy and corruption, backed by high unemployment, low wages and high inflation. The incidents in Tunisia prompted revolutionary action by the youth in Egypt and massive rallies, protests, strikes and civil disobedience followed. Wael Ghonim was released from police detention and joined the protests. Although the protests were all over Egypt and were carried out by almost all sections of people, the Tahrir Square in Cairo saw the largest gatherings, with hundreds of thousands of people giving voice to the protest. Though most of the protests were non-violent, the government did resort to use of force and several hundred protesters were killed and thousands wounded. Less than a month after the protests began, Mubarak stepped down.

In Egypt too, social media had a strong role to play in both the build-up to the revolution as well as during the organisation of the protests. Blogs created by individuals, as also Facebook pages, recorded the uneasiness and repressed mood of the public. The Facebook page created by Wael Ghonim was called 'We are all Khaled Saeed' referring to a Cairo man who had been beaten to death by the police. This page attracted a very wide following both inside Egypt and across the world, and also drew Western media attention to the imminent uprising. Since official media was controlled, Facebook and blog pages described the repressive nature of Mubarak's regime. (Like the deposed Tunisian dictator Ben Ali, Mubarak too was friendly towards the USA and Europe.) During the protests, Facebook, Twitter and SMS were used to organise rallies, create coordination mechanisms for continuous protests and also share news and information about the direct action. Many of the protests were video recorded and shown on YouTube.

Many argue that the protests in Egypt were spontaneous and provoked largely by the happenings in Tunisia, with online media having little to do with it. Like other developing countries, there is a large digital divide in Egypt too, with a large part of the population without access to the internet and without the knowledge to use it. Furthermore, much of the resistance and protests were in small towns and cities across Egypt without a central organising effort required at the Tahrir Square. However, it is also true that the depiction of violence and brutality in website pictures and videos did influence the outcome of the revolution by informing people of what was going on.

In a different vein, another type of protest and rioting happened in the UK, in London, in August 2011. The incident originated in the accidental shooting of Mark Duggan, a resident of Tottenham in London, by the police. Residents of Tottenham immediately went to the police station to protest the shooting, and soon someone created a Facebook page with the details of the shooting. There was a near instant response to this on social media, and within a few hours several areas in London were in flames as rioters took to the streets. The rioting continued for two nights with the targets being stores, public vehicles and buildings, which were set on fire or looted.

Subsequent inquiry by the police showed that most of the organising for the riots was done through the BlackBerry Messenger Service, a peer-to-peer messaging service that is encrypted and remains visible to only the recipients. The BlackBerry is very popular with young Britons, who are also fond of the messaging service as it is free and allows groups to be created for one-to-many broadcasts. The messages were focused and precise, asking peers to converge on a particular street at a given time to start the riots. One such message read as follows:

> Everyone from all sides of London meet up at the heart of London (central) OXFORD CIRCUS!! Bare SHOPS are gonna get smashed up so come get some (free stuff!!!) [*&%@] the feds we will send them back with OUR riot! >:O Dead the ends and colour war for now so if you see a brother... SALUT! if you see a fed... SHOOT!

Another sent out shortly before a riot read as, 'Everyone in edmonton enfield wood green everywhere in north link up at enfield town station at 4 o'clock sharp!'

The focus of the riots in London was not a revolutionary political change; it was an upsurge of anger at the shooting death of an innocent man, in this case a man of non-European origin. Commentators argue that there is repressed anger and frustration in the UK, as was the case in Egypt, which played out in the violence that targeted the symbols of wealth such as brand-name stores and well-known buildings. The rioters did not have a common political agenda but were motivated by a sense of outrage at the social conditions they have to endure owing to the policies of the government.

19.1 SOCIAL DYNAMICS OF THE INTERNET

The internet is a vast ocean of people, groups, organisations and even nations connected through electronic links. This constitutes perhaps the largest organising medium ever in history. It is also a social force that is bringing together hitherto diverse and unconnected groups of people and organisations. This social aspect of the internet is different from its commercial aspects discussed under issues such as e-commerce. The social aspect has its own dynamics and an impact that has to be understood differently.

The technology that the internet is built upon is that of the protocols (such as TCP and IP) discussed earlier. However, many applications have evolved, which address the needs of the society of the internet – technologies such as tagging, rating, wikis and mashups. These technologies enable particular kinds of services and social organising. Such services include search, social networks, blogs and so on. Each service provides a unique set of features and ways by which people and groups can interact.

The society created by the internet is different from ordinary society – it allows individuals to have multiple identities; it impacts the privacy of individuals and organisations and enables many to work in a transparent manner; and it impacts the media.

The following sections cover issues related to the society of the internet, beginning with the services that are available on the internet, the technologies that enable this and the issues that arise from people using the internet.

19.2 SERVICES OF THE INTERNET

19.2.1 Search

Search is possibly the most important service on the internet, as it allows people to look for and find what they are interested in, in the vast array of internet resources. The search service allows people to find information of their interest in a reasonable amount of time and with the expense of a reasonable amount of effort.

The first search services, such as Yahoo!, provided directories of sites on the internet, where users could look up sites and move to the relevant pages. However, this became insufficient as web pages had many links that led to other pages that would not necessarily correspond to the topic of the original page. It was then important to list pages according to their relevance to the user's search need. The first search services, such as AltaVista, provided such answers. In AltaVista, if a user searched for a phrase such as 'modern dance', the search service would list all pages, from different sites that it knew of, that had the phrase 'modern dance'.

AltaVista attempted to discover and list all possible pages that were available on the public internet and classify them according to their content. The *search engines*, as they were called, relied on finding pages and then exploring all possible links that the pages contained, moving on to other sites and exploring their content, which was indexed using a classification scheme. This was termed as *crawling* and was performed by automated programs that continuously searched the Web for pages and classified them.

The problem that such search services suffered from was that they determined relevance based on the frequency of occurrence of words and phrases on the pages. For example, say a user is looking for information on 'modern dance' and is interested in understanding the differences between modern dance and classical dance forms. A page that describes these differences may not use the phrase 'modern dance' much, and may use other phrases to describe the dance forms. However, a page talking about a music band with the name 'modern dance' may have a higher number of occurrences of the phrase 'modern dance' although it is not the most relevant page from the user's perspective. But, the search engine would give prominence to the music band page in its search results.

The search engine Google, one of the largest search engines today, solved the above problem differently. The founders of Google realised that a good way to find out whether a page was

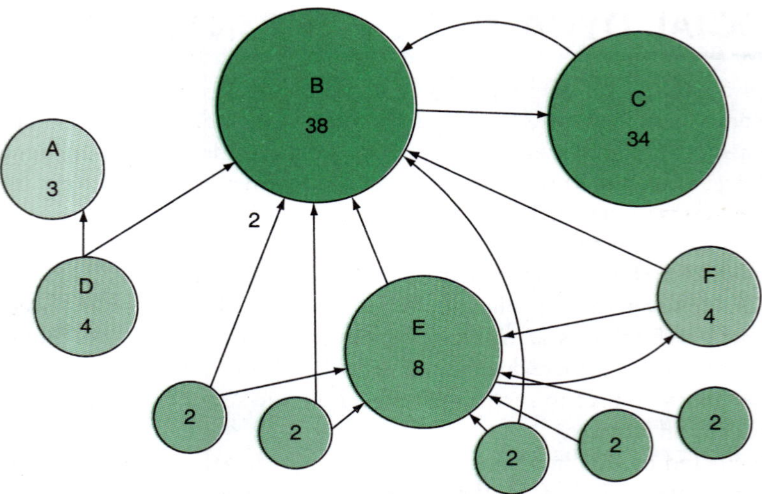

FIGURE 19.1 Google's Page Rank Method. Page B has the highest relative rank (38) as it has the highest number of pages pointing to it. Page C has only one page linking to it, which is Page B, but as Page B has a high rank, so Page C also has a high rank.

important for a particular topic was to see how many people pointed to it. For example, if there are two pages, page A and page B, which both talk about 'modern dance', and if it is known that a larger number of other pages link to B rather than A for the topic of 'modern dance' then B has higher relevance than A for this particular topic. Google was created with this broad philosophy and it turned out to be widely successful. A key point about this strategy of Google is relying on other sites and pages for pointing out the most relevant page for a particular topic.

Google's Page Rank method relies on using two methods to rank a page: one is the number of other pages linking to it regarding a particular topic, and the other is the weight of the pages that link to it. If a page that is already heavily ranked, on say 'modern dance', as a lot of other pages link to it, and it in turn links to other pages, these other pages too achieve a high rank (see Fig. 19.1). Such a method allows Google to rank pages that people find valuable and link to them, and further uses this ranking to rank other pages. This ranking method requires constant monitoring by the Google crawlers that frequently visit all the pages on their servers to explore whether others have created or deleted links to them.

Google lists billions of pages on its servers and is able to provide reliable searches almost instantly. As stated above, it also provides a ranking of the relevance of the pages for the search topic. Google maintained more than two million servers (in 2016) around the world that run web crawlers, which update the database of links. Google has found this strategy to be very successful and is one of the most powerful and popular internet search engines.

Google also provides search services on special subjects like academic papers and news items, as also for special digital objects such as images, maps and videos. These services allow the search engine to focus on a particular domain and not bring in all possible items from the Web into the search results. Special searches like these are very popular and have opened a separate line of business for Google.

There are also many other search engines that provide different types of search capabilities and features, the most notable of these being Duckduckgo.com, Bing.com, Dogpile.com, Ask.com, Exalead.com and so on. Duckduckgo.com does not track the searches on its site and hence respects the users' privacy. Ask.com allows users to type in their query in the form of a question. It interprets the question and provides possible answers.

Despite considerable advances in search technology, most users believe that the results from search engines are unsatisfactory. A Google search, for instance, does provide a host of pages and links to choose from, but in most cases the pages are not what users were seeking and they have to check many pages before they find their answers. Advances in search technology have addressed this problem. Summaries, visual maps, special knowledge about the search topic and other techniques are being used to narrow down the search results and provide more relevant and meaningful answers to users.

19.2.2 Blogs

Blogs are short for web logs or web pages maintained by individuals about their activities, interests or hobbies. Blogs are websites that enable individuals to easily and quickly write content in a web page and to add features such as images, videos and links to other sites. Each blog page has the name of the author and the pages are listed on a blog site such as Blogspot.com or Wordpress.com. Users create pages on these sites and then announce the address to their friends and acquaintances who can then read the content on the page. Pages are usually updated frequently and the readers return to their favourite pages to read the content provided. Readers can also leave comments on the write-ups.

Many famous personalities maintain blogs. The famous Bollywood film personality, Amitabh Bachchan maintains a blog that is actively read and followed (see http://srbachchan.tumblr.com/). Posts on his blog sometimes become front page news articles. Some famous journalists too maintain blogs. These are actively followed by their readers, as sometimes articles that are editorially removed from the regular news publications may be placed by these journalists on their blogs. Commentators say that blogs have become an alternative outlet for journalists and much of interesting breaking news about events first appears on blogs and later in news media.

Most blogs are created by ordinary citizens, many of whom are students, who write about their daily lives, their activities, their hobbies, their likes and dislikes, and publish them for their peers to read and comment upon. Blogs thus create a community that arises from the text and images on websites, where people with shared interests communicate and interact. Blogs are typically open to the world and can be accessed by anyone on the Web. They are also visible to search engines.

19.2.3 Social Networks

Social networks represent online web-based communities of people who share facilities similar to blogs. Social network facilities are provided by certain firms, such as Facebook and Microsoft. These facilities enable people to create their own web spaces using which they can selectively interact with others. These networks differ from blogs in that they do not allow everybody to see pages and they permit users to define what is public and what remains private.

In social network sites, users can create web pages with images, video, sound, text and other materials. They can then join a network of others, with explicit links to other pages, and a method by which they define access – for example, 'friends' have most access to the user's page and facilities, whereas 'acquaintances' have lesser access. The software enables all persons on a particular network to see who has logged in, what messages have been posted, who has asked for specific information via a phone call or an email, etc. It also allows users to play online games with each other. Online games are a particularly important feature of social networks and have drawn a large number of people to them, who play long and extensive games.

Social networks such as Linkedin.com are designed for professional use. People on LinkedIn use the network to seek professional contacts, information and services and also apply for job vacancies.

Social networks have evolved their own codes of conduct, where specific messages convey specific information that is coherent only to the users of the network. For example, a 'friend' request on a network is considered vital for many as it is an indication that the requester wants your attention. A delay in response or no response at all to such a request conveys different meanings. As most of the networks allow both synchronous and asynchronous communication, they provide a very rich environment for interaction and also for communicating both explicit and tacit messages.

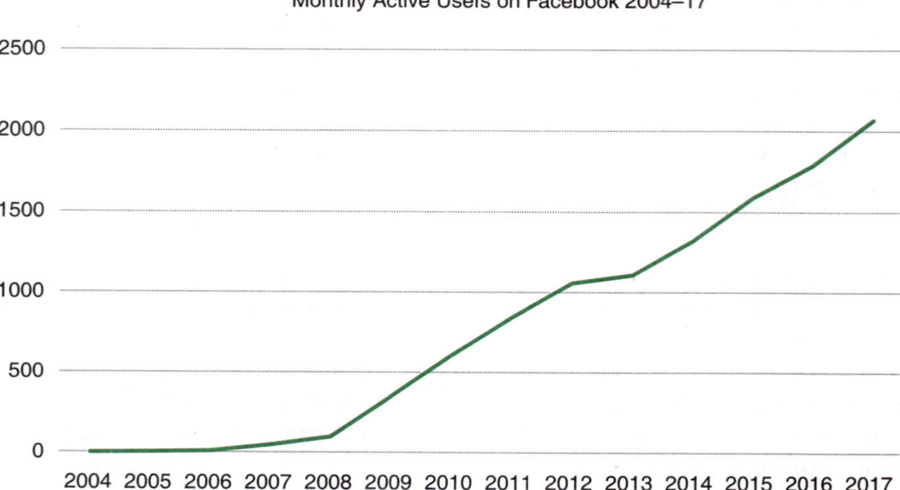

FIGURE 19.2 | Growth in the number of Facebook users in (millions).
Source: Facebook statistics.

Social networks have also been 'attacked' by spam messages and unwanted users. This has led to the decline of some networks, with users abandoning their sites owing to the large amount of irrelevant messages they have been subjected to. The social networking site Orkut suffered such a fate.

Social networking sites are subject to very strong network effects. The more the number of users on the site, the higher the value for individuals as they can interact with a lot more people (see Fig. 19.2 that depicts the growth of Facebook users, showing strong network effects). Strong positive feedback, obtained from exchanging messages and playing games, ensures that users stay with the network. However, negative feedback, in the form of spam messages, also acts to dissuade users from visiting the site and hence causes a mass decline in usage.

19.2.4 Peer-to-Peer Sharing

File sharing on the internet precedes the arrival of the World Wide Web. Enthusiasts interested in sharing files used to upload their files on the sites that were accessible by the File Transfer Protocol (FTP). These FTP sites, as they were called, were then made known to others through bulletin boards and email lists. Sometimes files were protected by passwords, and only selected members of lists who had access to the passwords could download the files, or they were made available through 'anonymous' users who did not need passwords. FTP sites were used extensively to share data, images and video files.

With the advent of the Web, the HTTP emerged as an easier method for sharing files, and people listed their data and multimedia files on websites that others can access and download. This is still popular as many users share their personal files with others through their blogs and social network pages.

Peer-to-peer file sharing evolved as a concept after the application initiated by a firm called Napster. Napster allowed users to store music files on giant servers, and these could be accessed and searched by others seeking music. Napster was unusual as a sharing site, as it was meant mainly for music files. The files used the MP3 format (this format allows music files to be compressed to a suitable size and also retain the original flavour of the music). Many users started converting their personal collection of files to this format to share them on Napster. Napster gained from positive network effects and became popular very quickly. Thousands of users started listing millions of songs on Napster's servers. Very soon the music industry realised that there were copyright infringements due to the sharing of files, and followed with a lawsuit to close down Napster. They were effective in doing so, and Napster was effectively shut down after being in operation for only about 3 years.

Napster's demise led to a number of innovations in file sharing without the use of a central server. Software such as BitTorrents, Gnutella, Kazaa, eDonkey and Limewire allowed users to share files directly with each other without the use of a central server. Each client in a *Torrent* sharing application is both receiving files from a client and also serving data to another. Typically, any client could be connected to many other peers in the network. There was no central coordination. The software was designed in such a manner as to encourage sharing, where the user who shared the most number of files and data also benefited from the highest speeds. Owing to copyright infringement lawsuits, sites such as Kazaa, eDonkey and Lime wire were forced to shut down.

File-sharing services led to the creation of many sites across the internet, which enabled users to easily search for different categories of files and then download them from the peer-to-peer clients. One such site was called The Pirate Bay and included music, video, audio books, images and software files. Many of these files were being shared in violation of copyright laws of various countries. The Pirate Bay site was sued by the owners of film and music companies and the case was concluded in Sweden with a prison term and a fine for the owners of Pirate Bay. The court decided that enabling others to distribute copyright material is in violation of Swedish laws even though the site itself did not contain any copyright material.

Other file-sharing sites, such as Rapidshare.com and Megaupload.com, directly stored and served files. They allowed users to store files to their servers and then ask others to download them. Rapidshare.com was very popular and stored millions of files that were downloaded and distributed by others. Sharing enthusiasts had also created websites that listed files stored on Rapidshare.com, thus enabling users to easily search and identify the files they wanted. Sites such as Rapidshare.com were able to version their products easily, where users who have paid higher amounts were afforded better speeds for accessing files. In other such sites too, versioning based on speed of access enabled the site owners to generate revenues directly from users. File-sharing software that work on a peer-to-peer basis did not have a model by which revenues could be directly extracted from users; instead, they relied on advertising on the pages that users saw.

There is pressure from the music and film publishing industry to shut down such download sites, and Rapidshare.com has had to de-list many files that it had on its site that violated copyright laws. Recently, such sites have also had to submit to authorities the login information and IP address of users, as copyright owners have charged these sites with violations. Both Rapidshare.com and Megaupload.com were forced by the legal authorities in the countries in which they were hosted to shut down their sites.

19.2.5 Streaming Sites

As access to the internet grew with the spread of smart phones, media streaming sites gained popularity. These sites enable users to hear or view files directly from the site without having to download any files. Streaming enables users to consume content, without the content files being located on their host devices. The main requirement for users is to have a strong internet connection that allows the data in the files to be downloaded easily and then displayed.

One of the most prominent streaming sites is YouTube, which has over 4 billion views every day of millions of video files on its site. YouTube was initiated in 2005 with the idea of allowing users to upload their own videos and publicly sharing the link so that others can view them by streaming onto their host devices – phones or computers. Users proceeded to actively upload their content and YouTube was populated by millions of videos. Subsequently, businesses and corporations started to upload their own videos, for marketing and outreach, followed by academic institutions, governments and other organisations. YouTube's popularity soared (and it was later acquired by Google) and competitor sites that also hosted video content were created, such as – Vimeo.com, Dailymotion.com, Veoh.com and many others.

The idea of streaming videos led to the creation of sites that streamed movies, such as Netflix.com, and also radio content, such as Tunein.com and Gaana.com. Netflix started out as a site that enabled users to rent movie DVDs on a subscription basis. As the penetration of the internet grew and access speeds and costs improved, they started to offer movies on a streaming basis and also popular television shows. By 2017, Netflix had a successful business that extended streaming to all forms of devices including smart televisions, mobile phones and computers. Other sites followed this success in streaming video content by offering popular movies and television programmes, and this included sites such as Amazon's Prime Video and Hotstar.com. These sites have become so popular that they are now producing their own video content (advertised as "originals") rivalling those produced by television studios. Their success has also dented the business revenues of traditional television stations and movie theatres.

Streaming sites such as YouTube, Vimeo, Soundcloud (for audio tracks) have created a facility for artists, film-makers, videographers, singers and composers to display their art or compositions to the world. It is common now for musicians, both new and established artists, to upload their compositions on the streaming platform for listeners to view or hear their productions. After seeing the initial response, artists may consider other modes of distributing their content for better revenues. Sites such as YouTube have evolved a revenue model where they pay artists for their content, based on the number of listeners or viewers they are able to attract and to whom advertisements are shown. Some film producers list their videos only on YouTube and rely in the revenues they are able to obtain from there.

19.2.6 Virtual Worlds

Some of the most popular applications on the internet have been online multi-user games that have drawn thousands of players from across the globe. In these games, players can join as individual elements of, say, a warring side, pick their own weapons and skills, and pitch their wits against the opposition that also consists of other players who have donned other roles. The roles are defined by particular images and shapes and sounds, and those of a given nation or type have similar characteristics. Games such as Warcraft are extremely popular and have attracted a large number of players. The social aspect of such games reflects in the manner in which players, who may be completely unknown to each other, join in the game from different parts of the world and try to coordinate their activities and strategies to win. The games have built-in elements of luck and chance, such as the appearance of a dangerous animal or enemy element, that shape the player's responses and chances of survival.

In each game, it is common for users to assume an *avatar* or a persona that is either human-like or of an entirely different form. Such avatars have a finite life, and require food and company of others to survive, in a weak imitation of real life. The avatars are also imbued with some skills that they could deploy to survive in the game and win points.

Caselet Second Life

In a social networking site initiated in 2003, called *Second Life* (see http://secondlife.com/), the creators took the essential ideas of multi-user games and avatars and created a world in which users could log in with their own avatars and participate in social interaction. There was no gaming element to Second Life (SL), but the avatars could engage in conversations, own property, exchange objects and money, interact in private or public and generally maintain a life in a digital space. SL's objective was to provide a virtual space in which avatars could interact as if in the real world and insisted that it was not merely to play games.

Second Life allowed people to own digital property on the site. It floated a currency of its own, called Linden dollars, which could be bought with real money. With Linden dollars, users could buy property in the different neighbourhoods and locations in SL, build homes or offices and start living there. Many started businesses that transacted entirely on SL, for example, they sold digital objects that could be used to construct other objects. Others started businesses that could assist with the real-world businesses, such as marketing of products and services. Large firms such as IBM and Dell set up stores and offices on SL. Many firms held private meetings and also job interviews on SL. Some universities offered courses on SL.

SL has gained immense popularity. In 2007 it had 7 million registered users and transacted business worth USD 500 million. Although SL is hosted by a US firm, its primary user base is not USA, and a majority are from other countries. The size of the physical land that SL simulates is similar to that of the nation of Singapore.

In a landmark event, Sweden opened an embassy in SL in 2007. This consulate had its own building where avatars could visit. The building had paintings of famous Swedes and also had a gallery where art displays. The embassy did not issue passports or visas and was meant to provide information about Sweden to interested visitors. The virtual embassy was closed in 2012.

Much of SL's success derives from the fact that the virtual social space presents a context in which interactions happen. Though people can interact on the Web by many channels – chatting, video streaming, email and exchange of files, SL created an environment in which specific objects had meaning. For example, objects like room, chair, window, etc. could be used to create a context. If a firm wanted to demonstrate a product to potential customers, it could create images and videos of it and send them to the customer to view, or it could create a simulation of the object (provided it can be simulated) on SL and demonstrate it with their SL avatars to its clients. SL too is subject to strong network effects and had gained popularity as more people joined it. However, since about 2010, SL has also experienced some negative feedback which has led to a decline in the number of active users.

19.3 TECHNOLOGY OF THE INTERNET

This section discusses some of the technologies that are used to create the society of the internet. Some elements of these technologies have been discussed in earlier chapters.

19.3.1 Web Pages

Web pages on the internet are created by using the HTML that enables pages to be rendered or viewed by the browser. Pages for the Web are written in plain text with markup commands that the browser reads to display the text. For example, the following command:

```
<html>Hello</html>
```

tells the browser, such as Mozilla Firefox, that the word '`Hello`' within the markup commands has to be rendered as text on a web page. Other commands include formatting commands, such as bold (<b>...</b>), italics (<em>...</em>), commands to link to other pages, commands to format the page, to position text or images and so on.

Web pages also allow embedding of scripts and code written in Java or other programming languages that allow complex computations. These scripts can also connect the web page to a server that provides data for computation or saves data entered on forms on the page. The HTML language provides the front end for displaying the page, whereas other languages can be used for quite complex applications.

19.3.2 Wiki

A wiki is also a web page, with a difference. A wiki page can be created and then modified by many authors. The idea of the wiki is to allow collaborative authoring of text on the web page. The wiki technology is similar to a Content Management System, where many people can write or upload content. The difference is that the wiki allows anybody to change the content at any time, and it maintains all past versions so that if an older version is required, it can easily be recovered.

One of the most famous examples of the use of a wiki to create content is the Wikipedia, an online encyclopaedia. Its originator, Jimmy Wales, initially wanted to create an online encyclopaedia that would have high-quality articles that could be freely accessible to anybody (in opposition to publications such as the Encyclopaedia Britannica, which have articles of very high quality but were very expensive and few could afford them). He started by contracting a few authors, those who were experts in their fields, and asked them to write articles for the encyclopaedia. This was not very successful as he was able to obtain only a few articles over many months. He was then struck by the idea of creating a site where anybody could write an encyclopaedia article, and with anyone else being able to critique and modify it. Wales envisioned that with a crowd of people getting together to create and edit articles, the quality was bound to be good, possibly very high.

Wales created a set of rules by which to write and modify articles and then opened up the Wikipedia site to the world. The response was tremendous as within a few months, thousands of articles appeared on the site with hundreds of authors and editors. The rules for creating the articles were:

1. No original research articles.
2. All citations had to be provided.
3. On matters of debate there would be a specified time period for discussion.
4. Conventions of writing/rewriting of articles would be followed.

Wikipedia articles gained popularity among readers in all parts of the world, and wiki articles in many other languages started appearing on the website. By February 2011, there were over 17 million articles on Wikipedia in 30 different languages. Other details about Wikipedia are given in Table 19.1.

The wiki technology allows network effects to take place. Those contributing to articles attract both readers and writers. The topics are not restricted, and this attracts a large number of people too as unlike traditional encyclopaedias, wikis touched casual topics of mass interest, such as popular films, film stars, popular music and culture. Contributors wrote articles on all types of subjects that took their fancy and that were likely to have interest among readers. The articles were permitted to be listed on Wikipedia as long as they met the editorial criteria.

Wikipedia is quite popular in India where it received over 13 million unique visitors a month in 2010. Wikipedia articles exist in many Indian languages but more than 98% of the traffic is directed at English articles. Table 19.2 shows the number of Wikipedia articles in major Indian languages.

The wiki technology is used by other sites too, to enable collaborative writing and document creation. Sites such as Wikispaces.com allow organisations to create private wikis, those open to the members of the organisation but not to the world, and use them to collaborate on projects, create documents and communicate with others. The wiki technology is built on open source components and can be accessed and used by anyone. Many organisations have set up internal wikis for collaboration and knowledge sharing.

Table 19.1 | Details about Wikipedia, as of December 2017

Number of articles in English Wikipedia	5.4 million
Number of Wikipedia language versions	288
Number of active community members	127 k
Number of articles in all languages	47 million

Source: Wikipedia.

Table 19.2 | Number of Wikipedia Articles in Major Indian Languages by December 2017

Language	Number of Articles on Wikipedia
Hindi	122,761
Telugu	68,330
Marathi	50,081
Tamil	114,509
Bengali	54,863
Malay	53,429

Source: Wikipedia.

19.3.3 Twitter

Twitter is one of the most successful social networking sites. It is a combination of a blog and a short messaging service (SMS) on a mobile phone. A user can post messages, called tweets, on the Twitter service, and the messages are then broadcast to all those who have enrolled with the user. Messages are necessarily short, less than 140 characters, the limit for SMS messages (this limit was extended to 280 characters in November 2017, for most languages). Once a twitter message is posted, it is listed on the user's Twitter page as a blog, and also sent out as a tweet.

The Twitter service was envisaged as a short but frequent blog service. Users send tweets about their everyday routine activities, about recent news, about sports scores or simply idle chatter. Since tweets can be received on mobile phones, the message receivers are not restricted to access through computers or websites. Short messages can increase in density and number and have a tendency to be very addictive for users looking for news on a topic of their choice.

Famous personalities too have started using twitter to update their fans or followers about their activities. The US presidential candidate Barack Obama used it effectively to keep in continuous touch with his supporters during his campaign in 2008. Many film personalities, elected officials and journalists too keep their fans updated through frequent tweets about their activities.

The Twitter technology is also subject to strong positive feedback and network effects. As messages are short and frequent, there is a tendency to continuously read and forward them. Furthermore, the Twitter website allows searching for terms and also aggregates the most frequently tweeted terms. These cause a feedback loop as users further seek and read about these items, and forward them through tweets.

19.3.4 Rating

With the very large number of sites on the internet and the massive scale of information, quite often users turn to rating services and agencies to provide them with reliable ranking of the information provided on various sites. The search services do this by providing their own rankings, such as the one provided by Google. Other services, such as Digg.com and Reddit.com rely on explicit user ratings of articles. Reddit allows users to rate all articles listed on its site, and the ones with the highest ratings are showed prominently. This rating is done by the user community and not by the employees of Reddit.com and thus is governed by the popularity of articles.

Sites such as Alexa.com rate websites by the number of users visiting them. Other websites rate celebrities, films, books, consumer products, software and hardware, jobs, companies, news magazines and so on. The technology may be as simple as choosing between two pictures and checking off which is better, or asking users to rate a product on the basis of a 5-point scale, with 1 point as the worst and 5 points as the best. The technology allows the aggregate rating to be updated immediately thus showing the user how his/her rating matches with others who have rated.

Websites such as Stumbleupon.com allow users to rate the sites they have listed, categorise them, and then provide the highest rated ones as surprise entries to those who visit the site. Stumbleupon relies on ratings provided by prior users to decide on what to offer to subsequent visitors. Stumbleupon has a very successful website based entirely upon preferences of users.

Successful e-commerce sites such as Flipkart.com and Amazon.com also rely on ratings. Flipkart relies on ratings of its products provided by buyers to inform potential buyers of the quality of the product they are considering buying. Flipkart's rating system is very successful as people are honest about their ratings and also rely on the ratings provided by others. Both Flipkart.com and Amazon.com allow users to rate items on the website itself. Users can also leave detailed comments about why they liked or disliked the item, thus justifying the rating they provided. Amazon further allows readers to rate the comments on products and say whether they found them useful, thus allowing the most useful comments to be displayed prominently.

Enabling the rating technology on websites explicitly enables feedback that is necessary for network externalities to function. Such facilities are able to ensure shortening of the feedback loop and hastening of the externality effects.

19.3.5 Tagging/Folksonomies

Some websites allow users to not only rate the quality of the content but also classify their contents. For example, a site on 'modern dance' may actually have a bulk of its content dedicated to fusion dance, with a blend of Indian classical and western dance. Some users, knowledgeable about such matters, could classify or tag the content appropriately. Such tagging can then be displayed for other users to check and use.

The site flickr.com, which facilitates sharing of photographs, uses tags to classify photos. The tags are provided by the users to broadly classify the images they upload to the site. The collection of tags on a site is sometimes called a 'tag cloud' where all the subjects are displayed for other users to access. Tag clouds are also graded, with the most visited tags getting the largest font size and the less visited ones getting smaller font sizes.

Creating taxonomies of sites and pages and content by the users of the sites are referred to as *folksonomies* that refer to the 'folk' nature of creating the taxonomies. These folksonomies show network effects, as the feedback provided by users serves to reinforce the category of the content. It is evident that the search engine Google.com also uses tagging created by users to classify and rate the content of websites.

19.3.6 Mashups

Some websites are created by joining up two technologies available on other sites. For example, some sites take map data from a particular site and join this with the wiki technology to enable maps that can be written upon and changed by users. One example of such a site is wikimapia.org, a site where users can update and change the maps available or add their own data. The sites that join two technologies are called 'mashups'.

Mashups rely on using the underlying interfaces of different technologies and joining them in such a manner as to make them amenable to manipulation. They provide a means by which sites and services can build upon existing facilities.

19.4 SOCIAL ISSUES

19.4.1 Identity

The society of the internet poses peculiar situations for individuals to maintain their identity. Every online service asks the user to create an 'account' or an identity that can be used by him/her. This account often has to be verified or supported by an email address of the user or, if it is a commercial site, by a real credit card. However, in many sites, the identity that a person uses does not have to be connected to the real person. So a person on Twitter, for example, can assume a different name, a different gender, a different age group and a different language. The person can present himself/herself in a manner that is in no way similar to his/her real identity. What is more, the person can maintain multiple identities on the same site or on different sites.

Such a facility allows a person to assume different roles and, possibly, play games or use some form of entertainment. However, for organisations, this is of interest as individuals can use various identities to resist changes, present unpopular views, challenge others, or even expose secrets or hidden issues. Such activities have always been present, in the form of anonymous messages and emails, leaking of information to rival organisations, etc. However, in the internet era, they have assumed a different significance and form. Organisations now have to set up procedures to identify or at least have an idea of the persons, real or virtual, they are dealing with.

19.4.2 Privacy

Most social networking sites such as Facebook allow users to create their own settings for privacy of their data, which means that users can specify what aspects of their personal details are visible to others. When users do not set many controls, it leads to a situation where all their documents, settings and activities are visible to others, and also the site is able to use the data for its own analysis. Even when users set tight privacy controls, some of the preferences they set and some of their activities are used as data by the system.

In some countries, individual data privacy is protected by laws. The data created by individuals on electronic networks is their property and cannot be shared, copied or distributed by others including those maintaining the networks. However, there are grey zones within these privacy protections. For example, Facebook users found that the books and movies they borrowed from a private service were being broadcast to their network of friends without their knowledge. This was contentious; although they had given permission to share data with their friends, they had specifically not permitted this transaction data to be shared. Facebook had to remove this feature upon demand from its users.

Many famous personalities, such as film stars, sports stars, authors, political leaders and journalists, have started revealing detailed aspects of their private lives on blogs and other social network sites. Film stars in India often reveal their whereabouts in Tweets they send out to their fans, as also the clothes they are wearing, the people they are with and other details. Some are careful about what they reveal, whereas others uncover details of an intimate, and possibly, insecure nature.

19.4.3 Media Impact

Social media is having a strong impact on traditional media. Prior to the internet era, the principal mode of communication for media was through broadcast means such as radio, television and newsprint. Individuals were recipients of news and opinions, and could occasionally inform such channels through letters, public interviews or talk shows. With the presence of social media, the tables have turned considerably. A large number of media channels, including print and television, are both influenced by and are influencing the social media.

Many social and political events, such as those depicted in the lead case, are now often first reported or listed on social media by ordinary citizens, which then creates the awareness that drives traditional media to them. Political commentators in India are now prone to publish a report on a blog or a Facebook page to draw public attention before writing or presenting the same in traditional media. Often, the only sources of information from some troubled areas, as was the case in Egypt and also during the tsunami strike in Japan in March 2011, are the posts, videos and images available on social media. Individuals with mobile phones or netbook computers are able to write and upload images using their own devices, which become the prime source of information.

Traditional media also becomes a source of activity on social media. When events such as military strikes against a nation or the suspension of civil rights in a country are reported by traditional media, they become the focus of attention of social media, who may oppose or support and spread the views. Many traditional media also maintain their presence on sites such as Facebook, Myspace and Twitter and encourage such responses.

19.4.4 Collaboration

The internet represents the largest collaboration platform in history. The collaboration is enabled not only for social and political action but also for creating software, encyclopaedic content, books and films. Wikipedia, discussed earlier, is a massive collaboration platform for over 100,000 individuals dispersed all over the globe to participate in creating content. The open source movement, discussed in the next chapter, has created billions of software modules and packages that are used by people all over the world. An open source package, like the operating system Linux, has thousands of developers around the globe who collaborate through the internet.

The phrase *crowdsourcing* is often used to describe projects that encourage collaboration. The term refers to the idea that a 'crowd' of people, not necessarily known to each other, participate in working on a project.

Many critics have argued that crowdsourcing works for some kinds of tasks, but for others it is not effective. For instance, it was initially argued that the quality of articles on Wikipedia was not as good as that available in a traditional encyclopaedia like Encyclopaedia Britannica. However, this turned out to be only partially true. In a comparison conducted by the *Nature* magazine, a well-respected science journal from UK, some experts were asked to rate 42 articles on scientific topics from both Wikipedia and Encyclopaedia Britannica. The results were that the experts found 162 errors in Wikipedia, whereas Britannica had 123 errors. Although Wikipedia did have a higher number of errors, it was striking that Britannica had such a high number too. This finding starkly put to rest the notion that some traditional media were far superior than new media.

A very unusual crowdsourcing effort is known as the Galaxy Zoo (available at www.galaxyzoo.org). The problem that Galaxy Zoo places before visitors is that of classifying images of galaxies, which are star constellations in the universe, obtained from the Hubble Space Telescope (see Fig. 19.3). The site is created by a consortium of universities that do research on studying the universe. One of the first tasks that the site put out was that of classifying the galaxy images into two groups - spiral and elliptical galaxies. Although the classification of images can be done by software such as Neural Networks, the researchers knew that humans were much better at this task. The project was initiated in 2007 with a million images of galaxies to be classified, and the organisers assumed it would take about 2 years to complete the task. However, the site

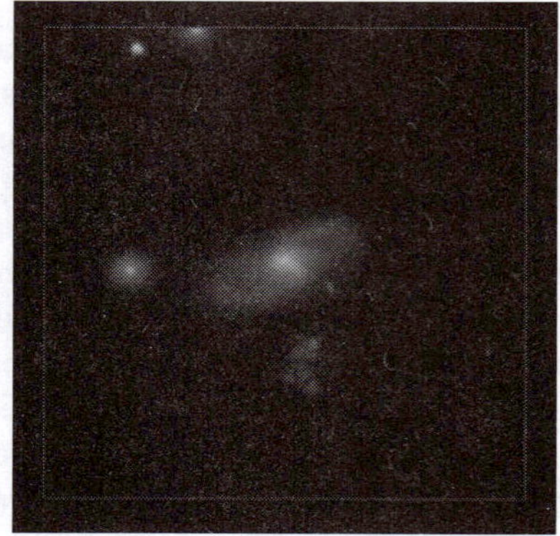

FIGURE 19.3 | Image of a galaxy classified on Galaxy Zoo. The grey object in the bottom is an unclassified element that prompted further research.

Source: www.galaxyzoo.org (reproduced under Creative Commons License).

started receiving 70,000 classifications an hour, and in 1 year received more than 50 million classifications (many galaxies were classified multiple times). The classified galaxies were then considered for further research. The participants in this crowdsourcing exercise were often school children and ordinary citizens, not necessarily scientists.

After the success of the first round, the site set up another project by taking images from the first classification effort, and asking more detailed questions about the images. Within 14 months, the site had received over 60 million classifications. Some volunteers of the site were also able to point to the objects in the images that were outside the scope of the task, which drove the researchers to examine these new objects and ask new questions - thus opening up new areas of research.

19.4.5 Emergence of Order

The openness of the internet collapses the traditional presence of hierarchy in societies. It is possible for an ordinary citizen of India to send an email to the Prime Minister or to visit the blog page of the President of another country and leave a message. Before the electronic era, this would have required the citizen to move through a protocol of controls and permissions to be even near a Prime Minister let alone talk to one; but, for the most part citizens simply did not have access to those at the top.

Collaboration over the internet has a flavour of democratic access where everybody can contribute equally and no one is barred. This leads, as many argue, to a chaotic situation where anybody can say anything and there is no focus or clarity. However, the evidence from sites such as Wikipedia and open source projects shows that there is an order that emerges from the chaos to create high-quality products.

When Wikipedia was opened up for contributions from the world at large, the premise was that people would collaborate to write articles. However, right from the start it became clear that there would be differences of opinion as to the content of articles, and as the wiki technology allows any number of revisions, the articles could possibly be changed endlessly. Wikipedia has discussion pages that support all articles, and maintain a record of all the discussions around the text that is written and edited, including a record of all the versions. These discussion pages allow contributors, who may participate in the writing of an article at different points of time, to see the history and reasoning behind the article and then build upon it. Discussions would range about the content of different contributors, their intentions, the overall goal of the article and how the article should be further edited. An example of a comment on a discussion page is as follows:

> This editor's contributions are always well provided with citations, but examination of these sources often reveals either a blatant misrepresentation of those sources or a selective interpretation, going beyond any reasonable interpretation of the authors' intent.

Articles were written and rewritten, and edited many times. Some articles continued to evolve over many months. Wikipedia had liberal editing and control norms to begin with, but to stem some of the difficult debates and contentions, it evolved a hierarchy of editors who would be in a position to resolve the differences. As Wikipedia began to grow, these editors, who were also volunteers, assumed greater powers and got entrenched in a hierarchy, largely of their own making. By 2006, when Wikipedia had over 3 million articles, some commentators called the strict hierarchy of editors 'digital maosim' referring to the almost dictatorial powers that some editors wielded. Wikipedia responded to this criticism by revising its policies to ensure more debate and discussion, but the structures of editorial staff remained. These structures represented an order that had emerged from the democratic anarchy.

19.5 SOCIAL NETWORKS IN THE ENTERPRISE

The services and technologies that constitute the society of the internet are used extensively by enterprises. Social networking sites like Facebook and LinkedIn are being used extensively by organisations for both marketing their products and also for recruiting personnel. Given the success of many technologies in the social space, enterprises have now incorporated them within their organisation. The idea is to use a wiki or a social networking platform, but within the organisation. These are often called *Enterprise 2.0* tools.

The use of social network tools within organisations poses many challenges and opportunities. One challenge is that these tools may not lead to productivity increase, as they may make employees fritter away their time on making posts and reading them. Studies show that organisations may lose much even if employees spend 20 min a day on social media sites. However, the opportunities that these sites provide are tremendous: the ability to create and sustain ad hoc groups to solve particular problems or work together on projects; the facility of searching quickly or asking someone about information and knowledge related to particular tasks (in other words, helping in knowledge management); and helping employees to know one another, particularly in large organisations with many divisions and departments.

Recognising and finding experts within the organisation is one of the primary benefits of social networking within organisations. Many organisation theorists argue that the most productive employees are so because they not only know their jobs very well and work hard, but also because they know who to ask for what information. The best employees maintain an informal network of contacts through which they can get their work done. Social networking technologies assist in helping employees find the best skilled people and retain links with them, thus helping them do their jobs better.

Managers have also found that by using Enterprise 2.0 tools they can know who is connected with whom, who all share skills and interests, and who can work with whom. This knowledge helps them put together teams for future projects.

Chapter Glossary

Search The ability to seek and find relevant information on the internet in reasonable time.

Blogs A web page or a log used by individuals to record their thoughts and opinions on the internet for everyone to view.

Social networks Internet facilities that enable communities of people to create web pages through which they selectively interact with others.

Peer-to-peer sharing File sharing between individuals on the internet without the facilities of a central server or website.

Avatar Online persona of an individual, assuming a human-like or other form.

Wiki A web page that can be authored and edited by many persons.

Tagging Classification of web pages by individuals or by communities.

Folksonomies Classification of pages and content by communities.

Mashups A combination of two or more internet technologies.

Crowdsourcing Enabling many people to contribute to pages, products, artistic creations and other artefacts on the internet.

Enterprise 2.0 Firms and organisations that have adopted social networking technologies within their organisation.

Review Questions

1. How is the Google search engine technology different from others?
2. What is a blog?
3. How are blogs different from social networking sites?
4. Are social networking sites, like Facebook, subject to network effects? How?
5. What are two different ways of sharing files through the internet?
6. How are virtual worlds different from regular websites?
7. What is the Wiki technology? Is it subject to network effects?

8. What is the Twitter technology? How is it different from SMS?
9. How are ratings used by e-commerce sites?
10. What is tagging?
11. What are folksonomies?
12. What are the issues of identity on the internet?
13. Why is privacy a concern for organisations?
14. How does crowdsourcing work? How is quality controlled when crowdsourcing is used?
15. How does the site Galaxy Zoo manage crowdsourcing?

Research Questions

1. What are some examples of use of social networking technologies for political campaigns in India?
2. How is crowdsourcing used for creating maps? Give some examples.
3. Do a search on a particular term, such as 'modern dance' on Google and then conduct a similar search on another search engine (Bing.com or others). Consider only the first 10 results from each search and examine them carefully to see which search engine gives better results.
4. Consier a scientific topic, such as 'alluvial soil', and read up about it on Wikipedia. Then look up the same topic in a relevant science book or another encyclopaedia. Carefully compare the two articles. Which source is more comprehensive and accurate?

Further Reading

1. Halliday, J. (2011) London riots: How BlackBerry Messenger played a key role, *The Guardian*.
2. Gustin, S. (2011) Defiant Google Exec Wael Ghonim Released From Egyptian Custody. The article is available at: *Wired.com*.
3. Noor, N. (2011) Tunisia: The Revolution that Started it All, *International Affairs Review.*
4. Pontin, J. (2011) What Actually Happened, *Technology Review India*.
5. Read article 'Alaa Abd Al Fattah Discusses New Media In Egypt', available at: www.npr.org (accessed on 7 October 2011).
6. Reagle, J.M. (2010) *Good Faith Collaboration: The Culture of Wikipedia*, The MIT Press, USA.
7. Special Reports on Social Networking, *The Economist*, 28 January 2010.

CHAPTER 20

Open Source Software

LEARNING OBJECTIVES

After completing this chapter, you will be able to:

- Understand the concept of open source software
- Get an overview of the history of free and open source software
- Learn about popular packages
- Get an overview of licences associated with open source software
- Learn about the use of open source in business and government
- Understand the concepts of open data standards and the open community

Open source software, also called free software, differs from proprietary software as it is made by a community of programmers who collaborate via the internet. The collaboration effort starts with an identified need for a software, an initial attempt at the design and conception of the software along with some working code, and then a call for others to join, contribute, test, re-design and distribute. Programmers create open source software to satisfy a personal itch, to fight against the control of proprietary software, to give and receive gifts of programs or to create a reputation for themselves. Open source software originated from a need to create free software that anyone could use, modify and distribute without any hindrance from software vendors. Such software has gained immense popularity across the world and is widely used. Popular open source packages include Linux, Firefox, Apache, GIMP and Open Office.

Open source and free software are distributed under different licences, the most popular of which is the GNU General Public Licence (GPL). The GPL permits creators of the software to retain copyright over their work, but allows users to use, modify, distribute as they please, while retaining the GPL. Other licences, such as BSD and Apache, allow different facilities. Business firms have evolved various models by which to draw revenues from open source software and services. Many governments have adopted open source as it enables them to reduce costs of IT and dependence on vendors; it allows them to experiment and also reduces piracy. Open source software also enables use of open data standards and promotes the culture of open collaboration and sharing, thus helping create the digital commons.

MIND MAP OF CHAPTER TOPICS

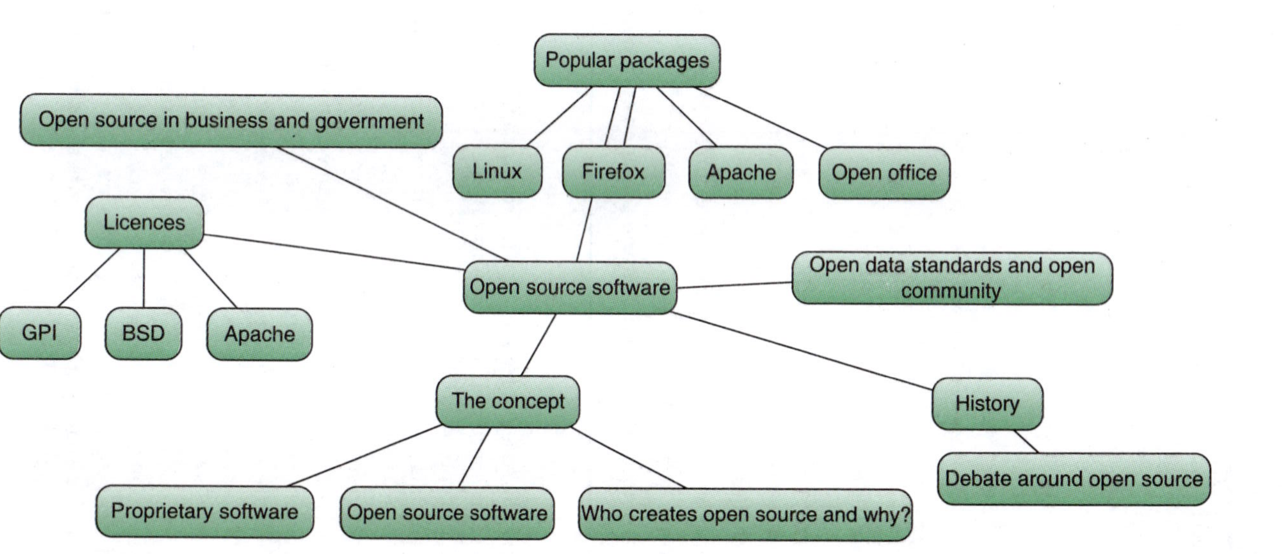

JustDial describes itself as a local search engine. It is a text- and speech-based service that allows users to call in and ask for a business or service in their locality. This could be a place where they can order a pizza or get in touch with a nearby dry-cleaning shop. JustDial operators can answer on the phone, after looking up the caller's location and searching for the business in their databases, or they can text the answer to the caller, which is usually the preferred mode. And, they need just 60 s to do all this.

The search engine market in India was valued at USD 100 million in 2008 and is expected to reach USD 600 million by 2015. Local web search constitutes 30% of the overall search. Local search has evolved from word-of-mouth and print directories to phone-based information services and online web directories. The prerequisites for an effective local search engine include comprehensiveness and updated information, the relevance of the search result in the context of local information, and the ease and speed of accessing information.

JustDial is one of the leading players providing services across multiple channels including a print directory (Yellow pages), a phone/voice search, web search (www.JustDial.com) and mobile phone search (SMS and WAP services). In 2010, the firm has very impressive statistics to boast, including a database comprising of 4 million companies, 125,000 small and medium enterprise (SME) advertisers, 25 million unique users and a spread across 240 cities, with 3500 staff. By 2015, its business had increased to over 15 million listings and over 10,000 employees.

The business model for JustDial is based on providing customers with people-assisted search data, which is information on local SMEs. The customers for JustDial are the end-users who are the audience for its data and the SMEs, whose data it stores. It obtains revenues from the listing fee local businesses pay for being on its database, the advertisements it includes on the website, and the banners it includes in text messages. JustDial also obtains revenues from sharing its database with partners, and also by participating in search queries of global database engines.

JustDial is in a highly competitive market as their business requires low capital investments, has very low switching costs for customers (as there is very little lock-in for them), and also has low lock-in costs for their clients (the SMEs). Its competition includes India-specific websites such as sulekha.com, practo.com, urbandap.com, zomato.com, khoj.com and asklaila.com; local players such as discoverbangalore.com and dialgurgaon.com; and global search engines such as Google and Yahoo. The one thing that gives JustDial strength is its existing database, which is hard to replicate, as the cost of generating local information on SMEs across hundreds of cities is prohibitive. However, for JustDial it is also essential that its database is constantly updated and provides relevant and current information. This is a strategic necessity.

With the increasing availability of the internet, more and more consumers are opting for web searches instead of accessing data through a phone. Global search engines, such as Google and Yahoo, which act as default search sites, are often used for local information search as well. Competition is also emerging from websites such as Asklaila, which are tying up with mobile network providers.

In light of the competition, it is imperative for JustDial to maintain a high quality of service, which would differentiate it from its competitors, and also provide search services that are superior to engines such as Google and Yahoo.

JustDial's choice to compete on the basis of technology meant that the IT systems it deployed had to be positioned at the cutting edge of technology. The technical requirements included:

1. Need for high reliability.
2. Accurate information that is constantly updated and relevant.
3. Fast response time (internal target of 95% of the calls to be addressed in less than 60 s). This needs the ability to digest the customer query, identify the information and retrieve it, communicate it to the customer, and do all of this in less than 60 s!
4. Almost instantaneous and guaranteed SMS response requiring a strong integration with the telecommunications service providers.
5. Instantaneous data extraction needing superior search engine capabilities.
6. Simple user interface on top of a superior technology at the back-end.

Given the diverse and critical needs for technology, JustDial chose open source software as their platform of choice for developing various IT systems. Vendor independence, flexibility, superior quality and scalability, in addition to cost advantage, were cited as the main reasons for adopting open source software.

Considering that there was a strong need for constantly evolving the system, JustDial could not afford any sort of vendor lock-in and sought the ability to change at will without being tied down to any external vendor. The independence provided by open source went beyond just cost and time implications, and allowed JustDial the freedom to innovate, flexibility to change and address their stringent time-to-market considerations.

Open source provided JustDial the ability to choose the hardware platform and build the software by mixing and matching several open source components that delivered flexibility and superior performance. In addition, the choice of these open source components provided JustDial the ability to scale up and support their aggressive growth targets.

The ability to view the source code that had contributions from a vast community of developers also provided the JustDial team a source of new ideas and the required impetus to constantly innovate.

The cost advantage inherent in open source also gave them the ability to do vast in-house development and build a superior technology platform to support the numerous business demands without the worry of astronomical IT development costs.

The open source platform deployed at JustDial was based on a CLAMP stack (C, Linux, Apache, MySQL and PHP). Red Hat Enterprise Linux was chosen for the servers and Ubuntu Linux was deployed on the workstations. The ability to customise Ubuntu with Mozilla Firefox integration so as to enhance the data extraction performance on the IRO's (Information Retrieval Officer) workstation was a major factor in support of the open source decision. The system was built by carefully evaluating and selecting software components based on specific business and technological needs. One example was the use of Sphinx, a full-text search engine that integrates well with an SQL database and is able to provide fast, relevant full-text search.

JustDial belongs to the elite list of rare companies who ventured to develop and use in-house IT systems and establish a market leadership in India based on the strength of their technical innovation. Based on the success of their model in India, JustDial attempted to expand their global footprint, launching their operations in the USA. This is perhaps an unusual case where an Indian company is looking at capturing the global market and competing on the basis of superior in-house built IT systems. That open source software is a central piece of this story underlies its growing importance as a strategic tool for organisations.

20.1 THE CONCEPT OF OPEN SOURCE SOFTWARE

20.1.1 Creation of Proprietary Software

Proprietary software that comes from large corporations is usually created by a team. Team members first create a design of the software that includes specifying its component parts, based on requirements they have obtained from a client or from the design of an existing software. These parts are then allocated to individual programmers who create the code by writing it from scratch, or by re-using existing modules if such modules are available. Programmers also test the portion of the software they are working on. The code modules are then handed over to testers who have specialised skills in creating a varied set of conditions under which the modules are tested, individually and in a combined manner. The tested code may be sent back to its programmer for further enhancements and fixes, or may be moved on and merged with other modules that have been created by other programmers in the team.

The team functions as a unit and usually works on the software entirely on its own without relying on support from other teams or outsiders. The idea is to create a unique software product that can bring revenues to the creator firm from sale or licencing.

Many argue that manufacturing software is more of a craft than an assembly line operation. Software even today cannot be made by creating component parts independently according to a design, and then assembling them. For, although it is technically possible, it still requires considerable effort on the part of the software creators to ensure that all the parts fit together and function coherently. During the writing of software, errors also creep in the code that is being created. For ensuring smooth working of the software, it has to be rid of bugs or debugged. This is a detailed process that requires skill and experience, and borders on being an art as much as it is a science.

The software created in the above manner is strictly controlled by licencing arrangements that ensure that only the firm that has created the software has rights to distribute, modify and extend it. Users are permitted to use the software but not change, distribute or share it. They do not get to see the source code that was used to create the binary version of the software. Since software is very easy to copy, the licencing the firm employs is designed to protect its interests and restrict use of the software to only those who have paid-up licences. In many cases, the licences too are temporary, and users have to renew them to continue using the software.

An important aspect of the software that is created and sold or distributed in this proprietary manner is that it is given away in compiled form. The detailed source code is compiled into a comprehensive package and then given to users and customers. The source code is not given away. Users may have the ability to customise and configure the software to their own needs but they cannot change what is compiled into the software.

Open source software differs from commercial or proprietary software in one essential aspect – the software source code is available to users. Open source software is given out in compiled form, and may be sold or commercially licenced, but the source code is always provided.

20.1.2 Creation of Open Source Software

Open source software is created by a large community of people who collaborate via the internet. These people are programmers or designers or testers who have a common interest in a particular type of software, either an application software, such as a word processor, or a system software such as a driver for a digital camera. These people collaborate through online websites such as Sourceforge (www.sourceforge.net).

A typical open source project is initiated by some person or group creating a project page on a website such as Sourceforge and then asking their contacts or others to join in. The design is settled upon by exchanging emails and messages, and by jointly working on the specifications. Coding for the design also begins and people submit their code to others to review and test. As the design and coding progress, others may join the project to provide assistance with testing, documentation, revisions and extensions.

At the time of initiation, the persons who originally started the project usually decide the language or platform on which the code will be created, the manner in which it will be distributed and what licencing policies they will follow. This allows those who join later to participate in a project whose ultimate goals are specified in advance. Within these specifications and constraints, the project team may experiment and create the software according to their desires and wishes.

KEY POINT

Open source software is created by a community of people who collaborate via the internet.

Many open source projects do not succeed. People start the projects with some goals, and then find that they cannot proceed with it, or others do not join them and there is no progress in building the software. Sometimes a project reaches a certain level of maturity, that is, a lot of software is created, tested and found to be functional. But then the project may be abandoned as the creators lose interest and stop working on it or the project is superseded by another that has a better design and potential.

In this sense, the creation of open source software is often compared to the *bazaar* where many players come to participate, some stay on and succeed while others leave. From this bazaar model, many powerful software packages have emerged that rival and sometimes outperform their proprietary counterparts. For example, many argue that the Apache web server, an open source package, is as good as or better than any proprietary web server.

20.1.3 Who Creates Open Source Software and Why?

Open source software is created by software enthusiasts, professionals, students, professors and hobbyists from all around the world. Many work part-time on projects, contributing to the code or testing or documentation as and when they can. Many students work on projects as part of their assignments in colleges or as part of their summer projects.

Many professional software programmers in large software companies such as Sun Microsystems and IBM also work on open source projects. These are highly paid professionals and experts in their craft. They work on some open source projects as their companies have an interest in those particular projects.

However, the vast majority of developers and programmers who participate in open source projects work part time. They may be employed as software or IT professionals in their day jobs, but find time to contribute to and work on projects as they are very much interested in a particular software. Many economists and psychologists have asked the question as to why so many software programmers, who are highly trained and skilled professionals, give so much of their time to create highly complex software knowing fully well that it will be given away to the community and they will not make any salary or profits from it. Some of the answers that have emerged are discussed below.

1. Programmers and developers work on open source to satisfy a personal *itch*. They may have a desire for a particular kind of software that works in a particular manner, and since they cannot find what they want in the vast amount of software already created, they set out to build their own. This itch is highly personal and individualised, and the developers seek to involve others, via the open source websites, to participate in their project, hoping they will have a similar itch.
2. Many work on open source software to create an alternative to proprietary software. Their objection is to the closed and un-free manner in which proprietary software is controlled and the restrictions placed on its manipulation and re-distribution. Open source software is a reaction to industry control. Programmers create high-quality software to rival the one produced by software companies and distribute it freely, thus diminishing the control of proprietary software.
3. Some argue that open source developers give away software as a gift. Their expectation is that others, who take their gift, will return the favour in kind. In this *gift economy*, the utility of creating and giving away complex software is derived from the return gifts obtained from the community. Open source programmers and developers use only open source products and platforms to build their own code that they give away. They maintain a reciprocity – that of taking and giving gifts.

4. For many young developers, students and starting professionals, participating in open source projects is a way of showing off their programming skills. It is well known that for famous projects, such as the Linux open source operating system, it is very difficult to write code that is finally included in the product. Programmers have to have very strong skills to be able to write code that survives the scrutiny of thousands of collaborators around the world. For those who are involved with projects, it is an achievement that they can boast of and include in their resumes, and this helps them professionally to obtain better and high-paying jobs.

20.1.4 History of Free and Open Source Software

When the first commercial computers were sold by companies such as IBM in the early 1950s, the hardware was accompanied by the instructions to run them, which was the software. The source code for the software was provided as sophisticated compilers had not been invented as yet, and code had to be carefully arranged to be run on the hardware. The computers were very expensive, and only a handful of firms and organisations could afford them. The main cost was for the hardware, and software was literally given for free to ensure that the hardware would run.

This trend continued, and later as the computer industry grew, more firms began making and selling hardware packaged with software. Hardware gained in sophistication with larger memories, greater speed, and better and faster secondary storage. Software too gained in sophistication, with the emergence of distinct categories of application software and systems software. Specialised departments were created within computer manufacturing firms that dealt with creating software alone. The discipline of software engineering evolved and an entire industry began to grow that focused exclusively on creating software that could be run on the available hardware. At this stage too, the revenues obtained from software were mainly linked to the hardware sale. Software was still not separately licenced and sold.

By the late 1970s, several companies, such as Commodore and Apple, had started to market personal computers, which came bundled with software, and were targeted mainly at individual users, not at large corporations. These computers were cheaper and were affordable by ordinary people interested in computing. In the early 1980s, IBM began marketing the first versions of desktop computers for commercial organisations that could use these in offices for all workers. IBM made these personal computers or PCs, as they are called, as highly modular component-based units that could be easily assembled and also upgraded. A large number of manufacturers were encouraged to make the components for PCs, which reduced their prices and made their market competitive. Software manufacturing too was given to vendors who could build and compete to sell their products. This gave rise to the PC software industry with a large number of players making software for the PCs. This initiated the idea of proprietary software, where software manufacturers would protect their source code by licences or by simply not giving them out.

The non-PC manufacturers, the mainframe manufacturers as they were now called, too had switched to the proprietary form of software for distribution by this time. When hardware was sold, the operating system and applications were given, with the users in some cases having to sign single-user agreements, preventing them from sharing the software or source code with others.

The idea of proprietary software was exploited extensively by Microsoft Corporation that created the most popular operating system for the PCs. Microsoft's strategy was to give away only the compiled code that was *bundled* with the PC hardware. Microsoft used software licences that permitted only use of the software by its owner, thus disallowing re-distribution or sharing. They also prevented changing the software code by not letting users have access to the source code.

As a reaction to this move in the industry, a pioneer of computing technology, Richard Stallman, started the Free Software Movement in 1983. Stallman was a graduate of the Massachusetts Institute of Technology (MIT) where he had also worked as a software programmer. He created a software licence known as the GNU General Public License (also known as the GPL) that explicitly allowed users of software to use, inspect, modify and re-distribute software. He used the term *free software* to identify with freedom. GPL gave users freedom to use and work with software as they wished. Stallman also created a host of applications, mainly consisting of utilities to build software that were given under GPL, thus allowing anybody to freely use the software.

Initially the free software created by Stallman and his collaborators was available to only those who had access to them physically, on media such as floppies or tapes, as those days the internet was restricted to a few universities, commercial organisations and government departments. Only employees of these organisations could get the free software off the internet. The growth of the free software movement and the internet are intertwined. In the 1990s, as the internet became commercial and available to people around the world, so too the free software movement grew and gained strength. Computer programmers from around the world could now access the free software created by others and build on these.

The operating system Linux originated on a call given by a Finnish graduate student to build such a system using tools already available under GPL. His call attracted a lot of developers to work on the system. Linux grew exponentially and further attracted a lot of users and developers. It started a trend of releasing updated software versions frequently, about every 6 months, and created a culture where users expected new versions frequently and looked forward to them.

By the mid-1990s, there was immense commercial interest in Linux as it was a very stable operating system and rivalled any of its proprietary competitors. Some entrepreneurs decided to create a business out of distributing and servicing Linux but decided to use a new term to describe the manner in which Linux was created and distributed. They chose the term *open source* to signify that Linux is always provided with the source code. Many industry analysts agreed that this provided a better *brand* for this kind of software and promoted open source actively.

Open source software, thus, is not very different from free software, and in fact most open source software use GPL as the user licence. Nowadays there are many licences that are used to distribute open source software and they are variants of the original GPL (some differ significantly). The idea of freedom of use, modification and re-distribution is, however, retained by most open source software, making them highly competitive in the commercial market.

By late 2010, open source software had gained immense popularity and was used around the world in a large number of organisations. Packages such as Apache and Firefox are very popular. Open source and free software are phrases that organisations and individual users around the world recognise as signifying both high quality of and low (or often zero) cost of software.

20.1.5 Debate Around Open Source Software

Open source software poses a competitive threat to proprietary software. It works on practically all types of hardware. Organisations can easily download open source software, distribute it freely to all employees and make modifications or changes to suit their needs. Faced with a threat to their business from open source software, some rival proprietary software firms have engendered a debate around the merits of open source software, arguing that the software may be free to acquire but its *total cost of ownership* is higher. The phrase 'total cost of ownership' refers to the final costs of acquiring, installing, customising, maintaining and upgrading software.

Those favouring proprietary software argue that open source software only reduces the initial cost of software acquisition, but finally organisations have to pay out more to use the software than they would if they used proprietary software. The genesis of this argument is in the fact that many organisations, which already use proprietary software, have a *lock-in* to it. Lock-in implies that the organisation has invested money in acquiring the software, trained its employees to use the software and created routines and processes that use the capabilities of the software, and may have extended contracts with service firms that help in maintaining the software. This investment constitutes a lock-in that is quite high in monetary value. The *switching cost* of moving to another software type, like open source, would be quite high as the organisation would have to re-learn the software, re-create its processes and re-train its employees.

Furthermore, the proponents of proprietary software argue, since proprietary software is used more on the desktop, more people are familiar with using and supporting it. For example, proprietary software such as Microsoft's Windows operating system has about 90% of the market share for desktop and laptop operating systems. There are a large number of service firms who

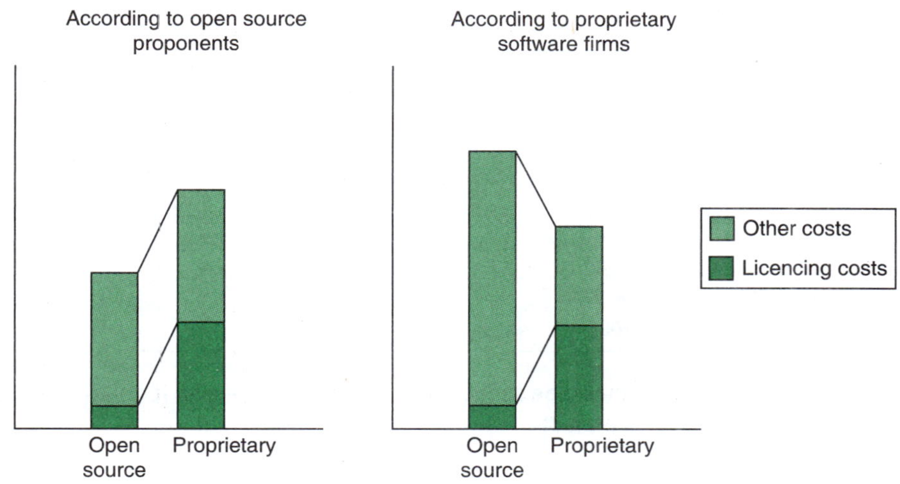

FIGURE 20.1 | Costs of owning open source versus proprietary software.

can help with using, installing, upgrading and maintaining Windows. This helps organisations reduce their costs of using the Windows software as opposed to open source software.

Proponents of open source software argue that the low initial costs of acquisition for the software, which is zero in most cases as the software can be downloaded free of cost, actually offsets the cost of getting support for and training users on the new software (see Fig. 20.1). Furthermore, the long-term costs of upgrades and maintenance are lower as support is available for free, albeit not immediately (support for open source software is available online on websites and mailing lists).

Possibly, the strongest argument for using open source for a desktop operating system is that of security. It is well known that the Windows operating system is susceptible to virus attacks. In 2008, there were more than a million known viruses for Windows. Comparably, for the Linux operating system, there are hardly any viruses and there is no need to use any anti-virus software either. For Windows users, virus-protection software costs a lot to acquire and maintain, but the most damaging aspect is the losses incurred by organisations that have been struck by viruses and lose hours and days of productivity.

Over the decades of its existence, the free software and open source movement has produced many highly stable and efficient programs that are widely used. Some of these packages are described in the sections below.

20.1.6 Popular Packages

20.1.6.1 Linux

The Linux operating system was initiated by Linus Torvalds, a Finnish graduate student, in 1991. Torvalds was keen to build an operating system of his own as the ones available at the time, to run on desktop computers, were either proprietary, such as the one sold by Microsoft, or were not powerful enough (such as an operating system called Minix). Torvalds wrote the basic structure of an operating system using free software tools built by Richard Stallman. He then sent out an email message on the Minix user group (a community of enthusiasts working with the Minix operating system) asking if anyone was interested in the operating system he was developing. A portion of the text he sent out is quoted below in Fig. 20.2.

The response to the message sent out was immense. Enthusiasts around the world responded to this call by first downloading the system Torvalds put out on a website and then by adding, commenting, testing and providing bug fixes to the code. The system was called Linux and became very popular.

```
Hello everybody out there using minix - I'm doing a (free) operating sys-
tem (just a hobby, won't be big and professional like gnu) for 386(486)
AT clones. This has been brewing since april, and is starting to get
ready.I'd like any feedback on things people like/dislike in minix, as my
OS resembles it somewhat (same physical layout of the file-system (due to
practical reasons) among other things). I've currently ported bash (1.08)
and gcc (1.40), and things seem to work.This implies that I'll get some-
thing practical within a few months, andI'd like to know what features
most people would want. Any suggestions are welcome, but I won't promise
I'll implement them :-)
```

Linus (torvalds@kruuna.helsinki.fi)

Linus Torvalds, 25 August 1991.

FIGURE 20.2 | Part of the message sent out by Linus Torvalds calling for participation in the Linux project.

By the late 1990s, many commercial firms starting showing interest in Linux, and companies such as RedHat and Caldera were formed that sold a commercial version of Linux. Although, Linux was still open source, and anybody could access all the code for free, these companies built some extensions on their own and also specialised them for certain kinds of applications for which customers were willing to pay their commercial price.

Linux continued to grow and many users and organisations around the world adopted it. Linux was made available in many languages and an extensive portfolio of applications was developed for it. Linux also grew into many distributions. These distributions essentially work on the same core kernel of the operating system, but they have built their own specialised user interfaces and applications depending on the needs of the community they are serving. Some details about Linux are provided in Box 20.1. Linux is now used in all variety of hardware: Servers, desktops, laptops, mobile phones, personal digital assistants and portable audio players.

Box 20.1 Some facts about Linux in 2016

1. The 5.0 version of Debian Linux had 323 million software lines of code in 2016.
2. The Linux core kernel had over 5000 contributors in 2016.
3. The estimated cost of developing the entire set of packages in Debian 5.0 is estimated to be USD 8 billion.

Source: Wikipedia and The Linux Foundation, www.linuxfoundation.org (accessed on July 2016).

It is used to create massive parallel processing supercomputers as also small devices that have embedded operating systems. Linux development continues at a rapid pace, with a new version of a kernel being released about every 6 months. The number of applications and packages that are available for Linux continue to multiply. A screenshot of a typicial Linux user interface is shown in Fig. 20.3.

20.1.6.2 *Mozilla Firefox*

Firefox is an open source browser that is used to view pages and multimedia content on the World Wide Web. Firefox is the second most popular browser in the world (in December 2017) with a market share of 14% (the most popular browser is Google Chrome, also an open source

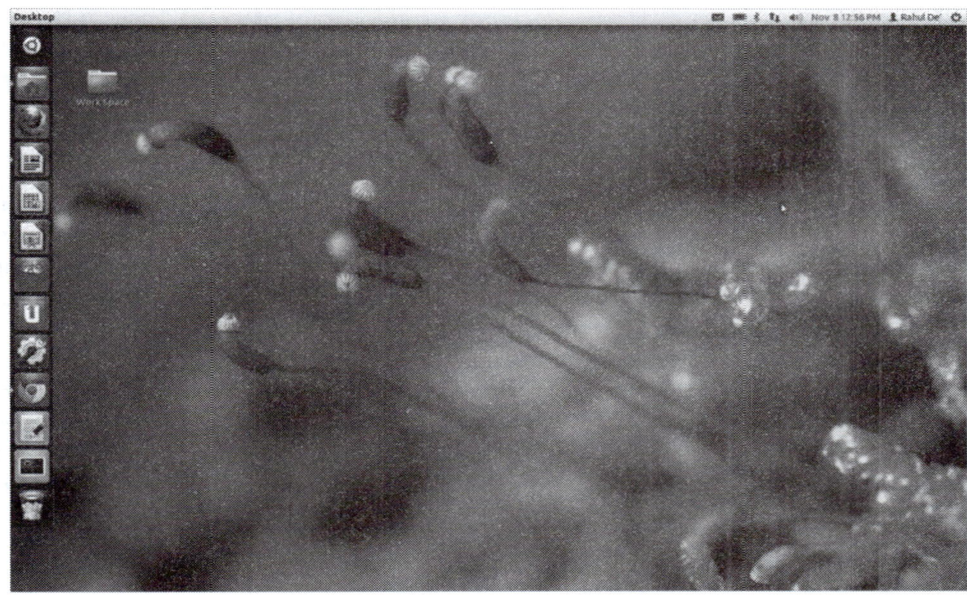

FIGURE 20.3 | Image of a Linux desktop.

browser released by the Google Corporation). Firefox runs on all the major desktop operating systems, including Windows, Linux and Mac. Firefox is also available in 91 languages.

The Mozilla Firefox browser derives from the erstwhile Netscape browser that was one of the first browsers created after the World Wide Web was launched. Netscape was very popular in the 1990s and was eventually replaced almost entirely by Microsoft's Internet Explorer. Netscape was one of the first projects, which started as a proprietary project and then was made open. After Netscape's code was made open source, it was sponsored and further developed by the Mozilla Foundation (a non-profit organisation), leading to the current version of the Firefox browser.

20.1.6.3 Apache

Apache is a web server, a software that allows websites to serve pages to visitors. Apache is arguably one of the most successful open source projects ever, as it is unrivalled in the proprietary software world. The Apache server is responsible for the initial rapid growth of the World Wide Web.

As such, the Apache server is an HTTP server, where HTTP is the hypertext transfer protocol, the protocol used to transmit data on the World Wide Web. An Apache server can be installed on any computer connected to the internet, and with an appropriate IP address, the machine can begin to act as a web server. The server is very easy to install and configure and can run on a wide variety of operating systems. It is maintained and updated by the Apache Software Foundation.

Apache, in 2016, hosted 46% of all websites in the world.

20.1.6.4 Libre Office

Libre Office is the name of an *office suite* software application. An office suite software consists of applications that are typically used in the office environment and include a word processor, a spreadsheet, a presentation software, a database, and some others such as a graphics creator and calendar. Libre Office being an office suite contains most of these applications.

Libre Office was forked from openoffice which was derived from a product called StarOffice that was owned by the firm Sun Microsystems. Sun spun off OpenOffice in 2000 to create an open source product as a direct competitor to proprietary office packages. (The name OpenOffice.org was used for the package as the phrase Open Office was already being used by another product.)

In 2009, OpenOffice.org had about 9 million lines of code in about 30,000 source files. It is available in 110 languages and had been downloaded 98 million times, with an estimate of 15–20% of the market share for desktop office applications.

One of OpenOffice.org's greatest strengths is that it is compatible with a number of other office applications, including Microsoft Office. It can open and create files in formats of other office products. On its own, it relies on open standards and formats for data files. For example, its word processor, Writer, saves files in the Open Document Text format (files with the extension .odt) which is a universal open standard for text files.

Due to the availability of the source code, a number of variations of the basic office suite have also been released. These products extend the basic functionality of OpenOffice.org in some manner, either by speeding up the programs, or by adding features that make them attractive to special kinds of users. One example is the IBM Lotus Symphony, which is released by IBM, and is based on the OpenOffice.org source. Symphony is packaged by IBM with other products from their portfolio, giving their customers a better bundle of packages.

20.1.6.5 GIMP

Gimp stands for the GNU Image Manipulation Program. It is an image manipulation and raster graphics program that is entirely open source and is used widely by professional graphic artists and amateurs alike. GIMP can be run on many popular operating systems and is currently available in about 50 languages. GIMP is widely perceived to be a free substitute for the professional quality proprietary program called Adobe Photoshop. Many use GIMP as such, as it can manipulate and touch up digital photographs. It uses advanced techniques of image manipulation. Many businesses have used the source code to modify GIMP for their own particular needs.

20.2 OPEN SOURCE LICENCES

20.2.1 GNU General Public Licence (GPL)

The GNU licence is one of the oldest and most used licences for software in the open source community. It stands as a guide for other licences, many of which have been inspired by it. GNU stands for Gnu is Not Unix, which is a recursive name given by Richard Stallman who created the licence.

The philosophy of the GPL is to allow free and unhindered usage of software, and to ensure that this is perpetuated. When any software is given the GPL, it ensures that anybody is free to use the software, see its source code, distribute to as many users as desired, and change the source code to suit one's needs. Seen differently, the GPL 'protects' users from anyone taking away these freedoms to use, distribute and modify the software.

One particular aspect of the GPL is regarding distributing modified software. When a software that is already under the GPL is modified, the new modified version is known as the *derived work*. The GPL states that if the derived software is distributed, it has to be distributed under the same licence. It cannot assume a new licence that violates GPL's essential freedoms. It is important to understand that if a person or organisation uses and then modifies GPL software, then they can continue to use the modified version as long as they like. If they choose to distribute the derived software then the GPL ensures that the source code has to be distributed also. This protects the freedom of the receiving entity to see, use and modify the source code.

The GPL does not impose any restrictions on sale of software. Software created under the GPL licence can be sold, provided the source code is distributed also. Furthermore, the author of the software can retain the *copyright* to the software under the GPL. This implies that organisations or individuals who create GPL software and distribute it retain possession of the intellectual content of the software (thereby preventing others from claiming the software as theirs).

The GPL allows copyright but prevents patenting of software. A *patent* is a special protection under the legal framework of most countries, where a patent holder has complete rights over the idea patented; anyone who may later want to use a similar or the same idea has to pay royalties to the original patent holder. Patents in software are highly restrictive and curb innovation. Many developers around the world are opposed to software patents. To understand why, consider a popular application that many people use – the word processor. When word processors were first developed, the idea of word processing was not patented. This allowed many firms and individuals to design and develop various kinds of word processors and either sell or distribute them freely. Had the first word processor been patented, none of the later developers would have had any incentive to create new and original word processors, as they would all have to pay royalties to the patent holder for any revenues they obtained for their own work.

20.2.2 BSD Licence

BSD stands for the Berkeley Software Distribution. This licence is one of the most permissive licences, which allows free distribution of the software and derived works with or without the source code. The licence specifies two main conditions for software users – the software may be distributed freely in source or binary form, but the copyright notice of the original copyright holder has to be retained, and the name of the copyright holder cannot be used to promote any derived works. Furthermore, the licence clarifies that there are no guarantees of performance or warranties associated with the software under the licence.

The BSD licence prompted many open source developers to adopt it as it allowed them to create software that they could distribute as they pleased. There are many variants of the BSD licence, which borrow the main ideas and then add some further clauses of their own. These variants include – the MIT licence, the NetBSD licence, the FreeBSD licence and so on.

20.2.3 Apache Licence

The Apache software licence is somewhat different from the above licences. This licence also allows free distribution, use and modification of the software to create derivative works. It further allows licencing of software along the lines of any other licence. Thus, those who use Apache licenced software can modify the code, create a new application, and then licence it differently. This extends further to create patent restrictions.

The main difference between Apache and the GPL is that the GPL explicitly forbids patenting of software derived from its licence, whereas Apache allows this. This has made Apache particularly attractive to many developers who want to take free software and extend it with their own work, but want to make it proprietary to extract revenues from it.

As with the others, the Apache licence does not warranty the performance of the software licenced by it, and also limits the liability arising from the use of the software. The latter provision means that if people download and use Apache licenced software and suffer some financial damages because of that (or related to the software), they cannot sue the software maker for the damages. This aspect of the licence is common for all the open source licences.

There are many other open source licences that are used by the community, including the GNU Affero General Public licence, the Mozilla Public Licence and the Common Public Attribution licence.

20.3 OPEN SOURCE IN BUSINESS AND GOVERNMENT

20.3.1 Open Source in Business

Open source software has been widely adopted in business and government. Many prominent information technology businesses such as IBM, Sun Microsystems (later a part of Oracle Corporation), Hewlett-Packard, Oracle and many others saw the value of open source quite early and adjusted their business models and products to accommodate the value and power of open source. IBM, for instance, actively supports the development of many open source products, and has contributed extensively to their growth and popularity. Some businesses such as Google and Yahoo that are very large internet-based businesses have developed a significant part of their infrastructure using open source software components.

Businesses not in the information technology industry use open source products quite widely. The OpenOffice software is used by businesses for the routine desktop activities, along with packages such as the Firefox browser and the Linux operating systems. There are also a large number of specialised open source packages that businesses use as low cost, high value and quality alternatives to proprietary software. Packages such as SugarCRM (a customer relationship management software), Compiere Open Source ERP (an enterprise resource planning software), GNU Cash (an accounting software) and MySQL (a database software) are quite popular.

Many firms have now set up business models based on open source software. Some examples of how firms are doing this are as follows:

1. **The Dual-Licencing Model:** In this business model firms create open source software that they release to the community under an appropriate licence such as GPL. Community members use and modify and extend the software, thereby contributing to its growth. The creators, however, retain the copyright and also sell the software on a second, proprietary, licence, which is a closed source (see Fig. 20.4). Businesses that want the open source software customised to their needs have the copyright holders modify the software and give it to them on a proprietary licence, thus protecting their business interests. MySQL, the open source database software, is managed by its creators on such a dual licence. Businesses that buy the proprietary version have an advantage of a customised software (which is of lower cost than other proprietary softwares); the firm selling the software has revenues; and the community benefits as it has a free version that it can use.
2. **The Service Model:** In this model, some firms take an open source software, like a database or an operating system, and create a highly specialised service package around it that they can sell. For instance, one firm contracts with large business organisations to support and maintain one particular distribution of Linux. The advantage to the client is that it has a skilled organisation supporting its needs across its offices spread around the world, and provides support for infrastructure.
3. **The Product Model:** In this model, firms create products based on extensions of open source software and sell them as commercial software. For example, RedHat Linux sells a portfolio of Linux distributions that it has created on its own. Its model is to sell the product and along with it a service that clients find very useful. RedHat generates revenues by creating, selling and supporting operating systems specialised for mission critical needs. RedHat

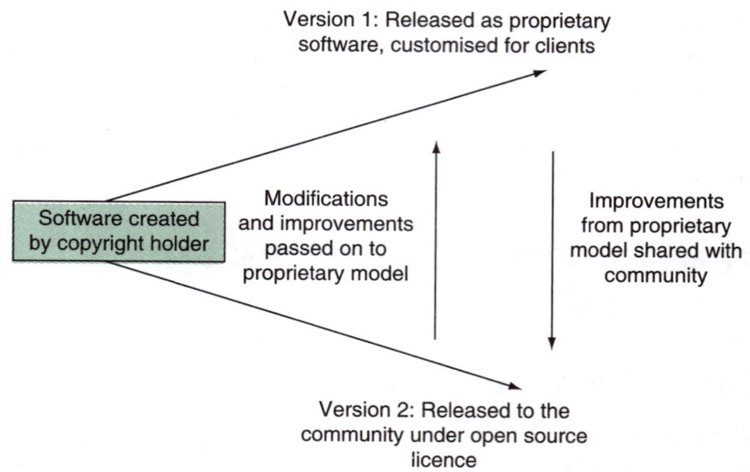

FIGURE 20.4 | Dual-licencing business model for open source software.

also maintains a basic community version of the software that it supports and extends. The benefit to the community is that it can draw on RedHat s immense contributions, and for RedHat the benefit is that it can draw on the community s extensions and features.

4. **The Hardware Model:** Some firms make or assemble specialised hardware that runs open source software. Their main revenue source is from the hardware sales, and they support users with the open source software which has been customised for their hardware. Examples of such firms include Nokia, the manufacturer of mobile phones, and Acer, the maker of laptops and desktop; both use open source operating systems for their hardware.

20.3.2 Open Source in Government

Governments in many parts of the world have sought out open source as a high-quality and low-cost alternative to proprietary software. In some cases, national governments have passed laws advocating use of open source software, wherever this is possible, over proprietary software. And in other cases, state, city and local governments have taken steps to adopt open source software.

In developing countries, in particular, open source software has found many adherents. For example, in many states in India, including Kerala, Assam and New Delhi, local governments have sought to not only adopt but also actively promote knowledge about and value of open source software. In China, Brazil, Indonesia, Philippines, Cambodia and Malaysia, support for open source software is quite strong and the governments actively promote its use. In Spain, Germany, the USA and Sweden, several state and local governments have clearly articulated policies to adopt open source software.

Government departments have found several advantages in adopting open source. Some of these are listed below:

1. Open source software is invariably of lower cost than proprietary software. This allows departments, which always operate on budgets, to allocate limited resources to more abundantly available software. In particular, costs of upgrading software and per seat licences are low, which helps reduce costs in the long run as departments grow.
2. Open source software for developing countries has an additional advantage related to lower cost, that of reducing the dependence on foreign goods, thereby reducing the outflow of foreign exchange.
3. Open source software allows easy experimentation. Many departments around the world have 'discovered' many things they could do with computerisation simply by trying out different things with open source software at a very low cost. This allows breaking out of rigid and bureaucratic processes by seeing the value of and experimenting with information technology.
4. Open source products are mainly based on open data standards and open formats (this is discussed below). For governments this is crucial as public data can be maintained on open standards across many departments, and state and local bodies. This data can be shared and maintained in perpetuity within a format that is open, and hence not tied to any particular vendor company's fortunes.
5. Owing to weak piracy prevention in many developing countries, open source represents a way to curb piracy and encourage users in all walks of the economy to use legal software. In China, one explicit goal for promoting open source was to curb the menace of piracy.

20.4 OPEN DATA STANDARDS AND THE OPEN COMMUNITY

20.4.1 Open Data Standards

Many software programs store data in a format that is specific to them. For example, a word-processed document that is created using the Microsoft Word program is stored in the .doc format. This format is specific to Microsoft Word. Other programs may read the .doc format, but to create files in this format, they would have to obtain a commercial licence from Microsoft.

A *standard* in data is a common format in which the data is stored in files. Standards are created by standard setting bodies. These bodies are constituted by the firms or organisations that are responsible for creating programs that use the standard. In software, many standards are maintained by the International Organisation for Standardisation that maintains the ISO standards. The ISO creates the bodies that create the standards and uphold them. Standard setting is a detailed and drawn out process in which many parties have to agree as to what the standard will be and how it will be maintained. Another organisation that also promotes standards is the Internet Engineering Task Force (IETF) that has standards related to the internet and its services.

KEY POINT

A data standard is a common format in which data is stored and shared.

Proprietary standards are those owned by some firms, and to use them others have to pay royalties. Open standards are those that are free to be used by anyone without paying royalties. Thus, many commercial firms, which create programs, are interested in creating proprietary standards to extract royalties. However, there is a risk that proprietary standards may not be widely adopted and so the firms could lose out. On the other hand, open standards may be widely adopted, but there is not much royalty income from them. Some firms work mainly with open data standards so that they are widely adopted, and the firms can then obtain revenues from complementary products.

One of the most popular data standards that is used for file sharing and exchange is the Portable Document Format or the pdf. Files that are named as 'Homework.pdf' are created with the pdf data standard. Pdf is an open standard though it was created and is owned by Adobe Incorporated, a commercial firm based in the USA. Adobe initially created the format, which was used by its own programs. Adobe also created a reader for pdf files, called the Adobe Acrobat Reader, that was a free download for all to use and that enabled the easy reading of pdf files. Pdf became a very popular method of exchanging files within organisations and also across the internet because of the availability of the free reader. Also, now that pdf is an open format, there are many open source and proprietary programs available that can create pdf files.

Open standards are important for organisations of all types. Data files created with open data standards can be maintained in *perpetuity*. This point is important. As has been seen with software of all kinds, the evolution and changes in them is fast and sometimes abrupt. Data files created with a certain kind of, say, a word processor are sometimes unreadable a few years later as the version of the word processor has changed and does not support the earlier data format. Also, the firm that created the word processor may go out of business and may not be able to create new versions of software that can read the old files. If the data is in a proprietary format then other software makers may not want to create programs that can read the old files, or may charge a very high price to do so. However, with open standards, it is possible for many firms to create readers and provide them at reasonable prices.

For governments, in particular, open standards are important as data can be conveniently stored in perpetuity. Governments have to maintain very large volumes of data, pertaining to transactions by the entire population, and hence need to have the assurance that the digital data they have will be readable in future by programs available at reasonable prices.

Another advantage of open standards is that they promote a culture of sharing. Readers can be created for different operating systems and in different human languages that allow data in open standards to be read. Multimedia data in audio, video, image and graphics applications can be shared easily if they are in open standard files.

It is also important to mention here that proprietary standards are also very popular. The best example is the MP3 data standard for audio files. MP3 audio files are almost universally known. Millions of MP3 files are available for sharing or purchase on the internet, and there are thousands of software programs and hardware players (such as the famous iPod) that play MP3 files. MP3 is a patented format, and to create players or encoders for it, firms have to pay a royalty to the owners of the patent (which is the Fraunhofer Institute in Germany). Many software and hardware vendors have sought to remove MP3 as the *de facto* standard for music files and promote other and better standards. However, the MP3 popularity is so high that its usage has grown and not declined. Open standards for music files such as Vorbis are also popular and are actively used and promoted by the open source community.

Open data standards allow many commercial firms to create and sell creators and readers of data files. This competition improves the quality of the programs available and also reduces the price of the products.

Open standards also enable the continuous evolution and growth of the data formats. With a community participating, as happens in open source, the number of varied interests and requirements is very high and that contributes to the growth of standards.

20.4.2 The Open Community

The open source community represents one of the largest open communities in the world, which participates in shared goals. This community spans across nations, geographies, languages, gender and economic differences. This community collaborates to engineer some of the most complex systems ever created. And yet, it remains largely physically invisible, amorphous and transient. This is an open community that is beginning to define, in many ways, the way we live, work and share.

It is argued that the open source movement represents a *digital commons*. The commons are a shared resource whose value lies in the fact that a single individual or group's consumption of the resource does not preclude others from using it. A city park is a commons, as those who go there to walk or play do not prevent others from doing so simultaneously (a private good, like a car, in contrast, if being used by the owner, cannot be used by others). The open source community has created a digital commons as it allows anyone to use and share the resources it creates; the use by one does not block anyone else from using the same. The philosophy of the GPL is to preserve this aspect of the commons.

Open standards too help sustain the digital commons. When data is in an open standard it can be shared with all. Many universities around the world have now opened their course content and materials for sharing over the internet. Many nations across the world, and including India, have passed laws mandating that data and information pertaining to government activities has to be made freely available to the public. All these efforts finally rely on open data formats by which data can be shared and easily read by all.

The Creative Commons (CC) Licence was established as a counterpart to a software licence for creative works. Under the CC licence, any creative work – a piece of prose, a video, an artwork, a musical piece – can be licenced to be in the public domain. This means that anyone can read, see and listen to the work, but there are restrictions on modifying or distributing it. The CC specifies that distribution of the work is possible, but the copyright and licence notice has to be retained, and further the distributed work cannot be modified in any way. However, there are many variations that are possible within the portfolio of CC licences that may allow (or disallow) modification, permit creating derivative works, or allow commercial distribution. The CC has been widely adopted by authors and artists across the globe. This is in the spirit of the commons, enabling the public to consume the works without restricting others from doing so.

The culture of digital commons has permeated in other areas of creative collaboration such as collaborative writing of books and making of movies. The idea that digital goods can be shared is infective and has been widely adopted. Many of the activities of collaborating across cultures and sharing are driven by a motive to learn. Individuals who participate want to learn about and contribute to what interests them, as much as they want to consume what is available. This aspect of the open community is the most valuable, also the most powerful.

Caselet | **Android Operating System**

The Android operating system was the most widely used operating system in the world in 2017. It is used extensively on a wide range of smart phones, made by manufacturers such as Samsung, HTC, Motorola, and also Google's Pixel phones, and many other manufacturers around the world. Android is an open source operating system as its source code is publicly available and it is also released under an Apache licence that allows anyone to modify and re-distribute the code. Google maintains and updates the Android kernel code and releases it to the community for further development. Smart phone manufacturers use the open source code to build their own, often proprietary, extensions to the operating system and then release it bundled with their hardware.

Android was originally developed in 2003 as a fork of Linux, with the intention of having an operating system that could be used with small, handheld devices which were aware of and made use of their location and user preferences. It was later acquired by Google and by 2008, with the wide gains in the market for smart phones, it was being installed on original equipment made by several manufacturers. Google distributed the source code but held the trademark of Android and licenced it to the manufacturers on a contractual basis, thus allowing it to obtain revenues. The availability of source code also helped to evolve an ecosystem of developers who built a variety of software to run on Android and also for it to run on a wide variety of hardware platforms. Other device makers, such as Amazon and Nokia, took the source code and built their own versions of the operating system for their own devices.

The core kernel of Android is Linux and thus has the GPL licence. Other software developed on top of the kernel largely uses the Apache licence. Both these licences are largely used for systems software that is used to drive the hardware. Application software that is run on the smart phone largely uses proprietary licences. Some commentators argue that because different types of licences, including open source and proprietary licences, are mixed within the Android ecosystem, the system cannot really be called an open source software. However, others argue that since the kernel software is open source and has a community of developers working on it, it relies on the principles of open source.

Though it had a small market share when it was launched in 2008, Android soon gained popularity and was the dominant operating system for mobile phones in 2013. It is estimated that about 3 billion Android smart phones were sold worldwide by 2014, since Android's launch. In some countries, Android had over 70% market share of mobile phones used to access the internet. The website statcounter.com estimated that in December 2017, Android had 40% of the market share for all operating systems in the world, followed by Windows (36%) and iOS (13%).

Inspite of the use of open source and a wide developer community, Android has encountered some challenges. Google follows the practice of first developing and deploying a major update for Android for its own Pixel line of phones and then releasing the source to the community. The other phone manufacturers then use the code to re-build and test their own extensions that they can then release as patches for their older models or on their new phones. This takes several months of development and testing effort, thus delaying the release of the new and updated software for various phone manufacturers. This delay is reflected in the application software also, which has to be modified to take advantage of the newer features available. Google has tried to address this problem by adding layers of software that will help other manufacturers develop their extensions faster and in a smoother manner.

Chapter Glossary

Proprietary software Software that is created by commercial firms and released under a licence that restricts the software use, sharing, modification and distribution. Such software is usually released in compiled form, and source code is not provided.

Bazaar model The open participation of many people around the world to develop open source software.

Personal itch Refers to the desire by programmers to create a software tailored to their special needs.

Gift economy A situation in which people give gifts with the expectation that others will in turn give them gifts too.

Free software Software that is licenced under the GNU General Public licence which assures that users of the software can have access to the source code, use it, modify it and distribute the modifications.

Open source Software that is released along with the source code, and usually carries a GPL or similar licence.

Total cost of ownership The costs incurred by organisations when they acquire and use software. In addition to the cost of buying the software or the licence, these costs include expenses on maintenance, training, support, upgrades and migration.

GPL Acronym for the GNU General Public Licence that ensures that software distributed with this licence is not patentable and allows the user to use, modify and distribute without any restrictions.

BSD Acronym for the Berkeley Software Distribution licences, which are a set of permissive licences allowing creators and users of software to freely distribute and use software, with the only restrictions of retaining copyright notices and of not having any warranties.

Dual-licencing A situation where creators of a software release it under both an open source and a proprietary licence.

Data standard An agreed upon and shared format by which data is stored in files.

Perpetuity Refers to an endless time horizon.

Creative commons licences A set of licences that allow works of art, such as books, poems, songs, to be released in the public domain for free viewing and consumption. The restrictions are on commercial use and modification.

Review Questions

1. What are the main differences in the manner by which proprietary and open source software are created?
2. Who are the people who participate in creating open source software?
3. Why do people create open source software?
4. What are the main arguments of the debate between the proponents of proprietary and open source software?
5. What are the main provisions of the GPL?
6. How is the BSD different from the GPL?
7. What are the provisions of the Apache licence?
8. What are the four main models of doing business with open source software?
9. Why do governments choose to use open source software?
10. What is an open data standard? Why is it preferable over a proprietary data standard?
11. What is the open community?

Research Questions

1. What are the different applications for which commercial firms have adopted open source software? Visit some local firms to do the research.
2. Read the JustDial case. What were the strategic reasons for which JustDial adopted open source?
3. The Android operating system has become very popular and is used widely on mobile phones and tablet computers. What licencing model does it follow and why has it become so popular?
4. Explore the business model of the RedHat firm that sells a Linux product by the same name. How does RedHat earn revenues? Why is it successful?

Further Reading

1. Read an article 'Computer viruses hit one million' available at: news.bbc.co.uk, 10-04-2008 (accessed on July 2009).
2. De, R. (2008) FOSS Business Models for Developing Countries in Asia, *IOSN South Asia Node Report*.

Objective Type Questions

Chapter 1 Organisations and Information Systems

A. Complete the Following

1. Organisations are collections of ____________ with shared ________.
2. Modern organisations have elements of ______________ built into their structure, functioning in a world of _____________ networks. They are highly _______________ and rely on ____________ workers largely.
3. ____________ order effects arise as a direct consequence of the introduction of information systems in an organisation.
4. A ________ is a set of steps required to accomplish a task and _____________ systems are widely used in organisations to support processes for all the functions that they perform.
5. The technology road map for an organisation is like an ____ plan of information systems in the organisation.

B. State True or False

1. A major task of modern organisations is to process information.
2. Modern organisations use a matrix structure where strict hierarchies are present.
3. Companies disperse their operations only to locate functions where resources such as skilled labour or raw material are available.
4. Before the advent of personal computers, the software used was automatically bundled with the hardware purchased.
5. Second-order effects of the introduction of information systems in organisations are designed outcomes that are visible or measurable in the short term.

C. Choose the Right Option from the List

1. An essential component of a modern-day organisation is an information system
   (a) which binds the organisation
   (b) which enables its interactions with the world through the Internet
   (c) both (a) and (b)
   (d) only (b)
2. In the 1980s, the Free Software Movement emerged, which advocated
   (a) free usage and sharing of software only
   (b) free modification of software by making the source code available
   (c) an opposition to locking software in licences that required to be bought
   (d) all of the above
3. Outcomes of the implementation of information systems in organisations are
   (a) largely positive
   (b) largely negative
   (c) positive or negative, depending on how the organisation adapts to the new system
   (d) negative in the short term and positive in the long run

4. Remaining on the network, requires the organisation to
   (a) sense the flow of information on the network
   (b) respond to the flow of information on the network
   (c) both sense and respond to the flow of information on the network
   (d) do nothing more, once added on to the network
5. IT is understood as artifacts while Information Systems (IS) is
   (a) the collection of all IT artefacts in the entire organisation
   (b) the manner in which IT artefacts in an organisation are used by its people
   (c) the collection of all IT artefacts used by various functions in an organisation, within the organisation
   (d) the collection of all IT artefacts used by various functions in an organisation, to respond to information on its network
6. One of the most popular forms of data exchange on the Internet is
   (a) chat
   (b) email
   (c) social networking
   (d) videos
7. Managing information systems in organisations is a challenge because
   (a) the organisation needs to respond to change in their business and economic environments
   (b) the organisation needs to respond to rapid changes in information systems
   (c) the organisation itself changes as employees gain more experience with the work environment
   (d) all of the above
8. Whether an information system implemented for an organisation is successful depends upon
   (a) the culture and the competitive environment of the organisation
   (b) the competitive environment and the competitive strategy of the organisation
   (c) the culture, the competitive environment and the competitive strategy of the organisation
   (d) the culture, the competitive environment, the competitive strategy and the structure of the organisation
9. Budgeting for an information system can be arrived at by
   (a) seeing how much competitors spend on similar systems and considering the strategic importance of the system
   (b) looking at best-in-class products that meet the requirements of the organisation
   (c) gauging the future income the system will provide after implementation and computing a return on investment.
   (d) all the above means
10. Knowledge workers differ from blue-collar workers
   (a) in that their responsibilities involve accessing and dealing with knowledge
   (b) in that their responsibilities involve repetitive labour related to production
   (c) in that their responsibilities involve decisions regarding the generation of revenues for the organisation
   (d) only marginally, as the two terms are often used interchangeably
11. ENIAC differed from earlier computers
   (a) because it was built entirely of electronic components
   (b) because it was general purpose in nature
   (c) because it was built in a university
   (d) because it was the first commercial computer to be built

Chapter 2 IT and Innovation

A. Complete the Following

1. Moore's law predicted that the number of ________ packed into integrated circuits would _______ almost every two years.
2. The consequence of Moore's law is a tremendous growth in the _______ and _________ of the basic computing hardware that drives innovation.
3. ____________________ means business creators strive to constantly innovate and bring forth new products and services that eventually crush existing products and services.
4. In Rogers' model, ________________ influence the thinking of their peers and are important for ideas to spread.
5. Innovation researchers describe the first appearance of an idea as that of _________ the ________.

B. State True or False

1. One implication of Moore's Law is that though the processing power of chips increased significantly, their costs also increased.
2. Digital cameras are an example of disruptive innovation as they replaced film cameras.
3. According to Rogers, innovators influence the thinking of their peers and are important for the ideas to spread.
4. After 1995, firms that invested heavily in enterprise systems and other systems, gained market share in comparison to others.
5. With the rise of digital innovation and increased competition, prices of goods and services have risen.

C. Choose the Right Option from the List

1. Moore's law predicted that the number of transistors packed into electronic circuits would
   (a) double every two years
   (b) halve every two years
   (c) double every four years
   (d) halve every four years
2. One implication of Moore's law is that with more transistors on the chips
   (a) the chips can achieve higher speeds at lower temperatures
   (b) the chips can accomplish more specialised tasks
   (c) the cost of the chips increased significantly
   (d) the chips became nearly impossible to produce
3. Creative destruction means
   (a) destruction of ideas is necessary for business
   (b) creative people destroy the older ways of doing business
   (c) older businesses and models destroy new and uncompetitive products
   (d) new products and business models destroy older businesses
4. Rogers' model of diffusion of innovation is based on
   (a) the communication of money within populations
   (b) the spread of email within populations
   (c) the communication of ideas within populations
   (d) the spread of digital media within populations
5. Early adopters of a technology or innovation
   (a) are usually risk takers and may or may not be financially secure
   (b) are usually financially secure, have social influence and carefully assess the innovation
   (c) are usually conservative in their thinking and may not have much social influence
   (d) are usually socially conservative and may have low finances
6. One tendency of firms that are high IT users is that
   (a) they have high turbulence in their rankings with regard to market share
   (b) they have low turbulence in their rankings with regard to market share
   (c) they have no turbulence in their rankings with regard to market share
   (d) they have high resistance to their rankings with regard to market share
7. Winner-take-all markets refer to firms that
   (a) win all the games with regard to IT and markets
   (b) win all the IT market share from their competitors
   (c) give winners preference for IT products in the market
   (d) gain tremendous market share from their rivals owing to their use of IT
8. Innovations can cause a ripple, by articulating an organising vision, which is
   (a) a universal norm of the innovators
   (b) a focal idea for the community
   (c) a contractual obligation for the innovators
   (d) a binding idea for the community
9. Plug-n-play innovations in digital products refer to
   (a) IT products that are plugged into mobile devices
   (b) games that can be played over innovative devices
   (c) adding or providing a product or service over the platform
   (d) innovations that can be played without plugging into platforms

10. With the increase in competition in digital products
    (a) there is an increase in the prices of goods and services
    (b) there is no change in the prices of goods and services
    (c) prices of goods and services fluctuate widely
    (d) there is a downward pressure on prices of goods and services

Chapter 3 Concepts of Management Information Systems

A. Complete the Following

1. ____________ and __________ are the key resources that have to be managed by organisations.
2. Examples of various kinds of memories used are ____________, __________________ and ___________.
3. Modern information systems are designed to support either ____________, ____________ or enterprise ____________.
4. Asynchronous communication between two parties is marked by the presence of a ______ in communication, which does not allow __________ communication between the two.
5. ____________ decisions made by the top managers of an organisation, relate to the vision and _________ of the organisation, has long-term scope and impact the nature of work the organisation does.
6. Radio receivers are examples of __________ devices.

B. State True or False

1. All major functions in an organisation collect data and create information resources that are used across the organisation.
2. Information can be treated as raw data if used for further processing.
3. Nowadays, organisations commonly have total storage capacities of many gigabytes.
4. The workers of an organisation have to decide on how to go about their work and such decisions are termed operational decisions.
5. Only the raw data collected by the organisation is stored in the internal storage of organisations called databases, while the information processed from raw data are not stored, but processed when required.
6. High levels of connectivity leads to an overload of communication information, which is a challenge faced by modern organisations.

C. Choose the Right Option from the List

1. Memory storage is referred to by
    (a) 8-bit byte units
    (b) 16-bit byte units
    (c) 32-bit byte units
    (d) 64-bit byte units
2. Duplex communication can be achieved through the use of
    (a) radio transmitters
    (b) email
    (c) radio receivers
    (d) phone networks
3. Duplex communications happen when persons can communicate with each other
    (a) both ways at the same time
    (b) both ways but not simultaneously
    (c) only in one direction
    (d) none of the above.
4. Operational decisions are decisions
    (a) made by managers based on aggregate data
    (b) observed to have a medium-term scope
    (c) often supported by decision support systems
    (d) all of the above
5. A phone conversation between two people is an example of
    (a) asynchronous, duplex communication
    (b) synchronous, simplex communication

(c) synchronous, half-duplex communication
(d) synchronous, duplex communication

6. The three types of Information technology in organisations are
(a) enterprise, network and functional information technology
(b) databases, operating systems and high-level applications
(c) transaction processing systems, executive decision-support systems and MIS.
(d) none of the above

7. Decision making is supported by communication networks as it aids
(a) data collection
(b) data and information collection
(c) dissemination of information
(d) all of the above

8. Executive support systems are MIS
(a) used by the highest level of the organisation
(b) that provide aggregated information of various activities of the organisation
(c) that provide details of the industry at large
(d) all of the above

9. Batch processing involves
(a) processing of data much after the transaction has completed
(b) processing of data as the transaction is happening
(c) both (a) and (b).
(d) processing of data as the transaction is happening, but from a batch storage

10. Transaction processing systems are also called online systems because
(a) they record all transactions as they happen in real time
(b) they record all activities of various lines and functions in an organisation
(c) they record and aggregate activities to report them online
(d) they record only online transactions of an organisation

11. Archiving involves
(a) storing large quantities of data in as-is format
(b) storing large quantities of data in compressed format, while reducing size but still preserving the content.
(c) storing raw data only, in compressed format
(d) storing raw data only

Chapter 4 IT Strategy and Digital Goods

A. Complete the Following

1. Firms choose partnerships as against keeping a function doing the same thing, within their own organisation, only when they incur lower _______ costs.
2. __________________ refers to a specific skill or set of skills which an organisation possesses, for making a product or doing business in a unique manner.
3. As more people in a group start using the same technology, network externalities result in benefits to the people using it, which is felt as an increase in the ________ of using that technology while the _____ of using it still remains the same.
4. A combination of _____________ and ______________ gives rise to tippy markets, where eventually only one product survives the competition.
5. In Porter's value chain model, __________ activities directly add value to the organisation's product while the _________ activities assist such activities.

B. State True or False

1. For modern businesses, transaction costs are not affected by the use of information systems.
2. Information systems, through the use of highly specialised systems, assist with creating barriers to entry of competition by linking firms closely, allowing partnerships to be created.
3. Substitutes are products that are very similar to the original, which serve the same function and hence can act as replacements.

4. Information technology cannot create businesses that did not exist before.
5. Information goods lend themselves to versioning easily.

C. Choose the Right option from the List

1. Firms generally partner to lower transaction costs, with
   (a) vendors only
   (b) utility firms and vendors only
   (c) banks, utility firms and vendors
   (d) banks, service providers, utility firms and parts vendors
2. In a competitive business environment, the firm is in a strong competitive position if
   (a) the firm depends solely on one supplier
   (b) the firm keeps switching between suppliers frequently
   (c) the firm depends on more than one supplier
   (d) none of the above.
3. Information systems reduce the bargaining power of buyers
   (a) because they reduce costs
   (b) by keeping out competition
   (c) by providing faster and more efficient service and exclusive online channels to buy from
   (d) all of the above
4. Information technology
   (a) can create and sustain substitute products
   (b) can create businesses that did not exist before
   (c) can create and sustain substitute markets
   (d) all of the above
5. Enterprise resource planning and production planning systems are very popular with manufacturing and services organisations because they
   (a) focus on primary activities
   (b) focus on support activities
   (c) focus on primary activities and support activities
   (d) assist inbound logistics
6. ________ help overcome technology lock-in
   (a) Transaction costs
   (b) Licencing costs
   (c) Switching costs
   (d) Exchange costs
7. Information goods are __________ to produce, very _______ to reproduce.
   (a) cheap, expensive
   (b) cheap, cheap
   (c) expensive, cheap
   (d) expensive, expensive
8. Firms that compete on differentiation adopt the stance of
   (a) low cost, limited quality
   (b) low cost, high volume sales
   (c) high costs, high quality
   (d) high costs, limited quality
9. Industry regulations can aid businesses to thrive through
   (a) friendly taxation policies and strict security and controls
   (b) facilitation of easy procurement and movement of goods, services, products and personnel
   (c) facilitation of use of specific resources that are critical to business
   (d) all of the above
10. In a highly competitive environment, barriers to entry of new players can be set up through the use of
   (a) patents
   (b) strong partnerships
   (c) specialised information systems
   (d) any of the above

Chapter 5 Electronic Commerce, Electronic Business, Electronic Governance

A. Complete the Following

1. During the Dotcom boom, one common theme running through startups was the belief in _______________.
2. One of the earliest protocols that was used for the purpose of sending emails across computers on a network was called ________.
3. Some email groups are ____________ which means the content is controlled and what is broadcast is __________ by someone.
4. The ___________ is a collection of networks connected together by common, shared standards of communication.
5. ________________________ is used to allow organisations to create a private network across the public Internet.
6. A _____________ is a single site that contains links to and information about other sites.

B. State True or False

1. An important property of email communication, which allows a message to be directed at an identified individual, is used even now to verify the identity of individuals.
2. Spam is unsolicited mail sent out by persons known to the recipient.
3. A 'click-and-mortar' e-commerce firm offers customers choices of buying online as well as physically from a book store.
4. The motivations for using e-governance are the same for both developed and developing countries.
5. Auction sites are not affected by network effects.

C. Choose the Right Option from the List

1. The main economic benefit of e-business is
   (a) convenience.
   (b) reduced transaction costs
   (c) ease of communication
   (d) it provides faster access
2. Setting up supply chains helps organisations
   (a) reduce the risk of doing their business
   (b) improve quality
   (c) provide better prices
   (d) all of the above
3. E-governance ________________ transaction costs for governments
   (a) reduces
   (b) increases
   (c) reduces or increases (depending on the nature and scale of the systems used)
   (d) does not largely impact
4. Aggregators allow _________________ to transact over the Internet.
   (a) end consumers and businesses
   (b) institutional buyers and sellers
   (c) governments and citizens
   (d) governments and businesses
5. The main challenge facing search engines is in understanding the context of pages and categorising them properly, which Google achieved by
   (a) looking at word counts for assigning weights
   (b) looking at links to a page as a measure of its worth
   (c) looking at the number of visitors to the page
   (d) looking at the number of recent hits the page has had
6. Examples of online payment services are
   (a) paypal and net banking
   (b) paypal, credit cards, net banking
   (c) paypal, cash cards, credit cards and net banking
   (d) paypal and e-vouchers

7. Electronic Data Interchange (EDI) standards allow organisations to link their offices together or to co-operate with other firms, often through proprietary standards
   (a) similar to the Internet
   (b) different from the Internet.
   (c) built on top of the Internet
   (d) none of the above
8. Examples of websites that allow buyers and sellers to meet over the Internet are
   (a) auctions only
   (b) search engines
   (c) auctions and aggregators
   (d) aggregators only
9. Hyperlinks are used to link
   (a) words and phrases only within a file
   (b) words and phrases within a file to another, but on the same computer
   (c) words and phrases within a file to those, anywhere else, including different computers on the Internet
   (d) one page to another on the same network
10. For the government, the use of electronic networks
    (a) helps reach out to thousands of citizens with reduced transaction costs
    (b) means reduced costs of physical infrastructure such as buildings, offices and personnel
    (c) has the potential to reduce errors committed during processing
    (d) has no benefits other than providing citizens with faster and easier access to information
11. B2B differs from B2C
    (a) in the nature and value of transactions involved, in that, B2C transactions are ad hoc, with one seller selling to customers in a single transaction of relatively low value compared to B2C, where transactions involve many buyers and many sellers who establish long-term contracts
    (b) as opposed to B2C, B2B markets do not have fixed prices and may involve auctions of goods
    (c) B2B delivery schedules and timings of goods purchased tie into supply chains of businesses and hence involve a high degree of commitment in terms of delivery
    (d) on all the above counts

Chapter 6 Managing Information Systems

A. Complete the Following

1. Data __________ is a key issue in centralised IT management; __________ and the ability to__________ are the key characteristics of decentralisation.
2. When an organisation has varied IT needs across departments and works with various fast-changing technologies that require differing levels of customisation, the _________ model is the preferred choice.
3. ______________________ is a numerical measure of the financial value of an investment.
4. Large vendors often work with ___________ IT management while small vendors prefer to deal with ______________ IT management.
5. A stark contrast is visible between the top performing firms and all the firms in the archetypes employed in the way __________ and ___________ are decided.

B. State True or False

1. Centralised IT management is always preferred over decentralisation as it is more economical in the long run.
2. In modern organisations, the threat to IT infrastructure from harmful software and internal security violations is insignificant.
3. There is a stark contrast between the best performing firms and the ones that do not perform as well, in terms of their IT governance.
4. Authentication addresses both external and internal threats to an organisation's security.
5. Managers can introduce IT to orchestrate organisational change like when they deliberately use IT to control departments in a strongly decentralised management culture.

C. Choose the Right Option from the List

1. Many government departments in India that have added IT to complement their processes have already realised
   (a) first-order effects
   (b) first- and second-order effects
   (c) first-, second- and third-order effects
   (d) none of the above effects yet
2. Employee participation in technology assessment and design is
   (a) possible more easily in centralised IT Management
   (b) possible more easily in decentralised IT Management
   (c) unaffected by the IT management model chosen
   (d) none of the above
3. High security in an organisation
   (a) slows down processes
   (b) leads to loss of privacy
   (c) entails cumbersome procedures
   (d) all of the above
4. The IT governance archetype marked by the pre-dominance of the head of the IT function in decision-making is called
   (a) the Feudal archetype
   (b) the Federal archetype
   (c) the IT Monarchy archetype
   (d) the IT Duopoly archetype
5. With centralised IT, procurement of IT benefits from
   (a) scale and standardisation
   (b) reduced prices
   (c) better support and inventory management
   (d) all of the above
6. Computing ROI for IT is difficult because
   (a) IT by itself does not contribute to revenue generation of non-IT businesses
   (b) IT effects improvements in organisational processes, which can in turn be hard to measure
   (c) it involves devising measures of productivity gains
   (d) all of the above
7. The CIO's responsibilities include
   (a) management of the IT infrastructure of the organisation
   (b) alignment of the IT infrastructure with the organisational goals
   (c) computing ROI on non-IT investments
   (d) both (a) and (b)
8. The information systems (IS) plan of an organisation is a document specifying at a high level how IT will support the organisational activities and is created by
   (a) the CIO of the organisation
   (b) jointly by the various business heads of the divisions of the organisation
   (c) the CEO of the organisation
   (d) the COO of the organisation
9. An industry best practice when examining bids from vendors
   (a) is to rule out vendors who do not meet technical criteria even though they have attractive commercial terms
   (b) is to look primarily at the commercial bid with the lowest bid
   (c) is to look at the bids of the vendors with highest rating
   (d) is to look at vendors with referrals from peers only
10. Service levels specified with vendors, for various types of technologies are often specified in terms of percentages of
    (a) turnaround time
    (b) downtime
    (c) uptime
    (d) transaction time

Chapter 7 Ethical and Social Issues

A. Complete the Following

1. From ___________ perspective, workplace monitoring improves productivity and morale of the workers, by ensuring there is no _______________ and by spotting ______________ for prompt rewards.
2. ______ are publicly accepted rules of behaviour and are determined by loose codes which _______ sharply encoded in texts, in sharp contrast to __________ issues.
3. ______________, _______________________ and _____________________ are examples of data and information relating to individuals that are collected by organisations, which could be of a sensitive nature.
4. Electronic monitoring is considered by experts, as a modern day equivalent of _____________, a much-debated 19th century concept.
5. Managements concerns of __________ are often over-ridden by the concern for ____________, hence justifying workplace monitoring.
6. ____________ creates an atmosphere of isolation and disorientation for workers in a workplace.

B. State True or False

1. Collection of personal data by Government departments and provision of unique identities for all citizens by the Government, do not challenge any of the rights of the citizens.
2. Workplace monitoring has only recently become a contentious issue because of the reach and ease of use of digital technologies.
3. Responsibility and authority structures in the organization are shaped by information systems.
4. Information systems have reduced paperwork for most offices.
5. De-skilling, as a result of computerisation, has minor, short-term impact on productivity.
6. E-waste is not a major problem in developing countries.

C. Choose the Right Option from the List

1. As the JSPL Case Study points out, workplace monitoring through video surveillance cameras, helps the organization
   (a) track unknown persons, reduce theft and damage, improving security
   (b) remotely monitor project progress, saving costs
   (c) remotely monitor project personnel, improving productivity
   (d) achieve all the above, going from a tactical solution to become a strategic management tool
2. The Right to Information law though strengthening democratic processes, tends to infringe on what rights of individuals?
   (a) Privacy Rights
   (b) Right to Education
   (c) Right to Freedom
   (d) Right to Equality
3. Ethics are moral rules and codes that individuals in a society follow, which are
   (a) derived by religion and community ethos
   (b) publicly accepted widely, forming loose codes and guidelines
   (c) both (a) and (b)
   (d) determined by an explicit set of laws
4. With pervasive use of information systems in organisations, the scale and precision of monitoring for certain tasks like 'back-office' tasks has
   (a) increased considerably
   (b) decreased considerably
   (c) remained the same
   (d) decreased marginally
5. Which of these are possible ways of electronic monitoring in organisations?
   (a) Use of access cards
   (b) Incoming and outgoing emails
   (c) Inactivity records on system logs
   (d) All the above
6. In modern organisations, the role of information systems professionals
   (a) has increased in importance owing to a heavy dependence on information systems
   (b) has increased due to the power they exercise over other users

(c) both (a) and (b)
(d) is not more important than other functions

7. To have the best possible situation for organisational decision making, full awareness of any exercise of power by systems professionals
   (a) is neither necessary for the systems users nor is it required of systems professionals
   (b) is required of systems professionals, so that they can guide the organisation towards better solutions
   (c) is required of systems users, so that they can ensure that sub-optimal solutions are not implemented by the organisation
   (d) is required of both systems users and systems professionals to ensure negotiations for mutually-acceptable solutions
8. For many commercial organisations, workplace monitoring is
   (a) a competitive necessity
   (b) a security imperative
   (c) a strategic management tool
   (d) all of the above
9. Alienation in the workplace results from
   (a) reduced social interaction among employees, due to computing, networks and social networks
   (b) de-skilling of employees
   (c) both (a) and (b)
   (d) neither (a) nor (b)
10. Telecommuting has many advantages and the following drawbacks:
   (a) employee alienation
   (b) security challenge
   (c) need for the employee to work longer to avoid being seen as 'slacking off'
   (d) all the above

Chapter 8 Managing Green IT and Smart Cities

A. Complete the Following

1. Industrial activity increases production of ______________ that cause global warming.
2. The measure of the carbon footprint is in _______ of _______ emissions per year.
3. Green IT refers to efficient and green _____ of IT and relying on IT for ensuring green _____.
4. One key role of IT is that of monitoring, measuring and managing ____________________ activities within the organisation.
5. Smart cities refers to regions that have invested heavily in ____ infrastructure to facilitate the management of the region for business and for ______ of life.

B. State True or False

1. IT does not contribute to carbon dioxide emissions around the globe.
2. Production of Green House Gases (GHGs) and global warming are related.
3. Manufacturing of IT components does not contribute as much to carbon emissions as its use does.
4. Since software design and use are based on hardware, they have no consequences for GHG emissions.
5. The concept of smart cities involves use of IT for sustainable environments and quality of life.

C. Choose the Right Option from the List

1. Green IT emphasizes two objectives for use of IT:
   (a) increased energy use with IT, but control of IT in other firm activities
   (b) control of energy use with IT, and control of IT costs in firms
   (c) reduced energy use for IT and use of IT to monitor other firm activities
   (d) increased control over costs in the firm, and competitive advantage
2. The concept of context-aware design implies
   (a) the context of the system is aware of the design
   (b) hardware sense and respond to local surroundings
   (c) the software is based on the context of the design
   (d) the hardware is designed to replicate the context

3. One way for users to reduce power consumption in hardware devices is to
   (a) increase hard disk usage
   (b) decrease reliance on the internet
   (c) obtain battery backup for the hardware
   (d) turn off or reduce brightness of monitors
4. Organisations are interested in adopting green IT practices to
   (a) reduce costs of operations, abide by laws and protect their reputation
   (b) ensure compliance with existing laws and green taxes
   (c) improve the quality of their products and services
   (d) improve their ability to compete in the market
5. A common aspect of the definitions of smart cities in India and Europe is
   (a) the emphasis on urbanisation and regional growth
   (b) the use of power saving methods to reduce energy costs
   (c) the reliance on political will and citizen motivation
   (d) the use of ICT for improving the quality of life of its citizens
6. Methods of monitoring traffic on roads include
   (a) police personnel with mobile cameras and reading devices
   (b) analysis of images from cameras and sensing of mobile phone usage in cell towers
   (c) analysis of traffic violation patterns
   (d) review of traffic density data obtained from pollution monitoring
7. Sensors in water pipes gauge the pressure of water to
   (a) ensure the pressure remains constant, to improve flows
   (b) ensure the pressure remains high, to reduce pollution
   (c) ensure the pressure is maintained at a lower level, to reduce leakages
   (d) ensure the pressure is maintained at a high level, to improve flows
8. Smart buildings use IT to
   (a) sense, monitor and control all energy consuming devices and services
   (b) ensure parking lots are available for the residents
   (c) sense the pressure and temperature in the water pipes
   (d) maintain a constant temperature in the building
9. Smart governance requires
   (a) educated and smart functionaries who can use IT effectively
   (b) collection of data from citizens and traffic
   (c) use of data to analyse patterns of citizen behaviour
   (d) collection of data for government functions from distributed and decentralised sources
10. Two key management concerns for building smart infrastructure are
   (a) ensuring the competition is not aware of the design
   (b) maintaining a database on consumers and competitors
   (c) maintaining privacy of individuals and the potential of surveillance
   (d) reducing costs of services and retaining employees

Chapter 9 Information Technology Infrastructure and Choices

A. Complete the Following

1. The IT __________ of an organisation is a technical design of the computing ecosystem of the organisation, consisting of hardware, software and networks that form the IT __________ of the organisation, where the latter is determined by the business and work needs of the organisation.
2. Software that is distributed only in the compiled, binary version is called ________ software, whereas software that is distributed with the source code is called __________ software.
3. A _______ is a software that is used extensively to manage a device.
4. ______________ chips have a large number of circuits to do different kinds of tasks, while ______________ chips have a smaller set of instructions.
5. Games and entertainment software rely on ______________ graphics hardware and software, which can render the complex images adequately on screen.

B. State True or False

1. There are few known viruses that infect Linux, and its protection levels have ensured that it is secure as a server.
2. Strong passwords improve security as they are relatively more difficult to crack.
3. Database applications are easily interchangeable and do not create a lock-in.
4. Open source software options are limited and not widely available for all kinds of applications.
5. Cloud computing does not impose restrictions on the type of operating system used or the type of computer used, as it is Internet-based.

C. Choose the Right Option from the List

1. Laptops typically have smaller renewal cycles as they are
   (a) more prone to physical shocks and mechanical wear
   (b) cannot be easily upgraded due to tight packing of components
   (c) cannot be easily interchanged or replaced
   (d) all of the above
2. Compact discs are used in applications where there is a need to
   (a) write data many times, and read many times
   (b) write data many times, and read once
   (c) write data once, and read once
   (d) write data once, and read many times
3. Almost all peripheral devices are now connected via the _________, which is now an industry standard.
   (a) MULTIBUS I
   (b) MULTIBUS II
   (c) SCSI Bus
   (d) Universal Serial Bus
4. Orphan products are technologies
   (a) that do not evolve further as the manufacturer does not provide a road map for the product
   (b) that typically force an organisation adopting it to support it themselves or abandon it for alternatives
   (c) both (a) and (b)
   (d) that are open source technologies, as the source code is available for all to use and modify
5. IT products are subject to ______________ obsolescence cycles.
   (a) rapid
   (b) long term
   (c) slow
   (d) seasonal
6. Before selecting cloud applications, organisations have to ensure
   (a) adequate connections to the Internet that is both reliable and of sufficient capacity
   (b) to protect their data from leaks by drawing up a security contract with the service provider
   (c) the cloud service provider can scale up easily to meet their growing business needs
   (d) all of the above
7. Virtualisation allows
   (a) many different servers to be consolidated into a single virtual server
   (b) easy sharing of resources like hard disk space, RAM, network connectivity, printers and other peripheral devices
   (c) better and more efficient utilisation of servers
   (d) all of the above
8. Embedded software is
   (a) used for special-purpose chips, which have limited instruction sets and small footprints
   (b) written in high-level languages and then compiled specially for the chip
   (c) resident on the chip in special memory modules
   (d) all of the above
9. Some of the issues related to the use of secondary storage are
   (a) security
   (b) scalability
   (c) disaster recovery
   (d) all of the above

10. Examples of some popular open source software are
    (a) Windows OS, Linux, OpenOffice
    (b) Oracle database, mySQL, Linux
    (c) Linux, Open Office, SAP ERP
    (d) Linux, Solaris, mySQL

Chapter 10 Cloud Computing and Internet-of-Things

A. Complete the Following

1. Cloud computing enables access to _______ facilities and infrastructure over the ______.
2. The main economic motivation to adopt the cloud computing is to shift from ________ expenses of purchasing IT assets to ______ expenses of renting services.
3. The Infrastructure-as-a-Service model of the cloud is based on providing ___________ facilities to clients over the internet.
4. The Platform-as-a-Service (PaaS) model builds on and extends the IaaS model, where special _____ is included over and above the infrastructure.
5. The Internet-of-Things (IoT) consists of a large number of ______ that are connected via the _______ to sense and respond to conditions in their environments.

B. State True or False

1. An organisation that employs cloud services has to maintain its own servers.
2. Scalability of IT infrastructure refers to the ability to address the needs of increase demand.
3. The main advantage of using a private cloud is that of security.
4. In the SaaS model of cloud service offering the users can install their own software.
5. The challenge of managing IoT systems is that of managing the massive volume, variety and flows of data.

C. Choose the Right Option from the List

1. Elasticity in the cloud model of services refers to
   (a) the ability to increase or decrease quality of computing services
   (b) the ability to expand the reach of computing services
   (c) the ability to expand and collapse services, based on demand
   (d) the ability to reduce the costs associated with services
2. A community cloud is
   (a) a facility, like a social network, that has diverse users
   (b) a shared cloud facility, whose users have common needs
   (c) a facility that is located in a community building
   (d) a facility that is maintained by the community, but used privately
3. In the Infrastructure-as-a-Service (IaaS) model of cloud service
   (a) the responsibility of maintaining the infrastructure is with the cloud provider
   (b) the responsibility of maintaining the infrastructure is with the user
   (c) the responsibility of maintaining the infrastructure is with the community
   (d) the responsibility of maintaining the infrastructure is with the government
4. The most widely used type of cloud service is
   (a) IaaS
   (b) PaaS
   (c) SpaaS
   (d) SaaS
5. Using the cloud makes most sense when
   (a) users have to be secured against virus attacks
   (b) applications have to be scaled quickly
   (c) governments have to protect privacy of citizens
   (d) smart cities have to provide security services
6. In Software Defined Networking
   (a) the data is moved to the cloud by the software
   (b) the definition of the control plane and the data plane are transparent

(c) the role and paths of routing are maintained on a private cloud
(d) the control plane decides on the routing and the data plane does the routing

7. Cloud computing shifts the spending required for creating and expanding IT infrastructure
(a) from low to high
(b) from high to low
(c) from capital expenses to operating expenses
(d) from operating expenses to capital expenses

8. The Internet-of-Things consists of four elements
(a) devices, data, the internet and software
(b) cloud, services, contracts and regulations
(c) investments, labour, services and capital
(d) devices, labour, metering and quality

9. The difference between IoT sensors and actuators is
(a) sensors are more expensive than actuators
(b) sensors detect events and changes and actuators cause change of state
(c) sensors sense the data and actuators convert data into states
(d) sensors collect data whereas actuators analyse the data

10. A basic architecture for managing IoT devices
(a) consists of two layers - applications and operations
(b) consists of two layers - hardware and software
(c) consists of four layers - devices, networks, management and applications layers
(d) consists of three layers - IaaS, PaaS and SaaS

Chapter 11 Networking and Telecommunication

A. Complete the Following

1. The Internet is a collection of protocols that enable various ___________.
2. ___________ services are faster than ________________ ones, but they are also less reliable.
3. Internet service providers closest to user organisations are called ______ service providers.
4. ___________ are computers on the network that host data or applications that can be shared by others.
5. Wireless devices are also called ___________.

B. State True or False

1. The layered nature of the protocols of the Internet and their relative independence allows for immense innovation in the services and protocols.
2. DHCP is more secure than static addresses since no particular IP address is tied to a computer making it a target of attacks.
3. Packets headed to the same address follow the same path through the Internet.
4. When an organisation arranges to buy an Internet service or bandwidth from an external provider, the router is the device to which the external provider will fix the Internet cables.
5. The protocol for web browsing, the Hypertext transfer protocol (HTTP) uses the port 25.

C. Choose the Right Option from the List

1. Problems plaguing rural network operators are
(a) low economic viability of setting up broadband Internet networks
(b) erratic supply of electricity and lack of access to trained personnel
(c) relatively small user base spread over remote areas
(d) all of the above

2. The last mile problem in providing Internet connectivity is solved
(a) through the use of telephone lines and dial-up and broadband DSL connections
(b) through the use of television cables and cable modems
(c) through radio waves using WiMax technology
(d) all of the above

3. Firewalls, like Proxies, act as filters for packets
(a) to filter out any traffic that is not of the right type
(b) to check for addresses that are permitted

(c) to effectively monitor all traffic
(d) all of the above

4. Proxies regulate
(a) packets going from the organisation to the outside
(b) packets coming into and going out of the organisation's network
(c) the speed of the packets going through them
(d) the size of the packets going through them

5. TCP's elaborate routines for handshaking and establishing connections
(a) makes it the most widely used protocol on the Internet
(b) uses strict, regulated procedures for data transfer ensuring transfer of complete information in the desired order
(c) also make it vulnerable for misuse in the form of DOS attacks
(d) all of the above

6. The TCP protocol along with IP protocol together constitutes TCP/IP, an Internet standard, where
(a) the former is connection-less while the latter is connection-oriented
(b) both protocols are connection-less
(c) both protocols are connection-oriented
(d) the former is connection-oriented while the latter is connectionless

7. The difference between hubs and switches is that when packets are sent to switches they are
(a) redirected to all the other ports, including the ones they are not intended for
(b) redirected only to the port for which they are designated
(c) handled similar to their handling by hubs, because hubs and switches are the same
(d) always sent out of the network

8. __________ protocol is used to transmit packets from sender to receiver in a fast, but unreliable manner, especially by multimedia applications
(a) TCP
(b) NAT
(c) TCP/IP
(d) UDP

9. World-wide IP addressing scheme is maintained by
(a) the United Nations Council for Internet Addresses (UNCIA)
(b) by a council of representatives from each country's nodal agencies
(c) ICANN located in the US, which runs the Internet Corporation for Assigned Names and Numbers (IANA)
(d) by the Defence department of the US.

10. Translation of Internet addresses (host names) into IP addresses is done by the __________.
(a) Network Address Translation Protocol
(b) Dynamic Host Control Protocol
(c) Domain Name Server Protocol
(d) Router Information Protocol

Chapter 12 Information Systems Security and Control

A. Complete the Following

1. A __________ is an autonomous software that finds security loopholes to penetrate computers and networks.
2. In public key encryption, ____________ is required to ensure that the keys are secure and obtained from a reliable source and also to ensure that no one can else impersonate the sender. The latter is achieved through the use of __________.
3. Malicious external software that pose a threat to the security of organisations are called __________, __________, ____________ and __________ are common and widely prevalent forms of such threats.
4. Cracking exploits either __________ or __________ weakness in the security of systems.
5. __________ firewalls can be used to protect home computers connected to the Internet through fixed IP addresses so that they are not captured to be used as zombies for DoS attacks.

B. State True or False

1. The need to send across the key is the weakness of symmetric key cryptography.
2. Countries like India and the UAE have threatened to disallow BlackBerry services within their boundaries citing security reasons, because the makers of BlackBerry hesitated to accede to their demands to allow access to the data, which is pushed in highly encrypted form through their push email servers in Canada.

3. Of the servers in an organisation, those most prone to attack by crackers are the database servers.
4. An important aspect of a security audit in a firm, other than to ensure compliance towards achieving the firm's security goals is risk assessment, which helps the management decide how much to spend on security infrastructure.
5. People are often the weakest link in the security chain as they do not always follow basic security rules.

C. Choose the Right Option from the List

1. Cracking and hacking, used interchangeably
   (a) refer to the same thing – the act of breaking into computers or networks illegally
   (b) refer to the same thing – the act of ethically breaking into computers or networks to expose weaknesses
   (c) are terms used to refer to the act of breaking into computers or networks; while cracking stems from a noble intent of exposing weaknesses rather than do any harm, hacking stems from a malicious intent to cause mischief or harm and is illegal
   (d) are terms used to refer to the act of breaking into computers or networks; while cracking stems from a malicious intent to cause mischief or harm and is illegal, hacking is used to signify expert or high-level programming which can be ethical, with an intent of exposing weaknesses rather than do any harm
2. To enable a secure IS infrastructure in an organisation, the following have to be ensured
   (a) confidentiality and authenticity
   (b) message integrity
   (c) access and availability
   (d) all of the above
3. __________ is a method of cracking, where crackers identify the kind and type of system that is being used and then uncover its security mechanism.
   (a) Social engineering
   (b) Identity theft
   (c) Phishing
   (d) Reverse engineering
4. The programmers' intent behind cracking is
   (a) mischief to show how clever they are at breaking secure systems
   (b) to steal information, digital resources or money
   (c) industrial and political espionage
   (d) all of the above
5. DoS attacks work
   (a) by stealing cycles from systems
   (b) by stealing identities
   (c) by exploiting the three-step handshake of connection-oriented protocols, where non-receipt of the third-step request keeps the server waiting till it times out
   (d) by all of the above means
6. Public-key cryptography overcomes the weakness of symmetric key cryptography
   (a) by encrypting the key itself
   (b) by having a pair of keys called the public and the private key
   (c) by having a pair of keys called the sender's key and the receiver's key
   (d) none of the above
7. A Virtual Private Network (VPN) is a technology that
   (a) relies on authentication and encryption and enables clients or employees who work outside the organisation's network to connect with the organisation securely
   (b) is a kind of 'tunnel' through which a secure, private connection is possible while using the public Internet
   (c) is a virtual network of home computers that allows setting up of a private network using the public Internet
   (d) both (a) and (b)
8. Radio Frequency Identification (RFID) technology can be used for identifying, tracking and sensing objects and people, but the challenge is
   (a) the signal needs to work within line of sight
   (b) the signal has a limited range (a few metres)
   (c) the signal penetrate through clothing and other accessories or packaging the RFID object may be kept in
   (d) both (b) and (c)
9. A wireless sensor network (WSN) consists of wireless sensors and wireless networking devices and can be used
   (a) for sensing and relaying war zone information
   (b) for monitoring and tracking physical and environmental conditions

(c) in precision agriculture for more effective treatment targeted at specific spots, reducing input costs and increasing crop yield
(d) all of the above

10. Which one of the following is correct?
(a) India is yet to enact a comprehensive IT Act
(b) India enacted the IT Act in 2000 with no amendments to it
(c) India enacted the IT Act in 2000 which was amended as the IT (Amendment) Act or ITAA in 2008
(d) India was among the first few to enact an IT Act in 1999

Chapter 13 Information Systems Development and Project Management

A. Complete the Following

1. ______________ refers to the increase in the requirements of a software module, much after the requirements phase is over.
2. ____________ refers to testing of software that is nearly complete, has all the features and can be conducted under conditions similar to the real environment for which it has been created.
3. ____________ outlines the fundamental propositions of the Agile methods.
4. ____________ and __________ are the alternatives to the waterfall software development life-cycle model.
5. Use cases are a part of the formalised software development methods known as ________________ and ____________.

B. State True or False

1. Function point analysis provides fairly accurate estimates of the size and complexity of an information system to be built, but it cannot account for changes such as project-based specificities like developer skill levels, platform availability, etc.
2. Extreme programming and Scrum are two well-known Agile methods.
3. The flowchart is used to illustrate the logic and flow of an algorithm.
4. A flowchart shows how a program will use data, decisions and processes to complete an activity, whereas a DFD captures the data flows of a system.
5. Agile methods suit all types of firms and projects.

C. Choose the Right Option from the List

1. The waterfall model is characterised by the following drawbacks:
(a) linear and bureaucratic method which ignores feedback
(b) it slows down small projects
(c) cost of identifying and rectifying errors is high
(d) all of the above
2. Rapid prototyping suffers from
(a) wastage of effort in the discarded initial prototype
(b) reduced documentation leads to a maintenance nightmare
(c) detailed or time-consuming analysis and design
(d) only (a) and (b)
3. The Scrum method relies on evolving the requirements for the project based on
(a) the project plan
(b) the basis of work completed
(c) clearly defined requirements
(d) none of the above
4. ____________ in Scrum is a record of backlogs that have been completed.
(a) Metaphor
(b) Gantt chart
(c) Burn down chart.
(d) Project plan
5. The difference between Scrum and Extreme programming lies in the way
(a) requirement changes are handled
(b) teams are composed

   (c) releases are handled
   (d) project prototyping is handled
6. The spiral model is a/an __________ to the waterfall model
   (a) enhancement
   (b) special case
   (c) better model at handling risks as compared
   (d) both (a) and (b)
7. One-time cutover to a new system
   (a) eliminates the old system in one go
   (b) ensures better adoption of new system
   (c) lets users to smoothly transition from the old system to the new one, over a period of time.
   (d) both (a) and (b)
8. CASE tools permit quick creation of software prototypes that are used to
   (a) freeze the requirements
   (b) validate and refine the design
   (c) both (a) and (b)
   (d) none of the above
9. Structured methodology helps document business processes
   (a) in a top-down, step-by-step manner
   (b) relying on many tools to focus on different levels of details
   (c) using many diagrammatic techniques for communication
   (d) all of the above
10. Refactoring, in Extreme programming implies
   (a) requirements factored into the system at the very beginning
   (b) continuous design improvement as the system evolves
   (c) neither (a) nor (b)
   (d) the system is fully integrated only towards the end of the SDLC

Chapter 14 Managing Data Resources

A. Complete the Following

1. A __________ is a data warehouse containing data pertaining to a particular domain.
2. __________ is the process of removing erroneous data from data warehouses.
3. As a form is to entry of data into tables, so is a _______ to read data from tables.
4. __________ is a special data structure to store metadata.
5. A __________ database is one whose tables are maintained on various different servers.

B. State True or False

1. Currently, tables can be normalised upto sixth normal form, based on the context of the application in which it is being used.
2. Normalisation of data reduces redundancy, but leads to inefficient processing.
3. The hierarchical model of organising data involves creating a tree-like structure to hold data, while the object-oriented model relies on structures that are objects.
4. Relational databases are those whose tables are associated through special links called joins.
5. Commercial databases are the most popular generic and specialised DBMS solutions.

C. Choose the Right Option from the List

1. __________ connects distributed databases to different client devices
   (a) Firmware
   (b) Software
   (c) Dataware
   (d) Middleware
2. Serious challenges for modern databases include
   (a) managing concurrency, security and recovery from crashes
   (b) size

(c) distributed access
(d) support for heterogeneous databases

3. Federated databases imply databases across a network that are
(a) the same
(b) heterogeneous
(c) centralised
(d) highly secure

4. __________ are special objects used within DBMS to present data and analysis in an appealing manner
(a) Queries
(b) Reports
(c) Pivots
(d) Forms

5. Personal databases are databases
(a) created by individual users for their personal use in organisations or at home
(b) contain the personal data of every employee of an organisation
(c) are highly tuned to the needs of the user and therefore not meant to be shared
(d) both (a) and (b)

6. The field that contains data that uniquely identifies a record is termed
(a) the primary key
(b) the private key
(c) the public key
(d) the secondary key

7. An E–R diagram essentially consists of
(a) data entities and relationships between them
(b) data entities, relationships between them and attributes that describe the entities and their relationships
(c) data entities and records
(d) data entities, records and tables

8. Attributes that are used to describe entities
(a) are always single valued
(b) are always multi-valued
(c) should have at least one value which must be unique, which constitutes the primary key for the table.
(d) none of the above

9. The order of a relationship between two entities is called
(a) multiplicity
(b) cardinality
(c) weight
(d) depth of the relationship

10. MySQL and PostgreSQL are examples of
(a) proprietary databases
(b) popular open source databases
(c) databases owned by Oracle corporation
(d) none of he above

Chapter 15 Business Process Integration and Enterprise Systems

A. Complete the Following

1. In the 1990s, enterprise systems like ____________, __________ and ____________ gained popularity as they enabled firms to bring together a number of______ systems within one platform.
2. The idea of managing supply chains originated in __________ manufacturing that gained popularity in the late 1980s.
3. ________________ effect refers to small fluctuations in demand at various points of the supply chain resulting in fairly high fluctuations in inventories at the end of the chain.
4. __________ are interfaces at which the marketing establishment of a commercial firm, interfaces with a current or _____ customer, either directly or indirectly.
5. Some special marketing tasks that the CRM system enables are that of_________, __________ and _________.

B. State True or False

1. The Y2K problem was one of the main factors that spurred deployments of enterprise systems.
2. Multinationals are headquartered in many countries and function independently in each country, while transnational companies maintain offices in many countries, while being headquartered in one country.
3. Enterprise systems force organisations to align their processes along industry best practices.
4. Business processes refer not necessarily to processes within the organisation, but to any process that is transformational in nature, taking inputs and producing outputs that are desired by the organisation.
5. The supply chain is also referred to as the logistics chain.
6. The current trend of providing enterprise services through the cloud model has lowered many of the implementation risks as also the costs.

C. Choose the Right Option from the List

1. JIT has the following advantages:
   (a) reduces costs, wastage and need for storage space
   (b) reduces dependence on accurate demand information and automation
   (c) forces forging stronger links with suppliers to reduce uncertainties in supply
   (d) both (a) and (c)
2. Enterprise systems are criticised for
   (a) diluting firms' competitive advantage by embodying industry practices in software, thereby levelling the playing field
   (b) dumbing down the innovation potential of employees
   (c) both (a) and (b). And for rupturing the organisational culture through the changes forced by these systems
   (d) both (b) and (c) only
3. Enterprise systems are popular because they address
   (a) problems of legacy systems with widely varying data formats
   (b) business process re-engineering needs
   (c) both (a) and (b)
   (d) needs to keep costs low and help manage change more easily
4. Outsourcing and off-shoring are decisions useful for an organisation in
   (a) reducing cost
   (b) acquiring expertise
   (c) both (a) and (b)
   (d) only (a)
5. Cross-selling is the act of offering
   (a) higher priced products to buyers and current clients
   (b) several products to a customer with a price discount
   (c) complementary products to buyers
   (d) products across multiple locations
6. A supply chain of an organisation consists of vendors and suppliers who provide ___________ to the organisation.
   (a) raw materials and parts
   (b) raw material and services
   (c) raw material, parts and services
   (d) parts and services
7. In the context of global markets and e-commerce-based marketing, the _______ production is beginning to dominate production.
   (a) supply-push
   (b) supply-pull
   (c) demand-push
   (d) demand-pull
8. The main issues to manage in an ERP implementation are
   (a) change management and customisation
   (b) top management support and cost control
   (c) project management and vendor selection
   (d) all of the above

9. An ERP package consists of
   (a) four fundamental modules (manufacturing, finance and accounting, sales and marketing and human resources) and a centralised database
   (b) modules that may be implemented independently, but with the same core database
   (c) all modules that bring best practices in terms of processes
   (d) all of the above
10. In a supply chain,
   (a) upstream and downstream partners are with reference to client organisation
   (b) tier-1 suppliers are those the organisation deals with directly, while tier-2 suppliers are those whom the tier-1 firm deal with directly
   (c) accuracy of demand information is critical
   (d) all of the above

Chapter 16 Decision Support Systems

A. Complete the Following

1. __________ is a set of graphical displays that show certain parameters in real time.
2. ___________ knowledge refers to knowledge that is codified in text or some tangible manner, while ________ knowledge refers to that which is known to humans in the form of insights and experiences, and that cannot be easily verbalised.
3. ___________ encode human knowledge and reasoning in a set of rules, pertaining to a domain, which can be applied to solve problems in the same domain.
4. __________________ refer to systems used to store and retrieve documents by any group within or outside the organisation.
5. Depending on the kind of data required and the kind of business problem to be solved, business intelligence techniques like _____________, ________________, ________ and ____________ are often used by businesses.

B. State True or False

1. A decision tree is used in a manner similar to neural networks, but only for prediction problems.
2. Clustering techniques are usually used to discover patterns, which may not be confirmed by other techniques.
3. Extreme data points or outliers, in data visualisation, need special attention and are difficult to spot by humans visually, whereas statistical techniques can easily pinpoint them.
4. High-performance expert systems can be modelled with just a set of rules, without the need for human expert models.
5. Declarative knowledge refers to invariant facts or descriptions while procedural knowledge refers to how things are done.

C. Choose the Right Option from the List

1. Mindmaps
   (a) are diagrams that depict a central node or theme around which are arranged through links, related concepts and themes
   (b) can be created and shared by a group
   (c) are maps of the various knowledge management systems in use in an organisation
   (d) both (a) and (b)
2. Knowledge needed by an organisation includes
   (a) knowledge about the external environment – the industry, the competitors, Government regulations, the economy and innovations that can affect the organisation
   (b) knowledge about the internal workings of the organisation
   (c) only (b) since it is the key to efficiency of the organisation as a whole
   (d) both (a) and (b)
3. MIS and DSS differ in that
   (a) MIS are used more regularly, while DSS are used more on an ad hoc basis
   (b) MIS reports are characterised by fixed output and are largely targeted at specific users, used especially by higher management, while DSS find use across the organisation

(c) MIS process data to present various views and summaries to enable managers to get a high-level view as well as deep, penetrating view whereas DSS process data to enable users to arrive at a decision and is largely decision-specific
(d) all of the above

4. The market model of knowledge management does not work well in a fast-changing environment where context changes rapidly because
   (a) the search costs are high
   (b) knowledge degradation is sharp
   (c) effort required to seek and understand the knowledge are high, as the knowledge is not explicitly coded for a context or a situation
   (d) all the above factors
5. The knowledge life cycle progresses through the following stages:
   (a) creation, development and degradation
   (b) creation and degradation
   (c) creation, development, use and reuse
   (d) creation, development, use and degradation
6. The contradiction at the heart of many failed efforts at knowledge management arises because
   (a) much of the competitive advantage enjoyed by employees of an organisation come from their superior knowledge about their work which leads to superior performance vis-a-vis the peers
   (b) sharing knowledge freely among peers dilutes this advantage
   (c) incentives for contribution to knowledge sharing are not comparable to promotion as an incentive
   (d) all the above
7. Bounded rationality
   (a) implies restricting the choices leading to a decision, so that the end result is satisfactory though not necessarily the best or most optimal
   (b) arises partly from the limits on the number of things that people can think about at a time
   (c) helps reach a decision even in complex situations involving many decision parameters and choices
   (d) all of the above
8. Training a neural network implies
   (a) use of a long stream of data in forecasting a number or value for future
   (b) use of past data to help classify an input
   (c) both (a) and (b)
   (d) neither (a) nor (b)
9. __________ analysis is used by firms that have large-scale ongoing transactions, through the use of a dashboard
   (a) Predictive
   (b) Structured
   (c) Unstructured
   (d) Real-time
10. The IDC model by Herbert Simon,
   (a) includes intelligence-design-choice as three essential stages of problem solving
   (b) includes ideation-deliberation-choice as three essential stages of problem solving
   (c) does not hold today
   (d) (a) and alongwith bounded rationality helps complex decision-making

Chapter 17 Artificial Intelligence

A. Complete the Following

1. The Turing test compares the performance of a ________ with that of ______ in a live interaction situation.
2. The basis of _______ and problem solving amongst humans was searching through a ________ of the problem.
3. Two broad categories of search methods are known as ______ and _________ search.
4. For general problem-solving systems ________ about the world, the representations of ______ and preconditions are encoded by humans.
5. The neural networks are __________ representations of ________ in brains and they are widely used to solve machine learning problems.

B. State True or False

1. The Turing test reveals whether a computer can imitate a human.
2. According to Simon and Newell, the Turing test is the basis of all intelligence.
3. Search means finding a path through possible states to find the goal state.
4. Learning in neural networks takes place while data is moved from the input nodes to the output nodes.
5. Decision trees enable drawing conclusions about data whose classification is unknown.

C. Choose the Right Option from the List

1. The Turing test is designed as a competition between
   (a) a computer and another computers
   (b) a human and another human
   (c) a human interrogator and a computer
   (d) a neural network and a computer
2. Problem-solving systems are based on rules about states and actions
   (a) that are coded by neural networks
   (b) that have to be coded by humans
   (c) that are created by machine learning algorithms
   (d) that are often contradictory and unsolvable
3. Backpropagation learning in neural networks (NNs) is based on
   (a) computing the weights of the network by using input data
   (b) computing the outputs of the network by using input data
   (c) comparing the input with the actual output of the network
   (d) comparing the actual output of the network with the target output
4. Deep neural networks are similar to NNs, but
   (a) where the training is not based on backpropagation
   (b) with a larger number of weights required for every node
   (c) with a larger number of layers and nodes in each layer
   (d) where the neurons are deeper and more mathematical
5. Decision trees are used to classify data in trees
   (a) where the leaf nodes show the classes
   (b) where the leaf nodes show the data
   (c) where the root node shows the classes
   (d) where the branch nodes show the data
6. In Bayesian learning new data is used to update
   (a) posterior probabilities about the classification of data
   (b) prior probabilities about the classification of data
   (c) known probabilities about the dependencies in data
   (d) unknown probabilities in the data set
7. The idea behind learning by analogies is that the class of the target example is found by
   (a) comparing with the average of the group
   (b) comparing with close and distant neighbours
   (c) random selection of samples
   (d) comparing with the closest neighbour
8. In genetic algorithms
   (a) a part of a solution is represented by a string of number or alphabets
   (b) an entire solution is represented by a string of numbers or alphabets
   (c) some of the states in the solution are represented by strings
   (d) only the goal state is represented by strings of numbers or alphabets
9. In reinforcement learning, an agent has to learn the best actions to take
   (a) to minimize the reward it receives
   (b) to min-max the reward it receives
   (c) to minimize and then maximize the reward it receives
   (d) to maximize the reward it receives
10. One limitation of machine learning systems is that
    (a) the basis for their computations is not known
    (b) the basis for their conclusions is not known

(c) the manner in which they learn is not known
(d) the manner in which data is input is not known

Chapter 18 ICT for Development and E-Governance

A. Complete the Following

1. __________ is the term used to refer to people using digital means to take part in a democracy, which is distinct from ____________, which refers to the use of electronic services by the government for its own use and __________ which refers to the use of digital technologies to assist in the governance of a state.
2. __________ refers to the difference in access to ICT services between peoples of nations and regions.
3. When government procedures and red tape give rise to bribery to 'speed up' that is termed ____________ corruption, in contrast to __________ corruption which refers to bribes being offered to overcome government procedures, rules or restrictions.
4. ____________, ______________, __________ and _________ are implementation challenges faced by e-governance projects.
5. Community radio is an example of an ICT intervention that is both _________ and ____________ in nature.

B. State True or False

1. When United Nations and World Bank refer to development, it is understood to refer to an improvement in the per capita (per person) income of a community or nation.
2. Countries like USA and Sweden are developed only because of higher levels of ICT penetration.
3. E-participation is very strong in India.
4. E-governance efforts being restricted by government restrictions, their success is based on the successful re-engineering that can be introduced for modification of processes.
5. A standard kiosk portfolio common across an entire region, state or many states is highly feasible.

C. Choose the Right Option from the List

1. Multilateral aid agencies divide the nations of the world into the following categories:
   (a) the first world and the third world
   (b) the developed countries and the developing countries
   (c) the less developing countries (LDCs), the developing countries and the developed countries
   (d) the political North and the political South
2. Transactional systems in developing countries are typically provided through
   (a) kiosks that are usually manned
   (b) websites only
   (c) mobile phones
   (d) mobile offices
3. Amartya Sen, the Nobel-prize winner, development economist argues that development
   (a) must be concerned with an improvement in per capita (per person) income of a community or a nation
   (b) is an end by itself and not a means to an end
   (c) does not concern itself with anything other than an increase in employment opportunities and income generation
   (d) is achieved by expanding certain human freedoms that enable citizens to live their lives in a fruitful and full manner.
4. Stakeholders are those impacted by a system or having an impact on the system, where the impact may be
   (a) through design and implementation
   (b) through use
   (c) through non-use
   (d) through any of the above means
5. Demand-side stakeholders of an e-governance system
   (a) are the direct beneficiaries of the system
   (b) are the project sponsors, project managers and co-ordinators and officials who oversee the initiation, funding and implementation of the system
   (c) are the direct beneficiaries as well as agencies that benefit from the usage of the system
   (d) are all citizens at large

6. E-governance development in nations has been observed to proceed in stages from
   (a) information to transaction
   (b) information to transaction via an interaction stage
   (c) information to one-way interaction to two-way interaction to transaction stage
   (d) information to transaction to political to educational and finally to sustenance stage
7. Systems that provide sustenance for rural populations have to be designed
   (a) such that a single approach works effectively with different segments
   (b) with clear choice of services for different classes, castes and professions of people
   (c) to address the needs of the local community and involve their active participation
   (d) both (b) and (c)
8. A big challenge in the design of e-governance systems arises out of the need to
   (a) customise the services to the local language
   (b) reach out to the non-literate, through the use of appropriate graphics
   (c) be conveniently and closely located to the communities, with access to basic amenities for continuous functioning and easy maintenance
   (d) all of the above
9. Reasons for resistance to e-governance projects are
   (a) fear of unknown technology, job loss or loss of skills
   (b) resistance to change
   (c) a perceived threat to power and prestige, particularly if their power derives from access or control of information
   (d) all of the above
10. Common data standards for e-governance projects
   (a) helps sharing and pooling of data
   (b) helps useful reports to be generated across projects
   (c) allows building complex applications based on the pooled data
   (d) all of the above

Chapter 19 The Society of the Internet

A. Complete the Following

1. __________, __________, ________ and ________ are a few examples of technologies of the Internet.
2. __________ is the most important service on the Internet.
3. _________ is used for classification of web pages by individuals or communities.
4. Sites that join two technologies are called __________.
5. ______________ evolved as a concept after the application initiated by a firm called Napster, which was closed down later following lawsuits filed against it by the music industry.

B. State True or False

1. Google's Page Rank method solved the problem of relevance of a page to a specific search, by relying on the number of other pages linking to it and the weight of the pages that link to it.
2. Most technologies of the Internet are subject to strong positive feedback and network effects.
3. Files can be shared without the use of a central server.
4. Inappropriate settings by users on social networking sites for privacy of their data, can lead to compromise of data security and data abuse.
5. In recent times, posts, videos and images available on the social media have often emerged as the only sources of information from some troubled areas.

C. Choose the Right Option from the List

1. _______ are rapidly becoming an alternative outlet for journalists and citizen reporters alike, where much of interesting and relevant breaking news about events first appear.
   (a) Wikipedia.
   (b) Peer-to-peer networks
   (c) Blogs and social networks
   (d) Email groups

2. The society of the Internet is different from ordinary society in that
   (a) it allows individuals to have multiple identities
   (b) it impacts the privacy of individuals and organisations
   (c) it enables many, even unrelated individuals to work in a transparent and collaborative manner
   (d) all of the above
3. With the advent of the web, ___________ emerged as an easier method for sharing files
   (a) FTP
   (b) TCP/IP
   (c) HTTP
   (d) SNMP
4. File sharing as a service on the Internet _________ the arrival of the World Wide Web
   (a) developed just a little after
   (b) developed at the same time as
   (c) precedes
   (d) developed much later, after
5. In recent times, social media have had a strong role to play in
   (a) mobilising mass support for causes
   (b) organising protests
   (c) citizen reporting
   (d) all of the above
6. Crowdsourcing has been found to work well, where there is need for
   (a) collaboration on simple tasks only
   (b) expert advice
   (c) collaboration, as long as the bigger task can be broken down into smaller chunks, irrespective of complexity
   (d) collaboration within a close-knit community
7. Collaboration on the Internet
   (a) collapses because of chaos that arises from its democratic access
   (b) works well, even in large projects, due to the emergence of an order, from the chaos, to create high-quality products
   (c) collapses because there is not sufficient motivation to collaborate
   (d) works because of patent-based incentives
8. Social media
   (a) has failed to impact traditional media
   (b) is strongly impacting traditional media
   (c) has emerged as a major source of information, particularly from troubled areas
   (d) both (b) and (c)
9. Enabling the rating technology on websites
   (a) explicitly enables feedback
   (b) shortens the feedback loop
   (c) hastens the network externalities effect
   (d) all of the above
10. Identity, in the society of the Internet
   (a) poses a challenge to organisations
   (b) poses a challenge to websites and e-businesses
   (c) poses a challenge to individuals
   (d) all of the above

Chapter 20 Open Source Software

A. Complete the Following

1. Proprietary software firms have engendered a debate around the merits of open source, largely arguing that the software may be free to acquire but its _________________ is higher.
2. A patent is a special protection under the legal framework of most countries, where a patent holder has complete ________ over the idea patented, and anyone who may later want to use a similar or the same idea has to pay _________ to the original patent holder.
3. The ________________ licence is one of the oldest and most used licences in the open source community.

4. Creative Commons Licences allow works of art, such as books, poems, songs, to be released in the public domain for free viewing and consumption with restrictions only on ____________ use and __________.
5. Governments benefit by adopting open source software because of lower ________, reduced outflow of ____________, easy ______________ and the ease of maintaining large amounts of data in ___________, besides curbing ______________.

B. State True or False

1. Open standards do not support or sustain digital commons.
2. In China, one explicit goal for promoting open source was to curb the menace of piracy.
3. GPL allows copyright but prevents patenting of software.
4. MySQL is available with copyright and as a closed source, commercial product.
5. The Hardware model where some firms make or assemble specialised hardware that runs open source software is still not very popular.

C. Choose the Right Option from the List

1. The growth of the Free Software Movement and the Internet
   (a) were in sequential order
   (b) were unconnected
   (c) were closely intertwined
   (d) took root in commercial firms
2. The strongest argument for using open source for a desktop operating system is
   (a) lower costs
   (b) stability
   (c) availability of applications
   (d) security
3. The phrase 'total cost of ownership' refers to the
   (a) costs of acquiring and maintaining software
   (b) costs of acquiring and installing software and per user licences for shared software
   (c) final costs of acquiring, installing, customising, maintaining and upgrading software
   (d) none of the above
4. One of the most successful open source software products, unrivalled by any proprietary equivalents, this software was responsible for the initial rapid growth of the World Wide Web
   (a) Netscape browser
   (b) Linux operating system
   (c) Mozilla Firefox
   (d) Apache web server
5. The Dual licencing model allows for firms to
   (a) create open source software to be shared with the community with appropriate licences
   (b) facilitate product extension and growth through the efforts of community members
   (c) retain copyright and sell software on a second, proprietary licence, which is closed source
   (d) all of the above
6. Open standards
   (a) are those that are free to be used by anyone without paying royalties
   (b) allow data to be maintained in perpetuity
   (c) encourage sharing
   (d) all of the above
7. The Product model
   (a) allows firms to create products and services based on open source software and sell them
   (b) allows firms to create two distinct versions of products for community use and commercial use
   (c) allows firms to create products based on open source software for freely sharing with community with appropriate licences
   (d) does not allow commercial use of open source software
8. Open source software and components are preferred by
   (a) small businesses
   (b) SMEs

(c) large Internet-based businesses
(d) all of the above

9. The main difference between the Apache and GPL is that
   (a) GPL disallows commercial use of derived versions without making source code available while Apache allows it
   (b) GPL explicitly forbids patenting of software derived from its licence whereas Apache allows this
   (c) GPL allows copyrights whereas Apache forbids copyrights to be associated with the software
   (d) these terms are not different and are used interchangeably
10. Patents in software
   (a) ensure protection of patent-holder's interests and ensure faster innovation
   (b) are highly restrictive and curb innovation
   (c) do not ensure royalties for sale of derived work obtained from the patented software
   (d) make sharing easier by concentrating all rights over the idea or product with the patent holders

ANSWER KEY

Chapter 1

A. Complete the Following

1. People/individuals, goals
2. Information technology, digital networks, dispersed, knowledge
3. First
4. Process, information systems
5. Evolution

B. State True or False

1. True
2. False
3. False
4. True
5. False

C. Choose the Right Option from the List

1. (c)
2. (d)
3. (c)
4. (c)
5. (b)
6. (b)
7. (d)
8. (d)
9. (d)
10. (a)
11. (b)

Chapter 2

A. Complete the Following

1. Transistors, double
2. Power, capacity
3. Creative destruction
4. Early adopters
5. Breaking, surface

B. State True or False

1. False
2. True
3. False
4. True
5. False

C. Choose the Right Option from the List

1. (a)
2. (b)
3. (d)
4. (c)
5. (b)
6. (a)
7. (d)
8. (b)
9. (c)
10. (d)

Chapter 3

A. Complete the Following

1. Data, information
2. Random Access Memory (RAM), secondary memory/hard disk, flash memory stick
3. Individuals, groups, functions
4. Time gap, simultaneous
5. Strategic, mission
6. Simplex

B. State True or False

1. True
2. True
3. False
4. False
5. False
6. True

C. Choose the Right Option from the List

1. (a)
2. (d)
3. (a)
4. (d)
5. (d)
6. (a)
7. (d)
8. (d)

9. (a)
10. (a)
11. (b)

Chapter 4

A. Complete the Following

1. Transaction
2. Core competence
3. Value, cost
4. Network externalities, positive feedback
5. Primary, support

B. State True or False

1. False
2. True
3. False
4. False
5. True

C. Choose the Right Option from the List

1. (d)
2. (c)
3. (d)
4. (d)
5. (c)
6. (c)
7. (c)
8. (c)
9. (d)
10. (d)

Chapter 5

A. Complete the Following

1. Network effects
2. SMTP
3. Moderated, edited
4. Internet
5. Virtual Private Network (VPN)
6. Portal

B. State True or False

1. True
2. False
3. True
4. False
5. True

C. Choose the Right Option from the List

1. (b)
2. (d)
3. (a)
4. (b)
5. (b)
6. (c)
7. (b)
8. (c)
9. (c)
10. (a)
11. (d)

Chapter 6

A. Complete the Following

1. Standardization, flexibility, innovate
2. Decentralised
3. Return on investment (ROI)
4. Centralised, decentralised
5. Business applications and IT budgets

B. State True or False

1. False
2. False
3. True
4. True
5. True

C. Choose the Right Option from the List

1. (a)
2. (b)
3. (d)
4. (c)
5. (d)
6. (d)
7. (d)
8. (b)
9. (a)
10. (c)

Chapter 7

A. Complete the Following

1. Management's, free-loading, best performers
2. Ethics, are not, legal
3. Email, network logs, work of employees
4. The Panopticon
5. Privacy, security
6. Alienation

B. State True or False

1. False
2. False
3. True
4. False
5. False
6. False

C. Choose the Right Option from the List

1. (d)
2. (a)
3. (c)
4. (a)
5. (d)
6. (c)
7. (d)
8. (d)
9. (c)
10. (d)

Chapter 8

A. Complete the Following

1. greenhouse gases
2. kilograms, carbon
3. use, practices
4. environmentally sustainable
5. ICT, quality

B. State True or False

1. False
2. True
3. False
4. False
5. True

C. Choose the Right Option from the List

1. (c)
2. (b)
3. (d)
4. (a)
5. (d)
6. (b)
7. (c)
8. (a)
9. (d)
10. (c)

Chapter 9

A. Complete the Following

1. Architecture, infrastructure
2. Proprietary, open source
3. Driver
4. RISC, CISC
5. High-performance

B. State True or False

1. True
2. True

3. False
4. False
5. True

C. Choose the Right Option from the List

1. (d)
2. (d)
3. (d)
4. (c)
5. (a)
6. (d)
7. (d)
8. (d)
9. (d)
10. (d)

Chapter 10

A. Complete the Following

1. computing, internet
2. capital, operating
3. datacenter
4. software
5. devices, internet

B. State True or False

1. False
2. True
3. True
4. False
5. True

C. Choose the Right Option from the List

1. (c)
2. (b)
3. (a)
4. (d)
5. (b)
6. (d)
7. (c)
8. (a)
9. (b)
10. (c)

Chapter 11

A. Complete the Following

1. Services
2. Connection-less, connection-oriented
3. Tier-3
4. Servers
5. Access points

B. State True or False

1. True
2. True
3. False
4. True
5. False

C. Choose the Right Option from the List

1. (d)
2. (d)
3. (d)
4. (b)
5. (d)
6. (d)
7. (b)
8. (d)
9. (c)
10. (c)

Chapter 12

A. Complete the Following

1. Worm
2. Authentication, digital certificates
3. Malware, viruses, worms, Trojans
4. Technological, human/social
5. Personal

B. State True or False

1. True
2. True

3. False
4. True
5. True

C. Choose the Right Option from the List

1. (d)
2. (d)
3. (d)
4. (d)
5. (c)
6. (b)
7. (d)
8. (d)
9. (d)
10. (c)

Chapter 13

A. Complete the Following

1. Scope creep
2. Beta testing
3. The Agile Manifesto
4. Rapid prototyping, the spiral model
5. Rational Unified Process (RUP), Unified Modelling Language (UML)

B. State True or False

1. True
2. True
3. True
4. True
5. False

C. Choose the Right Option from the List

1. (d)
2. (d)
3. (b)
4. (c)
5. (a)
6. (d)
7. (d)
8. (c)
9. (d)
10. (b)

Chapter 14

A. Complete the Following

1. Data mart
2. Data scrubbing
3. Query
4. Data dictionary
5. Distributed

B. State True or False

1. True
2. True
3. True
4. False
5. False

3. Choose the Right Option from the List

1. (d)
2. (a)
3. (b)
4. (b)
5. (d)
6. (a)
7. (b)
8. (c)
9. (b)
10. (b)

Chapter 15

A. Complete the Following

1. ERP, SCM, CRM, legacy
2. Just-in-Time (JIT)
3. The Bullwhip effect
4. Touchpoints, prospective
5. Cross-selling, up-selling, bundling

B. State True or False

1. True
2. False
3. True
4. True
5. True
6. True

C. Choose the Right Option from the List

1. (d)
2. (c)
3. (c)
4. (c)
5. (c)
6. (c)
7. (d)
8. (d)
9. (d)
10. (d)

Chapter 16

A. Complete the Following

1. Dashboard
2. Explicit, tacit
3. Expert Systems
4. Content Management System
5. Neural networks, decision trees, clustering and data visualisation

B. State True or False

1. False
2. False
3. False
4. False
5. True

C. Choose the Right Option from the List

1. (d)
2. (d)
3. (d)
4. (d)
5. (d)
6. (d)
7. (d)
8. (c)
9. (d)
10. (d)

Chapter 17

A. Complete the Following

1. program, human
2. intelligence, representation
3. breadth-first, depth-first
4. knowledge, actions
5. mathematical, neurons

B. State True or False

1. True
2. False
3. True
4. False
5. True

C. Choose the Right Option from the List

1. (c)
2. (b)
3. (d)
4. (c)
5. (a)
6. (b)
7. (d)
8. (b)
9. (d)
10. (b)

Chapter 18

A. Complete the Following

1. e-participation, e-government, e-governance
2. Digital divide

3. Exogenous, endogenous
4. Standards, legal issues, resistance, corruption
5. Political, educational

B. State True or False

1. True
2. False
3. False
4. True
5. False

C. Choose the Right Option from the List

1. (c)
2. (a)
3. (d)
4. (d)
5. (c)
6. (c)
7. (d)
8. (d)
9. (d)
10. (d)

Chapter 19

A. Complete the Following

1. Search, rating, wikis, mashups
2. Search
3. Tagging
4. Mashups
5. Peer-to-peer

B. State True or False

1. True
2. True
3. True
4. True
5. True

C. Choose the Right Option from the List

1. (c)
2. (d)
3. (c)
4. (c)
5. (a)
6. (c)
7. (b)
8. (d)
9. (d)
10. (d)

Chapter 20

C. Complete the Following

1. Total cost of ownership/TCO
2. Rights, royalties
3. GNU
4. Modifying, distributing
5. Costs, foreign exchange, experimentation, perpetuity, piracy

B. State True or False

1. False
2. True
3. True
4. True
5. False

C. Choose the Right Option from the List

1. (c)
2. (d)
3. (c)
4. (d)
5. (d)
6. (d)
7. (a)
8. (d)
9. (b)
10. (b)

APPENDIX B

Useful Online References

Chapter 1 Organisations and Information Systems

- http://www.thocp.net/ – An URL for history of computing project.
- http://www.computerhistory.org/ – An URL for computer history museum.
- http://topdocumentaryfilms.com/the-machine-that-changed-the-world/ – An URL for most comprehensive documentary about the history of computing ever produced, it is a whirlwind tour of computing before the Web. It is jointly produced by WGBH Boston and the BBC.
- http://topdocumentaryfilms.com/triumph-nerds-rise-accidental-empires/ – An URL for film chronicles the rise of the personal computer/home computer beginning in the 1970s.
- http://topdocumentaryfilms.com/download-true-story-internet/ – An URL for the technological, cultural, commercial and social revolution that has radically changed our lives.
- http://ei.cs.vt.edu/~history/ – An URL that has a collection of materials relating to the history of computing.
- http://www.bnet.fordham.edu/public/ics/msilver/itmodel.htm – An URL for the article 'The Information Technology Interaction Model: A Foundation for the MBA Core Course' by Silver, Marcus and Beath.

Chapter 2 IT and Innovation

- http://www.business-standard.com/article/technology/technology-is-core-for-olacabs-112082600001_1.html – Article on Ola Cabs' use of technology.
- http://www.computerworld.com.au/article/606253/understanding-blockchain-hype-why-much-it-nothing-more-than-snake-oil-spin/ – A critical look at Blockchain applications.
- http://www.nytimes.com/2015/05/13/opinion/thomas-friedman-moores-law-turns-50.html?_r=0 – Article on Moore's Law.
- https://blockgeeks.com/guides/what-is-blockchain-technology/ – Article on Blockchain technology.

Chapter 3 Concepts of Management Information Systems

- http://reflections-shivanand.blogspot.com/2011/11/ sam-pitroda-interviewhtml – An URL to view an interview with Sam Pitroda, where he dwells on the computerisation of Indian Railways and other stories.
- http://cris.org.in/CRIS/Home/Home – An URL for Center for Railway Information Systems.
- http://www.in.kpmg.com/pdf/Railway_Conf.pdf – An URL for International Railway Conference, New Delhi, 2007 – A background note.
- http://www.youtube.com/watch?v=4Zj7txoDxbE – An URL for RFID technology video.
- http://www.colorado.edu/geography/gcraft/notes/gps/gps_f.html – An URL for The Global Positioning System.

Chapter 4 IT Strategy and Digital Goods

- http://www.thehindubusinessline.com/todays-paper/tp-new-manager/article2507045.ece – Flipkart has grown from being a four products a minute company in 2010 to sixteen shipments a minute in October 2011. With a fairly flat structure and around 2500 employees (2011) whose average age is 27, it is an organisation of four or five teams with diverse skills. It has partnerships with around 12 courier service providers, yet it is slowly getting into delivery itself. With a transparent, vibrant work culture and a borderless office with liquid spaces, it encourages staff to contribute across functions.

- http://www.nasscom.in/ – An URL for the premier organisation setting the tone of public policy for the Indian software industry.

Chapter 5 Electronic Commerce, Electronic Business, Electronic Governance

- http://www.cio.in/case-study/balakrishnans-mobile-platform-opens-new-channels-revenue – An URL for a case study on mobile platforms.
- http://topdocumentaryfilms.com/nerds-brief-history-internet/ – An URL for Nerds 2.0.1 documents the development of ARPANET, the Internet, the World Wide Web and the dot-com bubble of the mid and late 1990s.

Chapter 6 Managing Information Systems

- http://www.networkmagazineindia.com/200204/200204cio.shtml – An URL for CIO Speak 'Managing IT assets'.
- http://www-935.ibm.com/services/in/cio/pdf/forrester_indian_cios.pdf – An URL for August 12, 2008 article 'Indian CIOs Excel As Chief Innovation Officers; Western CIOs: Emulate Business-Focused, Well-Networked Indian CIOs'.
- http://www.mckinsey.com/clientservice/bto/pointofview/pdf/MoIT11_ICICInterview_F.pdf – An URL for The CEO as CIO an interview with ICICI's K.V. Kamat.
- http://biztech2.in.com/interviews/business-processes/indian-cios-should-not-limit-their-focus-to-applications/26611/0 – May 2008, John Roberts, research VP and distinguished analyst, Gartner Inc. discusses with Biztech2.0 how the role of the CIO is being redefined in the Indian IT space.
- http://www.ciol.com/Enterprise/Enterprise/Interviews/Telescope-CIO-role-is-not-about-SAP-and-Oracle/151672/0/ – An URL for article 'CIO role is not about SAP and Oracle'.
- https://www14.software.ibm.com/webapp/iwm/web/signup.do?source=csuite-NA&S_PKG=2011CIOStudyUS – An URL for article 'IBM Global CIO Study 2011'.

Chapter 7 Ethical and Social Issues

- http://networkedblogs.com/qJqAe – An URL for Bengaluru Aadhar operators violating privacy.
- http://cartome.org/foucault.htm – An URL for Michael Foucault: Panopticism
- http://cartome.org/panopticon2.htm – An URL for article 'The Panopticon Writings' by Jeremy Bentham. Edited by Miran Bozovic, London: Verso, 1995, pp. 29–95.
- http://www.surveillance-and-society.org/articles1(3)/pathologisation.pdf – An URL for article 'Panoptic Power and the Pathologisation of Vision: Critical Reflections on the Foucauldian Thesis' by Majid Yar.
- http://home.fnal.gov/~annis/digirati/otherVoices/Lyon.html – An URL for article 'From Big Brother to Electronic Panopticon' by David Lyon.
- http://www.documentingreality.com/forum/f181/panopticon-all-seeing-eye-88980/
- http://www.ces.iisc.ernet.in/energy/paper/ewaste/ewaste.html – An URL for article 'Environmentally Sound Options for E-Wastes Management' by Ramachandra, T.V. and Saira Varghese K., Energy and Wetlands Group, Center for Ecological Sciences, Indian Institute of Science, Bangalore.
- http://moef.nic.in/downloads/rules-and-regulations/1035e_eng.pdf – An URL for 'Ministry of Environment and Forests Notification', 2011.
- http://www.business-standard.com/india/news/india-gets-first-e-waste-management-rules/438474/ – An URL for article 'India gets first e-waste management rules'.
- http://www.toxicslink.org/art-view.php?id=134 – An URL for article 'Sustainable e-waste management'.
- http://www.wipro.com/documents/insights/green-it-matters-at-wipro.pdf – An URL for article 'Green IT Matters at WIPRO Ltd'.

Sample e-waste policies

- http://www.tcs.com/about/corp_responsibility/Documents/tcs_sustainability_ewaste_policy.pdf – An URL for article 'TCS E-waste Management Policy'.
- http://www.assocham.org/events/recent/.../E_Waste_Recommendations.doc – Assocham

- http://www.efytimes.com/e1/fullnews.asp?edid=28426 – An URL for article 'Wipro supports e-waste law in India'. Greenpeace study finds that Wipro, HCL and Acer have effective takeback policy for their products.
- http://www.enn.com/pollution/article/38220 – An URL for article 'Report reveals flawed US e-waste policies' (September 2008).
- http://www.jindalsteelpower.com/ReportFile/File_2011_annual-report-2010-11.pdf – Latest Annual report of JSPL.

Chapter 8 Managing Green IT and Smart Cities

- http://www.livescience.com/37821-greenhouse-gases.html – Article on greenhouse gases and global warming.
- http://www.greenit.net/whygreenit.html – Portal for Green IT technologies and applications.
- http://fortune.com/2015/08/20/smart-traffic-signals/ – Article on smart signals and traffic management.
- https://www.wired.com/2011/03/cell-phone-networks-and-the-future-of-traffic/ – Article on use of cellular networks to monitor traffic in real time.
- http://www.libelium.com/smart_city_environmental_parameters_public_transportation_waspmote/ – Article on environmental monitoring in Serbia.
- http://datasmart.ash.harvard.edu/news/article/monitoring-air-quality-and-the-impacts-of-pollution-679 – Article on monitoring air quality in cities in the USA.
- http://www.rcrwireless.com/20160725/business/smart-building-tag31-tag99 – Article on smart buildings.

Chapter 9 Information Technology Infrastructure and Choices

- http://opensource.sys-con.com/node/1210012 – An URL for article 'Cloud Computing Basics' from Open Source Magazine.
- http://www.sei.cmu.edu/library/assets/whitepapers/Cloudcomputingbasics.pdf – An URL for article 'Basics About Cloud Computing'.
- http://www.techrepublic.com/article/introduction-to-server-virtualization/6074941 – An URL for article 'Introduction to Server Virtualization'.
- http://cioresearchcenter.com/2011/05/the-business-of-the-cloud-nitin-khanapurkar-kpmg/ – An URL for article 'The Business of the Cloud – Interview with Nitin Khanapurkar, KPMG'

Chapter 10 Cloud Computing and Internet-of-Things

- https://azure.microsoft.com/en-in/overview/what-is-azure/ – Discussion of Microsoft's Azure cloud services.
- https://www.swan-forum.com/resources/a-layered-view/ – Basic architecture of smart water networks.
- https://www.ibm.com/cloud/why-ibm – An introduction to IBM's cloud products and services.
- https://www.openstack.org/software/ – A description of OpenStack, an open source cloud platform.
- https://www.openshift.com/features/ – A description of OpenShift, a cloud utility that enables the use of self-contained containers, which are a method of virtualization.
- https://www.ibm.com/internet-of-things – IBM's Internet-of-Things product offering that is based on Watson.
- https://www.cisco.com/c/en_in/solutions/internet-of-things/overview.html – Use of IoT in different industries by Cisco.

Chapter 11 Networking and Telecommunication

- http://www.redbooks.ibm.com/redbooks/pdfs/gg243376.pdf – An URL for IBM's TCP/IP Tutorial and Technical Overview.
- http://www.youtube.com/watch?v=PBWhzz_Gn10 – An URL about warriors of the net movie describes the journey of an IP packet.

Chapter 12 Information Systems Security and Control

- http://topdocumentaryfilms.com/can-you-hack-it-hackers-wanted/ – An URL for top documentary film on 'Can you Hack It? – Hackers Wanted'
- http://topdocumentaryfilms.com/web-warriors/ – An URL for top documentary film 'Web Warriors'.
- http://www.pluggd.in/justbooks-takes-library-to-next-level-with-rfid-tagging-297/ – An URL for article 'JustBooks takes Library to next level with RFID Tagging'.
- http://justbooksclc.com/hooked – An URL for a look at the 'smart kiosk'.
- http://en.wikipedia.org/wiki/The_Information_Technology_Act,_2000
- http://www.cryptographyworld.com/ – An URL about cryptography basics.

- http://media.wiley.com/product_data/excerpt/94/07645487/0764548794.pdf - An URL of a chapter 'Cryptography Basics'.
- http://www.networkworld.com/news/64452_05-17-1999.html - An URL for article 'Public key encryption fordummies'.

Chapter 13 Information Systems Development and Project Management

- http://martinfowler.com/agile.html - An URL that includes the Agile Manifesto.
- http://www.scrumalliance.org/learn_about_scrum - An URL about Scrum primer.
- http://www.smartdraw.com/resources/tutorials/data-flow-diagrams/#/resources/tutorials/Context-Diagrams - An URL about introduction to data flow diagrams.
- http://www.getahead-direct.com/gwbadfd.htm - An URL for online tutorial on data flow diagrams.
- http://www.bredemeyer.com/use_cases.htm - An URL about introduction to Use Cases.
- http://gatherspace.com/static/use_case_example.html - An URL about writing effective Use Cases.
- http://www.waterfall-model.com/ - A site dedicated to the Waterfall Model.
- http://www.youtube.com/watch?v=p6vW84Pq-Uc - An interesting video on the Waterfall Model.
- http://www.dimap.ufrn.br/~jair/ES/artigos/SpiralModelBoehm.pdf - An URL for article 'A Spiral Model of Software Development' by Barry W. Boehm.
- http://agilemanifesto.org/ - An URL on the Agile Manifesto of software development.
- http://www.extremeprogramming.org/ - An URL on gentle introduction to extreme programming.
- http://scrummethodology.com/ - An URL on Scrum methodology.
- http://www.scrummethodology.org/ - An URL on introduction to Scrum methodology.

Chapter 14 Managing Data Resources

- http://freevideolectures.com/Course/2280/Database-Design/ - Introdution to Database systems - Free lecture IIT Madras Lecture Series.
- http://www.roseindia.net/jdbc/relational-database-concepts.shtml - An URL about basic concepts of relational databases.
- http://www.tutorialspoint.com/sql/sql-rdbms-concepts.htm - An URL about relational database concepts.
- http://docs.oracle.com/cd/B19306_01/server.102/b14220/intro.htm - Introduction to Oracle database.
- http://www.mysql.com/ - MySQL website.
- http://www.postgresql.org/ - Website of PostgreSQL.
- http://www.linuxinsider.com/story/70919.html - An URL about article on open source databases.
- http://databases.about.com/od/specificproducts/a/normalization.htm - An URL about article on database normalization.
- http://docs.oracle.com/cd/B10501_01/server.920/a96520/concept.htm - An URL about data warehouse concepts.
- http://www.datawarehousingconcepts.in/ - An URL about data warehousing concepts.

Chapter 15 Business Process Integration and Enterprise Systems

- http://www.brint.com/BPR.htm - An URL about good resources on business process reengineering.
- http://www.cio.com/article/40323/ERP_Definition_and_Solutions -An URL about ERP definitions.
- http://www.sap.com/india/index.epx - An URL about website of SAP in India.
- http://www.youtube.com/watch?v=PVRglXLWDHs - An URL about good video on ERP.
- http://www.youtube.com/watch?v=BMtv6sbmdLc - An interesting video on CRM.

Chapter 16 Decision Support Systems

- http://www.psy.cmu.edu/psy/faculty/hsimon/hsimon.html - An URL of a page on Herbert Simon, the originator of the Intelligence-Design-Choice model.
- http://dssresources.com/ - A website dedicated to decision support systems.
- http://35.8.121.127/MWDSSP-Templates/a2/index.asp - An example of a DSS for managing environmental resources.
- http://www.financenterinc.com/ - An online DSS for financial decisions.
- http://www-958.ibm.com/software/data/cognos/manyeyes/ - The Many Eyes site for data visualization.
- http://www.caida.org/tools/visualization/otter/ - A tool for visualizing networks.

- http://www.visualcomplexity.com/vc/ – An online collection of visualizations.
- http://www.mindmeister.com/ – An online mind-mapping tool.

Chapter 17 Artificial Intelligence

- https://futureoflife.org/background/benefits-risks-of-artificial-intelligence/ – The potential of Artificial Intelligence and what implications it has for society.
- https://www.aaai.org/ – Portal for the Association for the Advancement of AI; includes academic resources for AI.
- https://www.mckinsey.com/global-themes/artificial-intelligence – McKinsey's page on AI with many articles on applications.
- https://openai.com/ – A site dedicated to research and development of safe AI technologies.
- https://www.tensorflow.org/ – An open source machine learning framework for deep learning.
- https://www.h2o.ai/ – An open source AI toolkit, with many commercial applications.

Chapter 18 ICT for Development and E-Governance

- http://www.etuktuk.net/ – An URL of a page on the e-tuktuk project.
- http://portal.unesco.org/ci/en/ev.php-URL_ID=21987&URL_DO=DO_TOPIC&URL_SECTION=201.html – An URL about article 'etuktuk takes Internet and radio to Sri Lankan villages'.
- http://www.youtube.com/watch?v=Un_gXqN-XnY – An URL about eTuktuk – Kothmale Community Radio.
- http://bhoomi.karnataka.gov.in/ – An URL about the Bhoomi website.
- http://www.youtube.com/watch?v=ybVBZ4_Y3W0 – An URL about Karnataka Govt Headed e-Governance Way – Part 1
- http://www.youtube.com/watch?v=rlhZ6BXtd6o&feature=relmfu – An URL about Karnataka Govt Headed e-Governance Way – Part 2
- http://www.videovolunteers.org/ – Videovolunteers website – Empowering Community Vocies through training in critical thinking and creativity.
- http://www.youtube.com/user/VideoVolunteers – Videos generated by video volunteers.
- http://southasia.oneworld.net/fromthegrassroots/indias-first-rural-community-radio-station-goes-on-air – Sangham Radio
- http://www.youtube.com/watch?v=OywaiupafA0 – Introducing Radio Sangham.
- http://www.youtube.com/watch?v=DHHmBg0r2f4 – A video link on the Lokvani project of UP.
- http://www.youtube.com/watch?v=kw2OZ7Ozwt4 – A video link on 'ICT Facilitated Access to Information Innovations – South Asia', includes Jaankari of Bihar
- http://www.youtube.com/watch?v=k2c4PZ8GaWA – Jaankari on YouTube.
- http://www.webchutney.org/work/case-study-jaago-re-tata-tea/ – An URL about case study on Jaago Re.

Chapter 19 The Society of the Internet

- http://topdocumentaryfilms.com/inside-the-mind-of-google/ – An URL on top documentary films 'Inside the Mind of Google'.
- http://topdocumentaryfilms.com/hackers-outlaws-angels/ – An URL on top documentary films 'Hackers: Outlaws and Angels'.
- http://www.galaxyzoo.org/ – An URL on Galaxy Zoo.
- http://www.ox.ac.uk/public_affairs/case_studies/galaxy_zoo.html – Galaxy Zoo, a case-study
- http://topdocumentaryfilms.com/the-truth-according-to-wikipedia/ – A documentary film on Wikipedia.

Chapter 20 Open Source Software

- http://topdocumentaryfilms.com/revolution-os/ – An URL that traces the history of GNU, Linux, and the open source and free software movements.
- http://www.iimb.ernet.in/~rahulde/RD_FOSSRep2009.pdf – An URL about article 'Economic impact of free and open source software – A study in India' by Rahul De', IIMB, 2009.
- http://www.ibm.com/developerworks/opensource/ – An URL about article 'Open Source: Resources to open source development and implementation'.
- http://www.redhat.com/magazine/015jan06/features/tapia/ – An URL about article 'What does open source mean in India'.

- http://www.business-standard.com/india/news/open-source-software-can-save-india-2-bn/369858/ – An URL about article 'Open source software can save India $2 bn'.
- http://www.ciol.com/Developer/Open-Source/Feature/Indian-open-source-community-biggest-in-the-World/152545/0/ – An URL about article 'Indian open source community biggest in the world'.
- http://www.opensource.org/node/551 – An URL about article 'Indian open standards policy finalised'.
- http://www.deccanherald.com/content/26913/free-software-suited-ui-card.html – An URL about article 'Free software is best suited for UI card project'.
- http://news.cnet.com/India-leader-advocates-open-source/2100-1016_3-1011255.html – An URL about article 'India leader advocates open source'.
- http://www.informationweek.in/Open_Source/10-12-13/Indian_CIOs_open_up_to_open_source.aspx?page=6 – An URL about article on 'Indian CIOs open up to open source'.
- http://www.project-open.org/ – Open Source, web-based Project & Service Management/ERP system for companies with 3-3000 employees
- http://www.asiaosc.org/open-source-software-resources.html – An URL about article 'open source software resources'.
- http://www.ciol.com/Developer/Open-Source/Feature/Switching-to-FOSS-saves-money-MS-begs-to-differ/301009127092/0/ – An URL about article 'Switching to FOSS saves money? MS begs to differ'.
- http://nrcfoss.org.in/
- http://www.opensource.org/node/467 – An URL about artice 'Open source software can save India $2 BN/year – At least!' by Michael Tiemann.
- http://www.opensource.org/
- http://www.informationweek.com/news/47900215 – An URL about article 'Why the open source model can work in India'.
- http://www.opensourceresources.org/
- http://www.mayin.org/ajayshah/MEDIA/1998/free-sw.html

Index

A
Aadhaar scheme, 303–304
ABC Bank, 55–56
access points, 232
accounting function in an organisation, 46
account updating, 281
active state of software system, 154
actuators, 217
addiction, 143
aggregators, 100–101
Agile Methods, 292–295
Agricultural Market Information System (AMIS), 276
Aircel, 149–150
AirJaldi Networks, 225–226
Ali, Zine el-Abidine Ben, 429
Alibaba.com, 101
alienation, 138–139
Amazon.com, 70, 144
AMD Corporation, 72
Analytical Engine, 9
analytics, 35, 367–368
anarchy, 122
Android operating system, 463–464
Apache, 454, 457
Apache software licence, 459
Application Layer Protocols, 241
application server, 230
ArcelorMittal, 352
archiving, 44
arithmetic operations, 179
artificial Intelligence (AI), 10, 381
  breadth-first and depth-first search, 390
  general problem solving, 392
  history of, 385–386
  implications for managers, 401
  limitations, 400–401
  planning systems, 391–392
  representation and search, 387–390
  Turing test, 386–387
artificial neural networks (NNs), 392
Association for Democratic Reforms, 7
asynchronous communication, 56, 87
Atanasoff-Berry computer, 9
attributes, 323, 325
auctions, 100
authentication, 115, 259–260
automated teller machine (ATM), 49, 89, 266

B
Babbage, Charles, 9
bandwidth shaping, 235
Bangladesh bank heist, 261–262
bargaining power
  of buyers and customers, 67
  of suppliers, 66–67
barriers to entry, 68
Basel Convention regulation, of e-waste, 141
batch mode monitoring, 49–50
Bayesian learning, 397–398
Bayes' rule, 397
Bentham, Jeremy, 132
Berners-Lee, Tim, 11
Betamax, 75
Bhoomi land records system of Karnataka state, 409–410
Big Data, 328–331
  characteristic of veracity in, 330
  variety in, 330
  velocity of, 329
  volume of, 329
binary digits (bits), 43
BlackBerry Messenger Service, 430
Blockchain technology, 33, 354–355
blogs, 433
Bluetooth standard, 263
board on CPU, 183
botnets, 257
bounded rationality, 363
brand management, 365
breadth-first search, 390
Bring-Your-Own-Device (BYOD), 193–194
browser, 12
BSD Licence, 459
bus, 183
business continuity planning (BCP), 269
business intelligence techniques, 368–373
business processes, 337–340
  business process analyst, 277
  of buying a ticket online, 337–338
  data flow diagrams (DFDs) of, 279–282
  definition of, 277
  example of complex, 338–340
  life cycle models, 284–285
  tools for analysis, 277–279
  use cases of, 282–284
business process re-engineering, 340
'bust' of the dotcom bubble, 84
bus topology, 242–243

C

cables, 231–232
cache, 180
cache miss, 180
carbon-based wastes, 140
carbon footprint, 152–153
cardinality, 323–324
career paths of IT staff, 113–114
Carr, Jeffrey, 250
Cascading Style Sheets (CSS), 86
cash cards, 90
category 5 (CAT 5) cables, 231–232
category 6 (CAT 6) cables, 232
centralised computing, 142
centralised IT management, 110, 113
  innovations in IT, 112–113
  IT procurement, 113
  standardisation, 111–112
  vendors, 112, 116–118
central processing unit (CPU), 253
  components and their meanings, 180
Centre for Science and Environment (CSE), India, 140
change management, 351
Chevron Corporation, 133
Chief Information Officer (CIO), 18–19, 105, 114
  role and responsibilities of, 118–119
  vendor coordination and, 119
Christensen, Clayton, 28
ciphertext, 257
circuit switching, 229
Cisco Corporation, 352
Cisco Systems, 102
click-stream data, 328
client, securing of, 266–267
clients, 231
cloud computing, 20–21, 199
  advantages and features of, 204–207
  'anytime-anywhere' access, 206
  challenges of migrating to, 210–211
  definition, 203–204
  economic rationale for, 213
  elasticity, 204–205
  heterogeneity, 206
  infrastructure, 199, 207–208
  managed services, 205
  measurement of use of, 205
  reduced setup time, 206–207
  resource pooling using, 207
  scalability, 204
  service levels, 205–206
  service models, 208–210
  usage-based pricing, 205
cloud infrastructure, 199
cloud technologies, 211–212
clustering, 372
coal sales in India, 83
co-location facilities, 269
communication in organisations, 56–58
community cloud, 208
compact-fluorescent lamps (CFL), 150
competitive environment, 16, 65–69
  bargaining power, 66–67
  barriers to entry, 68
  industry regulations and, 69
  partnering for mutual benefit, 65–66
  product differentiation and, 70
  threat of substitutes, 68–69
competitive strategy, 16, 75–76
Complex Instruction Set Computing (CISC) chips, 180
computer architecture, 179
computing devices, history
  Electronic Numerical Integrator and Computer (ENIAC), 9–10
  Free Software movement, 10–11
  internet users, growth of (1993–2014), 12
  personal computing, 10
  Robotics, 10
conceptual exercise of power, 134
concurrency, 306
Conficker worm, 252–253
connectionless services, 238
connection-oriented services, 238
Containers, 199, 212
content management systems (CMS), 377–378
context-aware devices, 155
control, 54
controlling costs, 351
cookies, 130
Corruption Perceptions Index of the Transparency International, 422
crackers, 247
cracking, 253–254
creative innovation, 28
Crew Management System (CMS), 42
crowd sourcing, 35
culture of an organisation, 16
customer relationship management (CRM) system, 17–18, 31, 78, 175, 333, 341, 348–349
customisation, 351

D

data, 39, 301
  access, 306
  administration, 306
  classification of, 381
  click-stream, 328
  consistency, 306
  entity, 322–323
  independence, 305–306
  information and, 43
  mart, 327
  measuring, 43–44
  mining, uses, 327–328
  nature of, 128–129
  normalisation, 325–326
  online search, 328
  point-of-sale purchase, 328
  privacy and ownership of, 130
  real-time, 50
  redundancy, 306
  scrubbing, 327
  security, 184
  semi-structured, 330
  structured, 330
  text, 328
  unstructured, 330
  visualisation, 372–373
  warehouses, 326–328
database management systems (DBMS), 301
  application development, 307
databases, 43, 189
  basic architecture, 308–310
  client-server architecture of, 309
  commercial, 321–322
  concepts, 307–310
  design of, 311–320
  elements of, 312–320
  fields, 307–308
  files, 307–308
  forms, 312
  with homogeneous and heterogeneous architectures, 309–310
  metadata, 319–320
  personal, 309
  queries, 312–317
  records, 307–308
  reports, 319
  tables, 312
  workgroup, 309
database server, 230
data efficiency, 154–155
data flow diagrams (DFDs), 279–282

cautions while creating, 282
elements of, 280
example, 281–282
data management
challenge of, 305–307
history of, 305
managing concurrency, 306
managing security, 306–307
recovery from crashed servers, 307
data networks, 11
data standardisation, 111
Deccan Development Society (DDS), 415–416
de-centralised IT management, 110–113
decision making
with communication, 58
with MIS, 52–55
decision support systems (DSS), 52, 357, 361–364
database component, 364
decision making stage, 362–363
history of, 365–367
inputs and outputs for decision making, 361
model base, 364–365
types of decisions, 363–364
user interfaces, 365
decision trees, 370–371, 396–397
deep packet inspection (DPI), 261
Dell, 78
demilitarised zone (DMZ), 265
denial-of-service (DoS) attack, 241, 249, 255–257
depth-first search, 390
de-skilling, 138–139
desktop, 181
desktop firewalls, 266
despatch processing, 281
development, definition of, 411–412
dial-up connections, 236
Difference Engine, 9
differentiation, 70
diffusion of innovation, 29–30
digital cameras, 28
digital certificates, 259
digital distraction, 143
digital divide, 412–413
digital goods, 61
digital imaging and photography, 34
digital networks, 7
digital subscriber line (DSL) technology, 236
digital wallets, 90
Digit (Digit.in), 32
direct selling, 98–99
disaster recovery (DR) planning, 269
dispersed organisation, 8
disruptive innovation, 28
domain name server (DNS) protocol, 239
domain name servers (DNS), 240
dotcom boom and bust, 83–85
downstream firms, 102
drill-down procedure, 50
duplex communication, 57

E
early adopters, 30
early majority, 30
earth air tunnel (EAT) system, 150
eBay, 100
e-business, 101–102
e-commerce servers, 182
e-government, 423
electrical energy, 163
electronic commerce (e-commerce), 12, 16, 34, 63, 69, 96
B2B e-commerce, 100
B2C e-commerce, 100
dotcom bust and, 83–85
technology, 83
electronic data interchange (EDI), 89–90
electronic governance (e-governance), 81, 102–103, 407, 417–423
advantages, 103
development assessment, 419–420
economic implication of, 419
government to business (G2B) service, 103
government to citizen (G2C) service, 103
government to government (G2G) service, 103
implementation challenges, 420–423
stages of, 418–419
stakeholders of an, 419
Electronic Numerical Integrator and Computer (ENIAC), 9–10
email, 12, 86–88
email server, 230
embedded software, 191–192
employee relationship management (ERM), 349
empty cycles, 180
encryption, 257–258
endogenous corruption, 422–423
energy consumption, 151
energy management, 162–163
enterprise information technology, 48
enterprise resource planning (ERP) systems, 31–32, 78, 189, 194, 201, 333, 342–345
finance and accounting module, 343
human resource management module, 344
manufacturing and operations module, 344
sales and marketing module, 344–345
enterprise systems, 194, 340–341
challenges of implementations, 350–352
Enterprise 2.0 tools, 444
entities, 322–323
entity-relationship (ER) diagrams, 301, 322–324
environment, securing of, 267–268
E-Office, 424–425
e-participation, 423–424
espionage, 253–254
e-supply chains, 102
ethernet topologies, 242–243
ethical hacking, 253
ethical issues with IT
power over users, 133–135
privacy, 128–130
workplace monitoring, 131–133
e-tuktuk project, 417
e-waste, 140–142, 156
health effects of, 140
managing, 141–142
receiving cities in India and China, 141
regulation of exports, 141
execution cycle, 179
executive support systems (ESS), 50–51
exogenous corruption, 422
experience goods, 72
expert systems, 377
external security threats, 114
extranets, 89
Extreme Programming, 293, 295

F
Facebook, 74, 443
fair use policy statement at a university, 268
feudal political state, 121–122
fibre cables, 232
field, 307–308
files, 307–308
file server, 229–230

firewall, 260–261
firewalls, 227
firm-bank partnership, 66
first-order effects, 15–16, 109
five nines, 117
fixed storage, 183
flextime, 142
Flipkart.com, 34, 63–64, 70, 330–331
Ford Motors, 340
free email services, 12
“freemium” model, 201
Free Software Movement, 453
Free Software movement, 10–11
Freight Operation Information System (FOIS), 42
frequently asked questions (FAQ) documents, 375
function point analysis, 297

G

4G, 149
games and entertainment software, 191
Gartner Group, 177
generational difference, 137
genetic algorithms, 399
Gigahertz, 180
GIMP, 458
Giraff project, 215
Global Positioning System (GPS), 57, 262
Global System for Mobile Communication (GSM), 235
global warming, 151–152
Gmail, 88
Gnarus Solutions, 218–219
GNU General Public Licence (GPL), 447, 453, 458–459
Google, 86, 209, 227
Gostev, Alexander, 250
greenhouse gases (GHGs), 147, 151–152
green IT, 153
green practices
  challenges for managers, 165–166
  in hardware design and manufacture, 153–154
  IT for managing greening, 156
  in IT use, 155–156
  monitoring and managing greening activities, 156–157
  in software design, 154–155
  steps to reduce power consumption in laptop and desktop computers, 155
Group Decision Support systems (GDSS), 367

H

Hadoop, 330
half-duplex communication, 57
Hammer, Michael, 340
hard disk, 180, 183
hardware, 10, 171
healthcare with IoT, 215
heterogeneous systems, 206
hierarchy organisational structure, 16–17
host computers, 231
host names, 239
HSBC bank, 352
hubs, 232–233
human resource management, 344, 365
human resources function in an organisation, 47
hycrid cloud, 208
Hypertext Markup Language (HTML), 85–86, 427
Hypertext Transfer Protocol (HTTP), 11, 241, 255
Hyundai Motors India, 65

I

ICANN (Internet Corporation for Assigned Names and Numbers), 239
ICICI Bank, 107–108, 112
identity theft, 254
ID Fresh Foods, case study, 14–15
idle state of software system, 154
IDOS, 201–203, 207
ILOVEYOU worm, 252
inbound logistics, 77–78
Indian Institute of Management Bangalore (IIMB), 195
Indian IT Act 2000, 130, 260, 268
Indian Railways (IR), 41–42
  ticket booking website, 91–95
induction learning, 395–397
Industrial Internet-of-Things (IIoT), 214
industry regulations, 69
information
  data and, 43
  in organisational functions, 46–47
  as a resource, 44–45
information and communication technologies (ICT), 407
  challenges of remote areas, 413
  for development, 411–413
  in education, 414–415
  examples, 415–417
  for implementations of informational systems, 413–414
  interventions, 413–415
  for political interactions and participation, 414
  to provide sustenance to rural populations, 415
  for transactional systems, 414
information goods, 71–72
information systems, 39, 48–52
information systems in organisations
  challenges for manager, 18–21
  choosing and implementing information systems, 18
  competition and organisational traits, effects of, 16
  computing, brief history, 9–11
  definition of, 8–9
  first-order effects, 15–16
  fundamental need for an information systems (IS), 19
  level of safety and security, 20
  managing, 13–18
  managing Internet, 13
  organisational structure, effects of, 16–17
  role of Internet, 11–13
  second-order effects, 15–16
  technology road map for, 21
  third-order effects, 15–16
  using for competition, 69–70
information systems (IS), 3, 118–119
information technology
  career paths of IT staff, 113–114
  dark side of, 142–144
  effects of introducing, 109–110
  first-order, second-order, and third-order impacts, 15–16, 109
  for greening, 147
  impacts on the nature of business, 105
  intentional misuse of, 143
  modern IT environment, 109–110
  procurement, 113
  security, 114–115
  selecting, 115–116
  types of, 47–48
  unintentional misuse, 143
  work culture and, 113
information technology (IT) infrastructure, 171
  components, 178–192

- decisions, 176–178
- definition of, 175–176
- questions with regard to business needs, 176
- questions with regard to technology issues, 176–177
- solutions, 192–196

Infosys, 352
Infrastructure-as-a-Service (IaaS), 199, 208–209
infrastructure management, 78
InMobi.com, 34
innovations in IT, 23, 112–113
innovation theory
- business innovations with IT, 33–35
- challenges for managers, 35–36
- competitive advantage, 30
- creative innovation, 28
- diffusion of innovation, 29–30
- disruptive innovation, 28
- innovation impact, 30–33
- Moore's law, 27–28
- Rogers' model for managers, 29–30

innovation wave complex, 31–32
innovators, 29
instance-based learning or learning from analogies, 398
institution-specific email identities, 88
instruction cycle, 179
integrated circuit, 27
Integrated Coaching Management System (ICMS), 42
Intel Corporation, 27
internal security threats, 114
International Information Systems, 352–354
Internet Assigned Numbers Authority (IANA), 239
internet devices, 234–236
Internet Engineering Task Force (IETF), 462
Internet-of-Everything (IoE), 214
Internet-of-Things (IoT), 13, 28, 199
- architecture, 217–218
- definition of, 213–215
- example of, 215
- healthcare with, 215
- internet access challenges of, 220
- managing, 215–216
- privacy challenges of, 219
- security challenges of, 219

Internet Protocol (IP), 11, 238–239, 254
internet service provider (ISP), 231
internet users, growth of (1993–2014), 12
Interop (interop.com), 32
intranets, 89
Islam, Sirajul, 275–276
ISO standards, 462
IT architecture, 121
IT budgets, 121
IT Duopoly, 122
IT-enabled organisation, 7
IT governance, 120–123
IT Interaction Model, 13–18
IT monarchy, 121
IT outsourcing, 194–196
IT principles, 120–121
IT services, 121
ITZ Cash Card, 90

J

JavaScript, 86
Jeopardy!, 383–384
Jindal Steel and Power Ltd (JSPL), 127
JSON (Java Script Object Notation) language, 330
JustBooks, 264
JustDial, 449–450

K

Karnataka Land Reforms Act of 1951, 422
Karnataka Land Revenue Act of 1964, 422
keylogging, 254
Kindle e-Reader, 76–77
Kiviat diagram, 375
knowledge degrades, 375
knowledge development, 375
knowledge life cycle, 374–375
knowledge management (KM), 357, 373–378
- hierarchic approach to, 376
- identify knowledge needs, 375–376
- market approach to, 376–377
- strategies for, 375–377
- technologies for, 377–378

knowledge organisation, 8
knowledge use, 375
knowledge workers, 8, 137
Kuoni Travel India, 269
Kyoto Protocol, 151

L

laggards, 30
landfills, 140
laptops, 181–182
last mile problem, 236
late majority, 30
latency in CPU, 180
layers, 241–242
Libre Office, 457–458
life cycle models of business processes, 284–285
life of a packet, 227–228
light-emitting diode (LED) lighting, 150
LinkedIn, 443
links, 12
Linux, 187–188, 454–456
local area network (LAN), 89, 227–228, 231
logical operations, 179
logistics management with IoT, 215
Long Term Evolution (LTE), 149
Lovelace, Ada, 9
low-cost substitutes, 69–70

M

machine cycle, 179
machine learning (ML) methods, 381
- implications for managers, 401
- limitations, 400–401

MacOS, 188
maintenance activities, 78
Makemytrip.com, 34
malware, 114, 251–253
managed services, 205
management information systems (MIS), 49–52, 362
- decision making with, 52–55
- at different levels, 50–52

marketing function in an organisation, 47
Maruti Suzuki, 65
Marx, Karl, 28
mashups, 440
massive open online courses (MOOC) sites, 35
Material Resources Planning (MRP), 342
Matlab, 230
matrix organisational structure, 16–17
McAfee Avert Labs, 249
measurement of use of IT infrastructure services, 205
metadata, 330
metadata file, 308
metaljunction (mJunction), 83
metaphors, 293
Microsoft Corporation, 72

middleware, 310
mind map, 3–4, 378
Minitel network, 11
mirroring, 269
Mitra Biotech, 378–379
mobile commerce, 96
mobile phones, 185
modern IT environment, 109–110
modern manager, 3
modern organisation, 7–8
MongoDB, 330
monitoring, 115
Moore, Gordon, 27
Moore's law, 27–28
motherboard, 180
Mozilla Firefox, 86, 456–457
MP3 files, 462
multi-core chips, 182
multimedia software, 191
multinational organisations, 8
multinationals, 352
multi-tasking, 142
multi-threading, 154
MySQL open source database, 189

N

National Electronic Funds Transfer (NEFT), 56
natural language interfaces, 34
negative feedback, 74
net-banking service, 96
Netscape, 457
network, securing of, 265–266
networked organisation, 7–8
network externalities, 73–74
network information technology, 47
networking, 190
  components for, 231–234
  layers, 241–242
  management challenges in, 236–237
  in organisation, 228–231
network interface cards (NICs), 231
networks, 88–89, 192
neural networks, 369–370
  artificial, 392
  deep, 395
  layers of, 393
  learning in, 394–395
node, 392

O

octet, 239
office productivity applications, 190
off-shoring, 353–354
Ola Cabs, 25–26, 29, 34
online auctions, 100
online payment technologies, 90–96
online search data, 328
open community, 463
open data standards, 461–463
OpenOffice.org, 458
open source softwares, 188, 447
  in business, 459–461
  creation of, 451–452
  debate around, 454–455
  developers of, 452–453
  in government, 461
  history of, 453–454
  licences, 458–459
  open data standards and open community, 461–463
  popular packages, 455–458
OpenStreetMap, 164
operating system, 186–187
operational decisions, 52–53
optical fibre cables, 232
optional attributes, 323
order processing, 281
organisation, definition of, 3
organisation's knowledge base, 8
outbound logistics, 78
outsourcing, 353–354
Oxford book store, 335–336, 339

P

packet switching, 229
pair programming, 293
PAN card, 303
Panopticon, 132
partner relationship management (PRM), 349
Passenger Reservation System, 42
password, 187
password management, 266–267
Paypal, 90
Paytm, 96
peer-to-peer file sharing, 434–435
perimeter security, 265
peripherals, 184–185
personal computing, 10
phishing, 114, 254
photovoltaic panels, 163
Physical Layer, 241
plaintext, 257
planning, 54
Platform-as-a-Service (PaaS), 209
plug-and-play innovations, 34
point-of-sale purchase data, 328
political decision making, 122
pollution control, 162
Portable Document Format (pdf), 462
Porter, Michael E., 77
portfolio management, 365
positive feedback, 74
power and exercising power, 133–135
primary key, 303, 308
print server, 230
privacy of individuals, 125, 128–130, 166, 219
private cloud, 207
private key, 258–259
processors, 178–181
production, 78
programmable logic control (PLC) software, 249
project management, 351
proprietary programs, 191
proprietary software, 451
protocols, 11, 238–241
proxy server, 230–231
public addresses, 240
public cloud, 207–208
public-key cryptography, 258–260

Q

Qualcomm, 27

R

Radio Frequency Identification (RFID), 215, 263–264
Radio Sangham, 415–416
random access memory (RAM), 179, 183, 254
Rapid Prototyping, 290–291
rating services and agencies, 439–440
real-time gross transfer (RTGS), 56
real-time mirroring, 269
real-time monitoring, 49
record, 307–308
Reduced Instruction Set Computing (RISC), 180
regional internet registries (RIRs), 239
reinforcement learning, 381
reinforcement learning (RL), 399–400
relational database, 301
relationship management, 117
Reliance Telecommunications, 235
removable storage, 183
renewable and recyclable materials, 142
resistance to systems, 135–137, 422
return on investment (ROI), 19
  of technology, 119
revenue optimisation (RO), 359–360
reverse engineering, 253

Rikuzentaka, Japan, 165
Robotics, 10
robots, 10
Rolls Royce Company, 214
routers, 233–234

S
sales and marketing, 78
SAP, 189, 342–343
schema, 301
Schumpeter, Joseph, 28
scrubbed data, 327
Scrum, 293–295
ScrumMaster, 294
search engines, 97–98
secondary storage, 183–184
Second Life, 436–437
second-order effects, 15–16, 109
security, for handling threats
  encryption, 257–258
  firewall, 260–261
  public-key cryptography, 258–260
  virtual private network (VPN), 261
  wireless technologies, 262–264
security, for IS
  client, securing of, 266–267
  disaster recovery (DR) planning, 269
  environment, securing of, 267–268
  important features, 265
  network, securing of, 265–266
  security audit and risk assessment, 268–269
security audit and risk assessment, 268–269
security levels in IT, 114–115
security management, 247
semiconductors, 27
Sen, Amartya, 411
sensed information, 7
sensors, 162, 216–217
Seoul's Owl Bus Service, 160–161
servers, 182
  application, 230
  database, 230
  email, 230
  file, 229–230
  print, 230
  proxy, 230–231
  web, 230
service level agreements (SLAs), 117
service levels, 116–117
services of internet
  blogs, 433
  peer-to-peer file sharing, 434–435
  search, 431–433
  social networks, 433–434
  streaming sites, 435–436
  virtual worlds, 436
Simon, Herbert, 362–363
Simple Mail Transfer Protocol (SMTP), 241
simplex communication, 56–57
smart buildings, 163–164
smart cities, 157–165
  definitions of, 157
  facilities of, 158–160
  historical origins, 157–158
  sensing and measuring, 158–159
  smart transportation, 159–160
smart environment, 161–163
  energy management, 162–163
  pollution control, 162
  water conservation, 161–162
smart governance, 165
smart living, 164–165
smart technologies, 34
smart transportation, 159–160
SMTP (Simple Mail Transfer Protocol), 86
Snapdragon, 27
snooping, 254
social engineering, 252–254
social issues, 135–142
  changing work practices, 137–138
  de-skilling and alienation, 138–139
  e-waste, 140–142
  resistance, 135–137
  telecommuting, 139
  workplace behaviour and health, 135–138
social issues, of the internet, 431
  collaboration, 442–443
  emergence of order, 443
  identity, 440–441
  media impact, 441–442
  privacy, 441
social issues, with IS
  alienation, 138–139
  de-skilling, 138–139
  e-waste, 140–142, 156
  telecommuting, 139
  workplace behaviour and health, 135–138
social networking sites, 11
social networks, 433–434, 443–444
Social Security Number (SSN), 304
software, 10, 171
  application, 188–190
  development, 191
  Linux, 187–188
  MacOS, 188
  operating system, 186–187
  Solaris, 188
  Windows, 188
Software-as-a-Service (SaaS), 201, 209–210
Software Defined Networking (SDN), 199, 211–212
software project management, 295
  function point analysis, 297
  project estimation, 296–297
  team composition, 295–296
  top management support, 295
  vendor selection, 296
Solaris, 188
spam, 88
Spiral Model, 291–292
spyware program, 130
SQLSlammer, 252
Stallman, Richard, 10, 453
standard in data, 462
standardisation, 111–112
StarOffice, 457
star topology, 242–243
startups, 84
State Bank of India (SBI), 112
Steel Authority of India (SAIL), 83
storage area networks (SAN), 184
straightline.in, 83
strategic decisions, 54–55
streaming sites, 435–436
structural exercise of power, 134
structured decisions, 363
Structured Query Language (SQL), 320–321
Stuxnet, 249–250, 254
substitutes, threat of, 68–69
Supervisory Control and Data Acquisition (SCADA) systems, 250
supply chain management (SCM) system, 78, 341, 345–348
supply chain management (SCM) systems, 333
switches, 232–233
switching costs, 73
Symantec, 249
@ symbol, 86
symbolic exercise of power, 135
symmetric key cryptography, 258
synchronous communication, 56

T
tablet computers, 185
tactical decisions, 52

tagging/ folksonomies, 440
Taj Hotels Resorts and Palaces group, 359–360
Taobao, 101
tape drives, 183
Tata Consultancy Services (TCS), 112
Tata Motors, 5–6, 8, 65
Tata Steel, 83
Tata Teleservices, 235
Techmentor (tecnmentorevents.com), 32
technical bid, 116
technical exercise of power, 134
technology hype cycle, 177–178
technology lock-in, 72–73
technology of internet
  mashups, 440
  rating services and agencies, 439–440
  tagging/ folksonomies, 440
  Twitter, 439
  Web pages, 437
  wiki, 437–439
technology selection, 115–116, 119
technostress, 142–144
telecommunication industry in India, 149
telecommunication networks, 223
telecommuting, 139
Telnet, 260–261
text data, 328
third-order effects, 15–16, 109
threats to IS
  cracking, 253–254
  denial-of-service (DoS) attack, 255–257
  espionage, 253–254
  identity theft, 254
  malware, 251–253
  phishing, 254
Tier-1, 2 and 3 service providers, 235
tippy market, 75
top management support, 351
transaction costs, 66
transaction processing systems, 49–50
transistors, 178
Transmission Control Protocol (TCP), 240–241
transnational companies, 352
travelling salesman problem, 53–54, 363
Tribhovandas Bhimji Zaveri (TBZ), IT infrastructure of, 173–174
Tunisia uprising and revolution, 429–430
turbulence in markets, 31
Turing, Alan, 9, 386
Turing test, 386–387
Twitter, 439
two-factor authentication (TFA), 266

U

Ubuntu, 188
Unique Identification Number (UID) scheme, 303
United Nations Environment Programme (UNEP), 153
unshielded twisted pair (UTP) copper cables, 231
unstructured decision problems, 363–364
upstream firms, 102
usage-based pricing, 205
use cases, 282–284
User Datagram Protocol (UDP), 241
utilities, 190

V

Value Chain Model, 77–78
valuejunction, 83
values and beliefs, 135
Vasa story, 297–298
velocity of data, 329
vendors, 112
  contracts and service levels, 116–117
  management, 116–118
  retention or termination, 117–118
  selection of, 116, 351
venture capitalists, 84
versions, 71–72
VHS, 75
videoconferencing, 237
Video Volunteers (V V), 416–417
'village phone' (VP) ladies, 275
virtualisation, 142, 193
virtual private network (VPN), 89, 261
virtual worlds, 436
viruses, 88, 114, 247
vision and mission of organisation, 55
Visual Basic scripting language, 252
VMware vSphere 4, 173
Voice over Internet Protocol (VoIP) telephony services, 225

W

warehouses, 301
water conservation, 161–162
Waterfall Model, 273
  alternatives to, 290–292
  analysis of project, 286
  coding and testing, 288
  design of, 286–288
  implementation and integration of, 288–289
  maintenance phase, 289
  perspective, 289–290
  project requirements, 285
water pollution, 162
Web pages, 86, 437
web pages, 11–12
web portals, 97
web server, 230
wide area network (WAN), 231
Wi-Fi routers, 262–263
Wi-Fi (Wireless Fidelity), 232
wiki, 437–439
WiMax (Worldwide Interoperability for Microwave Access) technology, 236
Windows, 188
winner-take-all markets, 31
Wired (Wired.com), 32
wireless devices, 232
wireless sensor network (WSN), 264
wireless technologies, 262–264
work culture, 16, 113
workflow systems, 16–17
working capital, 50
workplace behaviour and health, 135–138
workplace monitoring, 131–133
  Chevron Corporation, case of, 133
  management's perspective, 131
  Panopticon effect, 132
  rationale for, 133
  types of, 131–132
workstations, 182
World Wide Web (WWW), 11–12
worms, 114, 247

X

XML (Extensible Markup Language), 86, 330

Y

Yahoo!, 12, 97, 100, 209, 227
Yahoo Mail, 88
YES Bank, 263–264
Y2K problem, 341

Z

Zoho Office (zoho.com), 21, 209
zombies, 257
Zuse, Konrad, 9